D0857633

Literary-Critical Approaches
to the Bible

Literary-Critical Approaches to the Bible

An Annotated Bibliography

Mark Minor

LOCUST HILL PRESS
West Cornwall, CT
1992

Library of Congress Cataloging-in-Publication Data

Minor, Mark.
   Literary-critical approaches to the Bible : an annotated
bibliography / Mark Minor.
   520p.   cm.
   Includes index.
   ISBN 0-933951-48-5 : $50.00
   1. Bible--Bibliography.   I. Title.
Z7770.M66   1992
[BS511.2]
016.2206'6--dc20   92-7469
                                  CIP

#25509820

Printed on acid-free, 250-year-life paper
Manufactured in the United States of America

Ad Patrem, et Ad Matrem Carissimae Memoriae

CONTENTS

ACKNOWLEDGMENTS

Anyone who attempts to compile a thorough bibliography in an institution with modest library resources will understand the crucial importance of inter-library loan. In this sense, my greatest professional debt is to Mrs. Evelyn Oltmanns, director of inter-library loan services at Teikyo Westmar University. Her patience with me and my project over the last three years, her dedication and ingenuity in tracking down requests for obscure materials have been amazing, easing my task innumerable times.

I certainly could not have finished in time without a good seminary library fairly nearby. The staff at the library of North American Baptist Seminary in Sioux Falls has been unfailingly helpful and friendly to a stranger in their midst. Other seminary or university libraries where I have received much assistance on research visits include, in the Chicago area, Garrett-Evangelical, Seabury-Western, Northwestern University, the Joseph L. Regenstein Library at the University of Chicago, Spertus College of Judaica, and Loyola University; in Wisconsin, the University of Wisconsin-Madison and Marquette University; in Iowa, Wartburg Theological Seminary, and the University of Dubuque; in South Dakota, the University of South Dakota-Vermillion; and in Nebraska, the University of Nebraska-Lincoln.

Because most of the work on this book was done without the aid of research or travel money, I owe a large debt to those persons who provided hospitality and in some cases transportation: Drs. Dwight and Linda Vogel; Rev. Lisa Luethye; Dr. Gary and Ann Brienzo; my mother-in-law and late father-in-law, Marvel and Warren Carncross; Leslie Sims; Elaine Hanks; and the Student Services staff at Sioux Falls College. After financial assistance became available from my institution during the last six months of work on this book, my Academic Dean, Dr. Leon Scott, and the directors of the academic divi-

sions at Teikyo Westmar approved my request for funds; I would like
to thank them for this and for other, more informal but equally
meaningful forms of encouragement. I am grateful to the Board of
Trustees at Teikyo Westmar for approving my sabbatical leave request for Fall, 1991, so that I could key the book into the computer
in time to meet my publisher's deadline. Dr. Gregory Clapper, a
former colleague, and Dr. Colin Holman, a current one, gave much
advice about word processing, and the latter also helped with
printing. Michael Kistner supplied photocopies of material not otherwise available to me.

Several colleagues from around the country sent material which
I might otherwise have missed: Roland Bartel, Robert M. Fowler,
Ann Hughes, Berel Lang, Gila Ramras-Rauch, and Guy Stern. While
I was not able to use everything they provided, their assistance in
identifying sources was invaluable. My students Bret Denekas and
Joseph Melnichak were of great help during a January Term course
in getting the raw materials organized and indexed. Any errors in
numbering which may have occurred are, however, entirely my doing, made after Bret and Joe had finished their part of the effort.
They also wrote a few of the entries, for which credit is given in the
appropriate places below.

Families of scholars engaged in extensive projects often bear a
difficult burden: time spent away from them which in normal circumstances would have been devoted to family. For all her support
over the years, in so many ways which cannot be mentioned here,
my greatest debt is to my wife, Joyce. The dedication page of this
book records both intellectual and personal sources of gratitude.

INTRODUCTION

Anyone who has examined biblical criticism published over the last two decades will have noticed that the methods of secular literary criticism are being applied to the Bible with increasing frequency. Some biblical critics argue that this development represents so fundamental a change in method that it amounts to a paradigm shift—an abandonment of the older historical-critical model dominant since the late nineteenth century in favor of a new, literary-critical one. For those who so argue, literary criticism is much more than an occasional means of clarifying an otherwise puzzling passage; it has become a new way of reading—perhaps even of thinking about—the Bible. Others, while acknowledging that this new approach is widely practiced, believe that historical criticism must and will remain the basis of biblical interpretation. Despite the differing opinions among scholars about the appropriateness of using literary criticism on the Bible, its explosive rate of growth in recent years is a "truth universally acknowledged"; as a result, even biblical critics who choose not to employ literary methods have had to take the presence and the influence of those methods into account. The importance as well as the sheer amount of literary-critical work done on the Bible since the 1960's makes the present bibliography both necessary and timely. I hope that this classification and analysis of published work will help critics of all persuasions understand how the relationship between biblical and literary studies has developed up to the present, and therefore how they themselves might contribute to the field.

The Literary-Critical Approach: A Brief History

Although the developments described above are relatively new, the idea of examining the Bible from a literary-critical point of view has in fact a considerable history. We know that courses in "The Bible as Literature" existed at Harvard before 1920.[1] In the mid-nineteenth century the English critic Matthew Arnold saw a literary criticism of the Bible as the only viable choice for modern readers. Yet the real beginnings in both Christianity and Judaism seem to lie much further back than that, perhaps in the ancient Mediterranean world. In the Jewish tradition, it is uncertain whether early post-biblical scholars read the Bible from a literary point of view.[2] Nevertheless, it is clear that the first writers of the Talmud (as early as 100–25 BCE) were influenced by Hellenistic rhetoric in their development of Jewish religious law. Indeed, a long and fruitful encounter between Jewish and Hellenistic cultures took place in the ancient world. Because the Greeks believed that the Hebrew Bible originated much of the profound wisdom present in their own culture, and because large portions of the Hebrew Bible were, like Homer, in narrative or poetic form, Hellenistic readers often allegorized the Jewish scriptures as they did Homer. This allegorizing, together with the Greek tendency to idealize poetry as of divine origin, made application within Greek culture of literary criticism to the Hebrew Bible seem only appropriate. For believing Jews, however, it was only with the flowering of Jewish culture in medieval Spain that a literary approach to their scripture became acceptable. Beginning in the tenth century, the development of Hebrew grammars stimulated interest in biblical style; and Greek literary ideas filtering through Arab culture also influenced Jewish writers, as did the rise of a literary criticism of the *Qur'an*.

In the Christian tradition, from the time of the earliest Church Fathers there is evidence of a continuing awareness of the relevance of Greco-Roman rhetoric to interpreting the New Testament (an awareness, ironically, which may have finally faded only about 1900 with the disappearance of rhetorical study from western universities, to be rediscovered in the 1970's). It has been argued that "the literary approach to the Bible is implicit in the biblical studies of Eusebius and Basil from the fourth century," and further,

"From the seventh through the thirteenth centuries such commentators as Cassiodorus, Alain de Lille, Isidore of

Seville, the Venerable Bede, Jonah ibn Janah, and Ulrich showed their appreciation of the parallelism, tropes, and metaphors of the Bible'spoetry and their admiration of the rhetorical excellence of its orations and exhortations as well as the simplicity and perspicuity of its narratives."[3]

In the middle ages, the analysis of metaphorical and allegorical levels of the Bible had, at times, a decidedly literary cast—or at least kept the notion of a "literal" reading of scripture as only one of several legitimate levels of interpretation. However, it was not until the advent of the Protestant Reformation that the literary-critical approach to the Bible began to develop something like a methodology. At that time a contro versy grew up over whether poetic and rhetorical ornamentation of any kind could be a vehicle of God's truth. Those who argued in the affirmative were able to point to significant portions of the Hebrew Bible (Old Testament) to support their view.[4] According to one scholar, this "intense concern with biblical imagery and biblical tropes" reflected the "Protestant view that the literal meaning of scripture is often conveyed through figurative language and so can be properly apprehended through rhetorical and poetic analysis."[5] The prose writings of John Milton show decided traces of interest in this kind of biblical analysis, while more direct and detailed defenses or explications of the literary method can be found in works of his contemporaries such as George Ballard, *The History of Susanna* (1638); Giles Fletcher, *Christes Victorie ...* (1632); Abraham Cowley, "Preface" to *Davideis* in *Collected Poems* (1656), and John Prideaux, *Sacred Eloquence: The Art of Rhetoric as it is Laid Down in Scripture* (1659). Even a scientist such as Robert Boyle wrote a book called *Some Considerations Touching the Style of Scripture*, published in 1668. However, literary criticism of the Bible in the seventeenth century was limited in two important ways: it seems to have been directed toward the books most obviously dependent upon a "poetic" language or form: *Song of Songs* and *Psalms* for the most part, with a lesser interest in *Proverbs* and *Ecclesiaste* [6]; and, much of it was meant to serve not so much the purposes of biblical exegesis, as it was the composition of original poetry.

We do not find the first attempts at developing a systematic literary theory of the Bible until literary criticism itself began to become systematized—i.e., not until near the end of the Enlightenment. In the second half of the eighteenth century in England and in Germany two pioneering books paved the way, albeit on quite different grounds. In England Bishop Robert Lowth (1710-1787) published his *De Sacra Poesi Hebraeorum* in 1753 (English translation 1787 as "The Sacred Poetry of the Hebrews"). Lowth argued that Christians owed the literature of their own faith the same aesthetic attention as that which they gave to the ancient Greek and Roman writings.[7] He held that biblical critics should learn how to judge Hebrew writing by its own standards, rather than by those of the Hellenistic world. This was the theoretical basis for the close literary analysis of biblical poetry which Lowth undertook in his enormously influential work. In Germany, the first important critic to take up the subject was Johann Gottfried Herder (1744-1803) in *Vom Geist der Ebraischen Poesie* ("The Spirit of Hebrew Poetry") published in 1783. Herder, too, wanted a standard for judging Hebrew poetry that was culturally appropriate. However, his motivation, unlike that of Lowth, derived not from religious conviction but from his view that poetry, whether biblical or secular, was "the mother tongue of the human race":

> "In human fashion must one read the Bible; for it is a book written by men for men: Human is the language, human the external means with which it was written and preserved; human finally is the sense with which it may be grasped, every aid that illumines it, as well as the aim and use to which it is to be applied."[8]

Lowth's method shows that his thinking was still firmly anchored in the Age of Reason, while Herder's indicates that he was already responding to the early currents of European romanticism. We should also note that as late as Samuel Johnson (1709-1784), the typical Protestant strategy was to separate biblical from secular poetics; only with Romantics such as Coleridge early in the next century did an understanding of biblical typology enter the mainstream of literary criticism.[9] A literary-critical approach to the Bible did not develop at once from seventeenth-century Protestantism's rediscovery of the relevance of poetics and rhetoric for interpreting scripture. Although something like a literary criticism of the Bible may have been brought into being in the ancient world by Hellenistic allegorizing, in the modern world it did not (and probably could not) finally emerge as an approach in its own right until the decline of allegory.

We may still wonder, though, why this way of reading the Bible, available in some recognizable form since the late eighteenth century, did not begin to have a strong and widespread influence on biblical studies until about twenty to thirty years ago. Here the brilliant work of Hans Frei may help us. Frei argues[10] that a crisis in the authority of the Bible as adequate description of the "real" world was a characteristic of the European Enlightenment. Out of this crisis appeared the first signs of what later came to be called the "historical-critical method" of explicating the Bible. This method (explained in more detail below) became a way of being scientific and yet unthreatening theologically. Ironically, however, the historical-critical method helped bring about the very condition it was designed to prevent. Because it involved a taking-apart of the biblical text to see what lay "behind" it, it encouraged the attitude that the text itself was not truth immutable, but a means to arrive at something else which was somehow "truer" than the text. Still, it had the advantage of seeming to ground itself in history, and thus was preferable to the "abandonment" of history which literary criticism was sometimes supposed to represent. Although some nineteenth-century critics practiced one form or another of literary analysis of the Bible, their efforts (with notable exceptions like Matthew Arnold's) were not conceived of as a challenge to the prevailing historical school, which was itself still developing. Not until the 1920's and 1930's did the literary-critical work of such biblical scholars as Amos Niven Wilder and James Muilenberg warn of trouble ahead for historical criticism. By then, for all its advantages over previous methods, the problems inherent in historical criticism were becoming too obvious to ignore. In encouraging scholars to be concerned with the forms and sources which are presumed to lie behind (i.e., historically prior to) the text of a passage or book, historical criticism largely ignored two crucial facts: that the final text is, after all, the only version we really have; and that whatever sources may lie behind it, and whatever its faults as a text, this final version was self-evidently the one which the ancient authorities regarded as "inspired." The tendency of historical criticism to focus on earlier forms, or on the rituals of a believing community which produced those earlier forms, also came to be seen as flawed because it stunted the overall reading experience: the sense readers need of the whole; the cumulative impact of verses, incidents and chapters as they move toward a climax and a resolution. The decline of the historical authority of the Bible is sometimes said to be the main cause of the rise of a biblical literary criticism over the last century or so—the implication being that, with faith in its historicity eroding, the only standard left for evaluating the Bible was an aesthetic one. Such a theory founders on the undoubted fact that historical criticism itself was a product of the Enlightenment: the historical-critical and the literary methods both emerged from the same cultural climate. (Indeed, many modern academic disciplines and methods have this origin). Realizing this helps us in turn see that a literary criticism of the Bible need not imply the abandonment of its theological significance.

Not only did these two criticisms appear as conscious methodologies at nearly the same historical moment; in their pre-Enlightenment manifestations they were always related in one way or another, and often developed in parallel. It is fair to say that literary criticism itself is in large part the creation of ancient and medieval biblical criticism, with its formula for reading a text on four levels: the moral, allegorical, anagogical and literal. Biblical criticism from the early Fathers on was, then, always potentially literary. Closer to our own time, historical criticism as practiced in seminaries over the last century and more derives in part from the literary criticism found in nineteenth century English departments; i.e., it is philological and textual—concerned largely with the stages of composition and transmission of the Bible. Not surprisingly, then, when literary criticism itself began to metamorphose in the 1950's and 1960's under the pressures of structuralism, linguistics, reader-response and *Receptionsaesthetik*, deconstruction, feminism and Marxism (to name only some of the prominent schools) biblical criticism shortly thereafter began to experience the same diversification. For that matter, once the limitations of the historical critical method became obvious, biblical studies could not have avoided even the less radical methods of close reading, of "explication de texte," dominant in literary studies from the 1930's to the 1960's and still widely practiced today, usually known as the "New" criticism. This is not to imply that biblical criticism always "follows" its literary cousin, only that theological interests may make it more resistant for a longer time than literary criticism to the kinds of pressures described above. The 1960's, we may remind ourselves, saw a number of humanistic disciplines move from consensus on method to a proliferation of competing methods where no one approach tended to dominate. In historical studies, for example, the older consensus that history must be written in narrative form, and that it must concern itself with the doings of political leaders, began to dissolve in the 1960's with the appearance of the "Annales" school of documenting "mentalities," and the "new social history."[11] In opening itself to a variety of literary-critical practices, biblical studies was undoubtedly responding, as it always has, to the times in which it found itself.

Defining the Literary-Critical Approach

The growing presence of modern literary interests within biblical studies has served to highlight the fact that, whatever their common origins, important differences exist between the two schools. Although some critics hold that historical and literary criticisms of the Bible can reinforce each other without conflict, to judge by the entries in this book that is far from being a majority view. As we have already seen, literary critics generally focus on the final form of the text, wanting to know how its parts interact to produce the whole which (if the Bible is our text) we call Psalm 51, the Gospel of Luke, the Letter to the Romans, or the "story" of Joseph in Genesis 37-50. Biblical critics, on the other hand, have been more interested in the supposed documentary history of the text as it may be located in oral traditions, in earlier versions still visible where they were joined ("redacted") to produce the present text, in rituals transformed into writing for wider audiences. There is, however, a deeper gulf between the two schools of criticism locatable in their different attitudes toward the role of language in writing. As Karl Plank puts it in *Paul and the Irony of Affliction* (#2123 below),

> "... the literary-rhetorical paradigm is essentially linguistically-based and systemic in character. As *linguistically-based*, the paradigm affirms language as a fundamental category: the language of a text does not grant access to some reality behind or beyond its own expression, but refers to the reality of its own creation. As *systemic*, the paradigm insists that a text's meaning does not emerge genetically in terms of its development or cause, but as created synchronically within a textual system of relations." (p. 7)

Plank probably overstates his case here—for example in ruling the genetic approach out of literary criticism, when in fact it constitutes an important methodological tool for many in the discipline. Also questionable is his assumption that the linguistic paradigm dominates, when in fact it is one among several accepted models; many literary critics practice methods where the text's ability to refer to "reality behind or beyond its own expression" is taken for granted. Nevertheless, Plank has isolated an important distinction between historical and literary approaches. What theologians call "form," "source," "redaction" and "tradition" criticisms do share the concept of language as a "window"—capable of revealing the truth of events, personalities, etc., referred to by the language. In contrast, literary critics do tend to see language more as a "mirror"—not so much revealing the truth about whatever is described as being in itself a part of the truth which the work embodies.

A second point of contrast between the two approaches is that historical criticism tends to view the form in which a biblical book or passage is written as largely a means to another end—e.g., the communication of information or persuasion leading to belief—whereas to a literary critic, form and content cannot be separated; one cannot exist without the other, and the "meaning" of a work "is" both form and content because the two are one. (Despite its title, "form criticism" is not an exception to this rule, as I hope is clear elsewhere in this introduction). Finally, we may note a third principle common to almost all types of literary criticism: that the finished work must be the foundation for whatever analysis is pursued on that work—especially when no previous published or manuscript versions are known. This principle does not make consideration of earlier stages entirely irrelevant, but they cannot be, as they often are in historical criticism, an end in themselves. These three principles, then:

(a) language as "mirror";

(b) the inseparability of form and content;

(c) the work primarily as a finished whole, rather than primarily as a deposit of earlier sources;

seem to represent a reasonable formula for defining the literary-critical approach, and thereby for distinguishing literary from historical criticism. It is this formula which has guided the selection of items included in this bibliography.

In spite of such differences in approach, these two camps can sometimes merge, as happens for example in a technique known as "Composition Criticism."[12] In composition criticism the critic focuses on how the author's (not the redactor's or editor's) theology transforms his materials into a new, seamless whole. The biblical book or portion thereof is viewed as an original composition with a theological message as its usual raison d'être, and with a form which is itself part of the content to be transmitted. The possible existence of source materials behind the present version may be admitted, but does not enter into the analysis since all authors have had sources of some sort behind their finished work. Composition criticism, the approach closest to traditional theological methods included in this book, is represented in these pages because in it we can clearly discern the second and third of our basic assumptions of literary criticism: that form and content are inseparable, and that the final version of the work is what matters most. Composition criticism may have another relevant and important role to play: it may help answer those who object that literary criticism is an alien discipline when applied to the Bible because it sidesteps the faith position from which the Bible has to be read to be finally understood. Already in the criticism of Lowth and Herder we saw evidence of a tension between those who apply literary criticism to the Bible because they believe it will redound to the greater glory of God, and those who do so without regard to theological results, simply because they believe that any narrative, any poem, any letter, can be analyzed using theories developed for that purpose. This tension has been visible in biblical studies ever since. Of course a critic may (and many critics do) occupy both camps. Those who emphasize that the literary approach is appropriate are often believing Jews or Christians who are confident that they, and we, can respect the claims of scholarship without fearing damage to their readers' faith from the results. Still, where literary criticism of the Bible has been resisted, the charge of irrelevance has often been coupled with that of the undermining of belief. The phrase "Bible as literature" (about which I have unrelated objections indicated below) really means, among other things, "the Bible as religious literature." That is, literary critics should recognize that the biblical books were written from within specific theologies, and therefore they cannot deal adequately with the Bible without taking those theologies into account. However, being aware of, and fair to, the faith of the biblical authors, and seeing the Bible from within a given faith position, are two different things. "The Bible as religious literature" surely means the former, but need not mean the latter. Readers of course must decide for themselves what they regard as a legitimate interpretation. Theological critics should not rule out an interpretation simply because it comes from outside a faith position, or because it attempts to be objective about faith and belief; likewise, literary critics approaching the Bible as another "text" must not assume that there is no difference between, say, a biblical narrative and a modern novel.

The Scope of This Book

The exclusion of traditional historical-critical methods from this bibliography has one exception: in selected cases, the "form" critics' attempts to isolate earlier "forms" and "genres" behind the present biblical text sometimes leads them to perform what amounts to "New Criticism" on the Bible: i.e., a close attention to style, structure, diction, genre, etc., of the biblical text as we have it. Where such is obviously the case in a given item, I have included it. I have also included as many examples as I could find of the technique known as "rhetorical" criticism; it originally grew out of form criticism, but more and more its methodology overlaps significantly with related literary-critical approaches. I have included as well discussions of the apparent influence of various pagan literary forms on the Bible, and of the influence of one part of the Bible on another—again, so long as the purpose of such discussion was not primarily to further a particular theological viewpoint about biblical predictions "coming true" later in the Bible itself. After all, literary critics now embrace intertextuality as readily as they do any of the other methodologies mentioned herein. Various experimental methods borrowed from other disciplines which have lately become a part of many literary critics' work are also included here; I refer to structuralism, folklore and myth criticism, feminism, linguistics, and post-structuralist methods such as deconstruction. I have included all of these I could find which take the Bible as their text, so long as they were employing literary criticism in some recognizable manner: e.g., structuralist studies which are primarily anthropological are omitted, whereas those which are primarily literary (however much dependent on social-scientific methods as a starting point) are included. I recognize that such decisions are finally subjective, but the lines have to be drawn somewhere, and I believe that this book is inclusive enough that those seeking to cross the lines between the historical, social scientific and literary methods will have no trouble doing so. Two other exclusions deserve notice: I have omitted book reviews except for a handful of cases where the discussion went significantly beyond an evaluation of that particular book; and there are very few biblical commentaries herein. Some commentaries have in recent years begun to reflect the impact of literary criticism, but as a whole commentaries have a synthesizing function such that they do not seem to be necessary in a book such as this one. Finally, readers should be aware that this bibliography is confined to works published in English. Some significant work in the field is being done in other languages, but as I am not competent in some of those languages, to have included that material would have delayed publication indefinitely. Many of the items in this book make reference to literary-critical work on the Bible in Hebrew, Dutch, etc., so readers needing to move into other languages will find much here of interest.

Users of this book should also note the first part of the title. It embodies a subtle but important distinction: it is "literary-critical approaches to the Bible," not "the Bible as literature." The problem with the latter phrase, popular as it may be, is that it can too easily be taken to mean that the Bible is "belles lettres," and that therefore books or passages lacking the belles-lettristic character are irrelevant to understanding the whole. The phrase becomes, in effect, an invitation to ignore, or at best to marginalize, the Bible's theological import. I chose my title because it seems to me a more accurate reflection both of what literary critics do and of what the Bible actually is. Any piece of writing, regardless of its origins, genre, etc., may be better understood using literary-critical methods. While it is true that the most powerful and accessible biblical narratives and poems (e.g., the Joseph and the Samson narratives, certain psalms, Job, the parables of Jesus) have attracted the lion's share of literary exegesis, many entries in this book demonstrate unmistakably that there is no part of the Bible which cannot be illuminated using literary criticism.

The pioneering (and only previous) bibliography of literary-critical approaches to the Bible was John H. Gottcent, *The Bible as*

Literature: A Selective Bibliography (Boston: G.K. Hall, 1979). As reviewers of that book pointed out, Gottcent's work had two shortcomings: selective coverage of the available literary-critical material; and the inclusion of a large number of works of theological criticism and historical background—perhaps on the assumption that what theologians and historians had done with the Bible had to be learned before literary critics could perform their task. Whatever the validity of this assumption, I have taken a different approach by including all the literary-critical work I could find published any time in the last hundred years, while eliminating the other matter since it is easily locatable by other means, should the critic so desire. If I have succeeded in finding somewhere near all the enormous amount of English-language work published just since Gottcent's book came out, and of filling in many of the gaps from earlier years, then the present book will prove its usefulness for a long time to come.

Notes

1. Amos N. Wilder, *The Bible and the Literary Critic* (Philadelphia: Fortress Press, 1991), p. 64. Given the textbooks designed for student use dating from well before 1900, such courses must have been taught in American universities during the nineteenth century.

2. In the historical sketch which follows, I am indebted to James L. Kugel, "The 'Bible as Literature' in Late Antiquity and the Middle Ages" (*HUSLA* 11: 1983, 20-70); Kugel, *The Idea of Biblical Poetry: Parallelism and its History* (New Haven and London: Yale University Press), 1981; David Daube, "Rabbinic Methods of Interpretation and Hellenistic Rhetoric" (*HUCA* 22: 1949, 239-264); Abraham Heschel, *The Prophets* (New York and Evanston: Harper and Row), 1962; Burton L. Mack, *Rhetoric and the New Testament* (Minneapolis: Fortress Press), 1990.

3. James H. Sims, "Milton, Literature as a Bible, and the Bible as Literature" in J. Max Patrick and Roger H, Sundell, eds., *Milton and the Art of Sacred Song* (Madison: University of Wisconsin Press, 1979), pp. 3-4.

4. Sims, pp. 15-16.

5. Barbara Kiefer Lewalski, *Protestant Poetics and the Seventeenth-Century Religious Lyric* (Princeton: Princeton University Press, 1979), Part One.

6. *Ibid.*

7. James L. Kugel, *The Idea of Hebrew Poetry: Parallelism and its History* (New Haven and London: Yale University Press, 1981), p. 274.

8. Quoted in Hans W. Frei, *The Eclipse of Biblical Narrative: A Study in Eighteenth and Nineteenth Century Hermeneutics* (New Haven and London: Yale University Press, 1974), pp. 183, 184.

9. Frye, *The Great Code: The Bible and Literature* (New York: Harcourt Brace Jovanovich, 1982), p. xix. See also Stephen Prickett, *Words and The Word: Language, Poetics, and Biblical Interpretation* (Cambridge: Cambridge University Press, 1986).

10. Frei, chapters 10-12. These chapters present a fascinating history of how and why the literary approach simply failed to develop, and should be required reading for anyone interested in the whole subject of "The Bible as Literature."

11. David Hackett Fisher, *Albion's Seed: Four British Folkways in America* (New York: Oxford University Press, 1989), vii-ix.

12. See the introduction to Stephen D. Moore, *Literary Criticism and the Gospels: The Theoretical Challenge* (New Haven and London: Yale University Press, 1989).

How to Use This Book

The basic organization of this bibliography is by books of the Hebrew Bible and the New Testament, and within each section on a book, alphabetically by author of the item listed. There are several further subdivisions and refinements of this basic arrangement which should be kept in mind. Before the listings on individual biblical books come several more general sections: First are books, edited collections, and articles which deal with literary criticism of the Bible in general, either without focusing on particular biblical books or passages, or by referring to a number of passages throughout the Bible. Next come books and articles on the Hebrew Bible as a whole, followed by ones on Hebrew Biblical Narrative, and then Hebrew Biblical Poetry. Books and articles are listed separately in all these categories because this is normally useful when a large number of items is to be presented. Following these are items on the individual sections and books of the Hebrew Bible in their traditional order; in cases where a large number of items on an individual book are included, and/or where natural subdivisions of a biblical book occur (Genesis being a good example), a further division of items is made on that basis, so that readers will not have to spend unnecessary time going through irrelevant material. Roughly the same arrangement is followed for the New Testament.

The cross-indexing arrangement throughout is also intended to make items more easily accessible. All items are numbered. If in order to illustrate its point a book or article uses biblical passages belonging to another part of the bibliography, a "see also" in the annotation, followed by one or more numbers, will direct the reader to the appropriate items. If, however, an item belongs about equally in more than one place, its number, author and title (but not its annotations) are repeated at each relevant location. Such repetition is indicated by an asterisk where the number normally would be, followed by the abbreviated information and a "See #....." to indicate where full bibliographical information and annotation may be found. Finally, the author index refers the reader to all items written or edited by that person. Occasionally, an item of particularly outstanding importance is indicated by two asterisks following the annotation. I have tried to confine my annotations to neutral summaries of contents; however, on a few occasions I have editorialized when I thought it necessary for clarity. Finally, I have tried to design the bibliography so that it can be more than a list of books and articles to be consulted after this one is put back on the shelf. The annotations have been written so as to make it possible to read through an entire section and get a good impression about where criticism has been, and is going, with regard to that particular topic about, or book of, the Bible.

Abbreviations

Periodicals and Annuals Frequently Cited:

ABR	*Australian Biblical Review*
AJBI	*Annual of the Japanese Biblical Institute*
AJSL	*American Journal of Semitic Languages & Literatures*
ATR	*Anglican Theological Review*
AUSS	*Andrews University Seminary Studies*
Bijdragen	*Bijdragen: Tijdschrift voor Philosophie en Theologie*
BJRL	*Bulletin of the John Rylands University Library*
BR	*Biblical Research*
B Sac	*Biblioteca Sacra*
BT	*The Bible Translator*
BTB	*Biblical Theology Bulletin*
BZAW	*Beheift zur ZAW*
BZNW	*Beheift zur ZNW*
CBQ	*Catholic Biblical Quarterly*
CL	*Christianity and Literature*
ET	*The Expository Times*
ETh	*Eglise et Theologie*
FFF	*Foundations and Facets Forum* (occasionally "Forum" with subtitle)
GTJ	*Grace Theological Journal*
HAR	*Hebrew Annual Review*
HJ	*Heythrop Journal*
HS	*Hebrew Studies*
HTR	*Harvard Theological Review*
HUCA	*Hebrew Union College Annual*
HUSLA	*Hebrew University Studies in Literature & The Arts*
JAAR	*Journal of the American Academy of Religion*

JANES	*Journal of the Ancient Near Eastern Society of Columbia University*
JBL	*Journal of Biblical Literature*
JETS	*Journal of the Evangelical Theological Society*
JJS	*Journal of Jewish Studies*
JNSL	*Journal of Northwest Semitic Languages*
JQR	*Jewish Quarterly Review*
JR	*Journal of Religion*
JSJ	*Journal for the Study of Judaism*
JSNT	*Journal for the Study of the New Testament*
JSOT	*Journal for the Study of the Old Testament*
JSS	*Journal of Semitic Studies*
JTS	*Journal of Theological Studies*
JTSA	*Journal of Theology for Southern Africa*
LB	*Linguistica Biblica*
LT	*Literature and Theology*
Nov T	*Novum Testamentum*
NTS	*New Testament Studies*
OPTAT	*OPTAT: Occasional Papers in Translation and Text Linguistics*
OS	*Oudtestamentiesche Studien*
OTE	*Old Testament Essays*
PEGL	*Proceedings of the Eastern Great Lakes Biblical Society* (later: *Proceedings of the Eastern Great Lakes and Midwest Biblical Societies*)
PRS	*Perspectives in Religious Studies*
PWCJS	*Proceedings of the World Congress of Jewish Studies* (number after the abbreviation indicates which Congress not which volume)
SBL	Society of Biblical Literature
SBLSP	*Society of Biblical Literature Seminar Papers*
SJOT	*Scandinavian Journal of the Old Testament*
SWJT	*Southwestern Journal of Theology*
SR	*Studies in Religion/ Sciences Religieuses*
TB	*Tyndale Bulletin*
TJ	*Trinity Journal*
TT	*Theology Today*
TZ	*Theologische Zeitschrift*
UF	*Ugarit Forschungen*
USQR	*Union Seminary Quarterly Review*

VE	*Vox Evangelica*
VT	*Vetus Testamentum*
WTJ	*Westminster Theological Journal*
ZAW	*Zeitschrift für die Alttestamentliche Wissenschaft*
ZNW	*Zeitschrift für die Neutestamentliche Wissenschaft*

Other Abbreviations:

BD	Annotations by Bret Denekas
HB	Hebrew Bible
JM	Annotations by Joseph Melnichak
NT	New Testament
OT	Old Testament
P	Press
Rpt	Reprinted
Tr	Translated by
U	University

Literary-Critical Approaches
to the Bible

THE BIBLE
(Hebrew Bible and
New Testament Together)

Authored Books

1. Brown, Stephen J., S.J. *Image and Truth: Studies in the Imagery of the Bible.* Rome (Officium Libri Catholici), 1955.

   A theory of imagery and a defense of metaphor against the charge that it cannot offer as direct or impressive a truth as can literal statement. Imagery in the OT; metaphor in the Gospels and in Paul; nature symbolism in the Bible.

2. Bullinger, E.W. *Figures of Speech Used in the Bible Explained and Illustrated.* London (Eyre and Spottiswoode), 1898; rpt Grand Rapids (Baker Book House), 1968.

   An exhaustive catalog of examples, with brief explanations based on classical Greek rhetorical terminology, e.g. enthymema; asyndeton; anadiplosis; pleonasm; periphrasis; metonymy; irony; anacoluthon; prosopopoeia; etc.

3. Detweiler, Robert. *Story, Sign, and Self: Phenomenology and Structuralism as Literary Critical Methods.* Philadelphia (Fortress P) and Missoula (Scholars P), 1978.

   How these methods interact, and how they provide an arena where interpreters of secular and religious texts can meet. Genesis 1-4; Mark 5; the passion stories; I Corinthians; John; parables.

4. Fischer, James A. *How to Read the Bible.* Englewood Cliffs (Prentice-Hall, Inc.), 1982 (1981).

   The quest for objectivity in reading the Bible is fruitless; we must instead allow the imagination legitimate play. Elements of biblical

3

narrative: plot, character, symbolism, tragedy, comedy, epic and historical narrative; Ruth as example. How to read legal and moral teachings, and reflective passages, e.g. Pauline letters, parts of Jeremiah and other prophets, Hebrews, Proverbs, and the parables.

5. Frye, Northrop. *The Great Code: The Bible and Literature.* New York (Harcourt Brace Jovanovich), 1981, 1982.

An outgrowth of Frye's earlier work on the Bible in *Anatomy of Criticism.* The Bible is not so much a great anthology as it is a great typology. It is thus a unity when studied in terms of its special modes of language (rhetoric), myth (narrative), metaphor (imagery), and typology (phases of revelation). **

6. Frye, Northrop. *Words with Power. Being a Second Study of The Bible and Literature.* San Diego (Harcourt Brace Jovanovich), 1990.

Illustrates and develops the argument of *The Great Code* that "the organizing structures of the Bible and the corresponding structures of 'secular' literature reflect each other." The Bible is held together by "an inner core of mythical and metaphorical structure." Therefore, it "demands the active and creative response that the imagination makes to literature and mythology; the faith that it calls for must be able to accept divergences from historical fact as one of its conditions." The Bible's structure arises from the four primary human concerns: to create, love, sustain life, and escape restraint—expressed in its myths of mountain, garden, cave, and furnace.

7. Gottcent, John H. *The Bible: A Literary Study.* Boston (G.K. Hall-Twayne), 1986.

Initial chapters on "The Bible: A Historical-Cultural Overview"; the importance of the Bible (including why we subject it to literary analysis); a short history of such analysis; chapters on individual books and episodes: Genesis 6-9; Moses (Exodus, Numbers 20; Deuteronomy 34); Judges 11, 13-16; I & II Samuel; I & II Kings; Jonah; Psalm 23; Job; Ruth; Ecclesiastes; in the NT: Luke 10, 15; Acts 1-15; Revelation 1-22. **

8. Grawe, Paul H. *Comedy in Space, Time, and the Imagination.* Chicago (Nelson-Hall), 1983.

Comedy says that humans will survive and carry on; it is a celebration of life. Chapter 17, on comedy in the OT: God is outside of space, time, and human limitation; OT concerned with survival of God's elect within the natural order (examples I and II Samuel). Chapter 18, on comedy in the Gospels: they transcend space and time, are concerned with survival in eternity. The great incongruities between Jesus' earthly humility and future glory are the basis of NT comedy.

9. Greenstein, Edward L. *Essays on Biblical Method and Translation.* Atlanta (Scholars P), 1989.

Chapter 1, "The State of Biblical Studies," argues for a synthesis of older historical and newer synchronic approaches, "to [be] open to new disciplines and conceptual models, ..." especially those which encourage us to examine our methods objectively.

10. Greenwood, David. *Structuralism and the Biblical Text.* Berlin, New York, Amsterdam (Mouton), 1985.

Explanation of structural procedures in general, and specific methodologies of Levi-Strauss, Roland Barthes, A.J. Greimas. Their application to the Bible by Edmund Leach, Daniel Patte, John Crossan, Dan O. Via; by Jean Calloud to Matthew 4; by Erhart Güttgemanns to the NT. Their applicability to the Bible is somewhat limited, as illustrated by discussions of Genesis 22 and Luke 15.

11. Henn, Thomas R. *The Bible as Literature.* New York (Oxford UP), 1970.

If we read the Bible from a literary standpoint, we see it as a "great and diverse epic," inviting "the response of all great literature: wonder, delight, exaltation, liberating the mind." Themes, language and style, imagery, poetry, "types of persuasion," Psalms, Job, Proverbs, character versus plot, problem of evil.

12. Innes, Kathleen E. *The Bible as Literature.* London (Jonathan Cape), 1930.

A general survey of literary forms and styles found in both OT and NT. The best-selling status of the Bible is due as much to its literary as to its theological and ethical qualities. OT stories (Ruth, Samson, Joseph); poetry; Song Of Songs, Proverbs, Job, Ecclesiastes; the prophets; parable and story in the NT; Pauline oratory; NT letters; Revelation.

13. Jones, Howard M. *Five Essays on the Bible.* New York (ACLS), 1960.

One chapter, "The Bible from a Literary Point of View," argues that the Bible does not have aesthetic unity, but is an anthology of often contradictory documents. Its incomparable stylistic power can make us ignore these discontinuities. It is a great, primary book with simple themes; its foremost tragic heroes are Saul and Jesus, though its characters do not develop as they do in Shakespeare or the Greeks.

14. Josipovici, Gabriel. *The Book of God: A Response to the Bible.* New
     Haven (Yale UP), 1988.

     The Bible's technique is more to show us truth than to tell it.
     "Elements of Rhythm": Genesis 1-2, 37-50; Judges (the latter counter-
     ing the rhythm of the Pentateuch); "Aspects of Speech": HB notions
     of memory, genealogy, repetition, and dialogue. "Configurations of
     Character": David, Jesus, and Paul as representing different under-
     standings of the self. The relationship of Hebrews to the HB.
     Methodology is generally but not exclusively literary-critical. Incor-
     porates #94. **

15. Kort, Wesley A. *Story, Text, and Scripture: Literary Interests in Bib-
     lical Narrative.* University Park and London (U Pennsylvania
     P), 1988.

     Narratives are crucially important as a mode of religious meaning.
     "Narrativity" and "textuality" are the defining characteristics of bibli-
     cal material. Plot, character, atmosphere, and tone applied to por-
     tions of Exodus, Judges, Jonah, Mark, and their relationship to re-
     cent developments in literary, myth, structural, and hermeneutical
     criticisms. A "literary doctrine of scripture" is possible and desirable,
     based on indispensability of narrative, textuality, and scripture as the
     centers out of which we are always speaking.

16. Lategan, Bernard C., and Willem S. Vorster. *Text and Reality:
     Aspects of Reference in Biblical Texts.* Philadelphia (Fortress P)
     and Atlanta (Scholars P), 1985.

     Literary criticism now directs us to the question: In what ways do
     texts refer to reality?, rather than to the historical critic's question:
     To what extent is there a congruence between text and reality? How
     we can understand this problem of referring. Meaning and reference
     in Mark 4: "parables refer as parables within their own narrative
     world"; reader-response and reference in II Samuel 12:7.

17. Lawton, David. *Faith, Text and History: The Bible in English.*
     Charlottesville (UP of Virginia), 1990.

     The Bible's "power to signify: not what it means, but what it can be
     and has been taken to mean"—i.e., the fact that "the history of a
     book's reception becomes part of our reading of that book." Literary
     theorists and Bible readers need to realize how much they owe each
     other. How the Bible has been read since ancient times; literary in-
     terpretations of HB narratives: Genesis, Ruth, Job; the Gospels, Song
     Of Songs, and apocalyptic: Daniel, Revelation.

18. Longman, Tremper III. *Literary Approaches to Biblical Interpreta-
     tion.* Grand Rapids (Zondervan), 1987.

History of literary-critical approaches to the Bible, classified as pre-cursors, author-, text-, reader-centered, and deconstructive. Benefits and dangers of the literary approach. Sample analyses of I Kings 22; Acts 10, 11; Exodus 15; Song Of Songs 5; Psalm 51; Micah 4; Luke 1.

19. Macky, Peter W. *The Centrality of Metaphors to Biblical Thought. A Method for Interpreting the Bible.* Lewiston, Queenston, Lampeter (Edwin Mellen), 1990.

The function and importance of various kinds of metaphors in the Bible. Metaphors which have "retired" to literal speech, or are oth-erwise hidden. Why biblical authors' concern to explore spiritual mysteries inevitably led them to figurative language, and how some God-language must have been literal. The frequently neglected func-tions of biblical metaphors as exploratory, transforming, and rela-tional.

20. McKnight, Edgar V. *The Bible and the Reader: An Introduction to Literary Criticism.* Philadelphia (Fortress P), 1985.

Given the crisis in historical criticism, we are best off turning to literary criticism, since it offers the most productive way of accom-modating the variety of models with which biblical critics will have to contend. The reader is the key, since it is the reader who makes meaning in texts. Bulk of the book explains basics of formalist and structuralist literary theory: Russian, Czech, American; specifically Roman Ingarden, Vladimir Propp, Claude Lévi-Strauss, A.J. Greimas, Roland Barthes, Wolfgang Iser.

21. McKnight, Edgar V. *Post-Modern Use of the Bible: The Emergence of Reader-Oriented Criticism.* Nashville (Abingdon), 1988.

The history of various approaches to the Bible since ancient times, and why a new one is needed. Modern historical-hermeneutical methods show the impossibility of finding any one "foundational" approach which can dominate and include all others. Structuralism and a reader-oriented criticism can best help us "image the sacred and actualize biblical discourse," though "no method can provide all the keys to all of [the text's] possibilities." Only a literary approach can guarantee the continued relevance of the Bible in and beyond the church. **

22. Morgan, Robert, with John Barton. *Biblical Interpretation.* Ox-ford (Oxford UP), 1988.

The relationship "between the rational methods used to under-stand the biblical writings and the religious interests which not only made them a subject of inquiry in the first place, but also drove some seekers after truth to press questions that threatened the fabric of traditional belief." Literary methods are appropriate for the Bible, although at the same time they are a "minefield" that is "dangerous for religion." Thorough survey of the history of such approaches, especially in the 1970's and 1980's.

23.   Moulton, Richard G. *The Literary Study of the Bible.* Revised Edition. Boston (D.C. Heath) and London (Isbister), 1899.

Basic literary forms of verse and prose; lyric poetry; history and epic; rhetorical literature (letters and Deuteronomy); wisdom literature; prophetic literature. Introduction discusses various kinds of literary interests, illustrated by Job.

24.   Poland, Lynn M. *Literary Criticism and Biblical Hermeneutics: A Critique of Formalist Approaches.* Chico (Scholars P), 1985.

"... the specific problems which the introduction of literary criticism poses for the task of biblical interpretation," since "the kinds of attention to the [Bible] ... which literary criticism of this kind makes possible is a significant and positive contribution to the process of biblical interpretation." The reasons biblical hermeneutics needs to be rethought if literary criticism is to be a part of it. We must move beyond the New Criticism, since its "assumptions are in many respects at odds with, or at least insufficient for, the full task of biblical interpretation."

25.   Polzin, Robert M. *Biblical Structuralism. Method and Subjectivity in the Study of Ancient Texts.* Missoula (Scholars P) and Philadelphia (Fortress P), 1977.

Definition of structuralism; how it compares to traditional historical critical methods; "an attempt at a structural analysis of Job": specifically its "framework," "code," and "message"; three classics of biblical criticism from a structuralist point of view by Wellhausen, von Rad, and Noth.

26.   Prickett, Stephen. *Words and 'the Word': Language, Poetics and Biblical Interpretation.* Cambridge (Cambridge UP), 1986.

The continuity in the relations among philosophy of language, literary theory, and biblical criticism during the last two centuries. Literary criticism can teach biblical scholars a greater respect for the "literality" and metaphoricity of the text than the historical critical approach allows, while biblical studies can remind literary criticism of the strange appeal to readers of a text which is literary but not secular. A number of comparative treatments of I Kings 19 illustrate the argument. **

27.   Ryken, Leland. *Words of Delight: A Literary Introduction to the Bible.* Grand Rapids (Baker Book House), 1987.

"Biblical Narrative": narrative elements, artistry, hero stories, epic, and tragedy. "Biblical Poetry": poetic elements, artistry, Psalms, Song Of Songs. "Other Literary Forms": encomium, proverb, satire, and drama. "Complete revision" of Ryken's 1974 *Literature of the Bible* (#186).

28.   Schneidau, Herbert. *Sacred Discontent: The Bible and Western Tradition.* Baton Rouge (Louisiana State UP), 1978.

The Bible's "sacred discontent" is its "mysterious probing energy" which constantly questions what it has just concluded. Its demythologizing tendency, its tendency to deconstruct itself, is what most sets it apart from writings of other ancient cultures. **

29.   Schökel, Luis Alonso. *The Inspired Word: Scripture in the Light of Language and Literature.* Tr Francis Martin. New York (Herder and Herder), 1965.

We need a reconciliation of theological and literary understandings of scripture. We must recognize that the Bible is the inspired word of God as much on the level of literary techniques and the psychology of artistic creation as it normally is on the level of theological propositions. Literary considerations may contribute to theological understanding.

30.   Shutter, Marion D. *Wit and Humor of the Bible. A Literary Study.* Boston (Arena Publishing Co.), 1893.

The sense of the ludicrous has its uses in the Bible as in every human activity. "... the literature of the Bible contains the same elements that in any other literature we call Wit and Humor." Character sketches of Alimelech, Samson, Nabal, Jonah, Absalom, and Simei; "touches of nature"; Jesus' sense of humor; proverbs and epigrams; repartee, wit and logic; ridicule in OT and NT.

31.   Wilder, Amos N. *The Bible and the Literary Critic.* Minneapolis (Fortress P), 1991.

"The way is open for a new postdogmatic appropriation of our biblical classics and heritage" through understanding how both historical and visionary poetics are involved. Evaluates contributions of George Steiner, Robert Alter and Frank Kermode to the growth of and objections to the literary-critical approach; surveys development of NT studies since 1920; assesses work of John Crossan concerning Wilder's career and on the parables; the relationship between reminiscence and history-writing; the rejection of history by postmodernism. Most sections reprinted from earlier journal articles.

Edited Collections

32. Abbott, Lyman, et al., eds. *The Bible as Literature.* New York (Thomas Y. Crowell & Co.), 1896.

    Essays mostly on individual books by twenty one scholars. Fourteen essays are literary-critical; these are analyzed separately as #s 275, 501, 890, 971, 1056, 1102, 1216, 1360, 1445, 1695, 1994, 2087, 2192, and 2252.

33. Alter, Robert and Frank Kermode, eds. *The Literary Guide to the Bible.* Cambridge (Belknap P of Harvard UP), 1987.

    Forty essays by a variety of critics: a general introduction; introduction to the OT; twenty two essays on individual books or groups of books in the OT (analyzed separately as #s 232, 257, 390, 494, 642, 662, 665, 678, 708, 791, 863, 893, 960, 987, 1023, 1096, 1223, 1308, 1339, 1373, 1429, 1443, 1466, 1474, and 1482). Introduction to the NT as a whole; eight essays on individual gospels, Acts, the Pauline letters, catholic letters, plus "general essays" on the HB and Canaanite literature; the NT and Greco-Roman writing; a structuralist approach; characteristics of ancient Hebrew poetry; midrash and allegory (analyzed separately as #s 1531, 1538, 1541, 1727, 1768, 1904, 1978, 2053, 2066, 2189, and 2240). **

34. Clines, D.J.A., David M. Gunn, and Alan J. Hauser, eds. *Art and Meaning: Rhetoric in Biblical Literature.* Sheffield (JSOT P), 1982.

    Twelve essays which share the method of rhetorical criticism and the "viewpoint ... that biblical authors were artists of language. Through their verbal artistry—their rhetoric—they have created their meaning. So meaning is ultimately inseparable from art...." Analyzed separately as #s 96, 527, 643, 649, 658, 667, 901, 923, 1137, 1260, 1923, and 2002.

35. Clines, David J.A., Stephen E. Fowl and Stanley Porter, eds. *The Bible in Three Dimensions: Essays in Celebration of Forty Years of Biblical Studies in the University of Sheffield.* Sheffield (JSOT P), 1990.

    Eighteen essays, of which seven offer a literary-critical analysis of particular books or passages, or otherwise explore issues raised by application of literary criticism to the Bible. Analyzed separately as #s 63, 341, 579, 895, 1435, 1738, and 1951.

36.   Collins, John J., ed. *Semeia 14. Apocalypse: The Morphology of a Genre.* Missoula (Scholars P), 1979.

Collins, "Towards the Morphology of a Genre." Collins, "The Jewish Apocalypses" (analyzed as #1450). Adela Y. Collins, "The Early Christian Apocalypses" (analyzed as #2234). Other essays dealing with ancient religious but non-biblical material.

37.   Detweiler, Robert, ed. *Semeia 23. Derrida and Biblical Studies.* [No city] (Scholars P), 1982.

Articles on Derrida's theories as they relate to interpreting the Bible, by Herbert Schneidau, John D. Crossan, and John P. Leavey, Jr. Two responses by Derrida.

38.   Draisma, Sipke, ed. *Intertextuality in Biblical Writings: Essays in Honour of Bas van Iersel.* Kampen (Uitgeversmaatschappij J.H. Kok), 1989.

Four essays by W.S. Vorster and others on intertextuality in the Bible, analyzed as #1648; essays on Isaiah, Genesis and the NT, Hebrews, Luke, Matthew 27, and Psalm 2 analyzed separately as #s 929, 1753, 1888, 1898, 1961, 2118, and 2187.

39.   Gros Louis, Kenneth R.R., ed., with James S. Ackerman and Thayer S. Warshaw. *Literary Interpretations of Biblical Narratives* [Vol. I]. Nashville and New York (Abingdon P), 1974.

Sixteen essays on both HB and NT texts, as well as on general interpretative issues arising from the use of literary criticism on the Bible. Analyzed separately as #s 137, 523, 524, 585, 628, 631, 634, 721, 869, 921, 1054, 1224, 1334, 1401, 1757, 1778, and 2238. **

40.   Gros Louis, Kenneth R.R., ed., with James S. Ackerman. *Literary Interpretations of Biblical Narratives.* [Vol. II] Nashville (Abingdon P), 1982.

Eighteen essays on both HB and NT texts, as well as on general interpretative and pedagogical issues arising from the use of literary criticism on the Bible. Analyzed separately as #s 87, 193, 493, 525, 564, 565, 605, 615, 666, 764, 776, 797, 823, 1342, 1361, 1723, 2005, and 2026. **

41.   Phillips, Gary A., ed. *Semeia 51. Poststructural Criticism and the Bible: Text/History/Discourse.* Atlanta (Scholars P), 1990.

Nine essays concerned "with biblical criticism in the wake of structuralism." Relevant authors are Gary A. Phillips, Fred W. Burnett, David Jobling, Kerry M. Craig and Margaret A. Kristjansson (on

Luke 11: see #1936), David H. Fisher, A.K.M. Adam, Irena
Makarushka, and Mark C. Taylor.

42. Prickett, Stephen, ed. *Reading the Text: Biblical Criticism and
     Literary Theory.* Oxford, England, and Cambridge, Mass.
     (Basil Blackwell), 1991.

     Essays by six scholars tracing the history of the interaction of bibli-
     cal and literary criticism from the Middle Ages to the present. The
     essays are "conceived as a single connected history of that subtly in-
     tertwined relationship." The "underlying argument" is that each type
     of criticism is dependent upon the other for its well-being. "A gen-
     uinely nonliterary criticism of the Bible (were that possible) would
     be as wrong-headed and futile as a genuinely secular and value-free
     theory of literary criticism."

43. Ricoeur, Paul. *Essays on Biblical Interpretation,* ed. Lewis Mudge.
     Philadelphia (Fortress P), 1980.

     "Analysis of religious discourse ought not to begin with ... theolog-
     ical assertions ... [but with] modalities of discourse that are most
     originary within the language of a community of faith; ... those ex-
     pressions by means of which the members of that community first in-
     terpret their experience for themselves and for others.... [T]he con-
     fession of faith [in the Bible] ... is directly modulated by the forms of
     discourse wherein it is expressed."

44. Russell, Letty M., ed. *Feminist Interpretation of the Bible.*
     Philadelphia (Westminster P), 1985.

     Three essays on "feminist critical consciousness"; five on "feminists
     at work"; three on "feminist critical principles," with introduction by
     Russell and postscript essay by Phyllis Trible. Essays by Sharon H.
     Ringe on Mark 7 and Matthew 15, and by T. Drorah Setel on Hosea
     analyzed separately as #s 1839 and 999.

45. Schwartz, Regina, ed. *The Book and the Text: The Bible and Liter-
     ary Theory.* Cambridge, Mass. and Oxford (Basil Blackwell),
     1990.

     Essays on various books or groups of books of the HB and NT, ana-
     lyzed separately as #s 143, 357, 500, 554, 627, 695, 715, 864, 1034,
     1346, 1552, 1645, and 2141. **

46. Tolbert, Mary Ann, ed. *Semeia 28: The Bible and Feminist
     Hermeneutics.* Chico (Scholars P), 1983.

     Three of the seven essays are relevant, on Exodus 1-2, Matthew,
     and Mark; analyzed separately as #s 641, 1702, and 1791.

47.   Tollers, Vincent, and John R. Maier, eds. *The Bible in its Literary Milieu. Contemporary Essays.* Grand Rapids (Eerdmans), 1979.

Essays reprinted from #s 29, 515 and 694; other reprinted essays analyzed separately as #s 112, 268, 417, 535a, and 1598.

48.   Tollers, Vincent L., and John Maier, eds. *Mappings of the Biblical Terrain: The Bible as Text.* (Bucknell Review). Lewisburg (Bucknell UP); London and Toronto (Associated University Presses), 1990.

An introduction and twenty four essays, of which twenty are literary-critical: fourteen on the HB, four on the NT, and two on both. Analyzed separately as #s 78, 84, 237, 256, 283, 335, 336, 550, 599, 625, 690, 720, 775, 894, 1109, 1341, 1692, 1982, 2241, and 2253.

49.   White, Hugh C., ed. *Semeia 41: Speech Act Theory and Biblical Criticism.* Decatur (Scholars P), 1988.

Essays on the relationship of speech act theory and literary criticism as applied to the Bible by White, Michael Hancher, Susan S. Lanser, Daniel Patte, Ronald L. Grimes, Martin J. Buss, Robert Detweiler and Charles E. Jarrett. Lanser and Detweiler discuss Genesis 2, 3.

Articles

50.   Albright, William F. "The Bible," in Francis H. Horn, ed. *Literary Masterpieces of the Western World* (Baltimore: Johns Hopkins UP), 1953, pp. 3-20.

"Much of the Old Testament was written and polished by skilled literary craftsmen, and their works continued in favor partly because of their literary excellence. The books of the New Testament were not written by literary craftsmen though they sometimes reached a high level of literary excellence. They must always stand high from a literary point of view because of the matchless simplicity and beauty of the Gospel narrative and because of the incredible fervor and deep poetic feeling of the Apostle Paul."

51.   Atkinson, David W. "The Literary Critic and the Religionist: The Common Ground of Experience." *Religious Studies and Theology* 9, #s 2 and 3 (May and September, 1989), 20-26.

The "religionist" and the literary critic have much in common: the former can learn much from the latter whenever he is prepared to abandon notions of being scientific and objective, and recognize that dialogue with the literary critic will help him learn how to make religious texts speak for themselves.

52.   Barr, James. "The Bible as Literature" in *The Bible in the Modern World.* New York (Harper and Row), 1973.

Various ways the Bible can be analyzed literarily, and the arguments for and against doing so. While such a method has distinct advantages, it is incomplete without a theological tie-in; yet it is not well-adapted to theological issues.

53.   Barr, James. "Reading the Bible as Literature." *BJRL* 56 (1973), 10-33.

Much of the objection to reading the Bible as literature lies in its being read solely that way. The method may serve as a bridge between religious and non-religious persons. Historical criticism has itself contributed to the decline of religious reading and to the decline in the authority of the Bible. Still, we must ask what the relationship is between recognizing the theological themes of the Bible and the beliefs of those who read it as the sacred text of their religion.

54.   Barry, Peter. "Exegesis and Literary Criticism." *Scripture Bulletin* 20 (1990), 28-33.

"... conflicts between the manifest and covert senses of texts can never be easily resolved, but some provisional conclusions can be drawn": e.g., that factors making for a plausible reading of a biblical passage are not always found in the text itself, and biased readings proliferate because there is no barrier to them. Biblical studies are taking to literary criticism to escape from two centuries of historical criticism.

55.   Barton, John. "Classifying Biblical Criticism." *JSOT* 29 (1984), 19-35.

Applies M.H. Abrams' four coordinates to biblical criticism in order to provide biblical critics with a map of various theories and methods important today. Canonical criticism represents a radical shift and thus belongs with literary criticism. Structural criticism is also a basic change in perspective. In any case, historical criticism should be ruled out, and various modern approaches substituted. Traditional secular and sacred critical methods tend to parallel each other.

56. Beentjes, Pancratius C. "Inverted Quotation in the Bible: A Neglected Stylistic Pattern." *Biblica* 63 (1982), 506-523.

Inverted quotation is a common but neglected feature of biblical style, of which a variety of examples can be found in both the OT and NT. It is not an "untidy" quotation, but is done quite deliberately. It must have functioned at least as an attention-getting device.

57. Berlin, Adele. "On the Bible as Literature." *Prooftexts* 2 (1982), 323-7.

Berlin (replying to James L. Kugel [see #98]: Kugel in *Prooftexts* 1 calls into question not only current literary criticism of the Bible, but "by implication all modes of biblical interpretation." He posits an artificial distinction between scripture and literature, and assumes, incorrectly, that literary criticism attempts to deny history. Kugel replies in this issue, pp. 328-332: Much modern literary criticism of the Bible is ingenious, but unfortunately tells us little about the Bible itself; it is often a modern invention.

58. Black, C. Clifton, II. "Rhetorical Criticism and Biblical Interpretation." *ET* 100 (1988-9), 252-8.

Reviews contributions of rhetorical criticism to biblical study in recent years, assessing its advantages and limitations. George Kennedy's definition of rhetorical criticism is the best one, although his assumptions about what we "know" about ancient generic theory, and about the universal applicability of rhetorical criticism, are questionable. Rhetorical criticism is valuable because it forces us to ponder the relationship of form and content.

59. Blank, G. Kim. "Deconstruction: Entering the Bible Through Babel." *Neotestamentica* 20 (1986), 61-7.

"The Bible is a problematical text.... There is nothing completely original in the Bible.... And like all texts it misuses, mistranslates, and misinterprets what other materials it has integrated.... [I]t is an especially difficult text [because] ... it is also an intertext with itself.... In other words, like all discourses it has fallen inwards under the weight of being writing."

60. Bloom, Harold. "Literature as the Bible." *New York Review of Books* 35, #5 (March 31, 1988), 23-5.

A true literary criticism of the Bible has proven very difficult to attain because of Christian bias and structuralist-feminist misreadings. This is shown by the history of the interpretation of such books as Genesis, John, and Revelation.

61. Boonstra, Harry. "Biblical Metaphor—More Than Decoration." *Christianity Today* 31, #6 (December 17, 1976), 22-3.

"God allowed the writers of Scripture to play seriously with language and make lively, at times even outlandish, comparisons. And part of our perception and learning comes from the indirection and suggestion of art. The songs, poetry, and metaphors of Scripture are a part of God's communicating his beauty and truth to us."

62. Brenner, Athalya. "Female Social Behavior: Two Descriptive Patterns within the 'Birth of the Hero' Paradigm." *VT* 36 (1986), 257-273.

The "birth of the hero" is a widely-known model in world folklore. It has two paradigms: two mothers who produce either one or two heroes; and one mother who produces either one or two heroes. The first paradigm is important in both HB and NT, as is shown by a number of passages from both. The different characterization of males and of females in these passages may have various explanations.

63. Brett, Mark G. "Four or Five Things to do with Texts: A Taxonomy of Interpretative Interests," in #35, pp. 357-377.

How "some competing approaches [to biblical interpretation] might learn to co-exist peacefully." There is no all-inclusive method, and therefore scholars using different ones should not see themselves as competing for the one truth, but as working independently and then comparing results in a spirit of openness. The basic methods are "emics," "etics," "synchronic," "diachronic," and "interests in the text as such" (especially literary discussions of plot, character, point of view, theme, style, etc).

64. Brown, Schuyler. "Biblical Philology, Linguistics and the Problem of Method." *HJ* 20 (1979), 295-8.

Philological and linguistic approaches to the Bible are in tension. The literary-critical approach is valuable, but that doesn't necessarily mean that historical criticism is out of date. "Certainly, any methodological monopoly is quite unjustified at the present time."

65. Brown, Schuyler. "Reader Response: Demythologizing the Text." *NTS* 34 (1988), 232-7.

Reader response is superior to older ways of reading the Bible because the reader is truly a reader, not a critic; i.e., he does not stand over against the text.

66. Cahill, P. Joseph. "Literary Criticism, Religious Literature, and Theology." *SR* 12 (1983), 51-62.

Literary criticism and theological discourse both emerge from religious literature, which is the "centre." Theology has proven incapable of dealing with the "growing acknowledgment that myth is a universal and necessary carrier of meaning in all cultures and at all times." Therefore, the best work is being done among those who make use of literary criticism.

67. Cary, Norman Reed. "Modern Biblical and Literary Criticism: An Overview of Trends and Portents." *Literature and Belief* 9 (1989), 30-46.

Biblical and literary criticism have moved along roughly parallel lines: historical, leading to denial of history, leading to a proliferation of approaches both historical and ahistorical. Biblical criticism, despite the growth of literary techniques, is still largely historical, since only a small minority of critics have tried structuralism or any other true literary-critical techniques. Biblical criticism is therefore more conservative than is literary criticism, and will not likely embrace deconstruction.

68. Coggins, Richard. "Keeping Up with Recent Studies: The Literary Approach to the Bible." *ET* 96 (1984-5), 9-14.

A number of recent books and articles on the literary approach show that it involves a shift away from historical interest. There are five key points of impact on biblical study: (a) seeing ourselves as others see us; (b) our tendency to avoid awkward questions; (c) the difficulty of knowing what the relationship is between historical and literary approaches; (d) lack of objective criteria in the method; and (e) the possibility that literary criticism is a barrier to belief.

69. Crossan, John Dominic. "Perspectives and Methods in Contemporary Biblical Criticism." *BR* 22 (1977), 39-49.

Biblical exegesis is in a state of revolutionary change. This change is best described as altering biblical studies from a single discipline to many (chiefly literary, anthropological, and sociological methods). Structuralist analysis is logically prior to historical analysis.

70. Crossan, John D. "Ruth Amid the Alien Corn: Perspectives and Methods in Contemporary Biblical Criticism," in Robert Polzin and Eugene Rothman, eds., *The Biblical Mosaic: Changing Perspectives* (Philadelphia: Fortress P; Chico: Scholars P, 1982), pp. 199-210.

The revolutionary change in biblical studies from one to many disciplines shows that the twin axes of the field are historical and structuralist. Although the latter is logically prior to the former, biblical studies must proceed along both axes at the same time.

71.   Crossan, John Dominic. "Stages in Imagination." *JAAR Thematic Studies* 48, #2: *The Archaeology of the Imagination* ed. Charles E. Winquist, pp. 49-62.

"Is it possible ... to have ethics or politics or theologies which are not simply new algebras engendered at the null point but which show the wounds of their origin in the syntactics, pragmatics, and semantics of their discourse?"

72.   Crossan, John Dominic. "Waking the Bible: Biblical Hermeneutic and Literary Imagination." *Interpretation* 32 (1978), 269-285.

The importance of a literary approach to the Bible, with a survey of many recent, important books and articles. Biblical studies must use literary criticism because language is the only metasemiotic system available to us.

73.   Crotty, R.B. "Changing Fashions in Biblical Interpretation." *ABR* 33 (1985), 15-30.

The rise of literary-critical approaches to the Bible has created two competing paradigms. It remains to be seen which paradigm will win out, or whether some compromise is possible.

74.   Culley, Robert C. "Some Comments on Structural Analysis and Biblical Studies." *VT* Supplement 22 (*Congress Volume Uppsala* 1971). Leiden (E.J. Brill, 1972), 129-142.

Biblical studies is obliged to come to terms with structuralism, though that word is not easily defined. The structuralism of Edmund Leach and Claude Lévi-Strauss is wanting in several respects, but it raises interesting questions about the life of texts in translation.

75.   Culpepper, R. Alan. "Commentary on Biblical Narratives: Changing Paradigms." *FFF* 5, #3 (September, 1989), 87-102.

The historical evolution of the "genre" of biblical commentary. The next generation of commentaries must "close the gap between narrative theory and commentary form," e.g., by emphasizing the unity of the text (a difficult thing), understanding the world of narrative (as distinct from that of the characters or the author), and alerting the reader to the text as a series of signals to the reader.

76. Dudek, Louis, et al. "The Bible as Fugue: Theme and Variations." *University of Toronto Quarterly* 52 (1982-3), 128-154.

There is a "cloud of awesome implication" in Northrop Frye's writing on the Bible, which leads to misunderstanding of his meaning. We can, however, penetrate the assumptions behind Frye's criticism. To follow him is to revise radically many aspects of orthodox Christianity. To make a mythopoeic thing out of the Bible is to "save it" from rationalism.

77. Dulles, Avery, S.J. "Symbol, Myth, and the Biblical Revelation." *Theological Studies* 27 (1966), 1-26.

The Bible employs a great variety of literary forms, but in "every book we find vivid and imaginative speech"; and vivid and majestic symbolism rather than a "collection of eternal and necessary truths." Myth is definable, valuable, expresses itself as imagery, and has continuing relevance for believers.

78. Edwards, Diane T. "From Garden to City: Closure in the Bible," in #48, pp. 102-117.

"Much of whatever unity we perceive in our reading of the Bible derives primarily from the arrangement of the texts, pronounced intertextual patterns of repetition, both verbal and thematic, and the sense of closure that these devices create." One of the main themes is that of the garden to which we can no longer return, and the city to which we are led forward.

79. Ellington, John. "Wit and Humor in Bible Translation." *BT* 42 (1991), 301-313.

"... the Bible is replete with examples of puns, irony, satire and a generally clever use of language" that must have caused original readers to laugh and at the same time to think seriously. Examples and definitions of devices and techniques; how to translate biblical humor.

80. Flanagan, James W. "Structuralism and Biblical Studies." *Horizons* 2 (1975), 245-6.

Argues the importance of this approach because "structure plays a major role in understanding the meaning intended by the biblical author." See also #108.

81. Fowler, Robert M. "Post-Modern Biblical Criticism." *PEGL* 8 (1988), 1-22.

There is an argument for applying reader response criticism to the Bible, though we ought to know its various hermeneutical branches.

The "one grand index of the postmodern [is] an increasing recognition that reading and interpretation is always interested, never disinterested; always significantly subjective ... always committed and therefore always political ... always historically bound...."

82. Fowler, Robert M. "Postmodern Biblical Criticism." *FFF* 5, #3, (1989), 3-30.
    Aichele, George, Jr. "On Postmodern Biblical Criticism and Exegesis." Pp. 31-5.
    Moore, Stephen D. "Postmodernism and Biblical Studies." Pp. 36-41.

    Debates among these three scholars about how postmodern biblical criticism should be defined, what it does or should include, and how it relates to traditional biblical criticism.

83. Frye, Northrop. "History and Myth in the Bible," in Angus Fletcher, ed., *The Literature of Fact: Selected Papers from the English Institute* (New York: Columbia UP, 1976), 1-19.

    "... the Bible demands a literary response from us.... No book could have had the Bible's literary influence without itself possessing a literary form, however many other things it may possess.... [A]s the mythical and metaphorical language spoken by literature is primary language, and the only means of reaching any spiritual reality beyond language, then ... works of literature themselves represent a practically untapped source of self-transforming power."

84. Fuchs, Esther. "Contemporary Biblical Literary Criticism: The Objective Phallacy," in #48, pp. 134-142.

    Patriarchal ideology informs not only the Bible itself, but modern literary criticism of it as well. It should instead be questioning this ideology. An emphasis on "receptivity" and "the reader's self-subjugation to the biblical text" are the reasons current literary criticism can do no better than the ancient writers did.

85. Geller, Stephen A. "Through Windows and Mirrors into the Bible: History, Literature and Language in the Study of Text," in *A Sense of Text: The Art of Language in the Study of Biblical Literature* (Winona Lake: *JQR* Supplement, 1982), pp. 3-40.

    We need a true literary criticism of the Bible, avoiding, however, the self-defeating practices of much modern literary criticism which separates reader from author and text. Historical and literary approaches should not be rivals.

86. Gill, Jerry H. "The Orphic Voice: Language, Reality, and Faith." *Encounter* 42 (1981), 235-245.

The relationship between speech and reality, and its bearing on "God-talk." Three issues are involved: poetic (metaphoric) speech; the fact that language creates reality; and the corollary that this language is therefore religious. Linguistic activity, and the self-conscious participation in it, is part of reality, and therefore of religious reality.

87. Gros Louis, Kenneth R.R. "Some Methodological Considerations," in #40, pp. 13-24.

There are various assumptions which literary critics make about a text, various questions which they ask. These assumptions and questions differ from those usually made and asked by theological critics. The literary approach can be illustrated by applying these assumptions and questions to Jesus' parables.

88. Hammond, Gerald. "The Bible and Literary Criticism." *Critical Quarterly* 25, #2 (Summer, 1983), 5-20.

Recent developments in literary criticism of the Bible, especially contributions by Northrop Frye, Robert Alter, James L. Kugel, Edmund Leach and Roland Barthes, are "part of a movement of impressive critical breadth...a shared concern with the nature and structure of narrative." #722 is a follow-up.

89. Hunter, J.H. "Deconstruction and Biblical Texts: Introduction and Critique." *Neotestamentica* 21 (1987), 125-140.

"Biblical scholars have to take serious[ly] the fact that their interpretation of the text does not start with something before the text ... but with a text in which the characters are part of textuality.... Meaning is thus not conveyed through the text from outside the text, but has to be discovered by considering their 'performance' in textuality." Deconstruction "probably means a rethinking ... of some of the most basic questions in the field of biblical studies...."

90. Jasper, David. "Hermeneutics, Literary Theory and the Bible," in *The Study of Literature and Religion: An Introduction* (Minneapolis: Fortress P, 1989), pp. 83-96.

The literary-theological implications of Milton's *Paradise Lost* and the theories of Ferdinand Saussure; modern reader-response criticism, structuralism, Paul Ricoeur and their hermeneutic results for reading the Bible. "But the privilege granted to the Biblical text must be hard-won, not least through a critical awareness of it as literary art and language. For the Bible, whether we like it or not, is art composed of that tricky stuff language...."

91.   Jobling, David. "Structuralism, Hermeneutics, and Exegesis: Three Recent Contributions to the Debate." *USQR* 34 (1978-9) 135-147.

Structuralism is the best available method of biblical interpretation. Reviews books by Edgar McKnight, Robert Detweiler, Daniel and Aline Patte (#s 1927, 3, and 1861). The next two tasks are to move into non-narrative parts of the Bible, and to tackle large pieces of it.

92.   Johnston, Robert. "How We Interpret the Bible: Biblical Interpretation and Literary Criticism," in *The Proceedings of the Conference on Biblical Interpretation* (Nashville: Broadman P, 1988), pp. 51-63.

Conflicting theories among evangelicals about how to read the Bible, as illuminated by M.H. Abrams' four approaches in *The Mirror and the Lamp.* "A 'principled eclecticism' can facilitate evangelical biblical interpretation today. Here is, perhaps, the primary lesson that literary criticism offers the evangelical reader of the Bible." Given the historical origins of the four methods, "interpreters should be leery of absolutizing their approaches."

93.   Johnston, Robert K. "Interpreting Scripture: Literary Criticism and Evangelical Hermeneutics." *CL* 32, #1 (Fall, 1982), 33-47.

Literary criticism can give to evangelical Christianity both an "historical analogue" and a "typological handle." It can help evangelicals sort out current debates about biblical interpretation. The literary theory of M.H. Abrams, its strengths and weaknesses; various evangelicals who fall into each of Abrams' four schools of criticism.

94.   Josipovici, Gabriel. "The Bible: Dialogue and Distance," in Michael Wadsworth, ed., *Ways of Reading the Bible* (Totowa: Barnes and Noble, 1981), pp. 133-153.

The ways in which the Bible invites and yet frustrates the reading/interpretive experience. It remains an "open" book despite our attempts to "close" the distance between us and God. An earlier version of part of #14. **

95.   Kessler, Martin. "An Introduction to Rhetorical Criticism of the Bible: Prolegomena." *Semitics* 7 (1980), 1-27.

Biblical critics must study literary criticism, while avoiding reliance on any single method. The basics of various schools and methods. The relationship of the New Criticism to earlier and later methods of both historical and literary criticism of the Bible.

96. Kessler, Martin. "A Methodological Setting for Rhetorical Criticism." *Semitics* 4 (1974), 22-36. Rpt #34, pp. 1-19.

The increasing interest in synchronic approaches to the Bible has forced significant modifications in form criticism, just as the increasing awareness of the role of language in creating meaning in all forms of writing is taking place. "In sum, rhetorical criticism deserves serious consideration as ... the leading ... synchronic criticism, particularly if ... [it includes] both classical rhetorical and the new rhetoric."

97. Kugel, James. "The 'Bible as Literature' in Late Antiquity and the Middle Ages." *HUSLA* 11 (1983), 20-70.

Far from ignoring the literary power and nature of scripture, theologians since antiquity were quite aware of the whole issue. Hellenistic allegorizing was the start of the literary-critical approach to the Bible. It is not true that secularization and modern critical distance were required before the literary aspect of the Bible could be noticed and appreciated.

98. Kugel, James L. "On the Bible and Literary Criticism." *Prooftexts* 1 (1981), 217-236.

A key problem with the Bible as literature is that in ignoring all but the final stage of the text, we ignore theological meanings, and we equate the Bible with modern novels. The "subterranean" purpose of such critics may be to remove the Bible as scripture. Present-day critics need greater awareness of the historical situation of what they practice. #57 replies.

99. Kunjummen, Raju D. "The Single Intent of Scripture—Critical Examination of a Theological Construct." *GTJ* 7 (1986), 81-110.

How the literary theories of E.D. Hirsch can aid evangelicals in interpreting scripture.

100. La Fargue, Michael. "Are Texts Determinate? Derrida, Barth, and the Role of the Biblical Scholar." *HTR* 81 (1988), 341-357.

Derrida teaches us to look not so much for the "meaning" of a text as for the "substantive content." Thus we should distinguish between items important in a reading competence of a biblical text, and evaluating the relevance of that text for today; we should use evidence appropriate to each task. Past restrictive models of rationality should not prevent us from rational inquiry.

101. Lasine, Stuart. "Indeterminacy and the Bible.: A Review of
      Literary and Anthropological Theories and Their Applica-
      tion to Biblical Texts." *HS* 27 (1986), 48-80.

      The common thread of recent literary-critical work on the Bible is
      "an interest in the meaning and function of indeterminacy in the
      Bible."

102. Leon-Dufour, Xavier, S.J. "Exegetes and Structuralists," in Al-
      fred M. Johnson, ed., *Structuralism and Biblical Hermeneutics*
      (Pittsburgh: Pickwick P, 1979), 91-107.

      The contributions of Roland Barthes to biblical interpretation.
      Why the critics of structuralism are wrong in their attacks.

103. Longman, Tremper, III. "Form Criticism, Recent Develop-
      ments in Genre Theory, and the Evangelical." *WTJ* 47
      (1985), 46-67

      The genre theory of Northrop Frye, E.D. Hirsch, Tsvetan Todorov,
      and others can help clarify the values and the limitations of form
      criticism. "There is no escape from genre analysis. The question ... is
      whether ... analysis will be conscious and methodical or unconscious.
      Whenever we read anything we make at least an unconscious genre
      identification which triggers a certain reading strategy in our mind."

104. Martin, James P. "Toward a Post-Critical Paradigm." *NTS* 33
      (1987), 370-385.

      The relationship between the dominant scientific paradigms and
      hermeneutical schemas current in biblical interpretation. Twentieth-
      century revolutions in physics, cosmology, theology, and biblical
      hermeneutics "together signify a basic shift from a Mechanical
      (critical) to a Holistic (post-critical) Paradigm."

105. McKnight, Edgar V. "The Contours and Methods of Literary
      Criticism," in Richard Spencer, ed., *Orientation by Disorienta-
      tion: Studies in Literary Criticism and Biblical Literary Criticism*
      (Pittsburgh: Pickwick P, 1980), pp. 53-69.

      A literary approach to the Bible grows logically out of the recent
      history of biblical criticism, while not demanding the abandonment
      of traditional historical criticism. Literary approaches "dissolve the
      distance between the ancient texts and the modern reader-critic,"
      and allow for integration and utilization of the historical-critical
      tradition.

106. Meyer, Ben F. "The Challenge of Text and Reader to the Historical-Critical Method," in Wim Beuken, et al., eds., *The Bible and its Readers* (*Concilium* 1991, #1), pp. 3-12.

As a result of positivism's loss of its dominant position since the 1950's, "the initiative in biblical scholarship [has] passed from theology to social scientific studies ... and to literary criticism." Literary criticism, especially reader response, challenges historical critics to "cut the last of their underground ties with positivism, ... [and] to attend intensely and consistently to the implied author or the voice of the text," and to the creativity of the open-ended text.

107. Miles, John A., Jr. "Radical Editing: *Redaktionsgeschichte* and the Aesthetic of Willed Confusion," in Baruch Halpern and Jon D. Levenson, eds., *Traditions in Transformation: Turning Points in Biblical Faith* (Winona Lake: Eisenbrauns, 1981), pp. 85-99.

The current state of historical, and especially redaction, criticism shows us that the "aesthetic of willed confusion" in modern literature provides the best model of how the Bible can and should be read in our day. Historical criticism has deconstructed the Bible, has not proved to be the science of sciences, and is not infallible. Critics are now freer to see the Bible in all of its sometimes contradictory and confusing state. Thus the literary sensibility may prove a helpful corrective to the historical.

108. Milne, Pamela and James W. Flanagan. "Dialogue on 'Structuralism and Biblical Studies.'" *Horizons* 3 (1976), 95-7.

Exchange between Milne and Flanagan concerning his editorial about structuralism and biblical studies in *Horizons* 2 [#80]. Milne: structuralism "does not attempt to reveal origins or originally intended meanings"; it looks not for any particular meaning but for how meaning is made possible. Flanagan: structuralists do in fact care what the text means.

109. Momigliano, Arnaldo. "Biblical Studies and Classical Studies." *Biblical Archaeologist* 45 (1982), 224-8.

Interpreting the Bible poses no problems that interpreting other ancient literature doesn't pose. Rhetoricians are wrong when they claim that ideological and rhetorical analysis shows there to be no way to distinguish between fiction and historiography in ancient literature.

110. Moore, Stephen D. "Narrative Commentaries on the Bible: Contexts, Roots, and Prospects." *FFF* 3, #3 (September, 1987), 29-62.

The phenomenon of the rise of narrative biblical commentaries, their use of various literary theories, and the difficulties they have experienced. There are three "primary bands on the spectrum" onto which these works fall: story, reader, and self-interrogative reading.

111. Moore, Stephen D. "The 'Post-'Age Stamp: Does it Stick? Biblical Studies and the Postmodern Debate." *JAAR* 57 (1989), 543-559.

"Postmodern" may be defined as "the renewal within critical discourse, through the agency of French poststructuralism, of the modernist revolution in the arts, exhausted and at an impasse by the 1960's...." This critical discourse is only now being "affected by the crisis of representation that marked the birth of modernist art and literature more than a century ago." European and American biblical scholarship are different; postmodernism is more an American concern, and much feminist biblical criticism is not postmodern at all.

112. Muilenberg, James. "Form Criticism and Beyond." *JBL* 88 (1969), 1-18. Rpt in #47, pp. 362-380.

Form criticism has made great contributions to biblical scholarship, but biblical critics must not neglect matters of literary structure and aesthetics, despite their fears that literary criticism is not systematic or scientific enough. We need what amounts to a rhetorical criticism of the Bible.

113. Nohrnberg, James. "On Literature and the Bible." *Centrum* 2, #2 (Fall, 1974), 5-43.

The Bible is a kind of literature, but not exactly a literary "work." It is a canon, and thus does not generate other works of its kind, as normal literature does. Literature is self-reflexive, whereas the Bible constantly refers us to something else. "... the Bible as literature ... may be a contradiction in terms. No doubt much that is useful can be done with this contradiction, once we turn it into a comparison."

114. Olsson, Birger. "A Decade of Text-Linguistic Analyses of Biblical Texts at Uppsala." *Studia Theologica* 39 (1985), 107-126.

Definition of the text-linguistic approach to biblical texts, based on M.H. Abrams' work. Several arguments for this approach, including that it is "a basic component of all exegesis.... [T]o handle the texts is as basic for our discipline as to handle words and sentences."

115. Ong, Walter J. "*Maranatha*: Death and Life in the Text of the Book." *JAAR* 45 (1977), 419-449. Rpt in *Interfaces of the Word* (Ithaca and London: Cornell UP, 1977).

Recent studies of textuality open new insights for study of the Bible. These theories show the status of a text to be a "monument" where "print is even more bound to death than writing is." Comparing the status of oral, written, and printed texts shows that the Bible has "an unusual relationship to textuality: it is not literature in the way other texts are. Fecundity of writing and print is achieved by passage through death."

116. Osborne, Grant. "Genre Criticism—*Sensus Literalis.*" *TJ* 4, #2 (Autumn, 1983), 1-27.

The concept of genre is crucial to biblical interpretation, but is nevertheless complex and elusive. A number of recent theories of genre in the Bible can help us, but do not clear up all the mysteries.

117. Parunak, H. Van Dyke. "Transitional Techniques in the Bible." *JBL* 102 (1983), 525-548.

Biblical texts use several transitional devices to join sections, having in common patterns of repetition and similarity. The kinds of repetition include morphological, lexical, syntactic, and rhetorical. The basic patterns may be called "keyword," "link," and "hinge." Passages illustrated are Genesis 11, Isaiah 53, Ezekiel (various), Psalm 19, Proverbs 3 and 9, John 5, Romans 8 and 14, I Corinthians 8, Hebrews 1 and 10, I John 2.

118. Payne, Michael. "Recent Studies in Biblical Literature." *Papers on Language and Literature* 23 (1987), 89-103. Paul L. Gaston. "Text and Textbook: The Bible as Literature." *Papers on Language and Literature* 23 (1987), 104-111.

Review of a number of new books in the field, including Northrop Frye (#5); Meir Sternberg (#320); Robert Alter (#s 303, 365); Frank Kermode (#1859); John Gabel and Charles Wheeler (#172). All of them are valuable in their own way, though the tendency of some to criticize each other is counterproductive. A different kind of tension—that between historical and literary critics—is likely to be more creative than destructive for future biblical scholarship.

119. Petersen, Norman R. "Literary Criticism in Biblical Studies," in Richard A. Spencer, ed., *Orientation by Disorientation: Studies in Literary Criticism and Biblical Literary Criticism* (Pittsburgh: Pickwick P, 1980), 25-50.

Form criticism and historical criticism of the Bible are a dead end, a "closed door." Another door was opened by Erich Auerbach and by literary criticism in general. What a literary criticism of the Bible should consist of. If this door is entered, biblical criticism will no longer be reductive, but restorative.

120. Petersen, Norman R. "On the Notion of Genre in Via's 'Parable and Example Story: A Literary-Structuralist Approach.'" *Semeia* 1 (1974), 134-181.

Via [#1693] misses the fact that genres are culturally shared media. He therefore needs a more comprehensive communication model, e.g. as could be supplied by Roman Jakobson. There are alternative structural models and suggestions to Via's which future biblical criticism could adopt.

121. Poland, Lynn. "The Bible and the Rhetorical Sublime," in #1517, pp. 29-47.

A "poetics of the sublime," which holds that the human word is discontinuous from divine rhetoric, is preferable to a "poetics of the beautiful," which holds that language, and therefore the superiority of unity over disunity, is justified and made possible by the Word. "It is language in its 'lawlessness,' in its failure to signify, that provides the occasion and the motivation to pass, experientially, through terror to assurance."

122. Polzin, Robert M. "Literary and Historical Criticism of the Bible: A Crisis in Scholarship," in Richard Spencer, ed., *Orientation by Disorientation: Studies in Literary Criticism and Biblical Literary Criticism* (Pittsburgh: Pickwick P, 1980), pp. 99-114.

The problem, or crisis, is the mistaken assumption that biblical critics should model themselves after science. Historical criticism is still valuable, even fundamental, but competent literary analysis of the Bible is necessary for even preliminary understanding; yet most biblical scholars lack even a small acquaintance with disciplined literary analysis.

123. Polzin, Robert. "Literary Unity in Old Testament Narrative." *Semeia* 15 (1979), 45-9.

A response to P.D. Miscall (#784), stressing the paradoxes of pure formalism. We can neither usurp the Bible's proclamation through criticism nor ideologically subjugate criticism to some institutionalized form of the biblical message.

124. Powell, Mark Alan. "The Bible and Modern Literary Criticism." *Summary of Proceedings: Annual Conference—American Theological Library Association* 43 (1989), 78-84.

Why literary criticism has become so popular among biblical critics. The major characteristics of literary criticism which differentiate it from historical criticism are that it emphasizes the finished form of the text, its unity, the text as end in itself, and readers more than authors.

125, 126. Poythress, Vern S. "Analyzing a Biblical Text: Some Important Linguistic Distinctions." "Analyzing a Biblical Text: What are We After?" *Scottish Journal of Theology* 32 (1979), 113-137, 319-331.

We need to distinguish among various types and levels of meaning to be gotten from a text. The difference between synchronic and diachronic analysis, and between "oral" and "graphic" and the relationship of speaker to audience in synchronic analysis; differences between "speaker" and "discourse" analysis. Types of analysis will differ, depending on the type of meaning we seek.

127. Poythress, Vern S. "Philosophical Roots of Phenomenological and Structuralist Literary Criticism." *WTJ* 41 (1978), 165-171.

The "hermeneutical crisis in biblical studies ... is promoting more hermeneutical self-consciousness in exegesis ... [particularly] phenomenological and structuralist ... principles." These methods are "empiricistic and mechanistic," and therefore reductive. Nevertheless, they often produce new and valuable insights, and therefore Christians can "learn [from them] while avoiding seduction."

128. Prickett, Stephen. "Towards a Rediscovery of the Bible: the Problem of the Still, Small Voice," in Michael Wadsworth, ed., *Ways of Reading the Bible* (Totowa: Barnes and Noble, 1981), pp. 105-117.

Their handling of I Kings 19 shows that modern translators are gripped by a "fundamental theological confusion" caused by their inability to recognize that the language of the Bible is often ambiguous, poetic, multilayered, and therefore cannot be naturalized. They lack, i.e., the ability at close reading which literary criticism teaches. An earlier version of chapter 1 of *Words and the Word* [#26].

129. Quinn, Arthur. "Rhetoric and the Integrity of Scripture." *Communio* 13 (1986), 326-341.

Rhetoric, a branch of literary criticism, restores respect for the received text, defending its integrity. How this approach works on various OT and NT texts, especially Judges 5.

130. Radzinowicz, Mary Ann. "How and Why the Literary Establishment Caught Up with the Bible: Instancing the Book of Job." *CL* 39, #1 (Autumn, 1989), 77-89.

"Literary criticism is insatiably hungry for analytical subjects. The interpretive community appropriates new texts ... when the themes, figures, or other literary features of the new texts can be approximated to the presuppositions of the criticism that reads them."

131. Reed, Walter L. "A Poetics of the Bible: Problems and Possibilities." *LT* 1 (1987), 154-166.

There are many benefits to be gained from a literary-critical approach to the Bible. However, there are also some potential problems: e.g., the biblical text is often impervious to the "probings of a poetics." Definition of the characteristic biblical "modes of utterance."

132. Ricoeur, Paul. "The Bible and the Imagination," in Hans D. Betz, ed., *The Bible as a Document of the University* (Chico: Scholars P, 1981), pp. 49-75.

Interpreting the Bible via the principle of intertextuality. Context is a concept of the imagination which sees the reader as participant in creating meaning. Several of Jesus' parables as examples.

133. Ricoeur, Paul. "Naming God." *USQR* 34 (1978-9), 215-227.

"It is the naming of God by the biblical texts that specifies the religious at the interior of the poetic." The levels of discourse involved in the word "God," and the extent to which naming God depends on the poetic word.

134. Rogerson, John. "Recent Literary-Structuralist Approaches to Biblical Interpretation." *The Churchman* 90 (1976), 165-177.

"Structuralist approaches may help us to understand some of our old methods more clearly," but an "irrational landslide" toward such approaches will be bad for biblical studies. The theories of Roland Barthes, Claude Lévi-Strauss, and Ferdinand Saussure. The advantages and disadvantages of the method for biblical interpretation.

135. Rossow, Francis C. "Dramatic Irony in the Bible—With a Difference." *Concordia Journal* 8 (1982), 48-52.

The Bible is not only the word of God, but great literature as well; as such, it needs to be approached with the tools of literary criticism. Dramatic irony occurs surprisingly often in the Bible, as witness, e.g., II Samuel 12, Psalm 88, Matthew 27, Luke 24, John 4 and 11, and Acts 28.

136. Ryken, Leland. "The Bible: God's Storybook." *Christianity Today* (October 5, 1979), 34-8.

To see the Bible as story is to see how it unites "imagination and reason, or mystery and fact.... Stories reveal some truths and experiences in a way that no other literary form does."

137. Ryken, Leland. "Literary Criticism of the Bible: Some Fallacies," in #39, pp. 24-40.

The field of the Bible as literature is plagued with several fallacies, the chief being that the Bible is not, and cannot be treated as, literature. These fallacies may be eliminated if instructors will assume textual unity rather than fragmentation; respond to the Bible with "a child's sense of awe"; realize the difference between literary criticism and traditional biblical scholarship; and, most importantly, leave questions of textual origins to the biblical scholars. (JM)

138. Ryken, Leland. "'With Many Such Parables': The Imagination as a Means of Grace." *B Sac* 147 (1990), 387-398.

We should not engage in a sacred-secular dichotomy in writing. Christians need to be versed in artistic values and forms because the imagination is one of the chief means to arrive at religious truth.

139. Ryken, Leland. "'Words of Delight': The Bible as Literature." *B Sac* 147 (1990), 3-15.

"Conservative biblical scholarship stands at something of a crossroads. In the larger world of biblical scholarship, literary methods are more prominent with every passing year. The methods of traditional literary criticism ... can significantly enrich the insights of evangelical scholars and preachers."

140. Schneidau, Herbert N. "Biblical Narrative and Modern Consciousness," in Frank McConnell, ed., *The Bible and the Narrative Tradition* (New York and Oxford: Oxford UP, 1986), pp. 132-150.

"The sheerest narrative is already an interpretation. In the Bible this is implicitly recognized, as is the consequence that *definitive interpretation* is a contradiction in terms.... The Deuteronomists reinterpret the old histories, the prophets and later Jesus reinterpret ethics and eschatology, and the Church reinterprets Jesus and the Old Testament, while the rabbis turn the narratives into a *logos*. But the process by which the Bible was started on its career of endless self-reinterpretation ... began before these well-known stages.... [A] revisionist dynamic inheres in the whole project, in accord with the uncapturability of Yahweh."

141. Schökel, Luis Alonso, S.J. "Hermeneutics in the Light of Language and Literature." *CBQ* 25 (1963), 371-386.

We can "formulate a coherent theory and efficacious methodology
... to interpret ... the literary reality" of the Bible by offering "a
broader and natural context for hermeneutical theory: namely, language and literature." Since sacred scripture is God's revelation in
language, we must know how language and literature operate to understand the Bible.

142. Schökel, L. Alonso. "Trends: Plurality of Methods, Priority of
     Issues," in J.A. Emerton, ed., *Congress Volume Jerusalem 1986*
     (Leiden: E.J. Brill, 1988), 285-292.

     The new literary and sociological trends in biblical scholarship,
     with examples of books employing narrative art (semiotic, Jamesian,
     and stylistic), and semantic approaches. The question of how much
     these trends "fully belong to biblical science" is a key one for the
     immediate future.

143. Schwartz, Regina. "Introduction," in #45, pp. 1-15.

     "... the Bible is now being subjected to the same theoretical ques-
     tions we ask of other texts. But ... doing just that signals a radical de-
     parture from business-as-usual in biblical studies, another genuine
     rupture in the history of interpreting the text." The application of
     the ideas of Barthes, Derrida, Lacan, feminist and Marxist criticism to
     the Bible will inevitably affect theological understanding of the Bible
     as well.

144. Segert, Stanislav. "Prague Structuralism in American Biblical
     Scholarship: Performance and Potential," in Carol L. Mey-
     ers and M. O'Connor, eds., *The Word of the Lord Shall Go
     Forth* (Winona Lake: Eisenbrauns, 1983), 697-708.

     How Prague structuralism entered and how it affected American
     scholarship generally; its virtues as contrasted with other schools,
     e.g., French structuralism. Its influence is not yet widespread, but
     there are various ways in which a "new and viable methodology" for
     biblical study can be constructed.

145. Shaffer, E.S. "The 'Great Code' Deciphered: Literary and Bib-
     lical Hermeneutics." *Comparative Criticism* 5 (1983), xi-xxiv.

     "... the interpretative community to which [Northrop] Frye ap-
     peals is the literary criticism of our own time.... The hermeneutical
     process in which the Great Code is grounded has been half con-
     cealed, yet only to render up a troubling vision of a structure no
     longer hospitable to its formerly indwelling communities."

146. Sheppard, Gerald T. "'Blessed Are Those Who Take Refuge in Him': Biblical Criticism and Deconstruction." *Religion in Intellectual Life* 5 (Winter, 1988), 57-66.

The "pragmatic, constructive implications" of deconstruction for biblical studies, using Psalm 2 as example. We must recognize that the decision to use any particular method on the Bible is rationally indefensible. Deconstruction shows us that biblical books are "arenas for interpretation," allowing us to see that our goal is not to control the text.

147. Sider, John W. "Nurturing Our Nurse: Literary Scholars and Biblical Exegesis." *CL* 32 (Fall, 1982), 15-21.

Consciously or not, Christians have always been indebted to secular literary theories in reading the Bible. The nineteenth century saw historical concerns bury literary ones in biblical study. We need a new dialogue between the two disciplines, though biblical scholars do not necessarily need a detailed knowledge of the latest developments in literary criticism.

148. Spencer, Aida Besancon. "An Apology for Stylistics in Biblical Studies." *JETS* 29 (1986), 419-427.

Stylistics provides us with more objective data with which to test our intuitions, in order to realize the potential of style to disclose meaning. How stylistics is defined; how it is done. It is appropriate for biblical studies because it aims at close, precise reading.

149. Spivey, Robert A. "Structuralism and Biblical Studies: The Uninvited Guest." *Interpretation* 28 (1974), 133-145.

Situating the text in its "set" or "system" is a helpful corrective to the historical exegete's exclusive search for "objectivity." Structuralism is a way of investigating "the human process by which we give meaning to phenomena." How a structuralist approaches biblical texts, e.g., Genesis 1 and 4, and Jesus versus John in the gospels. Structuralism has the advantage of avoiding the oppressive rigidity of much modern scholarship.

150. Sprinkle, Joe M. "Literary Approaches to the Old Testament: A Survey of Recent Scholarship." *JETS* 32 (1989), 299-310.

There is much of value in recent literary work on the Bible, though there are several aspects of it which evangelicals should be cautious about when they use it.

151. Steinmetz, David C. "The Superiority of Pre-Critical Exegesis." *TT* 37 (1980), 27-38.

"The medieval theory of levels of meaning in the biblical text, with all its undoubted defects, flourished because it is true, while the modern theory of a single meaning, with all its demonstrable virtues, is false. Until the historical-critical method becomes critical of its own theoretical foundations and develops a hermeneutical theory adequate to the ... text ..., it will remain restricted—as it deserves to be—to the guild and the academy, where the question of truth can endlessly be deferred."

152. Stock, Augustine, O.S.B. "The Limits of Historical-Critical Exegesis." *BTB* 13 (1983), 28-31.

Recent literary theory is forcing biblical scholars to re-examine their notions of text: e.g., the text is intelligible not because it corresponds to reality but because it respects certain internal structures. How semiotics, structuralist and post-structuralist theory can help biblical scholars solve the fragmentation caused by the historical-critical method.

153. Swanston, Hamish F.G. "Literary Categories and Biblical Imagery," in Paul Burns and John Cumming, eds., *The Bible Now: Essays on its Meaning and Use for Christians Today* (New York: Seabury P, 1981), 49-60.

The scientist Galileo understood that authorial intention in scripture "may be discerned only through and in literary forms and images that the author puts to use.... [Thus,] the range of forms and images in the scriptural writings is both an acknowledgment that the divine cannot be adequately expressed unless the literary devices of many peoples are brought into service, and an announcement that the order insinuated by such literatures is finally discoverable in Jesus."

154. Talmon, Shemaryahu. "The 'Comparative Method' in Biblical Interpretation—Principles and Problems." *Congress Volume Göttingen 1977. VT* Supplement 29. (Leiden: E.J. Brill, 1978), 320-356.

In assessing the method of comparing biblical with non-biblical material for solving sociological, historical, and literary exegetical problems, we can conclude that "the interpretation of biblical features ... with the help of inner biblical parallels should always precede the comparison with extra-biblical materials."

155. Tolbert, Mary Ann. "Protestant Feminists and the Bible: On the Horns of a Dilemma." *USQR* 43 (1989), 1-17; rpt Alice Bach, ed., *The Pleasure of Her Text: Feminist Readings of Biblical*

and Historical Texts (Philadelphia: Trinity Press International, 1990), 5-23.

The problems women readers have with an androcentric Bible, and various ways of overcoming these problems. We should recognize the relativity of all readings of biblical texts, and "retrieve the genuinely liberational ideology that gives to them their basic emotive power."

156. Vanhoozer, Kevin J. "A Lamp in the Labyrinth: The Hermeneutics of 'Aesthetic' Theology." *TJ* 8 (1986), 25-56.

The development of the "aesthetic turn" in twentieth-century history, theology and philosophy. Its most appropriate application is in the interpretation of literature. The various recent critical schools: new criticism, structuralism, post-structuralism have in common the use and interpretation of the Bible as an aesthetic object, "cut off from its original situation and from the authority of its author." Evangelicals should be concerned about its effect on their theology.

157. Vanhoozer, Kevin J. "The Semantics of Biblical Literature: Truth and Scripture's Diverse Literary Forms," in D.A. Carson and John Woodbridge, eds., *Hermeneutics, Authority, and Canon* (Grand Rapids: Zondervan, 1986), 53-104.

How literary forms in scripture affect the meaning and authority of the Bible. Instead of defending "propositional revelation," evangelicals should pay attention to certain important features of biblical literature. Devices, e.g., analogy, metaphor, symbol, and poetry "cannot be translated without risking cognitive loss into univocal and pseudo-scientific form."

158. Vogels, Walter. "Inspiration in a Linguistic Mode." *BTB* 15 (1985), 87-93.

How do new theories of semiotics and reader-response help us look at the notion of an inspired text in a new way? As a bridge between the producing and reading communities, inspiration is equally present in both. Thus it is continually being rewritten.

159. de Waard, Jan. "Biblical Metaphors and their Translation." *BT* 25 (1974), 107-116.

What we know about metaphor in ancient Greek and Hebrew culture. We need to be cautious about translating biblical metaphors too literally. We should if possible try to find an equivalent metaphor in the host language, rather than remove a figure altogether.

160. Walker, Steven C. "Deconstructing the Bible." *Literature and Belief* 9 (1989), 8-17.

Although "I am anything but a deconstructionist," this method of reading texts offers ways of getting at meaning which are not available to orthodox approaches. The Bible's paradox is its tendency to comment on, even to contradict itself. Multiple versions of the same event, dynamic characterization, "deliberate, persuasive ambiguity," all make deconstructive readings fruitful, even necessary.

161. Watson, Nigel. "Authorial Intention—Suspect Concept for Biblical Scholars?" *ABR* 35 (1987), 6-13.

New and post-new criticism help us understand that, while authorial intention cannot be accepted without qualification, it can be an important tool if used with appropriate caution.

162. Watson, Nigel. "Reception Theory and Biblical Exegesis." *ABR* 36 (1988), 45-56.

Reception theory is "a potentially valuable tool for the biblical scholar ... [because] it alerts us to the complexity of the process of communication ... as well as offering us a set of terms to help us unravel that complexity." For example, it clarifies intended versus subconscious meaning in texts, categories of author and reader, and how we distinguish empirical from theoretical authors and readers.

163. Wilder, Amos N. "The Rhetoric of Ancient and Modern Apocalyptic." *Interpretation* 25 (1971), 436-453. Rpt in #1669, pp. 153-168.

Since apocalyptic is an act of imagination and of language which breaks with the cultural patterns of its particular period, we should see its rhetoric "in terms that are more generic and fate-laden than those associated with more humanistic categories." The problem of the variety of levels, psychological and linguistic, through which the apocalyptic vision has been mediated. Its chief characteristics are: a sense of anomie or loss of a world; a rhetoric of panic and archetype; ecstatic disclosure; a sense of sheer immediacy; and numinous tension.

164. Wilder, Amos N. "Story and Story-World." *Interpretation* 37 (1983), 353-364.

We have a new respect for stories as stories, and a new awareness of their appeal for adults. The Bible and its authors and characters show many uses for stories. What makes a story "true."

Pedagogy and Preaching

165. Ackerman, James S., with Jane Strouder Hawley. *On Teaching the Bible as Literature. A Guide to Selected Biblical Narratives for Secondary Schools.* Bloomington (Indiana UP), 1967.

    "Old Testament background for the teacher." Brief literary analyses of seven HB narratives: Genesis (a number of chapters); Exodus 1-16, 19-21, 31-2; Joshua 6; Judges 13-16; I Samuel 17-18.

166. Ackerman, James S., et al. *Teaching the Old Testament in English Classes.* Bloomington (Indiana UP), 1973.

    Background information and plot summaries of key parts of Genesis, Exodus, Joshua, Judges, Samuel, Kings, Amos, Hosea, Isaiah, Micah, Jeremiah, Ezekiel, Ezra-Nehemiah, Ruth, Jonah, Esther, Daniel, Proverbs, Ecclesiastes, Job, Song Of Songs, Psalms. Questions for discussion which focus largely on literary-critical analysis of the books discussed.

167. Adar, Zvi. *Humanistic Values in the Bible.* New York (Reconstructionist P), 1967. Originally published in Hebrew in 1953.

    The standard approaches to teaching and studying the Bible in modern Israel are the "traditional religious," the "scientific," "the nationalistic," and the "socio-moralistic." Each has its values and its defects. On balance, we would be better off adopting a "humanistic-literary" approach. By eliminating the fallacies and limitations of the other approaches, the humanistic one combines the benefits inherent in each; sets before us a central and clear aim in teaching the Bible; and "restores the Book to its original status as a great, educative force."

168. Barr, David L. *New Testament Story: An Introduction.* Belmont (Wadsworth), 1987.

    A classroom introduction to the study of the NT, centered on rhetorical and literary approaches. The NT writings are "interacting stories, not ... discrete documents." The context of ancient Greco-Roman rhetoric, and the literary nature of each book (structure, narrative devices, etc.).

169. Barton, John. *Reading the Old Testament: Method in Biblical Study.* Philadelphia (Westminster P), 1984.

To introduce students of the OT to some critical methods and questions, and to "argue for certain convictions about the place of method in the general study of the Old Testament." Genre recognition; source, form, and redaction criticism, and how they work on Qohelet; canonical, structuralist, and New criticism. The search for one overall, perfect method is illusory, since all methods, while they have something to offer, are ultimately circular. **

170. Battenhouse, Roy, et al. [Forum on Teaching the Bible as Literature]. *CL* 31, #3 (Spring, 1982), 31-66.

Battenhouse, "The Tragedy of Absalom," pp. 53-7: How to teach a class that this story follows some of Aristotle's stipulations for tragedy; Hart, Dabney, "The Bible as Comparative Literature," pp. 31-6; Schwab, Gweneth B., "An Experimental Course, 'Jesus and the Quest," pp. 37-46; Longfellow, Allena, "Counterpoint: The Bible and Literature" pp. 47-52; Catlin, Janet Green, "Bugs in the Garden: Teaching 'The Bible as Literature' in Oklahoma," pp. 58-66.

*   Blackwell, John. *The Passion as Story: The Plot of Mark.* See #1848.

171. Boys, Mary C. and Thomas G. Groome. "Principles and Pedagogy in Biblical Study." *Religious Education* 77 (1982), 486-507.

New developments in biblical studies, including use of literary theory, and how they should affect how we teach the Bible. There are three main implications: we must acknowledge its ancientness; respect its literary character; and call on the specialists.

172. Gabel, John B., and Charles B. Wheeler. *The Bible as Literature: An Introduction.* 2nd edition. New York and Oxford (Oxford UP), 1990.

Initial chapters on the "literary forms and strategies in the Bible," the Bible and history, physical settings and canon formation; followed by chapters on broad groups of books: Pentateuch, prophets, wisdom literature, apocalyptic literature, apocrypha, gospels, letters, translation, and religious uses of the Bible. Both historical-critical and literary: much in it assumes the tenets of source, form, and redaction criticism.

173. Goitein, S.D. "Form and Spirit in Biblical Literature." *Judaism* 3 (1954), 68-75.

The values contained in the HB cannot be taught to students without attention to the literary forms in which they are expressed. We can get closer to deciding what a Hebrew poetics consisted of if we remember (a) that their prosody, even in the laws, was based on parallelism and stress patterns; (b) their traditionalism; (c) the necessity of reading aloud to get the full effect; (d) that there are no rigid forms in the HB; (e) that there are sociological reasons why the HB differs from other ancient literatures.

174. Gottcent, John H., et al. [Forum on Teaching the Bible as Literature]. *CL* 30, #1 (Fall, 1980), 80-102.

Articles by Gottcent, Leonard R.N. Ashley, and Nancy M. Tischler on how to remove students' fears; what students can learn from such a course; how to appeal to the non-humanities student at a state school.

175. Gottwald, Norman K. *The Hebrew Bible: A Socio-Literary Introduction.* Philadelphia (Fortress P), 1985.

The "profound shift and enrichment" in biblical studies introduced by new literary and social-scientific approaches with the older critical methods. Relevant chapters include 5 and 6; 20 (Moses); 23 (Joshua-Judges) 29 (Samuel, I Kings); 34, 37, 50 (the prophets); 52 (biblical poetry: Psalms, Lamentations, Song Of Songs); 53 (short stories: Ruth, Jonah, Esther); 54 (wisdom: Proverbs, Job, Ecclesiastes); 55 (apocalyptic: Daniel). **

* Gros Louis, Kenneth R.R. "Revelation." See #2238.

176. Hilkert, M.C. "Retelling the Gospel Story: Preaching and Narrative." *ETh* 21 (1990), 147-167.

Luke 24:13-35 seen from the standpoint of Ricoeur's theory of narrative is a process of threefold mimesis and extended metaphor. Narrative as extended metaphor has the power to effect conversion. The preacher as narrator; the hearer's sense of an ending in narrative and in liturgy; divine versus human narrators.

* Juel, Donald, with James S. Ackerman and Thayer S. Warshaw. *An Introduction to New Testament Literature.* See #1495.

177. Long, Thomas G. *Preaching and the Literary Forms of the Bible.* Philadelphia (Fortress P), 1989.

"... the literary form of a biblical text is hermeneutically important and should exert an influence in the production of a sermon." How to know what to expect from form in writing; how to "interrogate" a biblical text to discover genre; rhetorical function; literary devices;

how the sermon and the text interact; answers to objections about reading historical texts from a literary point of view. Application of the theory to preaching on Psalms, Proverbs, narratives, parables of Jesus, NT letters.

178. Ohlsen, Woodrow. *Perspectives on Old Testament Literature.* New York (Harcourt Brace Jovanovich), 1978.

Each section on a book of the Bible contains plot summary; several essays on the literary qualities and related interpretative issues; suggested readings; questions for discussion and writing. Books covered: Genesis, Exodus, Deuteronomy, Joshua, Judges, Samuel, II Kings, Amos, Isaiah, verse and poetry, Song Of Songs, Psalms, Proverbs, Job, Ecclesiastes, Esther, Ruth, Jonah.

179. Olshen, Barry N., and Yael S. Feldman, eds., *Approaches to Teaching the Hebrew Bible as Literature in Translation.* New York (Modern Language Association), 1989.

Various translations of the HB, recommended commentaries, reference works, literary criticism and aids to teaching. Four essays defining the field of study; eight essays exploring "pedagogical and theoretical perspectives" on the HB as a whole; eight essays on individual genres and texts: genealogies, Genesis 6-9, Exodus 32, prophetic books, Psalm 23, Job, Ruth, Song Of Songs. This last group of essays analyzed separately as #s 539, 563, 653, 682, 1141, 1249, 1325, and 1348 respectively.

180. Prince, Gilbert. "The Bible as Literature: Dealing with Presumptions." *The Council of Societies for the Study of Religion Bulletin* 19, #2 (April, 1990), 33, 35, 37.

Various problems which arise in teaching the Bible as literature, and how they can be solved by the teacher.

181. Ralph, Margaret Nutting. *"And God Said What?" An Introduction to Biblical Literary Forms for Bible Lovers.* New York and Mahwah (Paulist P), 1986.

The importance of knowing the literary forms in the Bible for grasping what it is and what it is not. Major forms are myth, legend, fiction, gospel, parable, allegory, letters, revelation.

182. Robinson, Bernard P. *Israel's Mysterious God: An Analysis of Some Old Testament Narratives.* Newcastle upon Tyne (Grevatt and Grevatt), 1986.

Generally literary-critical surveys of Genesis 37-50, I Samuel 8–I Samuel 2 (Saul), I Kings 17–II Kings 2 (Elijah), Job, Ecclesiastes, and

Jonah. Literary and theological "questions for discussion" at the end of each chapter.

183. Ryken, Leland. "'And it Came to Pass': The Bible as God's Storybook." *B Sac* 147 (1990), 131-142.

Those who teach and preach the Bible should pay more attention to its narrative dimension, since its widespread appeal is based on its combination (typical for all narrative) of the factual and the marvellous.

184. Ryken, Leland. *How to Read the Bible as Literature*. Grand Rapids (Zondervan), 1984.

The Bible "demands a literary approach because its writing is literary in nature ... [and] because it is through [literary devices] ... that the Bible communicates its message." Biblical narrative, poetry, proverb; the narrative world of the gospels; epistolary genre, satire, visionary literature; the various plot and character archetypes which create a unity.

185. Ryken, Leland. "'I Have Used Similitudes': The Poetry of the Bible." *B Sac* 147 (1990), 259-269.

The "dynamics of biblical poetry" and their implications for teaching and preaching. Too much biblical instruction is like Paul's (abstract), and not enough like Jesus' (concrete, poetic, anecdotal). Instead of the traditional three-part topical sermon, we should have the three-part strategy: interact with the text on literary terms, state the themes that emerge, apply the themes.

186. Ryken, Leland. *The Literature of the Bible*. Grand Rapids (Zondervan), 1974.

Types of biblical writing using major categories and theories of literary criticism as models. Genesis; I Samuel 17–II Samuel 16; Judges 6-8; Daniel 1-6; Ruth; Esther; Exodus; Numbers; Deuteronomy; Job; Psalms; Song Of Songs; Proverbs; Ecclesiastes; Jonah; Amos; Revelation, together with the genres (tragedy, pastoral, satire, lyric, epic, etc.) to which they belong. See #27.

187. Thompson, Leonard L. *Introducing Biblical Literature: A More Fantastic Country*. Englewood Cliffs (Prentice-Hall), 1978.

A guide to "the structure of biblical symbolism," focusing "almost entirely upon the language of the Bible and the fantastic world created through that language." General chapters on "the recurring patterns of relationships among stories, sayings, and songs in the Bible"; "time space, and movement" in the OT (especially historical books and Psalms); legal, proverbial, prophetic and apocalyptic sayings; the NT. **

188. Trawick, Buckner B. *The Bible as Literature: The New Testament.* 2nd edition. New York (Barnes and Noble), 1968.

Surveys each of the gospels, Pauline letters, Hebrews, the pastoral letters, and Revelation, summarizing purpose and plot or outline of each, themes, and style.

189. Trawick, Buckner B. *The Bible as Literature: The Old Testament and the Apocrypha.* 2nd edition. New York (Barnes and Noble), 1970.

Historical and geographical background. Surveys of prophetic literature, lyric poetry, "dramatic literature," "short stories and tales," wisdom literature, apocalyptic. Plot summaries of each individual OT book, brief comments on character, style, authorship, and sources.

190. Vogels, Walter. *Reading and Preaching the Bible: A New Semiotic Approach.* Wilmington (Michael Glazier), 1986.

A synchronic, semiotic method can fill in the gaps left by the historical-critical method for both readers and preachers of the Bible. How semiotic analysis works, with application in several "practical exercises" to Job, Genesis 2, 13, Luke 7, 19. "The real aim of the analysis is that the reader should come to respect the text and discover its richness."

191. Warshaw, Thayer S. "The Bible as Textbook in Public Schools." *Religious Education* 77 (1982), 279-299.

Brief review of current legal cases. Twelve propositions about "the interplay among public education, religion, and moral education." Suggestions about the use of the Bible "as," "in," and "and" literature in literature classes. The Bible should be taught in humanities and social science classes, but never as a substitute for science.

192. Warshaw, Thayer S. *Handbook for Teaching the Bible in Literature Classes.* Nashville (Abingdon P), 1978.

The importance of how one approaches a text with the potential for controversy. How to translate works of literary scholars on the Bible into classroom materials. Teaching aids, quiz questions throughout. Secondary school level.

193. Warshaw, Thayer S. "Some Pedagogical Considerations," in #40, pp. 25-34.

The differences between approaching the Bible as a religious document and as literature. Religious commitment need not interfere with literary analysis of the Bible. Pedagogy, however, is more complicated, because students approach the Bible with denominational or "semi-secular" prejudices about other groups, and because the Bible will always be read for more than artistic craftsmanship. Teachers "have a moral obligation to open the minds and spirits of their students and to foster our society's nobler commitment to a harmonious pluralism."

194. Wheeler, Charles B. "'But Where Did Cain Get His Wife?' Reflections on Teaching the Bible as Literature." *South Atlantic Quarterly* 80 (1981), 49-60.

Teaching the Bible as literature is fully justified on its own grounds. "Surely this most influential book of all, ... deserves a full and impartial critical study." How to deal with devout conservatives who don't like this approach, as well as with skeptics and those in between. An advantage is that students will be freed from the burden of uncritical worship of the Bible, and will thus get back to OT thinking. If critics, e.g., Northrop Frye, sometimes want a putative mythic unity in the Bible, we can forgive students who want a religious one.

See also: #s 1054, 1848, 1899.

THE HEBREW BIBLE

Authored Books

*   James S. Ackerman, et al. *Teaching the Old Testament in English Classes.* See #166.

195.   Armerding, Carl E. *The Old Testament and Criticism.* Grand Rapids (Eerdmans), 1983.

     Evangelical scholars can and should use modern methods of biblical criticism, including literary and related structuralist approaches. How structuralist analysis of biblical texts works.

196.   Aschkenasy, Nehama. *Eve's Journey: Feminine Images in Hebraic Literary Tradition.* Philadelphia (U of Pennsylvania P), 1986.

     Various aspects of patriarchal traditions in both the Bible and modern Jewish literature, and the diverse images of the Jewish woman in these works. Wishes to "follow an archetypal or prototypical feminine figure as it travels through generations and cultures." The "otherness" of the female characters, just as the Jew is the "other" in a gentile world. Sections on "Evil, Sex, and the Demonic"; "Woman as Mother"; "Woman and Oppression"; "Female Strategy" (i.e., tricks, anger, dissociation, retreat into the feminine).

*   Barton, John. *Reading the Old Testament: Method in Biblical Study.* See #169.

197.   Bigger, Stephen. *Creating the Old Testament. The Emergence of the Hebrew Bible.* Oxford, England and Cambridge, Mass. (Basil Blackwell), 1990.

45

We need to listen afresh to the words of the HB, freed from the selective reinterpretations of Christianity which have often "obscured ... some of the intrinsic value of the Hebrew books." We should "strike a balance between literary and historical methods, in the belief that each is essential to ... develop our understanding and appreciation of ... the Hebrew Bible."

198.   Bloom, Harold. *Ruin the Sacred Truths: Poetry and Belief from the Bible to the Present.* Cambridge, Mass. (Harvard UP), 1989.

Chapter 1, "The Hebrew Bible," attempts to explicate the Yahwist's vision of God in Genesis and elsewhere in the HB, distinguishing it from that of the Elohist, the Priestly writer, the Deuteronomist, and the prophets. This vision is so radical that, were we to absorb it, it would create "a spiritual and cognitive crisis throughout our culture, even among the most secular." Authors in the HB who resemble Genesis J in their criticism of Yahweh are Jeremiah, Job, and Jonah.

199.   Boman, Thorleif. *Hebrew Thought Compared with Greek.* Philadelphia (Westminster P), 1960.

These two may be compared with regard to type of thinking (dynamic versus static); impression and appearance (sense of the beautiful, lyric expression, imagery); concepts of time and space; symbolism and instrumentalism; logical and psychological understanding.

200.   Bruns, Gerald L. *Inventions: Writing, Textuality, and Understanding in Literary History.* New Haven and London (Yale UP), 1982.

"Secrecy and Understanding": the attitudes of the ancients toward texts, and how they may differ from modern attitudes: an emphasis on the "secrecy" of writing; acceptance of the idea of "correcting" a text in rabbinic commentary (while not altering its letters); the Torah as a combination of textual and oral traditions; the scriptures as not fully interpretable or translatable. All of these contrast with modern understanding of scripture with its categorical rejection of secrecy. **

201.   Caird, G.B. *The Language and Imagery of the Bible.* Philadelphia (Westminster P), 1980.

An approach to the Bible through semantics, "to set out systematically for the ordinary reader the questions he needs to ask if he is to enhance his understanding of the Bible...." How language means in the HB; how it is used and abused; how and why it may be vague or ambiguous. The Hebrew idiom and thought-patterns;

their sense of figurative and comparative language; Hebrew language of history, myth, and eschatology.

202.   Casanowicz, Immanuel M. *Paronomasia in the Old Testament.* Boston (Norwood P), 1894.

Paronomasia may be defined as any figure based on similarity of sound. Thus it includes, for the OT, alliteration, rhyme, puns, word-play in general, and assonance. Lists over five hundred examples. Paronomasia is "an element of higher style, that is, of poetical and prophetical diction." It occurs only occasionally in the historical books, but very frequently in the poetic books. It reaches its height in the prophetic books, where it "is meant to reflect the inner excitement and impress the hearer with the certainty and magnitude of an event...."

203.   Chase, Mary Ellen. *Life and Language in the Old Testament.* New York (Norton), 1955.

The "distinctive and peculiar habits of thought which marked the ancient Hebrews as a people...." Their conceptions of history and time, their sense of place, and qualities of mind. Greek and Hebrew narratives compared in style, length, subject matter, and imaginative ideas. The distinct periods of language and style of the OT.

204.   Chotzner, J. *Hebrew Humour and Other Essays.* London (Luzac and Company), 1905.

The use of satire, sarcasm, and puns is widespread in various books of the HB. The HB is the equal of ancient Greco-Roman writing in literary and aesthetic quality. This is especially true of its lyric poetry.

205.   Chotzner, Rev. Dr. [J]. *Humour and Irony of the Hebrew Bible.* Harrow (J.C. Wilbee), 1883.

The charm of the style and diction of the HB includes its variety of humor, irony, sarcasm, etc. The greatest humorist in the HB is Ecclesiastes. There is excellent satire in Isaiah, Jeremiah, several of the minor prophets, and even in many of the sayings of Moses.

206.   Clines, David J.A. *What Does Eve Do To Help? and Other Readerly Questions to the Old Testament.* Sheffield (JSOT P), 1990.

Genesis 1-3 is irredeemably androcentric, yet still can be a force for inspiration for feminist readers. The famous predictions in Genesis not only do not come true, but illustrate the general failure of prediction from Genesis to II Kings. We should recognize a "primary history" in Genesis-II Kings, and a "secondary history" from I Chronicles on—both distinct and unified literary compositions. The effects of deconstruction on our understanding of Job; the implications of seeing Nehemiah from a literary perspective as an autobiographical memoir.

207.   Coggins, Richard J. *Introducing the Old Testament.* Oxford (Oxford UP), 1990.

How a range of scholarly disciplines, including literary criticism and many of the social sciences, can shed light on the OT. The limitations of each discipline when applied to the OT. All of these disciplines share a dissatisfaction with the historical-critical method of traditional biblical criticism.

208.   Fishbane, Michael. *Text and Texture: Close Readings of Selected Biblical Texts.* New York (Schocken Books), 1979.

Stylistic-structural studies of HB passages, emphasizing intertextuality and the theological significance arising from these literary considerations. "Narratives and Narrative Cycles": Genesis 1-11, 25-35; Exodus 1-4; "Speeches and Prayers": Deuteronomy 6; Jeremiah 20; Psalms 19, 122. "Motifs and Other Textual Transformations": the "Eden" and "Exodus" motifs.

209.   Good, Edwin M. *Irony in the Old Testament.* 2nd edition. Sheffield (Almond P), 1981.

How we may identify irony in writing generally, and specifically in the OT. The extent and function of irony in Jonah, I Samuel, Genesis, Isaiah, Qohelet, Job. **

210.   Handelman, Susan A. *The Slayers of Moses: The Emergence of Rabbinic Interpretation in Modern Literary Theory.* Albany (State University of New York P), 1982.

"In the West, those thinkers who have meditated on the problems of the text have always done so within the context of the Biblical tradition, or in reaction to it." Recent theorists within the Jewish tradition who have challenged the "Greco-Christian" strain of interpretation include Harold Bloom, Jacques Derrida, Jacques Lacan, and Sigmund Freud. Rabbinic emphasis on the "divinity and endless interpretability" of the Text, versus the Greco-Christian emphasis on the specific meaning of the Word. The different ways in which ancient Greek and HB texts convey meaning, and the nature of Paul's allegorical interpretation of the HB. **

211.   Humphreys, W. Lee. *The Tragic Vision and the Hebrew Tradition.* Philadelphia (Fortress P), 1985.

The nature of the tragic vision, and its appearance in the *Gilgamesh Epic*, I Samuel 9-31, Judges 13-16, Genesis 2-4, 22, II Samuel 24, Jeremiah, Job, and Ecclesiastes. Sometimes the tragic vision is present only potentially, sometimes fully developed, sometimes affirmed but then transcended. "The Hebraic tradition did not produce tragedy in any sustained way.... But at their best, expressions of that tradition had behind them intimations of the tragic."

212. Jacobson, Dan. *The Story of the Stories: The Chosen People and its God*. New York (Harper and Row), 1982.

The "'real' yet wholly figurative actions, the ever-trembling, self-energizing *instability* of the relationship between the literal and the metaphysical in the Scriptures," especially the prophets. The overall "plot" of the HB, its appearance especially in poetic language, and the definition of poetic parallelism.

213. Joines, Karen Randolph. *Serpent Symbolism in the Old Testament*. Haddonfield (Haddonfield House), 1974.

Mostly historical-critical, but chapter 2, "The Serpent in Genesis 3," discusses the serpent as symbol of wisdom, of chaos, and of life.

214. Laffey, Alice L. *An Introduction to the Old Testament: A Feminist Perspective*. Philadelphia (Fortress P), 1988.

The entire OT by sections, concentrating on a number of excerpts analyzed from a feminist-literary perspective. How feminism might approach key themes found in each section.

215. MacDonald, Duncan Black. *The Hebrew Literary Genius, An Interpretation. Being an Introduction to the Reading of the Old Testament*. Princeton (Princeton UP), 1933.

The history of literary approaches to the OT from Robert Lowth, Johann Gottfried Herder, and the Romantics down to modern times. The nature of Hebrew poetry and its world view. The David stories; folk poetry; the prophets; the nature and types of Hebrew narratives. Wisdom literature, especially Proverbs and Ecclesiastes. The desirability of moving away from archaeological and historical factors in the OT, and toward literary ones.

216. Niditch, Susan. *The Symbolic Vision in Biblical Tradition*. Chico (Scholars P), 1983.

We need both diachronic and synchronic approaches, since the form of the symbolic vision seems to develop from Amos and Jeremiah to Zechariah to Daniel. Yet all these books are participants in a formal tradition whose stages flow into one another. These stages may be analyzed in detail in terms of content, form, and structure. The basic form adapts to meet changing thematic needs, evolving in a narrative direction.

217.   Patrick, Dale. *The Rendering of God in the Old Testament.* Philadelphia (Fortress P), 1981.

We need "to develop a theory of literary character applicable to the biblical depiction of God." Concepts of dramatic action form the basis of this theory. Biblical literature is a mimetic art, just as other literatures are. "... the biblical God is rendered as a character and his acts are represented as part of a dramatic setting which enlists the reader's participation." This fact has theological consequences.

218.   Patrick, Dale, and Allen Scult. *Rhetoric and Biblical Interpretation.* Sheffield (Almond P), 1990.

"... how the critic can encounter the text as a living discourse by investigating its rhetorical power to address audiences through the ages." How rhetorical criticism deals with genre; the persuasive purpose of biblical texts; the rhetorical purposes of the historical books of the OT. Job rhetorically analyzed as an example, also Genesis 1-3. The OT as a whole "was shaped to be read as one communication of God."

219.   Robertson, David. *The Old Testament and the Literary Critic.* Philadelphia (Fortress P), 1977.

How the literary approach can be justified and explained. There are many parallels between Exodus 1-15 and Euripedes' *The Bacchae* in plot and characterization. Literary analysis of Job [originally appeared as #1241]; a comparison of Psalm 90 and Shelley's "Hymn"; the prophets as poets.

220.   Sandmel, Samuel. *The Enjoyment of Scripture: The Law, The Prophets, and The Writings.* New York (Oxford UP), 1972.

A "purely literary appraisal" of the HB, but not an uncritical one, since some passages are abhorrent, or at best pedestrian, even if the majority of the HB is worthy of the high admiration it enjoys as literature. We need to learn how to deepen our comprehension of, and our emotional response to, scripture; historical criticism cannot help us with this task.

*   Trawick, Buckner B. *The Bible as Literature: The Old Testament and the Apocrypha.* See #189.

221.   Trible, Phyllis. *God and the Rhetoric of Sexuality.* Philadelphia (Fortress P), 1978.

Close attention to the patterns of figurative language in the HB demonstrates that our habit of reading scripture as showing that male dominance is endorsed by God is simplistic and misleading. The imagery for God in Genesis 1-4, Song Of Songs, and Ruth is as much female as male; these authors celebrate the equality and mutual interdependence of the sexes, despite the patriarchal character of much of scripture. To recognize these patterns is to understand God in new ways.

222.   Wakeman, Mary K. *God's Battle with the Monster: A Study in Biblical Imagery.* Leiden (E.J. Brill), 1973.

The HB's anti-mythological attitude is not just a polemic in Genesis 1, but a bible-wide response to "the language of Canaan." Summary of Near Eastern myths relating to battle; the battle myth in the HB compared to Ugaritic material. All "passages in which words possibly connoting 'monster' ... are found in the Old Testament ... their attributes and actions," whether having "mythological significance" or being "poetic hypostatizations."

223.   Weiss, Meir. *The Bible From Within: The Method of Total Interpretation.* Jerusalem (Magnes P); Winona Lake (Eisenbrauns), with subtitle: *The Literary Critical Foundations of Interpretation,* 1984.

"Total interpretation" defined as reading "what is written in the text, all that is written there, and only what is written there." The history of literary criticism and its influence on biblical studies. Examples from Isaiah 1, 6, 7; Jeremiah 2, 7, 25; Ezekiel 16; Amos 1, 7, 8; Joel 4; Hosea 8; Psalms 1, 8, 13, 46, 51, 73, 74, 104, 114, 116, 120; Job 4. Addendum by Yair Zakovitch on I Kings 21.

*   Westermann, Claus. *The Parables of Jesus in the Light of the Old Testament.* See #1668.

Edited Collections

224.   Anderson, Bernhard, ed. *The Books of the Bible I: The Old Testament/The Hebrew Bible.* New York (Scribners), 1989.

Essays on each book or small groups of books by a variety of different scholars, with considerable emphasis on literary-critical matters in each.

225.   Bal, Mieke, ed. *Anti-Covenant: Counter-Reading Women's Lives in the Hebrew Bible.* Sheffield (Almond P), 1989.

Introduction relating narrative theory to women's lives in the HB. Essays in three sections: two on Genesis 12-25; four on Judges 4; five on Judges 11 (also II Samuel 13, Genesis 19, 38), analyzed separately as #s 557, 743, and 747, respectively.

226.   Collins, Adela Yarbro, ed. *Feminist Perspectives on Biblical Scholarship.* Chico (Scholars P), 1985.

Relevant essays are: T. Drorah Setel, "Feminist Insights and the Question of Method"; Carolyn Osiek, "The Feminist and the Bible: Hermeneutical Alternatives"; Esther Fuchs, "Who is Hiding the Truth? Deceptive Women and Biblical Androcentrism"; and, analyzed separately, essays on the Jacob cycle (#614), and on "mothers and sexual politics," (#338).

227.   Deist, Ferdinand, and Willem Vorster, eds. *Words from Afar: The Literature of the Old Testament, Volume I.* Cape Town (Tafelberg), 1986.

A "text-theoretical" survey of the OT by six authors. Examination of the OT as both canon (in terms of writer or sender) and reading (in terms of reception-history) are necessary if we are to grasp the OT as a whole. Texts by groups: poetry, narrative, wisdom, prophecy, apocalypse, and law—each discussed in terms relevant to its history, e.g., character and plot, text and audience codes, language, form, communication contexts.

228.   Exum, J. Cheryl, ed. *Semeia 32: Tragedy and Comedy in the Bible.* 1985.

Four essays, analyzed separately, on "Isaac, Samson, and Saul" (#559); "Apocalypse as Comedy" (#1457); Hosea (#988); the latter prophets (#886); with responses by four other scholars not matched essay by essay.

229.   Exum, J. Cheryl, and Johanna W.H. Bos, eds. *Semeia 42: Reasoning with the Foxes: Female Wit in a World of Male Power.* 1988.

Essays using "various literary, folkloristic, sociological or anthropological approaches" to biblical texts. Relevant essays, analyzed separately, on Proverbs (#1293); Genesis 38, Judges 4, Ruth 3 (#608); Genesis 31 (#590); and on ancient Near Eastern myth (#337).

230.   Niditch, Susan, ed. *Text and Tradition: The Hebrew Bible and Folklore.* Atlanta (Scholars P), 1990.

Twenty one "responses" and "reflections" exploring connections between biblical and non-biblical traditional literatures by scholars in folklore, anthropology, comparative literature, biblical and Near Eastern studies. Relevance of folklore for study of the HB; definition of folklore; difficulty of judging between aesthetic and other characteristivs of the HB, and of defining the poetics of written versus that of oral literatures. Relevant essays are analyzed separately as #s 273, 278, 526, 668, 713, 754, 758, and 1318.

*   Ohlsen, Woodrow. *Perspectives on Old Testament Literature.* See #178.

*   Olshen, Barry N., and Yael S. Feldman, eds. *Approaches to Teaching the Hebrew Bible as Literature in Translation.* See #179.

231.   Radday, Yehuda T., and Athalya Brenner, eds. *On Humour and the Comic in the Hebrew Bible.* Sheffield (Almond P), 1990.

On humor in general in the HB; application; why we miss the humor when we read; semantic field of humor; humor in names; as a tool for exegesis. Other essays analyzed separately as #s 559, 684, 940, 1047, 1253, 1347, 1403, 1441.

Articles

232.   Alter, Robert. "Introduction to the Old Testament," in #33, pp. 11-35.

Problems of terminology (OT versus HB); the integral nature of the OT despite its "anthological diversity"; function of etiological tales; nature of narrative; defense of literary-critical methodologies against older historical-critical ones; continuity of Hebrew literary forms over a millenium of writing and compilation.

233.   Amit, Yairah. "The Dual Causality Principle and its Effects on Biblical Literature." *VT* 37 (1987), 385-400.

Applying modern literary criticism to the HB makes us ask why the biblical narrators preferred realism. The answer may lie in "dual causality": God causes history, but so do humans. This forces narrators to "secularize" history—as seen in plots, characterization, and time treatment. These stories "are distinctive in their poetics and they assume a prominent part in the struggle for a more abstract concept of God."

234.   Avishur, Y. "Studies of Stylistic Features Common to the Phoenician Inscriptions and to the Bible. *UF* 7 (1975), 13-47; 8 (1976), 1-22.

A number of different word-pairs in the HB, as well as literary phrases, similes, common idioms, with numerous examples of how they are used.

235.   Barton, John. "Reading the Bible as Literature: Two Questions for Biblical Critics." *LT* 1 (1987), 135-153.

Is historical criticism anachronistic? The history of literary theory and what kind critics should use on the Bible. Historical and literary criticism are mutually exclusive. Is there any literature in the OT? Our categories of what we call "literature" are too narrow; it has not always meant the same thing throughout human history. Biblical critics could avoid anachronism if they would employ literary criticism.

236.   Berlin, Adele. "Lexical Cohesion and Biblical Interpretion." *HS* 30 (1989), 29-40.

The frequency of this phenomenon and its potential for interpretation have gone largely unnoticed. "If we take seriously the *wording* of the biblical text, as literary interpreters must, then lexical cohesion belongs in our exegetical repertory."

237.   Boyarin, Daniel. "History Becomes Parable: A Reading of the Midrashic *Mashal*," in #48, pp. 54-71.

"[The rabbis] have often then represented on the surface of their hermeneutical texts precisely the ideological codes which allow and constrain their interpretation. The *mashal* is the most clearly defined of those codes which generate interpretation by narrative expansion. The *mashal* is a basic narrative structure ... [which is] thus the carrier of values and ideology in the culture. The biblical story ... is made to signify by being read with its rabbinic intertext. By this practice, history becomes parable."

238.   Breslauer, S. Daniel. "Literary Images of Women in the Jewish Tradition." *HS* 22 (1981), 49-57.

Literature allows us to glimpse "the interplay between symbol and reality in [a society's] ... cultural life." Biblical images of women are surprisingly positive and dynamic, though admittedly women are also frequently portrayed in the HB as "passive catalysts of destructive change." Thus the view of women in both Jewish and

Christian traditions is pluralistic. II Kings 4 provides a "dramatic example of the correlation of the image of woman and social realities"—the Shunammite woman is symbol both of a temptress who threatens the status quo, and of a classical biblical heroine.

239. Campbell, Antony F., S.J. "The Literary Approach to the Old Testament," in Eric Osborn and Lawrence McIntosh, eds., *The Bible and European Literature* (Melbourne: Academia P, 1987), 142-157.

Recent developments in literary criticism of the Bible are provocative and have changed the way we read, but their claim about the death of the historical-critical approach is exaggerated. Most of the OT is not historical in genre, but "reported story." Such a genre specializes in omitting less significant elements, since that is what the reporter would do—leave some things to the hearer's imagination.

240. Cassuto, Umberto, "Biblical and Canaanite Literature," in Cassuto, *Biblical and Oriental Studies, Vol. II: Bible and Ancient Oriental Texts.* Tr Israel Abrahams. Jerusalem (Magnes P), 1975, pp. 16-59. [Originally published in Italian in 1938].

Given the artistic finish of even the earliest Hebrew literature, and the insufficient time for such polish to have developed in Hebrew culture, the logical conclusion is "that Biblical literature was but the continuation of the *antecedent Canaanite literature*." Numerous examples from HB literary form, stylistic and rhetorical techniques which show these two cultures sharing a common tradition.

241. Clines, D.J.A. "Story and Poem: The Old Testament as Literature and Scripture." *Interpretation* 34 (1980), 115-127.

The distinction between the Bible as literature and the Bible as scripture is largely artificial. We can hear it properly as scripture only when we read it as literature. Examples from story: Jonah, David stories, Pentateuch, Esther; poem: Psalms 42, 43, Song Of Songs, Hosea 2.

242. Cooper, Alan. "On Reading the Bible Critically and Otherwise," in Richard Elliott Friedman and H.G.M. Williamson, eds., *The Future of Biblical Studies: The Hebrew Scriptures* (Atlanta: Scholars P, 1987), 61-79.

We need to adopt literary-critical methods of reading the HB as a counter-balance to the excesses of historical criticism. "... a new form of historical consciousness can emerge from the literary-critical model—so that biblical scholars might connect simultaneously

with the full history of their discipline, and with the broader world
of humanistic discourse they inhabit."

243.   Culley, Robert C. "Structural Analysis: Is It Done with Mir-
        rors?" *Interpretation* 28 (1974), 165-181.

        How structuralist analysis of biblical texts is understood, espe-
        cially in its "broader perspective" of author, reader, and text. Ap-
        plication to a series of "deception stories": Genesis 12, Exodus 1,
        Joshua 9, I Samuel 19, Judges 3, 4.

244.   Dauber, Kenneth. "The Bible as Literature: Reading Like
        the Rabbis." *Semeia* 31 (1985), 27-48.

        The HB is literature insofar as it resists showing a concept of Be-
        ing. It renders not the revelation of an existence but the estab-
        lishment of a certain relation. The Bible is not a text to be inter-
        preted, but, according to the rabbis, interpretation is the text
        itself.

245.   Driver, G.R. "Playing on Words." *PWCJS* 4 (1967), 121-9.

        Word-play is common in the HB. Kinds of word-play include as-
        sonance, double entendres, same word with different meanings in
        adjoining lines, persons' names as play on their qualities, etc. Such
        word-play "seems to have begun merely as a literary device to em-
        bellish or add point to a story, but it clearly comes to serve [the
        purpose] ... of imparting esoteric information to interested read-
        ers."

246.   Eilberg-Schwartz, Howard. "Israel in the Mirror of Nature:
        Animal Metaphors in the Ritual and Narratives of Ancient
        Israel." *Journal of Ritual Studies* 2 (1988), 1-30.

        "... the root metaphors of Israelite thought, which are drawn
        from animal husbandry and agriculture, gave rise to a number of
        religious practices and provide the interpretative context in which
        these practices can be understood," in both the HB and in Paul's
        letters.

247.   Engnell, Ivan. "The Figurative Language of the Old Testa-
        ment," in Engnell, *Critical Essays on the Old Testament*, tr
        and ed. John T. Willis (London: SPCK, 1970), 242-290.

        Various functions of figurative language in the OT, its original-
        ity, extent, and forms. Figurative language "is a necessary prerequi-
        site to any presentation of spiritual reality in speaking or writing,
        especially in conscious literary forms, whether prose or poetry...."

248.   Fishbane, Michael. "Inner Biblical Exegesis: Types and Strategies of Interpretation in Ancient Israel," in Geoffrey Hartman and Sanford Budick, eds., *Midrash and Literature* (New Haven: Yale UP, 1986), 19-37; rpt in Fishbane, *The Garments of Torah* (Bloomington: Indiana UP, 1989), 3-18.

Various examples of passages in later books of the HB glossing earlier ones; the loss of awareness of this fact in a "frozen canon" is very unfortunate. How traditions were transmitted, received, and revalued for new generations. How new teachings came through strategic revisions of earlier ones.

249.   Fox, Michael V. "The Identification of Quotations in Biblical Literature." *ZAW* 92 (1980), 416-431.

Robert Gordis was correct [see #1091] that the use of quotation is an authentic element of biblical literature. The question is, how is it to be used, since without guidelines it can lead to interpretive abuses. "I suggest as a working assumption that all words a speaker does not attribute (virtually or explicitly) to another person be taken as his own or as an expression of his own point of view."

250.   Gammie, John G. "Paraenetic Literature: Toward the Morphology of a Genre." *Semeia* 50 (1990), 41-77.

An attempt to "review and to clarify the definition and formal characteristics of several hortatory sub-genres and to suggest [how] ... they might be arranged hierarchically." Paraenetic literature is a major subdivision of Israel's wisdom literature; it has two major complex or composite genres: instructions, and paraeneses, as well as various sub-genres.

251.   Glück, J.J. "Paronomasia in Biblical Literature." *Semitics* 1 (1970), 50-78.

"Paronomasia was as common a figure in biblical literature as it has been in world literature ever since. In contrast with modern rhetorical concepts and with classical usage generally, the biblical paronomasia is no pun but an integral part of the elevated diction of the Bible." See also #204.

252.   Goitein, S.D. "Women as Creators of Biblical Genres." *Prooftexts* 8 (1988), 1-33.

The lives of women in ancient Israel related to various possible writings by them: perhaps Ruth, definitely some poetry since the poetry makes that claim, possibly laments as quoted in Ezekiel, Jeremiah, Isaiah 27, Judges 5, Proverbs, Psalms. All of these quote women's poetry, and read as though they could be by women, or show that women's oral/verbal expression was possible.

253.   Gordis, Robert. "On Methodology in Biblical Studies." *JQR*
        61 (1970), 93-118.

> Biblical scholarship is plagued by various "reductive fallacies....
> In some quarters the Bible becomes little more than a poorly
> transmitted corpus of Ugaritic literature." We need to keep in
> mind the basic clues to the literary structure of the Bible, e.g., the
> principle of association, which is "the basis for most of the rhetori-
> cal figures ... [and is] the basic mechanism underlying chiasmus
> ... the key to many difficult passages in biblical literature...."

254.   Gordon, Cyrus H. "Asymmetric Janus Parallelism." *Eretz Is-
        rael* 16 (1982), 80-81.

> Janus parallelism defined, with examples from Genesis 2, 49,
> Ruth 1, Exodus 33, Job 9, Hosea 1, 3. This device and related ones
> "do not merely yield new interpretations of individual passages but
> affect major aspects of biblical scholarship."

255.   Gordon, Cyrus H. "Homer and the Bible: The Origin and
        Character of East Mediterranean Literature." *HUCA* 26
        (1955), 43-108.

> The cultural and literary parallels between Homeric, biblical,
> and ancient Near Eastern civilizations. "... we [must] view Greek
> and Hebrew civilizations as parallel structures built upon the same
> East Mediterranean foundation," with the literary link being pro-
> vided by Ugarit.

256.   Gottwald, Norman K. "Literary Criticism of the Hebrew
        Bible: Retrospect and Prospect," in #48, pp. 27-44.

> To "assess the achievements of literary criticism of the HB,"
> while also "noting feedback from other forms of biblical criticism
> which may prove instructive for the literary-critical task." There are
> a number of "coordinate dimensions to biblical texts," all of which
> require one another for full interpretation, though in the past
> these methods have tried to isolate themselves. A satisfactory liter-
> ary theory to "frame and give intellectual warrant to" the interrela-
> tionships of the literary, social and theological dimensions is
> needed, and could be based on the work of Fredric Jameson and
> Terry Eagleton.

257.   Greenfield, Jonas C. "The Hebrew Bible and Canaanite Lit-
        erature," in #33, pp. 545-560.

> Biblical writers drew on the literary traditions of many Near
> Eastern cultures included Mesopotamian, Egyptian, and Hittite,
> but chiefly Canaanite. We know Canaanite literature mainly from
> texts at Ugarit revealed since 1929. The HB used four aspects of

this literature: its gods, its mythology, its literary styles and techniques, and facts of daily life.

258.   Greenwood, David. "Rhetorical Criticism and Formgeschichte: Some Methodological Considerations." *JBL* 89 (1970), 418-426

Form criticism has several limitations. We should view the literary units of the HB in Hebrew, not in European terms. We should analyze the structure of a biblical composition, which in turn will help us with connotative meanings. Rhetorical criticism is an art, and part of the larger world of literary criticism. To read the HB adequately, we must be able to account for its style and rhetorical techniques.

259.   Grossberg, Daniel. "Multiple Meaning: A Literary Device in the Hebrew Bible." *College Language Association Journal* 26 (1982), 204-14.

Several examples of multiple meaning within the context of other literary figures, e.g., paronomasia, metaphor, pivotal patterning, and coda.

260.   Hallo, William W. "Assyriology and the Canon." *The American Scholar* 59 (1990), 105-8.

"... for all its apparent and splendid isolation, Assyriology (along with Egyptology) can ... help open the study of the biblical canon to the literary approach ... help liberate the curriculum from a too exclusive preoccupation with Greek philosophy and its interpreters. And it can expand the canon—not only in its ethos, gender, and race but also in time, providing the perspective of a continuous literary and linguistic tradition that was already as venerable in Plato's time as Plato is today."

261.   Halperin, Sarah. "Tragedy in the Bible." *Dor-le-Dor* 9 (1980), 3-10.

The Bible's ability to make us see the struggles of its characters from both human and theological points of view "causes the turbulent effect of pity and fear as we watch the action of the hero and foresee the consequences." We then gain a new clarity of vision. Thus, Genesis, as well as other parts of the HB, adheres to Aristotle's definition of tragedy.

262.   Handelman, Susan. "'Everything is in It': Rabbinic Interpretation and Modern Literary Theory." *Judaism* 35 (1980), 429-440.

What modern literary theory of "troping" can tell us about how and why midrash interpreted scripture. Rabbis as "belated interpreters," as deconstructors of meaning in the HB. The views of Ferdinand de Saussure may not be inimical to the rabbinic method.

263.   Hardmeier, Christof. "Old Testament Exegesis and Linguistic Narrative Research." *Poetics* 15 (1986), 89-109.

Wishes to raise "basic questions of a historical-exegetical narrative analysis" of OT texts. For example, how are beginnings of the text rejected in its surface? Linguistic research should provide more reliable answers to such questions. Amos 7 as illustration of problems of text surface and narrative function.

264.   Honeyman, A.M. "*Merismus* in Biblical Hebrew." *JBL* 71 (1952), 11-18.

Various HB passages which illustrate "a comparatively simple and undeveloped form of merismus." How the term is defined. The theological ramifications of recognizing it in the HB. Merismus is "a frequent trope in Hebrew literature, both of prose and poetry," and is characteristic of a people not used to thinking in the abstract.

265.   Hughes, Ann. "City of Yahweh and Sister of Sodom: The City in Old Testament Literature." *Lamar Journal of the Humanities* 7, #2 (Fall, 1981), 61-73.

"A strong anti-urban theme appears in ancient Hebrew literature.... It is discernible in the earliest Genesis legends: by implication in the Cain-Abel story and its sequel, more clearly in the Tower of Babel legend, and obviously in the account of Sodom and Gomorrah." Reasons for this bias include the Hebrews' nomadic culture; the earliest cities of the region were Canaanite and thus pagan; and the fact that their bitterest enemies as a nation were city-oriented civilizations.

266.   Jacobson, Richard. "The Structuralists and the Bible." *Interpretation* 28 (1974), 146-164; rpt Donald K. McKim, ed. *A Guide to Contemporary Hermeneutics: Major Trends in Biblical Interpretation* (Grand Rapids: Eerdmans, 1986), 280-296.

Definitions and explanations of basic concepts of structuralism; how and why they have come to be applied to the OT; how their practitioners differ from anthropologists working on a primitive society. The weaknesses of structuralist theory; the importance of the French structuralists.

267. Kessler, Martin. "Inclusio in the Hebrew Bible." *Semitics* 6 (1978), 44-49.

An "orientation and overview" of inclusio, one of countless figures in classical rhetoric. There is still disagreement about how it is to be identified. How to compare it to, and distinguish it from, related figures, e.g., chiasmus, parallelismus membrorum, introversion, and keyword style.

268. Kramer, Samuel Noah. "Sumerian Literature and the Bible." *Analecta Biblica* 12 (1959), 185-204; rpt #47, 185-204.

Possible influences of Sumerian literature (myths, epics, hymns, wisdom literature) on the OT—or at least noticeable parallels between them: e.g., in stories about creation, paradise, flood, Tower of Babel, law, "Job," "Cain," plagues, etc.

269. Krašovec, Jože. "Merism: Polar Expression in Biblical Hebrew." *Biblica* 64 (1983), 231-9.

How "merism" may be defined, and what work has been done on it in languages other than English. Various examples from throughout the HB, and how they function to heighten meaning.

270. Landy, Francis. "The Case of Kugel: Do We Find Ourselves When We Lose Ourselves in the Text?" *Comparative Criticism* 5 (1983), 305-316.

Why we should defend the application of literary criticism of the Bible against the strictures of James Kugel (citing #378). Because literary-critical approaches to the HB often involve a form of decanonization, they can be terrifying; but contrary to Kugel, they do not ignore history. It is the literary critic, not the theologian, who most often renews our sense of the enormous pain in the HB, the "sheer quality of its evil," the "horror of [its] God." Yet the humanitity of the Bible redeems it, because "the characters ... are all imagined with a tact, sympathy and dispassionate insight indicative of the Bible's preoccupation with the mystery and wonder of man and the complexity of its writing." **

271. Lang, Dov B. "On the Biblical Comic." *Judaism* 11 (1962), 249-254.

Contrary to the usual assumption, the HB is filled with various types of humor: puns, "trickster" stories, and irony (especially in the prophets). It is wrong to assume that humor is inconsistent with serious or ultimate concerns. Since the Bible is about the distance between "is" and "ought," the actual and the possible, humor is relevant.

272.   Longman, Tremper. "The Literary Approach to the Study of the Old Testament: Promises and Pitfalls." *JETS* 28 (1985), 385-398; revised as part of #18.

We need to be more thoroughly and consciously literary and aesthetic in our approach to the OT, despite the danger of misreading ancient texts with modern methods, and of assuming that there is no determinant meaning.

273.   Lord, Albert B. "Patterns of Lives of the Patriarchs from Abraham to Samson to Samuel," in #230, pp. 7-18; Gunn, David M. "'Threading the Labyrinth': A Response to Albert B. Lord," in #230, pp. 19-24.

The "appearance of repeated narrative patterns and elements associated with the Lives of the patriarchs" to suggest an approach to the oral-traditional character of parts of the OT. The pattern begins with a genealogy, then prophecy of a miraculous birth (sometimes associated with an opposite twin), e.g., Isaac and Ishmael, Jacob and Esau, Joseph and his brothers. It reappears in Judges 13-16, (although there the "divine pair" is missing) and I Samuel 2.

Gunn: How are we to read such patterned stories? A great deal of Genesis through II Kings shows recurring patterns of family violence and rupture characteristic of much of the HB.

274.   Lund, N.W. "The Presence of Chiasmus in the Old Testament." *AJSL* 46 (1929-30), 104-126.

How OT writers use chiasmus for effect. Examples, with explanations of their meaning for textual criticism and for interpretation, from Leviticus 11, 14, 24; Isaiah 28, 55.

275.   Moulton, Richard G. "The Bible as Literature," in #32, pp. 3-11.

The HB contains a great variety of literary forms and types. As a collection, its intrinsic worth, its beauty and aesthetic power make it second to none among the literatures of the world.

276.   Mounin, Georges. "Hebraic Rhetoric and Faithful Translation." *BT* 30 (1979), 336-340.

We must learn respect for formal structures in the Bible, which means we must study Hebrew rhetoric. Examples from HB and NT, including chiasm in Isaiah 60.

277.   Muilenberg, James. "The Literary Approach—The Old Testament as Hebrew Literature." *Journal of the National Association of Biblical Instructors* 1 (1933), 14-22.

The large number of books on the literary approach since the turn of the century shows that "the background and materials for competent aesthetic literary study [of the OT] are present today as they have never been before." Various questions which must be addressed by future scholars—e.g. literary and poetic styles and techniques, and conventions of history-writing in ancient Israel.

278. Oden, Robert A., Jr., Joseph Falaky Nagy, Burke O. Long, Robert Coote, Margaret Mills. "Reflections on the Hebrew Bible and Folklore: A Conclusion," in #230, pp. 217-241.

Major methodological issues raised by the rest of the essays in Susan Niditch, ed. *Text and Tradition: The Hebrew Bible and Folklore* [#230] which suggest further avenues of inquiry. These might include the biblical tendency to pass back and forth between oral and written traditions; whether "self-canonization" ever fully succeeds; the importance of the actual message of the biblical writers, however multilayered; the difficulty of reconstructing actual cultural settings of ancient writings; and the need to examine the sources of our responses as readers.

279. Parunak, H. van Dyke. "Some Axioms for Literary Architecture." *Semitics* 8 (1982), 1-16.

Why do certain surface structures, or literary architectural patterns, occur? Are they based on more fundamental principles? Four axioms help us with these questions: biblical literature is essentially aural; biblical writers could recognize two passages as similar or dissimilar; they wrote in paragraphs; more than one pattern may be active in a passage at a time.

280. Rabinowitz, Isaac. "Towards a Valid Theory of Biblical Hebrew Literature," in Luitpold Wallach, ed., *The Classical Tradition* (Ithaca: Cornell UP, 1966), 315-328.

A theory of biblical Hebrew literature requires more than that it is an art of communication, since to the ancient Hebrews, words had other functions beyond expression and communication. The failure to take this into account is the chief defect of modern literary study of the Bible. For the ancient Hebrews, literature "could affect the world directly and immediately ... through influencing human minds and hearts."

281. Rabinowitz, Isaac. "'Word' and Literature in Ancient Israel." *New Literary History* 4 (1972), 119-139.

We must know a society's traditional beliefs about nature and the power of words to know what it considers to be literature. To ancient Israel, words had a broader range of functions than the Greeks appear to have allowed. Words were not only a means of communication, but objects with power. The character of Hebrew literature is traceable to this second assumption. Literary consequences of this belief included the avoidance of pejorative statements about God; the setting up of the order of books in the HB as we have it now; and the tendency to take words of hope as ones of accomplishment.

282.   Ramras-Rauch, Gila. "The Myth of Man in the Hebraic Epic." *Analecta Husserliana* 18 (1984), 175-183.

Ways in which the OT differs from epics of other ancient Mediterranean cultures: its emphasis on a covenant; retention of sanctity; emphasis on more than story-telling; the "newness" of the situations into which protagonists are thrust; the more fully human nature of its heroes; and its avoidance of the ironic and the tragic.

283.   Rosenbaum, S.N. "In the Beginning is the Word," in #48, pp. 92-101.

Only a careful knowledge of Hebrew can enable us to understand the HB. Its trilateral root system, word play and number symbolism are often ignored. Translation is not a substitute since Semitic languages cannot be adequately translated into Indo-European ones. A "semantic field theory" approach is best, although despite intentions to the contrary this may inhibit appreciation of the Bible as literature. "I ask only that in our haste to encompass the whole, we do not stint on the naming of parts."

284.   Rosenberg, Joel. "Biblical Tradition: Literature and Spirit in Ancient Israel," in Arthur Green, ed., *Jewish Spirituality: From the Bible Through the Middle Ages* (New York: Crossroad, 1987), 82-112.

We cannot grasp biblical tradition apart from "the ways it was appropriated and refashioned [by] ... postbiblical interpreters." The emergence of the "postbiblical reader"; what the modern reader sees in the HB. The advantage of a literary approach is that it "has shown effectively ... that we are confronting in the Hebrew Bible ... various types of human discourse, each with its own genres, rules, and conventions...." How the HB is organized, its poetic versus its prose traditions, its use of irony and quotation, the importance of narrative, its main characters, the relation of literary to theological interests. **

285.   Rosenberg, Joel. "The Feminine Through a (Male) Glass Darkly: Preface to a Demythology." *Response* 9 (Winter, 1975-6), 67-88.

Ways in which the Torah may have anticipated the liberation of women include signs of awareness of their pivotal place in the life of the nation; our misreadings of Genesis 2-3; the power of women in Judges 4-5; the woman as metaphor for Israel in the prophets; and Songs Of Songs as blueprint for the next stage of male-female relationships in the twentieth century.

286. Rosner, Dov. "The Simile and its Use in the Old Testament." *Semitics* 4 (1974), 37-46.

Scholars differ on the correct definition of "simile," though it is found in every book of the OT. There are two main types: the brief, lucid, popular simile from the Wisdom tradition; and the well-elaborated simile with analogy.

287. Sanders, James A. "The Integrity of Biblical Pluralism," in #318, pp. 154-169.

We need a canon criticism which recognizes the HB's "internal dialogues," its intertextuality. We would then neither completely harmonize divergent traditions nor claim that they are contradictory. Instead, we would realize that the "integrity of reality ... can never be fully contained by doctrine.... To go back and read all the parts in the light of the whole would revolutionize reading of the text ... would for most people amount to a rewriting of the text but without changing a single word preserved on leather, parchment, and papyrus."

288. Sandmel, Samuel. "The Bible as Literature." *Central Conference of American Rabbis Journal* 20, #2 (Spring, 1973), 57-71.

Only by studying the Bible as literature can we give credit to the ancient Hebrew writers' sense of their own material, their creativity and their writing abilities. Only then can we recognize that the historicity of many passages matters less than their narrative or artistic qualities. The author(s) of the Pentateuch and of other major sections of the HB had clear ideas what they were about—ideas which can only be seen in an overview which historical criticism does not allow.

289. Sandmel, Samuel. "The Enjoyment of Scripture: An Esthetic Approach." *Judaism* 22 (1973), 455-467.

Aesthetic appreciation helps us respond to scripture as other, more formal types of criticism cannot. Scholarship has dealt with the literature of Bible as though it were anything but literature. We need to know what the author is saying, and how he says it. The HB is a "wedding of lofty poetry and lofty ideas." Examples from I Samuel, Judges 3, Jonah, Esther, Deuteronomy, Genesis.

290.   Schökel, Luis Alonso. "Hermeneutical Problems of a Literary Study of the Bible." *VT* Supplement 28 (1974), 1-15.

Why is it that, since we all accept that many OT narratives are literature, few of us accept that they should be studied as literature? Is it because such study is not scientific? Or because form distracts us, or diminishes the text? The solution is to realize that form is not pure, but is a part of meaning; therefore they are one, and cannot be separated. While a literary approach is called for, the value of structuralism as part of this study is doubtful.

291.   Talmon, Shemaryahu. "The 'Desert Motif' in the Bible and in Qumran Literature," in Alexander Altmann, ed., *Biblical Motifs: Origins and Transformations* (Cambridge, Mass: Harvard UP, 1966), 31-63.

A careful tracing of the "desert motif" through the Pentateuch and the prophets shows that, contrary to those who believe that the desert is idealized in the OT, almost the opposite is true.

292.   Talmon, Shemaryahu. "Literary Motifs and Speculative Thought in the Hebrew Bible." *HUSLA* 16 (1988), 150-168.

Why the almost total absence of systematic conceptualizing in the HB? Examination of its literary conventions "will show that such patterns, particularly motifs, are in fact condensed signifiers of speculative thought." This can be shown, e.g., in the motif of the barren wife.

293.   Trible, Phyllis. "De-Patriarchalizing in Biblical Interpretation." *JAAR* 41 (1973), 30-48.

The biblical God "is not on the side of patriarchy." Even the myth of the Fall challenges patriarchy. Various passages from the HB, e.g., from Song Of Songs, Genesis 2-3, and Exodus demonstrate a de-patriarchalizing principle in the HB, operating within scripture itself rather than imposed by exegetes.

294.   Tsumura, David Toshio. "Literary Insertion (A X B Pattern) in Biblical Hebrew." *VT* 33 (1983), 468-482.

Defined as a word, phrase, clause or discourse inserted within an otherwise composite unit which limits the unit as a whole grammatically or semantically. It has hitherto been largely unnoticed as a literary pattern. Seeing this pattern enhances our understanding of various OT texts.

295.   Tsumura, David Toshio. "Literary Insertion (A X B Pattern) in Biblical Hebrew." *PWCJS* 8 (1982), 1-6.

Definition and examples of this "almost unnoticed" phenomenon.

296.   Vorster, W.S. "The In/compatibility of Methods and Strategies in Reading or Interpreting the Old Testament." *OTE* 2, #3 (1989), 53-63.

Neither structuralist nor post-structuralist methods of reading the Bible are compatible with the historical-critical method. Nevertheless, this should not prevent us from employing all available analytical strategies on the Bible.

297.   West, Gerald. "Can a Literary Reading Be a Liberative Reading?" *Scriptura* 35 (1990), 10-25.

"... by viewing [Phyllis Trible's] literary readings of the Old Testament as deconstructions of patriarchy, we have a theoretical framework for grounding a literary biblical hermeneutics of liberation." Biblical studies should "move away from the notion of ... the pursuit of disinterested truth to something more human and transformative, something which is shaped by a self-critical solidarity with the victims of history."

298.   Whallon, William. "Biblical Poetry and Homeric Epic," in Whallon, *Formula, Character, Context. Studies in Homeric, Old English, and Old Testament Poetry* (Washington, D.C.: Center for Hellenic Studies, 1969), 214-240; rpt #47, 318-325.

Erich Auerbach is correct in seeing that biblical and Homeric writing are different. His metaphors of "background versus foreground" and "vertical versus horizontal" are valid for both prose and poetry. However, his assertion that the Judaeo-Christian tradition knows no separation of styles is incorrect.

299.   Worden, T. "The Literary Influence of the Ugaritic Fertility Myth on the Old Testament." *VT* 3 (1953), 273-297.

Fourteenth-century B.C. Ugaritic texts of North Canaan containing fertility myths were an important influence on OT imagery, expression, and thought patterns. This can be seen especially in ritual laments.

300.   Wright, Addison G. "The Literary Genre Midrash." *CBQ* 28 (1966), 105-138, 417-457.

There is a growing recognition that a number of biblical passages must be assigned to this genre. The origin and content of midrash; types of midrash, purposes, techniques, and primary characteristics. It is possible that certain NT passages are *midrashim* on OT ones.

301.   Zaborski, Andrzej. "Structural Methods and Old Testament
        Studies." *Folia Orientalia* 15 (1974), 263-8.
        There is an urgent need for biblical scholars to familiarize them-
        selves with linguistics and semiotics.

See also: #s 1, 14, 166, 173, 175, 1151, 1500, 1844.

Hebrew Biblical Narrative

Books

302.   Adar, Zvi. *The Biblical Narrative.* Tr Misha Louvish. Jerusalem
        (Department of Education and Culture of the World
        Zionist Organization), 1959.
        There are five stages in HB narrative, in ascending order: short
        tale, cycle of stories, long story, book, and the biblical narrative as
        a whole. Examples of tale include Judges 9, I Samuel 1 and 25,
        Genesis 22; of the cycle: Judges 13-16; Genesis 12-25; I Kings 17-19,
        21, II Kings 1-2; of the long story: II Samuel 15- 19; of the book: I
        and II Samuel. Each of these stages has its own way of viewing hu-
        man nature and conduct.

303.   Alter, Robert. *The Art of Biblical Narrative.* New York (Basic
        Books), 1981.
        Literary art plays a crucial role in the shaping of biblical narra-
        tive. This art is "finely modulated ..., determining in most cases
        the minute choice of words and reported details, the pace of
        narration, the small movements of dialogue, and a whole network
        of ramified interconnections in the text." Biblical narrative as
        prose fiction; type scenes; the function of dialogue; techniques of
        repetition; characterization; "composite artistry"; point of view.
        Includes revised forms of #s 323, 324, 326, 770. **

304.   Bal, Mieke. *Lethal Love: Feminist Literary Readings of Biblical
        Love Stories.* Bloomington (Indiana UP), 1987.
        The Bible is neither a feminist nor a sexist manifesto. How does
        the Bible express and reflect its culture's "articulation of gender"?
        We need a dialogue between modern feminist and narrative

theory and the ancient text, rather than assuming the dominance of one and irrelevance of the other. Fourth essay, "One Woman, Many Men" (pp. 89-103): problem of the link, if any, between the Tamar-Judah story and the rest of the Joseph novella. Tamar is a bringer of insight to Judah, and therefore to the reader. First, second, third and fifth essays analyzed separately as #s 513, 755, 829, and 1311.

305.   Bar-Efrat, Shimon. *Narrative Art in the Bible.* Sheffield (Almond P; Sheffield Academic P), 1989.

Formal and structural aspects of the HB, techniques, design, and types of narration. How the narrator is used, including omniscience, gaps, and bias; devices that reveal character; chiasmus and other parallel construction of plot, and how they underscore the theme; importance of time over space; stylistic devices, especially in I Kings 1, II Samuel 17. How all of these techniques show up in II Samuel 13. **

306.   Berlin, Adele. *Poetics and Interpretation of Biblical Narrative.* Sheffield (Almond P), 1983.

Biblical narrative is a form of literary art, and thus demands a poetics to illuminate it. This poetics should be based chiefly on characterization and point of view. Why the literary, or synchronic, approach is superior to the historical-critical, or diachronic approach. Extensive analysis of Ruth, with briefer interpretations of I Samuel 25, II Samuel 6, 11, I Kings 1-2. **

307.   Brenner, Athalya. *The Israelite Woman: Social Role and Literary Type in Biblical Narrative.* Sheffield (JSOT P), 1985.

Part II, "Literary Paradigms of Female Types and Behaviour," on the hero's mother, positive and negative temptresses, foreign women and ancestress types in the HB: Genesis 2, 19, 39; Exodus 2; Proverbs 1-9; Judges 4-5, 14-16; Ruth; and in the NT briefly: Matthew, Luke. All such analysis should proceed through four stages: identification-definition of the female model; compilation of type features; identification of departures from type; identification of similar models from elsewhere in the HB.

308.   Church, Brooke Peters. *The Golden Years: The Old Testament Narrative as Literature.* New York and Toronto (Rinehart and Company), 1947.

Treating the OT only as a religious book has increased the tendency to ignore its contributions to, and power as a part of, world literature. Themes, forms, and literary techniques of the narrative portions of the OT, and a running comparison with ancient Greek literary practices. Reprints of narrative portions of Genesis, Exodus, Numbers, Deuteronomy, Judges, I, II Samuel, I, II Kings, Ruth, Esther, Tobit in order to isolate the "literary" qualities of the OT.

309.   Crossan, John D. *The Dark Interval*. Allen, Texas (Argus Communications), 1975.

A juxtaposition of Ruth, Jonah, Jesus' parables, and the fiction of Kafka and Borges enables us to see that myth and parable are opposite poles of language and story. Myth mediates irreducible opposites, while parables are fictions and thus agents of change, not of stability. Parable is story grown self-conscious and self-critical. Parables are in both OT and NT poised against the legal and prophetic traditions (Ruth, Jonah), against the wisdom tradition (Ecclesiastes); Jesus' parables show he was an upsetter. Since parables shatter our accepted world by showing us the relativity of story, they cannot be allegorized successfully; they prepare us to receive God and his word.

310.   Culley, R.C. *Studies in the Structure of Hebrew Narrative*. Philadelphia (Fortress P) and Missoula (Scholars P), 1976.

Part III, "Structure in Some Biblical Narratives": If we juxtapose stories with similar themes and structures, we see patterns and general conclusions emerging which would not otherwise be visible. Genesis 4; Exodus 15, 17; Numbers 11, 21; I Kings 17; II Kings 2, 4, 6.

311.   Damrosch, David. *The Narrative Covenant: Transformations of Genre in the Growth of Biblical Literature*. San Francisco (Harper and Row), 1987.

The conflict between historical and literary criticisms of the Bible results from the tendency of each to turn the other into a caricature. We need instead a biblical criticism combining the two methods because they mutually illuminate. Ancient Mesopotamian epic and historical writing helps us explore the development of Israelite literary-historical consciousness, and the writing which resulted. Not only the ancient texts, but Icelandic sagas, Montaigne's essays, and the *Thousand Nights and a Night* can also illuminate the composite artistry of the HB. Chapter 6 appears also as #662. **

312.   Frei, Hans W. *The Eclipse of Biblical Narrative: A Study in Eighteenth and Nineteenth Century Hermeneutics*. New Haven and London (Yale UP), 1974.

Survey of the decline in the authority of the Bible as *the* truth about the world; how eighteenth- and nineteenth-century critics missed the opportunity to develop a true narrative criticism of the Bible. In Germany, interest in the subject developed into the historical-critical method, while in England it was channelled into the realistic novel. The work of Robert Lowth, Johann Gottfried Herder, Friedrich Strauss, and the "myth" critics. **

313.   Green, Garrett, ed. *Scriptural Authority and Narrative Interpretation.* Philadelphia (Fortress P), 1987.

Relevant section: "Theoretical Considerations." Charles M. Wood: attention to narrative affects how we inquire about the relationship between a text's scriptural status and its interpretation. The decision to regard something as scripture does not mean surrendering our critical freedom. Ronald E. Thiemann: *contra* many literary critics, biblical narratives do depict a followable world, inviting the reader into the tale. Kathryn E. Tanner: linking scriptural authority to its narrative meaning has encouraged a flexible and self-critical use of the Bible. Garrett Green: we need to reconsider what it means to call a text "fiction," since fiction-like narrative contains its own truth. Stephen Crites: the concept of narrative space helps us grasp what it means to say that stories tell the truth. The plain sense of biblical tales is not history but narrative meaning.

314.   Licht, Jacob. *Storytelling in the Bible.* Jerusalem (Magnes P), 1986.

Mimetic and aesthetic aims and devices in biblical narrative; basic scene structures; role of repetition and time; how more complex narrative units differ from shorter ones. Why scholars have shied away from literary analysis of the HB narratives, and why doing such analysis is nevertheless important.

315.   Limburg, James. *Old Stories for a New Time.* Atlanta (John Knox P), 1983.

Believers can better understand the relevance of OT narratives for modern times if they learn how they functioned then and function now as stories. Genesis 24, 37-50; Judges 6-8, 13-16; Ruth; Esther; Jonah.

316.   Long, Burke O., ed. *Images of Man and God: Old Testament Short Stories in Literary Focus.* Sheffield (Almond P), 1981

Six essays, five of which are relevant: on Genesis 37-50: #621; on Moses (Exodus): #657; on Judges 13-16: #768; On Saul (I Samuel): #799; and on David and his sons (II Samuel): #843.

317.   Milne, Pamela J. *Vladimir Propp and the Study of Structure in
        Hebrew Biblical Narrative.* Sheffield (Almond P), 1988.

        Previous attempts to apply Propp's theories to HB narrative have
        been uneven, depending on how well they grasped the purpose
        and limitations of the model, e.g., its genre-specific nature. Propp
        can be of value in two ways: as a useful tool for describing structure
        in some HB narratives; and as a new perspective for addressing
        problems of genre. Extensive discussion of Daniel 1-6 as example.
        Proppian analysis works best on narratives which remain close to
        oral forms. It can account for many, but not all, of the structural
        features of Daniel 1-6.

*   Robinson, Bernard P. *Israel's Mysterious God: An Analysis of
        Some Old Testament Narratives.* See #182.

318.   Rosenblatt, Jason P., and Joseph C. Sitterson, Jr. *"Not In
        Heaven": Coherence and Complexity in Biblical Narrative.*
        Bloomington and Indianapolis (Indiana UP), 1991.

        Ten essays: nine of them on narratives in the HB, and one on
        Mark 6 and 8; based on the idea that "we can accept that our own
        complexity as readers might parallel the sometimes irreducible
        complexity of narrators...." Analyzed separately as #s 287, 328, 536,
        553, 576, 577, 622, 792, 1440, and 1831.

319.   Savran, George W. *Telling and Retelling: Quotation in Biblical
        Literature.* Bloomington (Indiana UP), 1988.

        The poetics of dialogue in biblical narrative. Quotation is impor-
        tant because it is at once direct speech of the present and recollec-
        tion of prior words; because the quoter is both teller and subject;
        and because it is rereading or respeaking the past in a new con-
        text. This is why the HB so often repeats phrases where summariz-
        ing would have sufficed. How this change in language affects
        meaning; how quotation functions as a device in characterization.
        Law, and Former Prophets.

319a.   Ska, Jean Louis. *"Our Fathers Have Told Us": Introduction to the
        Analysis of Hebrew Narratives.* Rome (Editrice Pontificio Is-
        tituto Biblico), 1990.

        Definitions of basic terminology of narrative analysis, including
        semiotic, structuralist, and reader-response as well as more tradi-
        tional narrative theories. How these terms and concepts have been
        or may be applied to a variety of narratives in the HB. Story versus
        discourse; time; plot; narrator and reader; point of view; character-
        ization.

320. Sternberg, Meir. *The Poetics of Biblical Narrative. Ideological Literature and the Drama of Reading.* Bloomington (Indiana UP), 1985.

"... biblical narrative emerges as a complex, because multifunctional, discourse. Functionally speaking, it is regulated by a set of three principles: ideological, historiographic, and aesthetic." The "drama of reading" comes from the reticence of biblical narrative: its knowledge gaps, play of multiple perspective, temporal discontinuity, ambiguity of characterization, and complex levels of repetition. Texts analyzed in detail: Genesis 24, 27, 37-50; Judges 4-5; II Samuel 11. **

321. Trible, Phyllis. *Texts of Terror: Literary-Feminist Readings of Biblical Narratives.* Philadelphia (Fortress P), 1984.

The methodology of literary criticism and the perspective of feminism to analyze four "sad stories" or "texts of terror" about helpless female victims in the HB: Hagar (Genesis 16, 21); Tamar (II Samuel 13); a Bethlehem concubine (Judges 19); and Jephthah and his daughter (Judges 11). The relationship between these texts and violence against women today. Intended as a follow-up to #221. Chapter Four also appears in #753.

322. Williams, James G. *Women Recounted: Narrative Thinking and the God of Israel.* Sheffield (Almond P), 1982.

Reading biblical narrative as a "dynamic mode of thinking whose aesthetic properties support and enhance the process of arriving at knowledge." Its main characteristic is tolerance of moral ambiguity. May be compared to aphorism, historical thinking, and myth. Women important in Israel's genesis and destiny: Sarah, Rebecca, Rachel, Moses' mother and Pharaoh's daughter, Zipporah, Samson's mother, and Hannah. Other feminine figures including Eve, Deborah, Jael, Judith, Esther, Mary, Ruth, Potiphar's wife, Delilah, and the "Alien Woman" of Proverbs.

Articles

323. Alter, Robert. "Biblical Narrative." *Commentary* 61, #5 (May, 1976), 61-7.

The use of repetition in biblical narrative to show how literary scholarship deepens appreciation of the HB as both literature and religion. Previous explanations were inadequate because they failed to notice whether the repetition was word-for-word or had

variations—which can be a clue to character, theme, or plot interpretation. Numbers 22-24; Judges 13; I Samuel 15; I Kings 1. Revised as part of #303.

324.   Alter, Robert. "Biblical Type-Scenes and the Uses of Con-
        vention." *Critical Inquiry* 5 (1978), 355-368.

        We will have difficulty perceiving the artistry of the HB unless we
        know its conventions. We notice, e.g., the seeming repetition of
        the "same" story over and over. This phenomenon can be ex-
        plained by the concept of the "type-scene" borrowed from Home-
        ric scholarship. Good examples are scenes at the well: Genesis 24,
        29; Exodus 2; Ruth; Judges 14. Aborted or absent type-scenes. Re-
        vised as part of #303.

325.   Alter, Robert. "How Conventions Help Us Read: The Case
        of the Bible's Annunciation Type-Scene." *Prooftexts* 3
        (1983), 115-130.

        The literary approach tends to create anxiety about moderniz-
        ing the Bible. If anything, the literary approach helps us recognize
        biblical conventions as they were, rather than as some modern log-
        ical sequence would have them. It is well worth the trouble to re-
        cover what we can of the ancient literary code. Genesis, I Samuel,
        II Kings.

326.   Alter, Robert. "Sacred History and Prose Fiction," in
        Richard Elliott Friedman, ed., *The Creation of Sacred Litera-
        ture* (Berkeley: U California P, 1981), 7-24.

        We need to view biblical narrative as a kind of "prose fiction."
        This has the advantage of "latitude for the exercise of pleasurable
        invention for its own sake," from sound play to characterization,
        which the hermeneutical perspective cannot allow for. Rpt as
        Chapter Two of #303.

327.   Bar-Efrat, Simon. "Some Observations on the Analysis of
        Structure in Biblical Narrative." *VT* 30 (1980), 154-173.

        Biblical narrative operates on verbal, narrative technique, narra-
        tive world, and conceptual content levels. It can also be described
        in terms of character, events (plot structure and dramatic struc-
        ture), and chiasm. However, the interpretation of structure is
        much more prone to subjectivity than is its mere description. Gen-
        esis 24, 27, 32, 33; I Samuel 1, 25, 29; II Samuel 11, 13; Job 1; Ruth.

328.   Berlin, Adele. "Literary Exegesis of Biblical Narrative: Be-
        tween Poetics and Hermeneutics," in #318, pp. 120-128.

The "discovery of verbal and/or thematic similarities in two distant narratives," leading to the interpretation of one in the light of the other, "has obscured the distinction between the strategies that the Bible uses to interpret them." Therefore, two principles follow: "(1) We must be cautious in using literary analysis for purposes of dating texts, [and] (2) We should not mistake hermeneutic principles for compositional techniques."

329.   Berlin, Adele. "Point of View in Biblical Narrative," in Stephen A. Geller, ed., *A Sense of Text: The Art of Language in the Study of Biblical Literature* (Winona Lake: Eisenbrauns, 1983), 71-113.

Biblical narrative is characterized by a variety of narrative points of view. Its range of techniques includes juxtaposition of accounts by various characters; retelling some information and comments by the narrator—all resulting in a narrative with depth and sophistication. The reader thus is an active participant because he must reconcile gaps and conflicts.

330.   Blenkinsopp, Joseph. "Biographical Patterns in Biblical Narrative." *JSOT* 20 (1981), 27-46.

Vladimir Propp's morphology of the folktale can be an important tool for analyzing HB narrative, showing us how the narrative structure can be taken seriously "as a bearer of meaning and message."

331.   Borgman, Paul. "Story Shapes That Tell A World: Biblical, Homeric, and Modern Narrative." *Christian Scholar's Review* 9 (1980), 291-316.

Biblical narratives tell us that the world is open and full of surprises, where "the inevitable often seems to happen purely by chance, and ... the real has an air of the absurd." By contrast, Homeric epic portrays "a world in which only the expected happens." The world of contemporary cinema, like that of many modern novels, is more like the Homeric than the biblical one, where "serious attention is paid to portraying as clearly as possible what *can* be expected." I Samuel 16-26.

332.   Culley, Robert C. "Themes and Variations in Three Groups of *OT* Narratives." *Semeia* 3 (1975), 3-13.

Relationships among the stories in three groups: miracle, deception, and punishment stories. These themes generally concern death, and the movement between life and death. Miracle stories: Exodus 15, 17; I Kings 17; II Kings 2, 4, 6. Deception stories: Genesis 12, 19, 38; Exodus 1; Joshua 9; Judges 3; I Samuel 19. Punishment stories: Genesis 4; Numbers 11, 12, 21; I Kings 20; II Kings 2, 20.

333.   van Dijk, P.J. "The Function of So-Called Etiological Elements in Narratives." *ZAW* 102 (1990), 19-33.

Many such narratives are not etiological at all, but "serve a rhetorical function to affirm the narrative (and its symbols) and to heighten its entertainment value."

334.   Doron, Pinchas. "The Art of Biblical Narrative." *Dor-Le-Dor* 17 (1978), 1-9, 91-96.

Almost all biblical narratives display three layers: one of plot nearest the surface; one of emotional and mental attitudes of the characters; and the deepest layer containing the writer's general ideas and world-view. HB narratives are told with a minimum of ornamentation and physical description, with only two to three characters appearing at a given time. Thus these narratives are intellectually more advanced than those of the Babylonians, Hindus, and Greeks; at the same time they are simpler, more human and universal.

335.   Engar, Ann W. "Old Testament Women as Tricksters," in #48, pp. 143-157.

Trickster characters in the OT are generally female. They are generally admirable characters, sometimes even grasping God's will better than male characters do. Genesis 24-25, 29-30, 32, 38; Exodus 1, 2; Joshua 2; Judges 4, 5; II Samuel 14; Ruth; Esther.

336.   Eslinger, Lyle. "Narrational Situations in the Bible," in #48, pp. 72-91.

"It is this existential gap between God and man that is the mainspring of much biblical narrative and it is the genius of biblical authors to have developed a narratorial vehicle—the external unconditioned narrator—to explore what would otherwise be a no-man's-land of misconception and ignorance. The key to understanding biblical narrative ... is neither history nor literary history, but an appreciative acceptance of those extraordinary narrators. Without them, ... we will fail just as miserably as the human characters in their stories to understand the way of God with man." Genesis 1; Judges 2; I Samuel 8-12; Nehemiah 1.

337.   Fontaine, Carol. "The Deceptive Goddess in Ancient Near Eastern Myth: Inanna and Inaras." *Semeia* 42 [#229], 84-102.

Folklore shows us that "the deceptive female characters of the Hebrew Bible have counterparts in the 'goddess literature' of the surrounding cultures." This type of character appears frequently in both Jewish and Near Eastern literatures in contexts of sexual exchange, drunkenness and feasting. Genesis 19; Judges 5, 14; II Samuel 13; Esther 5, 7; Ruth 3.

338.   Fuchs, Esther. "The Literary Characterization of Mothers and Sexual Politics in the Hebrew Bible," in #226, pp. 117-136; rpt *Semeia* 46 (1989), 151-166.

Feminist literary analysis of partriarchal strategies in the Bible is rare beyond Genesis 2-3. The mother-figures in the type-scenes of Genesis 17, 21, 30, and II Kings 4 remain flat characters because they are seen as part of an institution, and thus not experiencing complexity in their lives.

339.   Gerhart, Mary. "The Restoration of Biblical Narrative." *Semeia* 46 (1989), 13-29.

Questions of theory and methodology in literary analysis of biblical narrative have been hampered by "a thicket of unexamined assumptions." Theory of genre and of narrative, with evaluations of recent books in the field of biblical narrative.

*   Gräbe, Ina. "Theory of Literature and Old Testament Studies—Narrative Conventions as Exegetic Reading Strategies." See #1037.

340.   Gunn, David M. "New Directions in the Study of Biblical Hebrew Narrative." *JSOT* 39 (1987), 67-75.

The recent impact of various forms of literary criticism on the study of biblical narrative. Such study is now entrenched; historical studies still dominate, but their position is fast eroding. Literary criticism raises many disturbing questions about the texts. Predictions about likely future avenues of exploration.

341.   Gunn, David M. "Reading Right. Reliable and Omniscient Narrator, Omniscient God, and Foolproof Composition in the Hebrew Bible," in #35, pp. 53-64.

Meir Sternberg is incorrect [in #320] when he assumes that reading a text can be an ideologically neutral activity, that there can be only one biblical poetics if we read carefully. Thus, even "reliable," "omniscient," and "foolproof" are heavily loaded terms.

342.   Kort, Wesley A. "Narrative and Theology." *LT* 1 (1987), 27-38.

There is a "need to take the narrative coherence of biblical discourse seriously." Three notions underlie this need: that narrative is a primary form of discourse; that it is complex, with its own laws (plot, character, tone, etc.); and that it is "inevitably related to mystery and belief."

343.   Kurzweil, Baruch. "Is There Such a Thing as Biblical Tragedy?" in Israel Cohen and B.Y. Michali, eds., *An Anthology of Hebrew Essays in Two Volumes*. Vol. I (Tel Aviv: Institute for the Translation of Hebrew Literature and Massada Publishing Company, Ltd., 1966), 97-116.

Attempts to find tragedy in biblical narrative only come from confusion, since they must "lift the biblical narrative out of its context, out of its world, and impose on it by force the subjective approach of the secular, uncommitted artist." We call some books and characters "tragic" only by abandoning the religious meaning of the narrative.

344.   Long, Burke O. "Framing Repetitions in Biblical Historiography." *PWCJS* 9, Vol. I (1986), 69-76.

Notions of narrative tense, mood, and voice demonstrate that "framing repetitions were not simply a matter of clumsy editing or violations of chronology. More often, they were devices by which an ancient narrator manipulated the reader's experience to shape sympathies, attitudes, and perceptions. With ... framing repetitions, the narrator could sharpen characterization, provide ironic perspective, or comment on the story with didactic intent."

345.   Martin, W.J. "'Dischronologized' Narrative in the Old Testament." *VT* Supplement 17 (1968), 179-186.

"Dischronologized narrative" denotes a seemingly random dispersal of events in a narrative. It is not the absence of chronology, but chronology of a different order. It is a rhetorical device, a vehicle of bias, and thus anti-historical. It is part of the art of writing history. II Samuel 4, 12; I Kings 1, 11, 18; II Kings 24; the Gospels; Egyptian and Assyrian documents.

346.   Megged, Aharon. "Stories Without Heroes: The Singularity of the Hebrew Short Story." *Partisan Review* 51 (1984), 417-423.

Despite the supposed parallels with myths in other ancient cultures, the distinctive literary qualities of HB narrative come from that specific language and milieu. The most important difference is that HB narrative does not contain heroes: this is why it is "a theater of the soul rather than a theater of fate." This imperfectness of Hebrew protagonists in turn makes them more individualized and thus more interesting.

347.   Moberly, R.W.L. "Story in the Old Testament." *Themelios* 11 (1986), 77-82.

Lack of historicity does not detract from the truth or relevance of an OT book. While the Bible is more than literature, it clearly *is* literature among other things, and therefore has to be read with the tools of literary criticism.

348.   Perry, Manaham, and Meir Sternberg. "The King Through Ironic Eyes: Biblical Narrative and the Literary Reading Process." *Poetics Today* 7 (1986), 275-322.

A theory of gaps and of gap-filling by the reader to help explain the way HB narrative works. The story of David, Bathsheba, and Joab (II Samuel) as example. Parts revised and incorporated into #320.

*   Polzin, Robert. "Literary Unity in Old Testament Narrative: A Response." See #123.

349.   Prickett, Stephen. "The Status of Biblical Narrative." *Pacifica* 2 (1989), 26-46.

The problematic status of biblical narratives still troubles biblical scholarship. "Neither proposals that they be treated as 'history' nor as 'fiction' address the fact that our modern concepts of both history and ... fiction are themselves derived to a surprising degree from those narratives themselves." Rather, we should investigate what it means that we are no longer able to read those narratives on their own terms.

350.   Radday, Yehuda T. "Chiasmus in Hebrew Biblical Narrative," in John W. Welch, ed., *Chiasmus in Antiquity* (Hildesheim: Gerstenberg, 1981), 118-168.

The sequence of events in narrative passages of all lengths in the HB is governed by chiastic principles, with the main idea always located at the center. The study of chiasmus turns us toward the central message of a narrative, and away from its periphery.

351.   Robertson, Edward. "Old Testament Stories: Their Purpose and Their Art." *BJRL* 28 (1944), 454-476.

Understanding the narrative art of OT stories is a pre-requisite for grasping their theological import. The characteristic features of OT storytelling. Hebrew literature was distinct from other literatures surrounding it.

352.   Rosenberg, Joel. "Biblical Narrative," in Barry W. Holtz, ed.,
        Back to the Sources: Reading the Classic Jewish Texts. (New
        York: Summit Books, 1984), 31-81.

        The various literary qualities which make narratives in the HB
        accessible to modern readers. Adequate reading of these narratives
        involves both analytic and synthetic visions. Characteristics of the
        narrative technique include word play, ambiguity, understatement,
        use of type scenes, and symmetrical structure. How these tech-
        niques convey the themes and ideology of HB narratives. Genesis
        2-3.

353.   Savran, George. "The Character as Narrator in Biblical Nar-
        rative." *Prooftexts* 5 (1985), 1-18.

        The reader must understand the world of the story in order to
        grasp its deeper narrative strategy. The relationship between the
        narrator as storyteller and the character as narrator. Genesis 37-50.

354.   Schwartz, Regina. "Free Will and Character Autonomy in
        the Bible." *Notre Dame English Journal* 15, #1 (1983), 51-74.

        Past approaches have focused on the issue of narrative silence,
        but we must first ask how free biblical characters are in a providen-
        tial design. Patriarchal legends present a strong sense of Yahweh's
        hand in human affairs. This creates a tension because it tends to
        militate against character autonomy while mimesis tends to grant
        it. Biblical narrative shows that freedom lies in obedience.

355.   Simon, Uriel. "Minor Characters in Biblical Narrative."
        JSOT 46 (1990), 11-19.

        Minor characters are very important in biblical narrative, espe-
        cially since OT narrators normally eschew value judgments. These
        characters further plot, indirect characterization, and evaluation
        of the protagonist mainly through comparison and contrast and
        ironic reversal of social conventions.

356.   Spero, Shubert. "Multiplicity of Meaning as a Device in Bib-
        lical Narrative." *Judaism* 34 (1985), 462-473.

        "... an attempt to demonstrate the usefulness of perceiving mul-
        tiplicity of meaning as an effective literary device consciously re-
        sorted to by the Biblical narrator." Genesis 24, Exodus 7-10, Num-
        bers 22.

357.   Sternberg, Meir. "Time and Space in Biblical (Hi)story
        Telling: the Grand Chronology," in #45, pp. 81-145.

        The HB's use of "mimetic chronology" is an important narrative
        device; consequently, contemporary literary theory loses some-

thing valuable by privileging fictional over history-like narrative structures. How this mimesis works, and why it is misleading to assume that straight chronology is the simpler approach to narration.

358. Sternberg, Meir. "The World From The Addressee's Viewpoint: Reception as Representation, Dialogue as Monologue." *Style* 20 (1986), 295-318.

There is a distinction between "seeing" and "hearing" in the HB, as various passages show. The Bible is a great exploiter of the loophole between "truth" and the "whole truth," which makes biblical mimesis different from modern.

359. Talmon, Shemaryahu. "The Presentation of Synchronicity and Simultaneity in Biblical Narrative." *Scripta Hierosolymitana* 27: J. Heinemann and S. Werses, eds., *Studies in Hebrew Narrative Art Through The Ages* (Jerusalem: Magnes P, 1978), 9-26.

The problem facing all narrative and epic literatures is that of presenting synchronous events in a linear medium. Biblical writers solved this with the technique of "splicing and resuming," as numerous examples from both historical and prophetic books demonstrate.

360. Vater, Ann M. "Narrative Patterns for the Story of Commissioned Communication in the Old Testament." *JBL* 99 (1980), 365-382.

This pattern may be defined as "that direct speech in a specific narrative situation in the first person of the sender, with the second person referring to the addressee, sent ... by means of a messenger." There are basically four types of commissioning messages: double scene, commissioning only, delivery only, and citation of message. It is one of many techniques which biblical narrators employ.

361. Vater, Ann M. "Story Patterns for a Sitz: A Form- or Literary-Critical Concern?" *JSOT* 11 (1979), 47-56.

"... my approach is of course diachronic, not synchronic, and urges rhetorical criticism to return to a more diachronic approach. The *distinctive* medium of the biblical authors and a full understanding of the distinctive character of biblical narration is a worthy goal in which we all can participate...."

362. White, Hugh C. "French Structuralism and OT Narrative Analysis: Roland Barthes." *Semeia* 3 (1975), 99-127.

Barthes' method compared to that of Hermann Gunkel's "traditional literary criticism." Whereas historical criticism tries to determine authorship and to reconstruct the literary and historical process through which the text was produced, Barthes "focuses upon the narrative text and the way in which its structure produces meaning."

363.   White, Hugh C. "A Theory of the Surface Structure of the Biblical Narrative." *USQR* 34 (1979), 159-173.

The semantic process which informs the structure of the biblical narrative and provides its meaning may arise from a surface phenomenon: speech events not reducible to logical terms. We must distinguish between performative speech and logical statements. In classical narrative the latter is dominant, while in biblical narrative direct discourse of the divine voice forces the former to be dominant. The consequences for the description of God and of human characters. There is a tension, then, between the closed meanings of logic and the open meaning of performative speech.

364.   Williams, James G. "The Beautiful and the Barren: Conventions in Biblical Type-Scenes." *JSOT* 17 (1980), 107-119.

The explanation for the existence of type-scenes lies not in historical or sociological data but in recognizing archetypal literary conventions. They are closer to myth than to history, and provide a symbolic understanding of the origins of Israel. They also function to set up expectations by providing codes. Four types of matriarchal type-scenes are: wife as sister; betrothal; contest of the barren wife; and promise to the barren wife. Genesis 12, 16, 18, 24, 29, 30; Exodus 2; Judges 13; II Samuel 1; II Kings 4; Luke 1.

See also: #s 23, 123, 165, 177, 264.

Hebrew Biblical Poetry

Books

365.   Alter, Robert. *The Art of Biblical Poetry.* New York (Basic Books), 1985.

Style, parallelism, and structure of HB poetry. How these devices and characteristics function in Job, Psalms, the prophets, Proverbs, and Songs Of Songs. "The choice of the poetic medium ... was not merely a matter of giving weight and verbal dignity to a preconceived message but of uncovering or discovering meanings through the resources of poetry.... [T]he spiritual, intellectual, and emotional values of the Bible that continue to concern us so urgently are inseparable from the form they are given in the poems." Incorporates #s 391, 392, and 1278. **

366.   Avishur, Yitzhak. *Stylistic Studies of Word-Pairs in Biblical and Ancient Semitic Literatures.* Kevelaer (Butzon Verlag and Bercker) and Neukirchen-Vluyn (Neukirchener Verlag), 1984.

Word-pairs are one of the most important techniques for constructing poetic parallelism. They are prosodic phenomena, many of which are common to biblical and other ancient Semitic literatures and languages. Stylistic and textual questions which the existence of word-pairs raises.

367.   Berlin, Adele. *The Dynamics of Biblical Parallelism.* Bloomington (Indiana UP), 1985.

The definition of parallelism is broader than "semantic or grammatical equivalent," and it occurs in places other than just between or within two lines. It can exist on many levels, from words and phrases to groups of lines. We cannot comprehend a poem's structure and unity until we have discovered which things it equates and which contrasts. Parallelism may be morphological, syntactic, lexical, semantic, or phonological.

*   Burney, C.F. *The Poetry of Our Lord. An Examination of the Formal Elements of Hebrew Poetry in the Discourses of Jesus Christ.* See #1566.

*   Cloete, Walter Theophilus Woldemar. *Versification and Syntax in Jeremiah 2-25.* See #939.

368.   Cobb, William Henry. *A Criticism of Systems of Hebrew Metre: An Elementary Treatise.* Oxford (Clarendon P), 1905.

Various facts upon which any "inductive" theory of Hebrew poetic meter must be based. Various theories proposed in England and Germany from the mid-eighteenth century to 1900. Hebrew poetry is sometimes metrical and sometimes not, but no theory so far proposed adequately accounts for its features.

369.   Collins, Terence. *Line-Forms in Hebrew Poetry: A Grammatical Approach to the Stylistic Study of the Hebrew Prophets.* Rome (Biblical Institute P), 1978.

A grammatical approach to biblical Hebrew poetry shows that grammar plays a "neglected ... yet ... important part in the composition of poetic lines." It should be complementary to previous work on the semantic (parallelism) and phonetic (metre) layers. This approach as well ties in with current theories of stylistics. Biblical poetry shows a unified tradition with considerable freedom, and provides criteria for recognizing poetic passages.

370.   Fisch, Harold. *Poetry with a Purpose: Biblical Poetics and Interpretation.* Bloomington and Indianapolis (Indiana UP), 1988.

The Bible is literature, but also anti-literature, because its authors were conscious of needing to question, even to condemn, all merely literary effects. The paradox is that biblical passages often gain tension and power from the very devices which they renounce. Esther, Job, Latter Prophets, Exodus, Song Of Songs, Psalms, Hosea, Qohelet. **

371.   Follis, Elaine, ed. *Directions in Biblical Hebrew Poetry.* Sheffield (JSOT P), 1986.

On the general area of Hebrew poetry, and on specific poems or poetic books in the HB. Latter analyzed separately as #s 404, 478, 632, 645, 1030, 1070, 1185, 1192, 1211, and 1286. Former are: David Noel Freedman on how prose and poetry can in fact be distinguished; Michael O'Connor on "pseudosorites" in Hebrew verse; Elaine Follis on the theme of "the holy city as daughter," which occurs in both Greek and Hebrew verse traditions, tied up with the notion of a divinely-chosen people in their own land.

372.   Freedman, David Noel. *Pottery, Poetry, and Prophecy: Studies in Early Hebrew Poetry.* Winona Lake (Eisenbrauns), 1980.

Reprints of a number of essays initially published in journals and other edited collections. Relevant items reprinted are #s 376, 414, 415, 417, 1140, 1189.

373.   Gevirtz, Stanley. *Patterns in the Early Poetry of Israel.* Chicago (U of Chicago P), 1963.

We need to pay close attention to minute details of style before we can grasp biblical poetry. Biblical poets are dependent upon, and artfully deploy, a traditional literary diction. General statement on parallelism in Hebrew poetry; studies of poetry in Genesis 4, 27; Numbers 23; I Samuel 18; II Samuel 1.

374.   Gilfillan, George. *The Bards of the Bible.* New York (Harper and Brothers), 1851.

We can learn to prize the Bible for its literary qualities as we already do for its religious truth. The "beauty of the poetic utterance of the Bible rather than its theology or rituals." General characteristics of Hebrew poetry, varieties, types. Poetry in the Pentateuch, Job, historical books, Psalms, Song Of Songs, most of the NT.

375.   Gordis, Robert. *Poets, Prophets, and Sages: Essays in Biblical Interpretation.* Bloomington (Indiana UP), 1971.

Relevant chapters are 3: "The Structure of Biblical Poetry" (stich, change of meter, parallelism, types of order); 15: "The Song of Songs" (structure, as lyrical anthology, motifs, patterns, symbolism, aesthetics, style).

376.   Gray, George Buchanan. *The Forms of Hebrew Poetry: Considered with Special Reference to the Criticism and Interpretation of the Old Testament.* Prolegomenon by David Noel Freedman. [New York] (KTAV Publishing House), 1972. [Originally published 1915].

Definition and analysis of parallelism and rhythm in Hebrew poetry. The strophe as embodiment of rhythm. Application to Lamentations 4, Nahum, Psalms 9, 10. Prolegomenon: Although Gray's views, especially on meter, are still accepted, they are not entirely adequate. Gray has been most influential in arguing that rhythm is more basic than parallelism, in subjecting previous theories to rigorous analysis, and in decrying conjectural emendations to the text when a literary approach would show the integral nature of the questioned line or word.

377.   Krašovec, Joze. *Antithetic Structure in Hebrew Poetry.* VT Supplement 35. Leiden (Brill), 1984.

Antithesis as a rhetorical-stylistic form in ancient literatures generally, and Hebrew poetry specifically. Reasons for its frequency in Hebrew literature. The relationship between stylistic devices and belief: e.g., the verticality of Yahweh versus the horizontality of human disobedience. Judges 5; Psalm 73; Jeremiah 10, 12, 17, 18, 30; Ezekiel; Job 14, 28, 29.

378.   Kugel, James L. *The Idea of Biblical Poetry: Parallelism and its History.* New Haven and London (Yale UP), 1981.

How parallelism functions in the HB. History of ideas about, and definitions of, parallelism (as well as Hebrew poetry in general) from the ancient rabbis through the eighteenth century. There is no such thing as poetry in the HB, since every characteristic so far identified in biblical poetry can also be found in biblical prose. In fact, the very notion of "poetry" is foreign to ancient Hebrew culture, so we only confuse the issue by importing this idea from pagan literatures; we then compound the problem by looking for, and finding, "rhyme," "rhythm," "lines," "stanzas," etc. See also #436.**

379.   Kugel, James L., ed. *Poetry and Prophecy: The Beginnings of a Literary Tradition.* Ithaca and London (Cornell UP), 1990.

The first three of ten essays, by Kugel and by Alan Cooper, debate the complicated relationships in the HB between poetry and prophecy: whether prophets were thought of as poets; whether the poetic and prophetic imaginations are identical, or even similar; how in the later books of the HB, David acquired a reputation as both prophet and poet.

380.   Loretz, Oswald, and Ingo Kottsieper. *Colometry in Ugaritic and Biblical Poetry: Introduction, Illustrations and Topical Bibliography.* Altenberge (CIS Verlag), 1987.

Colometry could provide a better grasp in the future of Hebrew biblical metrics. The "diversity of colometric problems ... [in] biblical poetic texts": Isaiah 30; Amos 2; Joel 2; Psalms 19, 29, 33, 72, 77, 114; Proverbs 5, 9.

381.   Lowth, Robert. *Lectures on the Sacred Poetry of the Hebrews.* Tr George Gregory. 2 Vols. London (Joseph Johnson), 1787; rpt Hildesheim (Georg Olms Verlag), 1969.

To explain the impact of Hebrew poetry "by demonstrating the congruity of artistic means and moral ends." Generic classification of ancient theory: elegiac, didactic, lyric, idyllic, prophetic and dramatic poetry. Thirty four lectures: III–XVII on general matters of style, metrics, imagery, allegory, figures, sublimity; XVIII–XXX on prophetic poetry, elegy, and didactic poetry; XXXI–XXXIV on Job.

382.   van der Moor, Willem, and Johannes C. de Moor, eds. *The Structural Analysis of Biblical and Canaanite Poetry.* Sheffield (JSOT P), 1988.

Eight essays by various scholars using structuralism as a literary-critical tool to understand biblical poetry, analyzed separately as #s 431, 710, 906, 1043, 1058, 1077, 1271, and 1432.

383.   O'Connor, M. *Hebrew Verse Structure.* Winona Lake (Eisenbrauns), 1980.

A manual of Hebrew verse structure; previous descriptions of Hebrew verse from Lowth to the present. Structure should be seen as being based on parallelism, repetition, syntax, and diction. Genesis 49; Exodus 15; Numbers 23, 24; Deuteronomy 32, 33; Judges 5; II Samuel 1; Habakkuk 3; Zephaniah; Psalms 78, 106, 107.

384.   Pardee, Dennis. *Ugaritic and Hebrew Poetic Parallelism: A Trial Cut.* VT Supplement 39. Leiden (E.J. Brill), 1988.

"... I utilize, explain, compare, and criticize several of the most important systems of analysis of these poetries which have been proposed in the last decade.... I propose a systematic analysis of parallelism as a structural device which permeates all levels of a Ugaritic or Hebrew poem ... a systematic notation of the types of parallelism [repetitive, semantic, grammatical, phonetic] over a given poem." Analysis by bi- and tri-cola is obsolete; we need instead application of more traditional literary criticism. Extensive analysis of Proverbs 2, and of the theories in #s 369 and 383.

385.   Robinson, Theodore H. *The Poetry of the Old Testament.* London (Gerald Duckworth), 1947.

The importance of form in distinguishing poetry from prose. How parallelism has been defined from Lowth to Gray; meter and stanza forms are in fact present in OT poetry; thematic analysis of Job, Psalms, Proverbs, Song Of Songs, Lamentations.

386.   Schökel, Luis Alonso. *A Manual of Hebrew Poetics.* Rome (Editrice Pontificio Istituto Biblico), 1988.

Brief historical survey of previous treatments from ancient times. Definitions of poetic genres, sound devices, rhythm, parallelism, synonymy, antithesis, imagery, figures of speech, dialogue, themes and motifs. Which of these were available to the ancient Hebrews, and which may be modern inventions without an ancient foundation.

387.   Smith, George Adam. *The Early Poetry of Israel in its Physical and Social Origins.* London (British Academy), 1912.

How Hebrew poetry works in terms of rhythm, parallelism, and structure. How Hebrew poetry is related to the national and cultural characteristics of the ancient Hebrews.

388.   Stuart, Douglas K. *Studies in Early Hebrew Meter.* Missoula (Scholars P for Harvard Semitic Museum), 1976.

There is a continuity evident between Ugaritic and early Hebrew poetry. Both descend from a common poetic tradition and thus share a number of features. It is mostly formulaic in composition; scansion should be based on overall quantity of syllables per colon, though "many problems and uncertainties remain." Genesis 4, 49; Exodus 15; Numbers 21, 23, 24; Deuteronomy 33; Judges 5; II Samuel 1, 22 (Psalm 18); Amos.

389.   Watson, Wilfred G.E. *Classical Hebrew Poetry: A Guide to Its Techniques.* Sheffield (JSOT P), 1984, 1986.

The methods and results of current scholarship, with guidelines for further study. How to analyze a poetic passage; what structural devices were available to a Hebrew poet; how Hebrew poetry resembles, and differs from, Ugaritic and Akkadian poetry; the importance of style in any analysis. We must first isolate individual features, then show how they interrelate to make the complete poem. Oral/epic poetry, meter, parallelism, stanza, strophe, verse patterns, sound devices, imagery, rhetorical devices. Outstanding bibliography, with many foreign items. **

*   William Whallon. "Biblical Poetry and Homeric Epic." See #298.

Articles

390.   Alter, Robert. "The Characteristics of Ancient Hebrew Poetry," in #33, pp. 611-624.

The role poetry plays in giving form to the biblical religious vision. Semantic parallelism is its "prevalent feature." Syntactic parallelism, also important at times, is a parallelism of rhythmic stresses. Parallelism is not synonymy, but "dynamic equivalence," where something new should be constantly looked for.

391.   Alter, Robert. "The Dynamics of Parallelism." *HUSLA* 11 (1983), 71-101.

How parallelism works in biblical poetry, and how poets convert its limitations into strengths. Revised as part of #365.

392.   Alter, Robert. "From Line to Story in Biblical Verse." *Poetics Today* 4 (1983), 615-637.

The greatest peculiarity of Hebrew biblical poetry is its avoidance of narrative. Definition of parallelism, and how it leads from one point to another by semantic development. Revised as part of #365.

393. Andersen, T. David. "Problems in Analyzing Hebrew Poetry." *The East Asis Journal of Theology* 4, #2 (1986), 68-87.

History of the prose-poetry debate in HB studies. The "significance of meter and parallelism, ... and ... the features of prose particles, acrostics and strophic structure." While some metric and rhythmic regularity does exist in biblical poetry, it is not consistent or general. Parallelism is fundamental to the poetry, though admittedly a feature of prose as well in less intense fashion. Biblical poetry shows no strophic structure; it may be that "information units" are its most fundamental component.

394. apRoberts, Ruth. "Old Testament Poetry: The Translatable Structure." *PMLA* 92 (1977), 987-1004.

OT poetry is translatable because of parallelism's "remarkable degree of overlap of form and content.... The field is rich for structuralist studies ... the psalm structure is a model of totality, transformability, and self-regulation, an 'instrument of coherence' which may in turn constitute a subunit of a larger structure."

395. Arnold, William R. "The Rhythms of the Ancient Hebrews," in Robert Francis Harper, et al., eds., *Old Testament and Semitic Studies in Memory of William Rainey Harper*, Vol. I (Chicago: U of Chicago P, 1908), 165-204.

The many attempts in the nineteenth century to pin down the rhythmic principles of biblical poetry, especially in the work of Eduard Sievers. Our best help comes from the ancient Greeks, however, particularly the writings of Aristoxenus of Tarentum. The rhythm of biblical poetry is divided into two equal parts, in a ratio of 1:1, 2:3, or 1:2; it is without exception dactylic; its measures are quadruple, sextuple, or octuple.

396. Avishur, Y. "Addenda to the Expanded Colon in Ugaritic and Biblical Verse." *UF* 4 (1972), 1-10.

Completes a survey begun by S.E. Loewenstamm [in #441]. Examples from Judges 5, Isaiah 25 and 65, Jeremiah 2, Ezekiel 22 and 30, and various psalms, "stress the great variety in the form of the expanded colon ... in biblical literature."

397. Berlin, Adele. "Motif and Creativity in Biblical Poetry." *Prooftexts* 3 (1983), 231-241.

General guidelines for entry into reading biblical poetry are contents, structure, diction, grammar, sound, and rhetorical devices, e.g., repetition and imagery. Four "separate but thematically-related passages" sharing the motif of creation which illustrate these guidelines are Isaiah 40, Psalm 104, Proverbs 8, Job 38-39.

398.   Berlin, Adele. "Parallel Word Pairs: A Linguistic Explana-
          tion." *UF* 15 (1983), 7-16.

          Purpose is "to show that linguistics can provide a better way of
          understanding word pairs, and ultimately a better way of under-
          standing parallelism." There are several "paradigmatic rules"
          which show that word pairs "were not especially invented to enable
          the composition of parallel lines."

399.   Berlin, Adele. "Shared Rhetorical Features in Biblical and
          Sumerian Literature." *JANES* 10 (1978), 35-42.

          The Bible is rarely compared with Sumerian texts in the area of
          rhetoric. To do so is to see that they share rhetorical features; vari-
          ous kinds of parallelism in these texts and in the Bible demon-
          strate the truth of this contention.

400.   Breck, John. "Biblical Chiasmus: Exploring Structure for
          Meaning." *BTB* 17 (1987), 70-74.

          Chiasmus should be distinguished from various forms of paral-
          lelism "in order to stress its focus upon a thematic center or
          'pivot'.... [R]ecognition and analysis of chiasmus is indispensable
          for a proper understanding of the theological message...."

401.   Broadribb, Donald. "A Historical Review of Studies of He-
          brew Poetry." *Abr Nahrain* 13 (1972-3), 66-87.

          "... to review, chronologically and thematically, the basic steps
          taken over the past centuries to formulate the nature of classical
          Hebrew poetry." From Josephus in the ancient world through
          Lowth to the modern theorists, the stress has been mainly on par-
          allelism, meter, and strophe. Despite all this work, little advance
          has been made in understanding the subject.

402.   Bronzwick, Norman M. "'Metathetic Parallelism'—An Un-
          recognized Subtype of Synonymous Parallelism." *HAR* 3
          (1979), 25-39.

          An object or predicate belonging to one stich may be inter-
          changed at times with that of the corresponding stich, resulting in
          a "strangely striking synonymous parallelism." Isaiah (various chap-
          ters); Amos 6, 8; Psalms 25, 35, 50, 90, 105; Micah 2; Proverbs 18;
          Job 13, 30, 38.

403.   Clifford, Richard J. "Rhetorical Criticism in the Exegesis of
          Hebrew Poetry." *SBLSP* 1980, 17-28.

          Rhetorical criticism grew out of form criticism, but must be dis-
          tinguished from it in that the former concentrates on typical form

and setting, the latter on unique interpretations and aims of each author and work. Isaiah 41, Psalms 78, 89, Proverbs 9.

404. Clines, D.J.A. "The Parallelism of Greater Precision: Notes from Isaiah 40 for a Theory of Hebrew Poetry," in #371, pp. 77-100.

A hitherto unnoticed feature of parallelism in HB poetry which may help us revise our understanding of the nature of parallelism: the second half of a parallelistic couplet is often more precise or specific than the first half. If we compare other aspects of parallelism already known with this new feature we find that they reinforce parallelism of precision, or at least do not contradict it. The general relationship of "A" to "B" is above all unpredictable.

405. Cloete, W.T.W. "Verse and Prose: Does the Distinction Apply to the Old Testament?" *JNWSL* 14 (1988), 9-15.

This is still a controversial question. A majority of recent contributions to the debate hold that the OT does distinguish between prose and verse despite our occasional difficulty in separating the two. Our still unsatisfactory knowledge of the ancient Hebrew system of versification.

406. Collins, Terence. "Line-Forms in Hebrew Poetry." *JSS* 23 (1978), 228-244.

There is no agreed-upon metrical account of Hebrew poetry. This problem can be solved by "an analysis of lines based on grammatical structures"—i.e., a syntactical rather than semantic or phonetic explanation. "Perhaps the major benefit of our study is the light it throws upon the obscure yet significant phenomenon of poetic tradition among the prophets." All examples from the Latter Prophets.

407. Craigie, Peter C. "Biblical and Tamil Poetry: Some Further Observations." *SR* 8 (1979), 169-175.

Interpreting the similarities between religions or between literatures is fraught with difficulties because we often cannot know if the similarities result from actual influence, archetypal human patterns, or sheer coincidence. Examples from Song of Songs and Isaiah used by Chaim Rabin [see #1382] demonstrate that some of his evidence is very general, and weakens his case because it does not require an historical explanation.

408. Craigie, P.C. "A Note on 'Fixed Pairs' in Ugaritic and Early Hebrew Poetry." *JTS* n.s. 22 (1971), 140-143.

Theory of fixed pairs as set forth in the recent work of Stanley Gevirtz and others. While useful, this theory has dangers because of its "extreme subjectivity."

409.   Craigie, P.C. "The Problem of Parallel Word Pairs in Ugaritic and Hebrew Poetry." *Semitics* 5 (1977), 48-58.

Mitchell Dahood's theory is that word pairs in Ugaritic and Habrew poetry enable us to recover 'the Canaanite thesaurus from whose resources the Ugaritic and Hebrew poets alike drew,' and that this fact is valuable for literary criticism of HB poetry. The theory is questionable because Dahood's data have to be used "with considerable caution."

410.   Crim, Keith R. "Translating the Poetry of the Bible." *BT* 23 (1972), 102-109.

Two fallacies exist about HB poetry: that all of it must be put into verse form when translating; and that translators have no obligation to create great poetry when they translate. The characteristics of Hebrew poetry, and the tension between finding an equivalent poetic form and distorting the semantic content.

411.   Culley, R.C. "Metrical Analysis of Classical Hebrew Poetry," in J.W. Wevers and D.B. Redford, eds., *Essays on the Ancient Semitic World* (Toronto and Buffalo: U Toronto P, 1970), 12-28.

A descriptive method which measures "some of the characteristics relevant to metre, without introducing concepts like 'feet' or 'beats'.... Even the question of the existence of metre at all is held in suspension." The theory rejects matters of stress, number of words per line or cola, while choosing syllables as a measuring device, with all its defects. Numbers 23, 24; Job 6, 9; Psalms.

412.   Dahood, Mitchell, S.J. "A New Metrical Pattern in Biblical Poetry." *CBQ* 29 (1967), 574-9.

The presence of a previously unnoticed "double-duty modifier" in Hebrew poetry. Some thirty examples have been recognized to date. How to scan the pattern, especially its generally chiastic structure. Examples from Psalms.

413.   Fisch, Harold "The Analogy of Nature, A Note on the Structure of Old Testament Imagery." *JTS* n.s. 6 (1955), 161-173.

Modern literary criticism is concerned with keywords, concepts, and images, the ambiguities in their use and the "fundamental antitheses" which the work poses and resolves. Various "iterative" themes, images and symbols in the OT might be analyzed to see what kinds psalmists, prophets and historians used. Images of vine, bride/groom, and "natural order" are important. To analyze these images, we must first abandon our "immanence: transcendence" terminology.

414. Freedman, David Noel. "Acrostics and Metrics in Hebrew Poetry." *HTR* 65 (1972), 367-392. Rpt in #372.

Detailed statistical analysis of acrostic poems in the HB, using syllable and line counts, frequency and distribution of anomalous features. There are two different acrostic structures in Hebrew poetry.

415. Freedman, David Noel. "The Broken Construct Chain." *Biblica* 53 (1972), 534-6. Rpt in #372.

Recognizing the presence of this poetic phenomenon enables us to understand certain passages more completely. Definition of the broken construct chain, with examples from Isaiah 10, Habakkuk 3, Hosea 14.

416. Freedman, David Noel. "Deliberate Deviation from an Established Pattern of Repetition in Hebrew Poetry as a Rhetorical Device." *PWCJS* 9, Vol. I (1986), 45-52.

Deviations are not unintended errors, but part of the poet's strategy. We still have a lot to learn about Hebrew poetry. Genesis 49 and Deuteronomy 33; Jeremiah 51; Amos 1-3, 4, 6; Jeremiah 51.

417. Freedman, David Noel. "Pottery, Poetry, and Prophecy: An Essay on Biblical Poetry." *JBL* 96 (1977), 5-26. Rpt in #47 and #372.

Poetry in the Bible demands serious attention because of its bulk, quality, and difficulty. Form, style, and word order "all play a vital role in conveying content, meaning, and feeling." The character of HB poetry and "its function as a vehicle of revelation." The terms "prophet" and "poet" should be thought of as interchangeable.

418. Garr, W. Randall. "The Qinah: A Study of Poetic Meter, Syntax and Style." *ZAW* 95 (1983), 54-74.

The interrelationship of meter, syntax, and poetic style in the *Qinah,* and the general rules for understanding them. Deviations, including how we classify and explain them stylistically and metrically, how we analyze their structure and determine the syntactic features which produce the well-known "sobbing effect." The *Qinah* poet had considerable flexibility within the rules.

419.   Geller, Stephen A. "The Dynamics of Parallel Verse: A Po-
        etic Analysis of Deuteronomy 32: 6-12." *HTR* 75 (1982),
        35-56.

        "... to show the great richness of a system of verse which
        employs parallelism." The only obligatory structure of parallel
        verse is the couplet. Parallelism, as Deuteronomy 32 shows, is
        complex: it operates at phonetic, grammatical, and semantic levels,
        with no one level predominant. "The constant reanalysis of
        structure lies at the heart of the experience of parallelism."

420.   Geller, Stephen A. "Theory and Method in the Study of
        Biblical Poetry." *JQR* 73 (1982), 65-77.

        A review of the books by Michael O'Connor and James L. Kugel
        [#s 383 and 378, respectively] shows that we need a dual method
        of analyzing biblical poetry: through linguistics, and through per-
        ception or aesthetic effect.

420a.   Glück, J.J. "Assonance in Ancient Hebrew Poetry: Sound
        Patterns as a Literary Device," in I.H. Eybers, et al., eds. *De
        Fructu Oris Sui: Essays in Honour of Adrianus van Selms*
        (Leiden: E.J. Brill, 1971), 69-84.

        The ancients "regarded assonance as a single figure of
        rhetoric.... They were mostly guided ... by the ear, and their sense
        of rhythm.... Some of the Biblical poets reveal an exquisite taste in
        poetry when they sacrifice easy rimes for the internal balance of
        echoing rhythm. Assonance occurs everywhere in the Old Testa-
        ment, both in the poetry and in the prose sections, and it is invari-
        ably appropriate. Examples from Genesis, Isaiah, Job, Proverbs.

421.   Good, Edwin M. "Ezekiel's Ship: Some Extended Metaphors
        in the Old Testament." *Semitics* 1 (1970), 79-103.

        How metaphor functions generally, and specifically in the OT.
        Types of metaphors to be found there, and in poetry generally.
        Imagery, and allegory versus metaphor. Ezekiel 27; Isaiah 5, 51;
        Song Of Songs 4; Joel 2; Hosea 2.

422.   Greenfield, Jonas C. "The 'Cluster' in Biblical Poetry."
        Maarav 5-6 (Spring, 1990), 159-168.

        Word pairs or epithets used to construct a complex poetic struc-
        ture or to create background were devices available to both
        Canaanite and biblical poets. Psalms, Job.

423.   Greenstein, Edward L. "Aspects of Biblical Poetry." *Jewish
        Book Annual* 44 (1986-7), 33-42.

"... experts cannot agree on whether there is poetry in the Bible at all, let alone reach consensus on what it is that characterizes biblical poetry." Various recent attempts to solve this problem in terms of language, meter, lines and couplets, and word pairs. We can in fact identify two indirect indicators of meter in biblical verse: couplets, and the deletion of syntactic elements from second lines of couplets with substitution of other words to fill out the line. "The quasi-metrical balancing of line-length ... is the major agent of parallelism in line balance."

424. van Grol, H.W.M. "Paired Tricola in the Psalms, Isaiah and Jeremiah." *JSOT* 25 (1983), 55-73.

The frequency of paired tricola argues its importance as a verse/strophe form in ancient Hebrew poetry. Verse-lines "occur in richly-shaded groups," their function "uncommonly absorbing." We need more than an inventory of poetic forms; we also need a sense of their function.

425. Grossberg, Daniel. "Multiple Meaning: Part of a Compound Literary Device in the Hebrew Bible." *The East Asia Journal of Theology* 4 (1986), 77-86.

The HB abounds in word play, including paronomasia, metaphor, pivotal patterning, climax order, repetition with variants, and coda. How these various devices interact.

426. Haran, Menahem. "The Graded Numerical Sequence and the Phenomenon of 'Automatism' in Biblical Poetry." *VT* Supplement 22 (1971), 238-267.

How this phenomenon functions in poetry throughout the HB, as arranged in a climax order.

427. Hillers, D.R. "A Convention in Hebrew Literature: The Reaction to Bad News." *ZAW* 77 (1965), 86-90.

"The poet's use of traditional literary formulae prevents us from drawing any conclusions as to his individual psychological reaction." Examples from the Latter Prophets.

428. Hrushovski, Benjamin. "Notes on the Systems of Hebrew Versifications," in T. Carmi, ed., *The Penguin Book of Hebrew Verse* (New York: Viking, 1981), 57-72.

Hebrew biblical poetry used a system of "free accentual meter" based on "varying semantic-syntactic rhythmic parallelism in phrase groups."

429.   Isaacs, Elcanon. "The Origin and Nature of Parallelism."
         AJSL 35 (1919), 113-127.

         Parallelism is not simply repetition. Two main kinds are syn-
         onymous and deferred. The role of meter.

430.   Kaddari, M.Z. "A Semantic Approach to Biblical Paral-
         lelism." *JJS* 24 (1973), 167-175.

         Terms like "synonymous" and "antithetic" parallelism are mis-
         leading, and need to be replaced with more precise terms. Non-
         poetic texts, for example, show evidence of semantic parallelism.
         To read parallelism, we need to consider the whole semantic field
         of the example.

431.   Korpel, Marjo C.A., and J.C. de Moor. "Fundamentals of
         Ugaritic and Hebrew Poetry," in #382, pp. 1-61.

         How both Ugaritic and Hebrew poetries were structured to
         allow growth through "building blocks."

432.   Kosmala, Hans. "Form and Structure in Ancient Hebrew
         Poetry." *VT* 14 (1964), 423-445; rpt *Studies, Essays and Re-
         views*, Vol. I (Leiden: E.J. Brill, 1978), 84-106.

         In Hebrew poetry, metrical/semantic analysis shows that there is
         a "perfect beauty and strict correspondence between outward form
         and inner structure." The basic element of HB poetry is the word-
         or thought-unit irrespective of beats and stresses.

433.   Kraft, Charles F. "Some Further Observations Concerning
         the Strophic Structure of Hebrew Poetry," in Edward C.
         Hobbs, ed., *A Stubborn Faith* (Dallas: Southern Methodist
         UP), 1956.

         Studies of parallelism will in future profoundly affect our under-
         standing and appreciation of Hebrew poetry. We know a great deal
         about parallelism, but less about strophes and stanzas. How to dis-
         tinguish them, how it has been done badly in the past, the fact of
         its subjectivity. The existence of strophic structure is indisputable;
         the poet's freedom in adapting it suggests we should be cautious
         when analyzing it, however. It can provide insight into the genius
         of the Hebrew poetic mind. Proverbs 8; Psalms.

434.   Kselman, John S. "Design and Structure in Hebrew Poetry."
         SBLSP (1990), 1-16.

         How the surface structure of some HB texts reveals the way "the
         poet has built the *microstructure* of *parallelismus membrorum* into

larger complexes." Isaiah 2, 35, 38; Hosea 8, 9; Zephaniah 3; Micah 4; Psalm 21.

435. Kselman, John S. "Semantic-Sonant Chiasmus in Biblical Poetry." *Biblica* 58 (1977), 219-223.

Semantic-sonant chiasmus is not exactly consciously intended on the poet's part, "but seems to occur to the poet as a melody may to a composer. It combines chiasmus and assonance. It is found in a variety of HB books, e.g., Genesis, II Samuel, Jeremiah, Ezekiel, Psalms, Proverbs, Qohelet, Lamentations.

436. Landy, Francis, Wilfred Watson, and Patrick Miller. [Discussions of James L. Kugel's *The Idea of Biblical Poetry* (#378)]. *JSOT* 28 (1984), 61-117.

Landy: Kugel ignores genre, as well as larger structural units in biblical poetry. Miller: Kugel also ignores the figurative dimension of (biblical) poetry. Kugel, "Some Thoughts on Future Research": replies to criticisms of these and other critics in print elsewhere.

437. La Sor, William Sanford. "An Approach to Hebrew Poetry Through the Masoretic Accents," in Abraham I. Katsh and Leon Nimoy, eds., *Essays on the Occasion of the Seventieth Anniversary of Dropsie University (1909-1979)*. (Philadelphia: Dropsie University, 1979), 327-353.

Accents in the Masoretic text are a valid division of the biblical text; they "indicate a kind of poetic structure in [poetic] passages...." They help us see that western notions of "meter" and "feet" are misapplied to Hebrew poetry and to ancient semitic poetry in general, thus giving that poetry more flexibility than Greek, Latin, or English poetry.

438. La Sor, William Sanford. "Samples of Early Semitic Poetry," in Gary Rendsburg, et al., eds., *The Bible World: Essays in Honor of Cyrus H. Gordon* (New York: KTAV, and Institute of Hebrew Culture and Education of New York University, 1980), 99-121.

In attempting to understand Hebrew poetry, we should give priority to materials from the ancient Semitic world—i.e., pre-Masoretic. Possible avenues of study illustrated by samples from Akkadian, Ugaritic, Aramaic (Daniel 2), Qumran Hebrew, early Arabic, and Sumerian poetries.

439. Lichtenstein, Murray H. "Biblical Poetry," in Barry W. Holtz, ed., *Back to the Sources: Reading the Classic Jewish Texts* (New York: Summit Books, 1984), 105-127.

There is an abundance of poetry in the HB. Its chief characteristics, and the large amount we do not yet know about ancient Hebrew concepts of poetry. How poetry in the HB differs from prose, and is integrated with it. Questions of form and content; why poetry appears where it does in the HB.

440.   Lichtenstein, Murray H. "The Poetry of Poetic Justice: A Comparative Study in Biblical Imagery." *JANES* 5 (1973), 255-265.

It is natural to wish "to discern patterns in the use of imagery." There are two distinct sets of images using the theme of poetic justice in the HB: those of entrapment, and those of physical striking.

441.   Loewenstamm, Samuel E. "The Expanded Colon in Ugaritic and Biblical Verse." *JSS* 14 (1969), 176-196.

Biblical poetry uses the same devices as does Ugaritic poetry, but it is not so rigidly bound by formal rules, not as archaic or as simple. The expanded colon, e.g., is employed in the HB with considerable variation. It can be found mostly in Psalms, but also in Song of Songs.

442.   Longman, Tremper III. "A Critique of Two Recent Metrical Systems." *Biblica* 63 (1982), 230-254.

The effectiveness of two contemporary approaches to Hebrew meter. Neither one—syllable counting, syntactic-accentual—can be seen as unequivocally positive. We might even question the validity of trying to find meter at all in Hebrew poetry.

443.   Meek, Theophile James. "Hebrew Poetic Structure as a Translation Guide." *JBL* 59 (1940), 1-9.

"... more careful regard for the poetic structure of a passage will often lead to a translation quite different from that generally accepted and one much more faithful to the original." Micah 7 (prose); Lamentations 2 (poetry, *qinah* rhythm, ascending parallelism); Psalm 90 (poetry).

444.   Meek, Theophile James. "The Structure of Hebrew Poetry." *JR* 9 (1929), 523-550.

We can have confidence that the work of scholars on the structure of Hebrew poetry, despite many unsolved problems, has borne fruit. Characteristics of Hebrew poetry include poetic diction, love of archaic words, use of chiasm much more frequently than rhyme, alliteration, parallelism, and distich lines. Discussion of sound values and rhythm—the latter being almost always regular. "[The Hebrew poet] was cramped by no poetic structure that was meticulously exact or artificially regular."

445.   Melamed, Ezra Z. "Break-up of Stereotype Phrases as an Artistic Device in Biblical Poetry," in Chaim Rabin, ed., *Scripta Hierosolymitana 8: Studies in the Bible* (Jerusalem: Magnes P, 1961), 115-153.

Two halves of the verse are so interdependent as to form frequently a single syntactic structure. They break up compound linguistic stereotypes into their two components, one in each half of the verse, the two halves becoming still more tightly interlocked. Categories of such phrases include divine names, place names, names of living creatures, hendiadys, and compound nouns. Some stereotyped phrases, e.g., "son of man," have become so overused as to be "transformed out of all recognition."

446.   de Moor, Johannes C. "The Art of Versification in Ugarit and Israel. I: The Rhythmic Structure," in Yitschak Avishur and Joshua Blau, eds., *Studies in Bible and the Ancient Near East* (Jerusalem: E. Rubenstein, 1978), 119-139.

"In Ugraitic and Hebrew poetry the smallest structural unit was not the syllable but the word or the cluster of words bearing a main stress.... It is fairly certain that Ugaritic and Hebrew poetry were based not on metre, but on a free rhythm similar to that of Jewish cantillation and Gregorian chant."

447.   de Moor, Johannes C. "The Art of Versification in Ugarit and Israel. II: The Formal Structure." *UF* 10 (1978), 187-217.

Application of the principle of expansion/contraction to the *stichos*. Examples from Psalms.

448.   de Moor, Johannes C. "The Art of Versification in Ugarit and Israel. III: Further Illustrations of the Principle of Expansion." *UF* 12 (1980), 311-316.

Further examples of the principle "that especially on the level of smaller structural units ... the singers were allowed a certain freedom to expand or contract their text." Judges; II Kings; Isaiah; Jeremiah; Ezekiel; Micah; Zechariah; Hosea; Joel.

449.   Muilenberg, James. "A Study in Hebrew Rhetoric: Repetition and Style." *VT* Supplement I (1953), 97-111.

Purposes of repetition in the OT. Its roots were deeply embedded in the language and literature of Israel. Isaiah; Jeremiah; Psalms. **

450.   O'Connor, Michael. "The Pseudo-Sorites in Hebrew Verse,"
        in Edgar W. Conrad and Edward G. Newing, eds., *Perspec-
        tives on Language and Text* (Winona Lake: Eisenbrauns,
        1987), 239-253

        The pseudo-sorites is a means of rupturing ordinary prose struc-
        tures; a strategy that apes the sorites (a chain of propositions) in a
        negative rather than a positive form—a "way of encoding every-
        thing by encoding its negative."

451.   Rankin, Oliver Shaw. "Alliteration in Hebrew Poetry." *JTS*
        o.s. 31 (1930), 285-291.

        Review of recent work on sound values in Hebrew poetry finds
        alliteration to be a significant device with many functions. It is a
        rhetorical, not strictly a poetic, device.

452.   Revell, E.J. "Pausal Forms and the Structure of Biblical Po-
        etry." *VT* 31 (1981), 186-199.

        Pausal forms are a clue to understanding biblical poetry's struc-
        ture because they were an important guide for the poets them-
        selves. Short passages from Psalms, Job, Proverbs.

453.   Robinson, Th.H. "Anacrusis in Hebrew Poetry," in Paul
        Volz, et al., eds., *Werden und Wesen des Alten Testaments:
        BZAW* 66 (Berlin, 1936), 37-40.

        While anacrusis is technically an impossible occurrence in He-
        brew verse, it does in fact appear as a "parallel phenomenon"—or
        at least where, if we do not assume an anacrusis, the line loses
        force and even becomes nonsense.

454.   Robinson, Theodore Henry. "Basic Principles of Hebrew
        Poetic Form," in Walter Baumgartner, et al., eds., *Fest-
        schrift Alfred Bertholet zum 80 Geburtstag* (Tübingen: J.C.B.
        Mohr, 1950), 438-450.

        Recognition of parallelism by Robert Lowth was the beginning
        of modern study of Hebrew poetic form. It creates, by ideas rather
        than by sounds, an "expectancy." Various attempts after Lowth to
        understand Hebrew parallelism. As in all poetry, Hebrew poetry
        shows an intertwining of form and content. Common forms are
        lines of either two units plus two units and three plus two, or three
        plus three plus three, etc. Since structure was controlled by mean-
        ing, not sound, units must be sense units.

455.   Robinson, T.H. "Hebrew Poetic Form: The English Tradi-
        tion." *VT* Supplement 1 (Copenhagen, 1953), 128-149.

History of theories about Hebrew poetic form; disagreements about the existence of Hebrew poetry. The principles discovered by Robert Lowth are still our best guide, as "modified in the light of later research ... will lead us to a reasonably consistent system, and help us to read Hebrew poetry as the poets meant it to be read."

456.   Robinson, Th.H. "Some Principles of Hebrew Metrics." *ZAW* 54 (1936), 28-43.

The important points made and conclusions reached by past work on Hebrew meter. How parallelism probably developed in ancient Hebrew poetry, and why meter cannot be ruled out.

457.   Roth, Wolfgang M.W. "The Numerical Sequence x/x+1 in the Old Testament." *VT* 12 (1962), 300-311.

The numerical sequence "x/x+1" can be used in the OT (and in ancient Near Eastern literature generally) in two different ways: in poetry it can be distributed over the two verse halves, forming distinctively biblical parallelism; and as a stylistic device common in poetry and prose the world over.

458.   Schramm, Gene M. "Poetic Patterning in Biblical Hebrew, in Louis L. Orlin, ed., *Michigan Oriental Studies in Honor of George G. Cameron* (Ann Arbor: Department of Near Eastern Studies, University of Michigan, 1976), 139-166.

How the Hebrew language forms patterns; types of poetic construction, e.g., parallelism, lack of rhyme; importance of format and length in determining poetic patterning; "parallelism of ambiguity." Examples of this last pattern can be found in Isaiah 5; Ezekiel 29; Psalm 23; Lamentations 1; of parallelism generally: Psalms 145, 147.

459.   Segert, Stanislav. "Problems of Hebrew Prosody." *VT* Supplement 7 (1959), 283-291.

Hebrew biblical poetry developed over more than one thousand years, and uses different prosodic systems as a result. There are many problems about Hebrew prosody yet to be solved.

460.   Segert, Stanislav. "Symmetric and Asymmetric Verses in Hebrew Biblical Poetry." *PWCJS* 9, Vol. I (1986), 33-7.

Asymmetric poetry appears occasionally in the HB, and seems to be a characteristic of early poetry, before parallelism and other symmetrical tendencies gained the victory. Its most common use is in elegiac poetry and mockery. It was probably still in use during the middle period of poetic development in ancient Israel.

461.   Shoshany, Ronit. "Prosodic Structures in Jeremiah's Poetry." *Folia Linguistica Historica* 7 (1986), 167-206.

"... how a variety of linguistic features—phonological, morphological, syntactic and semantic—reflect the prosodic regularities at different levels of structure: from line to quatrain." This theory differs from others in assuming a hierarchy of prosodic structures, and in finding prosodic material in any feature of the words and their combinations. Application of the theory to various passages in Jeremiah. "... repetition, parallelism, semantic containment and God are regular markers in Jeremiah's poetry. The rest are idiosyncratic markers."

462.   Smalley, William A. "Restructuring Translations of the Psalms as Poetry," in Matthew Black and William A. Smalley, eds., *On Language, Culture, and Religion: In Honor of Eugene A. Nida* (The Hague and Paris: Mouton, 1974), 337-371

The best theory of translating Hebrew poetry would be one of "dynamic equivalence." Such a theory holds promise for greater understanding of the poetry as well. Psalms 2, 5.

463.   Stek, John H. "The Stylistics of Hebrew Poetry: A (Re)New(ed) Focus of Study." *Calvin Theological Journal* 9 (1974), 15-30.

Happily, there are signs of reawakened interest in the subject of stylistics in HB poetry. Illustrates "somewhat at random, a few of the more interesting phenomena, some long noted, others but recently recognized": parallelism, chiasmus, other forms of symmetry, and *inclusio.*

464.   Sterk, Jan P. "Bible Poetry in Translation." *OPTAT* 3, #1 (1989), 36-49.

Those who translate biblical poetry need to remember that there are several philosophies or approaches, e.g., functional equivalence, and common language. They also should remember that poetic meaning is rooted in linguistic structures, and that poetic meaning *is* real meaning.

465.   Tsumura, David Toshio. "Literary Insertion, AxB Pattern, in Hebrew and Ugaritic." *UF* 18 (1986), 351-361.

This pattern, "within a context of 'poetic parallelism,' is an important phenomenon of the Hebrew and Ugaritic grammar and style. The existence of this seemingly ungrammatical or 'unusual' word order is caused by the very nature of poetry, in which the principle of 'similarity' is more dominant than that of 'adjacency.'"

466.   Wansborough, John. "Hebrew Verse: Apostrophe and Epanalepsis." *Bulletin of the School of Oriental and African Studies* 45 (1982), 425-433.

Disagreements with the work of Samuel E. Loewenstamm, based on the likelihood that his criteria are inappropriate to Hebrew poetic language.

467.   Wansborough, John. "Hebrew Verse: Scansion and Parallax." *Bulletin of the School of Oriental and African Studies* 45 (1982), 5-13.

The current state of our knowledge of parallelism in Hebrew poetry. Linguistics has been of great benefit to the study of this poetry through attention to imagery, grammatical and semantic detail. We need a "redescription" of the familiar details of Hebrew poetry—ultimately an epistemological issue.

468.   Watson, Wilfred G.E. "Chiastic Patterns in Biblical Hebrew Poetry," in John W. Welch, ed., *Chiasmus in Antiquity* (Hildesheim: Gerstenberg, 1981), 169-182.

The general function of chiasm in biblical poetry is to break the monotony of persistent parallelism. The overall chiastic structure; its expressive purpose is to achieve certain effects.

469.   Watson, Wilfred G.E. "Internal or Half-Line Parallelism in Classical Hebrew Again." *VT* 39 (1989), 44-66.

New examples of internal parallelism have been identified since the previous article was published [#470]. Most of these examples occur in Genesis, Isaiah, Psalms, Proverbs.

470.   Watson, Wilfred G.E. "Internal Parallelism in Classical Hebrew Verse." *Biblica* 66 (1985), 365-384.

No comprehensive study of internal parallelism exists, and it was not covered in Watson, *Classical Hebrew Poetry* [#389]. What it is; how it operates within lines and clusters; its structural patterns and rhetorical functions. #469 a follow-up.

471.   Watson, Wilfred G.E. "The Pivot Pattern in Hebrew, Ugaritic and Akkadian Poetry." *ZAW* 88 (1976), 239-253.

Additional examples of a phenomenon discovered by Mitchell Dahood [see #412]. How the pivot pattern is defined; its function as providing a powerful ending to a poem; its roots in oral composition.

472.   Watson, Wilfred G.E. "Trends in the Development of Classical Hebrew Poetry: A Comparative Study." *UF* 14 (1982), 265-277.

Much work has been done in recent years on Hebrew poetry, though little has focused on its development; we have, e.g., no relative chronology based on technique. Stylistic criteria used to date Hebrew poetry need to be reassessed. The age of a poem may be judged on the basis of acrostic, expansion, inversion, degree rhyme is used, allusions, and imagery.

473.   Watson, W.G.E. "Verse-Patterns in Ugaritic, Akkadian and Hebrew Poetry." *UF* 7 (1975), 483-492.

To "establish which metrical patterns were used by the poets in their respective languages." These patterns include tricola, sorites, pivot patterns, redundancy, and economy.

474.   van der Westhuizen, J.P. "Hendiadys in Biblical Hymns of Praise." *Semitics* 6 (1978), 50-57.

To "investigate and clarify the figure of speech of 'hendiadys' ... in an attempt to determine its development in the literature of the O.T." It was not widely used, perhaps because it developed into parallelism. Exodus 15; Deuteronomy 32; Judges 5; Isaiah; Jonah; Psalms; Job.

*   Whallon, William. "Biblical Poetry and Homeric Epic." See #298.

475.   Whallon, William. "Formulaic Poetry in the Old Testament." *Comparative Literature* 15 (1963), 1-14.

Prophets and psalmists did not show greater originality because their diction was derived from oral tradition. Creating parallelism was difficult; the answer to the difficulty was numerous word pairs which became national property. Parallelism in Hebrew poetry corresponds to Homer's formulaic epithets and Old English formulaic kennings.

476.   Whallon, William. "Old Testament Poetry and Homeric Epic." *Comparative Literature* 18 (1966), 113-131.

Erich Auerbach in *Mimesis* ignored poetry, and thus half of the HB. The true generic analogue of Homeric epic is not prose but poetry. On the basis of style, the Hebrew mind or world view cannot be distinguished from that behind the *Odyssey* or the *Iliad*. Examples from Jeremiah, Psalms, Job.

477. Whitley, C.F. "Some Aspects of Hebrew Poetic Diction." *UF* 7 (1975), 493-502.

Criticizes #445 as "failing to carry conviction"; #1100 as "offering valuable insight"; #441 as offering illuminating parallels. Recognition of the extended colon enables us to appreciate Hebrew poetry more fully.

478. Willis, John T. "Alternating (ABA'B') Parallelism in the Old Testament Psalms and Prophetic Literature," in #371, pp. 49-76.

Alternating parallelism, where lines 1 and 3 balance each other, and so do 2 and 4, is a newly-discovered kind. Examples from Psalms and the prophets. Ways this phenomenon is used to convey the author's message. Meter, syllable, word, and letter count cannot be left out as irrelevant. There are certain themes, ideas, and emotions which authors tend to use this form of parallelism to express. It is in fact quite prevalent in biblical poetry.

479. Yaron, Reuven. "The Climactic Tricolon." *JJS* 37 (1986), 153-9.

The climactic tricolon functions as an emphatic formulation to assist memory, especially through terseness and repetition. There are three types to be distinguished. Proverbs, Deuteronomy.

480. Yoder, Perry B. "A-B Pairs and Oral Composition in Hebrew Poetry." *VT* 21 (1971), 470-489.

Both Ugaritic and Hebrew poets relied on a stock of fixed word pairs in composing their parallelistic lines. These pairs were a traditional stylistic feature of their poetry.

See also: #s 12, 23, 112, 175, 178, 204, 215, 264, 298, 1111, 1175.

LAW

481. Clines, D.J.A. *The Theme of the Pentateuch.* Sheffield (JSOT P), 1976.

The Pentateuch is a unity in its final shape; thus a theme can be deduced for even so large a unit as this. This theme is "the partial fulfillment ... of the promise to or blessing of the patriarchs ... both the divine initiative where human initiatives always lead to disaster, and a reaffirmation of the primal divine intentions for man." This promise has three elements: posterity (Genesis 12-50); divine-human relationship (Exodus, Leviticus); and land (Numbers-Deuteronomy).

482.   Conroy, C. "Hebrew Epic: Historical Notes and Critical Reflections." *Biblica* 61 (1980), 1-30.

Whether portions of the Pentateuch deserve the name "epic" in the general literary sense as the ancient world understood the term. Epic was not a genre as such at that time, but it did describe certain literary qualities, e.g., tone, range, and objectivity. This issue, whatever the answer, is a fundamental one.

483.   Levenson, Jon D. "The Eighth Principle of Judaism and the Literary Simultaneity of Scripture." *JR* 68 (1988), 205-255.

Moses Maimonides' eighth principle takes "legitimacy and authority of the Torah out of the realm of history altogether." Contradictions do not undermine the authority of scripture. No Jewish theology can be built on "smaller literary and historical contexts."

484.   Mann, Thomas W. *The Book of the Torah: The Narrative Integrity of the Pentateuch.* Atlanta (John Knox P), 1988.

The Torah is both composite and unity, so both traditional historical criticism's emphasis on sources and newer literary-critical emphasis on the whole are needed. The unity of the Torah derives from both narrative and non-narrative types of literature, and is created by sophisticated literary aesthetic *and* by the monotheistic revolution.

485.   Moye Richard H. "In the Beginning: Myth and History in Genesis and Exodus." *JBL* 109 (1990), 577-598.

The story of the Pentateuch is one of man's fall and exile. "That story is revealed by the movement ... from historicized myth to mythicized history. That is, the incorporation of independent mythical narratives into a forward-moving, linear narrative through a complex thematic and structural interrelation of mythical form and the historicizing form of genealogy makes 'history' of 'myth,' while the subsequent narration of the Patriarchal 'history' and of the exodus through the interpretive patterns of the original myths makes 'myth' of 'history.'"

*   Olson, Dennis T. *The Death of the Old and the Birth of the New: The Framework of the Book of Numbers and the Pentateuch.* See #671.

486.   Rosenberg, Joel. "Meanings, Morals, and Mysteries." *Response* 9, #2 (Summer, 1975), 67-94.

"... the Bible's value as a religious document is intimately and inseparably related to its value as literature. This proposition requires that we develop a different understanding of what literature is, one that might—and should—give us trouble." The Torah itself is a *midrash* (a critique on the idea of God). All literature in a sense interprets its readers.

*   Savran, George W. *Telling and Retelling: Quotation in Biblical Literature.* See #319.

487.   Whybray, R.N. *The Making of the Pentateuch: A Methodological Study.* Sheffield (JSOT P), 1987.

"The Pentateuch, then, it may be suggested, is an outstanding but characteristic example of the work of an ancient historian: a history of the origins of the people of Israel, prefaced by an account of the origins of the world. The author ... had at his disposal a mass of material, most of which may have been of quite recent origin and had not necessarily formed part of any ancient Israelite tradition. Following the canons of the historiography of his time, he radically reworked this material, probably with substantial additions of his own invention, making no attempt to produce a smooth narrative free from inconsistencies, contradictions and unevennesses. Judges by the standards of ancient historiography, his work stands out as a literary masterpiece."

See also: #s 206, 214, 241, 291, 319, 518, 1500.

GENESIS

488.   Baker, D.W. "Diversity and Unity in the Literary Structure of Genesis," in A.R. Millard and D.J. Wiseman, eds., *Essays on the Patriarchal Narratives* (Winona Lake: Eisenbrauns, 1980, 1983), 197-215.

Structural indicators in the Bible can be of three kinds: syntactical indications of discontinuity; structural framework seen in headings, summaries, or repeated patterns; and rhetorical devices.

The presence of these indicators in Genesis demonstrates "a well-structured literary document," not an amalgam of disparate sources.

489.   Brisman, Leslie. *The Voice of Jacob: On the Composition of Genesis*. Bloomington and Indianapolis (Indiana UP), 1990.

A literary investigation of the writing of Genesis based on the theories of Harold Bloom. Literary models for biblical study should be intertextual, not sociological; agonistic, not typological. The authors of Genesis were "in inspired competition for divine benediction—or readers' allegiance." This competition consisted of a later "J" writer reacting to a composite "E" and "P" text, rather than the reverse as is usually assumed.

490.   Carroll, Michael P. "Leach, Genesis, and Structural Analysis: A Critical Evaluation." *American Ethnologist* 4 (1977), 663-677.

Edmund Leach's classic analysis of the Genesis myth is correct in finding binary oppositions in the narrative, but incorrect in saying that these oppositions are mediated. Nevertheless, structural analysis can be fruitfully applied to Genesis, since a common structure underlies at least six stories from that book: the Fall, Cain and Abel, Noah, Lot, Jacob, and Joseph.

491.   Cohn, Robert L. "Narrative Structure and Canonical Perspective in Genesis." *JSOT* 25 (1983), 3-16.

We should combine literary and canonical criticism "to examine how the literary shaping of Genesis conditions its theological meaning.... The Narrative units which comprise Genesis exhibit increasingly tighter structures which correlate with increasingly more sophisticated depictions of the divine-human relationship."

492.   Dahlberg, Bruce T. "On Recognizing the Unity of Genesis." *Theology Digest* 24 (1976), 360-367.

We need not just a collaboration with, but an integration of, higher criticism and literary criticism of the Bible. Genesis is "a unitary composition thematically developed and integrated from beginning to end," regardless of the presence of smaller units within it, or of its presence within larger units in the OT.

493.   Dahlberg, Bruce T. "The Unity of Genesis," in #40, pp. 126-133.

Some critics see Genesis as a prologue to the OT; others more specifically argue that the Joseph narrative is a bridge between Genesis and Exodus. While the "bridge" theory may be valid, Genesis is a complete book unto itself. Its beginning and ending have several things in common, e.g., fall of man versus redemption of man. (BD)

494.   Fokkelman, J.P. "Genesis," in #33, pp. 36-55.

"As readers of Genesis, we must fully respect and explore the large variety in shape and structure, tone and length, which the literary units display": e.g., sudden shifts from narrative flow to elevated, poetic style; use of different genres (myths, genealogies, laws, blessings, etc.); differences in length; and interruptions of the narrative for other narratives. Yet at the levels of genre, theme, plot, content, and key words, "powerful means of integration are used" to unify the book.

495.   Fokkelman, J.P. *Narrative Art in Genesis. Specimens of Stylistic and Structural Analysis.* Assen (Van Gorcum), 1975.

We should perform structural (synchronic) work on a biblical text first, and only then worry about genetic (diachronic or historical critical) analysis. Genesis narratives are literary works of art, notwithstanding their differences from works of fiction in Western literature, since they use "historicity" and "story" synonymously. They were conscious shapers of their material, making extensive use of chiasmus.

496.   Fox, Everett. "Can Genesis Be Read as a Book?" *Semeia* 46 (1989), 31-40.

Rhetorical criticism, specifically its discussion of plot, character development, theme and style, show Genesis to have had a "final shaping consciousness" or author. They also demonstrate that the book is structured around four literary motifs in a "carefully-elaborated chiastic plot structure."

497.   Frye, Northrop. *Creation and Recreation.* Toronto, Buffalo, and London (U of Toronto P), 1980.

Genesis is one of a series of literary creation myths in the form of a Yeatsian "double gyre": a double consciousness descends to creation, and a human consciousness ascends toward being in the image of God. Typological view of the Bible and of subsequent Christian literature [developed more fully in #5]. This new way of reading the Bible, based on a "world-wide community of action and charity," is the only way to ascend toward the image of God.

498.   Gevirtz, Stanley. "Of Patriarchs and Puns: Joseph at the Fountain, Jacob at the Flood." *HUCA* 46 (1975), 33-54.

Numerous examples of hitherto unnoticed "geopolitical word-play" in Genesis, especially in chapters 25-50.

499.   Gunkel, Hermann. *The Legends of Genesis: The Biblical Saga and History.* New York (Schocken Books), 1964; originally published 1901.

Largely source and form criticism; however, chapter III gives extensive consideration to techniques of characterization, style, theme, and plot in Genesis, and how they differ from examples in modern literature.

500.   Nohrnberg, James C. "The Keeping of Nahor: The Etiology of Biblical Election," in #45, pp. 161-188.

The "language of genealogical inquiry" mainly in Genesis, and a few passages in Exodus and Deuteronomy. "... if Genesis is a revelation, it is a revelation of kinship."

501.   Peters, John P. "Literary Aspects of Genesis," in #32, pp. 15-31.

The various narratives of Genesis, their plots and possible sources. These narratives "are the work of skilful raconteurs, and some of them ... are among the most finished pieces of the raconteur's art which have been handed down in any language."

502.   Radday, Yehuda T., and Haim Shore. *Genesis: An Authorship Study.* Rome (Biblical Institute P), 1985.

The documentary hypothesis concerning the authorship of Genesis is shown by linguistic-statistical and literary analysis to be wrong. While Genesis may consist of layers of tradition blended together, the author's work should in reality be divided into Narrator's, Human, or Divine speech. This, and not historical criticism's "JEDP" divisions, is a proper guide to the structure of Genesis, and "provide[s] ... some congenial tools for investigating and appreciating Biblical literature *qua* literature."

503.   Robinson, Robert B. "Literary Function of the Genealogies of Genesis." *CBQ* 48 (1986), 595-608.

The genealogies have been neglected in comparison to the narratives, which have in recent years been privileged by literary theorists. There is a basic orderliness in the Genesis genealogies—in "profound and productive tension with the untidy economy of the narrative." The density and depth of Genesis comes from this tension, and from the ways in which narratives and genealogies reinforce each other.

504. Sarna, Nahum M. "The Anticipatory Use of Information as a Literary Feature of the Genesis Narratives," in Richard Elliott Friedman, ed., *The Creation of Sacred Literature* (Berkeley: U of California P, 1981), 76-82.

A little-known device that recurs frequently: "The sudden introduction in a text of certain information which is extraneous to the immediate context but which is later seen to be crucial to the understanding of a subsequent episode or theme." Significantly, this device "crosses all conventional source-critical divisions," and therefore contributes to the "literary structure and ultimate unity" of Genesis.

505. Sarna, Nahum M. *Understanding Genesis*. New York (McGraw-Hill), 1966.

"... source differentiation ... is inadequate to the appreciation of the Bible as a religious document.... [A]n awareness of the existential human predicament [is] an essential prerequisite for the understanding of the biblical message that addresses itself precisely to this predicament." Primarily religious, cultural, and political background analysis, though continual reference to literary-critical matters in the character-by-character analysis.

506. Steinberg, Naomi. "The Genealogical Framework of the Family Stories in Genesis." *Semeia* 46 (1989), 41-50.

"The application of Todorov's design for analyzing narrative leads us to conclude that the family stories of the book of Genesis must be read in the context of the genealogies of Israel's ancestors. The genealogies are of great importance; they are not merely a skeleton for the narratives. It is toward this goal of genealogy that the stories move. The plot of the book of Genesis, therefore, is genealogy."

507. Steinmetz, Devora. *From Father to Son: Kinship, Conflict, and Continuity in Genesis*. Louisville (Westminster/John Knox P), 1991.

Kinship "as a structure that symbolizes narrative concerns and conveys narrative meaning" in Genesis. The cultural heritage is the source of conflict among the patriarchs' sons in each generation as they seek their father's blessing. Lexical patterns and broad narrative structure reinforce awareness of this conflict and its meaning for the emerging Israelite national consciousness. Abraham and Jacob are the most successful at doing what fathers must do: understand their place in the passing on of the blessing of God (though even they succeed only after coming perilously close to failing to grasp their role).

508.   Turner, Laurence A. *Announcements of Plot in Genesis.*
        Sheffield (JSOT P), 1990.

        The ways in which Genesis alerts readers to what will come in
        the plot, or helps them make sense of what they have already read.
        Each of the four major narrative blocks employs these
        "announcement" techniques, though with varying results. Thus the
        announcement governing chapters 1-11 does not translate into
        fulfillment; that for 12-24 is often vague and only partially fulfilled;
        or, as in 25-36 and 37-50, shown to the reader as almost guarantee-
        ing non-fulfillment no matter what God wants. Thus Genesis itself
        warns readers not to place too much faith in seemingly authorita-
        tive statements.

509.   White, Hugh C. *Narration and Discourse in the Book of Genesis.*
        Cambridge (Cambridge UP), 1991.

        A "functional narrative theory in the form of a typology of narra-
        tive functions and modes" can "show how the overarching narra-
        tive structure of Genesis and the style of a number of separate sub-
        narratives relate to this typology, and how the reader is affected by
        the defamiliarization experience produced by the unique configu-
        ration of third person narration and direct discourse in each nar-
        rative." Part published earlier as #629.

510.   White, Hugh C. "Word Reception as the Matrix of the
        Structure of the Genesis Narrative," in Robert Polzin and
        Eugene Rothman, eds., *The Biblical Mosaic: Changing Per-
        spectives* (Philadelphia: Fortress P; Chico: Scholars P,
        1982), 61-83.

        A structuralist-semiotic approach to Genesis is needed. This
        method, characterized by "open subjectivity," explains aspects of
        biblical narrative which no other one can. Structuralism may be a
        generative matrix for the entire tradition of biblical narrative writ-
        ing.

See also: #s 17, 60, 165, 166, 178, 198, 206, 289, 325, 435, 469, 470,
2027.

Genesis 1-11

511.   Aichele, George, Jr. *The Limits of Story.* Philadelphia
        (Fortress P) and Chico (Scholars P), 1985.

The "infinitely undecidable self-referentiality of language" means that story is "inevitably incomplete, and ... must be completed by belief." Chapter 2: "Form and World": spatial and temporal form in Genesis 2-3, and in the creation myths of other religions.

512. Andersen, Francis I. "On Reading Genesis 1-3," in Michael P. O'Connor and David Noel Freedman, eds., *Backgrounds for the Bible* (Winona Lake: Eisenbrauns, 1987), 137-150.

The ability to comprehend a biblical text "includes a capacity to manage the literary structure." The various lexical, grammatical, and folk-literary aids outside the text of Genesis 1-3 which readers may need. How and why readings become obsolete; why no reading is definitive. We must keep up a dialogue between micro- and macro-readings.

513. Bal, Mieke. "Sexuality, Sin, and Sorrow: The Emergence of Female Character (A Reading of Genesis 1-3)," in Susan Rubin Suleiman, ed., *The Female Body in Western Culture: Contemporary Perspectives* (Cambridge, Mass.: Harvard UP, 1986), 317-328. Rpt from *Poetics Today* 6 (1985), 21-42, and in #304.

Passages from Genesis 2-3 which concern "the creation of the female body, the transgression, and its consequences." The tradition of sexist readings of this passage is in error, as are the illogical conclusions about female subservience often drawn from such readings. Close reading argues against seeing a contradiction in the two creation stories. The story rather concerns "creation, by differentiation, of humanity, of character."

514. Barré Lloyd M. "The Poetic Structure of Genesis 9:5." *ZAW* 96 (1984), 101-4.

If we juxtapose Genesis 9:5 with 1:27, the similarities become immediately apparent, confirming analysis of 9:5 as being interrelated with other passages through synonymous parallelism.

515. Burke, Kenneth. *The Rhetoric of Religion: Studies in Logology.* Boston (Beacon P), 1961.

"On Words and The Word": Six analogies between words and Scripture, which exist because humans are symbol-making animals. "The First Three Chapters of Genesis" (shorter version in *Daedalus* 87, #3 (1958), 37-64; rpt Rollo May, ed., *Symbolism in Religion and Literature* [New York: Braziller, 1960], 118-151): a "logological" (linguistic) meditation on the idea of order in Genesis 1-3, as embodied in its narrative style. The biblical concern for temporality versus the cyclic nature of pagan myth.

516.   Burns, Dan E. "Dream Form in Genesis 2.4b-3.24: Asleep in the Garden." *JSOT* 37 (1987), 3-14.

Study of literary theory and of secular literary works helps illuminate the structure and themes of Genesis 2-3. Adam and Eve leave the garden literally "dis-enchanted"; their "fall" is better understood as an awakening. "The future, and the imaginative experience of life which we call literature, lie before them."

517.   Christensen, Duane. "Janus Parallelism in Genesis 6:3." *HS* 27 (1986), 20-24.

Careful reading proves the existence of Janus parallelism in this verse.

518.   Clines, D.J.A. "Theme in Genesis 1-11." *CBQ* 38 (1976), 483-507.

Assuming that Genesis 1-11 is a unified composition, we can find two alternative possibilities for the theme of these chapters; both of these possibilities closely parallel the theme of the entire Pentateuch. Genesis 1-11 may be an amalgam, but it is one which achieves a new unity and meaning independent of the meanings found in its sources.

519.   Collins, John J. "The Rediscovery of Biblical Narrative." *Chicago Studies* 21 (1982), 45-58.

The new, literary-critical approach represents a radical, profound paradigm shift for biblical studies. The historical-critical method with its "negative results," has led us to literary criticism. Genesis 2-3 is a test case of how we may say that biblical stories are "true." Biblical narratives "do not provide absolute truths, but illustrations of human experience."

*   Forman, Charles C. "Koheleth's Use of Genesis." See #1393.

520.   French, R.W. "Reading the Bible: The Story of Adam and Eve." *College Literature* 9 (1982), 22-29.

The story of Adam and Eve is the best known in the Bible, but also "least known in significant detail and hence the most misunderstood." Significant details include the lack of narrative comment, the place of humans in the events, the truthful character of the serpent, and the proper conduct of Adam and Eve. The story is a "tribute to humanity."

521. Frymer-Kensky, Tikva. "The Atrahasis Epic and its Significance for Our Understanding of *Genesis* 1-9." *Biblical Archeologist* 40 (1977), 147-155.

Recent discovery of the Babylonian epic (written no later than 1700 BCE) "enables us to appreciate the major themes of this great cycle (Genesis 1-9) from a new perspective.... The composer of Genesis 1-9 had reinterpreted the cosmology and early history of Man ... [using] a framework that is at least as old as the Epic of Atrahasis, the framework of the Primeval History of Creation—Problem—Flood—Solution, and has retold the story in such a way as to reinterpret an ancient tradition to illuminate fundamental Israelite ideas...."

522. Gordon, Cyrus H. "Build-Up and Climax," in Yitschak Avishur and Joshua Blau, eds., *Studies in Bible and the Ancient Near East* (Jerusalem: E. Rubenstein, 1978), 29-34.

Study of Ugaritic has shown that repetition in the HB does not necessarily indicate combining of multiple sources; rather, traditional compositional style called for repetition with variants. Reading Genesis 1:1-2:4 in this light shows that the two creation stories are both supposed to be there as part of one climactic story.

523. Gros Louis, Kenneth R.R. "The Garden of Eden," in #39, pp. 52-8.

The process of character development in Genesis 3 directly through word choice and action, and indirectly through implication. (JM)

524. Gros Louis, Kenneth R.R. "Genesis I and II," in #39, pp. 41-51.

Overfamiliarity with the Creation story is a barrier to the objectivity necessary for effective literary criticism. In Genesis 1, word choice showing a marked lack of metaphor and simile is used to establish the conception of a transcendent and omnipotent God. Such a view of God may have helped leaders defend traditions, rituals, and hierarchies against criticism. In Genesis 2, however, portrayal of God shifts from transcendent to immanent, from "conservative" to "liberal," from "distant" to "philanthropic." (JM)

525. Gros Louis, Kenneth R.R. "Genesis 3-11," in #40, pp. 37-52.

Literary criticism enables us to ask the reasons for some of the "small" details in the Adam and Eve story: e.g., Where does the serpent come from? Why does it tempt Eve? What happens when Adam and Eve's eyes are opened? and so on. We also notice interesting parallels with the Noah story: the pattern of gift, sin, punishment, and mercy; a pattern also found in the Abraham narrative. (BD)

526.   Hasan-Rokem, Galit. "And God Created the Proverb ... Inter-Generic and Inter-Textual Aspects of Biblical Paremiology—or the Longest Way to the Shortest Text," in #230, pp. 107-120. Roland Murphy, "Proverbs in Genesis 2?" in #230, pp. 121-5.

Genesis 2:18 and 2:24 provide instances of proverbs in narrative. The poetics of such usage shows that these proverbs "were inserted at the point when the most extreme experience of ambivalence appears in the text." Thus these sayings influence the meaning of the surrounding text: its concern with moral choice and mortality. Murphy: The sayings in these verses are probably not proverbs at all, which in turn raises doubts about our ability to respond appropriately to biblical narrative texts.

527.   Hauser, Alan Jon. "Genesis 2-3," in #34, pp. 20-36.

The theme of intimacy developed in chapter 2 is shattered by the alienation in chapter 3: Adam and Eve from each other, and both from God. Their language, especially syntax and word-play, in 3:14-19, provides the clue that their alienation is complete.

528.   Hauser, Alan J. "Linguistic and Thematic Links Between Genesis 4:1-6 and Genesis 2-3." *JETS* 23 (1980), 297-305.

"The story of Cain and Abel in Gen 4:1-16 is structurally, linguistically and thematically interwoven with the narrative of Genesis 2-3." This was not done by a clever editor, but by "one highly-skilled writer who has interwoven all major aspects of the two stories so that ... they form one unit."

529.   Hendel, Ronald S. "Of Demigods and the Deluge: Toward an Interpretation of Genesis 6:1-4." *JBL* 106 (1987), 13-26.

Myth criticism shows the narrative of Genesis 6 proceeding dialectically, generating and then resolving oppositions while sketching a transition from mythical nature to human culture. The Yahwist has isolated a fragment from its traditional context and integrated it into the structural and thematic framework of the early part of Genesis.

*   Hesse, Eric W. and Isaac M. Kikawada. "Jonah and Genesis 1-11." See #1041.

530. Jobling, David. "Myth and its Limits in Genesis 2.4b–3.24," in *The Sense of Biblical Narrative: Structural Analyses in the Hebrew Bible* (Sheffield: JSOT P, 1986), 17-43.

Genesis 2:4-3:24 from both structuralist-semantic and feminist perspectives. The model for narrative shape should be "a man to till the ground," not "creation and fall." Ambiguity in the characterization of Yahweh. The passage is folk-tale, not myth.

531. Kessler, Martin. "Rhetorical Criticism of Genesis 7," in Jared J. Jackson and Martin Kessler, eds., *Rhetorical Criticism: Essays in Honor of James Muilenberg* (Pittsburgh: Pickwick P, 1974), 1-17.

There are duplications in the Flood narrative, but they are mutually related. It is a theological narrative which displays considerable artistic sophistication. Its chief narrative techniques include repetition of roots, formulaic word pairs, repetition as a framing device, thematic coherence and inversion, all of which demonstrate the unity of Genesis 7, and therefore call into question the traditional source divisions into "J" and "P."

532. Kikawada, Isaac M. and Arthur Quinn. *Before Abraham Was: The Unity of Genesis 1-11*. Nashville (Abingdon P), 1985.

The author of Genesis was so much in charge of his materials that it makes no sense to speak of him as an editor. In Genesis 1-11, evidences for this include the unity of the Noah chapters in style and motif through parody, chiasm, and vocabulary; the structural-thematic parallels between Genesis 1-11, Exodus 1-2, Matthew 1-3, Genesis as a whole and the Pentateuch; thematic unity derived from disagreement with the older Atrahasis epic; and genealogies showing the author's love for variety. Repetition was both typical of ancient Near Eastern style, or necessary for rhetorical emphasis.

533. Kikawada, Isaac M. "Literary Convention of the Primeval History." *AJBI* 1 (1975), 1-21.

The form of Genesis 1-11 versus that of the Old Babylonian Atrahasis epic. While their ideologies are antagonistic, Genesis borrows the form of the other work, as in fact do Exodus 1-2 and Matthew 1-3.

534. Kikawada, Isaac M. "A Quantative Analysis of the 'Adam and Eve,' 'Cain and Abel,' and 'Noah' Stories," in Edgar W. Conrad and Edward G. Newing, eds., *Perspectives on Language and Text* (Winona Lake: Eisenbrauns, 1987), 195-203.

The interrelationships among these three stories "reflects a progressive dramatic development in three stages...." Their significance is increased when they are viewed together—analogous to synonymously parallel tricola in Hebrew poetry.

535.   Kikawada, Isaac M. "The Shape of *Genesis* 11:1-9," in Jared J. Jackson and Martin Kessler, eds., *Rhetorical Criticism: Essays in Honor of James Muilenberg* (Pittsburgh: Pickwick P, 1974), 18-32.

If we can recover the "underlying ... unifying principles of organization that have fashioned the story of ... 'The Tower of Babel' into a particular shape," then we can observe its rhetorical features and structural devices, and the ways they influence understanding and appreciation of the story. These devices include balancing of episodes, chiasmus, introversion, inclusio, linear progression, sequential repetition, broken symmetry and irony as organizing principle.

535a.   Lambert, W.G. "A New Look at the Babylonian Background of Genesis." *JTS* 16 (1965), 287-300; rpt #47, pp. 285-297.

We need to be cautious about assuming Akkadian influence on the OT. Similarities and differences between Babylonian-Assyrian and biblical creation and flood stories "make the study of possible influences very complicated." In any case, parallels do not automatically mean influence. The biblical Flood story was probably borrowed, but the creation stories from the ancient Near East "had less obvious influence" on the OT.

536.   Levinson, Bernard M. "The Right Chorale: From the Poetics to the Hermeneutics of the Hebrew Bible," in #318, pp. 129-153.

Meir Sternberg in *The Poetics of Biblical Narrative* [#320] makes the error of assuming narrative to "be" the Hebrew Bible. He thus ignores the legal corpora, as well as the reality of diachronic dimensions of the HB. The stories of Noah in Genesis 6 and 7 illustrate the need for a "proper hermeneutics of the Hebrew Bible"—one which would recognize the impact on the ancient Israelite scribe of mutually exclusive traditions. The scribe attempted in Genesis 7 a harmony of conflicting accounts, thus calling attention to the Bible's own textuality, and revealing its tendency to deconstruct itself.

537.   Longacre, Robert E. "The Discourse of the Flood Narrative." *JAAR* 47 Supplement B (March 1979).

Discourse analysis demonstrates that the Flood narrative is a unity, and yet also explains its stylistic variations as different genres within the narrative: e.g., procedural, instructional, and predictive. Repetitions are due to the rhetorical device of "overlay," which is well-attested to in non-Western literatures.

538. Longacre, Robert E. "Interpreting Biblical Stories," in Teun A. Van Dijk, ed., *Discourse and Literature* (Amsterdam and Philadelphia: John Benjamins, 1985), 169-185.

The "tensions, contradictions, and repetitions" of Genesis 6-9 are not signs of separate sources but are better explained as "literary artistry of a high order." An "action profile" of plot, as seen by discourse analysis.

539. Maier, John. "The Flood Story: Four Literary Approaches," in #179, pp. 106-9.

Genesis 6-9 can be used to illustrate four different approaches to a literary work: literary history, rhetorical criticism, structuralism, and symbolism. This narrative in Genesis is a particularly useful example of how scholars apply various tools, and of the profound philosophical questions prompted by reading Genesis.

540. McEvenue, Sean E., S.J. *The Narrative Style of the Priestly Writer.* Rome (Biblical Institute Press), 1971.

Application of the New Criticism to the writings of the Priestly writer. Three passages may be used for this purpose: Genesis 6-9, 17, and Numbers 10 and 13-14. "P" "tends to replace action with theology, suspense with symmetry, interiorly motivated conflict with objective tableau."

541. McKenzie, John L., S.J. "The Literary Characteristics of Genesis 2-3." *Theological Studies* 15 (1954), 541-572.

"By the literary characteristics of Gen 2-3 I mean the literary species of the passage as a whole, its relation to extra-biblical literature, and its unity." The significance which this narrative may have had for the Israelites as "an idealized account of the origin of sex and of the perversion of sexual life from its primitive integrity."

542. Miller, Patrick D., Jr. *Genesis 1-11: Studies in Structure and Theme.* Sheffield (JSOT P), 1978.

The structure and motifs of Genesis 1-11 as a unified narrative, with theology weaving thematic strands together. Motifs include the divine versus the human world, and human participation in the world of deity; the correspondence of sin and judgment; and the *adamah* motif: how humans are involved with the earth.

543.   Milne, Pamela J. "The Patriarchal Stamp of Scripture: The Implications of Structuralist Analyses for Feminist Hermeneutics." *Journal of Feminist Studies in Religion* 5, #1 (Spring, 1989), 17-34.

The structuralist method raises serious questions about the viability of feminist biblical criticism, as illustrated by Genesis 2-3, since it reinforces our prior suspicions that the Bible cannot be rehabilitated as a spiritual resource for women because it is incurably patriarchal throughout.

544.   Miscall, Peter D. "Jacques Derrida in the Garden of Eden." *USQR* 44 (1990), 1-9.

Literary critics too often read Genesis 1-2 as an overall unity, ignoring the fundamental differences, the "dramatic shifts in style, form, and content" between 1:1-2:4a and 2:4b-25. Instead, we should focus on reading them together "as parts of the same text." We read them with "shifting, difference, division, leaving, and expulsion.... A river flows ... from Eden to water the garden; from there it goes into the world and divides into the literary and the real. That division has no solution."

545.   Niditch, Susan. *Chaos to Cosmos: Studies in Biblical Patterns of Creation.* Chico (Scholars P), 1985.

"... how the Hebrew myths of chaos, creation, and cosmos have informed the lives of various generations and how in the process the myths themselves have been transformed and renewed." Five creation themes may be traced: chaos, order and paradise, emergence of reality, overrating/underrating of family members, and genealogical catalogue. These themes as they appear first in Genesis 1-11, and as they relate to the whole of Genesis, to prophetic literature, and to Christian literature (especially Paul).

546.   Patte, Daniel, ed. *Semeia 18: Genesis 2 and 3: Kaleidoscopic Structural Readings.* Chico (Scholars P), 1980.

Articles by Patte, Robert C. Culley, David Jobling, Judson F. Parker, Hugh C. White, and Thomas E. Boomershine, with responses by Arno Hutchinson, James G. Williams, Glendon E. Byrne, Robert Detweiler, J.D. Crossan, Gary Phillips, Brian Watson Kovacs, and Clarence H. Snelling.

547.   Porten, Bezalel, and Uriel Rappaport. "Poetic Structure in Genesis IX 7." *VT* 21 (1971), 363-9.

"Sensitivity to structure and design and awareness of the a-b-c-b sequence enables us to appreciate better the meaning and context of Gen. ix 7." The context of this verse is found not only in immediately surrounding verses, but also later in Genesis, and even in Exodus.

* Rosenberg, Joel. *King and Kin: Political Allegory in the Hebrew Bible.* See #847.

548. Trible, Phyllis. "Eve and Adam: Genesis 2-3 Reread." *Andover Newton Quarterly* 13 (1973), 251-8; rpt Carol P. Christ and Judith Plaskow, eds., *Womanspirit Rising: A Feminist Reader in Religion* (San Francisco: Harper and Row, 1979), 74-83

"... we need no longer accept the traditional exegesis of *Genesis* 2-3. Rather than legitimating the patriarchal culture from which it comes, the myth places the culture under judgment. And thus it functions to liberate, not to enslave. This function we can recover and appropriate. The Yahwist narrative tells us who we are (creatures of equality and mutuality); it tells us who we have become (creatures of oppression); and so it opens possibilities for change, for a return to our true liberation under God. In other words, the story calls female and male to repent."

549. Walsh, Jerome T. "Genesis 2:4b–3:24: A Synchronic Approach." *JBL* 96 (1977), 161-177.

Genesis 2:4b–3:24 is a "highly structured unit" whose principal arrangement is concentric in seven "scenes," each in turn also carefully patterned. On a narrative level, the passage communicates anthropological, moral-theological, and parenetic points about sin and man's relation to God.

550. Wenham, G.J. "The Coherence of the Flood Narrative." *VT* 28 (1978), 336-348.

Form criticism makes a mistake when it separates these chapters of Genesis into J, E, D, and P, because then we miss the coherence of the narrative. Chiasm, or palistrophe, is the key to the unity of the Flood narrative.

551. Westbrook, Deeanne. "Paradise and Paradox," in #48, pp. 121-133.

Harold Bloom identifies a crucial element in the Yahwist as "the uncanny" or "antithetical"—a characteristic which lends a "rich ambiguity" but no one meaning to his work. The "unresolved antitheses" of the garden and the fall in Genesis 2-3 are symbolized most crucially by the two trees: life and death, fortune and misfortune: a message both nostalgic and repugnant. Adam is dust, Eve is life; together they create new life, having themselves both been created by a God who is both love and death.

552.   van Wolde, E.J. *A Semiotic Analysis of Genesis 2-3. A Semiotic Theory and Method of Analysis Applied to the Story of the Garden of Eden.* Assen/Maastricht (Van Gorcum), 1989.

Application to Genesis 2-3 of a semiotic approach to narrative texts based on the work of A.J. Greimas, modified from ideas of Charles Sanders Pierce to allow for interaction of text and reader. "Expression forms"; semantic analysis (network linked by the reader to the text: e.g. God-man, man-earth, man-animal, male-female, life-death); discursive analysis.

See also: #s 3, 5, 7, 14, 49, 117, 149, 190, 192, 206, 211, 213, 218, 221, 222, 254, 270, 293, 304, 307, 310, 311, 332, 336, 338, 352, 373, 388, 490, 556, 700, 1088, 1210, 1215, 1393, 1644.

Genesis 12-24

553.   Alter, Robert. "Biblical Imperatives and Literary Play," in #318, pp. 13-27.

Hebrew biblical narrative is characterized by a "fine excess," a "dimension of imaginative free play," revealing the "covenantal urgency of the biblical authors [which] impelled them on a bold and finally impossible project: ... to use literature to go irrevocably beyond itself...." This trait is revealed in the laughter of Sarah in Genesis 18, the helplessness of Barak and Sisera before Deborah and Jael in Judges 4, and in the "sexual and political comedy" of Esther.

554.   Alter, Robert. "Sodom as Nexus: The Web of Design in Biblical Narrative," in #45, pp. 146-160.

The use of Sodom in Genesis 17-21 as an example of "the juxtaposition of disparate materials that are purposefully linked by motif, theme, analogy and, sometimes, by a character who serves as a bridge between two different narrative blocks otherwise separated in regard to plot and often in regard to style and perspective or even genre." The Sodom story "is crucial not only to Genesis but to the moral thematics of the Bible as a whole ... because it is the biblical version of anti-civilization."

555. Auerbach, Erich. "Odysseus' Scar," in *Mimesis: The Representation of Reality in Western Literature*. Tr Willard Trask (Princeton: Princeton UP, 1953), 3-23.

Contrasting an episode from the *Odyssey* with Genesis 22 shows that the two episodes are fundamentally different: Homer foregrounds everything, Genesis leaves much in the background and unexplained. The "problematic psychological situation" of biblical characters allows a respect for everyday experience which is impossible in ancient Greek literature. Homer "seek[s] to make us forget our own reality for a few hours," while Genesis "seeks to overcome our reality." **

* Block, Daniel I. "Echo Narrative Technique in Hebrew Literature: A Study in Judges 19." See #717.

556. Crenshaw, James. "Journey into Oblivion: A Structural Analysis of Genesis 22:1-19." *Soundings* 58 (1975), 243-256; rpt Susan Wittig, ed., *Structuralism: An Interdisciplinary Study* (Pittsburgh: Pickwick P, 1975), 99-112.

The plot movements of Genesis 12 and 22, with especially important questions which the reader will ask about plot, character, and theme. The syntagmatic structure of Genesis 22, its syntactic features, and mythical (deep) structure, all of which are similar to that of Isaiah 7.

557. Delaney, Carol, and Ann Marmesh. "The Legacy of Abraham: Dubious Male Dominance and Female Autonomy." Part I of #225.

Narratological/feminist analysis in two essays, both on Genesis 12-37.

557a. van Dyk, P.J. "The Function of So-Called Etiological Narratives." *ZAW* 102 (1990), 19-33.

Many of these narratives are not etiological at all; rather, they are probably rhetorical devices whose function is "to affirm the narrative (and its symbols) and to heighten its entertainment value." Such theological and political symbols occur in Genesis 16: Hagar as Egyptian, Ishmael as wild ass, e.g., which serve to demarcate boundaries between "us" (Israelites) and "them" (Egyptians and Ishmaelites).

558. Edgerton, W. Dow. "The Binding of Isaac." *Theology Today* 44 (1987), 207-221.

Genesis 22 as illustration of how reader-response theory can extend and deepen interpretation of scripture. "... the relationship between interpreter and text is intimate.... The Word is to be found neither in the text nor the reader, but in relationship where the two meet."

559.   Exum, J. Cheryl, and J. William Whedbee. "Isaac, Samson, and Saul: Reflections on the Comic and Tragic Visions." *Semeia* 32 [#228] (1985), 5-40; rpt #231, pp. 117-168.

Three stories: Genesis 22, Judges 13, I and II Samuel, "to illustrate the characteristic patterns of comedy and tragedy in the Bible." Although Saul's is a tragic story, the dominant vision in the Bible is comic.

560.   Fokkelman, J.P. "Time and the Structure of the Abraham Cycle." *OS* 25 (1989), 96-109.

"... the organization of time offers us the key to the proper articulation of the Abraham cycle." The genealogical and age data "has its own order and invites systematic attention." The Abraham cycle has chiasmic structure overall, showing "the polarity of individual new life and collective death."

561.   Fuchs, Esther. "Structural and Patriarchal Functions in the Biblical Betrothal Type Scene: Some Preliminary Notes." *Journal of Feminist Studies in Religion* 3, #1 (Spring, 1987), 7-13.

In three betrothal type-scenes: Genesis 24 and 29, and Exodus 2, "the differences between the various bride figures are helpful hermeneutical keys to one of the structuring ideologies of the betrothal type-scenes." The structure and ordering devices of such scenes, particularly repetition, omission, information gaps and dialogue, "can be decoded as patriarchal strategies."

562.   Gordis, Daniel H. "Lies, Wives and Sisters: The Wife-Sister Motif Revisited." *Judaism* 34 (1985), 344-359.

The type-scene in Genesis 12, 20, and 26. History of the treatment of these scenes from Hermann Gunkel to Robert Alter. In each scene a specific theme predominates. How these scenes are constructed "so as to beg comparison."

563.   Greenstein, Edward L. "Genealogy as a Code in Genesis," in #179, pp. 102-5.

Analytical approach to genealogy which may be used as a model for classroom presentation. The "genealogical associations in Genesis [are] ... a code representing the relations that ancient Israel bore toward the various nations among whom Israelites lived." Abrahamic genealogies as example.

564. Gros Louis, Kenneth R.R. "Abraham: I," in #40, pp. 53-70.

Patterns in the Adam and Noah narratives, and how they relate to the Abraham narratives. Four basic steps in the pattern: gift, sin, punishment, and mercy. How these patterns fit into the overall structure of Genesis 12-19. (BD)

565. Gros Louis, Kenneth R.R. "Abraham: II," in #40, pp. 71-84.

We must be concerned with the narrative context of the Abraham and Isaac story. "And by that I mean not only the episodes that precede and follow it, but also that entire 'previous history' of Abraham...." How the character of Abraham is developed in Genesis 12-19, and how that in turn affects our interpretation of Genesis 20-24, especially of chapter 22. (BD)

566. Hackett, Jo Ann. "Rehabilitating Hagar: Fragments of an Epic Pattern," in Peggy L. Day, ed., *Gender and Difference in Ancient Israel* (Minneapolis: Fortress P, 1989), 12-27.

The similarities often noticed between the two Hagar stories, as well as their incongruities, can be explained better by comparing them not to each other as being from J and E strands of Genesis, but to similar patterns in other ancient Near Eastern epics. This will tell us more about what an ancient audience would have seen in Hagar and her story. There is, e.g., the type scene of the insulted goddess who demands revenge, with the less powerful person being the hero. Such a comparison enables us to see tension in the plot, to feel sympathy for the female characters, and to grasp the biblical author's sensitivity to issues of power and gender.

567. Jeansonne, Sharon Pace. *The Women of Genesis: From Sarah to Potiphar's Wife.* Minneapolis (Fortress P), 1990.

Application of narrative criticism to Genesis 12-50 in terms of character, dialogue, narrator's versus characters' perspectives, type-scenes, diction, and setting: to "uncover the narrator's perspective of the role that these women played in Israel's origins." In general, they are portrayed respectfully and paradigmatically: the trials of Sarah, Rachel and Rebecca underscore God's role in Israel's survival; that of Tamar illustrates the effects of the covenant on the community.

568. Kikawada, Isaac M. "The Unity of Genesis 12:1-9." *PWCJS* 6 (1973), 229-235.

Rhetorical criticism can describe the compositional units of Genesis 12 so as to demonstrate the unity of this chapter. Devices providing unity include antithetical themes, well-defined structure, *inclusio,* and key-words as linking terms. Chapter 12, then, acts as a fitting introduction to the entire patriarchal history (Genesis 12-50).

569.   Landy, Francis. "Narrative Techniques and Symbolic Trans-
        actions in the Akedah";
570.   Fokkelman, J.P. "On the Mount of the Lord There is a Vi-
        sion: A Response to Francis Landy Concerning the
        Akedah," in Cheryl Exum, ed., *Signs and Wonders: Biblical
        Texts in Literary Focus* [no city or publisher] (Scholars P?),
        1989, 1-40, 41-57.

The "split voice" in Genesis 22 compared with Job's "reworking of the Akedah motif" and correlations with Greek myths of initiation. Attention to point of view shows "how every detail and especially redundancy focus[es] attention on Abraham's unvoiced subjectivity." The interplay of space and time, "subversion of narrative sequence," "mystification of the place"; symbolic transactions; the context "of the theme of child sacrifice throughout the Hebrew Bible and as an inversion of the wife-sister stories in the Patriarchal narratives."
Landy is substantially correct, though a few of her details need modification. Her application of A.J. Greimas' actantial model is not completely correct; she offers inappropriate interpretation of the "lamb-ram" opposition; I Samuel 14 has greater relevance to Genesis 22 than Landy allows.

571.   Mazor, Yair. "Genesis 22: The Ideological Rhetoric and the
        Psychological Composition." *Biblica* 67 (1986), 81-88.

The "rhetorical and compositional layers" of the Abraham-Isaac story. Literary criticism illuminates not only its artistic devices but also its ideology, theology, and psychology. The story shows an impressive, intricate balancing of plot-character development and ideological purpose, so that neither overwhelms the other.

572.   McEvenue, Sean E. "A Comparison of Narrative Styles in
        the Hagar Stories." *Semeia* 3 (1975), 64-80.

Genesis 16 and 21 are told in three parallel accounts. Stylistic analysis of these accounts shows that P minimizes conflict and emphasizes genealogy; J dramatizes Sarah's inner conflicts; E offers a poignant tale of human grief and divine concern for human beings.

*   McEvenue, S.E., S.J. *The Narrative Style of the Priestly Writer.*
        See #540.

573. Miscall, P.D. *The Workings of Old Testament Narrative.*
Philadelphia (Fortress P) and Chico (Scholars P), 1983.

The richness, complexity, and elusiveness of OT narrative. It offers both too few and too many details. It gives rise to many contradictory readings because interpretation is often undecidable. As we can see in Genesis 12 and I Samuel 16-22, this complexity seems to be deliberate. Readings of these (or of any OT narrative) cannot go to the "center" of meaning because the text in fact undermines itself.

574. Petersen, David L. "A Thrice-Told Tale: Genre, Theme, and Motif." *BR* 18 (1973), 30-43.

By examining the categories of theme and motif in Genesis 12, 20, and 26, we realize that our genre classifications for biblical narrative need rethinking. To do so, we must be aware simultaneously of plot, character, setting, and theme. In these chapters of Genesis, the "wife-sister" motif is the key one.

575. Polzin, Robert M. "'The Ancestress of Israel in Danger' in Danger." *Semeia* 3 (1975), 81-98.

Two important transformations within three versions of the "same" story (Genesis 12, 20, 26): wealth and progeny transformed into adultery; and lies transformed into the truth discovered by a monarch. Traditional historical-critical, diachronic approaches will not discover this; only literary, synchronic ones will.

*   Rosenberg, Joel. *King and Kin: Political Allegory in the Hebrew Bible.* See #847.

576. Sternberg, Meir. "Double Cave, Double Talk: The Indirections of Biblical Dialogue," in #318, pp. 28-57.

Genesis 23 (the exchange between Abraham and the Hittites over the former's request for a burial place for Sarah) is a simple narrative on the surface. Yet its dialogue contains sophisticated, subtle and complex interweaving of motifs and characterization. It acts as "not just a sequel but a companion piece to the Binding of Isaac.... Each brings to a crisis one of the grand elements of the Promise. Each shows the Patriarch heroically rising to the challenge, doing what he must without a murmur...."

577. Trible, Phyllis. "Genesis 22: The Sacrifice of Sarah," in #318, pp. 170-191.

Using scripture to interpret scripture, we can expose "how the biblical depiction works to expose patriarchy in Genesis 22, how that exposure alters the meaning of the story, and how the resultant interpretation challenges faith. A feminist hermeneutic takes over the rhetorical analysis to yield a different reading.... The attachment of Genesis 22 to patriarchy has given us not the sacrifice of Isaac ... but the sacrifice of Sarah," whom patriarchy has marginalized.

578.   Trible, Phyllis. "The Other Woman: A Literary and Theological Study of the Hagar Narratives," in James T. Butler, et al., eds., *Understanding the Word: Essays in Honor of Bernhard W. Anderson* (Sheffield: JSOT P, 1985), 221-246.

Rhetorical criticism applied to Genesis 16 and 21 reveals parallels of structure and content which provide continuity as well as highlighting the differences between the two accounts: the first Hagar plot is circular (bondage-flight-bondage), the second linear (bondage-expulsion-homelessness). Her story illustrates oppression of nationality, class, and sex; she is thus a pivotal figure in Israelite religion.

579.   Turner, Laurence A. "Lot as Jekyll and Hyde: A Reading of Genesis 18-19," in #35, pp. 85-101.

How the narrative portrays Lot, and how Abraham's actions in chapter 18 form the context for that portrayal. Lot is presented as complex, with a variety of favorable and unfavorable traits. Close similarities between the Flood and Sodom episodes invite comparison of Lot with Noah, in whom we find two quite different characters.

580.   Vogels, Walter. "Lot in his Honor Restored. A Structural Analysis of Gn 13:2-18." *ETh* 10 (1979), 5-12.

Structural analysis helps us see that the reading which attributes generosity to Abraham in this situation is not the only possible interpretation. "... Abraham, by suggesting division, has trespassed his [Yahweh's] rights.... [T]he structure of the story shows that if anybody is to blame, it is Abraham rather than Lot."

581.   Waldman, Nahum. "Genesis 14—Meaning and Structure." *Dor Le Dor* 16 (1988), 256-262.

Genesis 14 has an intricate chiastic structure which "emphasizes the dramatic power of Abraham's recognition of the only God and his absolute rejection of the dependency which human overlordship imposes upon vassal and lord."

See also: #s 10, 206, 211, 243, 273, 302, 307, 315, 321, 322, 324, 332, 337, 338, 353, 356, 364, 619, 684, 727, 728, 747.

Genesis 25-36

582. Alter, Robert. "Scripture and Culture." *Commentary* 80, #2 (August, 1985), 42-48.

Literary approaches to the Bible can be defended as narrowing the gap between reader and text, while historical criticism widens that gap. How literary criticism illuminates Genesis 33, in contrast with other approaches. Literary criticism represents both a step in the long process of secularizing scripture and "a means of getting in touch again with the religious power of Scripture...." **

583. Andriolo, Karen R. "A Structural Analysis of Genealogy and Worldview in the Old Testament." *American Anthropologist* 75 (1973), 1657-1669.

The structural pattern inherent in OT genealogy, and its relationship to the ancient Hebrew world view. The Jacob narrative reveals this pattern and this relationship clearly.

584. Barthes, Roland. "The Struggle with the Angel: Textual Analysis of *Genesis* 32:23-33", in Roland Barthes, et al., *Structural Analysis and Biblical Exegesis: Interpretational Essays* (Pittsburgh: Pickwick P, 1974), 21-33; rpt *Image, Music, Text*, tr and selected by Stephen Heath (New York: Hill and Wang, 1977), 125-141; and in *The Semiotic Challenge* (New York: Hill and Wang, 1988), 246-260.

Structuralism is not a science or a discipline, but an investigation; it produces not findings or method, but a manner of proceeding. Most interesting in the structural analysis of character in Genesis 32 are "the interactions, the disruptions, the discontinuities of legibility." We should pursue not the "truth" of the text but the "reading" of it, to strengthen the "symbolic explosion" of the text so that it is not reduced to a signification, but "maintains its full significance."

585. Bland, Kalman P. "The Rabbinic Method and Literary Criticism," in #39, pp. 16-23.

We need a more traditional criticism in line with the rabbinic approach which investigates every word and its juxtaposition, not dismissing any word or phrase as an embellishment or excessive rhetorical verbiage. The Jacob and Joseph narratives offer prime examples of the benefits of rabbinic criticism.

586.   Caspi, Mishael Maswari. "'And His Soul Clave Unto Dinah'
         (Gen. 34)—The Story of the Rape of Dinah, the Narrator
         and the Reader." *AJBI* 11 (1985), 16-53.

         The "unseen struggle that exists between the reader and the
         narrative" in interpreting Genesis 34. "By careful juxtaposition of
         ideas and information with the content of the story, the reader is
         exposed to a process of crystallization of values and viewpoints."

587.   Curtis, Edward M. "Structure, Style and Context as a Key to
         Interpreting Jacob's Encounter at Peniel." *JETS* 30
         (1987), 129-137.

         "Literary structure and style of the Biblical narrative often pro-
         vide ... subtle but extremely effective clues to the interpretation of
         events recounted in the text." There are a number of rhetorical
         devices in Genesis 32-33 which help us interpret these chapters.

*   Delaney, Carol, and Ann Marmesh. "The Legacy of Abra-
         ham: Dubious Male Dominance and Female Autonomy."
         See #557.

588.   Fewell, Danna Nolan and David M. Gunn. "Tipping the Bal-
         ance: Sternberg's Reader and the Rape of Dinah." *JBL*
         110 (1991), 193-211.

         Meir Sternberg's notion of reading competence, while powerful
         and influential, does not handle ambiguity well, and leaves him
         prey to the limitations of a particular ideology. A literary-feminist
         reading of Genesis 34 offers quite different conclusions, emphasiz-
         ing "culpable neglect of responsibilities" by Simeon and Levi; sym-
         pathy rather than contempt for Jacob, Hamor, and Shechem; and
         sees Dinah not as a helpless girl needing rescue, but as a woman
         capable of making her own choices.

589.   Fishbane, Michael. "Composition and Structure in the Ja-
         cob Cycle (Gen. 25:19-35:22)." *JJS* 26 (1975), 15-38.

         The key to understanding the Jacob cycle is its overall chiastic
         structure. Revised as chapter 3 of #208.

590.   Fuchs, Esther. "'For I Have the Way of Women': Deception,
         Gender, and Ideology in Biblical Narrative." *Semeia* 42
         (1988) [#229], 68-93.

         "... gender is a primary factor which determines the literary pre-
         sentation of deception in the biblical narrative." Genesis 31 shows
         three major strategies: suppression of motivation, absence of au-
         thorial judgment, and absence of closure. Such narrative gaps

rarely appear around male characters, suggesting the importance of gender-sensitive readings.

591.   Gammie, John G. "Theological Interpretation by Way of Literary and Tradition Analysis: Genesis 25-36," in Martin J. Buss, ed., *Encounter With The Text: Form and History in the Hebrew Bible* (Philadelphia: Fortress P and Missoula: Scholars P, 1979), 117-134.

Three approaches to literary analysis of the HB help determine the main concerns and features of a given narrative: motif, structure, and style. In Genesis 25-36, the motif of strife predominates; structure is concentric, with ironic reversals: 25-30 chiasmic with 30-36; and style is dominated by play upon proper names.

592.   Geller, Stephen A. "The Struggle at the Jabbok: The Uses of Enigma in a Biblical Narrative." *JANES* 14 (1982), 37-60.

We can attain "a scientific hypothesis in literary garb" about Genesis 32. This chapter can be understood as "a paradigmatic example of [the Russian formalists'] 'device of making strange' ... of defamiliarization."

*   Gevirtz, Stanley. "Of Patriarchs and Puns: Joseph at the Fountain, Jacob at the Ford." See #498.

*   Gordis, Daniel H. "Lies, Wives, and Women: The Wife-Sister Motif Revisited." See #562.

593.   Hendel, Ronald S. *The Epic of the Patriarch. The Jacob Cycle and the Narrative Traditions of Canaan and Israel.*[Harvard Semitic Monographs 42]. Atlanta (Scholars P), 1987.

Analysis of Genesis 25-36 from "the stance of the narrative, cultic, and cultural traditions presumed by the original audience of the written text, in short, the world-view of ancient Israel." Brief history of interpretation of the Jacob cycle since Herder. The Jacob and Moses stories share an episodic pattern which originated in oral tradition in Israel and Canaan. Biblical characters and events exhibit a number of similarities with characters and events from Egyptian, Babylonian, and Canaanite epics.

594.   Jagendorf, Zvi. "'In the Morning, Behold, It Was Leah': Genesis and the Reversal of Sexual Knowledge," in David H. Hirsch and Nehama Aschkenasy, eds., *Biblical Patterns in Modern Literature* (Chico: Scholars P, 1984), 51-60.

Genesis is interested in ironic reversals whereby women become agents of re-creation on earth. Genesis 29 and 38 are both classic

examples of this reversal pattern. "The seed that left Jacob's body
under the control of the *thought* of Rachel achieves its aim, finally,
... the Patriarch is saved from sin."

*   Jeansonne, Sharon Pace. *The Women of Genesis: From Sarah to
           Potiphar's Wife.* See #567.

*   Landy, Francis. "Gilead and the Fatal Word." See #751.

595.   Martin-Archard, Robert. "An Exegete Confronting *Genesis
           32: 23-33*," in Roland Barthes, et al., *Structural Analysis and
           Biblical Exegesis: Interpretational Essays* (Pittsburgh: Pickwick
           P, 1974), 34-56.

           Supports Barthes [see #584] in refusing to impose a creed on
           the biblical text. We must use several disciplines, starting with his-
           torical criticism (reconstruct the original state of Genesis 32); then
           form criticism (origins and transformations of literary genres); fi-
           nally, examining the context in the rest of Genesis as a collection
           of related stories—e.g., the decisive test which Jacob encounters as
           a clue to his stubbornness, and as a symbol of his people's relation-
           ship with God.

596.   Matthews, Victor H., and Frances Mims. "Jacob the
           Trickster and Heir of the Covenant: A Literary
           Interpretation." *PRS* 12 (1985), 185-195.

           The Jacob cycle in relation to the "trickster" motif or figure. The
           ancient Hebrew audience would have recognized and applauded
           Jacob because of the popularity of such figures, whereas we feel
           more ambiguous about him.

597.   Maxwell-Mahon, W.D. "'Jacob's Ladder': A Structural Analy-
           sis of Scripture." *Semitics* 7 (1980), 118-130.

           The basics of structuralist analysis and its most influential theo-
           ries. A structuralist analysis of Genesis 28.

598.   Miscall, Peter D. "The Jacob and Joseph Stories as Analo-
           gies." *JSOT* 6 (1978), 28-40.

           The Jacob and Joseph stories are analogous—i.e., they exhibit
           the "feature of Hebrew narrative 'through which one part of the
           text provides oblique commentary on another.'" They have com-
           mon plot structures, characterization, and themes concerning the
           nature of divine intervention and human forgiveness.

*   Petersen, David L. "A Thrice-Told Tale: Genre, Theme, and
           Motif." See #574.

*   Polzin, Robert M. "'The Ancestress of Israel in Danger' in
        Danger." See #575.

599.   Ramras-Rauch, Gila. "Fathers and Daughters: Two Biblical
        Narratives," in #48, pp. 158-169.

        Can a female be regarded as a biblical protagonist in the fullest
        sense? Such a protagonist will have four typifying aspects: promise,
        trial, dialogue, and exile. Biblical women are part of the divine
        scheme, parallel the male protagonists in this respect, and are
        therefore protagonists themselves. Dinah in Genesis 34 and Jeph-
        thah's daughter in Judges 11 are protagonists; like all such charac-
        ters, they are "moored in their humanity, their vulnerability and
        mortality ... part of the complex interplay between divine design
        and human purposiveness."

600.   Roth, Wolfgang. "Structural Interpretations of 'Jacob at the
        Jabbok' (*Genesis* 32:22-32)." *BR* 22 (1977), 51-62.

        Four kinds of structuralist analysis of Genesis 32: sequential,
        based on Roland Barthes; functional, based on Vladimir Propp; ac-
        tantial, based on A.J. Greimas; and mythical, based on Lévi-Strauss.
        All four of these types of analyses are interrelated.

601.   Roth, Wolfgang M.W. "The Text is the Medium: An Inter-
        pretation of the Jacob Stories in Genesis," in Martin J.
        Buss, ed., *Encounter with the Text: Form and History in the He-
        brew Bible*" (Philadelphia: Fortress P, and Missoula: Schol-
        ars P, 1979), 103-115.

        Application of Paul Ricoeur's methodological synthesis to the
        Jacob tradition. Outline of the structure of these narratives; "the
        text as interplay of language"; "the text as invitation," following
        Martin Heidegger.

602.   Terino, Jonathan. "A Text Linguistic Study of the Jacob
        Narrative." *VE* 18 (1988), 45-62.

        The structure of Genesis 25-36 centers on two concentric circles,
        one inside the other, moving "from estrangement to reconcilia-
        tion," and posing the "question of blessing in connection with the
        divine promises," through a plot of conflicts. The whole is carefully
        built on chiasm.

603.   Thompson, Thomas L. "Conflict of Themes in the Jacob
        Narratives." *Semeia* 15 (1979), 5-26.

        The Jacob narratives are probably to be understood as literary
        fictions in both individual narrative segments and in development

of the larger complex tales. Thus these narratives do not reflect the lived sociological structures of pre-monarchical Israel.

604.   Williams, James G. "The Comedy of Jacob: A Literary Study." *JAAR* 46, Supplement B (June, 1978).

Genesis 25-35 is a comedy because of three characteristics: incongruity and paradox with eventual reconciliation of the protagonist and his world; incongruity of events; and humorous wordplay. The story is characterized by paradox and ambiguity.

See also: #s 3, 5, 206, 229, 273, 324, 327, 335, 338, 364, 373, 490, 560, 561, 574, 575, 822, 993, 1314, 1546.

Genesis 37-50

605.   Ackerman, James S. "Joseph, Judah, and Jacob," in #40, pp. 85-113.

The importance of doubling in the Joseph narrative, in terms of both events and characters. Opposing roles of Reuben and Judah. Important themes of the narrative are favoritism and deception. (BD)

606.   Alter, Robert. "Joseph and His Brothers." *Commentary* 70, #5 (November, 1980), 59-69.

It is just as useful and accurate to think of the narrative sections of the HB as fictions as to think of them as sacred history. Fiction, though play, is a form of knowledge as well: knowledge of human nature and of divine intentions. Characterization in the Joseph narrative as seen in hints about their motivations, and of knowledge gaps for both the reader and the characters.

607.   Bird, Phyllis A. "The Harlot as Heroine: Narrative Art and Social Presupposition in Three Old Testament Texts." *Semeia* 46 (1989), 119-139.

The interrelationship of narrative art and social presupposition in Genesis 38, Joshua 2, and I Kings 3. Each of these three texts requires as a presupposition a view of the harlot as marginal: tolerated but despised. The harlot herself is powerless to resolve this ambivalence toward her on the part of the other characters.

608. Bos, Johanna W.H. "Out of the Shadows: Genesis 38; Judges 4:17-22; Ruth 3." *Semeia* 42 (1988) [#229], 37-67.

The roles of Tamar, Yael and Ruth as challenges to patriarchy from within patriarchal structures: male initiative alone advances God's promises; female identity derives from male identity; a betrothal alliance will be decided by males.

609. Caine, Ivan. "Numbers in the Joseph Narrative," in Ronald A. Brauner, ed., *Jewish Civilization: Essays and Studies*, Vol. I (Philadelphia: Reconstructionist Rabbinical College, 1979), 3-17.

The possible significance of various numbers, particularly 2 and 5, in Genesis 37-50. They may hint at an unusual theme: "the action of Joseph is construed as the cause of the enslavement of the Hebrews. Since Joseph had, in effect, sold the Egyptians while protecting his family, it is poetic justice that his family's seed should have been sold, in effect, into slavery."

610. Cassuto, Umberto. "The Story of Tamar and Judah," in *Biblical and Oriental Studies Vol. I: The Bible*, Tr Israel Abrahams (Jerusalem: Magnes P, 1973), 29-40. Originally published in Hebrew, 1929.

Genesis 38 is an integral part of chapters 37-50, and 37-50 are in turn part of the larger unity of the whole of Genesis.

611. Coats, George W. *From Canaan to Egypt: Structural and Theological Context for the Joseph Story*. Washington, D.C. (Catholic Biblical Association of America), 1976.

Plot and structure of the Joseph narrative show that it has a remarkable unity and integration of elements, producing satisfactory tension and denouement. The principle structural focus is a shift from Jacob in Canaan to Israel in Egypt.

612. Coats, George W. "The Joseph Story and Ancient Wisdom." *CBQ* 35 (1973), 285-297.

The argument claiming a connection between Genesis 37-50 and the Wisdom tradition is inaccurate. The story as a whole in terms of genre and its complexity as a work of art. Donald Redford's description [see #623] of it as a novella is correct.

613. Emerton, J.A. "An Examination of a Recent Structuralist Interpretation of Genesis XXXVIII." *VT* 26 (1976), 79-98.

Edmund Leach's structuralist interpretation of Genesis 38 must be rejected for several reasons: it exaggerates the editing influence of Ezra and Nehemiah; its arguments are difficult to verify; its dating is problematical; it uses anglicized names; and it is not supported by details in the text.

614.   Furman, Nelly. "His Story and Her Story: Male Genealogy and Female Strategy in the Jacob Cycle," in #226, pp. 107-116; rpt *Semeia* 46 (1989), 141-149.

The meaning and function of garments in the Jacob cycle, especially in the scene between Joseph and Potiphar's wife. For male characters, garments have fixed meanings and symbolic value; for female characters they "are signifiers open to a variety of meanings, ... the channel they use to insert themselves into the exclusively male communicative process."

*   Gevirtz, Stanley. "Of Patriarchs and Puns: Joseph at the Fountain, Jacob at the Ford." See #498

615.   Greenstein, Edward L. "An Equivocal Reading of the Sale of Joseph," in #40, pp. 114-125.

Three interpretations of the divergences in Genesis 37 exist: some critics believe that the inconsistencies prove separate authors, with an editor; others feel that one version should simply be ignored; still others try to combine the two versions because they do not wish to deal with, or even acknowledge, the existence of discrepancies. Literary criticism shows that it is not so important how Joseph got to Egypt, but that he did get there and that this reveals to the author the actions of divine providence in history. (BD)

616.   Hollis, Susan Tower. "The Woman in Ancient Examples of the Potiphar's Wife Motif, K2111," in Peggy L. Day, ed., *Gender and Difference in Ancient Israel* (Minneapolis: Fortress P, 1989), 28-42.

The function of the "destructive female seducer" motif from folk literature in ancient Egyptian, Babylonian, and biblical forms (Genesis 39). This character also plays a positive role in the outcome of these stories: by placing the male protagonist in what turns out to be a rite of passage, an apparently destructive female act has longer-term positive consequences.

617.   Humphreys, W. Lee. *Joseph and His Family: A Literary Study.* Columbia (U of South Carolina P), 1988.

Genre, plot, characterization, basic rhetorical techniques, and theological perspective in Genesis 37-50. Hypotheses about how the Joseph material grew into its present form.

618. Irvin, Dorothy. "The Joseph and Moses Narratives," in John H. Hayes and J. Maxwell Miller, eds., *Israelite and Judaean History* (Philadelphia: Westminster P, 1977), 180-209.

   Folklorist analysis of Genesis 37-50 and Exodus 3-4. Both these narratives show many similarities with contemporary ancient Near Eastern legends.

* Jagendorf, Zvi. "'In the Morning, Behold, It Was Leah': Genesis and the Reversal of Sexual Knowledge." See #594.

* Jeansonne, Sharon Pace. *The Women of Genesis: From Sarah to Potiphar's Wife.* See #567.

619. Josipovici, Gabriel. "Interpretation versus Reading: From Meaning to Trust." *Salmagundi* #78-79 (1988), 228-254.

   Some problems inherent in interpreting seemingly marginal incidents in biblical narrative, e.g., Genesis 37:12-18 and Mark 14: 51-2. As readers, we prefer enigma to muddle. Both passages "bring us face to face with characters who cannot be either interpreted or deconstructed.... All our attempts to do more with them than the biblical text itself does will end in either distortion or failure."

620. Longacre, Robert E. *Joseph: A Story of Divine Providence. A Text Theoretical and Textlinguistic Analysis of Genesis 37 and 39-48.* Winona Lake (Eisenbrauns), 1989.

   "... careful textlinguistic or 'discourse' analysis ... can account for almost all the 'internal tensions,' 'contradictions,' and 'duplications' on which source criticism was originally based." This method applied to the Joseph narrative in terms of speaker, hearer, message, situation, macrostructure, texture, constituent structure, and the monitoring/processing efforts of speaker and hearer.

621. McGuire, Errol. "The Joseph Story: A Tale of Son and Father," in #316, pp. 9-25.

   We need to "assess and portray more adequately its distinctive literary and mythic features." Thematic outline of the episodes of Genesis 37-50; the narrative as serious comedy with sub-myths of a rite of passage. It has perfect structural symmetry.

* Miscall, Peter D. "The Jacob and Joseph Stories as Analogies." See #598.

622.   Nohrnberg, James C. "Princely Characters," in #318, pp. 58-
         97.

         Joseph and David are "hinge" characters in the HB—i.e., they
         are "prominently and analogously located at critical junctures of
         the biblical narrative taken as a whole...." They exemplify how
         character in the Bible differs from that in other literature: "they
         are always constrained by their election to their role." Thus their
         passions and motivations are not studied for their own sake.

623.   Redford, Donald. *A Study of the Biblical Story of Joseph.* Leiden
         (E.J. Brill), 1970.

         Largely form-critical treatment of Genesis 37-50, except for "The
         Joseph Story as Literature," which discusses the narrative as
         novella, and in terms of plot symmetry, irony, and motifs.

624.   Rendsburg, Gary A. "Literary Structures in the Qur'anic
         and Biblical Stories of Joseph." *The Muslim World* 78
         (1988), 118-120.

         The similarities in the chiasmic structures of these two versions
         of the Joseph story shows that there may have been a Near Eastern
         literary tradition upon which they both drew.

625.   Rendsburg, Gary A. "Redactional Structuring in the Joseph
         Story: Genesis 37-50, in #48, pp. 215-232.

         The standard source-critic's division of Genesis 37-50 into J, E,
         and P strands should be discarded. Literary criticism shows that
         the entire narrative is told in a careful chiastic structure with
         Joseph's disclosure to his brothers as the pivotal point.

626.   Savage, Mary. "Literary Criticism and Biblical Studies: A
         Rhetorical Analysis of the Joseph Narrative," in Carl D.
         Evans, et al., eds., *Scripture in Context: Essays on the Compar-
         ative Method* (Pittsburgh: Pickwick P, 1980), 79-100.

         Theories of narrative, especially structuralist and rhetorical, ap-
         plied to Genesis 37-50. The unity of the narrative (possibly except-
         ing chapter 38); how it differs in social realism and narrative tech-
         nique from other narratives; why *ethos* and *pathos* must be part of
         the definition of the genre.

627.   Schwartz, Regina. "Joseph's Bones and the Resurrection of
         the Text." *PMLA* 103 (1988), 114-124; rpt in #45, pp. 40-
         59.

         Remembering is "persistently linked to survival" in the Bible. "In
         the Joseph story, and by extension, in the Hebrew Bible, interpret-

ing is depicted as an activity of repressing and reconstructing, of forgetting and remembering, and that activity, by its very nature, resists completion.... [W]hat is at stake in his narrative is not truth ... but survival." **

628. Seybold, Donald A. "Paradox and Symmetry in the Joseph Narrative," in #39, pp. 59-73.

The narrative structure of Genesis 37-50 is controlled by three sets of dreams which become reality; four sets of analogous relationships into which Joseph enters; and variations on the "pit" episode which serve both narrative and symbolic purposes. These episodes "become the central repositories of paradox as well as provide links of concatenation through which the other elements combine into final and deeper significance...." (JM)

629. White, Hugh C. "The Joseph Story: A Narrative Which 'Consumes' Its Content." *Semeia* 31 (1985), 49-70.

A fundamental tension in narratives between direct discourse of characters and indirect discourse of narrative framework is rooted in the two axes of the sign: communicative and referential. In Genesis 37-50, direct discourse ultimately consumes or subordinates the referential system of meaning developed in the indirect discourse, preventing the story from attaining closure.

630. White, Hugh C. "Reuben and Judah: Duplicates or Complements?" in James T. Butler, et al., eds., *Understanding the Word: Essays in Honor of Bernhard W. Anderson* (Sheffield: JSOT P, 1985), 73-97.

Reluctance to move toward a more literary analysis of Hebrew narrative has been due to uncertainty about appropriate criteria for analyzing large units of text. The dilemmas of literary critics' assumption of a unified text versus evidence to the contrary is illustrated in the history of interpretation of the Joseph story. The work of Stanley Fish on dialectical versus rhetorical narrative presentations is a "suggestive theory" for illuminating Genesis 37-50.

See also:
  For the Joseph narrative as a whole: #s 12, 14, 182, 273, 304, 315, 353, 490, 1088, 1434, 1467;
  For Chapter 38: #s 332, 335, 594, 747, 781, 1314, 1316;
  For other individual chapters: #s 14, 254, 307, 383, 388, 416, 557, 1029.

EXODUS

631.   Ackerman, James S. "The Literary Context of the Moses
       Birth Story (Exodus 1 and 2)," in #39, pp. 74-119.

       Chapters 1 and 2 anticipate the rest of the epic by foreshadow-
       ing events and themes "... [in] structure and symbolism [which]
       point beyond Moses' early years.... [T]hrough Moses and Israel ...
       God will reshape and re-create the world." (J.M.)

632.   Anderson, Bernhard W. "The Song of Miriam Poetically
       and Theologically Considered"; Brueggemann, Walter. "A
       Response to 'The Song of Miriam' by Bernhard Ander-
       son," in #371, pp. 285-296, 297-302.

       Anderson: Literary criticism and theology can combine to dis-
       cuss the interplay of content, style and form in Exodus 15:21. Re-
       semblance of this passage to Psalm 117 is evident.
       Brueggemann: Anderson's connecting of speech event to histor-
       ical event is his key methodological innovation, since poetic libera-
       tion must precede political liberation. Anderson is properly more
       interested in what lies "in front of" the text than in what lies
       "behind" it.

633.   Auffret, Pierre. "The Literary Structure of Exodus 6.2-8";
       Magonet, Jonathan. "The Rhetoric of God: Exodus 6.2-8."
       JSOT 27 (1983), 46-74.

       Auffret: The passage is chiasmic in structure, embodying the
       message of the doubly compromised oath whose meaning appears
       in a double liberation. Magonet: Implications of the structure of
       verses 7-10 for the "problematic issue of the names of God in verse
       3." It prepares us for the transition from the covenant with Abra-
       ham to the complex covenant with the people.

634.   Barzel, Hillel. "Moses: Tragedy and Sublimity," in #39, pp.
       120-140.

       If we compare the Moses story to classical Greek tragedy, and to
       the definitions of tragedy found in German philosophy, we must
       conclude that Exodus does not meet those criteria, though it does
       evoke "a tragic emotion." The concept of sublimity, while foreign
       to classical Greek literature, is one of the tools necessary to com-
       prehend the HB. (JM)

635.   Boyarin, Daniel. "Voices in the Text: Midrash and the Inner
       Tension of Biblical Narrative." *RB* 93 (1986), 581-597.

Contradiction and opposition are "built into the very structure" of Exodus 16—i.e., the two voices, one approving Israel's conduct, one disapproving. "The voices in the midrash ... are a literary representation and doubling of the antithetical voices to which the Author, Himself has given speech within the Torah itself." The inner-textual dialogue is not an "arbitrary and awkward combination of documents, but ... the representation of ambivalence and equivocation."

636.   Brichto, Herbert Chanan. "The Worship of the Golden Calf: A Literary Analysis of a Fable on Idolatry." *HUCA* 54 (1983), 1-44.

Exodus 32-34 presents innumerable problems of form versus content, coherence and consistency, especially when analyzed by the historical-critical method. Literary criticism, however, shows us the episodic narrative technique in its construction, its "exemplary rhetorical achievement" in presenting a theological principle, and its careful echoing of Exodus 23. Its theological message is iconoclastic: "you cannot represent YHWH in any natural likeness ... for you saw no image when he revealed himself to you."

637.   Carmichael, Calum M. *Law and Narrative in the Bible: The Evidence of the Deuteronomic Laws and the Decalogue.* Ithaca and London (Cornell UP), 1985.

Contrary to the usual historical-critical assumption, OT laws do not issue from real-life situations. Rather, the laws in Exodus and Deuteronomy must be linked to various Pentateuchal narratives. They are literary fictions which served various legal and ethical purposes.

638.   Chirichigno, G.C. "The Narrative Structure of Exod 19-24." *Biblica* 68 (1987), 457-479.

The awkward surface structure of Exodus 19-24 can be explained by examining the sequence structure, particularly the device of resumptive repetition. The result if we do this is better awareness and comprehension of the distinct perspectives which the text offers.

639.   Chirichigno, G.C. "The Use of the Epithet in the Characterization of Joshua." *Trinity Journal* 8 (1986), 69-79.

Discussions of the epithet as a means of characterization by Adele Berlin and Naomi Steinberg can be applied to the epithets used of Joshua in Exodus 17, 24, 33; Numbers 11; and Joshua 1. This enables us to understand both direct and indirect characterization of Joshua whenever he appears.

640.   Dozeman, Thomas B. "Spatial Form in Exod 19:1-8a and in the Larger Sinai Narrative." *Semeia* 46 (1989), 87-101.

In Exodus 19, spatial rather than temporal narrative forms are used. Moses' repetitive movements "provide the narrative context for the promulgation of distinct legal codes ... now all anchored in the one revelation on Mount Sinai. Each scene, therefore, now provides a different perspective on the same core event...."

*   Enz, Jacob J. "The Book of Exodus as a Literary Type for the Gospel of John." See #1972.

641.   Exum, J. Cheryl. "'You Shall Let Every Daughter Live': A Study of Exodus 1:8-2:10." *Semeia* 28 (1983) [#46], 63-82.

"Exodus 1:8-2:10 tells of three unsuccessful attempts of pharaoh to stem the growth of the chosen people, two of these are stories of defiance on the part of women.... The subtle disobedience of the midwives is followed by the open defiance of Moses' mother and the pharaoh's own daughter.... In the refusal of women to cooperate with oppression, the liberation of Israel from Egyptian bondage has its beginnings."

642.   Fokkelman, J.P. "Exodus," in #33, pp. 56-65.

Like Genesis, Exodus "provides a foundation for the whole Bible" whose themes recur regularly in later books. The overall structure of Exodus; importance of repetition in establishing meaning; its continuity with Genesis, yet its distinctiveness as beginning the theme of the establishment of Israel.

643.   Gunn, David M. "The 'Hardening of Pharaoh's Heart': Plot, Character and Theology in Exodus 1-14," in #34, pp. 72-96.

The source of this key plot element would be important for understanding the narrative. In turn, character depiction is closely tied up with plot. In such analysis, themes emerge "that, by the very nature of this story of interaction between God and man, will be theological." The main theme is that of freedom versus control, with complex dimensions of that problem hitherto unnoticed.

644.   Hamlin, E. John. "The Liberator's Ordeal: A Study of *Exodus* 4:1-9," in Jared J. Jackson and Martin Kessler, eds., *Rhetorical Criticism: Essays in Honor of James Muilenberg* (Pittsburgh: Pickwick P, 1974), 33-42.

Exodus 4:1-9 has been unjustly neglected. The three signs mentioned therein are not merely previews of what will follow, but important in their own right. The setting of this passage as cultic drama brings the artistic dimension to our attention. It is organized by three ordeals which carry great symbolic weight.

645.　Hauser, Alan J. "Two Songs of Victory: A Comparison of Exodus 15 and Judges 5," in #371, pp. 265-284.

These passages are the two oldest pieces of poetry in the HB, and the only two extensive victory songs. They show many differences, as well as many similarities. Probably neither one was modelled after a "victory song type," which would have been known in early Israel. The two songs may be compared and contrasted in terms of their use of the divine name, a water motif, mocking of the enemy, and motif of falling.

*　Hendel, Ronald S. *The Epic of the Patriarch. The Jacob Cycle and the Narrative Traditions of Canaan and Israel.* See #593.

646.　Hendrix, Ralph E. "A Literary Structural Analysis of the Golden-Calf Episode in Exodus 32:1-33:6." *AUSS* 28 (1990), 211-217.

"The Golden-Calf episode in Exodus 32:1-33:6 displays an inverted parallelism or chiastic structure," with Moses' offer of repentance as the structural and thematic center of the judgment process.

647.　Hepner, Mark. "Some Observations on the Structure and Poetics of Exodus 1 and 2." *OPTAT* 2, #2 (1988), 39-52.

"... the author has structured his narrative ... around the recurring structural motif Proposal, Execution, Outcome, and Situation Continues Unresolved. He has used this structure to great effect in moving his story through a series of events towards a climactic conclusion." Other parts of Exodus will probably be found to use this same structural motif.

648.　Howell, Meribeth. "Exodus 15, 16-18: A Poetic Analysis." *Ephemerides Theologicae Lovanienses* 65 (1989), 5-42.

How the various poetic devices "interact within the poem to reveal, or to contribute to, its structure." We may follow Wilfred Watson [#389] in dividing this passage into parts, noting word repetitions, analyzing various kinds of parallelism, meter, figures, and the chiastic structure of some verses. The declarative alternating with the descriptive most determines the strophic arrangement.

*　Irvin, Dorothy. "The Joseph and Moses Narratives." See #618

649.   Isbell, Charles. "Exodus 1-2 in the context of Exodus 1-14: Story Lines and Key Words," in #34, pp. 37-61.

Exodus 1:8–2:25 functions as a prelude to the whole of chapters 1-14 by setting out important story lines and indicating key themes to be developed later on. Conclusions from this recognition are that Moses is not in fact a heroic figure in the usual ancient Near Eastern epic sense of the word; 1:18–2:25 is closely related to 13:17–14:31; and the whole story is tightly integrated.

650.   Kikawada, Isaac M. "Some Proposals for the Definition of Rhetorical Criticism." *Semitics* 5 (1977), 67-91.

The rhetorical method is "the study of the interaction of various units of compositional elements in a hierarchy of context." How it helps illuminate Exodus 2.

*   Kselman, John S. "Psalm 77 and the Book of Exodus." See #1169.

651.   Lawton, Robert B., S.J. "Irony in Early Exodus." *ZAW* 97 (1985), 414.

The subtle irony in Exodus 1-2 is often missed. For example, the irony aimed at Pharaoh, which when noticed enables us to grasp the writer's message about Pharoah's descendants.

652.   Leach, Edmund, and D. Alan Aycock. *Structuralist Interpretations of Biblical Myth.* Cambridge (Cambridge UP, 1983.

How can structuralist analysis, which is superior to the historical method, help us progress from the superficial, manifest meaning of the Bible to the deeper meaning? Various mythological patterns in the Bible; that of Moses and his sister in Exodus 2-3 is often repeated in both OT and NT.

653.   Levine, Herbert J. "The Narrative Mirror of Exodus 32: A Critique of the Philosophers' God," in #179, pp. 110-113.

Mistaken preconceptions that the HB posits an immutable God can be removed by a study of Exodus 32. Juxtaposition of the views of Moses Maimonides with those of Abraham Heschel on this chapter helps reveal how God wanted Moses to see Him as involved in the idolatry of the people through his anger. **

654.   Magonet, Jonathan. "The Bush That Never Burnt (Narrative Techniques in Exodus 3 and 6)." *HJ* 16 (1975), 304-311.

In Exodus 3 "the narrator has used a technique whereby the reader sees both the 'reality' of what is happening, and the way it is experienced by Moses, thus giving an ironic perspective to all subsequent events and Moses' reaction to them." This also throws light onto Exodus 6, where similar problems for the reader occur. In fact, these two passages "were composed in conscious relationship to each other and represent complementary parts of a skilful didactic-narrative composition."

655. Moberly, R.W.L. *At The Mountain of God: Story and Theology in Exodus 32-34*. Sheffield (JSOT P), 1983.

Combination of literary, theological and historical exegesis in a detailed exposition of Exodus 32-34. We discover a unified narrative in terms of plot, theme, use of foreshadowing, irony, suspense, and symbolism.

656. Muilenberg, James. "A Liturgy on the Triumphs of Yahweh," in *Studia Biblica et Semitica Theodoro Christiano Vriezen* (Wageningen: H. Veenman and Zonen N.V., 1966), 233-251.

This liturgy forms a literary climax in Exodus which is related to the extensive literature of the sea in the OT and other ancient Near Eastern literatures. It shows numerous stylistic, rhetorical and linguistic affinities with Accadian and Ugaritic epics and poems. Its structure is movement from past to future, memory to expectation, turbulence to peace and security. Details of the poetic structure, form, and imagery.

657. Nohrnberg, James. "Moses," in #316, pp. 35-57.

"Moses: a hero whose individuality is dissolved in his office, and whose life is almost totally conscripted by the history of Israel." A typology of the Moses hero-pattern as one of four possible kinds; "the more complete the cycle, the more something larger than the advent of the individual hero is betokened." How the Moses hero-pattern differs from the Joseph and Noah ones; implications of Moses' career as a type of Israel's.

* Smith, Robert H. "Exodus Typology in the Fourth Gospel." See #1997.

658. Vater, Ann M. "A Plague on Both Our Houses: Form- and Rhetorical-Critical Observations on Exodus 7-11," in #34, pp. 62-71.

Form and rhetorical criticisms are complementary. "... a study of the narrative patterns for oracle communication in this story does provide certain form-critical and stylistic clues to the questions of overall story form, structure and development of the Plagues story.... It is the overall mood, situation, and communication patterns of this story type which provides the impression of literary unity...."

659. Vogels, Walter W.F. "The Literary Form of the 'Question of Nations.'" *ETh* 11 (1980), 159-176.

The "question of nations" schemata in Exodus 12-15, Deuteronomy 6, and Joshua 4. These schemata show a close link for these writers between history, response to God, and blessings or curses which result.

660. Wicke, Donald W. "The Literary Structure of *Exodus* 1:2– 2:10." *JSOT* 24 (1982), 99-107.

The Exodus verses are intended as a unit with symmetry and balance to reinforce that sense. 1:1-14 balances 2:1-10, with 1:15-22 as bridge between them.

See also:
For Exodus as a whole: #s 7, 15, 27, 165, 166, 175, 178, 219, 293, 327, 500, 547, 914, 1305, 2027;
For specific chapters: #s 5, 18, 46, 243, 254, 307, 310, 322, 324, 332, 335, 356, 383, 388, 437, 474, 532, 533, 561, 1007, 1744, 1982.

LEVITICUS

661. Baker, David W. "Division Markers and the Structure of Leviticus 1-7," in E.A. Livingstone, ed., *Studia Biblica 1978 I: Papers on Old Testament and Related Themes* (Sheffield: JSOT P, 1979), 9-15.

The "formal structural parallels between biblical and cognate literatures, especially division markers within a text." The ritual instructions of Leviticus 1-7 and their function. This passage exhibits various linguistic formulae, e.g., casuistic introductions (content markers), and demonstrative pronouns as indicators of formal divisions within the text. These seem to have parallels with non-biblical ancient ritual texts.

662.   Damrosch, David. "Leviticus," in #33, pp. 66-77; appears in
       slightly different form in #311, pp. 261-298.

       Neglecting HB legal material as nonliterary and unattractive is a
       mistake because it "misses the central literary concern of the
       Priestly writers ... which was precisely the interweaving of law and
       history. Far from interrupting the narrative, the laws complete
       it...." Leviticus shows the effort of the Pentateuch "to subsume nar-
       rative within a larger symbolic order." It displays a complex artistry
       of prophetic reintegration of man and God on a different plane
       from that of Genesis.

663.   Magonet, Jonathan. "The Structure and Meaning of Leviti-
       cus 19." *HAR* 7 (1983), 151-167.

       The structure of Leviticus 19 is seen through its repeated
       phrases, sequence of topics, and their content. There are five sec-
       tions in a chiastic arrangement dramatizing the problem of
       boundaries.

664.   Schwartz, Baruch J. "A Literary Study of the Slave-Girl Peri-
       cope—Leviticus 19:20-22." *Scripta Hierosolymitana* 31
       (1986), 241-255.

       Literary-critical procedures successfully applied to the study of
       biblical narrative and poetry can also be used on legal literature.
       Leviticus 19, for example, can be analyzed using the close reading,
       holistic approach.

See also: #s 274, 311, 2027, 2192, 2209.

NUMBERS

665.   Ackerman, James S. "Numbers," in #33, pp. 78-91.

       Writers clearly assumed that life in the Exile of the sixth and
       fifth centuries, BCE, was analogous to life during the wandering in
       the wilderness. Thus, they reinterpreted the wilderness traditions
       "by arranging a sophisticated collage of diverse materials into a
       new literary context." Numbers has a thematic unity: the anxieties
       of preparing for the journey; establishing "spatial structures and
       hierarchies of personnel" to carry on contact with God; divine
       guidance; flesh versus spirit; successes and failures of leadership;
       anticipation of life in the promised land.

*   Chirichigno, G.C. "The Use of the Epithet in the Character-
           ization of Joshua." See #639.

666.   Clark, Ira. "Balaam's Ass: Suture or Structure?" in #40, pp.
           137-144.

           "... the story of Balaam's ass, that funny folktale seemingly at
           odds with God's previous grant, is not the crude suture of a bum-
           bling redactor; instead, it is a tale-teller's entertaining structural
           emphasis on the main issue of a three-part story with a single im-
           pact." Its three sections progressively elaborate the central point of
           view of Israel as God's chosen people.

667.   Coats, George W. "Humility and Honor: A Moses Legend in
           Numbers 12," in #34, pp. 97-107.

           Numbers 12 is not, as is usually thought, a disunity, but a unity
           in genre and structure which overshadows its disjointed facets.
           That is, a "rebellion" tradition has been transformed into a unified
           legend on the virtues of Moses.

668.   Culley, Robert C. "Five Tales of Punishment in the Book of
           Numbers"; Ben-Amos, Dan. "Comments on Robert Cul-
           ley's 'Five Tales of Punishment in the Book of Numbers.'"
           in #230, pp. 25-45.

           Numbers 11, 12, 20, and 21 all recount a pattern of punishment,
           though each differently depending on who complains, who is pun-
           ished or rewarded. While this pattern reinforces the notion that
           Yahweh cannot be crossed, the variations blur the pattern. Ben-
           Amos: It is more important to see how oral material is transformed
           through writing than to note a tale's traditional style. Structural
           analysis of sequence thus misses the point, because it ignores the
           speaker's ideology.

669.   Jobling, David. "'The Jordan a Boundary'; A Reading of
           Numbers 32 and *Joshua 22*." *SBLSP* 1980, 183-207.

           A "report on work in progress" on a long-term project to find "a
           mode of structural exegesis adequate to the Old Testament and ...
           to its narrative parts." We need to find ways to bridge historical
           and literary criticisms of the Bible. How this might be done in
           reading Numbers 32 and Joshua 22.

*   Jobling, David. *The Sense of Biblical Narrative. Three Structural
           Analyses in the Old Testament (I Samuel 13-31, Numbers 11-
           12, I Kings 17-18).* See #820.

*   Mc Evenue, S.E. *The Narrative Style of the Priestly Writer.* See
          #540.

670.   Newing, Edward G. "The Rhetoric of Altercation in Num-
          bers 14," in Edgar W. Conrad and Edward G. Newing,
          eds., *Perspectives on Language and Text* (Winona Lake:
          Eisenbrauns, 1987), 211-228.

          Considerable rhetorical skills are displayed in the chiasm of
          Numbers 14. Verbal linkages were worked out so as to be unique
          for each combination of speeches: each part being separate yet in-
          terlinked with, and dependent upon, the other parts.

671.   Olson, Dennis T. *The Death of the Old and the Birth of the New:*
          The Framework of the Book of Numbers and the Pentateuch.
          Brown Judaic Studies 71. Chico (Scholars P), 1985.

          Source, tradition-history, chronology, or geography criticisms do
          not work on the structure of Numbers because they tend to ignore
          content, or "fail to seek the conceptual unity of the book." The
          boundaries of Numbers are consciously shaped to fit into the Pen-
          tateuch, and are based on the census lists of chapters 1 and 26.
          The theme of Numbers, like that of the Pentateuch as a whole, is
          "the death of the old and the birth of the new"; God wrestling with
          his people.

672.   Sakenfield, Katharine Doob. "Feminist Biblical Interpreta-
          tion." *Theology Today* 46 (1989), 154-168.

          Numbers 27 and 36 illustrates three approaches to current dis-
          putes over feminist readings of biblical texts: the literary approach
          (largely New Critical); a second literary one (text as product of its
          culture); and the historical approach. These three have proceeded
          in parallel, rather than in intersecting ways. Practitioners of one
          method should be open to the others.

673.   Tosato, Angelo. "The Literary Structure of the First Two
          Poems of Balaam (Num XXIII 7-10, 18-24)." *VT* 29
          (1979), 98-106.

          These verses of Numbers 23 were composed according to the
          stylistic principle of concentric symmetry, with chiastic strophes
          often ignored by translators. This symmetry has interpretative con-
          sequences.

See also: #s 7, 310, 311, 323, 332, 356, 373, 383, 388, 411, 437, 684,
820, 2027.

DEUTERONOMY

* Carmichael, Calum M. *Law and Narrative in the Bible: The Evidence of the Deuteronomic Laws and the Decalogue.* See #637.

674. Christensen, Duane L. "Prose and Poetry in the Bible: The Poetics of Deuteronomy 1, 9-18." *ZAW* 97 (1985), 179-189.

 A reading of the Hebrew text of Deuteronomy 1 "reveals poetic features at several levels of analysis.... Inclusion, concentric framing devices, and inversion...." It was also written in a clearly metrical language which shows studied parallelism—yet clearly is a prose text—or perhaps we should call it narrative poetry.

* Eslinger, Lyle. *Into the Hands of the Living God.* See #700.

675. Freedman, David Noel. "The Poetic Structure of the Framework of Deuteronomy 33," in Gary Rendsburg, et al., eds., *The Bible World: Essays in Honor of Cyrus H. Gordon* (New York: KTAV, and Institute of Hebrew Culture and Education of New York University, 1980), 25-46.

 We should concentrate on the "structural components, metrical and rhythmic factors, and prosodic devices which link the several parts of the framework, the Opening, the Midsection, and the closing," to see if progress can be made in understanding the framework of Deuteronomy 33 (as opposed to that of the "blessing of Moses").

* Geller, Stephen A. "The Dynamics of Parallel Verse: A Poetic Analysis of Deuteronomy 32:6-12." See #419.

676. Labuschagne, Casper J. "On the Structural Use of Numbers as a Composition Technique." *JNWSL* 12 (1984), 87-99.

 "... Deuteronomy and Psalm 79 are carefully constructed numerical compositions governed by certain symbolic numbers.... [Claus] Schedl's logotechnical analysis is the appropriate method to detect the real structure of the text."

677. Leeuwen, Raymond C. Van. "On the Structure and Sense of Deuteronomy 8." *PEGL* 4 (1984), 237-249.

 The structure of Deuteronomy 8 is "interwoven linear" and chiastic, with clichés playing a key role. This structure, plus parallels with other biblical and ancient Near Eastern works, show that the reference is to "a multivalent, all-encompassing divine 'word,'" rather than the modern reading of spiritual versus material.

678. Polzin, Robert. "Deuteronomy," in #33, pp. 92-101.

Deuteronomy is the "opening frame and panoramic synthesis" of the entire history of Israel recounted from Joshua to II Kings. The implied reader's "spatial and temporal perspective" resembles that of Moses' audience. Its "superficial distinction of voices" seems at first to serve an underlying ideological unity—i.e., the notion that, in effect, Moses and the narrator are one. Yet there is much evidence that such unity is only apparent, since Deuteronomy "as a whole consists of an extended dialogue on a number of key ideological issues."

679. Polzin, Robert M. *Moses and the Deuteronomist: A Literary Study of the Deuteronomistic History, Part One: Deuteronomy. Joshua. Judges.* New York (Seabury), 1980.

The central problem is identifying the deuteronomist's main ideological stance. As we move through these books, we find an increasing tendency both to elevate and identify Moses' word with God's, and paradoxically to deconstruct the earlier deuteronomist's ideology. This is due to the narrator's admitted failure to be able to account for Israel's continued existence **

680. Skehan, Patrick W. "The Structure of the Song of Moses in Deuteronomy (Deut. 32:1-43)." *CBQ* 13 (1951), 153-163.

We can discover the pattern on which the writer of Deuteronomy deliberately constructed the Song of Moses. The chapter shows traces of "alphabetic thinking," though it is clearly not an acrostic. It is a "rich and vigorous" poem.

* Vogels, Walter W.F. "The Literary Form of 'The Question of Nations.'" See #659.

See also: #s 5, 7, 178, 214, 383, 437, 474, 659, 1546, 1905, 1942, 2113
  On Deuteronomy 33 specifically: #s 23, 289, 388, 416, 479, 500, 704, 1881, 1928, 2027.

PROPHETS

681.   Barton, John. "History and Rhetoric in the Prophets," in
        #1517, pp. 51-64.

        There is much more artifice in the classical prophets than is
        commonly noticed. They took "the highly recalcitrant facts of his-
        tory, whose religious and moral implications were in fact extremely
        ambiguous, and ... [interpreted] these facts [so as to] convince
        people not only that the hand of God could be seen in them, but
        that the operations of the divine hand were entirely comprehensi-
        ble in human moral categories.... Prophetic rhetoric is designed,
        that is to say, to make the contingencies of history look like divine
        necessities." How Jeremiah, Amos, and Isaiah influenced the later
        writing of the Deuteronomistic history.

682.   Berlin, Adele. "The Prophetic Literature of the Hebrew
        Bible," in #179, pp. 114-119.

        A literary approach—analysis of themes, motifs, and rhetorical
        strategies—is the best way to begin to grasp the power of the
        prophets' message. Isaiah 1 is a good example of prophetic
        rhetoric, but we find it throughout Jeremiah, Amos, Ezekiel, and
        Jonah as well.

683.   Cantalupo, Charles. "Religio Poetae." *Renascence* 36 (1983-
        4), 139-146.

        "Prophets were poets or *vates*, who wrote scripture." The ten-
        sions and interplay among the historical, spiritual, psychological,
        and literary levels of truth in the Bible.

684.   Carroll, R.P. "Is Humour Also Among the Prophets?" in
        #231, pp. 169-189.

        Reader-response analysis of prophetic books "can highlight the
        saving humour with which many of the stories are told." We can
        find it, e.g., in Genesis 20, Numbers 22-24, I Samuel, and I Kings
        17 to II Kings 2 (all by the Deuteronomistic historian). There is
        very little humor, however, in the latter prophets; at best, a certain
        amount of irony.

685.   Carroll, Robert. "Poets Not Prophets." *JSOT* 27 (1983), 25-
        31.

The prophets were in fact poets, and intellectuals. Given that undoubted fact, we will have to rewrite the history of prophecy.

686. Dick, Michael Brennan. "Prophetic *Poiesis* and the Verbal Icon." *CBQ* 46 (1984), 226-246.

"... the developed prophetic polemic against the human artisan's presumption in creating a divine image was a 'self-consuming artifact.'" The prophet himself thus became vulnerable to his own strictures against a human crafting a divine image." We can notice three phenomena in this connection: developed prophecy is a product of the writer's craft; it embellishes the parody against making cult images almost to baroque proportions; it then verges on extinction.

687. Fishelov, David. "The Prophet as Satirist." *Prooftexts* 9 (1989), 195-211.

"... the high correlation between the satirical mode and biblical poetic forms found in the prophets is not merely an accidental one. Biblical poetic forms seem to provide the most effective means for accomplishing the satirical goals of the prophets...."

688. Heschel, Abraham. *The Prophets*. New York and Evanston (Harper and Row), 1962.

Chapter 22: prophetic and poetic inspiration are not the same thing. History of the Bible as literature from ancient times to the eighteenth century. The origins of this method may be traced in Judaism to Longinus, though the literary approach does not become systematic and respectable until the eleventh century. In Christianity, it remains isolated and fragmentary until the Enlightenment, when, "in a sense, aesthetic appreciation became a substitute for the belief in divine inspiration."

689. Hillers, Delbert R. "The Effective Simile in Biblical Literature." *Journal of the American Oriental Society* 103 (1983), 181-5. Republished with other articles in this issue as Jack M. Sasson, ed., *Studies in Literature from the Ancient Near East* (New Haven: American Oriental Society, 1984), same pagination.

Magical texts in Akkadian and Hittite "abound in similes." These sometimes resemble biblical similes, e.g., in Isaiah 55, Hosea 13, and Psalm 68. These biblical similes relate to the symbolic action of the prophets because of its relationship with analogy.

690. Jeffrey, David Lyle. "How to Read the Hebrew Prophets," in #48, pp. 282-298.

The main approaches to reading the prophets over the last one hundred years; how these have led to various kinds of misreadings of the texts. The characteristics of prophetic rhetoric, as well as style and mood (especially dramatic shifts in mood) in various books.

691.   Jemielity, Thomas. "The Prophetic Character: Good, Heroic, and Naive." *LT* 5, #1 (March, 1991), 37-48.

The prophets, to counter criticism, "fashion a favorable character for themselves ... [similar to all] satiric self-presentation: namely, that the prophets appear as good and heroic persons, occasionally even as naive."

692.   Jemielity, Thomas. "Prophetic Voices and Satiric Echoes." *Cithara* 29 (1989), 30-47.

Prophets often construct a self-image which "resembles the satirist's frequently assumed role as the good or heroic man," and often as both.

693.   Keshet, Yeshurun. "Literature and Prophecy," in Israel Cohen and B.Y. Michali, eds., *An Anthology of Hebrew Essays in Two Volumes.* Vol. I (Tel Aviv: Institute for the Translation of Hebrew Literature and Massada Publishing Co. Ltd.), 1966.

Modern secular literature differs fundamentally from the Hebrew prophetic books in that the latter offers a "synthesis between the real and the spiritual world" as its core. "...prophetic literature, unlike secular literature, is concerned with the physical world not as an end in itself but as a means of achieving the ideal which transcends it...."

694.   Lindblom, Johannes. *Prophecy in Ancient Israel.* Oxford (Blackwell), 1962; Philadelphia (Fortress P), 1965.

Largely an examination of prophecy from social, psychological, and religious viewpoints, but admirably sensitive throughout to literary-critical issues, with extensive foreign bibliography. **

695.   Marks, Herbert. "On Prophetic Stammering," in #45, pp. 60-80.

"The rhetoric of obscuration which follows upon the prophetic call demonstrates—like the rhetoric of threat—the prophet's identification with the blocking agent that *he himself* has constructed in a reaction against the indefinite magnitude which threatens to overwhelm him.... [T]his central moment of blockage ... is represented by the prophetic stammer...."

696. Payne, D.F. "A Perspective on the Use of Simile in the Old Testament." *Semitics* 1 (1970), 111-125.

    Various types of similes used in the OT. Similes are most widely and most creatively used by the OT prophets.

697. Rofé, Alexander. "The Classification of the Prophetical Stories." *JBL* 89 (1970), 427-440.

    Classification of literary material in the Bible (biography, historiography, didactic legend, parable, martyrology) cannot be done by form criticism; we must trace the creative activity which expanded those original genres. How this can be done in some of the stories about prophets in II Kings.

698. Rofé, Alexander. *The Prophetical Stories: The Narratives About the Prophets in the Hebrew Bible[,] Their Literary Types and History.* Jerusalem (Magnes P), 1988.

    Problems of genre, date, authorship, character, and extent of these narratives: mainly I and II Kings, Jeremiah 25-45, with short sections of other books. "... first and foremost a historical study of the literary genre of the prophetical narratives, their growth and evolution." Plot; characterization; theme; "implicit motive and explicit purpose."

699. Sawyer, John F.A. "A Change of Emphasis in the Study of the Prophets," in Richard Coggins, et al., eds., *Israel's Prophetic Tradition: Essays in Honour of Peter R. Ackroyd* (Cambridge: Cambridge UP, 1982), 233-249.

    Definition and evaluation of newer methods of reading the prophets, especially semantic and structuralist literary methods, and canon criticism. These new methods can interact fruitfully with older, historical ones.

See also: #s 4, 12, 202, 212, 215, 285, 291, 545, 1500.

Former Prophets

700. Eslinger, Lyle. *Into the Hands of the Living God.* Sheffield (Almond P), 1989.

Narratological reading of the Deuteronomistic history, Deuteronomy to II Kings. There was a single deuteronomist as author of this history. How various parts of the history are structured; how the narrative makes evaluations of events and characters. Detailed focus on I Samuel 8-12 and Judges 2 and, outside the Deuteronomic history, on Genesis 1 and Nehemiah 1.

701.   Fontaine, Carol R. *Traditional Sayings in the Old Testament: A Contextual Study.* Sheffield (Almond P), 1982.

"... the form, style, content, and contextual use of a representative number of traditional sayings which occur in the Old Testament outside the corpus of wisdom literature." "Context" means their relationship to themes found *in* the wisdom literature. Based on studies in folklore, structuralism, and paroemiology about the traditional saying. Judges 8; I Samuel 16, 24; I Kings 20.

702.   Machinist, Peter. "Literature as Politics: The Tukulti-Ninurta Epic and the Bible." *CBQ* 38 (1976), 455-482.

There is a suggestive series of functional parallels between the Tukulti-Ninurta Epic and the experience of the united monarchy of Israel. Tracing these parallels allows a sharper focus on issues David and Solomon faced, and greater appreciation of the intimate relationship between literature and politics.

703.   Pollard, William G. *The Hebrew Iliad. The History of the Rise of Israel Under Saul and David.* Tr David H. Pfeiffer. New York (Harper and Brothers), 1957.

The style, and historical and religious background of this narrative. We determine which material in the HB is a part of it by "extricating it [sections of Judges, I and II Samuel, I Kings] from the other later material with which it has become intermixed ... to present to the general reader an ancient epic that ... ranks alongside the great epics of other civilizations ... to release ... the literary treasures of the Bible for general study and appreciation by students of the humanities."

704.   Polzin, Robert. "Reporting Speech in the Book of Deuteronomy: Toward a Compositional Analysis of the Deuteronomic History," in Baruch Halpern and Jon D. Levenson, eds., *Traditions in Transformation: Turning Points in Biblical Faith* (Winona Lake: Eisenbrauns, 1981), 193-211.

The "various points of view that make up its compositional structure." The deuteronomic history is a unified literary work, with the Deuteronomist as implied author. "Reported speech" is a key device in the Deuteronomist's literary technique: the reported word of God being found within the reporting word of the narrator. A competing dialogue can be detected even with the various utterances of God, whether reported or interpreted by the narrator.

*   Savran, George W. *Telling and Retelling: Quotation in Biblical Literature.* See #319.

705.   Seters, John Van. *In Search of History: Historiography in the Ancient World and the Origins of Biblical History.* New Haven and London (Yale UP), 1983.

   Comparison of the literary and investigative techniques in the historiography of Greece, Mesopotamia, the Hittites, Egypt, and ancient Israel. Form and source critics' concentration on hypothetical earlier collections, and on the presence of earlier works in the HB, is misguided. Israel's history writing "represents the development of a narrative style" with a carefully-designed thematic unity, sense of genre, and sophisticated sense of corporate history. This historiography must have strongly influenced the Yahwist and Priestly writers.

See also: #s 206, 214, 319, 678.

JOSHUA

*   Bird, Phyllis A. "The Harlot as Heroine: Narrative Art and Social Presuppositions in Three Old Testament Texts." See #607.

*   Chirichigno, G.C. "The Use of the Epithet in the Characterization of Joshua." See #639.

706.   Culley, Robert C. "Stories of the Conquest: Joshua 2, 6, 7 and 8." *HAR* 8 (1984), 25-44.

   The presence of "story" in the account of the conquest found in Joshua 1-11, especially from the viewpoint of narrative action. It has a reasonably clear structure, bound together by action sequences and the intermingling of divine and human viewpoints. We must account for both coherence and tension in a biblical text, not ignoring one in favor of the other.

707.   Giblin, Charles H., S.J. "Structural Patterns in Jos 24, 1-25."
       CBQ 26 (1964), 50-69.

       "Our limited aim is to draw attention to certain remarkable fea-
       tures of composition which help articulate its basic unity and
       which serve ... as a check on the tendency to eliminate more and
       more of the text as secondary." The numerical patterns discovered
       are not mere memory devices, but "help articulate the theology of
       the text...."

708.   Gunn, David M. "Joshua and Judges," in #33, pp. 102-121.

       Out of the "static, administrative prose" of Joshua "arises a pow-
       erful sense of the myriad elements that constitute 'the people.'"
       Joshua appears to have a "recognizable, if loosely-constructed
       plot.... Judges coheres less obviously in linear or cause-and-effect
       terms." The unity of Judges is through "rhetorical connectives," "a
       pervasive chronological scheme," "spatial coherence," and the-
       matic connections. Individual episodes of Judges from this per-
       spective.

*   Jobling, David. "'The Jordan a Boundary': A Reading of
       Numbers 32 and *Joshua* 22." See #669.

709.   Koopmans, William T. *Joshua 24 as Poetic Narrative.* Sheffield
       (JSOT P), 1990.

       Previous interpretations of, and research on, Joshua 24 from
       textual, archeological, source and form perspectives have almost
       totally ignored its literary structure. Detailed structural analysis of
       Joshua 24 must be systematic and methodological, "with careful at-
       tention to parallelism, formal ... strophic division, content ...," etc.
       These devices enable us to identify passages that are truly
       "narrative poetry."

710.   Koopmans, William T. "The Poetic Prose of Joshua 23," in
       #382, pp. 83-118.

       The "micro" and "macro" structures of Joshua 23 refute the
       widely-held notion that it is based on the treaty or covenant form.

*   Malamat, Abraham. "The Danite Migration and the Pan-Is-
       raelite Exodus-Conquest: A Biblical Narrative Pattern."
       See #726.

*   Polzin, Robert M. *Moses and the Deuteronomist.* See #679.

711.   Radday, Yehuda T. "Chiasm in Joshua, Judges and Others."
       LB 27/28 (1973), 6-13.

Chiasm as a help in explicating especially Joshua, as well as the minor judges and Samson in Judges; and, to a lesser extent, Jonah, Ruth, Ezra-Nehemiah and Chronicles.

* Vogels, Walter W.F. "The Literary Form of 'The Question of Nations.'" See #659.

712. Younger, K. Lawson, Jr. *Ancient Conquest Accounts: A Study in Ancient Near Eastern and Biblical History Writing.* Sheffield (JSOT P), 1990.

Techniques of written conquest accounts from Assyria, the Hittites, Egypt, and Joshua. Through semiotic analysis we find extensive and important similarities between Joshua and the other accounts: a "common transmission code that is an intermingling of the texts' figurative and ideological aspects."

713. Zakovitch, Yair. "Humor and Theology or the Successful Failure of Israelite Intelligence: A Literary-Folkloric Approach to Joshua 2";
Cross, Frank Moore. "A Response to Zakovitch's "Successful Failure of Israelite Intelligence,'" in #230, pp. 75-104.

Joshua 2 is both a "spy story" type and a "woman who rescues a man" story type—both from the world of folklore. The former is fundamentally masculine, the latter a woman's story- type. Both served the author well in creating the story and its message; their juxtaposition assured maximum effectiveness. The author toned down the sexual element "in order to accommodate the story to the conservative nature of the biblical narrative and to make even further fun of the men...."

See also: #s 165, 166, 175, 178, 182, 243, 332, 335, 659, 705, 860.

JUDGES

714. Amit, Yairah. "The Story of Ehud (Judges 3:12-30); The Form and the Message";
Jobling, David. "Right-Brained Story of Left-Handed Man: An Antiphon to Yairah Amit," in J. Cheryl Exum, ed., *Signs and Wonders: Biblical Texts in Literary Focus* [no city or publisher] (Scholars P?), 1989, 97-131.

"... how the text directs the reader to see the connection between human tactics and divine salvation." The reader is led to conclude that Ehud's success can only be the result of God's involvement. "Thus, the construction of the story in its details, ... serves to express its message...." Jobling: Objections to Amit's work include "her accounting for [multiple causality] ... entirely in terms of the intentional skill of a 'narrator.'" We need a theory of multiple causality in Judges 3 more in keeping with the intersection of political liberation and deconstruction.

715.   Bal, Mieke. "Dealing/With/Women: Daughters in the Book of Judges," in #45, pp. 16-39.

The "structure of violence" by and against women in Judges, especially three cases, seen in the light of narrative theory and of "condensation" (Freud): Deborah, Jephthah's daughter, and the concubine (chapters 5, 11, and 19). "It is only when the disciplines that study ancient texts are open to interdisciplinary collaboration ... that we can hope to undermine the language of power, and restore to the anonymous women the power over language."

716.   Bal, Mieke. "The Rape of Narrative and the Narrative of Rape: Speech Acts and Body Language in Judges," in Elaine Scarry, ed., *Literature and the Body: Essays on Populations and Persons* (Baltimore and London: Johns Hopkins UP, 1988), 1-32.

"The Meaning of the book is generated by the characters' speech acts, not by the narrator's discourse. The story is not told, it is *done*.... Kallah's death, Bath's sacrifice, and Beth's utter destruction string the episodes together. Beth's rape is the climax of the violence and of the narrative. If we can conceive of the ... book as one narrative at all, it is thanks to, not in spite of, chapter 19—the chapter that critics tend to eliminate, teachers to skip, and believers to disbelieve."

717.   Block, Daniel I. "Echo Narrative Technique in Hebrew Literature: A Study in Judges 19." *WTJ* 52 (1990), 325-341.

Echo narrative technique is the "deliberate employment of pre-existent accounts or segments thereof to shape the recounting of a new event." Judges 19 as an echo of Genesis 19, though which passage echoes which is an open question; probably Judges echoes Genesis for the purpose of conveying to the Israelites that they have arrived in a kind of Sodom, have come full circle without advancing spiritually.

718.   Brettler, Marc. "The Book of Judges: Literature as Politics." *JBL* 108 (1989), 395-418.

Much of the strangeness of Judges disappears if we read it as a political allegory fostering the Davidic monarchy. That is, it is a pro-southern, anti-northern-kingdom book. Literary devices of various kinds are used to communicate this message, e.g., repetition, characterization, symbolism, and re-use of Sodom motifs. Thus, in Judges literary tropes have been used to further socio-political ends.

719. Exum, J. Cheryl. "The Centre Cannot Hold: Thematic and Textual Instabilities in Judges." *CBQ* 52 (1990), 410-431.

A coherent literary interpretation of Judges is possible if we focus on "the increasingly problematic character of its human protagonists," and on "the increasingly ambiguous role of the deity." Thus interpreters who seek stable meaning from one part of Judges to another will be frustrated.

720. Globe, Alexander. "'Enemies Round About': Disintegrative Structure in the Book of Judges," in #48, pp. 233-251.

"... several nonsequential rhetorical, thematic, and symbolic patterns can coexist in a complex text. All of the themes and patterns in the Book of Judges cohere to emphasize the author's belief that the era disintegrated because of the Israelite failure to establish a religion uncontaminated by foreign influences.... The disintegration intimated in ... [the] prologue colors the rest of the book, with its ring structure heightening the contrast between Judah's victories at the beginning and northern ungodliness at the end."

721. Gros Louis, Kenneth R.R. "The Book of Judges," in #39, pp. 141-162.

We should look for unifying themes and patterns in a biblical book, not local fragments and isolated episodes. The basic plot pattern of Judges is: Israel does evil, God punishes them, they repent, a judge is chosen to save them, peace comes, then Israel does evil again. "... implicit in Judges [is] ... a conviction of the worth of every human gift and human characteristic.... Even ... human treachery is not all bad under certain circumstances." (JM)

* Gunn, David M. "Joshua and Judges." See #708.

722. Hammond, Gerald. "The Bible and Literary Criticism, Part II." *Critical Quarterly* 25, #3 (Autumn, 1983), 3-15.

The narrative qualities of Judges 19; how modern literary theory has treated the chapter. "By reading this way, with attention to dialogue and character and being prepared to sense narrative irony," we penetrate closer to its basic meaning than we would have via the older historical-critical method.

723.   Janzen, J. Gerald. "A Certain Woman in the Rhetoric of
         Judges 9." *JSOT* 38 (1987), 33-37.

         Earlier work on the narrative features of Judges 9 is satisfactory
         in terms of method, though we disagree on the issue of retribu-
         tion. Judges 9 discloses a "finesse ... in the wedding of narrative
         form to doctrinal implication," by "elevat[ing] stock expressions to
         nuanced rhetorical significance."

724.   Klein, Lillian R. *The Triumph of Irony in the Book of Judges.*
         Sheffield (Almond P), 1988.

         Not an interpretation of Judges but an attempt "to set forth the
         ironic and literary structure of the book and to show how they
         function in the text." Judges is a tour-de-force of irony, its devel-
         opment being progressive. That is, irony gradually increases in
         amount and complexity as we move forward from the opening
         chapters, until the resolution, which is "thick" with irony.

725.   Lilley, J.P.U. "A Literary Appreciation of the Book of
         Judges." *TB* 18 (1967), 94-102.

         The literary structure, and other literary features reveal how
         Judges fits together. The structure in turn shows us the author's
         view of history.

726.   Malamat, Abraham. "The Danite Migration and the Pan-Is-
         raelite Exodus-Conquest: A Biblical Narrative Pattern."
         Biblica 51 (1970), 1-16.

         The accounts of this migration given in Judges 18 and Joshua 19
         are "a sort of diminutive model of a ... pattern ... in the Exodus
         and pan-Israelite Conquest cycles." Structural analysis reveals ten
         "typologically relevant" narrative patterns common to both. This
         does not mean one copied the other, but that both probably fol-
         lowed "a basic pattern which had evolved for biblical narratives of
         campaigns and inheritance."

727.   Niditch, Susan. "The 'Sodomite' Theme in Judges 19-20:
         Family, Community, and Social Disintegration." *CBQ* 44
         (1982), 365-378.

         Judges 19 and Genesis 19 reflect themes of hospitality toward
         travelling strangers common in folklore. They share content pat-
         terns and "provide a potentially interesting case-study for issues
         such as oral composition in the OT and inner-biblical midrash, lit-
         erary dependence, and independent variation."

*   Polzin, Robert M. *Moses and the Deuteronomist.* See #679.

728. Unterman, Jeremiah. "The Literary Influence of 'The Binding of Isaac' (Genesis 22) on 'The Outrage at Gibeah' (Judges 19)." *HAR* 4 (1980), 161-5.

Linguistic, thematic, and ideological evidence all demonstrate that the author of Judges 19 intentionally used Genesis 22 when writing about the incident at Gibeah.

729. Webb, Barry G. *The Book of the Judges: An Integrated Reading.* Sheffield (Sheffield Academic Press), 1987.

Literary analysis of Judges guided by two "basic questions": "How is the text structured?" and "What does it mean as a complex whole?" The fundamental issue addressed by Judges is the non-fulfillment of Yahweh's oath to give Israel the whole land. Related themes—e.g., Israel's apostasy and Yahweh's freedom of action—are progressively developed, and climax in the Samson episode. The outlook of Judges is not, however, one of reward for virtue and punishment for apostasy, but resembles that of the book of Job.

See also: #s 7, 14, 15, 27, 165, 175, 178, 243, 289, 302, 315, 321, 332, 336, 448, 700, 705, 711, 860.

Judges 4-5

* Alter, Robert. "Biblical Imperatives and Literary Play." See #553.

730. Amit, Yairah. "Judges 4: Its Contents and Form." *JSOT* 39 (1987), 89-111.

Whatever the original version of this chapter, it was so rewritten that "the complex of ... the scenes and structure, the plot and characters, the narrator's judgment, the style and themes—form the guidelines of the redaction."

731. Bal, Mieke. "The Bible as Literature: A Critical Escape." *Diacritics* 16, #4 (Winter, 1976), 71-9.

Recent contributions of Robert Alter, Meir Sternberg and Phyllis Trible all engage in one form or another of critical escapism, as illustrated by their treatment of Judges 4-5. All three critics undermine their own critiques by begging questions. Their concept of gender is modern, offering no check against anachronism. They are all confused about the Bible, employing confusing terminology and uncritical methods.

732.   Bal, Mieke. *Murder and Difference: Gender, Genre, and Scholarship on Sisera's Death.* Tr Matthew Gumpert. Bloomington (Indiana UP), 1988.

When scholars in history, theology, anthropology and literary criticism have interpreted Judges 4-5, their disciplinary codes often reveal the faulty, specifically sexist, assumptions underlying their readings. The literary and "transdisciplinary" codes of theme and gender are more powerful interpretive tools, albeit still subject to sexism. Close reading of the many differences between chapters 4 and 5, since they are two quite different versions of the same event. **

*   Bos, Johanna W.H. "Out of the Shadows: Genesis 38; Judges 4:17-22; Ruth 3." See #608.

733.   Brenner, Athalya. "A Triangle and a Rhombus in Narrative Structure: A Proposed Integrative Reading of Judges iv and v." *VT* 40 (1990), 129-138.

The "operating structure of the cast of characters, and the central imagery," since the key to understanding Judges 4 and 5 lies in the structural/thematic affinities between the two chapters, not in their chronological relationships. They share a basic pattern, differing in the "specific articulation of their respective structures as well as in their ideological-social point of view."

734.   Coogan, M.D. "A Structural and Literary Analysis of the Song of Deborah." *CBQ* 40 (1978), 143-166.

Structure and style, rather than history, are the key to Judges 4-5. The author was disciplined and sophisticated, not primitive and naive: "metrical structure, use of chiasm, parallelism, paronomasia, and repetition all point to a careful and self-conscious literary technique." Analysis must be stanzaic, rhetorical, and formulaic.

735.   Craigie, P.C. "Deborah and Anat: A Study of Poetic Imagery (Judges 5)." *ZAW* 90 (1978), 374-381.

Is there one specific poetic technique in Judges 5 whereby the poet "sought to set the events in a larger perspective"? The imagery, which for an ancient audience would have evoked ideas of Anat, the Canaanite goddess of love and war, "has been used in Judges 5 to dramatize and impart religious significance to the role of Deborah in the Canaanite war."

736.   Craigie, P.C. "The Song of Deborah and the Epic of Tukulti-Ninurta." *JBL* 88 (1969), 253-265.

Similarities between Judges 5 and the Mesopotamian epic of Tukulti-Ninurta, which was Assyrian, and slightly earlier than Judges 5. Specific similarities of content, characterization, structure, and style. Possibilities of Assyrian influence.

737.   Fewell, Danna Nolan, and David M. Gunn. "Controlling Perspectives: Women, Men, and the Authority of Violence in Judges 4 & 5." *JAAR* 58 (1990), 389-411.

Readers' and characters' perspectives in Judges 4-5, read as a single story. Importance of gender roles, with two different women acting independently of patriarchal norms. Gender and politics placed Yael in jeopardy, and even her deliverance "is conditioned by the violence that confers authority in patriarchy." Yet, contrary to most interpretations, "Deborah appears, by the song's end, to be more trapped—trapped in the very value system which we imagine her to be subverting," because the story ultimately justifies the authority of violence.

738.   Gerleman, Gillis. "The Song of Deborah in the Light of Stylistics." *VT* 1 (1951), 168-180.

Style is one of the most neglected fields of OT exegesis. Hebrew poetic style compared to that of other ancient Near Eastern writing; narrative prose style, technique, role of the narrator, chiasm, and parallelism. In a sense, the prose version (Judges 4) is the more sophisticated artistically, the more advanced.

739.   Globe, Alexander. "The Literary Structure and Unity of the Song of Deborah." *JBL* 93 (1974), 493-512.

Judges 5 appears to be a literary unity, with a carefully-composed structure employing a significant number of recurring literary forms.

740.   Globe, Alexander. "The Text and Literary Structure of Judges 5:4-5." *Biblica* 55 (1974), 168-178.

The poet in Judges 5 seeks a variety of both poetic and theological comments on the significance of the battle against Sisera. The poet uses these comments to remind us of another "victory" on a mountain: the covenant between Yahweh and Israel.

741.   Hauser, Alan J. "Judges 5: Parataxis in Hebrew Poetry." *JBL* 99 (1980), 23-41.

Concentrating on parallelism and meter are insufficient; we need to discuss poetic style in a more inclusive sense: e.g., imagery, figures, sequencing techniques, keywords as unifiying devices, etc. Parataxis is probably the best clue: it is suited to the presentation of action as well as of unpredictable emotions and drives. Paratactic analysis shows Judges 5 to be a brilliant piece of poetry in no need of emendation, relying on repetition, allusion, onomatopoeia, assonance, consonance, and varied rhythms.

*   Hauser, Alan J. "Two Songs of Victory: A Comparison of Exodus 15 and Judges 5." See #645.

742.   Lindars, Barnabas, SSF, MA, DD. "Deborah's Song: Women in the Old Testament." *BJRL* 65 (1983), 158-175.

Judges 4 and 5 in terms of plot, style, characterization, irony, and their contrasting concepts of woman's role.

743.   Merideth, Betsy, et al. "Until I Arose: The Effect of Effective Women." Part II of #225.

Merideth: the ways that Judges 4 and Judith carry the same ideological representation of women and of female sexuality. Rasmussen: narratological analysis shows the elimination of Deborah's warrior role in Judges 4 as it passed from earlier to later rescensions. Hanselman: "Narratological mapping" of Judges 4 shows that "Both women act to achieve thematic resolution by means of exploiting the identity of the opponent's counterpart...." Women are portrayed as "full actants." Shaw: Why two recent attempts to analyze Judges 4 fail through stereotyping women.

744.   Murray, D.F. "Narrative Structure and Techniques in the Deborah-Barak Story." *VT* Supplement 30 (1979), 155-189.

Judges 4 has not received the concentrated attention given to the poem of Judges 5, largely because of the tendency to regard prose as "just history." Judges 4 is in fact "a unified narrative which displays a very high degree of technical competence and artistic finish." All of its elements serve plot and theme. The narrator's interests were literary, not historical.

745.   Niditch, Susan. "Eroticism and Death in the Tale of Jael," in Peggy L. Day, ed., *Gender and Difference in Ancient Israel* (Minneapolis: Fortress P, 1989), 43-57.

"... language in Judges 5:27 is double, evoking simultaneously death and eroticism.... Jael's image in Judges 4 and 5 partakes of the same liminal cross-culturally evidenced archetype, and ... the sexual subduing of the defeated male warrior, the play on 'sex and slaughter,' is typical of epic battle language, linked in the imagination of those who portray and create warrior figures.... It is of importance that an Israelite author of an early period imagines the 'womanization' of the enemy to be accomplished by a woman assassin. The author identifies with her even while employing an archetype dripping with phantoms of male fears and insecurities."

746.   Stek, John H. "The Bee and the Mountain Goat: A Literary Reading of Judges 4," in Walter C. Kaiser, Jr. and Ronald F. Youngblood, eds., *A Tribute to Gleason Archer* (Chicago: Moody Press, 1986), 53-86.

The narrative structure of Judges 4; various literary devices used therein; its theme. The structure is concentric with reinforcing verbal links which underscore the plot reversal. Literary devices include figurative language, evocative personal names, balanced sentences, parallel plot events, all contributing to the author's theological purpose.

See also: #s 129, 243, 252, 285, 307, 322, 335, 337, 377, 383, 388, 396, 437, 474, 715, 1386.

Judges 11

747.   Dijk-Hemmes, Fokkelien van, et al. "Commemmorating the Dead: Sacrificed Women and Readings of Revenge." Part III of #225.

Narratological analysis from a femininist perspective of Judges 11, with comments on Genesis 19 and 38, and II Samuel 13.

748.   Exum, J. Cheryl. "Murder They Wrote: Ideology and the Manipulation of Female Presence in Biblical Narrative." *USQR* 43 (1989), 19-39.

Judges 11 and II Samuel 6 are two stories of women (Jephthah's daughter and Michal) submerged in men's stories. The task of feminist literary criticism of the Bible is to deconstruct the dominant male voice and ideology of these stories in order to reconstruct this submerged woman's voice. Both women are victims of "literary murder."

749.   Exum, J. Cheryl. "The Tragic Vision and Biblical Narrative in the Case of Jephthah";
Humphreys, W. Lee. "The Story of Jephthah and the Tragic Vision: A Response to J. Cheryl Exum," in J. Cheryl Exum,

ed., *Signs and Wonders: Biblical Texts in Literary Focus* [no
city or publisher; Scholars P?, 1989], 59-83 and 85-96.

"... the text itself [should] shape our notion of the tragic." The
narrative of Judges 11 does not question the underlying causes of
Jephthah's misfortune; "its tragedy lies primarily in the conjunc-
tion of circumstances ... and in the divine silence, the refusal of
the deity to take a position vis à vis these events."

750.   Fuchs, Esther. "Marginalization, Ambiguity, Silencing: The
        Story of Jephthah's Daughter." *Journal of Feminist Studies in
        Religion* 5, #1 (Spring, 1989), 35-45.

        In Judges 11, the narrative "both expresses and suppresses, pre-
        sents and erases the daughter. The ambiguity functions ... as a
        kind of apology, a subtle justification of Jephthah's behavior." This
        focus on Jephthah as tragic victim, when it should really center on
        his daughter, is a literary strategy designed to serve a male ideol-
        ogy.

751.   Landy, Francis. "Gilead and the Fatal Word." *PWCJS* 9, Vol.
        I (1986), 39-44.

        Judges 11 is linked to Genesis 31 through echoes of father-
        daughter relationships, as well as various similarities and differ-
        ences in their treatment of themes of isolation and community. In
        both episodes, something is communicated across a boundary,
        from lawlessness into community, transforming energy into mem-
        ory and ritual.

752.   Mullen, E. Theodore, Jr. "The 'Minor Judges': Some Liter-
        ary and Historical Considerations." *CBQ* 44 (1982), 185-
        201.

        Major and minor judges are treated in two different literary
        styles, which "serves to reinforce the narrative purpose and theo-
        logical reflections of the deuteronomistic historian." That is, these
        "accounts of the 'minor' judges are used to 'frame' and hence
        draw attention to the critical story of Jephthah"—the theological
        focus of the book of Judges.

*   Ramras-Rauch, Gila. "Fathers and Daughters: Two Biblical
         Narratives." See #599.

753.   Trible, Phyllis. "A Daughter's Death: Feminism, Literary
        Criticism, and the Bible." *Michigan Quarterly Review* 22, #3
        (Summer, 1983), 176-189; rpt in slightly different forms
        in Michael P. O'Connor and David Noel Freedman, eds.,
        Backgrounds for the Bible (Winona Lake: Eisenbrauns,

1987), 1-14; as chapter 4 of #321; *USQR* 36 (1981), 59-73 under the title, "Meditation in Mourning."

We need to combine "the discipline of literary criticism with the hermeneutics of feminism" to reinterpret the story of Jephthah's daughter. It is a "story of terror" which echoes in various later biblical and apocryphal books.

See also: #7, 321, 715.

Judges 13-16

754.   Alter, Robert. "Samson Without Folklore";
         Bynum, David E. "Samson as a Biblical φὴρ ὀρεσκῷος" in
         #230, pp. 47-73.

         "The Samson story abounds in folkloric motifs and patterns, but an awareness of the folkloric backgrounds of the biblical text should not deflect us from attending to the subtlety with which traditional materials have been given literary articulation. The use of thematic key-words, variation in near-verbatim repetition, and nuanced dialogue are prime instances of such articulation. The literary recasting is not merely a matter of giving aesthetic finish to folkloric materials but of redefining their meanings." Bynum: We cannot fully understand Samson without placing him in the context of other comparable characterizations in the traditional literatures of a wide range of cultures (even if we omit folklore as such).

755.   Bal, Mieke. "Delilah Decomposed: Samson's Talking Cure and the Rhetoric of Subjectivity," in #304, pp. 37-67.

         Why Samson is not a hero, and how attempts to make him into one have led to misreading his character and the story. Psychoanalytic theory can illuminate Samson's gradual growth to maturity, with the temptations as symbols.

756.   Bal, Mieke. "The Rhetoric of Subjectivity." *Poetics Today* 5 (1985), 337-376.

         We should approach the problem of reality in fiction within the framework of the basic subjectivity of all fiction. That is, there is no basic difference between history and fiction. The mistake made by traditional readings of the Samson story is that they ignore contradictions and fill in gaps.

757.   Blenkinsopp, J. "Structure and Style in Judges 13-16." *JBL* 82
        (1963), 65-76.

    To understand the Samson story we must examine it as a whole.
    Its structure reveals a carefully-designed plot which revolves
    around an age-old motif in literature: the broken vow. The stylistic
    techniques of Hebrew dramatic, nondiscursive narrative are also
    important, particularly the use of climactic sequence.

758.   Camp, Claudia V. and Carole R. Fontaine. "The Words of
        the Wise and their Riddles";
        Slotkin, Edgar. "Response to Professors Fontaine and
        Camp," in #230, pp. 127-159.

    Samson's riddle of Judges 14 in terms of performance analysis,
    specifically from three perspectives: interaction situation, riddle
    situation, and context situation. "... this riddle is a carefully-crafted
    traditional form ... expertly used as a piece of crafty diplomacy by
    Samson, ... available to him from the linguistic and metaphorical
    resources of the culture.... [O]ne demonstrable purpose of this
    sage's story is to teach the construction, use, and final limitations
    of riddle performance in Israel." Slotkin: the point of this riddle
    may not so much be whether it can be solved, as that it is a com-
    mentary on the lack of communication and shared community be-
    tween Samson and the Philistines.

759.   Carmy, Shalom. "The Sphinx as Leader: A Reading of
        Judges 13-16." *Tradition* 14, #3 (Spring, 1974), 66-79.

    "The secret of Samson's career is hidden in the depths of his
    tormented, defeated psychology. The secret of Samson's leader-
    ship is tangled in the complex of his time. On one hand, Samson
    is the weakness of his time incarnate; on the other hand, he engi-
    neers, precisely through his frailty, ... a religious thrust that tran-
    scends the Judges' society."

760.   Crenshaw, James L. *Samson: A Secret Betrayed, a Vow Ignored.*
        Atlanta (John Knox P), 1978.

    "Literary and Stylistic Traditions": the story uses various tradi-
    tional motifs; its stylistic features include contrast, humor, repeti-
    tion, and hyperbole; the place of the story within the book of
    Judges and the Former Prophets. "Passion or Charisma": The pri-
    mary themes are those of competing loyalties and broken vows, ac-
    complished mainly through the characterization of female figures.
    "Riddles": as in all ancient literature, in Judges 13-16 they are
    proof of the hero's mental agility. "Tragic Dimension": The ulti-
    mate theme is the mystery of divine compassion for barren women
    and fallen heroes. It is the height of Israelite narrative art.

761.   Crenshaw, James L. "The Samson Saga: Filial Devotion or
         Erotic Attachment?" *ZAW* 86 (1974), 470-504.

         Judges 13-16 is the finest narrative in the OT. The conflict is
         within the hero's soul, and has devastating power. Close literary
         reading shows it to be not a collection of loosely connected and
         grossly editorialized traditions, but a unified narrative.

762.   Exum, J. Cheryl. "Aspects of Symmetry and Balance in the
         Samson Saga." *JSOT* 19 (1981), 3-29.

         Judges 13-16 shows superb literary artistry: solid literary pattern-
         ing, a narrative arrangement connecting events, characters, and
         themes. There is, e.g., a thematic symmetry between 14-15 and 16;
         a balance between 14 and 15; and an interplay of narrative art and
         theological purpose in 15:9-19.

*   Exum, J. Cheryl, and J. William Whedbee. "Isaac, Samson,
         and Saul: Reflections on the Comic and Tragic Visions."
         See #559.

763.   Exum, J. Cheryl. "Promise and Fulfillment: Narrative Art in
         Judges 13." *JBL* 99 (1980), 43-59.

         How form and content interrelate in Judges 13. The narrative
         seems intent on stressing the woman's role and importance; the
         narrative is chiastic in shape.

764.   Freeman, James A. "Samson's Dry Bones: A Structural Read-
         ing of Judges 13-16," in #40, pp. 145-160.

         The Samson story has vexed readers for three thousand years
         because it defies the normal structures of narratives, with some
         claiming it has no structure at all. Literary analysis in fact shows
         that the story does have a carefully-developed structure. (BD)

765.   Greenstein, Edward L. "The Riddle of Samson." *Prooftexts* 1
         (1980), 237-260.

         The "literary peculiarities" of the Samson story require a special
         interpretive procedure. The story should be read as a riddle, with
         the solution surfacing at various points within the text. Many fea-
         tures of the surface narrative symbolize aspects of the Israelite
         myth.

766.   Halperin, Sarah. "Tragedy in the Bible." *Semitics* 7 (1980),
         28-39.

         "... there is still room for tragedy in the Bible. I will show that
         actual stories in the Bible conform with the conception of tragedy

and comply with the principles of the classical theory of tragedy."
Judges 13-16 is an example.

767.   Matthews, Victor H. "Freedom and Entrapment in the Sam-
        son Narrative: A Literary Analysis." *PRS* 16 (1989), 245-
        257.

        The theme of freedom is central to Judges 13-16. Various vows,
        plans, and traps act as attempted counters to this desire for free-
        dom.

768.   Vickery, John. "In Strange Ways: The Story of Samson," in
        #316, pp. 58-73.

        "[Judges 13-16 gives us] a much sharper sense of the ways in
        which fiction is rooted in the ancient narrative world of folk tale
        and myth as well as a keener realization of the Old Testament's as-
        pirations to the narrative, structural, and thematic sophistication
        of technique found in what today we call literature." The Samson
        story differs from modern ones in divine intervention in human af-
        fairs, and in Samson being an improbable and unsympathetic
        character, and as well a type of Israel.

769.   Waldman, Nahum N. "Concealment and Irony in the Sam-
        son Story." *Dor Le Dor* 13 (1984-5), 71-80.

        Concealment and irony both play a major role in Judges 13-16,
        as does deception. Irony is itself a form of concealment. It may be
        that through these devices the narrator is showing criticism of the
        "nazirite or charismatic" leadership.

See also: #s 7, 12, 27, 165, 211, 273, 302, 304, 307, 315, 322, 323,
    324, 337.

SAMUEL

*Note: Readers should be aware that many scholars regard at least
the first two chapters of I Kings as being closely related to I and
II Samuel; thus, I Kings 1 and 2 is often treated as the conclusion of a narrative begun in Samuel. Accordingly, many items in
this bibliography relating to Samuel also pertain to I Kings, and
vice versa.*

770.   Alter, Robert. "Character in the Bible." *Commentary* 66, #4
        (October, 1978), 58-65.

"How does the Bible manage to evoke such a sense of depth and complexity in its representation of character with what would seem to be such sparse, even rudimentary means?" A series of related passages in the story of David, who is the "most complex and elaborately presented of biblical characters." The Bible's "artful selectivity produces both sharply defined surfaces and a sense of ambiguous depths in character...."

771.   Berlin, Adele. "Characterization in Biblical Narrative: David's Wives." *JSOT* 23 (1982), 69-85.

The four wives of David are characterized quite differently. Sometimes they are types, sometimes individuals. Both of these techniques also produce indirect characterization of David.

772.   Cook, Albert. "'Fiction' and History in Samuel and Kings." *JSOT* 36 (1986), 27-48.

How fictional character portrayals contribute to presentation of history. The narrative of Samuel proceeds by typology, analogy, and with David as model. Saul's failure is due to his incapacity (historical) rather than to God's caprice (tragedy). The tendency of some literary critics to see Samuel in terms of foreshadowing, irony, ambiguity, etc., oversimplifies a complex and intricate interaction of history and character.

*   Exum, J. Cheryl, and J. William Whedbee. "Isaac, Samson, and Saul: Reflections on the Comic and Tragic Visions." See #559.

773.   Fokkelman, J.P. *Narrative Art and Poetry in the Books of Samuel: A Full Interpretation Based on Stylistic and Structural Analyses. Vol. II: The Crossing Fates.* Assen/Maastricht and Dover (Van Gorcum), 1986.

I Samuel 13-31 and II Samuel 1. "... the intersection of Saul's downfall and David's rise and ... that conflict carefully and in stages." Saul's demise "satisfies all the conditions required to merit the predicate tragic in the strict sense." See also #s 774, 835. **

774.   Fokkelman, J.P. *Narrative Art and Poetry in the Books of Samuel: A Full Interpretation Based on Stylistic and Structural Analyses. Vol. III: Throne and City.* Assen/Maastricht and Dover (Van Gorcum), 1990.

II Samuel 2-8, 21-24. "Acts Nine, Ten, and Fifteen" of an "overall schema" of close stylistic and structural reading of I and II Samuel, as Vol. II above (#773) represents "Acts Four, Five, Six, Seven, and Eight."

775.   Frontain, Raymond-Jean. "The Trickster Tricked: Strategies of Deception and Survival in the David Narrative," in #48, pp. 170-192.

"The drama that is played out in 1 and 2 Samuel might be called the drama of 'reading.' Men and events must be assessed and interpreted insofar as men's limited means permit." Early on, David is a trickster in order to survive and to preserve his people; once sure of himself, his "trickster" behavior comes close to the ruthlessness in kings against which Samuel warned. Then other characters trick David, perhaps as a check on him.

776.   Gros Louis, Kenneth R.R. "King David of Israel," in #40, pp. 204-219.

In several important instances, David's personal desires come into conflict with his public duty. "We see him pursued and pursuing, in God's favor and out, in the hearts of his people and out, triumphant and downcast." David's multiple roles "... as giant-slayer, shepherd, musician, manipulator of men, outlaw, disguised madman, loyal friend and subject, lover, warrior, dancer and merrymaker, father, brother, son, master, servant, religious enthusiast and king," make him one of the most interestingly developed characters in the Bible. (BD)

777.   Gunn, David M. "David and the Gift of the Kingdom." *Semeia* 3 (1975), 14-45.

The structural and thematic coherence of the David story in II Samuel 2-4, 9-20, and in I Kings 1-2. The narrator's attitude toward his characters and the events of the plot contribute substantially to that coherence. Revised as part of #836.

778.   Gunn, David M. *The Fate of King Saul: An Interpretation of a Biblical Story.* Sheffield (JSOT P), 1980.

Saul's tragedy must be seen as combining the "character" and "fate" models. I Samuel 13-15 forces us to reexamine not Saul's conduct, but Yahweh's. Theme, characterization, and language as a trap for Saul in I Samuel 8–II Samuel 2. On balance, Saul's fall is due more to external circumstances than to flaws in his character.

779.   Gunn, David M. "From Jerusalem to the Jordan and Back: Symmetry in 2 Samuel XV-XX." *VT* 30 (1980), 109-113.

A particular example of a general contention [in #836] that recognition of the artistry of a story is of prime significance for its interpretation. "... schematic analysis of ... component scenes" in II Samuel 15-20 to underline the contribution of irony, tone, and chiastic structure to understanding David's character.

780. Gunn, David M. "In Security: The David of Biblical Narrative," in J. Cheryl Exum, ed., *Signs and Wonders: Biblical Texts in Literary Focus* [no city or publisher] (Scholars P?, 1989), 133-151.

Asks "Who is David?" and "seeks to hear some voices in the text. And, lest it silence them, it attempts to come to no certain conclusion." David's story "has a way of shifting out from under us," and shows that it "encodes ... key parameters of a relationship between Yahweh and humankind that is still 'plausible' for the reader...." #1479 replies.

781. Gunn, David M., ed., and David E. Orton, tr. *Narrative and Novella in Samuel. Studies by Hugo Gressman and Other Scholars 1906-1923*. Sheffield (Almond P), 1991.

Four pioneering works by German critics who were among the first to take the literary character of Samuel seriously: Hugo Gressman, "The Oldest History Writing in Israel" (II Samuel 10-26, I Kings 1-2); Wilhelm Caspari, "The Literary Type and Historical Value of II Samuel 15-20"; Bernhard Luther, "The Novella of Judah and Tamar and Other Israelite Novellas" (Genesis 38, II Samuel 5 and 10, I Samuel 22, 27, 29); Alfons Schultz, "Narrative Art in the Books of Samuel."

782. Martin, John A. "The Literary Quality of 1 and 2 Samuel." *B Sac* 141 (1984), 131-145.

The author of Samuel used two prominent literary devices to communicate his points: juxtaposition of characters, and the reversal-of-fortune motif structured in seven plot conflicts.

783. Miscall, Peter D. *I Samuel: A Literary Reading*. Bloomington (Indiana UP), 1986.

A "deconstructionist" literary reading based on the notion that the OT is different from Western literature, classical to modern, though it is just as complex and sophisticated as any Western poetry or narrative. I Samuel should be read as part of a larger work from Genesis to II Kings, held together by plot, characters, and theme. The varying roles of God; relationship of poetry and prophecy; themes of retributive justice versus mercy and of holy war.

784. Miscall, P.D. "Literary Unity in Old Testament Narrative." *Semeia* 15 (1979), 27-44.

Intended to extend and generalize the structural analyses of other scholars on Genesis 12, 20, and 26 (patriarch and wife in the promised land) by showing how we can include other material, e.g., I Samuel 25 and II Samuel 11, as well as other thematic emphases. "... a large part of Old Testament narrative can comprise a lengthy, complex work which must be dealt with as a literary unity." For reply, see pp. 45-50, and #123.

785.   Niccolls, S. Thomas. "The Comic Vision and the Stories of David." *Encounter* 42 (1981), 277-283.

Comic theory, including types of comic plots, applied to the David story. Thus, we can "appropriate the stories in such a fresh way that their continuing relevance may be appreciated...."

786.   Not used.

*   Nohrnberg, James C. "Princely Characters." See #622.

787.   Perdue, Leo G. "'Is There Anyone Left in the House of Saul ...?' Ambiguity and the Characterization of David in the Succession Narrative." *JSOT* 30 (1984), 67-84.

Recent interpretations of the character of David differ greatly from each other. The difficulty lies in the type of narrator, who does more showing than telling. The narrator's characterization of David is intentionally ambiguous in order to demonstrate David's complexity. This in turn reflects Israel's ambiguity about the monarchy in general.

788.   Petersen, David L. "Portraits of David: Canonical and Otherwise." *Interpretation* 40 (1986), 130-142.

The modern portrait of David by Marc Chagall can suggest the rich and complex biblical "portrait." This richness and complexity are suggested by passages from Samuel, Psalms and Chronicles, juxtaposed with other modern works of visual art. Even Chronicles as a book is more complex than it is usually given credit for being.

789.   Preston, Thomas R. "The Heroism of Saul: Patterns of Meaning in the Narrative of the Early Kingship." *JSOT* 24 (1982), 27-46.

I Samuel and I Kings 1-2 put the kings in the familiar OT pattern of "rise of the lowly—fall of the mighty." It also attempts to relate the fortunes of the major characters to each other, making the fortunes of each comment on those of the others.

790.   Radday, Yehuda T. "Chiasm in Samuel." *LB* 9/10 (1974), 21-31.

Chiastic structure, very widely used in OT narrative, can aid in discovering the author's main idea, since in Samuel as elsewhere, chiasm always places the most important idea at the physical center of the chiastic structure.

791.   Rosenberg, Joel. "1 and 2 Samuel," in #33, pp. 122-145.

Making sense of Samuel (the character's) role goes a long way toward defining the literary nature, character, and argument of I and II Samuel. These two books resemble Genesis in its "preoccupation with founding families" and as foci of historical change. The author of Samuel unfolded history on many planes, skilfully interweaving complementary theological, characterological, geographic, sacerdotal, demographic, and familial codes.

792.   Schwartz, Regina M. "The Histories of David: Biblical Scholarship and Biblical Stories," in #318, pp. 192-210.

"The writing of history in the Bible and the writing of history in biblical scholarship ... are so often and ... so dangerously blurred." Nineteenth-century German notions of national development influenced biblical criticism by seducing scholars into identifying the story of Germany with that of Israel. That is, "development" must imply successive stages of religious tradition still visible in the text; these must then be smoothed over into a "straightforward" reading. This is unfortunate, since as I and II Samuel demonstrate, biblical historiography is one of contradiction, confusion, and multiple perspectives. **

793.   Sternberg, Meir. "The Bible's Art of Persuasion: Ideology, Rhetoric, and Poetics in Saul's Fall." *HUCA* 54 (1983), 45-82.

A reading of I and II Samuel based on tensions among rhetoric (the pressure for consensus), ideology (pressure to uphold the law), and poetics (intricate character and history). "With preaching ruled out, the control strategy turns on an artful network of relations."

See also: #s 8, 27, 166, 175, 178, 182, 241, 289, 302, 311, 325, 348, 684, 705, 789, 814, 872, 1644.

I Samuel 1-15

794.   Brueggemann, Walter. "I Samuel 1: A Sense of a Beginning." *ZAW* 102 (1990), 33-48.

The opening chapter of I Samuel is not only a birth narrative, but shows a rhetorical strategy which transposes the birth narrative to become an "intentional beginning point for the larger Samuel-Saul-David narrative."

795.   Eslinger, Lyle M. *Kingship of God in Crisis: A Close Reading of I Samuel 1-12.* Sheffield (Almond P), 1985.

The narrative of I Samuel 1-12 "can be studied as an integral unit treating the causes and consequences of initiating a monarchy in theocratic Israel." It has a clear, "logically progressive plot." The narrator's voice structure is an essential ingredient in achieving this unity.

796.   Eslinger, Lyle. "Viewpoints and Points of View in 1 Samuel 8-12." *JSOT* 26 (1983), 61-76.

Neglect of point of view has made chapters 8 to 12 seem fragmented, even contradictory. Thus the confusions and incompleteness of historical-critical readings of the passage.

797.   Fishbane, Michael. "I Samuel 3: Historical Narrative and Narrative Poetics," in #40, pp. 191-203.

The formal structure and narrative stylistics of I Samuel 3. "The stereotypical repetition of Samuel's call ... controls the reader's perceptions of time; provides a fixed counterpoint to the developmental nature of the incidents; organizes the tensions of the action; and provides the neutral ground against which stylistic variations can be perceived.... [I]n the Hebrew Bible historical narrative is always narrative history, and so is necessarily mediated by language and its effects. It is thus language in its artistic deployment that produces the received biblical history."

798.   Gnuse, Robert Karl. *The Dream Theophany of Samuel: Its Structure in Relation to Ancient Near Eastern Dreams and its Theological Significance.* Lanham (University Press of America), 1984.

"... this section is a late literary creation with little historical value for that earlier period. The roles assigned to Samuel and the actions he performed are created according to the theological intentionality of the author or authors."

799.   Gunn, David. "A Man Given Over to Trouble: The Story of King Saul," in #316, pp. 89-112.

The people's rejection of God, and God's rejection of Saul, are somehow interrelated. Saul as "plaything of Fate"—i.e., of God. Yet Saul is also Fate's agent, however unwittingly. He cannot win, regardless of what he does. He remains of interest in the modern world partly because his struggle is our struggle.

800.   Hallberg, Calinda Ellen. "Storyline and Theme in a Biblical Narrative: 1 Samuel 3." *OPTAT* 3, #1 (1989), 1-35.

The strengths and weaknesses of two kinds of discourse analysis, and their application to I Samuel 3. Analysis of tension manifested in plot structure, "highlighted structures," and "statistical measures of unusualness of constructions." The approach of Robert Longacre "gives the overall surface structure and notional (plot) structure of the text," while the approach of Robert Bergen gives "marked constructions [which] carry primarily background information...."

801.   Humphreys, W. Lee. "The Tragedy of King Saul: A Study of the Structure of I Samuel 9-31." *JSOT* 6 (1978), 18-27.

Saul may occasionally disappear from sight in these chapters, but "he reappears again at critical points that underscore the structural framework for [this narrative]." The "distinctive literary function" played by the figure of Samuel, and the general literary structure of chapters 9 to 31 as a unified narrative.

*   Hurvitz, Avi. "Originals and Imitations in Hebrew Poetry: A Comparative Examination of 1 Sam 2:1-10 and Ps 113:5-9." See #1177a.

802.   Kahn, Sholom J. "The Samuel-Saul Story as Drama." *Judaism* 4 (1955), 3-12.

If we visualize these chapters as a "living drama," and analyze characterization, plot, etc., dramatically as part of a unified work of art (following the lead of Erich Auerbach), we learn a great deal about I Samuel 8-15 which we would otherwise not know.

803.   Long, V. Philips. *The Reign and Rejection of King Saul: A Case for Literary and Theological Coherence.* Atlanta (Scholars P), 1989.

Literary, historical, and theological issues in biblical texts are inseparable; literary approaches inevitably illuminate the history and the theology. Direct thematic links between I Samuel 10 and 13. An "integrated reading" of chapters 13 to 15 shows that "attempts to pinpoint Saul's offense ... can be resolved simply by recognizing the narrator's ability to describe Saul's failings on different levels of abstraction." Contrary to form criticism's conclusion that the Saul narrative is fragmented, it is in fact a unity, as can be seen in the anticipation of 9-11 of Saul's failure in 13-15.

804.   Miller, Patrick D., Jr, and J.J.M. Roberts. *The Hand of the
        Lord: A Reassessment of the 'Ark Narrative' of I Samuel.* Balti-
        more (Johns Hopkins UP), 1977.

        Various existing interpretations of I Samuel 2 and 4-7. A combi-
        nation of form and literary criticism is the best approach to these
        chapters. Theme and structure should be the main concern.

805.   Polzin, Robert. "On Taking Renewal Seriously: 1 Sam 11: 1-
        15," in Lyle Eslinger and Glen Taylor, eds., *Ascribe to the
        Lord: Biblical and Other Studies in Memory of Peter C. Craigie.*
        (Sheffield: JSOT P, 1988), 493-507.

        Puzzles of I Samuel 11 can be cleared up if we notice that the
        characterization of Samuel in that chapter is very uncomplimen-
        tary, implicating him "in the people's royal sin more devastatingly
        than anywhere else in the story."

806.   Polzin, Robert. *Samuel and the Deuteronomist: A Literary Study
        of the Deuteronomic History. Part Two: 1 Samuel.* San Fran-
        cisco (Harper and Row), 1988.

        Perspective, narrative voice structure and its ideological perspec-
        tive, characterization, and the functions of repetition in I Samuel.
        Compositional relationship of different parts of the narrative. "To
        make people marvel, to provoke humanity toward an ever-present
        quest for truth, even as we are disposed to recognize our relative
        ignorance—this is the fundamental perspective of this new kind of
        narrative."

807.   Polzin, Robert. "The Speaking Person and His Voice in 1
        Samuel." *VT* Supplement 36 (1985), 218-229.

        Bakhtin's philosophy of language and literary stylistics applied
        to I Samuel in order to reveal and explicate the various voices
        heard in chapter 1. We should "cease seeing biblical words, ...
        chapters, ... forms, etc. as smooth single language unities," but
        rather should hear "the profound speech diversity" of its unique
        style.

808.   Ritterspach, A. David. "Rhetorical Criticism and the Song of
        Hannah," in Jared J. Jackson and Martin Kessler, eds.,
        Rhetorical Criticism: Essays in Honor of James Muilenberg
        (Pittsburgh: Pickwick P, 1974), 68-74.

        I Samuel 2:1-10 shows strophic divisions which are remarkably
        similar in structure. The "Song of Hannah" lies somewhere be-
        tween a hymn and a song of thanksgiving. It is a powerful and pas-
        sionate statement, as shown by its form, structure, and diction:
        profoundly theological and at the same time intensely human.

809. Rooy, H.F. van. "Prophetic Utterances in Narrative Texts, with Reference to 1 Samuel 2:27-36." *OTE* n.s. 3 (1990), 203-218.

The utterance of the unknown man of God is an example of a "narrative with blanks," and also of "a narrator's alternation of the techniques of telling and showing in order to focalize in his narrative. In doing this, he supplements his own point of view...."

810. Rosner, Dov. "Irony in I Samuel Chapters 8-15." *Dor le Dor* 6 (1977), 17-26.

There are many ironic incidents, speeches and expressions in these chapters—indeed, the whole story is "an ironic episode." That is, Saul's admission that he failed as king because he feared the people is the ultimate irony, given what he has been chosen to do.

811. Watson, Wilfred G.E. "The Structure of 1 Sam 3." *Biblische Zeitschrift* 29 (1985), 90-93.

"... intended principally to lay bare the bones of narrative structure.... [N]arrative patterns were not linked rigidly to set texts. Rather, different oral traditions could make use of identical plots and end up with different versions of the same story." This is equally true whether the Masoretic text or a reconstructed text is used.

812. Willis, John T. "Samuel vs. Eli: I Samuel 1-7." *TZ* 35 (1979), 201-212.

In contrast to the historical critical approach, the literary approach shows that the narrator of I Samuel 1-7 could not "naturally" deviate from his account just to bring in material not relevant to his main concern: the crisis of the former regime.

See also: #s 209, 273, 302, 323, 336, 570, 700, 820.

I Samuel 16-31

813. Bach, Alice. "The Pleasure of Her Text." *USQR* 43 (1989), 41-58. Rpt from #46, pp. 25-44.

A reading of I Samuel 25 "concerned with woman as reader of male-produced literature, and with the way the hypothesis of a female reader changes our understanding or vision of a text by exploring the significance of its sexual codes." A close examination of these codes "shows Abigail to be more subversive than her male authors have understood."

814.   Brueggemann, Walter. "An Artistic Disclosure in Three Dimensions," and "Sport of Nature." *The Cumberland Seminarian* 28 (Spring, 1990), 1-8, 9-25.

In the Samuel books "Israel practiced ... an artistic rendering of social public reality.... [It] takes seriously providence, power, and personality, is narrative that does not claim to be eyewitness to personalities in dialogue, and that does not claim to speak directly about God." Close reading of I Samuel 18 in this light.

815.   Brueggemann, Walter. "Narrative Intentionality in 1 Samuel 29." *JSOT* 43 (1989), 21-35.

Close reading of this chapter not only shows a convincing alibi so David will not be blamed for Saul's death, but a "more subtle, and more important intention": David's being acquitted of guilt on several interacting levels, in which the narrator brackets the many "ifs" which will occur to the reader: a "teasing rhetorical intentionality," in an "artful, intentional, and subtle" narrative.

816.   Ceresko, Anthony R. "A Rhetorical Analysis of David's 'Boast' (1 Samuel 17:34-37): Some Reflections on Method." *CBQ* 47 (1985), 58-74.

The isolation of historical, literary, textual, sociological, and other methods from each other can be ended, in part by using rhetorical criticism to throw new light on style and structure, as can be illustrated in I Samuel 17.

817.   Gordon, Robert P. "David's Rise and Saul's Demise: Narrative Analogy in I Samuel 24-26." *TB* 31 (1980), 37-64.

Verbal, structural, and other narratological considerations demonstrate the intricate, complex unity formed out of the various individual episodes in I Samuel 24-26.

*   Gunn, David. "A Man Given Over to Trouble: The Story of King Saul." See #799.

*   Humphreys, W. Lee. "The Tragedy of King Saul: A Study of the Structure of I Samuel 9-31." See #801.

818.   Jason, Heda. "The Story of David and Goliath: A Folk Epic?" *Biblica* 60 (1979), 36-70.

Ethnopoetic analysis of I Samuel 17. Its narrative syntax, an-
thropomorphic aspects, genre (heroic fairy tale versus romantic
epic). The David-Goliath episode "is a short, prose record of an
ethnopoetic epic work (real or imitated) which was possibly composed in verse form; its genre is the romantic epic ... a subgenre of
the historic epic."

819. Jobling, David. "Jonathan: A Structural Study in I Samuel."
SBLSP (1976), 15-32.

The significance of Jonathan from structuralist and literary perspectives. These show that Jonathan's importance is to be found
through his function in the narrative, and only secondarily from
the assessment of history. The use of the character of Jonathan
provides the only plausible affirmation of the legitimacy of David's
kingship.

820. Jobling, David. *The Sense of Biblical Narrative: Three Structural
Analyses in the Old Testament (I Samuel 13-31, Numbers 11-
12, I Kings 17-18).* [Vol. I]. 2nd Edition. Sheffield (JSOT
P), 1986.

The problem of the status of kingship in I Samuel is solved by
means of the character of Jonathan: he is "character emptied into
plot," the transition from Saul to David. Narrative and structuralist-
semantic analysis of Numbers 11-12. Narrative analysis to explore
the "exchange of meaning" between text (combat on Mount
Carmel) and context (the drought) in I Kings 17-18.

* Keller, Joseph. "Biblical Literary Criticism: Logical Form
and Poetic Function." See #1331.

821. Kessler, Martin. "Narrative Technique in I SM 16:1-13." *CBQ*
32 (1970), 543-554.

These verses form a "tendentious pericope," but one with sophisticated literary technique, showing terseness, variety of pace,
etc. Study of the artistry of the passage is a valuable aid to exegesis,
since form and content are intimately connected.

822. Lawton, Robert B., S.J. "1 Samuel 18: David, Merob, and
Michal." *CBQ* 51 (1990), 423-5.

There seems to be a deliberate echo of the Leah-Rachel story of
Genesis 29 in I Samuel 18; it was apparently intended to underscore David's lack of love for Michal. "Merob, in the few verses
dealing with her, helps us to understand something of David's
character and of biblical artistry as well."

823.   Levenson, Jon D. "I Samuel 25 as Literature and as History."
        CBQ 40 (1978), 11-28; rpt in #40, pp. 222-242.

The story of Nabal, using the techniques of Robert Alter; and
reconstructing the political significance of "this brilliantly recounted tale." Why chapter 25 is located where it is; the artistry of
the narrator. It can be seen as a narrative analogy with David's attempt to kill Uriah, and also as a foreshadowing of the later David
of II Samuel.

*   Miscall, P.D. *The Workings of Old Testament Narrative.* See
        #573.

824.   Polak, Frank. "Literary Study and 'Higher Criticism' Ac-
        cording to the Tale of David's Beginning." *PWCJS* 9
        (1986), 27-32.

To reconcile literary and historical criticism of the Bible, we
must first distinguish between objective and subjective evidence in
the text, and between correspondence which is accidental and that
which is significant because related to theme and content. The
"conflicting" stories of David's beginnings illustrate these principles. From a literary standpoint, the apparent double exposition is
not redundant at all, but thematically appropriate.

825.   Rose, Ashley S. "The 'Principles' of Divine Election: Wis-
        dom in I Samuel 16," in Jared J. Jackson and Martin
        Kessler, eds., *Rhetorical Criticism: Essays in Honor of James
        Muilenberg* (Pittsburgh: Pickwick P, 1974), 43-67.

I Samuel 16 is an introduction to the extensive literary work describing relations between the old and new orders in Israel. It emphasizes the principles of divine election uniquely, by using
literary features similar to those found in traditional wisdom
literature. Thus the author of I Samuel's interpretation of the
Davidic monarchy is quite different from that of, e.g., II Samuel 7
and Psalm 89. The chapter's structure is a series of didactic
utterances followed by notices of responses to them.

826.   Sakenfield, Katharine Doob. "Loyalty and Love: The Lan-
        guage of Human Interconnections in the Hebrew Bible."
        Michigan Quarterly Review 22, #3 (Summer, 1983), 190-204;
        rpt Michael P. O'Connor and David Noel Freedman, eds.,
        Backgrounds for the Bible (Winona Lake: Eisenbrauns,
        1987), 215-229.

How understanding the meanings of individual words in Hebrew narrative contributes to appreciating the stories, and in turn
how careful reading of the stories helps us recognize subtleties in

the words. For example, *hesed* in I Samuel 18-23 and in Ruth has no precise English equivalent, but has "surprising connotations." We must of course know general vocabulary and basic social institutions of ancient Israel, "but it is the narrators' art which finally gives the words their power."

827.   Simon, Uriel. "A Balanced Story: The Stern Prophet and the Kind Witch." *Prooftexts* 8 (1988), 159-171.

The episode at Endor in I Samuel 28 "begins with the king's donning a disguise and denying his values; it ends with his restoration to his true identity and ... true self.... Thanks to the compassion ... [plus] strict justice in this balanced story, the humanity of the witch combined with the heroism of Saul are able to illuminate the morbid darkness of the king's last night."

See also: #s 7, 165, 211, 243, 303, 306, 313, 327, 331, 373, 701, 781.

II Samuel

See note to "Samuel."

828.   Ackerman, James S. "Knowing Good and Evil: A Literary Analysis of the Court History in 2 Samuel 9-20 and 1 Kings 1-2." *JBL* 109 (1990), 41-60.

How Meir Sternberg's thesis about the "epistemological gap"as chief characteristic of biblical narrative can be further substantiated through a reading of the "court history." The gap is our (and the characters') difficulty in knowing good characters from evil ones. "Using the Davidic house as its focus, the text is a profound meditation on how life works, envisioning an intricate balance between human freedom and divine sovereignty."

829.   Bal, Mieke. "The Emergence of the Lethal Woman, or the Use of Hermeneutic Models," in #304, pp. 10-36.

Various readings of the David-Bathsheba story in terms of one particular passage: the seemingly irrelevant detail about Abimelech's death during the siege at the hands of the woman of Thebez. It reveals why Uriah really dies: because he does not side with the men against the women, as does Joab.

830.   Bal, Mieke. "The Semiotics of Symmetry, or the Use of Hermeneutic Models." *Versus* 35/36 (1983), 7-36.

The range of interpretive possibilities for reading II Samuel 11 offered by three models: frame theoretical, formal semiotic, and narratological. While the question is only partly decidable, the frame theoretical model seems most satisfactory. Even if the situation is left ambiguous, such discussion is valuable because it forces us to reflect on how we read texts.

831.   Bar-Efrat, Shimon. "Literary Modes and Methods in the Biblical Narrative in View of 2 Samuel 10-20 and I Kings 1-2." *Immanuel* 8 (1978), 19-31.

The narrator of these chapters is an integral part of the narrative. He is omniscient, offering few intrusions to lessen the verisimilitude. Further, he offers characterization, skillful time shifts, and dialogue.

*   Battenhouse, Roy. [Forum on Teaching the Bible as Literature]. See #170.

832.   Coats, George W. "Parable, Fable, and Anecdote: Storytelling in the Succession Narrative." *Interpretation* 35 (1981), 368-382.

In order to interpret a biblical narrative adequately, we must correctly recognize its genre. We may wonder if II Samuel 11-12 is a parable, but if so there are problems with its structure. The solution may be to recognize how these chapters function as an "ironical hedge" in the larger story.

833.   Conroy, Charles. *Absalom, Absalom! Narrative and Language in 2 Samuel 13-20*. Rome (Pontifical Biblical Institute Press), 1978.

How the literary excellence of II Samuel 13-20 is manifested in its narrative techniques and use of language. Close readings of structure, plot, character, point of view, and narration in chapters 13 and 17. II Samuel 13-20 as a whole along the same lines; the dominant narrative patterns of these chapters together and within identifiable sections.

*   Exum, J. Cheryl. "Murder They Wrote: Ideology and the Manipulation of Female Presence in Biblical Narrative." See #748.

834.   Fokkelman, J.P. "A Lie, Born of Truth, Too Weak to Contain It. A Structural Reading of 2 Sam. 1.1-16." *OS* 23 (1984), 39-55.

The structure of II Samuel 1, and of the story within the story, both show concentricity, even down to the balancing of words in the word-count. The various "rings" or levels of the text, and their relation to theme and plot. Semiotics enables us to see the various "levels of meaning" in a text.

835.   Fokkelman, J.P. *Narrative Art and Poetry in the Books of Samuel: A Full Interpretation Based on Stylistic and Structural Analyses. Vol. I: King David.* Assen (Van Gorcum), 1981.

The narrative of II Samuel 9-20 and I Kings 1-2 is "a consummate whole well-suited to synchronic reading." The good reader of this material must be open and unbiased, totally committed on behalf of the text. The theme of this narrative centers on a series of polarities: whole/divided, unity/duality, self/ego, appearance/concealment, being weak/acting strong, father/king. See also Vols. II and III: #s 773, 774.

*   Gunn, David M. "David and the Gift of the Kingdom (2 Sam 2-4, 9-20, I Kgs 1-2)." See #777.

*   Gunn, David M. "From Jerusalem to the Jordan and Back: Symmetry in 2 Samuel XV-XX." See #779.

836.   Gunn, David M. *The Story of King David: Genre and Interpretation.* Sheffield (JSOT P), 1978.

The "Succession Narrative" as story constitutes its primary character. Previous views of its genre are inadequate: it is "traditional story," showing the influence of the techniques of oral composition. The narrative deliberately interrelates the personal and the political, and the resulting tension is central to the outcome. Its theme is the gaining and bequeathing of status and authority. The author has a powerful yet sympathetic sense of man's frailty.

837.   Hagan, Harry. "Deception as Motif and Theme in II Sam. 9-20, I Kings 1-2." *Biblica* 60 (1979), 301-326.

Deception is the basic theme of the "Succession Narrative." In fact, deception is an implied theme throughout the OT, allied to the theme of loyalty. Each episode shows deception perpetrated to obtain a woman, a kingdom, or to restore order.

838.   Halperin, Sarah. "Absalom's Story—Drama and Tragedy." *Dor Le Dor* 11 (1982), 1-14.

General literary analysis and appreciation of II Samuel 13-18, emphasizing how well Absalom fits Aristotle's definition of the tragic hero.

839.   Jackson, Jared J. "David's Throne: Patterns in the Succession Story." *Canadian Journal of Theology* 11 (1965), 183-195.

The Succession Narrative "is a masterpiece of the narrator's art, fashioned and polished in every detail, the structure imposed upon the events exactly fitting and giving perfect expression to the internal design of his work." It is "true history writing."

840.   Kleven, Terence. "Rhetoric and Narrative Depiction in 2 Sam 1:1-16." *PEGL* 9 (1989), 59-73.

"The stylistic arguments ... used to support an historical reconstruction of the passage have arisen from inadequate accounts of the style. If the historical David is different than the depiction of David in the narrative, the historical David is inaccessible to us and attempts to reconstruct his actions and motives are speculative." Aspects of style in this pasaage "are used intentionally by the author to create the story," and thus cannot be used to decide what the historical David thought or did through attempts to locate "sources."

*   Lasine, Stuart. "Fiction, Falsehood, and Reality in Hebrew Scripture." See #980.

841.   Lasine, Stuart. "Judicial Narratives and the Ethics of Reading: The Reader as Judge of the Dispute Between Mephibosheth and Ziba." *HS* 30 (1989), 49-69.

The "ethics of reading" means determining when readers are called on to make moral judgments, and when they should refrain from making them. The ethics of reading in II Samuel 16 and 19 suggests that we are called upon by the narrator to judge David negatively in these chapters.

842.   Lasine, Stuart. "Melodrama as Parable: The Story of the Poor Man's Ewe Lamb and the Unmasking of David's Topsy-Turvy Emotions." *HAR* 8 (1984), 101-124.

There is still disagreement about basic aspects of Nathan's story in II Samuel 12. It can be called a parable only by virtue of its incompleteness as melodrama. The actual effects on David of Nathan's story, and the author's use of it as a continued condemnation of David.

843.   Long, Burke O. "Wounded Beginnings: David and Two Sons," in #316, pp. 26-34.

II Samuel as "the beginning of anxiety about the kingdom.... But where events touch our deeper passions, the tale tells of twisted human relationships and wounded beginnings, as though from brokenness comes wholeness, a larger pattern more satisfying to the soul."

844.   McCarthy, Dennis, S.J. "II Samuel 7 and the Structure of the Deuteronomic History." *JBL* 84 (1965), 131-8.

The final section of the history reproduces the first two sections. A number of passages tie the complex Deuteronomic history together (in Joshua, Judges, I Samuel, I and II Kings). We should now add II Samuel 7 to this list because it not only acts as a tie-in, but also "sets in relief a carefully worked out over-all structure in the history as a whole."

845.   Ridout, George. "The Rape of Tamar: A Rhetorical Analysis of 2 Sam 13:1-22," in Jared J. Jackson and Martin Kessler, eds., *Rhetorical Criticism: Essays in Honor of James Muilenberg* (Pittsburgh: Pickwick P, 1974), 75-84.

Probably the foremost device for rhetorical critics to pay attention to is repetition. Extensive repetitions in II Samuel 13 of the words "brother" and "sister" carry structural and thematic weight. The structure of this chapter is chiastic.

846.   Rosenberg, Joel. "The Institutional Matrix of Treachery in 2 Samuel 11." *Semeia* 46 (1989), 103-116.

The physical and logistic details in the opening lines of II Samuel 11, though often analyzed in personal terms, in fact have extensive political ramifications: David the criminal, and the nation both accomplice and victim. Literary analysis shows "the role of story in political history." Adapted from material in #847.

847.   Rosenberg, Joel. *King and Kin: Political Allegory in the Hebrew Bible.* Bloomington (Indiana UP), 1986.

"... seeks to demonstrate the shape, style, and argument of three narrative complexes taken from the larger continuous narrative of Genesis through II Kings—namely, the Garden story, the Abraham cycle, and the Davidic history—to show their interrelation.... Genesis is ... a companion work to II Samuel, a 'midrash,' if you will, upon the Davidic history, adumbrating the dichotomies articulated in the historical work by appeal to legend, myth, and primordial history." Semiotic and deconstructionist analyses help us see these points. **

848.   Roth, Wolfgang. "You are the Man! Structural Interaction in 2 Samuel 10-12." *Semeia* 8 (1977), 1-13.

John D. Crossan's method can help us see that myth and polemic are also types of story. Ways in which they interact with parable; how the actantial model of A.J. Greimas explains the interaction of structural components in these chapters.

849.   Sacon, Kiyoshi K. "A Study of the Literary Structure of the 'Succession Narrative,'" in Tomoo Ishida, ed., *Studies in the Period of David and Solomon and Other Essays* (Winona Lake: Eisenbrauns, 1982), 27-54.

We must analyze at the paragraph level, which is the most basic unit of thought in a literary work. These chapters are largely chiastic in structure, which reinforces the themes and the build-up of narrative tension. The author wished to show the interrelationship of public and private affairs. The narrative is "an eloquent representation of a contradictory process in full tension between the external national expansion ... and the internal insecurity ... and uncertainty shortly after Solomon's succession."

850.   Seters, John Van. "Problems of Orality in the Literary Analysis of the Court History of David." *JSOT* 1 (1976), 22-29.

This passage may reflect traditional oral composition and historical traditions, but the important point is that the theme is antitraditional, and the whole crafted with great literary skill.

851.   Shea, William H. "David's Lament." *American Schools of Oriental Research Bulletin* #221 (February, 1976), 141-4.

The basic analysis of this passage from II Samuel 1 offered by David Noel Freedman is acceptable, but we must modify his treatment of verses 19-27 to illustrate the use of bi- and tri-cola, and inclusio.

852.   Smith, Jenny. "The Discourse Structure of the Rape of Tamar (2 Samuel 13:1-22)." *VE* 20 (1990), 21-42.

Close reading of the discourse structure of this episode yields the atmosphere which the original hearers would have perceived, and illuminates some of the difficulties of the text. How this pericope is delimited; the notional surface structures of each episode. Verse 15, the center of an elaborate chiasm, forms as well the story's "notional climax."

853.   Vorster, Willem S. "Readings, Readers and the Succession Narrative. An Essay on Reception." *ZAW* 98 (1986), 351-362.

The reader contributes meaning to a text; complexity exists because readers exist both inside and outside the text. II Samuel 9-20 plus I Kings 1-2, the so-called "Succession Narrative," is a hypothetical construct by modern scholars, though convincing nevertheless. These chapters do not show the influence of the Wisdom tradition, but do exhibit many characteristics of careful narrative shaping of plot and character. Why some responses to texts such as this one are inadequate.

854. Whybray, R.N. *The Succession Narrative: A Study of II Sam 9-20 and I Kings 1 and 2*. Naperville (Allenson), 1968.

This extended narrative is in effect a novel of political propaganda, but not a national epic or religious or moral tale. It was probably written early in Solomon's reign, and shows sophisticated thematic unity, structure, characterization, and style. Its resemblance to Genesis 37-50 and Proverbs suggests that it was influenced by the wisdom tradition rather than by I Samuel.

855. Yee, Gale A. "Fraught with Background: Literary Ambiguity in II Samuel 11." *Interpretation* 42 (1988), 240-253.

Narrative ambiguity in II Samuel is a deliberate stylistic device to engage the reader's imagination, creating interaction with the characters in a way that a more explicit account would not. There is ambiguity between action and motive, between the same words applied to different characters, and in the variation between narration and dialogue.

See also: #s 7, 16, 135, 211, 302, 304, 305, 306, 321, 327, 335, 337, 345, 373, 383, 388, 390, 435, 747, 781, 913, 1007, 1184, 1386.

KINGS

See note under "Samuel."

856. Cohn, Robert L. "Convention and Creativity in the Book of Kings." *CBQ* 47 (1985), 603-616.

Type scenes in four episodes involving the death of kings: Jereboam (I Kings 14), Ahaziah (II Kings 1), Ben-hadad (II Kings 8), and Hezekiah (II Kings 20).They show a formal structure referred to by another scholar as "prophetic inquiry schema," though each of the four episodes stretches the genre in some way. The author may have intended each succeeding episode to be read against its predecessors.

*   Cook, Albert. "'Fiction' and History in Samuel and Kings."
            See #772.

857.   Culley, Robert C. "Punishment Stories in the Legends of
            the Prophets," in Richard Spencer, ed., *Orientation by
            Disorientation* (Pittsburgh: Pickwick P, 1980), 167-181.

            Narrative structure in I Kings 13, 20, 21; II Kings 1, 2, 5. We
            must ask: How may action in narrative be understood? What do
            the structures of these six stories have in common? There were
            strong literary forces shaping these stories: they either create or
            they re-make reality.

858.   Long, Burke O. "Artistry in Hebrew Historical Narrative."
            PWCJS 8 (1982), 29-34.

            Parataxis in regnal frameworks in I and II Kings. They exhibit
            "simple beauty, reversals, and transformations."

859.   Long, Burke O. "Historical Narrative and the Fictionalizing
            Imagination." *VT* 35 (1985), 405-416.

            How the author of Kings used imaginative creativity to present a
            picture of Israel's past. He was not simply reporting the events he
            discussed, nor were his reasons simply theological. He was more
            interested in developing an ironic perspective. He used direct dis-
            course, prophets' speeches, and type-scenes in order to create an
            ideological drama. That is, he wrote literary fiction. It is too simple
            to rank narratives as archival, historical, or popular legend, be-
            cause these combine different rhetorical styles, and because to do
            so shows naivety about how language works.

860.   McConville, J.G. "Narrative and Meaning in the Book of
            Kings." *Biblica* 70 (1989), 31-49.

            The book of Kings has "a unified conception ... with a single fi-
            nal author in the exilic period." While most scholars see Joshua
            and Judges in contrast to Kings, these books must be read to-
            gether. "Kings allows for hope that exile might not be God's final
            word to his people."

861.   Nelson, Richard D. "The Anatomy of the Book of Kings."
            JSOT 40 (1988), 39-48.

            Modern readers tend to miss much of the richness of Kings be-
            cause it seems so relentlessly "history-like." A better model for un-
            derstanding it might be the Gospels. We need to try to grasp Kings
            as a whole, and apply to it such concepts as point of view and im-
            plied author.

862.   Radday, Yehuda T. "Chiasm in Kings." *LB* 31 (1974), 52-67.

Chiastic structure was compulsory for early narrators of the HB, but later disappeared. It can be used to discover an author's purpose or main idea. It exists on several levels in Kings: in the list or succession of kings; and in compositional principles. We can observe it at work especially in the Elijah and Solomon cycles, as well as in I and II Kings overall.

*   Roth, Wolfgang. *Hebrew Gospel: Cracking the Code of Mark.* See #1805.

863.   Savran, George. "1 and 2 Kings," in #33, pp. 146-164.

We must evaluate an historian's "narrative strategies" if we are to understand his point of view. The author of Kings was highly biased: using black and white standards for judging Israelite kings, offering categorical disapproval of northern rulers. All this was part of the Deuteronomic history's view of the reasons for Israel's existence and prosperity. Kings shows a chiastic structure, with subtle techniques of characterization and moral judgment. Its themes are the covenant with David, the building of the temple, and "oracle and fulfillment."

See also: #s 166, 182, 325, 448, 697, 705, 1644, 1805.

I Kings
See note to "Samuel."

*   Ackerman, James S. "Knowing Good and Evil: A Literary Analysis of the Court History in 2 Samuel 9-20 and 1 Kings 1-2." See #828.

*   Bird, Phyllis A. "The Harlot as Heroine: Narrative Art and Social Presuppositions in Three Old Testament Texts." See #607.

*   Brodie, Thomas Louis. "Towards Unravelling Luke's Use of the Old Testament: Luke 7.11-17 as an *Imitatio* of I Kings 17.17-24." See #1921.

864.   Bruns, Gerald L. "The Hermeneutics of Midrash," in #45, pp. 189-213.

Midrash "is not a method but a critique of method ... is haphaz-ardly, even disdainfully studied, and often misunderstood as a re-sult." Examples of its treatment of I Kings 5:12. Modern theory holds conflict of interpretations to be a defect, whereas midrash welcomes it. The rabbis see themselves as participating in Torah, not just analyzing it.

865.   Childs, Brevard S. "On Reading the Elijah Narratives." *Inter-pretation* 34 (1980), 128-137.

In studying a biblical narrative such as I Kings 18, we need to be careful of too easy parallels with pagan literature (e.g., Canaanite myths); pay attention to the shape of stories and of whole biblical books, and to the place of a given episode in the larger work. We may use whatever tools we like, so long as we preserve the integrity of the narrative and have an open mind about contemporary ap-plications.

866.   Cohn, Robert L. "The Literary Logic of I Kings 17-19." *JBL* 101 (1982), 333-350.

These chapters have a rich structural and thematic texture. As the story develops in a linear fashion, it also establishes three paral-lel episodic sequences, creating a network of patterns and associa-tions through which meaning is communicated. Source criticism, on the other hand, destroys the unity of this "sacred biography," since the scenes derive their meaning from their context.

867.   Cohn, Robert L. "Literary Technique in the Jereboam Nar-rative." *ZAW* 97 (1985), 23-35.

Literary artistry sets human behavior against divine purpose in I Kings 11-14. It is composite artistry with a generally chiastic shape. The Jereboam story is skillfully woven into the preceding Solomon story, yet is clearly distinguished from it. Thus, despite multiple sources, it functions as a literary whole, with the chiasm nicely un-dergirding a story of rise and fall.

868.   Conroy, Charles. "A Literary Analysis of I Kings 1: 41-53, With Methodological Reflections." *VT* Supplement 36 (1985), 54-66.

We need to work toward a "responsible integration" of literary and historical criticism of the Bible. The literary-narrative structure of I Kings 1; how it can modify the results of historical-critical analysis.

*   Fokkelman, J.P. *Narrative Art and Poetry in the Books of Samuel.* Vol. I. See #835.

869.   Gros Louis, Kenneth R.R. "Elijah and Elisha," in #39, pp.
        177-190.

   The purposes of the narrative are to establish Yahweh as more
   powerful than Baal, and to relate the "human aspects" of the
   prophets. Comparison of characterizations of the two prophets,
   and of both to Hamlet in Shakespeare's play. The miracles performed by the two prophets are strikingly similar in execution and
   in means employed. This similarity is in fact a literary device in order to create emphasis, confer a similar status on both prophets,
   and to assert God's primacy.

870.   Hauser, Alan J., and Russell Gregory. *From Carmel to Horeb:
        Elijah in Crisis.* Sheffield (Almond P), 1990.

   Hauser: The author of I Kings 17-19 was a skilled literary artist
   whose work shows "variety of imagery, ... intricacy of narrative
   structure, ... and wealth of ideas.... [He] skillfully interweaves the
   struggle between Yahweh and Baal with the struggle between Yahweh and death." Gregory: I Kings 19 is dominated by irony, and an
   ironic view of Elijah. The irony lies in both the structure and the
   theme of these chapters.

*   Jackson, Jared J. "David's Throne: Patterns in the Succes-
        sion Story." See #839.

*   Jobling, David L. *The Sense of Biblical Narrative, Vol. I.* See
        #820.

871.   Lasine, Stuart. "Solomon, Daniel, and the Detective Story:
        The Social Function of a Literary Genre." *HAR* 11 (1987),
        247-266.

   "The ideology of this story [I Kings 3:16-27], and the kind of
   comforting message it might have carried to ... ancient Israel, can
   be better understood by viewing it in terms of ... the classical detective story," with Solomon as hero-detective.

872.   Marcus, David. "David the Deceiver and David the Dupe."
        Prooftexts 6 (1986), 163-7.

   It is important to know the functions of, and motivations for,
   deceit in a biblical narrative. Deception in Davidic narrative shows
   two important trends: (a) he is successful at deceiving others and
   at the same time avoiding it being visited on him in return early in
   his career, but (b) he is not successful at these when at the peak of
   his career. Knowing this especially aids us in interpreting Uriah's
   actions, and the events of I Kings 1.

873.   Miscall, Peter D. "Elijah, Ahab and Jehu: A Prophecy Ful-
        filled." *Prooftexts* 9 (1989), 73-83.

        The intertextual allusions in I Kings 14-22. "In my reading
        prophecy and fulfillment are not a set pattern to order the text
        and to serve as a firm anchor for an interpretation, but are one en-
        trance among many into the labyrinthine ways of the Bible."

874.   Parker, Kim Ian. "Repetition as a Structuring Device in 1
        Kings 1-11." *JSOT* 42 (1988), 19-27.

        These chapters of I Kings are often viewed as a mix of materials
        and sources, but should rather be seen as a unified narrative by a
        single author. The narrative is written so as to allow us to focus on
        two sides of Solomon's character.

875.   Porten, Bezalel. "The Structure and Theme of the Solomon
        Narrative." *HUCA* 38 (1967), 93-128.

        Despite its heterogeneity, I Kings 3-11 is a well-structured, uni-
        fied narrative. The structure is the key to its meaning, not just as
        "artificial or literary elegance."

*   Vorster, Willem S. "Readings, Readers and the Succession
        Narrative. An Essay on Reception." See #853.

See also: #s 7, 18, 26, 128, 166, 175, 223, 302, 305, 306, 310, 323,
332, 345, 684, 701, 789, 820.

II Kings

*   Brodie, Thomas L., O.P. "Luke 7,36-50 as an Internalization
        of 2 Kings 4, 1-37: A Study in Luke's Use of Rhetorical Im-
        itation." See #1920.

876.   Cohn, Robert L. "Form and Perspective in 2 Kings V." *VT* 33
        (1983), 171-184.

        II Kings 5 is an especially apt example of a biblical narrative in
        which art and theology are symbiotically related. The author
        needed a three-part tale at this point for rhetorical effect.

877.   Cohn, Robert L. "Reading in Three Dimensions: The Im-
        perative of Biblical Narrative." *Religion and Intellectual Life*
        6 (1989), 161-172.

The Bible is distinctive in its magnetic hold on our culture because its truth is three dimensional: literary, theological, and historical. The narrative in II Kings 2 about Elisha illustrates this coordination of esthetic ordering with historical and theological aims.

878. Eslinger, Lyle. "Josiah and the Torah Book: Comparison of 2 Kgs 22:1–23:28 and 2 Chr 34:1–35:19." *HAR* 10 (1986), 37-62.

Because we commonly assume causality in temporal sequences, biblical (like modern) authors often can manipulate readers without actually stating cause and effect. II Kings 22-23 and its "daughter text," II Chronicles 34-35 is "an extended illustration of plot structuring using parallel sequencing *to imply* causality.... Here its strength lies in ... scenic parallelism ... and in *Leitwort* connections between the parallels."

879. Garcia-Treto, Francisco O. "The Fall of the House: A Carnivalesque Reading of 2 Kings 9 and 10." *JSOT* 46 (1990), 47-65.

Various senses of the "house" motif in II Kings 9 and 10, using Bakhtin's concept of "carnivalized" narratives: temporary upsetting of all normal hierarchical, bodily, spatial, and sacred relationships. With this concept we learn to see much more in the text than simple hostility to the Samaritans or to Ahab.

880. Heins, Barbara Doolan. "From Leprosy to Shalom and Back Again: A Discourse Analysis of 2 Kings 5." *OPTAT* 2, #1 (1988), 20-33.

The stages of II Kings 5 as an episodic narrative with extensive and intricate chiastic structure; various narrative features which make it cohesive; and a "single climactic narrator." Discourse analysis is especially useful and necessary for works such as the Bible which were written in different languages and cultural settings from our own.

881. Hobbs, T.R. "2 Kings 1 and 2: Their Unity and Purpose." *SR* 13 (1984), 327-334.

How the incidents in these chapters are arranged in a chiastic structure. How they derive from the first sentence of II Kings which sets the thematic tone for the entire book. The theme appears here because of the problem of prophetic succession.

882. Licht, Jacob. "Story-Telling in the Bible." *Immanuel* 7 (1977), 21-4.

Basic features of biblical story-telling which appear when we analyze II Kings 6 include mimesis in characterization; clever anecdotal structure; creation and resolution of tension; dialogue and the showing of direct action; and brevity.

883.   Moore, Rick Dale. *God Saves: Lessons from the Elisha Stories.* Sheffield (JSOT P), 1990.

A "literary-aesthetic analysis" of each of the Elisha stories in II Kings 5-7 in order to reveal their internal features and their dynamics; followed by a socio-historical analysis of the same material. They are "didactic salvation stories set against the Aramean military threat of ninth-century Israel."

884.   Olyan, Saul. " *Hāšālôm*: Some Literary Considerations of 2 Kings 9." CBQ 46 (1984), 652-668.

"The writer's careful employment of certain key words and phrases has created a story of great depth, laced with irony, suspense, and pathos." The key to interpretation is verse 26. Analysis bears out Erich Auerbach's contention that certain parts of style in Hebrew narrative are brought into high relief, others left obscure with an unexpressed background quality.

See also: #s 7, 238, 338, 364, 684, 1892, 1919, 2041.

Latter Prophets

885.   Geller, Stephen A. "Were the Prophets Poets?" *Prooftexts* 3 (1983), 211-221.

It is legitimate to ask if the prophets can be poets. There has always been tension between prophecy and poetry. Certainly the prophets can be poets, though whether they are causes exegetes problems because historical critics think of the text as transparent.

886.   Gottwald, Norman K. "Tragedy and Comedy in the Latter Prophets," in #228, pp. 83-96.

Plot, theme, and stylistic patterns in the latter prophets, and the "role of the hero," in terms of "comic and tragic literary categories." These fifteen books "are structured as comedy rather than tragedy, since salvation has the last word over judgment."

887. Jemielity, Thomas. "Prophets or Projectors? Challenges to Credibility in Hebrew Prophecy." *Studies in Eighteenth Century Culture* 18 (1988), 445-478.

Hebrew prophecy was markedly satiric, as William Blake already understood two centuries ago. Their satiric range is wide, "from witty invective ... to fantasies of gargantuan sexual excess ...quasi-allegorically figuring, as in Ezekiel, the religious apostasy of Israel and Judah.... Hebrew prophecy, much like satire, records an intrafraternal conflict ... that poses a need for a rhetoric of credibility." Hebrew prophets, like later satirists, were frequently accused of being "mad, malignly motivated, and treasonably subversive of the public order."

* Kugel, James L., ed. *Poetry and Prophecy: The Beginnings of a Literary Tradition.* See #379.

888. Sims, James H. "The Major Literary Prophecy of the Old Testament." *Dalhousie Review* 61 (1981), 447-468.

"Because of their peculiar function of reinterpreting Israel's past and present as well as foretelling her future, there is no other part of the Old Testament that is quite as crucial to understanding the whole as the literary prophets." Isaiah, Jeremiah, Ezekiel, and Daniel.

889. Williams, James G. "Irony and Lament: Clues to Prophetic Consciousness." *Semeia* 8 (1977), 51-74.

Prophetic experience and consciousness are integrally related to the forms and devices of prophetic utterance. Forms of lament, repetition of images, and other poetic devices all contribute to the effect. The "ironic poetry" which they wrote was indicative of their sense of being caught between God and people. It was a comic irony whose use was exposing pretensions of imposters, since God needs a "joyous ending" and a new Israel. Isaiah 1, 5, 10, 28-31; Jeremiah; Amos 5, 6; Micah 2.

See also: #s 175, 214, 370, 421.

ISAIAH

890. Cobb, William H. "A Study in Isaiah," in #32, pp. 147-160.

The "vast reach of Isaiah's thought," his leading themes, and the qualities of his style, e.g., humor, compression, vividness, sublimity.

891.   Conrad, Edgar W. "The Royal Narratives and the Structure of the Book of Isaiah." *JSOT* 41 (1988), 67-81.

The royal narratives, e.g., the "fear not" oracles so frequent in Isaiah, offer clues to understanding the structure of the book. These and the "war oracles" show that a certain progression (not just repetition) occurs—as, e.g., from Isaiah 7 compared with Isaiah 41; the latter chapter is deliberately placed in a strategic location in the book.

892.   Kosmala, Hans. "Form and Structure in Ancient Hebrew Poetry (Continued)." *VT* 16 (1966), 152-180; rpt *Studies, Essays and Reviews* I (Leiden: E.J. Brill, 1978), 107-135.

These structures (see #432) are of special interest to demonstrate that the approach can come nearer than other kinds of criticism to showing how additions have been made to Isaiah.

893.   Schökel, Luis Alonso. "Isaiah," in #33, pp. 165-183.

Isaiah is a "collection of collections" which "brings into focus centuries of historical experience and poetic concerns." There were at least three authors, but it is still one book. Stylistic elements in chapters 1-39, and the "poetic world" of chapters 40-66. Isaiah is "classic" poetry: objective, unlyrical, showing formal perfection and stylistic distance. Nevertheless, it is intensely rhetorical. Close reading of some passages in terms of genre, style, figures, and themes. Chapters 40-55 are the height of its poetry.

894.   Steinberg, Theodore L. "Isaiah the Poet," in #48, pp. 299-310.

Isaiah as a unified whole. The imaginativeness, development, and logic of its imagery, plus elaborate word play make it true poetry. All of the prophets were in fact poets.

895.   Webb, Barry G. "Zion in Transformation: A Literary Approach to Isaiah," in #35, pp. 65-84.

"The transformation of Zion is the key to both the formal and the thematic structure of the book as a whole.... The holy seed, the Immanuel child, the foundation stone, the messianic figure and the suffering servant figure are all metaphors for the faithful remnant ... which is the key to Zion's transformation, and hence to the transformation of the cosmos."

896.   Wojcik, Jan. "The Uncertain Success of Isaiah's Prophecy: A Poetical Reading," in Jan Wojcik and Raymond-Jean Frontain, eds., *Poetic Prophecy in Western Literature* (Ruther-

ford, Madison, Teaneck: Fairleigh Dickinson UP, 1984), 31-9.

The "endlessly varying rhetoric" of Isaiah. Its "disconcerting shifts and obscurities" may result either from "impassioned delivery or deliberate editing." The prophet does not presume the power to regulate or even to observe the response of the reader. In his indefatigable willingness to take up the pen repeatedly, "we can read with pleasure and gratitude the incomparable words of a poet who refuses, whatever the cost, to restrict his inspiration or to impose a meaning on it. His persistence is the poem's simple and capacious story."

See also: #s 166, 178, 205, 209, 402, 407, 424, 448, 449, 474, 681, 685, 888, 1088, 1454, 2209.

Isaiah 1-39

*   Beavis, Mary Ann. *Mark's Audience: The Literary and Social Setting of Mark 4. 11-12.* See #1823.

897.   Chisholm, Robert B., Jr. "Structure, Style, and the Prophetic Message: An Analysis of Isaiah 5:8-30." *B Sac* 143 (1986), 46-60.

Rhetorical and form-critical approaches to Isaiah 5 "reveal several overlapping structures that testify to the author's literary and rhetorical artistry." The structure of the message "contributes to its rhetorical force and highlights its central theme.... Several literary devices ... especially irony and word-repetition ... express the theme of poetic justice."

898.   Evans, Jeanne. "Paul Ricoeur's Biblical Hermeneutics: An Application to the Text of Isa. 14:4b-20b," in John V. Apczynski, ed., *Foundations of Religious Literacy* (Chico: Scholars P, 1983), 59-74.

The function of myth in Isaiah 14 "through the notion of metaphoric process." Ricoeur's theory of metaphor is "a form of predication, ... the dynamic process of language that enables metaphor to display new meanings beyond the literal through the interplay of differing contextual fields." The narrative structure of Isaiah 14 as "several unfolding dramatic scenes" in which "the myth, ... the inner taunt song, is essential to shaping the narrative action of the poem's plot."

899.   Exum, J. Cheryl. "Isaiah 28-32: A Literary Approach." *SBLSP*
        1979, Vol. II, pp. 123-151.

    These chapters need to be read as a whole, whether originally a
collection of fragments or not. They "display an essential development from confusion to clarity, ... and [are] concerned to
demonstrate the wisdom of Yhwh."

900.   Exum, J. Cheryl. "Of Broken Pots, Fluttering Birds, and Vi-
        sions in the Night: Extended Simile and Poetic Tech-
        nique in Isaiah." *CBQ* 43 (1981), 331-352.

    The literary tropes and rhetorical features we find in Isaiah 1-39
"are not just embellishments but rather mediums of persuasion." It
is a false idea that a literary work has meaning apart from its form.
The "fundamental quality of poetic discourse, its metaphorical
character." Isaiah 29, 30, and 31.

901.   Exum, J. Cheryl. "'Whom Will He Teach Knowledge?' A
        Literary Approach to Isaiah 28," in #34, pp. 108-139.

    Themes, style, imagery, and figures prominent in Isaiah 28.
Verses 1-6, like chapters 28-32 as a whole, moves "from judgment
to promise," and "displays an essential development from confusion to clarity," as well as numerous other points of contact between the chapter and the "whole prophetic collection" of chapters 28-32.

902.   Gitay, Yehoshua. "Isaiah and His Audience." *Prooftexts* 3
        (1983), 223-230.

    Reader-response theory applied to chapters 1-8 shows that
"rhetorically, the first cycle of speeches is tied together by the
common argumentative matrix. Each speech has its function, and
together they aim to influence the audience, either by warning, by
reinterpreting the present situation, or by depicting the possibility
of a bright future."

903.   Gray, G. Buchanan. "The Strophic Division of Isaiah 21:1-10
        and Isaiah 11:1-8." *ZAW* 32 (1912), 190-198.

    Exploring previous analyses of verse form in these chapters and
the textual emendations suggested therefrom, we conclude that "if
strophic and rhythmical divisions do not coincide with sense-divi-
sions and parallelism, the rhythm and strophe-divisions ... ought
not to govern the arrangement of a translation."

904.   Irwin, William H. "Syntax and Style in Isaiah 26." *CBQ* 41
        (1979), 240-261.

Various structural devices, e.g., chiasm, as well as stylistic ones, e.g., metonymy and paronomasia, and their contribution to our grasp of the chapter.

905. Jackson, Jared Judd. "Style in Isaiah 28 and a Drinking Bout of the Gods," in Jared J. Jackson and Martin Kessler, eds., *Rhetorical Criticism: Essays in Honor of James Muilenberg* (Pittsburgh: Pickwick P), 1974.

Appreciation of the prophets' poetic diction has been neglected in biblical criticism. The major "sense units" of Isaiah 28. The chapter is held together not only by content but also by repetition of key words and "inclusion." It exhibits extensive use of poetic diction. All three of its units have very carefully constructed strophes.

906. Korpel, Marjo C.A. "The Literary Genre of the Song of the Vineyard (Isa. 5:1-7)," in #382, pp. 119-155.

Rhyme and assonance are relevant to structure in this passage. We find three levels of interpretation: literal, metaphorical (vineyard as beloved woman) and metaphorical (vineyard as Israel). Despite previous critical opinion, these verses are not a fable; it is rather aimed at forcing an allegorical reading: a genre which enabled the author to disguise his intention.

907. Magonet, Jonathan. "The Structure of Isaiah 6." *PWCJS* 9 (1986), 91-97.

Devices of three-fold repetition are clues to the basic literary structure through the use of root-words. Structural analysis reveals the thematic center of the chapter to be the prophet's attempt to mediate between God and man, and the frustrations which result.

908. Muilenberg, James. "The Literary Character of Isaiah 34." *JBL* 59 (1940), 339-365.

"Qinah" meter can be found throughout Isaiah 34:1-10, and 3'3' meter in 34:11-17. The literary features of this chapter are "clear, striking, numerous, and varied," with parallelism and euphony carefully worked out; a diverse and highly-conscious style. One also finds paronomasia, assonance, word-pairs, careful repetition and climactic order.

909. O'Connell, Robert H. "Isaiah XIV 4B-23: Ironic Reversal Through Concentric Structure and Mythic Allusion." *VT* 38 (1988), 407-418.

Isaiah 14 makes extensive use of irony. It shows a chiastic structure with ironic reversal as a means of structuring its elements, and mythic allusions (apparently evoking Gilgamesh) in its attack on the Mesopotamian tyrant who attempts to usurp God himself.

910.   Popper, William. "Parallelism in Isaiah, Chaps 1-10." *University of California Publications: Semitic Philology* 1, #3 (August 6, 1918), 267-444.

Parallelism in Isaiah 1-10 from stylistic and linguistic perspectives, in order to explain its extent and its effect, and how it contributes to meaning. Its effect also on textual matters.

911.   Popper, William. "Parallelism in Isaiah: Chaps 11-35 (and 37:22-35.)" *University of California Publications in Semitic Philology* 1, #4 (April 7, 1923), 445-552.

Literary form in these passages for its own sake, and in relation to theme and meaning. The extent and effect of parallelism, its contribution to meaning, and its effect on textual matters.

912.   Wiklander, Bertil. *Prophecy as Literature: A Text-Linguistic and Rhetorical Approach to Isaiah 2-4.* Uppsala (C.W.K. Gleerup), 1984.

The coherence, unity, organization of meaning, type and intention of these chapters. Syntactic analysis shows an audience-oriented characteristic, an oratorical style, and an attempt to appeal to a mass audience. Semantic analysis enables us to grasp the whole through the metaphor of the treaty between Yahweh and Judah.

913.   Yee, Gale A. "The Anatomy of Biblical Parody: The Dirge Form in 2 Samuel 1 and Isaiah 14." *CBQ* 50 (1988), 565-586.

II Samuel 1 shows the established form of the dirge; Isaiah 14 deliberately parodies the form in David's lament, "in order to ridicule the tyrant and foretell his ignominious defeat." Thus, parody exists within the HB itself.

See also: #s 223, 252, 274, 380, 396, 415, 421, 434, 458, 460, 556, 682, 889, 1823.

Isaiah 40-55

914.   Anderson, Bernhard W. "Exodus Typology in Second Isaiah," in Bernhard W. Anderson and Walter Harrelson, eds., *Israel's Prophetic Heritage: Essays in Honor of James Muilenberg* (New York: Harper and Row, 1962), 177-195.

Second Isaiah interpreted what was happening in his own day in light of his understanding of the original Exodus. He heightens the exodus typology, since to him the events of the new exodus supersede the old. He creates a "historification of mythological motifs."

915.   Berlin, Adele. "Isaiah 40:4: Etymological and Poetic Considerations." *HAR* 3 (1979), 1-6.

Semantic and poetic analysis of this verse. Linguistic analysis of its "echoing parallelism" shows a "complete and symmetrical" image.

916.   Boadt, Lawrence. "Isaiah 41:8-13: Notes on Poetic Structure and Style." *CBQ* 35 (1973), 20-34.

Investigation of the structure of Isaiah 41 reveals "a prolific use of poetical devices: chiasm, parallelism, word-repetition, inclusions, metrical changes, reversal of fixed pairs...." It is a great poem which uses these devices to support and enhance the religious message.

917.   Clines, David J.A. *I, He, We, and They: A Literary Approach to Isaiah 53*. Sheffield (JSOT P), 1976.

Rhetorical criticism of the form of Isaiah 53 as a source of meaning in that chapter. The function of the four personae wholly occupies Isaiah 53, with "he" at the center of these relationships. Speech act theory also can contribute to this analysis, while historical criticism cannot be of help.

*   Curtis, John Briggs. "Elihu and Deutero-Isaiah: A Study in Literary Dependence." See #1263.

918.   Fokkelman, J.P. "Stylistic Analysis of Isaiah 40:1-11." *OS* 21 (1981), 68-90.

We can suggest a verse form for Isaiah 40, based on close stylistic analysis. Its lasting appeal lies in the interaction between text and reader which historical criticism can neither discover nor explain.

919.   Freedman, David Noel. "The Structure of Isaiah 40:1-11," in
        Edgar W. Conrad and Edward G. Newing, eds., *Perspectives
        on Language and Text* (Winona Lake: Eisenbrauns, 1987),
        167-193.

        Isaiah 40:1-11 achieves dramatic intensity and literary intricacy
        by a single switch, an interchange of parts I and III (as they are
        now known), and by transferring the concluding line to the center
        of the poem.

920.   Gitay, Yehoshua. *Prophecy and Persuasion: A Study of Isaiah 40-
        48.* Bonn (Linguistica Biblica), 1981.

        "The object of this study is to show the complex relationship in
        Isaiah 40-48 between the prophet's pragmatic goal—to persuade
        his audience of his divine message—and the literary forms he em-
        ploys to this end ... the relationship between the prophetic mes-
        sage and the audience, presenting the prophetic speech as insepa-
        rable from its audience's condition."

921.   Gros Louis, Kenneth R.R. "Isaiah: Chapters 40-55," in #39,
        pp. 208-225.

        Chapters 40-55 constitute a "single, coherent statement" with its
        focal point in 40:30-31. The rest of Second Isaiah "constantly
        echoes this great poem." The key literary questions of Second Isa-
        iah are: "Is it persuasive?", "Does it comfort?" and "Can it rally a
        people?" (JM)

922.   Holmgren, Frederick. "Chiastic Structure in Isaiah LI 1-11."
        VT 19 (1969), 196-201.

        "... the themes of the distribution of key terms in Isaiah 51:1-11
        exhibit a chiastic form. This pattern makes any revision of the text
        unlikely and argues forcefully for consideration of li 1-11 as a liter-
        ary unit."

923.   Kuntz, J. Kenneth. "The Contribution of Rhetorical Criti-
        cism to Understanding Isaiah 51:1-16," in #34, pp. 140-
        171.

        "To grasp the literary unit of 51:1-16 in its entirety," and to do
        close rhetorical analysis of its individual strophes. Chapter 51 is a
        moving and eloquent literary creation, realizing its theme in a
        number of different ways: Yahweh in first person; imagery; repeti-
        tion of key words and phrases; rhetorical questions; contrast; and
        direct quotation. Second Isaiah's "intense lyricism vividly conveys
        his assurance of impending salvation."

924.   Merrill, Eugene H. "Isaiah 40-55 as Anti-Babylonian Polemic." *GTJ* 8 (1987), 3-18.

Isaiah appropriated and adapted the "self-predication formula" of Sumerian-Akkadian hymns as a polemic device with which to exalt Yahweh as opposed to the Babylonian gods—in effect, a unique example of the HB using a foreign literary device to lambast the very culture that produced the device.

925.   Paul, Shalom. "Literary and Ideological Echoes of Jeremiah in Deutero-Isaiah." *PWCJS* 5, Vol. I (1969), 102-120.

Although Isaiah 40-66 was influenced by a number of biblical and non-biblical sources, Jeremiah is the predominant influence. This is proven by a number of parallels of various kinds. Jeremiah is, then, "a very important source for the literary creativity of deutero Isaiah."

926.   Raabe, Paul R. "The Effect of Repetition in the Suffering Servant Song." *JBL* 103 (1984), 77-81.

Repetition of key words is very noticeable in Isaiah 52-53, and "serves to highlight two important thematic contrasts: ... between the servant's humiliation and his evaluation and ... between what the speakers mistakenly believed and what was really the case...."

927.   Sacon, Kiyoshi K. "Isaiah 40:1-11: A Rhetorical-Critical Study," in Jared J. Jackson and Martin Kessler, eds., *Rhetorical Criticism: Essays in Honor of James Muilenberg* (Pittsburgh: Pickwick P, 1974), 99-116.

In studying the poetry of Isaiah 40, sentence-units should be used as the basis for structural analysis, with such other devices as inclusio, repetition, chiasmus, alliteration, and assonance being understood in sentence-unit terms.

928.   Spykerboer, Hendrik Carel. *The Structure and Composition of Deutero-Isaiah: With Special Reference to the Polemics Against Adultery*. Meppel (Krips Repro B.V.), [n.d.: dissertation accepted Gröningen, 1976].

Deutero-Isaiah is, contrary to form-critical assumptions, a unified, primarily literary work rather than a collection of oral utterances, with a theological proclamation presented "as one continuous message." The author used literary forms with great freedom and originality, with an eye to continuity.

See also: #s 117, 274, 396, 397, 403, 404, 421, 689, 1143, 1263.

Isaiah 56-66

929.   Beuken, Wim. "Does Trito-Isaiah Reject the Temple?" in
        #38, pp. 53-66.

        Various arguments that Isaiah 66 is not a unity are fallacious.
        This chapter in fact interacts with various other passages both
        within and outside of chapter 66.

930.   Clifford, Richard J. "Narrative and Lament in Isaiah 63:7-
        64:11," in Maurya P. Horgan and Paul J. Kobelski, eds., *To
        Touch the Text: Biblical and Related Studies in Honor of Joseph
        A Fitzmyer, S. J.* (New York: Crossroads, 1989), 93-102.

        We can affirm the unity of Isaiah 63:7-64:11 by pointing out
        hitherto neglected features of its genre and its rhetoric. It belongs
        to the genre of "historical recital" within the communal lament.

*   Fischer, James A. "Biblical Spirituality/ The Feminine Fac-
        tor." See #1182.

931.   Kosmala, Hans. "Form and Structure of Isaiah 58." *Annual
        of the Swedish Theological Institute* 5 (1967), 69-81; rpt in
        Studies, Essays and Reviews I (Leiden: E.J. Brill, 1978), 84-
        106.

        A literary study of the poetry of Isaiah 58, using the techniques
        from #432.

932.   Webster, Edwin C. "The Rhetoric of Isaiah 63-65." *JSOT* 47
        (1990), 89-102.

        The distinctive patterns of two poems: Isaiah 63:7-64:11, and Isa-
        iah 65. They both have triadic structures with verbal repetitions as
        links between sections.

See also: #s 276, 396.

JEREMIAH

933. Aitken, Kenneth T. "The Oracles Against Babylon in Jeremiah 50-51: Structures and Perspectives." *TB* 35 (1984), 25-63.

These chapters are not a loose conglomerate of amorphous thematic elements tacked together at random, but a unit with structure and coherence. The organization is chiastic, with speeches and sayings playing the most prominent structural role.

934. Anderson, Bernhard W. "'The Lord Has Created Something New': A Stylistic Study of Jer 31:15-22." *CBQ* (1978), 463-478; rpt Leo G. Perdue and Brian W. Kovacs, eds., *A Prophet to the Nations* (Winona Lake: Eisenbrauns, 1984), 367-380.

The structure, style, and rhetoric of these verses, and the unity which they create.

935. Brueggemann, Walter. "Israel's Sense of Place in Jeremiah," in Jared J. Jackson and Martin Kessler, eds., *Rhetorical Criticism: Essays in Honor of James Muilenberg* (Pittsburgh: Pickwick P, 1974), 149-165.

The motif of "space" in the OT has been neglected by critics, compared with that of "time." Imagery in Jeremiah 2, 3, 4, and 12 which carries the motif of "space"; how other motifs in Jeremiah derive from this one; the various thematic meanings which concepts of space, land, etc., have in Jeremiah.

936. Brueggemann, Walter A. "Jeremiah's Use of Rhetorical Questions." *JBL* 92 (1973), 358-374.

"Utilization of the double rhetorical question *h -˒m* reveals remarkable diversity and provides an important tool for understanding the poetry of Jeremiah." Its root is partly sapiential, but Jeremiah has altered it significantly for his own purposes.

937. Callaway, Mary Chilton. "Telling the Truth and Telling Stories: An Analysis of Jeremiah 37-38." *USQR* 44 (1991), 253-266.

This part of Jeremiah resembles "realistic narrative, yet it resists a straightforward historical reading. It is a rich and evocative narrative...." Its organizing principle "is not chronology or plot, but it may be the repeated use of a well-known story form. A narrative constructed of similar episodes repeated several times, linked largely by parataxis, invites a ... circular rather than a linear reading.... When we look behind this biblical narrative, what we see most clearly is not a historical event, ... but another story."

938.   Castellino, G.R. "Observation on the Literary Structure of Some Passages in Jeremiah." *VT* 30 (1980), 398-408.

Defining the guiding principle of Jeremiah 1-25 is not easy. Careful analysis shows not a lumping together of haphazard compositions, but a three-phase structure: subjective perception of impending disaster, objective vision of nature's havoc, and the impact of that disaster. Jeremiah 4, 9, 14, 25.

939.   Cloete, Walter Theophilus Woldemar. *Versification and Syntax in Jeremiah 2-25*. Atlanta (Scholars P), 1989.

Poetry can and should be distinguished from prose in the OT, even though scholars differ on how to describe the OT system of versification. Syntactic approaches offer the best hope for describing Hebrew verse because they are colometrically oriented. And among these, only M. O'Connor's syntactic description is really reliable. In Jeremiah 2-25, "repetition, clause initial particles and semantic considerations ... form part of the techniques used ... to combine cola."

940.   Davies, Philip R. "Joking in Jeremiah 18," in #231, pp. 191-201.

"... Jeremiah 18 *is* a joke, i.e., ... it is a funny story, and ... the story itself is *about* a joke." However, that is not to say that Jeremiah 18 was intended as a joke, even if the chapter does contain numerous features actually or potentially humorous. Three such features deliver the humor: reversal of the roles of deity and audience; changes in the relationship between prophet and Yahweh; and the rhetoric of potter and pot.

941.   Davies, Philip R. "Potter, Prophet and People: Jeremiah 18 as Parable." *HAR* 11 (1987), 23-33.

Historical criticism cannot explain Jeremiah 18, whereas rhetorical criticism can. We must assume that "parable" does not have a single, objective meaning, and that the significance of a parable lies in its "total picture and not in its individual details." The text of Jeremiah 18 contains three explanations of the parable, which can be understaood by analyzing the figurative language and the linguistic markers.

942.   Diamond, A.R. *The Confession of Jeremiah in Context: Scenes of Prophetic Drama.* Sheffield (JSOT P), 1987.

"... the crisis over the proper context in which the confessions [Jeremiah 11, 15, 17, 18, 20] are to be interpreted ... i.e., how is a valid reading to be achieved?" Part One: "... the foregrounding of each confession against lament poetic tradition from the standpoint of structure, diction, imagery, and thought...." Part Two: Jeremiah 11-20 as an integrated whole. The author of Jeremiah has placed the confessions in a "double-axis pattern," as part of the Deuteronomistic theodicy argument.

*   van Grol, H.W.M. "Paired Tricola in the Psalms, Isaiah and Jeremiah." See #424.

943.   Hobbs, T.R. "Some Proverbial Reflections in the Book of Jeremiah." *ZAW* 91 (1979), 62-72.

Jeremiah was well-acquainted with the proverbial rhetoric of the wise, though he always subordinates the reflectiveness of the wisdom tradition to the urgencies of the prophetic task.

944.   Hobbs, T.R. "Some Remarks on the Structure and Composition of the Book of Jeremiah." *CBQ* 34 (1972), 257-275; rpt Leo G. Perdue and Brian Kovacs, eds., *A Prophet to the Nations* (Winona Lake: Eisenbrauns, 1984), 175-191.

The clear message and structure of Jeremiah must be the work of an individual theologian, not the "'floating together' of traditional complexes" argued by other scholars.

945.   Holladay, William L. *The Architecture of Jeremiah 1-20.* Lewisburg (Bucknell UP) and London (Associated U Presses), 1976.

Rhetorical criticism analyzes the structure of Jeremiah 1-20 in terms of the relationship of a given passage to larger units, the presence of inclusio, etc. It looks for repetitions, parallels, contrasts in words, phrases, syntax and other structures. The establishment of the structure is entirely separate from theories about which passages are "original" and which are later insertions.

946.   Holladay, William L. "Prototypes and Copies: A New Approach to the Poetry-Prose Problem in the Book of Jeremiah." *JBL* 79 (1960), 351-367.

Many of the characteristic phrases of the prose sections of Jeremiah are a reshaping of phrases original to Jeremiah's poetry. How analysis of the prose style demonstrates this fact.

947.   Holladay, William L. "Style, Irony, and Authenticity in Jeremiah." *JBL* 81 (1962), 44-54.

Vocabulary, style, and thought of Jeremiah as they help us clarify and/or authenticate certain puzzling passages. Jeremiah is almost alone in Hebrew poetry in using chiasmus; we also see double meanings, heightened diction, striking metaphors, irony, and abrupt changes of speaker or mood.

948.   Isbell, Charles D. and Michael Jackson. "Rhetorical Criticism and Jeremiah VII 1–VIII 3." *VT* 30 (1980), 20-26

Builds on the analysis of Jeremiah found in #945. The interrelationship among sections is governed by an envelope structure. Holladay's case can be made even stronger by following out more thoroughly the implications of the method he employs.

949.   Kaiser, Barbara Bakke. "Poet as 'Female Impersonator': The Image of Daughter Zion as Speaker in Biblical Poems of Suffering." *JR* 67 (1987), 164-182.

Analysis of Jeremiah 4 and Lamentations 1 and 2 "suggests that distinctively female experience was regarded highly enough to function as the chief metaphor through which the poet expressed his agony over Jerusalem's fate and encouraged community catharsis."

950.   Kessler, Martin. "New Directions in Biblical Exegesis." *Scottish Journal of Theology* 24 (1971), 317-325.

Definition of the rhetorical approach to biblical texts. Applied to Jeremiah 41, it isolates key words as clues to the significant motifs in the chapter.

951.   Kessler, Martin. "Rhetoric in Jeremiah 50 and 51." *Semitics* 3 (1972), 18-35.

The function of anaphora, epiphora, anadiplosis, consonant and vowel patterns, and cacophonous sound in Jeremiah 50 and 51.

952.   Lewin, Ellen David. "Arguing For Authority: A Rhetorical Study of Jeremiah 1.4-19 and 20.7-18." *JSOT* 32 (1985), 105-119.

How Jeremiah "develops a persuasive argument in a situation of controversy"—i.e., not only how Jeremiah affected his audience but how they affected him and his message. The connection between chapters 1 and 20 of Jeremiah.

953. Lundbom, Jack R. *Jeremiah: A Study in Ancient Rhetoric.* Missoula (Scholars P), 1975.

Priorities are to define the limits of the literary unit, and to determine the structure of the composition as a whole. Previous investigations of Jeremiah have especially failed in analyzing its structure. The two controlling structural devices are inclusio and chiasmus.

954. Lundbom, Jack R. "Rhetorical Structures in Jeremiah 1." *ZAW* 103 (1991), 193-210.

Jeremiah 1 is neither a unity nor a fragmented collection. "... if Jeremiah 1 is to be understood properly, and the larger chronological and historical issues associated with Jeremiah's call and the beginning of his career are to find satisfactory resolution, the macrostructures in chapter 1 must be recognized as being rhetorical in nature.... Simple but nevertheless effective techniques of Hebrew rhetoric lie embedded in the text, their function being to enhance the reception of the text before its ancient audience."

955. Magonet, Jonathan. "Jeremiah's Last Confession: Structure, Image and Ambiguity." *HAR* 11 (1987), 303-317.

Jeremiah 20:7-18 has a chiastic structure. This structure is related to the ambiguity of its putative optimism as a challenge to the reader.

956. Martens, Elmer A. "Narrative Parallelism and Message in Jeremiah 34-38," in Craig A. Evans and William F. Stinespring, eds., *Early Jewish and Christian Exegesis: Studies in Memory of William Hugh Brownlee* (Atlanta: Scholars P, 1987), 33-49.

The stylistic technique of narrative parallelism is probably a key to understanding the present arrangement of materials in Jeremiah. Chapters 34-5 and 36-8 form two sets of parallel accounts of the people's obstinacy and the rightness of justice which God visits on Jerusalem.

957. Nasuti, Harry P. "A Prophet to the Nations: Diachronic and Synchronic Readings of Jeremiah 1." *HAR* 10 (1986), 249-266.

A primarily synchronic reading of the structure and themes of Jeremiah 1, and of its place in the book as a whole. This chapter "is the result of Israel's wrestling with the significance of the words and figure of Jeremiah as well as with its ongoing historical situation."

958.   Patterson, Richard D. "Of Bookends, Hinges, and Hooks: Literary Clues to the Arrangement of Jeremiah's Prophecies." *WTJ* 51 (1989), 109-131.

Contrary to much historical-critical scholarship, Jeremiah does show evidence of single authorship and careful, deliberate authorial design, as demonstrated by its symmetry and placement of themes.

959.   Polk, Timothy. *The Prophetic Persona: Jeremiah and the Language of the Self.* Sheffield (JSOT P), 1984.

The prophetic "I" is more prominent in Jeremiah than in any other prophet. We have failed until now to recognize the metaphorical nature of Jeremiah's "language of the heart." Jeremiah shows a "self in progress." It is inadequate to identify Jeremiah's "I" with the community, or with his private historical experiences. His message is rather his life as expressed in language, the prophet as paradigm. The confessions of chapters 17 and 20 are "patently poetic," though ambiguous. Wolfgang Iser's theory of the reader works well on Jeremiah.

960.   Rosenberg, Joel. "Jeremiah and Ezekiel," in #33, pp. 184-206.

The poetic oracles, prose sermons, biographical prose of Jeremiah. The book has a chiastic structure, as do chapters 20-40 by themselves. The expository structure of Ezekiel. The latter book is "a remarkable fiction, ... anticipating in imaginative power and in boldness of allegorical vision the major works of Dante, Milton, and Blake...." Its style and structure reflect the "extreme desperation" of the era that produced it.

961.   Selms, A. Van. "'Whate'er My God Ordains is Right'—A Figure of Style in the Book of Jeremiah." *Semitics* 5 (1977), 1-8.

A stylistic construction found in both the prose and poetry of Jeremiah, and probably nowhere else in the OT. Its presence helps to reinforce the argument for the book's integrity.

*   Shoshany, Ronit. "Prosodic Structures in Jeremiah's Poetry." See #461.

962.   Snaith, J.G. "Literary Criticism and Historical Investigation in Jeremiah Chapter xlvi." *JSS* 16 (1971), 15-32.

Jeremiah 46 contains much imagery derived from Egyptian culture, interpreting the struggle between Babylon and Egypt in terms of Yahweh versus Pharaoh. Historical hints place the chapter in the Babylonian occupation shortly after 605 BC. Its imagery is "particularly suited to that particular period in history," showing that "study of the imagery and structure ... in Jeremiah xlvi and investigation of the historical background may combine to lead to a deeper appreciation of the poems."

963.   Trible, Phyllis. "The Gift of a Poem: A Rhetorical Study of Jeremiah 31:15-22." *Andover-Newton Quarterly* 17 (1977), 271-280.

"Jeremiah 31:15-22 is a drama of voices.... Its five strophes form a chiasmus with the voice of Ephraim at their center.... This encircling pattern mirrors the relationship between female and male throughout the poem and thus provides a vision of both the parts and the whole."

964.   Willis, John T. "Dialogue Between Prophet and Audience as a Rhetorical Device in the Book of Jeremiah." *JSOT* 33 (1985), 63-82.

Lundbom [#953] recognized the importance of inclusio and chiasmus in the structure of Jeremiah; to these we must add a third: dialogue between prophet and audience.

See also: #s 4, 5, 166, 198, 205, 211, 216, 223, 252, 377, 416, 424, 435, 448, 449, 476, 681, 682, 684, 698, 888, 889, 925, 969, 1143, 1454, 1753.

EZEKIEL

965.   Allen, Leslie C. "Ezekiel 24:3-14: A Rhetorical Perspective." *CBQ* 49 (1987), 404-414.

These verses of Ezekiel 24 are an oracle. They show various rhetorical techniques and complex interrelationship of parts (verses), metaphor, and imagery. The style is especially characterized by the use of inclusio.

966.   Boadt, Lawrence. "Rhetorical Strategies in Ezekiel's Oracles
        of Judgment," in Johan Lust, ed., *Ezekiel and His Book: Tex-
        tual and Literary Criticism and Their Interrelation* (Leuven:
        Leuven UP, 1986), 182-200.

        Ezekiel is probably very highly structured, but that structure is
        not likely to be amenable to rational arguments. Other puzzles
        about the book include its relationship to Jeremiah; the role of
        repetition, imagery, and myth; its possible thesis; and whether it is
        the result of written or oral composition. The oracles (chapters 1-
        32) are unified by various literary devices, and seem intended not
        only for rhetorical effect but also to prove Ezekiel's charge against
        Zedekiah. Ezekiel reworks the myth of Israel "in order to re-estab-
        lish the authority and power of Yahweh.... Thus the mythological
        language is not merely mythopoetic...."

967.   Boadt, Lawrence. "Textual Problems in Ezekiel and Poetic
        Analysis of Paired Words." *JBL* 97 (1978), 489-499.

        Study of poetic techniques in oracles can give valuable assistance
        in uncovering intentional repetition in Ezekiel. Use of paired
        words in 30, 31, 2, and 29 help make this "prose" in fact quasi-po-
        etry: carefully-patterned repetition, chiasmus, parallelism, word-
        pairs, and rhythmic balance between lines.

968.   Bodi, Daniel. *The Book of Ezekiel and the Poem of Erra*. Göttin-
        gen (Vandenhoeck and Ruprecht), 1991.

        There is "a definite relationship between impressions, themes
        and motifs in the Book of Ezekiel and the Poem of Erra." It is
        therefore likely "that in the formulation of certain themes and mo-
        tifs in the Book of Ezekiel, its author or redactor knew and used
        [this] contemporary Akkadian song."

969.   Brownlee, William H. "Ezekiel's Poetic Indictment of the
        Shepherds." *HTR* 51 (1958), 191-203.

        The style and structure of Ezekiel 34 make it one of the most
        beautiful chapters in the OT. Its supposed relationship to
        Jeremiah. The poetry in Ezekiel is much more extensive than has
        been supposed; recognizing it changes our sense of Ezekiel's
        themes, and affects theories about his locale.

970.   Bruns, Gerald L. "Canon and Power in the Hebrew Scrip-
        tures." *Critical Inquiry* 10 (1983-4), 462-480.

        Concepts of the status and authority of the HB from ancient
        times to some recent literary criticism. The tendency of Hebrew
        scripture to "actualize," or update itself. "The whole fate of
        prophecy is contained in this figure of Ezekiel eating the scroll

[Ezekiel 2:8–3:3]: one could not assert the power and authority of written texts more dramatically than this."

971.　Curtiss, Samuel Ives. "Ezekiel and His Times," in #32, pp. 183-203.

"With a good knowledge of men and public affairs, he [Ezekiel] was much of a recluse and a dreamer, a John Bunyan, who wrote a Pilgrim's Progress adapted to his time, whose allegories, visions, and descriptions are as ideal as those of the English dreamer. His new Jerusalem is not to be taken more literally than the celestial city of the Bedford tinker."

972.　Davis, Ellen Francis. "Swallowing Hard: Reflections on Ezekiel's Dumbness";
Darr, Katheryn Pfisterer. "Write or True? A Response to Ellen Frances Davis," in J. Cheryl Exum, ed., *Signs and Wonders: Biblical Texts in Literary Focus* [no city or publisher given] (Scholars P?, 1989), 217-247.

"... Ezekiel's patterns of thought and public speech were shaped by habits of reading and writing, and ... through him Israelite prophecy for the first time received its primary impress in a consciously literary mode. Ezekiel's eating of the scroll and subsequent dumbness are ... figures for the new conditions and constraints imposed upon communication by the move toward textualization of the prophetic tradition." Darr: Davis's "intriguing and insightful suggestions" help solve a key problem in Ezekiel. Some of her conclusions, however, are questionable: her contention that hermeneutics became vital when writing was introduced; her lack of clarity on the relationsip of Ezekiel to writing; and her assumption that scroll-eating and dumbness are figures for textuality when it is more likely that they show "the need to distinguish between true and false prophecy."

973.　Davis, Ellen F. *Swallowing the Scroll: Textuality and the Dynamics of Discourse in Ezekiel's Prophecy.* Sheffield (Almond P), 1989.

"... to what sort of communicative task is narrative discourse particularly suited, and how does Ezekiel exploit its potential in the service of prophecy?" Prophetic literature after Ezekiel.

974.　Durlesser, James A. "The Sinking of the Ship of Tyre (Ezek 27): A Study of Rhetoric in Hebrew Allegory." *PEGL* 7 (1987), 79-93.

Rhetorical criticism applied to this metaphorical narrative reveals a unified, three-part oracle, with one common theme and no

drastic structural shifts. It also shows that even the prose trade list
has a literary role, and it discovers various rhetorical devices, e.g.,
inclusio, repetition, and verbal aspect shifts. The praise of Tyre in
this chapter is metaphorical, not ironic or satiric.

975.   Fox, Michael V. "The Rhetoric of Ezekiel's Vision of the
        Valley of the Bones." *HUCA* 51 (1980), 1-15.

   Dramatic imagery and verbal devices in Ezekiel 37. How this imagery and these devices relate to Ezekiel's argument and goals.

976.   Garfinkel, Stephen. "Another Model for Ezekiel's Abnor-
        malities." *JANES* 19 (1989), 39-50.

   Ezekiel's account of his temporary dumbness (3:22-27) may have
   been borrowed from Akkadian incantation literature, which contains parallels with Ezekiel's account of his aphasia, the Lord's
   hand being upon him, and the binding of his hands and feet.

977.   Greenberg, Moshe. "Ezekiel 17: A Holistic Interpretation,"
        in Jack M. Sasson, ed., *Studies in Literature from the Ancient
        Near East* [*Journal of the American Oriental Society* 103, #1]
        (New Haven, 1984), 149-154.

   The various verbal and thematic links between Ezekiel 16 and
   17. Detailed outline of its literary structure as "a spiraling progress
   of characters and planes."

978.   Greenberg, Moshe. "The Vision of Jerusalem in Ezekiel 8-
        11: A Holistic Interpretation," in James L. Crenshaw and
        Samuel Sandmel, eds., *The Divine Helmsman: Studies on
        God's Control of Human Events, Presented to Lou H. Silberman*
        (New York: KTAV, 1980), 143-164.

   "The diverse material of chapters 8-11 is organized into a single
   visionary experience whose complexity indicates considerable literary effort." A holistic interpretation attempts to imagine what
   Ezekiel's ideal reader would have found in the book: the tensions
   as evidence of a visionary experience, not necessarily of multiple
   sources. The main theme and its echoes show analogous structure
   and content in a chiastic arrangement.

979.   Klein, Ralph W. *Ezekiel: The Prophet and His Message.*
        Columbia (U of South Carolina P), 1988.

   Literary and theological analysis of Ezekiel. "It attempts to take
   seriously the present shape of the book, to decipher its imagery, to
   comment on its technical vocabulary, and to relate its several parts
   to one another."

980. Lasine, Stuart. "Fiction, Falsehood, and Reality in Hebrew Scripture." *HS* 25 (1984), 24-40.

The term "fiction" does not accurately describe biblical literary art. The relationship between fiction and reality in sacred texts. Analysis of Ezekiel 30:30-33 and II Samuel 12 "indicates that fiction is not well suited to create the kind of readers appropriate for scripture."

981. Lieb, Michael. "Ezekiel's Inaugural Vision as a Literary Event." *Cithara* 24, #2 (May, 1985), 22-39.

The problems with the text of Ezekiel are what distinguish it as a literary event—the vision embracing its own disruptions. "... the vision exists by means of those qualities that might otherwise appear to undermine it." Structure and motif in Ezekiel 1. The vision imposes itself on the exegete, not vice versa.

982. Newsom, Carol A. "A Maker of Metaphors: Ezekiel's Oracles Against Tyre." *Interpretation* 38 (1984), 151-164.

Ezekiel's skill in manipulating the power of metaphor to illuminate reality shows us his subtlety and force. We all perceive the realities of national power through metaphors; Ezekiel shows us how to critique them.

983. Parunak, H. Van Dyke. "The Literary Architecture of Ezekiel's *MAR'ŌT'ELŌHÎM.*" *JBL* 99 (1980), 61-74.

The structure of Ezekiel's three visions of God (chapters 1 to 3, 8 to 11, and 40 to 48). Their interrelationships through shared motifs which are nevertheless adapted in each vision to suit the immediate message. The intricacy and skill shown by the final redactor.

984. Rooy, H.F. van. "Parallelism, Metre and Rhetoric in Ezekiel 29:1-6." *Semitics* 8 (1982), 90-105.

The whole of Ezekiel 29:3-16 is poetry, which is demonstrated by its strophic framework, parallelism, distribution of elements, and overall structure. The whole passage shows unity and cohesion of thought.

* Rosenberg, Joel. "Jeremiah and Ezekiel." See #960.

985. Tromp, Nicholas J. "The Paradox of Ezekiel's Prophetic Mission: Towards a Semiotic Approach of Ezekiel 3, 22-27," in Johan Lust, ed., *Ezekiel and His Book: Textual and*

Literary Criticism and Their Interrelation (Leuven: Leuven UP, 1986), 201-213.

Syntactical semiotic analysis of Ezekiel 3 according to the method of A.J. Greimas. "... God's voice is suggested to have become the prophet's voice. Our text illustrates with suggestive penetration what the formula 'And God spoke through the mouth of his prophet' is about.... [T]his prophetic speech is tied speech."

See also: #s 117, 166, 223, 377, 396, 421, 435, 448, 458, 682, 684, 888, 1143, 1454, 2209.

THE TWELVE

*   Gottwald, Norman K. "Tragedy and Comedy in the Latter Prophets." See #886.

986.   House, Paul R. *The Unity of the Twelve.* Sheffield (Almond P), 1990.

Formalistic analysis, narratology, archetypal criticism, and genre theory all help us decide whether The Twelve is a unity, and if so, how that unity functions. Theological ideas as major structural devices; the presence of an "organized plot"; characterization of Yahweh and of the prophets; the implied author, narrator, and implied audience of The Twelve.

987.   Marks, Herbert. "The Twelve Prophets," in #33, pp. 207-233.

Since it was composed over five centuries, it is a heterogeneous book that presents problems and opportunities similar to that of the Bible as a whole. Its arrangement and contents show signs of Deuteronomistic shaping, although two books: Jonah and Malachi, seem at odds with the rest. Voice, structure, and style in The Twelve. A kind of "phantasia" characterizes some of the Twelve, especially Zechariah, which is a transitional book toward Daniel.

See also: #s 205, 973.

Hosea

988.   Buss, Martin J. "Tragedy and Comedy in Hosea." *Semeia* 32
        (1985), 71-82.

   Both tragedy and comedy play their part in Hosea, "by representing the quality of actual and potential forms of existence":
   tragedy arouses sympathy for the nation, while comedy "make[s]
   fun of the people's foolishness and express[es] joy in a new relation with God."

989.   Cassuto, Umberto. "The Second Chapter of the Book of
        Hosea," in *Biblical and Oriental Studies, Vol. I: Bible.* Tr Is-
        rael Abrahams (Jerusalem: Magnes P, 1973) [originally
        published in Hebrew in 1929], 101-140.

   Considerations of structure, theme, and context argue that
   Hosea 2 is a compositional unity. The symmetry, stylistic beauty
   and power of this chapter.

990.   Clines, David J.A. "Hosea 2: Structure and Interpretation,"
        in E.A. Livingstone, ed., *Studia Biblica 1978 I: Papers on Old
        Testament and Related Themes* (Sheffield: JSOT P, 1979), 83-
        103.

   The problem of structure from three angles: formal (proper sequence of verses); conceptual; and plot or narrative structure.
   There is general agreement on the stylistic and thematic coherence of Hosea 2. The conceptual structure of verses 4-25 shows "a
   delicate network of ideas, closely integrated but worked out with
   subtle variations ...," chiefly with regard to the concept of
   "belonging." The plot structure shows powerful narrative movement.

991.   Dijk-Hemmes, Fokkelien van. "The Imagination of Power
        and the Power of Imagination: An Intertextual Analysis of
        Two Biblical Love Songs: The Song of Songs and Hosea
        2." *JSOT* 44 (1989), 75-88.

   A "re-examination" of the similarities between the Song of Songs
   and Hosea 2. How the Hosea text uses motifs borrowed from the
   Song of Songs to convey its own message. Evidence of gender-
   specific relationships among reader, text, and author.

992.   Gnuse, Robert. "Calf, Cult, and King: The Unity of Hosea
        8:1-13." *Biblische Zeitschrift* 26 (1982), 83-92.

Contrary to the findings of historical criticism, Hosea 8 is a literary unity, "an intricate oracle wherein the prophet posits [that] Israel's own rebellious deeds have brought upon her imminent destruction."

993.   Holladay, William L. "Chiasmus, The Key to Hosea xii 3-6." *VT* 16 (1966), 53-64.

These verses of Hosea echo passages in Genesis 35, using a chiastic pattern to preserve precisely the order of events in the Genesis chapter.

994.   Kruger, P.A. "Prophetic Imagery. On Metaphors and Similes in the Book Hosea." *JNSL* 14 (1988), 143-151.

"No other Old Testament prophetic book makes more use of the stylistic form of imagery in such limited space (14 chapters) than Hosea." Various strategies of presenting images including wordplay; metaphorical fields of images; historical and religious contexts of images; formal structures of the similes concerning Yahweh. Imagery in Hosea is "an intrinsic feature of the prophetic manner...."

995.   Lundbom, Jack R. "Poetic Structure and Prophetic Rhetoric in Hosea." *VT* 29 (1979), 300-308.

Inclusio as guide to the poetic structure of Hosea 4 and 8. Hosea could assume that his readers would put these examples together in their minds. Inclusio here is an argumentative device, restoring focus and emphasizing key points.

*   Marks, Herbert. "The Twelve Prophets." See #987.

996.   Mazor, Yair. "Hosea 5.1-3: Between Compositional Rhetoric and Rhetorical Composition." *JSOT* 45 (1989), 115-126.

Structural and rhetorical criticism of Hosea 5 reveal the deep structure of this passage affecting the reader's perception of the argument. There is a "dialectic interplay between structure and rhetoric," synthesized to heighten the argument.

997.   Paul, Shalom M. "The Image of the Oven and the Cake in Hosea vii 4-10." *VT* 18 (1968), 114-120.

The oven in Hosea 7 is a "figure for the people's regicidal fury," while the inert cake is a figure for Ephraim's ineptness.

998.   De Roche, Michael. "Structure, Rhetoric, and Meaning in Hosea IV:4-10." *VT* 33 (1983), 184-198.

Use of rhetorical criteria on Hosea 4 help clear up thematic confusions found in earlier historical criticism of this chapter. Two distinct oracles emerge, each with its own structure.

999. Setel, T. Drorah. "Prophets and Pornography: Female Sexual Imagery in Hosea," in #44, pp. 86-95.

The "objectification of female sexuality" in the Bible and in Western culture. In Hosea, female sexual imagery plays a central thematic role separate from, and in negative relationship to, male experience. In Hosea (and in other prophets) this imagery may signal increasing separation of rich and poor, ritual and ethics, in Israelite society.

See also: #s 223, 241, 254, 370, 415, 421, 434, 448, 684, 689, 1454.

Joel

1000. Bliese, Loren F. "Metrical Sequences and Climax in the Poetry of Joel." *OPTAT* 2, #4 (1988), 52-84.

The book of Joel has a "remarkable overall chiastic outline," as well as various smaller chiasms which constitute individual poems within the book. These "metrical chiasms" nicely correspond in build-up and climax with thematic concerns in the book. The non-metrical climax markings include repetition, use of divine names, rhetorical questions, and metaphors.

1001. Garrett, Duane A. "The Structure of Joel." *JETS* 28 (1985), 289-297.

Careful study of the divisions of Joel shows it to be unified in its original form, and not unified by a redactor. Its structure is chiastic.

1002. Mallon, Elias D. "A Stylistic Analysis of Joel 1:10-12." *CBQ* 45 (1983), 537-548.

Analysis of each line of Joel 1:10-12 separately, and how they contribute to the structure of the entire poem.

* Marks, Herbert. "The Twelve Prophets." See #987.

1003. Thompson, John A. "The Use of Repetition in the Prophecy of Joel," in Matthew Black and William A. Smalley, eds.,

On Language, Culture, and Religion: In Honor of Eugene A. Nida (The Hague and Paris: Mouton, 1974), 101-110.

Study of repetition in Joel shows that the book is the product of conscious literary art with its artistic unity demonstrated, its themes revealed.

See also: #s 223, 380, 421, 448.

Amos

1004.   Christensen, Duane L. "The Prosodic Structure of Amos 1-2." HTR 67 (1974), 427-436.

The first six oracles of Amos fall into three pairs, with the fourth pair (indictment) being treated separately in 2:12.

1005.   Eslinger, Lyle. "The Education of Amos." *HAR* 11 (1987), 35-57.

Rhetorical analysis of the "vision" series (Amos 1-2, 7-9), shows why Amaziah's prose intrusion is not a sign of a breakdown of unity. "Proceeding through this balanced intricacy of interwoven visions, ... the reader, like Amos himself, gains an education through the vehicle of this literary creation on the necessity of judgment. But only when Amaziah's intervention is left to stand where the author of the book put it...."

1006.   Gitay, Yehoshua. "A Study of Amos's Art of Speech: A Rhetorical Analysis of Amos 3:1-15." *CBQ* 42 (1980), 293-309

We "must attempt to understand the prophet's activity as a rhetorical process. Amos seeks conviction (whose goal is truth) rather than persuasion (whose goal is activity)."

1007.   Jackson, Jared Judd. "Rhetorical Criticism and the Problem of Subjectivity." *PEGL* 2 (1982), 34-45.

"How are we to know that one person's rhetorical study of a passage is correct and another's is faulty?" Amos 3, II Samuel 15, Exodus 6 and 23 as examples of the usefulness of rhetorical criticism, and of the possibilities of arriving at objective criteria for analysis.

1008.   Landy, Francis. "Vision and Poetic Speech in Amos." *HAR* 11 (1987), 223-246.

The "capacity for subversion," "stylistic openness" of biblical poetry, and "anti-poetic in poetry, its artlessness," as found in Amos. "In the sequence of visions (7:1-9:3), ... where the metaphor shows itself without the mediation of words ... we reach the limits of poetry: what can be said of our contact with everything trans-human."

1009. Limburg, James. "Sevenfold Structures in the Book of Amos." *JBL* 106 (1987), 217-222.

There is a question as to whether these groupings in Amos are arranged thus for stylistic reasons, or as an indication of completeness. They often show a "7+1" arrangement. Those that are central to Amos appear to be stylistic devices to build toward a climax. However, this does not rule out the use of seven to indicate completeness in other cases.

* Marks, Herbert. "The Twelve Prophets." See #987.

1010. Newman, Louis I. "Parallelism in Amos." *University of California Publications: Semitic Philology* 1, #2 (August 6, 1918), 57-265.

Parallelism originates in the human love of repetition. In ancient cultures it progressed from reiteration to incremental repetition to artistic parallelism. Hebrew parallelism grew out of that found in Babylonian and Assyrian writing. Parallelism occurs everywhere in Amos, showing many shadings between poetry and prose, with extensive use of the typical Hebrew "couplet." All this has implications for the state of the text of Amos and the stages through which it may have passed.

1011. Paul, Shalom M. "Amos 3:3-8: The Irresistible Sequence of Cause and Effect." *HAR* 7 (1983), 203-220.

"By means of a series of rhetorical questions characterized by analogies drawn from common experience and well-known empirical phenomena, the prophet Amos logically and skillfully draws his unexpecting audience into the flow of a persuasive and penetrating presentation of the inextricable relationship of all events and happenings."

1012. Smalley, William A. "Recursion Patterns and the Sectioning of Amos." *BT* 30 (1979), 118-127.

Discourse analysis can be used to reveal the structure of Amos. Recursion of meaning occurs chiastically in Amos: in the book as a whole, and within many sections.

1013.   Super, A.S. "Figures of Comparison in the Book of Amos."
        Semitics 3 (1972), 67-80.

        Examination of the metaphoric structure of Amos shows it to be
        far more powerful a force in the book than is parallelism.

1014.   Terrien, Samuel. "Amos and Wisdom," in Bernhard W. An-
        derson and Walter Harrelson, eds., *Israel's Prophetic Her-
        itage: Essays in Honor of James Muilenberg* (New York:
        Harper and Row, 1962), 108-115.

        Amos was influenced by wisdom literature of the HB, rather
        than vice versa, as is shown by his terminology and his style.

1015.   Tromp, N.J. "Amos V 1-17: Toward a Stylistic and Rhetorical
        Analysis." *OS* 23 (1984), 56-84.

        We must distinguish between "rhetorics" and "stylistics" when
        analyzing the HB (as a study of classical rhetoric will help us un-
        derstand). The redaction of Amos 5; the rhetorical effects of verses
        1-17 in their totality. Rhetorical analysis helps illuminate the inter-
        action of orator and audience.

1016.   de Waard, J. "The Chiastic Structure of Amos V:1-17." *VT* 27
        (1977), 170-177.

        In order to clarify the complex structure of Amos 5:1-17, it is es-
        sential to see its sub-units, and to notice that they are chiastic
        within the chiasm. This analysis helps clarify the meaning of the
        verses as well.

1017.   Wal, Adri van der. "The Structure of Amos." *JSOT* 26
        (1983), 107-113.

        Analysis based on the dominant role of inclusio in Amos 1-6
        shows that religious and social aspects of these chapters are not, as
        is usually thought, contradictory, but complementary.

1018.   Weiss, Meir. "The Pattern of Numerical Sequence in Amos
        1-2." *JBL* 86 (1967), 416-423.

        "The fire of God burning in [the prophet] could not consume
        the conventional literary patterns ... but it could bend and shape
        them into a personal mold. This type of composition, not being a
        creation *ex nihilo,* was yet an *ad hoc* one...."

1019.   Wendland, Ernst R. "The 'Word of the Lord' and the Orga-
        nization of Amos." *OPTAT* 2, #4 (1988), 1-51.

        Discourse and structural analysis of Amos demonstrates that lex-
        ical-semantic recursion seems to be the key to understanding its

structure. Accompanying stylistic features include similarity-contrast, form-meaning, linear-concentric, and horizontal-hierarchical. The uses of inclusio, anaphora, and epiphora provide the clues to this structure.

1020. Wicke, Donald W. "Two Perspectives (Amos 5:1-17)." *Currents in Theology and Mission* 13 (1986), 89-96.

Comparison of the historical and literary perspectives on Amos 5, to discover how each perspective determines what we see in a biblical passage. While the historian seeks to get behind the text to its prehistory, the "litterateur" assumes artistic unity and works from there, exploring the interaction of form and theme. The question is not which perspective is true, but which is more helpful.

See also: #s 178, 223, 263, 380, 388, 402, 416, 460, 681, 682, 684, 889, 1088, 1362.

Obadiah

*   Marks, Herbert. "The Twelve Prophets." See #987.

1021. Snyman, S.D. "Cohesion in the Book of Obadiah." *ZAW* 101 (1989), 59-71.

While we cannot conclude that Obadiah is a thorough-going unity, there is ample evidence of careful chiastic structure which provides cohesion to the book as a whole.

Jonah

1022. Abramson, Glenda. "The Book of Jonah as a Literary and Dramatic Work." *Semitics* 5 (1977), 36-47.

"... an ironic tale which has all the stylistic qualities of a carefully constructed and, above all, a carefully thought out, literary composition." Its dramatic qualities, use of irony and related figures, of suspense and paradox.

1023. Ackerman, James S. "Jonah," in #33, pp. 234-243.

The differences between Jonah and all the other minor and major prophets as literature. There is no critical consensus as to its genre; perhaps it should be called a "short story," with some elements which bring it close to classical satire. Plot, character development, word play, structure, and symbolism.

1024.   Ackerman, James S. "Satire and Symbolism in the Song of Jonah," in Baruch Halpern and J.D. Levinson, eds., *Traditions in Transformation* (Winona Lake: Eisenbrauns, 1981), 215-246.

Traditional biblical criticism has had much difficulty with Jonah's song, wishing to separate it from the main body of the narrative. While literary critics are correct that the song is an integral part of the book, they have failed to see its function as part of the satiric purpose of Jonah. The "protagonist's misguided attempts to avoid certain enclosures, which he perceives negatively, by searching for other shelters that he perceives as sources of security.... Jonah's song plays a central role in the patterning of these symbols so that major thematic statements of the story can be articulated."

1025.   Alexander, T. Desmond. "Jonah and Genre." *TB* 36 (1985), 35-59.

Jonah is not a historical, but an imaginative, literary creation, though its author intended it to be read as "didactic history," not as fiction.

1026.   Band, Arnold J. "Swallowing Jonah: The Eclipse of Parody." *Prooftexts* 10 (1990), 177-195.

"... Jonah was originally a masterwork of parody ... [which] was eclipsed in the exegetical process which thus allowed for its canonization. Unlike the Song of Solomon which was converted through allegorization, ... Jonah was reconverted by interpretation—or misinterpretation—to the genre which it was designed to parody. A parody of a prophet's career became a prophetic book with a prophetic message."

1027.   Ben-Yosef, I.A. "Jonah and the Fish as a Folk Motif." *Semitics* 7 (1980), 102-117.

The folk story of "the man in the belly of a fish" is widely disseminated throughout the world, though only his being swallowed; Jonah's sojourning there and subsequent disgorging are rare additions. This transformation of monster into benevolent fish is "a monotheisation and de-mythologisation of the original story."

1028.   Burrows, Millar. "The Literary Category of the Book of
        Jonah," in Harry T. Frank and William L. Reed, eds.,
        Tranlating and Understanding the Old Testament (Nashville
        and New York: Abingdon, 1970), 80-107.

        Despite other attempts to explain Jonah, and despite the prob-
        lems which classifying it as a satire presents, "satire" is nevertheless
        the best generic identification because it avoids the most misinter-
        pretations.

1029.   Christensen, Duane L. "Anticipatory Paronomasia in Jonah
        3: 7-8 and Genesis 37:2." *Revue Biblique* 90 (1983), 261-3.

        Jonah 3:7-8 provides objective means of examining literary pun-
        ning on the structural level. It occurs here at the center of a chi-
        asm, as does another one in Genesis 37:2.

1030.   Christensen, Duane L. "Narrative Poetics and the Interpre-
        tation of the Book of Jonah," in #371, pp. 29-48.

        There is no agreement on the genre of Jonah, but at least we
        can see that Jonah is poetry rather than prose. It consists of 48
        verses, plus the "psalm" in 2:3-10 which is of a different genre than
        the rest of the book. Detailed analysis of its poetic structure, plus
        full translation. Its verse shows a rough equivalent to rhythm or
        metrical beat. The theological concerns of its author are reflected
        in the architectural design of the narrative. Thus, 2:3-10 becomes
        integral to the whole, not a secondary insertion as is usually
        thought.

1031.   Christensen, Duane L. "The Song of Jonah: A Metrical
        Analysis." *JBL* 104 (1985), 217-231.

        "... the prose framework of Jonah's psalm is in fact an integral
        part of the song itself, particularly from a metrical point of view."

1032.   Craig, Kenneth M., Jr. "Jonah and the Reading Process."
        JSOT 47 (1990), 103-114.

        The author of Jonah gives insufficient, even misleading informa-
        tion at key points in order to "invite the reader to stabilize the ac-
        tion as it unfolds," and to reconstruct the "projected world" of the
        story through "informational suppression."

1033.   Cross, Frank M. "Studies in the Structure of Hebrew Verse:
        The Prosody of the Psalm of Jonah," in H.B. Huffmon, et
        al., eds., *The Quest for the Kingdom of God: Studies in Honor of
        George E. Mendenhall* (Winona Lake: Eisenbrauns, 1983),
        159-167.

The psalm of Jonah has a complex verse structure. It is classic Hebrew poetry, characterized by intricate semantic and grammatical parallelism.

1034.   Eagleton, Terry. "J.L. Austin and the Book of Jonah," in #45, pp. 231-6.

Jonah is a "surrealist farce." In J.L. Austin's terms: Jonah's prophetic utterances are "constantive" in their surface grammar but "performative" in their deep structure. "What they get done is to produce a state of affairs in which the state of affairs they describe won't be the case." As the work of Paul de Man and J. Hillis Miller helps us see, "Jonah has to find some way to live with the fact that he can never know whether he is doing anything or not, which was perhaps the point of the whole futile narrative after all."

1035.   Fretheim, Terence. *The Message of Jonah: A Theological Commentary.* Minneapolis (Augsburg P), 1977.

Composition criticism of the book of Jonah. Literary structure; Jonah as narrative and as parable; the function and importance of irony; development of theme through these and through characterization.

1036.   Goitein, S.D.F. "Some Observations on Jonah." *Journal of the Palestine Oriental Society* 17 (1937), 63-77.

Since Jonah is a story, "the truth contained in it is not given explicitly, but has to be deduced, or felt, by the reader." Biblical stories "carry an everlasting stimulus to interpretation and reinterpretation." Jonah is concerned with two interrelated problems: the relationship between God and man, and the prophetic office. God is a flexible character, Jonah a rigid one. The theme is that "between man's atonement and God's grace there is an interdependence which is veiled from human comprehension."

1037.   Gräbe, Ina. "Theory of Literature and Old Testament Studies—Narrative Conventions as Exegetic Reading Strategies." *OTE* n.s. 3 (1990), 43-59.

"... it is especially sophisticated text-orientated models for reading literature that could best provide an Old Testament scholar with theoretical tools whereby the problematisation of the relation between signifier and signified in both poetic language and narrative structure may be analyzed." The indeterminacy of its message helps explain the universality of the Jonah narrative to questions of divine-human relationships.

1038. [Group from Rennes, France]. "An Approach to the Book of Jonah: Suggestions and Questions." *Semeia* 15 (1979), 85-96.

Syntactic and discursive analysis of Jonah. The former involves a "program" and its "anti-program" whose opposition is not resolved. The latter involves a more extensive list of oppositions in various structural codes.

1039. Halpern, Baruch, and Richard Elliott Friedman. "Composition and Paronomasia in the Book of Jonah." *HAR* 4 (1980), 79-92.

Jonah is "replete with word-play," offering "a unique example of the contribution that formal artistry makes to the impact of the final work." Repetition of key words, puns, and "frolic" (semantic ambiguity)—much of it for thematic and theological reinforcement.

1040. Hauser, Alan Jon. "Jonah: In Pursuit of the Dove." *JBL* 104 (1985), 21-37.

"The element of surprise is the key structural device employed by the writer of Jonah. Before 3:10–4:1, the writer misdirects the readers, leading them to picture Yahweh as a God of wrath...."

1041. Hesse, Eric W. and Isaac M. Kikawada. "Jonah and Genesis 1-11." *AJBI* 10 (1984), 3-19.

Jonah is chiastically parallel to Genesis 11, with verbal echoes and other allusions to it as well. This demonstrates that Jonah intended a radical revision of the Mosaic covenant to include all human beings everywhere.

1042. Holbert, John C. "'Deliverance Belongs to Yahweh!': Satire in the Book of Jonah." *JSOT* 21 (1981), 59-81.

We need a more specific generic designation for Jonah than "short story." Definition of satire, and why the term applies to Jonah, especially chapters 1 and 2. Satire is in fact the "hallmark" of the narrative art of Jonah.

1043. de Hoop, Raymond. "The Book of Jonah as Poetry: An Analysis of Jonah 1:1-16," in #382, pp. 156-171.

Structural analysis reveals parallelism, inclusio, and concentric structure in Jonah 1. The chapter is a unity, and uses devices indigenous to poetry.

1044.   Jauss, Hans Robert. "The Book *Jonah*—A Paradigm of the 'Hermeneutics of Strangeness.'" *Journal of Literary Studies* 1 (1985), 1-19.

Events and characters in Jonah seem especially strange to modern secular readers. "This intricate text, having technical similarities with the contemporary novel, emanates from an extraordinary and competent narrator and can be seen as the prototype of the modern novel." This is chiefly because it presents not answers but the process of deliberation, multiple reversals in action, and inevitable but unforeseen resolution. "... it can certainly be regarded as the first novel in world literature."

1045.   Magonet, Jonathan. *Form and Meaning: Studies in Literary Techniques in the Book of Jonah.* Sheffield (Almond P), 1983

Structure of smaller and larger units, including repetition and interrelationship of chapters. Quotations or reminiscences in Jonah from Joel, Ezekiel, Psalms 107 and 139, Exodus 14 and 32, Deuteronomy 21, I Kings 19, Jeremiah 26 and 36. Integral function of the psalm of Jonah in the rest of the book. Chiastic structure. Theme of Jonah is the freedom of God to be beyond any definition by which man would limit him. Good foreign-language bibliography.

*   Marks, Herbert. "The Twelve Prophets." See #987.

1046.   Mather, Judson. "The Comic Art of the Book of Jonah." *Soundings* 65 (1982), 280-291.

Jonah contains rich comic invention that merits appreciation as art. The ways in which its aesthetic form shapes its content (particularly in its themes of iconoclasm and mercy) and the story invites interplay with the reader. It is essentially satirical, especially in the idealized picture of God who lacks flexibility, initiative, and surprise. The reader has been taken in by the author, as Jonah was taken in by God.

1047.   Miles, John A. "Laughing at the Bible: Jonah as Parody." *JQR* 65 (1975), 168-181; rpt #231, pp. 203-215.

Realizing that Jonah is parody and satire helps us understand it better by enabling us to see its unity.

1048.   Pelli, Moshe. "The Literary Art of Jonah." *HS* 20/21 (1979-80), 18-28.

Close reading of Jonah, stressing the roles of characterization, structure and plot.

1049. Potgieter, J.H. "Jonah—A Semio-Structuralist Reading of a Narrative." *OTE* n.s. 3 (1990), 61-69.

Narrative theory of Gérard Genette applied to Jonah, especially the temporal relations between narrative, text and story. The network of relations in Jonah is achieved by various kinds of repetitions: of motifs, *leitwörter*, themes, action-sequences, and type-scenes. The "integration [of relations] into the structure of the book demonstrates the author's artistic-aesthetic ability to tell a story."

1050. Rauber, D.F. "Jonah—The Prophet as Schlemiel." *The Bible Today* 49 (1970), 29-38.

Literary-critical study of the Bible has been both sadly misunderstood and neglected. Barriers to it include the idea of the Bible as a monument. We need to approach Jonah through its humor to find "a sound reading of the work, one which is responsive to the style and method of the art."

1051. Roffey, John W. "God's Truth, Jonah's Fish: Structure and Existence in the Book of Jonah." *ABR* 36 (1988), 1-18.

Application of the hermeneutical critique of structuralism to Jonah identifies three forms of biblical discourse: prophetic, narrative, and wisdom. In situating Jonah within these forms, we find all three present there. Jonah as prophetic setting and narrative structure.

1052. Segert, Stanislav. "Syntax and Style in the Book of Jonah: Six Simple Approaches to their Analysis," in J.A. Emerton, ed., *Prophecy: Essays Presented to Georg Fohrer on his Sixty-Fifth Birthday 6 September 1980* (New York and Berlin: Walter de Gruyter, 1980), 121-130.

The six methods which involve the least subjectivity are: dependency syntax; clause length (clause and cola boundaries); word categories (narratives versus direct speech in Jonah); semantic areas (repetition as clue to artistic variety); functional sentence perspective; and narrative worlds. Use of Psalm 29 as further illustration of the method.

1053. Walsh, Jerome T. "Jonah 2,3-10: A Rhetorical-Critical Study." *Biblica* 63 (1982), 219-229.

Formal analysis worth close reading, and discussion of overall structural pattern of Jonah 2. Motif analysis, especially of spatial movements; textual and reader-level interpretations of its message.

1054.   Warshaw, Thayer S. "The Book of Jonah," in #39, pp. 191-207

Jonah is a satire. It teaches the reader by teaching the hero that love is a higher value than justice and that God's love is universal. "Its structure, careful plotting and interwoven motifs reinforce the theme of the priority of mercy over retributive justice." How Jonah might be taught to a high school class. (JM)

1055.   West, Mona. "Irony in the Book of Jonah: Audience Identification with the Hero." *PRS* 11 (1984), 233-242.

Jonah is best labelled a short story, if we do so cautiously. Types of irony in Jonah, and their functions. "The incongruities and opposition draw the audience into a dynamic encounter with the message of the book."

1056.   Whiton, James M. "The Book of Jonah," in #32, pp. 223-234.

Jonah is "the most individualistic book in the Bible," written in a "simple and striking ... narrative of successive incidents." It opened the way to a humanizing of religion which Christianity in turn retarded again by developing the dogma of Hell.

See also: #s 7, 15, 166, 176, 178, 182, 198, 209, 241, 289, 309, 315, 474, 682, 684, 711, 1434.

Micah

1057.   Hagstrom, David G. *The Coherence of the Book of Micah: A Literary Analysis.* Atlanta (Scholars P), 1988.

Micah is not a collection of pericopes, but a unified, coherent literary whole. This coherence is expressed through concrete literary devices and features, and has important implications for interpreting the book.

*   Marks, Herbert. "The Twelve Prophets." See #987.

1058.   de Moor, Johannes C. "Micah 1: A Structural Approach," in #382, pp. 172-185.

Although parts 1 and 2 of Micah were written at different times, a careful structural analysis of its literary devices shows it to be a unified literary work. Therefore, Micah himself must have been responsible for writing both parts of the book.

1059. Smith, John Merlin Powis. "The Strophic Structure of the Book of Micah." *AJSL* 24 (1908), 187-208.

Analysis of the *Qínah* movement of Micah, and the ways in which the structure of the book varies in adherence to strict strophic principles.

1060. Watson, Wilfred G.E. "Allusion, Irony and Wordplay in Micah 1,7." *Biblica* 65 (1984), 103-5.

The poet in Micah 1:7 alludes to an Ugaritic snake tradition, plays on words, and uses irony—all in the service of a polemic against idols.

1061. Willis, John T. "The Structure of the Book of Micah." *Svensk Exgetisk Årsbok* 34 (1969), 5-42.

The essential literary unity of Micah is achieved through a carefully crafted chiastic structure.

See also: #s 18, 166, 402, 434, 443, 448, 889.

Nahum

1062. Christensen, Duane L. "The Acrostic of Nahum Reconsidered." *ZAW* 87 (1975), 17-30.

The prosodic structure of the acrostic poem of Nahum 1:2-8. It displays highly-developed assonance, repetitive parallelism, chiasm, inclusio, "near-perfect metrical balance," and many mythological allusions. Various reasons why the acrostic might be incomplete.

1063. Christensen, Duane L. "The Acrostic of Nahum Once Again: A Prosodic Analysis of Nahum 1,1-10." *ZAW* 99 (1987), 409-415.

A new theory of metrical analysis allows a correction of the earlier analysis of this poem [#1062]. It eliminates the necessity for most of the earlier emendations, "and achieves a perfectly symmetrical metrical structure which extends through ten verses of text." This new method combines counting of syllabic subdivisions and syntactic-accentual stresses.

1064. Christensen, Duane L. "The Book of Nahum as a Liturgical Composition: A Prosodic Analysis." *JETS* 32 (1989), 159-169.

"Like the Song of Songs, the book of Nahum displays a remarkable structure: intricate in detail, with repeated metrical refrains and almost perfect symmetry in terms of total mora-count and syntactic-accentual stress units."

*   Marks, Herbert. "The Twelve Prophets." See #987.

1065.   Patterson, Richard D., and Michael E. Travers. "Literary Analysis and the Unity of Nahum." *GTJ* 9 (1988), 45-58.

Careful attention to literary matters, e.g., theme, structure, and style, shows the essential unity of Nahum. The literary devices are a necessary and integral part of the theme and structure, and show that Nahum rivals any other OT prophetic book in literary skill and artistry.

1066.   Patterson, Richard D. and Michael E. Travers. "Nahum: Poet Laureate of the Minor Prophets." *JETS* 33 (1990), 437-444.

To ignore literary features of scripture is to misread it, to make it incomplete, since the Bible is a literary book. Structural devices, stylistic features, and exegetical concerns in Nahum all elevate, rather than debase, the biblical text.

See also: #376.

Habakkuk

1067.   Cassuto, Umberto. "Chapter iii of Habakkuk and the Ras Shamra Texts," in *Biblical and Oriental Studies Vol. II: Bible and Ancient Oriental Texts,* Tr Israel Abrahams (Jerusalem: Magnes P, 1975 [originally published in Italian, 1938]), 3-15

How structural, thematic and stylistic parallels between Habakkuk 3 (the enigmatic "Psalm of Habakkuk") and certain newly-discovered Canaanite poems mutually illuminate each other.

1068.   Gowan, Donald E. "Habakkuk and Wisdom." *Perspective* 9 (1968), 157-166.

Like Proverbs, Ecclesiastes, and many psalms, Habakkuk seems "to ignore covenant, cult, and *Heilsgeschichte.*" This means that we should probably reassess its theology to account for the pervasiveness of wisdom in Israelite life, rather than vice versa.

1069. Haak, Robert D. "'Poetry' in Habakkuk 1:1–2:4?" *Journal of the American Oriental Society* 108 (1988), 437-444.

Semantic parallelism is found in Habakkuk 1 and 2, but that is not by itself sufficient to establish these chapters as poetry. However, its "interplay of semantic and grammatical parallelism in both near and more distant contexts" does make the text poetic. Rather than abandoning parallelism as a way of understanding poetry, we should pay attention to the variety of parallelism that is present.

1070. Hiebert, Theodore. "The Use of Inclusion in Habakkuk 3," in #371, pp. 119-140.

Previous attempts to find a coherent literary structure in Habakkuk 3 have failed to take "inclusion" into account. Also called cyclic, ring, or envelope composition, in this chapter it marks discrete sections and gives shape to the whole. It is evident here in repetition of motifs, key words and phrases, in syntactic patterns, parallelism, and phonetic elements.

1071. Kelly, Fred T. "The Strophic Structure of Habakkuk." *AJSL* 18 (1901-2), 94-119.

All three chapters of Habakkuk are in fact poetic, and show those characteristic connections between strophic structure and thematic function.

* Marks, Herbert. "The Twelve Prophets." See #987.

1072. Peckham, Brian. "The Vision of Habakkuk." *CBQ* 48 (1986), 617-636.

Habakkuk is a definite compositional unity of text and commentary, with logical features of argumentation (commentary) and lament (text). How these two parts form "an intricate unity," while each is "distinguished from the other by its structure, organization, language, style...."

1073. Tsumura, David Toshio. "Ugaritic Poetry and Habakkuk 3." *TB* 40 (1989), 24-48.

Those who see a connection between Ugaritic mythology and Habakkuk 3 are mistaken.

1074. Walker, H.H., and N.W. Lund. "The Literary Structure of the Book of Habakkuk." *JBL* 53 (1934), 355-370.

Habakkuk consists of a "closely knit chiastic structure throughout." Explication of this structure as it works itself out overall, and
in individual strophes.

See also: #s 383, 415.

Zephaniah

1075.   Ball, Ivan Jay, Jr. *A Rhetorical Study of Zephaniah* [cover reads:
        Zephaniah: A Rhetorical Study]. Berkeley (BIBAL P), 1988.

        The "literary structure and meaning" of Zephaniah as revealed
        by rhetorical criticism. Inclusio is the most obvious rhetorical fea-
        ture of Zephaniah as a whole, with parallel structure between
        chapters 1 and 3 also an important device contributing to its unity.
        Close reading of various stylistic and rhetorical devices in individ-
        ual lines, verses, and sections.

1076.   Ball, Ivan J., Jr. "The Rhetorical Shape of Zephaniah," in
        Edgar W. Conrad and Edward G. Newing, eds., *Perspectives
        on Language and Text* (Winona Lake: Eisenbrauns, 1987),
        155-65.

        Detailed rhetorical analysis of Zephaniah 2:1-7 demonstrates the
        unity of the entire book. This passage imitates the structural and
        thematic shape of the whole, and vice versa.

1077.   van Grol, Harm W.M. "Classical Hebrew Metrics and
        Zephaniah 2-3," in #382, pp. 186-206.

        Examples from Zephaniah of classical Hebrew rhythm confirm
        the theory of strophic structure. Still, this theory "is not yet a full
        explanation of verse structure."

1078.   House, Paul R. *Zephaniah: A Poetic Drama*. Sheffield (Al-
        mond P), 1988.

        The genre of Zephaniah is the major factor in determining its
        literary character. Its structure is created by a series of alternating
        speeches; its plot has a definite conflict and resolution based on
        the "day of Yahweh"; and "an almost totally dramatic point of view
        pervades the book." In classical terms, Zephaniah is a drama, its
        mode being "prophetic-comic."

1079. Kapelrud, Arvid S. *The Message of the Prophet Zephaniah: Morphology and Ideas.* Oslo-Bergen-Tromsø (Universitetsforlaget), 1975.

> Historical-critical analysis of Zephaniah, followed by close reading of diction, style, theme, structure, and their relation to the ideas presented in the book of Zephaniah.

* Marks, Herbert. "The Twelve Prophets." See #987.

See also: #s 383, 434.

Haggai

* Marks, Herbert. "The Twelve Prophets." See #987.

1080. Pierce, Ronald W. "Literary Connectors and a Haggai/Zechariah/Malachi Corpus." *JETS* 27 (1984), 277-289.

> These three books form a "meaningful literary unity," tied together by several literary connectors to form a coherent whole in the literary as well as the thematic sense. The theme is essentially negative in tone.

1081. Pierce, Ronald W. "A Thematic Development of the Haggai/Zechariah/Malachi Corpus." *JETS* 27 (1984), 401-411.

> The unified message or theme alluded to in the previous article [#1080] is the need for the people to confess their failure before Yahweh, since election does not guarantee favor.

1082. Whedbee, J. William. "A Question-Answer Schema in Haggai 1: The Form and Function of Haggai 1:9-11," in Gary A. Tuttle, ed., *Biblical and Near Eastern Studies* (Grand Rapids: Eerdmans, 1978), 184-194.

> There is greater depth and richness to Haggai's prophetic message than is usually assumed. Haggai's question-answer schema is used to enhance his didactic intention, and was probably influenced by the Deuteronomistic school. Haggai concentrates on the Temple, unlike other prophets, because "the honor of Yahweh" is for him the pivotal issue.

Zechariah

*   Collins, John J., ed., *Semeia 14: Apocalypse: The Morphology of a Genre.* See #36.

1083.   Kline, Meredith G. "The Structure of the Book of Zechariah." *JETS* 34 (1991), 179-193.

The later chapters of Zechariah are "structurally interlocked" with the earlier ones "by means of an intricate triple-hinge mechanism.... Such a curious overall structuring is rather clearly to be attributed to an original master plan for the whole work, not to a secondary redactional development.... The formal structure was evidently designed to highlight the figure of the coming Christ...."

*   Marks, Herbert. "The Twelve Prophets." See #987.

*   Pierce, Ronald W. "Literary Connectors and a Haggai/Zechariah/Malachi Corpus." See #1080.

*   Pierce, Ronald W. "A Thematic Development of the Haggai/Zechariah/Malachi Corpus." See #1081.

*   Strand, Kenneth A. *Interpreting the Book of Revelation: Hermeneutical Guidelines, with Brief Introduction to Literary Analysis.* See #2247.

Appendix by Philip Payne outlines the chiastic structure of Zechariah.

See also: #s 216, 448, 987, 1080, 1081, 1143, 1753, 2247.

Malachi

1084.   Berry, Donald K. "Malachi: A Dramatic Reading." *PEGL* 4 (1984), 77-86.

No one mode of speaking or writing dominates Malachi. Rather, its unity is found "as a conglomerate of images and ideas." Recognizing the book as dramatic (though not theatrical) allows it to be read as both prophetic and priestly writing. Its style made it suitable for temple reading, and it is drama in the truest sense.

1085. Fischer, James A. "Notes on the Literary Form and Message of Malachi." *CBQ* 34 (1972), 315-320.

We need to try to locate the focal point in the literary form of Malachi. The introductory statements in each of the six oracles contain the essentials of Malachi's teaching. This teaching is not, as is usually assumed, in combating the fertility cult, but in the narrow view of Yahweh as rewarder and punisher, as embodiment of love.

*   Marks, Herbert. "The Twelve Prophets." See #987.

1086. Ogden, Graham S. "The Use of Figurative Language in Malachi 2.10-16." *BT* 39 (1988), 223-230.

A literal reading of Malachi 2:10-16 is anomalous; it only makes sense figuratively as a series of metaphors for attacks on priestly relationships.

*   Pierce, Ronald W. "Literary Connectors and a Haggai/ Zechariah/Malachi Corpus." See #1080.

*   Pierce, Ronald W. "A Thematic Development of the Haggai/Zechariah/Malachi Corpus." See #1081.

WRITINGS

1087. Crenshaw, James L. *Old Testament Wisdom: An Introduction.* Atlanta (Scholars P), 1981.

Defining wisdom, its tradition, and its world. Proverbs, Job, Ecclesiastes, Sirach, Wisdom of Solomon, wisdom psalms, and the legacy of wisdom.

1088. Crenshaw, James L., ed. *Studies in Ancient Israelite Wisdom.* New York (KTAV), 1976.

Essays by various scholars relating wisdom literature to Isaiah, the Joseph narrative, Amos, Psalms, Genesis 2-3. How to go about determining the presence and degree of such influence.

1089.   Denning-Bolle, Sara J. "Wisdom and Dialogue in the Ancient Near East." *Numen* 34 (1987), 214-234.

"The search for Wisdom occupied the ancient mind as much as our own, if not more.... [T]he ancients ... could converse with each other about wisdom across national boundaries...." The role played by proverbs, scribal and folk traditions. The instruction of wisdom literature is concrete, its mode dialogic. How it compares to wisdom from Mesopotamia.

1090.   Forman, Rev. Charles C. "The Context of Biblical Wisdom." *Hibbert Journal* 60 (1961-2), 125-132.

"The context of Hebrew wisdom ... is to be found in an oriental literary tradition," and need not be explained by the growing Hellenism of the area occupied by the ancient Israelites.

1091.   Gordis, Robert. "Quotations as a Literary Usage in Biblical, Oriental, and Rabbinic Literature." *HUCA* 22 (1949), 157-219.

The use of quotations was an authentic element of the wisdom books, as well as of non-biblical literature of the ancient world. Ignorance of this usage leads to a failure to grasp the spirit of this literature. The quotations bring awareness of the "lively conflict of ideas" in wisdom literature.

1092.   Scott, R.B.Y. *The Way of Wisdom in the Old Testament.* New York and London (Macmillan), 1971.

General introduction to Proverbs, Job, and Qoheleth. Their chief literary forms and the international context of these forms. The general poetic nature of these books, and their relationship to the prophetic books; their theological outlook.

See also: #s 23, 175, 214, 701, 1088.

PSALMS

1093.   Alden, Robert L. "Chiastic Psalms. A Study in the Mechanics of Semitic Poetry in Psalms 1-50." *JETS* 17 (1974), 11-28.

The use of chiasm in individual verses and whole psalms is widespread. This knowledge "can evoke a new appreciation for the ancient poets...."

1094. Alden, Robert L. "Chiastic Psalms. A Study in the Mechanics of Semitic Poetry in Psalms 51-100." *JETS* 19 (1976), 191-200.

See #1093.

1095. Alden, Robert L. "Chiastic Psalms (III): A Study in the Mechanics of Semitic Poetry in Psalms 101-150." *JETS* 21 (1978), 199-210.

Examples of chiasm from a number of these psalms. Being aware of this device increases our appreciation of the literary genius of these poets; it also forms a powerful argument for the integrity and unity of the Psalms.

1096. Alter, Robert. "Psalms," in #33, pp. 244-262.

We understand the kind of literary activity in the Psalms better if we recall that they were common in the ancient world; that precise dating is impossible; that they are stylistically conservative; that the question of authorship is unsolvable; and that the book was organized late in the process of compiling the Bible. Genre is fluid (mainly supplication and praise); style is characterized by "pointed and poignant traditionalism." There is much figurative language, but less word play than is usual in Hebrew poetry. The structure is mainly chiastic. Psalms 6, 12, 48, 85, 88, 91, 107, 121.

1097. Barnes, W. Emery. "Hebrew Metre and the Text of the Psalms." *JTS* o.s. 33 (1932), 374-382.

There is a question as to whether available evidence points to rigid or to approximate meter in the Psalms. We need to be aware of the danger of emending the text in order to force the poem into a more rigid meter.

1098. Bazak, Jacob. "Numerical Devices in Biblical Poetry." *VT* 38 (1988), 333-7.

Various numerical devices in Psalms 23, 34, 81, and 92 prove that "the Psalmists deliberately employed numerical devices in order to emphasize central sentences...."

1099. Collins, Terence. "Decoding the Psalms: A Structural Approach to the Psalter." *JSOT* 37 (1987), 41-60.

Various "hidden structures" in Psalms lead us to conclude "that the book has an inner cohesion, despite the random surface arrangement of elements.... [It] shares the myth-like narrative framework and eschatological 'drift' with other major sections of the scriptures."

1100.   Culley, Robert C. *Oral Formulaic Language in the Biblical Psalms.* [Toronto] (U of Toronto P), 1967.

The theory and the research behind the idea of oral-formulaic composition of poetry in various primitive cultures. Numerous examples from Psalms demonstrate that there is ample reason for believing the psalms to have been composed and recorded in this manner.

1101.   Curtis, A.H.W. "The 'Subjugation of the Waters' Motif in Psalms; Imagery or Polemic?" *JSS* 23 (1978), 245-256.

This motif is important in the Psalms (probably more so than that of God as creator). It probably originated in a context between Yahweh and Baal within Israelite life, and in the psalmist's anxiety to show Yahweh as sole purveyor of fertility.

1102.   Dyke, Henry Van. "The Poetry of the Psalms," in #32, pp. 91-102.

Definition of parallelism. The individual psalms may vary considerably in literary quality, but at their greatest they evince "a deep and genuine love of nature, ... a passionate sense of the beauty of holiness, ... [and] an intense joy in God."

1103.   Goldingay, John. "Repetition and Variation in the Psalms." *JQR* 68 (1978), 146-151.

Errors we make in interpreting Psalms because of uncritical modern assumptions about how and where poems repeat, and about what is repetition and what is not in Hebrew poetry.

1104.   Greenstein, Edward L. "How Does Parallelism Mean?" in *A Sense of Text: The Art of Language in the Study of Biblical Literature* (Winona Lake: Eisenbrauns; *JQR* Supplement, 1982), 41-70.

The issue of how parallelism "means" may be clarified by applying transformational-generative analysis to some of the Psalms (as to much other ancient Hebrew Poetry).

*   van Grol, H.W.M. "Paired Tricola in the Psalms, Isaiah and Jeremiah." See #424.

1105.   Grossberg, Daniel. "The Disparate Elements of the Inclusio in Psalms." *HAR* 6 (1982), 97-104.

There is growing awareness of the importance of inclusio. It is not mere repetition as such, but "an inverted, reversed, or somehow opposed and varied relationship of the two parts." Psalms 26,

29, 47, 82 and 97 demonstrate its aesthetic and rhetorical effects, and its widespread use in Psalms.

1106.   Kodell, Jerome, O.S.B. "The Poetry of the Psalms." *BT* 65 (1973), 1107-1113.

The nature of poetry; how the eighteenth century came to recognize the existence of OT verse; some basic poetic devices in Psalms.

1107.   Kraft, Charles Franklin. *The Strophic Structure of Hebrew Poetry: As Illustrated in the First Book of the Psalter.* Chicago (U of Chicago P), 1938.

History of the discussion of strophic structure; various definitions of its presence in Hebrew poetry. "The existence and nature of poetic divisions above the line, the basic unit of the strophe," through examination of the first forty-one psalms. The presence of strophic structure is unmistakable, almost invariably in either couplets or triads; there is no uniform pattern of strophes moving into stanzas.

1108.   Kuntz, J. Kenneth. "The Canonical Wisdom Psalms of Ancient Israel: Their Rhetorical, Thematic, and Formal Dimensions," in Jared J. Jackson and Martin Kessler, eds., *Rhetorical Criticism: Essays in Honor of James Muilenberg* (Pittsburgh: Pickwick P, 1974), 186-222.

A comprehensive study of Psalms requires some consideration of the Israelite wisdom traditions, and vice versa. A "select overview of previous wisdom psalms research, identifying rhetorical and thematic elements [typically found] in psalmic wisdom." Nine of the Psalms certainly belong in this category: 19, 25, 32, 37, 49, 55, 119, as perhaps do a few others.

1109.   Levine, Herbert J. "The Dialogic Discourse of Psalms," in #48, pp. 268-281.

The work of Mikhail Bakhtin may help us find "one of the stylistic hallmarks of the biblical Psalms," except that where Bakhtin sees only a monologic voice in lyric poetry, we can find a "contest of quotations: a Bakhtinian 'ideological becoming' of human beings, seen in the 'process of selectively assimilating the words of others.'" These "words of others" with which the psalmist is in dialogue are either external words from a political struggle, or internal words from a quarrel "over the nature and power of God."

1110.   Lewis, C.S. *Reflections on the Psalms.* New York (Harcourt, Brace, and Co.), 1958.

"Most emphatically the Psalms must be read as poems; as lyrics, with all the licences and all the formalities, the hyperboles, the emotional rather than logical connections, which are proper to lyric poetry. They must be read as poems if they are to be understood...." Meditations on various topics arising out of the Psalms, from a Christian theological perspective.

1111.   Longman, Tremper III. *How to Read the Psalms*. Downers Grove and Leicester (Intervarsity P), 1988.

An overall "Christian" reading of the Psalms. Definitions of OT poetry, parallelism, imagery. Explication of Psalms 30, 69, and 98.

1112.   Lund, N.W. "Chiasmus in the Psalms." *AJSL* 49 (1932-33), 281-312.

Peculiarities of synonymous parallelism in Psalms. We need to admit the independence of Hebrew poetry from Greek and Roman classical poetry, and not let prosody color our analysis of biblical verse.

1113.   Mays, James Luther. "The David of the Psalms." *Interpretation* 40 (1986), 143-155.

It is legitimate to be interested in the David of the Psalms, even if he is only a literary reality. Literature shapes and therefore creates reality. A literary portrait of David drawn from I Samuel, Chronicles, and Psalms, each book having its own emphasis. We must read all three to get the full picture.

1114.   Miller, Patrick D., Jr. "Synonymous-Sequential Parallelism in the Psalms." *Biblica* 61 (1980), 256-260.

We should recognize an unusual form of parallelism which combines parallel and non-parallel elements—i.e., some elements are synonymously parallel and others sequential or continuous. This form deserves further investigation.

1115.   Mowinckel, Sigmund. *Real and Apparent Tricola in Hebrew Psalm Poetry*. Oslo (Aschehoug and Co.), 1957.

Previous scholars identified a number of tricola in Hebrew verse, almost all of them in Psalms. Except for a few cases, these can be resolved into other devices and forms, or are probable textual corruptions.

1116.   Raabe, Paul R. "Deliberate Ambiguity in the Psalter." *JBL* 110 (1991), 213-227.

Hebrew psalmists often deliberately created lexical, phonetic, and grammatical ambiguity. This ambiguity was not intended to deceive, but to amuse and to sustain the interest of the hearers. It demonstrates the psalmists' "mastery of the language, ... sense of humor and ... delight in the creative use of language." Most importantly, this ambiguity encourages reader interaction with the text, leading readers "to recognize the truth of the various possible interpretations."

1117. Raabe, Paul R. *Psalm Structures: A Study of Psalms with Refrains.* Sheffield (JSOT P), 1990.

The "basic building blocks" of a psalm, especially larger units such as strophes and stanzas. Psalms 42-3, 46, 49, 56, 57, 59 mainly, and also 39, 67, 80, and 99 show clear evidence of a refrain. They are not written in meter, but some regularity is evident within the considerable diversity of colon/verse length. Stanza/section divisions are primary over strophe divisions. Psalms show so much symmetry, primarily chiasmic, that "recognizing the stanzas of a psalm is essential for understanding the meaning of a psalm."

1118. Ridderbos, Nic H. "The Psalms: Style-Figures and Structure (certain considerations with special reference to Pss. xxii, xxv, and xlv)." *OS* 13 (1963), 43-76.

"... biblical science has scarcely even begun to develop a method for objectively investigating this subject of style." The stylistic device of repetition: refrains, beginning/ending correspondence, stairlike rhythm, and keywords. Strophes and other structural devices are also present. The sophisticated correspondence of form and content in Psalms is quite deliberate. Psalms 22, 25, 45.

1119. Ryken, Leland. "Metaphor in the Psalms." *CL* 31, #3 (Spring, 1982), 9-29.

Like Shakespeare, the poets of the Psalms thought metaphorically. Metaphors in the Psalms from four angles: as rhetorical figure; in relation to the reader; in relation to the poet; and in relation to reality.

1120. Simpson, D.C. *The Psalmists: Essays on their Religious Experience and Teaching, their Social Background, and their Place in the Development of Hebrew Psalmody.* Oxford and London (Oxford UP), 1926.

Seven essays, of which two are literary-critical. Godfrey Driver: resemblances between Hebrew and Babylonian poetry in meter, parallelism, chiasm, acrostics, diction, theology) are coincidental, and influence negligible. Aylward M. Blackman: Hebrew-Egyptian literary connections worked both ways, as various thematic parallels illustrate.

1121.   Willis, John T. "The Juxtaposition of Synonymous and Chiastic Parallelism in Tricola in Old Testament Hebrew Psalm Poetry." *VT* 29 (1979), 465-480.

Previously unnoticed structures in tricola, illustrated from various psalms. While bicola are usually thought to dominate, this evidence shows that tricola are frequent enough to be taken seriously, and are independent of bicola.

1122.   Youngblood, Ronald. "Divine Names in the Book of Psalms: Literary Structures and Number Patterns." *JANES* 19 (1989), 171-181.

Divine names as a technique are like chiasmus and inclusio: part of the literary stock in trade of biblical authors, and in fact each technique can incorporate the others.

1123.   Zevit, Ziony. "Psalms at the Poetic Precipice." *HAR* 10 (1986), 351-366.

History of the analysis of biblical poetry in this century. The insights of Roman Jakobson as means of exploring "the outer limit of biblical poeticity, ... the point at which the poetic function of the language totters on the brink of dissolution." Psalms 125, 133, 134, and briefly other psalms.

See also: #s 11, 27, 166, 175, 177, 178, 187, 252, 370, 396, 411, 412, 422, 424, 433, 435, 441, 447, 449, 452, 460, 469, 474, 476, 478, 788, 1088, 1454, 1500.

INDIVIDUAL PSALMS

Psalm 1

1124.   Bullough, Sebastian. "The Question of Metre in Psalm I." *VT* 17 (1967), 42-9.

Contrary to all previous explications of Psalm 1 as verse, it is in fact "plain rhythmic prose."

1125.   Crumpacker, Mary M. "Formal Analysis and the Psalms." *JETS* 24 (1981), 11-21.

Formal literary criticism gives us new tools for analyzing biblical poetry, as can be illustrated by examining Psalms 1, 51.

1126. Vogels, Walter. "A Structural Analysis of Ps 1." *Biblica* 60 (1979), 410-416.

To discern the structure of Psalm 1, we need to look at the cognitive level, with the help of A.J. Greimas's notion of several levels within the structure of a text. Chiasm (surface structure), narrative structure, discursive structure in the psalm.

1127. Willis, John T. "Psalm 1: An Entity." *ZAW* 91 (1979), 381-401.

Many scholars argue that Psalms 1 and 2 form one poem. However, analysis of the strophic structure of Psalm 1 shows it to be a separate poem.

See also: #s 223, 377.

Psalm 2

1128. Auffret, Pierre. *The Literary Structure of Psalm 2.* Sheffield (JSOT P), 1977.

Explication of style and content of each verse. The psalm shows a parallel and concentric structure. Psalms 1 and 2 may be read in parallel.

See also: #s 146, 462, 1898, 2197.

Psalm 3

1129. Kselman, John S. "Psalm 3: A Structural and Literary Study." *CBQ* 49 (1987), 572-580.

Continues for Psalm 3 the work of Pierre Auffret on Psalm 2 [#1128]. Psalm 3 is "an ideal candidate for a literary study" because of its use of traditional poetic formulae. Its "artistry and accomplishment ... [are] considerable."

Psalm 5

See #s 7, 462.

Psalm 6

See #1096.

Psalm 7

See #1258.

Psalm 8

See #223.

Psalm 9

See #376.

Psalm 10

See #376.

Psalm 13

See #223.

Psalm 15

1130.   Barré, Lloyd M. "Recovering the Literary Structure of Psalm
        XV." *VT* 34 (1984), 207-210.

        Psalm 15 can be analyzed as a chiasmus on both formal and se-
        mantic bases. The latter means the correspondence between struc-
        turally-related members.

1131.   Miller, Patrick D., Jr. "Poetic Ambiguity and Balance in
        Psalm XV." *VT* 29 (1979), 416-424.

        A "new" analysis of the structure of Psalm 15, in terms of how its
        poetry creates form and conveys meaning.

Psalm 18

1132.   Kuntz, J. Kenneth. "Psalm 18: A Rhetorical-Critical Analysis." *JSOT* 26 (1983), 3-31.

A rhetorical-critical analysis is of significant help in understanding the message of Psalm 18, and in order to appreciate this poet's talents, which are of the highest rank. Strophic structure, power of style and diction, unity, rhetorical effect, and spatial imagery.

See also: #1386

Psalm 19

*   Barrett, Cyril. "The Language of Ecstasy and the Ecstasy of Language." See #1345.

1133.   Glass, Jonathan T. "Some Observations on Psalm 19," in Kenneth G. Hoglund, et al., eds., *The Listening Heart: Essays in Wisdom and the Psalms in Honor of Roland E. Murphy, O. Carm.* (Sheffield: JSOT P, 1987), 147-159.

Psalm 19 as a literary unity through theme, interrelationship of parts, parallel structures, and figures. The psalm presents "a dialogue between humanity and the heavens ... and a dialogue between humanity and the Torah...."

1134.   Sager, Steven G. "'Sun' and 'Light' Imagery in Psalm 19," in Ronald A. Brauner, ed., *Jewish Civilization: Essays and Studies, Vol. I* (Philadelphia: Reconstructionist Rabbinical College, 1979), 33-40.

"... sun and light imagery pervade the entire psalm.... [It] is multipurposed, describing ... the Creator, and the law as well, weaving a radiant and light-filled hymn, all of whose elements contribute to a magnificent and quite intelligible whole...." Such imagery was common in the literary and religious traditions to which the poet was heir, and gives evidence of the psalm's unity of theme and structure.

1135.   Sarna, N. "Psalm XIX and the Near Eastern Sun-God Literature." *PWCJS* 4 (1967), 171-5.

The biblically unique personification of the sun as a mythological figure, combined with a hymn to the Torah, can be explained if we see Psalm 19 as "an anti-pagan polemic, specifically, an anti-

sun-god polemic, that has made use of the standard terminology of
the Near Eastern sun-god literature to combat the sun-cult
ideologically...."

See also: #s 5, 105, 380, 1108.

Psalms 20, 21

1136.   Kuntz, Kenneth J. "King Triumphant: A Rhetorical Study of
         Psalms 20 and 21." *HAR* 10 (1986), 157-176.

         What can we know about the context and function of Psalms 20
         and 21? What is their strophic structure? and, "as artful poems,
         how is their rhetorical achievement to be spelled out?" Rhetorical
         criticism has its problems in interpreting Psalms, despite its capac-
         ity to "sharpen our perception of the resourcefulness of the an-
         cient Israelite poets...." Psalm 21 continues and generalizes the
         military metaphor of Psalm 20.

See also: #434.

Psalm 22

1137.   Kselman, John S. "'Why Have You Abandoned Me?' A
         Rhetorical Study of Psalm 22," in #34, pp. 172-198.

         The rhetorical features, structures of its sections, themes which
         run through the whole psalm, and its unity. How the apparent
         contradictions of despair and faith expressed therein can be rec-
         onciled. "... this carefully constructed and developed psalm
         demonstrates the high degree of artistry of which the Hebrew po-
         ets are capable."

See also: #1118.

Psalm 23

1138.   Ahroni, Reuben. "The Unity of Psalm 23." *HAR* 6 (1982),
         21-34.

         Psalm 23 is not simple and homely, but tormented. Its unity is
         not prosodic or thematic or imagistic or rhythmic or syntactic.
         Rather, its unity is "subtle and implicit," a unity of style and emo-
         tional impressionism, of reverberating metaphors.

1139.   Foley, C.M. "Pursuit of the Inscrutable: A Literary Analysis of Psalm 23," in Lyle Eslinger and Glen Taylor, eds., *Ascribe to the Lord: Biblical and Other Studies in Memory of Peter C. Craigie* (Sheffield: JSOT P, 1988), 363-383.

Psalm 23 is best understood in terms of its various patterns of binary opposition and its exploration of the resulting tensions caused by this polarity.

1140.   Freedman, David Noel. "The Twenty-Third Psalm," in Louis L. Orlin, ed., *Michigan Oriental Studies in Honor of George G. Cameron* (Ann Arbor: Department of Near Eastern Studies, U of Michigan, 1976), 139-166. Rpt in #372.

"... there is an underlying theme which integrates the disparate elements of the poem and provides a framework for the bold and striking images used by the poets." The structure of the psalm is metrical, strophic, and thematic, and depends on inclusio. Verse-by-verse explication, with references to other parts of the HB.

1141.   Frontain, Raymond-Jean. "Teaching Psalm 23," in #179, pp. 120-123.

We need to read each biblical text both within and without the context created for it by the Bible proper. Four different translations of Psalm 23 compared in order to demonstrate qualities of imagery, simplicity of language, and temporal sequence.

1142.   McCarthy, David Paul. "A Not-So-Bad Derridean Approach to Psalm 23." *PEGL* 8 (1988), 177-191.

How to deconstruct Psalm 23, and why we should do so. We should realize that there are many possible deconstructive readings of Psalm 23, just as there are many possible logocentric ones: "double, contradictory, undecidable values always derive from the syntax."

1143.   Milne, Pamela. "Psalm 23: Echoes of the Exodus." *SR* 4 (1974-5), 237-247.

If we start with structure and vocabulary of Psalm 23, rather than with imagery as is usually done, we find a unity of structure and theme. "The central theme is the exodus, and it was employed by the biblical poet to offer the exiles in Babylon hope based on Israel's past experience of liberation from bondage in Egypt." The "God as shepherd" references always occur in the HB in a context of exile; e.g. Isaiah 40, 48; Jeremiah 23; Ezekiel 34; Zechariah 10, 11.

1144.   Pardee, Dennis. "Structure and Meaning in Hebrew Poetry: The Example of Psalm 23." *Maarav* 5-6 (1990), 239-280.

Psalm 23 tests a previously-published theory of poetic structure because its structure seems to fit poorly, and because it tests the poetry/prose borderline. Parallelism and other devices in the psalm show that it is as thoroughly poetic as any biblical poem that fits the usual formula.

1145.   Smith, Mark S. "Setting and Rhetoric in Psalm 23." *JSOT* 41 (1988), 61-6.

The problem of the relationship between verses 1-4 and 5-6 of Psalm 23 can be answered if we see it as a pilgrim psalm.

See also: #s 192, 458, 1098.

Psalm 25

See #s 400, 1108, 1118, 1188.

Psalm 26

See #1105.

Psalm 29

1146.   Craigie, P.C. "Psalm XXIX in the Hebrew Poetic Tradition." *VT* 22 (1972), 143-151.

Psalm 29 is a Hebrew victory hymn, at a midpoint in a particular tradition of Hebrew poetry which begins with Exodus 15 and ends with Psalms 47, 93, and 96-99. This tradition shows a strong Canaanite element, though decreasing as the tradition developed.

1147.   Freedman, David Noel, and C. Franke Hyland. "Psalm 29: A Structural Analysis." *HTR* 66 (1973), 237-256.

"... a structural analysis of the psalm ... points to some complex and sophisticated techniques of Hebrew poetry." Tabulated metrical data illustrate an analysis of verses and strophes and the psalm's envelope structure.

1148.   Fullerton, Kemper. "The Strophe in Hebrew Poetry and Psalm 29." *JBL* 48 (1929), 274-290.

The debate about stanzaic structures in Hebrew poetry should remind us that the main controversy is over their frequency, not their existence, and over the extent of regularity in these forms. Often, when an exegetical difficulty is cleared up, we find a rhythmic difficulty has also been solved, and the frequent emergence of a stanza form. Psalm 29 shows the "feeling for symmetrical form among Hebrew poets," and a "rare beauty" as a result.

See also: #s 380, 1052, 1105.

Psalm 30

See #1111.

Psalm 31

1149.   Dion, Paul E. "Strophic Boundaries and Rhetorical Structure in Psalm 31." *ETh* 18 (1987), 183-192.

We should always prepare for analysis by establishing the text-critical status of the pericope, its philological problems and versification. Psalm 31 has two main parts, its main body being chiastic. Definition of its cola; the links in the chiasm of verses 2-21, and the relationship of verses 22-25 to the main body of the poem.

1150.   Laberge, Leo. "A Literary Analysis of Psalm 31." *ETh* 16 (1985), 147-168.

The use of a variety of grammatical persons, inclusio, and overall structure of the psalm. Verse-by-verse explication; relationship of the literary devices to purpose and theme; tonal shifts and use of clichés.

Psalm 32

See #1108.

Psalm 33

See #380

Psalm 34

1151.   Fisch, Harold. "Bakhtin's Misreadings of the Bible." *HUSLA*
        16 (1988), 130-149.

> Literary study of the Bible, for example of such Psalms as 34 and
> 137, and others, could benefit from Bakhtinian theories of "social
> dialogism." Bakhtin's only misreading is to assume that readers do
> not internalize (i.e., make contemporary) their encounter with the
> text.

1152.   Liebreich, Leon. "Psalms 34 and 145 in the Light of their
        Key Words." *HUCA* 27 (1956), 181-192.

> Buber's contention that "the recurrence of the key-words is a ba-
> sic law of composition in the Psalms" is valid. His law "has a poetic
> significance ... as well as a hermeneutic one."

See also: #s 1098, 1188.

Psalm 35

See #402.

Psalm 37

See #s 1108, 1188.

Psalm 40

*   Danker, Frederick W. "The Literary Unity of Mark 14:1-25."
        See #1853.

1153.   Ridderbos, Nic. H. "The Structure of Psalm XL." *OS* 14
        (1965), 296-304.

> We must agree that Psalm 40 shows an original unity, assuming
> the theory about Psalmic structure discussed earlier [#1118]. The
> "aphoristic style" and "style of repetition" of the psalm.

See also: #1853.

Psalms 42-43

1154. Rowley, H.H. "The Structure of Psalm XLII-XLIII." *Biblica* 21 (1940), 45-50.

The irregularity of form in Psalm 42-43, and its changes of thought, "belong ... to the very artistry of the poem." It is written in Qinah meter, with three strophes and refrain. 42:9 is the center, with two double pentameters on either side; it functions as thematic reminder of "divine ministry even in the midst of distress."

1155. Schökel, Luis Alonso. "The Poetic Structure of Psalm 42-43." *JSOT* 1 (1976), 4-11.

"With its wealth of structure, its dynamics, its lyrical and dramatic intensity, this psalm exceeds mere classification."

See also: #s 241, 1117.

Psalm 45

See #1118.

Psalm 46

1156. Kelly, Sidney. "Psalm 46: A Study in Imagery." *JBL* 89 (1970), 305-312.

The imagery of this psalm shows an organic relationship between the two motifs of the glory of Zion and of Yahweh's universal victory over the nations of the earth; form criticism has tended to try, incorrectly, to separate these two themes.

1157. Tsumura, David Toshio. "The Literary Structure of Psalm 46, 2-8." *AJBI* 6 (1980), 29-55.

These verses have a chiastic structure. It is important to know this because scholars have long observed that Psalm 46 "does not follow the ordinary literary types."

1158. Tsumura, David Toshio. "Twofold Image of Wine in Psalm 46: 4-5." *JQR* 71 (1981), 167-175.

While the overall literary structure of Psalm 46 has yet to be explained, the "wine" image in verses 4-5 is a key one for understanding the poem. The "wine" image in various texts in the HB, both in and outside of the Psalms.

See also: #s 223, 1117.

Psalm 47

1159.   Beuken, W.A.M. "Psalm XLVII: Structure and Drama." *OS* 21 (1981), 38-54.

The semantic/grammatical structure of the psalm, analyzed in detail, reveals the underlying "drama" of the poem: i.e., the "dialogue of different voices" in the psalm.

1160.   Muilenberg, James. "Psalm 47." *JBL* 63 (1944), 235-256.

Structure, theme, and poetic diction of the psalm. It is a characteristic Hebrew poem in both form and style: symmetry and balance, aversion to stereotype, fondness for concrete imagery, euphony, and the scenic, and a sense of the dramatic.

See also: #s 1105, 1117.

Psalm 48

See #1096.

Psalm 49

1161.   De Meyer, F. "The Science of Literature Method of Prof. M. Weiss in Confrontation with Form Criticism, Examplified [sic] on the Basis of Ps 49." *Bijdragen* 41 (1979), 152-168.

Old historical and new literary methods can mutually illuminate a text, e.g., Psalm 49. Its repetitions, imagery, and figurative language all contribute to its theme: the conviction that the fate of the arrogant wealthy will be different from that of the pious poor.

See also: #1073

Psalm 50

1162. Allen, L.C. "Structure and Meaning in Psalm 50." *VE* 14 (1984), 17-37.

Previous attempts to decipher the structure of Psalm 50 have failed to see that chiastic parallelism is the key. This device brings out the theme of divine honor, the necessary intertwining of divine and human covenant; it also helps us identify the strophes and the inclusio.

See also: #418.

Psalm 51

1163. Dalglish, Edward R. *Psalm Fifty-One in the Light of Ancient Near Eastern Patternism.* Leiden (E.J. Brill), 1962.

Survey of Egyptian and Sumero-Accadian penitential literature. Outline of the poetic and strophic structure of Psalm 51. It exhibits many parallels with Near Eastern poetry in both style and content. Its significance is both literary and theological.

See also: #s 18, 223.

Psalm 55

See #1108.

Psalm 56

See #1117.

Psalm 57

See #1117.

Psalm 59

See #1117.

Psalm 68

1164.   Fokkelman, J.P. "The Structure of Psalm lxviii." *OS* 26
        (1990), 72-83.

        The feature of closure in Psalm 68 shows the first strophe to be
        part of the poem, and therefore that the psalm is a "well-ordered
        composition," a literary unity. Its structure is in three sections, with
        closely-connected strophes and stanzas "produced by parallelism
        on the strophic level." The psalm contains structurally "a modest
        form of development along the syntagmatic axis."

See also: #689.

Psalm 69

1165.   Allen, Leslie C. "The Value of Rhetorical Criticism in Psalm
        69." *JBL* 105 (1986), 577-598.

        "Stylistic aspects of the Psalm need to be taken seriously as yield-
        ing insights into the intricate exegetical development of the Psalm.
        They shed light upon the Psalmist's handling of standard forms,
        upon the major and minor pauses.... In the quest for meaning,
        style is an invaluable guide."

See also: #1111.

Psalm 72

1166.   Kselman, John S. "Psalm 72: Some Observations on Struc-
        ture." *American Schools of Oriental Research Bulletin* #220
        (December, 1975), 77-81.

        Psalm 72 shows an overall chiastic structure, inclusio, and
        smaller chiasms within certain sections.

See also: #380.

Psalm 73

1167.   Allen, Leslie C. "Psalm 73: An Analysis." *TB* 33 (1982), 93-
        118.

Rhetorical criticism (stressing the individuality of a work) and form criticism (stressing the work's type) on Psalm 73. Repetition is the key to unlocking its structure, with units formed by verses 1-4, 5-12, 13-17, 18-20, and 21-28. Its style is partly characterized by a "revolutionary vocabulary."

See also: #223.

Psalm 74

1168. Sharrock, Graeme E. "Psalm 74: A Literary-Structural Analysis." *AUSS* 21 (1983), 211-223.

Analyzing the structure of this psalm helps us grasp its three themes: religious rhetoric at times of national crisis; the community's self-identity; and concern for the name of God. The structure is chiastic, with one paragraph corresponding to each theme, and a climax order. The status of God's name and reputation becomes the primary theme.

See also: #223.

Psalm 77

1169. Kselman, John S. "Psalm 77 and the Book of Exodus." *JANES* 15 (1983), 51-8.

The style and structure of Psalm 77 echo those of Exodus 34. "Psalm 77 is a unity, a composition by a gifted poet who called upon the traditions and the sacred past of the people of Israel to answer the questions that distressed both poet and people."

See also: #380.

Psalm 78

1170. Clifford, Richard J. "In Zion and David A New Beginning: An Interpretation of Psalm 78," in Baruch Halpern and Jon D. Levenson, eds., *Traditions in Transformation: Turning Points in Biblical Faith* (Winona Lake: Eisenbrauns, 1981), 121-141.

In the long argument about the genre, structure, and purpose of Psalm 78, not enough attention has been paid to its rhetoric; i.e., how it works as a piece of liturgical poetry. How the narrator's perspective arranges history for effect; what this may tell us about the purpose of the poem and its date.

1171.   Greenstein, Edward L. "Mixing Memory and Design: Reading Psalm 78." *Prooftexts* 10 (1990), 197-218.

Psalm 78 is not a historical condemnation but an exercise in rhetoric. "The psalmist ... practices memory, not to recount the past, but to prompt the kind of remembrance that leads to change."

See also #s 383, 403.

Psalm 79

*   Labuschagne, Casper J. "On the Structural Use of Numbers as a Composition Technique." See #676.

Psalm 80

1172.   Tromp, N.J. "Psalm LXXX: Form of Expression and Form of Content." *OS* 25 (1989), 145-155.

Structuralist analysis of the link between "form of expression and form of content." There is a homological relationship between limits and non-limits and other related "figurative isotopies" in this psalm in which "guilt does not fit."

Psalm 81

See #1098.

Psalm 82

1173.   Handy, Lowell K. "Sounds, Words and Meanings in Psalm 82." *JSOT* 47 (1990), 51-66.

Psalm 82 is carefully constructed using parallelism in a variety of ways: meanings and sounds are both used to structure the poem. Many of its words have multiple meanings; recognizing this word-play is necessary for grasping the meaning. It has a chiastic, five-part structure.

See also: #1105.

Psalm 85

See #1096.

Psalm 88

See #s 135, 1096.

Psalm 89

1174. Ward, James M. "The Literary Form and Liturgical Back-
        ground of Psalm LXXXIX." *VT* 11 (1961), 321-339.

        The complexity of form and content in Psalm 89 should not
        blind us to its literary unity and integrity. It is "the deliberate com-
        position of a skillful poet who knew exactly what he was doing." It
        has no precise, fixed strophic arrangement, though "there are dis-
        cernible groups of lines ... which can be called strophes in the
        broad sense." Investigation of its liturgical setting reinforces the
        sense of its unity derived from literary criteria.

See also #403.

Psalm 90

See #s 219, 402, 443.

Psalm 91

See #1096.

Psalm 92

1175. Berlin, Adele. "Grammatical Aspects of Biblical Paral-
        lelism." *HUCA* 50 (1979), 17-43.

        Literary analysis of word pairs, grammar, parallelism (including
        morphological and syntactic parallelism) in Psalm 92.

*   Magonet, Jonathan. "Some Concentric Structures in
        Psalms." See #1198.

See also: #437, 1098.

Psalm 94

See also: #1108.

Psalm 97

See #1105.

Psalm 98

See #1111.

Psalm 104

See #223, 397, 1188.

Psalm 105

1176.   Ceresko, Anthony R., O.S.F.S. "A Poetic Analysis of Ps 105,
        with Attention to its Use of Irony." *Biblica* 64 (1983), 20-
        47.

        Structure of Psalm 105; various literary devices including chias-
        mus, merismus, inclusio, "distant parallelism," and especially
        irony. Irony is used to underscore the theme of the "land."

1177.   Clifford, Richard J. "Style and Purpose in Psalm 105." *Biblica*
        60 (1979), 420-427.

        Several rhetorical features illuminate its purpose: repetition of
        key words, e.g., "servant," "land," and "word"; parallel phrasing; re-
        arrangement of old historical traditions.

*   Hill, Andrew E. "Patchwork Poetry or Reasoned Verse?
        Connective Structure in 1 Chronicles XVI." See #1478.

See also: #403.

Psalm 106

See #383.

Psalm 107

See #s 383, 448, 1096.

Psalm 110

See #2197.

Psalm 111

See #1188.

Psalm 112

See #1188.

Psalm 113

1177a. Hurvitz, Avi. "Originals and Imitations in Hebrew Poetry: A Comparative Examination of 1 Sam 2:1-10 and Ps 113:5-9," in Ann Kort and Scott Morschauser, eds., *Biblical and Related Studies Presented to Samuel Iwry* (Winona Lake: Eisenbrauns, 1985), 115-121.

The scholarly consensus has been that "elaboration" and "more complex patterning" are necessarily later characteristics in Hebrew biblical poetry than a simple structure. On the contrary, they may be "pseudo classicisms indicative of a relatively late linguistic phase in the historical development of B[iblical] H[ebrew]." Thus, Psalm 113 is probably not an archaic composition antedating I Samuel 2.

Psalm 114

See #s 223, 380, 1188.

Psalm 116

1178.   Barré, Michael L. "Psalm 116: Its Structure and its Enigmas." *JBL* 109 (1990), 61-78.

Deciphering the structure of Psalm 116 has proven difficult, as has the fact that it derives from Psalms 18 and 56, and the strangeness of verse 15. Breakdown into sections and cola, and how themes reinforce this structure.

See also: #223.

Psalm 117

See #632.

Psalm 119

*   Thompson, P.J. "Psalm 119: A Possible Clue to the Structure of the First Epistle of John." See #2214.

See also: #s 437, 1108.

Psalms 120-134

1179.   Grossberg, Daniel. *Centripetal and Centrifugal Structures in Biblical Poetry*. Atlanta (Scholars P), 1989.

Analysis of Psalms 120-134, Song of Songs, and Lamentations "in terms of the particular structural tensions at work in each." Centripetal poems are "marked by a prevailing uniform structure and tight pattern"; centrifugal poems show "a disparate and a predominantly loose composition." Psalms 120-134 are examples of the former; Song of Songs of the latter; and Lamentations strikes a balance between these two tendencies. **

Psalm 120

See #223.

Psalm 121

See #1096.

Psalm 122

See #5.

Psalm 125

See #1123.

Psalm 127

1180.   Estes, Daniel J. "Like Arrows in the Hand of a Warrior (Psalm CXXVII)." *VT* 41 (1991), 304-311.

"... the arrow simile in *vv* 4, 5a provides a plausible thematic key to the total psalm.... Whatever the precise history of the composition of the psalm may have been, the figure of the arrow links the two superficially disparate segments into a profound statement on human significance."

Psalm 130

1181.   Marrs, Rick R. "A Cry From the Depths (Ps 130)." *ZAW* 100 (1988), 81-90.

Psalm 130 exhibits several poetic features worthy of note; the foremost are parallelism, semantic and syntactic repetition, all of which create a unified poem.

Psalm 131

1182.   Fischer, James A. "Biblical Spirituality/The Feminine Factor." *Studies in Formative Spirituality* 4 (1983), 207-15.

The question of the presence of feminine factors in spirituality is best approached from the viewpoint that story rather than history is "the principal carrier of theology in the Bible." Rhetorical criticism is most useful for analyzing feminine images in the HB, and specifically the mood, tension, and structure of poems, e.g., Psalm 131 and Isaiah 66.

Psalm 132

1183.   Brekelmans, Chr. "Psalm 132: Unity and Structure." *Bijdragen* 44 (1983), 262-5.

Various thematic doublings in Psalm 132 indicate the presence of a chiastic structure, so that all elements of the psalm are seen to have their appropriate place in this structure.

1184.   Huwiler, Elizabeth F. "Patterns and Problems in Psalm 132," in Kenneth G. Hoglund, et al., eds., *The Listening Heart: Essays in Wisdom and the Psalms in Honor of Roland E. Murphy, O. Carm.* (Sheffield: JSOT P, 1987), 199-215.

Psalm 132 shows evidence of strophic structure, "marked by grammatic, semantic and lexical parallelisms." Recognizing this structure "helps to resolve some interpretive problems with the psalm," e.g., its thematic similarity to II Samuel 6, 7; the call to Yahweh in verse 8 to defend but not to enter Jerusalem; and the ways in which some lines clarify obscurities in other lines.

Psalm 133

1185.   Berlin, Adele. "On the Interpretation of Psalm 133," in #371, pp. 141-7.

The psalm contains a "word chain": word A in verses 1,2; word B in verses 2,3; word C in verses 3,4; etc. Word chains have not been hitherto identified in the Bible. They serve to aid our perceiving the relationships between parts of the discourse. The presence of such a chain in Psalm 133 may have led to misinterpretations of its structure.

1186.   Tsumura, David Toshio. "Sorites in Psalm 133, 2-3a." *Biblica* 61 (1980), 416-17.

A hitherto unrecognized literary device in verses 2-3 is explained: it is climax, or gradation, which enhances the parallelism in the verse.

See also: #1123.

Psalm 134

1187. Auffret, Pierre. "Note on the Literary Structure of Psalm 134." *JSOT* 45 (1989), 87-9.

The chiasmus of verses 1 and 2 "forms part of the grand rhythm of days and nights."

See also: #1123.

Psalm 136

1188. Bazak, Jacob. "The Geometric-Figurative Structure of Psalm CXXXVI." *VT* 35 (1985), 129-138.

Some biblical poems are "figure" or "pattern" poems, "shaped by an impressive aesthetic figure, composed of carefully balanced symmetric geometric patterns which help to clarify the message." The triangle visual pattern of Psalm 136 corresponds to the thematic emphasis on heavens and earth, day and night, with four parts of equal size and shape closely interrelated. Also Psalms 25, 34, 37, 111, 112, 114, 145.

Psalm 137

1189. Freedman, David Noel. "The Structure of Psalm 137," in Hans Goedicke, ed., *Near Eastern Studies in Honor of William Foxwell Albright* (Baltimore and London: Johns Hopkins UP, 1971), 187-205. Rpt in #372.

"A study of the Psalm, with particular regard for its stylistic devices and metrical structure, should provide us with some insight into the state of the art in the sixth century, during the last great period of classic Hebrew poetry."

1190. Halle, Morris. "A Biblical Pattern Poem," in Nigel Fabb, et al., eds., *The Linguistics of Writing: Arguments Between Language and Literature* (New York: Methuen, 1987), 67-75.

A vowel-counting meter used in the composition of some OT verse, chiefly instanced here in Psalm 137. The regularities observed in OT poems using this method imply written rather than oral composition. "The psalm therefore is the creation of a literate poet writing for a literate audience exploiting possibilities provided by the fact that his medium is simultaneously both phonetic and graphic." Such pattern poems can be found in many other ancient as well as modern cultures and languages.

1191.   Halle, Morris, and John J. McCarthy. "The Metrical Structure of Psalm 137." *JBL* 100 (1981), 161-7.

Proposed metrical analysis of Psalm 137 based on a "specific syllable counting algorithm" valid at least for this poem, though not necessarily for other OT verse. The theory takes the work of David Freedman [#1189] as starting point, but differs from him in some particulars.

1192.   Lenowitz, Harris. "The Mock-śimhâ of Psalm 137," in #371, pp. 149-159.

The term seems to denote a specific type of song: the song of joy. Such a mock-song of joy lies at the center of Psalm 137. Since it is aimed at the Babylonians and Edomites who do not speak Hebrew, the poet can engage in mockery undetected.

*   Magonet, Jonathan. "Some Concentric Structures in Psalms." See #1198.

1193.   Shea, William H. "*Qînāh* Meter and Strophic Structure in Psalm 137." *HAR* 8 (1984), 199-214.

Through a "new structural analysis" we can prove the presence of *Qînah* meter in Psalm 137: in its five central bicola, in its serving as framing device in strophes II and IV, in the meter of strophe III, and in couplets and strophic groups.

See also: #s 1151, 1258.

Psalm 138

1194.   Holman, J. "Semiotic Analysis of Psalm cxxxviii (LXX)." *OS* 26 (1990), 84-100.

The theories of A.J. Greimas applied to the "discoursive syntax" of Psalm 138 (Septuagint) shows that the transformations are found on the level of actorialization: the actors "I" and "Thou." Its theme is "a spiritual growing process of the "I" within an I-Thou relationship. Analysis of surface and of deep structures.

Psalm 139

1195. Holman, Jan. "The Structure of Psalm CXXXIX." *VT* 21 (1971), 298-310.

Psalm 139 shows a strong unity of thought apparent in, among other characteristics, its use of inclusio and antithesis. The poem may have served as an *apologia* if the poet was being questioned about pagan sun-worship.

Psalm 145

1196. Berlin, Adele. "The Rhetoric of Psalm 145," in Ann Kort and Scott Morschauser, eds., *Biblical and Related Studies Presented to Samuel Iwry* (Winona Lake: Eisenbrauns, 1985), 17-22.

Linguistic and structural clues in the psalm "in order to elucidate its purpose and to show how it achieved this purpose." Its use of acrostic, inclusio, key words, major subdivisions, verbal shifts and movement.

* Liebreich, Leon. "Psalms 34 and 145 in the Light of their Key Words." See #1152.

1197. Lindars, Barnabas. "The Structure of Psalm cxlv." *VT* 39 (1989), 23-30.

Psalm 145 is one of several "alphabet" psalms. Variations in their structure may be caused by artistic considerations. Relationship between structure and meaning; use of other devices with visual appeal.

1198. Magonet, Jonathan. "Some Concentric Structures in Psalms." *HJ* 23 (1982), 365-376.

Concentric structures in Psalms 145, 92, and 137; the value of such an approach in interpreting these psalms.

See also: #s 458, 1188.

Psalm 147

See #458.

Psalm 149

1199.   Ceresko, A.R. "Psalm 149: Poetry, Themes (Exodus and Conquest), and Social Function." *Biblica* 67 (1986), 177-194

Psalm 149 has presented difficulties because of a seemingly contradictory combination of peace language and war language. The question is: how does the psalm promote aspects of the social model of early Israel through its literary devices?

Psalm 151

1200.   Storfjell, J. Bjørnar. "The Chiastic Structure of Psalm 151." *AUSS* 25 (1987), 97-106.

The Qumran text is from an alternate tradition to the Septuagint. Its chiasmus is not limited to the structure, but includes thematic elements also: a contrast-of-ideas approach which is able to address abstract philosophical questions.

JOB

1201.   Albertson, R.G. "Job and Ancient Near Eastern Wisdom Literature," in William W. Hallo, et al., eds., *Scripture in Context II: More Essays on the Comparative Method* (Winona Lake: Eisenbrauns, 1983), 213-230.

The Job motif "in the context of its own biblical setting and in that of Ancient Near Eastern Wisdom Literature ... similarities and differences, continuity and creative variation, contribute to the discovery of its integrity as a Biblical book."

1202.   Baker, John Austin. "The Book of Job: Unity and Meaning," in E.A. Livingstone, ed., *Studia Biblica 1978 I: Papers on Old Testament and Related Themes* (Sheffield: JSOT P, 1979), 17-26.

We cannot eliminate portions of Job—e.g., the Prologue, Epilogue, or Eliphaz speeches, since they are all necessary parts of a unified work. Its unity lies chiefly in its being "a magnificently sustained piece of dramatic irony," and knowledge of this fact is a prerequisite for grasping its suspense and its message. The meaning of Job is that, though human life is morally random, "this randomness has within it the greatest of all possibilities for us, the opportunity to do what is right and good whether or not it is for our advantage."

1203. Barr, James. "The Book of Job and its Modern Interpreters." *BJRL* 54 (1971-2), 28-46.

The literary significance of Job in terms of its structure; nature and importance of the dialogue; characterization; and theme. Survey of previous research on Job. Its theme is not about suffering, but is contained in our answer to the question: What does God mean in 42:7?

1204. "Symposium: Paul Ricoeur and Biblical Hermeneutics." *Biblical Research* 24-25 (1979-80).

An issue devoted to the "contributions, implications, and promise of Paul Ricoeur's writings for biblical interpretation." Essays by André Lacocque on Job, John D. Crossan on the parables, and Lewis Mudge on Ricoeur's work in general.

1205. Cook, Albert. *The Root of the Thing: A Study of Job and the Song of Songs.* Bloomington (Indiana UP), 1968.

The Bible is literature, but a special form which cannot be treated simply on the aesthetic level. There is drama all thoughout the Bible, but it exists in its purest form in Job and Song of Songs. The book of Job does not ask why Job had to suffer in order to perceive; rather it dramatizes his coming to understanding through suffering. The Song of Songs may be distant from the rest of the Bible in letter, but is close to it in spirit. Its "eros" somehow transcends eroticism and speaks of love.

1206. Cooper, Alan. "Narrative Theory and the Book of Job." *SR* 11 (1982), 35-44.

Study of the Bible as literature has always been comparative, since we possess no ancient Hebrew "Poetics." Recent attempts to apply genre theories to Job argue that Job is comic, ironic, or absurd, but this is erroneous. The plot structure of Job is chiastic. Job's blasphemy requires an appropriate response from God. God is absurd only if we assume he is supposed to answer Job's complaints.

1207. Daiches, David. "God Under Attack," in *God and the Poets* (Oxford: Clarendon P, 1984), 1-25.

"What emerges [from Job] is that the only real answer to Job's question is that there is no answer. The universe is more complicated than man can ever hope to understand, so he had better refrain from discussing the principles on which it is run."

1208.   Dion, Paul E. "Formulaic Language in the Book of Job." *SR* 16 (1987), 187-193.

Formulaic language in Job is not only echoed in other OT books, but in other ancient Near Eastern literature as well. Much of this language is laden with irony.

1209.   Feinberg, Charles L. "The Poetic Structure of the Book of Job and the Ugaritic Literature," in John F. Walvoord, ed., *Truth for Today: Biblioteca Sacra Reader* (Chicago: Moody P, 1963), 133-142.

Review of previous work on Hebrew metrics, and on poetry in Job. Job is an epic poem with a "3 + 3" meter. Other poetic devices in Job. The book of Job seems to have "definite points of contact" with Ugaritic poetry.

1210.   Fisch, Harold. "Job as Modern Archetype." *HUSLA* 11 (1983), 102-114.

Job as a creation poem which is a "visionary antithesis" of Genesis 1-2. In fact, it offers "a questioning of all stability and order whatever." Its literary form is not dialogue or monologue but "speech suspended in a void." Modern examples of Hebrew writers "for whom Jobian archetype is central."

1211.   Fontaine, Carol. "Folktale Structure in the Book of Job: A Formalist Reading," in #371, pp. 205-232.

Two important problems concerning Job are its genre, and the relationship between its prose and poetic sections. This poetry-prose juxtaposition seems to exist throughout the ancient Near East in both literary and folk forms. The Prologue and Epilogue of Job exhibit structural features of a folktale. The poetic sections "also follow and continue that folktale in structure, thus providing a key to ... several intriguing features." The theories of Vladimir Propp help us with the morphology of Job. The book is a "victim-hero" type of poeticized folktale.

1212.   Freedman, David Noel. "The Book of Job," in William Henry Propp, et al., eds., *The Hebrew Bible and its Interpreters* (Winona Lake: Eisenbrauns, 1990), 33-51.

Job is a forceful literary unity, despite the rough transitions between its parts. The book shows, as does the HB generally, that "the evidence points to a mystery at the center of the human person, a mystery that even God respects so that the ultimate truth of

human commitment can only be decided by time and testing....
One of the few conclusive points of the book [is that] friends
should be friends, not judges."

1213. Frieden, Ken. "Job's Encounters with the Adversary." Rpt
Harold Bloom, ed., *The Book of Job: Modern Critical Interpre-
tations* (New York, New Haven and Philadelphia: Chelsea
House, 1988), 91-102, from *Response* 14 (1975), 91-102.

"... Job is essentially a book about questions and assertions, a
book that leads us to consider the significance of theological questioning." Close reading of chapters 1, 4, 10, 13, 37, 38, 40, and 42.
There are echoes in Job from other books of the HB. When God
appears, he reaffirms not facts or dogmatic assertions but "the necessity of questions." "Job learns, most profoundly, a way of approaching God through language and its annulment."

1214. Frye, J.B. "The Use of Mašal in the Book of Job." *Semitics* 5
(1977), 59-66.

No one generic identification of Job is totally convincing. We
must recognize that its use of *masal* is important in the rhetoric of
the book as "the rhetoric of appeal to established reason," even
though it is not the dominant legal mode of the speeches in the
book.

1215. Gardner, Helen. "Tragedy in the Ancient World," in *Religion and Literature* (London: Faber and Faber, 1971), 38-
60.

The literary qualities of Genesis 1-2 and Job, among other texts.
Contrary to those who would see the Prologue and Epilogue of Job
as not integral to the rest of the book, Job in fact has literary integrity. Genesis 1-2 is a "tremendous leap of the imagination."

1216. Genung, John F. "The Book of Job as Literature," in #32,
pp. 77-87.

Like all of the world's greatest literature, Job deals profoundly
with the problem of suffering. "Its melody is solemn and sublime,
requiring the chastened ear to hear; but, rightly heard, it strikes
the deepest chords of the human and the divine."

1217. Glatzer, Nahum N., ed. *The Dimensions of Job: A Study and Selected Readings*. New York (Schocken), 1969.

Glatzer surveys the history of the interpretation of Job and the
chief issues involved; other sections of "selected modern readings"
of Job: Judaic traditions, Christian traditions, humanist readings,

the issue of theodicy, "The Ways of God Are Mystery," "Job as Lesson in Faith."

1218.   Good, Edwin M. *In Turns of Tempest: A Reading of Job, with a Translation.* Stanford (Stanford UP), 1990.

"Job turns back on itself, weaves from side to side in search of never-found certainty, and ends at a more ambiguous place than it began." The book "steadfastly refuses to reveal any unitary truth to us.... If we are to find truth in Job, it must come from the whole book, it must be ringed around with doubt and uncertainty, and it must be something other than the truth with which we came to the book."

1219.   Good, Edwin M. "Job and the Literary Task: A Response." *Soundings* 56 (1973), 470-484.

Despite much that is original and compelling in the interpretation of David Robertson [see #1241], it does not work as well as mine because his methodology is faulty: it is too much concerned about historical-critical (source-critical) terms. It also commits the intentional fallacy. His argument about the significance of Job's curses in chapters 29-31 is new and revealing, but his conclusion that both God and Job are frauds won't do.

1220.   Gordis, Robert. *The Book of God and Man: A Study of Job.* Chicago (U of Chicago P), 1965.

Job is not, as some think, an attack on basic Israelite religious concepts. Its major theme is that the residuum of the unknown in this world shouldn't force us to conclude that faith in the basic moral goodness of the universe is misplaced. Its secondary theme is that suffering can serve as a source of moral discipline, and is thus a spur to moral perfection. The background of Job in the law and the prophets; connections with biblical and Near Eastern wisdom literatures; plot and structure; language and style, use of quotations, and Job's "rhetoric of allusion and analogy"; provenance and date. **

1221.   Gordis, Robert. "The Temptation of Job—Tradition Versus Experience in Religion." *Judaism* 4 (1955), 195-208.

We must recognize the strong intellectual content of Job. Its theme is "the conflict between the accepted tradition of the group and the personal experience of the individual." Job's tragedy is an existential one; he has an "unswerving allegiance to the truth" of his own experience.

1222. Gordis, Robert. "Traumatic Surgery in Biblical Scholarship: A Note on Methodology." *JJS* 32 (1981), 195-9.

James Barr's review of my *Book of Job* would have benefitted from a consideration of my theory of virtual quotation in the HB. It is a stylistic device related to allusion and analogy which reveals the unity of Job to us.

1223. Greenberg, Moshe. "Job," in #33, pp. 288-304.

The chief literary problem of Job is whether it possesses coherence; how the prose and poetry are related, and how the Elihu section fits. Its literary complexity "is consistent with and appropriate to the nature of the issues with which it deals." We should not exaggerate the prose-poetry differences in content or style. Explication of structure and theme. Poetic quality.

1224. Gros Louis, Kenneth R.R. "The Book of Job," in #39, pp. 226-266.

Job presents a "stunningly timeless situation." It is a dialogue, whether or not it might be a drama or a poem. There are two threads in its dialogue: the earthly discussion of the problem of evil and suffering; and the shifts in Job's attitude toward God. It develops many themes, including disinterested righteousness; suffering of the innocent; limitations of religious dogma; inscrutability of God; and the necessity of turning away from evil, no matter what God is like.

1225. Grossvogel, David I. "Conclusion: Job and the Unendurable Mystery," in *Mystery and its Fictions: From Oedipus to Agatha Christie* (Baltimore and London: Johns Hopkins UP, 1979), 181-7.

Our "awareness of our non-awareness and our refusal to accept it are as old as our race." God expresses approval of Job but not of the friends because Job is aware of the ultimate mystery of existence whereas the friends think that easy answers are all we need." Job represents a sublime thrust, the furthest extension and frustration of the human will to understand."

1226. Habel, Norman C. *The Book of Job: A Commentary*. Philadelphia (Westminster P), 1985.

Introduction (pp. 21-73) discusses literary issues concerning Job: narration, plot, imagery, structure, parallelism, repetition, allusion, irony, metaphors, analogy, and theme.

1227. Hoffman, Yair. "Irony and the Book of Job." *Immanuel* 17 (1983-4), 7-21.

Irony is a problem in religious writing, given its tendency to deflect the message or make its expression complex and thus easy to miss. Irony occurs in the wisdom literature, and is especially prevalent in Job in three ways: remarks by the characters; between author and reader; and the author's self-irony. The Prologue is especially important "in structuring the work and shaping its ironic tone." Without irony and dialectic, Job's suffering would not affect us.

1228.   Irwin, William A. "Job and Prometheus." *JR* 30 (1950), 90-108.

Comparison of Job with Aeschylus' tragedy shows that the author of Job did not flinch from life's brutality; that he equals Aeschylus in "candor of criticism," and surpasses him in "comprehensiveness."

1229.   Kallen, Horace M. *The Book of Job as a Greek Tragedy.* 2nd edition. New York (Hill and Wang), 1959 [1st edition, 1918].

In its original form, Job was a Greek tragedy written in the manner of Euripides. The author was "aware of Euripides' tragic form, but un-Greek in his emulation of it; ... he followed the Greek precedent by framing his heresy in orthodox events and symbols.... [T]he form that he gave his tragedy was scrambled from the dramatic to the narrative when Job was added to the canonical Scriptures...."

1230.   Koops, Robert. "Rhetorical Questions and Implied Meaning in the Book of Job." *BT* 39 (1988), 415-423.

Analysis of the rhetorical questions in Job based on intentionality, reader-response, and speech-act theory. Levels of inference in the book. Job "illustrates the wide variety of rhetorical devices and discourse features that are present in many of the Hebrew Scriptures," though unfortunately much is lost on many readers in translation, and due to their unfamiliarity with rhetoric.

1231.   Lichtenstein, Aaron. "Irony in the Book of Job." *Dor le Dor* 13 (1984-5), 41-2.

The central puzzle in Job is: since the author confirms the righteousness of Job, why does a just God punish him? The Prologue provides the answer, since we know, while Job does not, that it is all to test Job.

1232.   Lichtenstein, Aaron. "Toward a Literary Understanding of the Book of Job." *HS* 20/21 (1979-80), 34-5.

Analysis based on the idea that the central puzzle in Job is the question of how a just God can torment Job.

1233. Miller, Ward S. "The Structure and Meaning of Job." *Concordia Journal* 15 (1989), 103-120.

Use of antitheses and contrasts in Job, including positive and negative themes and their interaction, and in characterization. The symmetry of the book; its masterful literary skill.

1234. Murphy, Roland E. *Wisdom Literature: Job, Proverbs, Ruth, Canticles, Ecclesiastes, and Esther*. Grand Rapids (Eerdmans), 1981.

Commentary which devotes considerable space to questions of genre, style, literary devices, and form.

1235. Parsons, Gregory W. "Literary Features of the Book of Job." *B Sac* 138 (1981), 213-229.

Job does not belong to any one genre, but interweaves three major ones: lawsuit, lament, and controversy dialogue. The author employs irony and mythopoeic language to show that man's relationship to God is not that of a business contract binding in court.

1236. Parsons, Gregory W. "The Structure and Purpose of the Book of Job." *B Sac* 138 (1981), 139-157.

The structure of Job is based on the symmetry of enclosed poetic body in the Epilogue and Prologue. The fact of a lack of symmetry at the end of the third cycle of speeches focuses the reader's attention on the futility of this dialogue with the friends, and on the need to resolve the main problem: the proper relationship between man and God.

1237. Penchansky, David. *The Betrayal of God: Ideological Conflict in Job*. Louisville (Westminster/John Knox P), 1990.

Read through the literary theories of Fredric Jameson and Pierre Macherey, Job becomes "a powerful example of the disparate text, an act of literature that is characteristically unstable, a place of conflict. Elements of Job come from differenmt genres; and the juxtaposition of parts produces obvious seams and gaping fissures in the text, in style, and in theological concern." Instead of trying to harmonize or stabilize the work to make it conform to some ideology, the critic should reflect upon those aspects of the text which resist his own reading.

1238. Polzin, Robert. "The Framework of the Book of Job." *Interpretation* 28 (1974), 182-200.

A central concern of Job is the contradiction between what a member of society should believe and what he actually believes. Parts of Job should not be separated from the whole, since the inconsistencies are part of the message: the contradiction between what we are taught to believe about God and what we experience in our daily lives.

1239.   Richards, I.A. *Beyond.* New York and London (Harcourt Brace Jovanovich), 1973, 1974.

The relationship of the Prologue and Epilogue to the poems, especially the usually ignored inconsistencies. Job compared to Plato's *Republic* on the question of the source of evil: "... it is clear that the contrast as to the source of evil ... could hardly be greater."

1240.   Ricoeur, Paul. "The Reaffirmation of the Tragic," in *The Symbolism of Evil* (New York: Harper and Row, 1967), 310-326.

The movement from the Adamic myth to the tragic myth "rests on the ethical vision itself ... [where] suffering emerges as an enigma." Tragedy was "killed twice, by the philosophical Logos and by the Judeo-Christian Kerygma, [but] it survived its double death.... The theme of the wrath of God" remained and remains.

1241.   Robertson, David. "The Book of Job: A Literary Study." *Soundings* 56 (1973), 446-469.

A variety of critical approaches to Job is necessary. The unfolding of the plot against the reader's expectations; the poet's deliberate reversals. God seems to think in the same "either-or" terms as do the friends; this "makes God the object of ... bitter irony." God is finally a tyrant, and showing this is the poet's way of curing our fears. See #1219.

1242.   Rowley, H.H. "The Book of Job and its Meaning." *BJRL* 41 (1958-9), 167-207.

We must reject the various proposals which would see some part(s) of Job as not original to the book. The qualities of different parts of the dialogue with the friends and with God. The meaning of Job lies in "the wresting of profit from the suffering through the enrichment of the fellowship of God."

1243.   Sawyer, John F.A. "The Authorship and Structure of the Book of Job," in E.A. Livingstone, ed., *Studia Biblica 1978 I: Papers on Old Testament and Related Themes* (Sheffield: JSOT P, 1979), 253-7.

There are two pieces of hitherto neglected evidence that Job is a "creative composition rather than arbitrary compilation": its variety of material is typical of the OT, even to the point of exhibiting considerable stylistic differences within one work; and the overall structure shows symmetry and dramatic unity. How chapter 28 fits, and confirms the structural pattern.

1244. Scafella, Frank. "A Reading of Job." *JSOT* 14 (1979), 63-7.

"Thus the literary classic ... will marshal ... the entire sensibility of the willing reader and march him forward into regions of human experience ... where he comes to understanding.... Then he is ready to take up and consider questions of history, myth, theology and cultic practice."

1245. Schökel, Luis Alonso. "Toward a Dramatic Reading of the Book of Job." *Semeia* 7 (1977), 45-61.

Imaginative staging of Job to discover the interplay of the characters among themselves and with the audience. Themes of ignorance, irony, and commitment emerge through this exercise. The tension between two conceptions of divine justice in Job. Responses by James L. Crenshaw, James G. Williams, and William J. Urbrock, pp. 63-9, 135-143, 147-154.

1246. Seeskin, Kenneth. "Job and the Problem of Evil." *Philosophy and Literature* 11 (1987), 226-241.

"... indignation and awe are as close as we will ever get to a 'solution' to the problem of evil.... The book suggests they are capable of existing together in the person of the prophet.... [He] is able to live with himself and attain a measure of dignity ... who even in agony can rise to heroic proportions."

1247. Selms, A. van. "Motivated Interrogative Sentences in the Book of Job." *Semitics* 6 (1978), 28-35.

Such sentences are a frequent stylistic device in Job, though they are not typical of wisdom literature but of the language of the *rîb*: stating a case by a person who has been wronged when preparing his formal *dîn* before the judge.

1248. Sewall, Richard B. "The Book of Job," in *The Vision of Tragedy*. New edition enlarged. New Haven (Yale UP), 1980, 9-24.

"... we can see with striking clarity in the writings of the ancient Hebrews the vision which we now call tragic, and in the book of Job the basic elements of the tragic form, [although] ... the rebellious Job was not typical" of ancient Hebrew heroes.

1249. Simmons, Robert E. "Ways of Teaching Job," in #179, pp. 124-6.

William Blake's illustrations to Job may be used for various reasons: their intrinsic interest, complexity and detail; their symbolic/allegoric reading of Job; and their ability to spark debate about issues which Job raises.

1250. Smick, Elmer B. "Architectonics, Structure Poems, and Rhetorical Devices," in Walter C. Kaiser, Jr., and Ronald F. Youngblood, eds., *A Tribute to Gleason Archer* (Chicago: Moody Press, 1986), 87-104.

The overall structure of Job is chiastic. Close reading of chapters 13-14, 27, 28-31, and 38-41 "reveal[s] a drive toward symmetry" in their structure.

1251. Tsevat, Matitiahu. "The Meaning of the Book of Job." *HUCA* 37 (1966), 73-106; rpt #1088, pp. 341-374.

"From the contradictions of Job there is a way to truth, from the consistencies of the friends, none." This understanding is arrived at by considering the demythologizing tendency of Job and of the entire HB. The literary nature of Job determines its means of presenting its theological insights.

1252. Urbrock, William J. "Job as Drama: Tragedy or Comedy?" *Currents in Theology and Mission* 8 (1981), 35-40.

The history of attempts to interpret Job as drama, especially as tragedy. To approach it as drama is to "find ourselves running the gauntlet between the ridiculous and the sublime, the tragic and the comic." To do so is to penetrate its innermost secrets of life.

1253. Whedbee, J.W. "The Comedy of Job." *Semeia* 7 (1977), 1-39; rpt #231, pp. 217-249.

The problem of the dominant genre of Job is perennial and frustrating. The most apt designation is comedy, based on three definitional criteria: perception of incongruities and irony; a basic plot line which ends with a harmonious society; and the presence of caricature and parody. Responses by David Robertson, James G. Williams, and William J. Urbrock, pp. 41-44, 135-143, 147-154.

1254. Whybray, R.N., et al. [Discussions of Robert Alter's *The Art of Biblical Narrative* (#303)]. *JSOT* 27 (1983), 75-117.

Application of the principles enunciated in Alter's book to Job, among other topics discussed.

1255.   Williams, James G. "Job's Vision: The Dialectic of Person and Presence." *HAR* 8 (1984), 259-272.

Job experiences simultaneously the otherness and the nearness of God, his differentness and yet his similarity to God.

1256.   Zuckerman, Bruce. *Job the Silent: A Study in Historical Counterpoint.* New York and Oxford (Oxford UP), 1991.

The study of Job offers us two conundrums: Why the tradition of the patient Job, when he is anything but patient? and, "How can one make sense of the literary structure of Job when it actually seems to be strained by its thematic contraries to the point of collapse?" The answer lies in the concept of thematic counterpoint: Job began as an attack upon tradition, but ended by embodying it. Each new reading forces the original themes into new combinations.

See also: #s 7, 11, 12, 17, 23, 25, 130, 166, 175, 178, 182, 190, 198, 206, 209, 211, 218, 219, 370, 381, 422, 452, 476, 1087, 1092, 1546.

Job 1-37

1257.   Bakon, Shimon. "The Enigma of Elihu." *Dor le Dor* 12 (1983-4), 217-228.

The character of Elihu forms an appropriate transition to the epiphany of God in Job 38-41. Elihu may well have been a real person, and perhaps even the author of Job.

1258.   Blank, Sheldon H. "An Effective Literary Device in Job XXXI." *JJS* 2 (1951), 105-7.

Chapter 31 is a crucial point in Job, for here he sums up his case before God; he does so by means of the literary device of the oath. Normally the oath-taker evades and suppresses the actual calamity which befalls him. There are only three examples of oaths in the HB with nothing suppressed: Psalms 7 and 137, and Job 31. This chapter is intended as a dramatic climax, and shows that the author thought Job innocent.

1259.   Clark, David J. "In Search of Wisdom: Notes on Job 28." *BT* 33 (1982), 409-13.

Examination of the poetic structure of a biblical book can help
translators by showing them the general flow and outline, how similar verses are related, and a greater appreciation of the literary
skills of biblical authors.

1260. Clines, David J.A. "The Arguments of Job's Three Friends,"
        in #34, pp. 199-214.

        There are three rhetorical elements in the friends' speeches rel-
        evant to their coherence and distinctiveness. The speeches are dis-
        tinct from one another, with each exhibiting coherence. Detection
        of these qualities is assisted by noticing the rhetorical features of
        the speeches: tonality, *topoi*, and verb modality, among others.
        Thus the static style of the friends' arguments matches the lack of
        development in their thinking as the dialogue proceeds.

1261. Clines, D.J.A. "False Naivety in the Prologue to Job." *HAR* 9
        (1985), 127-136.

        Contrasts between the language of the Prologue, which is severe
        and seemingly artless, and that of the rest of the book. This is,
        however, a "false naivety [which] exploits the appearance of art-
        lessness to convey a subtle message." That message concerns the
        inexplicability of Job's suffering in human eyes, but not in God's.
        Job suffers for God's sake.

1262. Cooper, Alan. "Reading and Misreading the Prologue to
        Job." *JSOT* 46 (1990), 67-79.

        There are three basic ways of reading Job, and each will be
        rooted in sympathy for one of the three characters in the Pro-
        logue: Satan, Job, and God. The Prologue is, by design, the intro-
        duction to all three possible readings.

1263. Curtis, John Briggs. "Elihu and Deutero-Isaiah: A Study in
        Literary Dependence." *PEGL* 10 (1990), 31-8.

        "... the author of the Elihu speeches is fully conversant with Isa-
        iah 40-55 and makes frequent use of ideas from Deutero-Isaiah, al-
        ways freely adapting these ideas to the needs of the Job story." The
        author "seems to have sought to present Elihu as reinforcing ...
        certain Deutero-Isianic ideas while correcting and purifying those
        concepts ... inadequately treated by Deutero-Isaiah." The key one
        is the idea of the Servant.

1264. Curtis, John Briggs. "Why Were the Elihu Speeches Added
        to the Book of Job?" *PEGL* 8 (1988), 93-99.

        The dramatic differences in style between the Elihu speeches
        and that of the rest of Job are quite deliberate on the part of the

original author, who wished to present Elihu as the "reductio ad absurdum" of traditional theology. Once he has spoken, traditional dogma can no longer be defended. We can only wait to see what God can say in his own behalf.

1265. Forrest, Robert W.E. "The Two Faces of Job: Imagery and Integrity in the Prologue," in Lyle Eslinger and Glen Taylor, eds., *Ascribe to the Lord: Biblical and Other Studies in Memory of Peter C. Craigie* (Sheffield: JSOT P, 1988), 385-398.

We can see the unity of the Prologue and dialogue in Job by noting the "ironic level of discourse in the poem," and the implication that, even in the Prologue, "underneath his integrity Job may wish to curse God...."

1266. Habel, Norman C. "The Role of Elihu in the Design of the Book of Job," in W. Boyd Barrick and John R. Spencer, eds., *In the Shelter of Elyon* (Sheffield: JSOT P, 1984), 81-98.

Attempts to fit Elihu into the literary design of Job have failed because their focus has been theological, not literary. Elihu in fact plays an important role, even if he were found to be saying nothing new. The author of Job had Elihu appear at the point where Job has called for a formal public hearing before God. Even though God later criticizes Elihu, he is important as representing a younger generation's mistaken attempt to defend God. Thus he is not just repeating the three friends' arguments.

1267. Hoffman, Yair. "The Relation Between the Prologue and the Speech-Cycles in Job: A Reconsideration." *VT* 31 (1981), 160-170.

The Prologue and the speeches are "essential and original components in one integral artistic work...." Various theories which argue the contrary and their shortcomings. The ambivalence between Prologue and speeches is not a sign of separate authorship, but a conscious literary device and an expression of the author's dialectic approach to the problems he raises. He aimed the book at both believing and skeptic readers.

1268. Holbert, J.C. "'The Skies Will Uncover His Iniquity': Satire in the Second Speech of Zophar." *VT* 31 (1981), 171-9.

Contrary to most commentators' views, Zophar does answer Job's speech in chapter 19. His reply provides "additional and powerful proof" that Job's cry for a vindicator is not for God but for a third party. Satire is the key to grasping the relationship between Job's speeches and those of his friends.

1269. Holland, J.A. "On the Form of the Book of Job." *Australian Journal of Biblical Archaeology* 2 (1972), 160-177.

The form of Job and of Aristophanic comedy are analogous. The model of the Alazon in this comedy is close enough to the Elihu speeches to provide attractive answers for many of the "chief conundrums" (often structural ones) which have bothered commentators on Job since ancient times. The *agon* of Job is chapters 3-21, and probably 3-31. The absurdity of Job's problems and of his restoration to fortune become clear. At a minimum, bringing in Aristophanic comedy helps us see the unity of Job.

1270. van der Lugt, Pieter. "Stanza-Structure and Word Repetition in Job 3-14." *JSOT* 40 (1988), 3-38.

Each chapter of Job from 3 to 14 comprises an individual poem; each poem is constructed of two or three stanzas, with other recognizable poetic structuring devices present as well. This analysis of structure reveals hitherto unnoticed connections among these chapters.

1271. van der Lugt, Pieter. "Strophes and Stanzas in the Book of Job: A Historical Survey" and "The Form and Function of the Refrains in Job 28: Some Comments Relating to the 'Strophic Structure' of Hebrew Poetry," in #382, pp. 235-293.

Problems the critic encounters in deciding on the structure of Job 28, as shown by recent critical work. Chapter 28 shows "a very rigid poetic framework," though with a vivid flow of ideas and verbal repetitions supporting strophic structures.

1272. Moore, Rick D. "The Integrity of Job." *CBQ* 45 (1983), 17-31.

The interpretation of Job pivots on the issue of whether the prose and poetry form an integrated whole. The poet sought not thematic continuity between poetry and narrative, but disjunction. That is, Job 3 is a negative commentary on 1:21. Job's existential honesty receives God's rebuke but the poet's sympathy. Canon-makers, however, wanted the two together as part of their "dialectic between the real and the ideal" from which faith springs.

1273. Perdue, Leo G. "Job's Assault on Creation." *HAR* 10 (1986), 295-315.

Wisdom texts, silent about salvation history, covenant, etc., greatly emphasize myths of creation: cosmology and anthropology. Job 3 destabilizes and negates these creation myths and the metaphors which express them. Because these myths and metaphors are at the center of creation traditions, Job's attack is far more than personal.

1274. Selms, Adrianus van. "A Composition Device in the Book of Job." *Semitics* 10 (1989), 1-9.

The "dichotomic elaboration of a dual theme" in Job, where the development of the second theme is delayed or suspended beyond where we expect it. It occurs in chapters 3 and 7, and the whole of 14, 23, 30, 36 and 37. It is found in no other books of the HB, and is necessary to be aware of if we are to grasp the meaning of these key passages in Job.

1275. Webster, Edwin C. "Strophic Patterns in Job 29-42." *JSOT* 30 (1984), 95-109.

Analysis of the strophic patterns of chapters 29-42, using using the same criteria as in #1276 below.

1276. Webster, Edwin C. "Strophic Patterns in Job 3-28." *JSOT* 26 (1983), 33-60.

Detailed analysis of these patterns show that they are what create the basic integrity of the book of Job by providing various numerical, concentric, and quotational links.

1277. Weiss, Meir. *The Story of Job's Beginning. Job 1-2: A Literary Analysis.* Jerusalem (Magnes P), 1983.

How form and content interrelate in the prose prologue to Job. The Prologue is a literary unit, functioning much like the first act of a play: it establishes "the dramatic situation from which all that is contained in the book develops and proceeds." The author's genius is shown just as much in chapters 1-2 as preparation for what follows as it is in the powerful poetry of chapters 3-39. Satan as destroyer of the distributive justice worldview.

See also: #s 223, 254, 327, 377, 402, 411, 437.

Job 38-42

1278. Alter, Robert. "The Voice from the Whirlwind." *Commentary* 77, #1 (January, 1984), 33-41. Rpt as chapter 4 of #365.

Everyone knows the power of the book of Job, but its structure has been a puzzlement. How the resources of poetry are marshalled in Job 38 and 41 to give intimation of the divine perspective.

1279. Brenner, Athalya. "Job the Pious? The Characterization of Job in the Narrative Framework of the Book." *JSOT* 43 (1989), 37-52.

The absence of the Satan from the Epilogue of Job is part of an overall literary strategy to signal the author's differences with the ideology in his sources. The prose-poetry contrast is also itself an intentional literary strategy, not just a respect for traditional style; it shows the author's integrity as well as "the subtlety and sophistication of [his] literary technique...."

1280. Clines, David. "Deconstructing the Book of Job," in #1517, pp. 65-80.

The Epilogue of Job deconstructs the rest of the book because it shows distributive justice in operation, even though 3:1–42:6 had emphasized that such a theory is "naive, dangerous, inhuman and above all, false." The Epilogue also deconstructs itself because, though Job's suffering is an experiment in causality, and therefore the reason for his suffering is never the reason for anyone else's, our instincts impel us in the opposite direction—i.e., toward believing that Job's sufferings illuminate ours.

1281. Crossan, John Dominic, ed., *Semeia 19: The Book of Job and Ricoeur's Hermeneutics.* Chico (Scholars P), 1981.

Six essays by various scholars on Ricoeur and the book of Job, particularly on his interpretation of chapter 38. Six shorter responses to these essays by other scholars.

1282. Jamieson-Drake, David W. "Literary Structure, Genre and Interpretation in Job 38," in Kenneth G. Hoglund, et al., eds., *The Listening Heart: Essays in Wisdom and the Psalms in Honor of Roland E. Murphy, O. Carm.* (Sheffield: JSOT P, 1987), 217-235.

Previous literary-critical analyses of Job 38-41 are helpful but lacking in the control provided by attention to literary structure. Proposes "a literary structure for Job 38 that passes both the formal and the functional tests." The goal is to move from there to identify the literary genre of Job, and in turn the thematic emphases of Job 38.

1283. Lang, Berel. "Job's Penitence." *Bucknell Review* 13 (1965), 102-112.

"Job can never again be what he has been or have what he had had. Job's penitence, the silence into which he subsides, includes now an enduring sense of loss, a new sense of the corrosive texture of experience—a sense which he shares, we have reason to believe, with the God who communicated it to him."

1284. MacKenzie, R.A.F., S.J. "The Purpose of the Yahweh Speeches in the Book of Job." *Biblica* 40 (1959), 435-445.

The author of Job had created a problem for himself with his portrait of Job and our expectations that when God appears He will explain something. Chapters 38-39 show originality in style, especially irony, though sustaining this over seventy verses proves difficult. God's anger is therefore pretended; he is not really mad at Job. How meaning in Job emerges from these speeches. Both God and Job are justified by the end.

1285. MacKenzie, R.A.F., S.J. "The Transformation of Job." *BTB* 9 (1979), 51-57.

Job at the end of the book is a nobler, more admirable character than he was at the beginning, and more fully a man.

1286. Scholnick, Sylvia Huberman. "Poetry in the Courtroom: Job 38-41," in #371, pp. 185-204.

What the "underlying artistic structure which unifies God's words with Job's" is constitutes a critical problem in the book, as does the question, "In what way is the creation poetry in Job 38-41 an adequate response to the hero's complaints...?" God accepts accountability in a human court of law, but also in his "creation poetry" he enlightens Job about a far more complex and awesome system of justice.

*   Webster, Edwin C. "Strophic Patterns in Job 29-42." See #1275.

1287. Williams, James G. "Deciphering the Unspoken: The Theophany of Job." *HUCA* 49 (1978), 59-72.

Job 38-41 in the context of the rest of the book; relationship of form and content, use of irony and of allusions to the rest of Job. The vision of the book is amoral. "Job discloses a profound view of human existence in an uncanny world and does so in a literary style that is superb and perfectly matched to the complexities and ironies of existence itself."

1288. Williams, James G. "'You Have Not Spoken Truth of Me: Mystery and Irony in Job." *ZAW* 83 (1971), 231-255.

The paradox of Job 42:7. The significance of the frame story is its juxtaposition against the dialogue and God's speeches. Thus the poet calls into question the world of retributive justice that is presupposed elsewhere in the work. The relevance of irony, and of the *alazon* and *eiron* characters from Greek comedy. Thus the poet takes the Epilogue seriously only as it enhances the irony of the theophany and the dialogue.

See also: #s 397, 402, 1275.

PROVERBS

1289.   Bryce, Glendon E. "Another Wisdom 'Book' in Proverbs." *JBL* 91 (1972), 145-157.

Proverbs 22:17–24:22, previously thought of as a loose collection of sayings, is in fact an actual wisdom-book, modelled on a foreign type.

1290.   Bryce, Glendon E. "The Structural Analysis of Didactic Texts," in Gary A. Tuttle, ed., *Biblical and Near Eastern Studies: Essays in Honor of William Sanford La Sor* (Grand Rapids: Eerdmans, 1978), 107-121.

Structural analysis of Proverbs 25 based on the theories of Vladimir Propp and A.J. Greimas. Such analysis does not merely confirm the form critics' theory of the existence of discursive units, but brings "into sharp focus the transformational elements that do not appear on the surface of the text but that [help determine] ... the way in which meaning is realized in the text."

1291.   Byington, Steven T. "A Mathematical Approach to Hebrew Meters." *JBL* 66 (1947), 63-77.

A count of accents, syllables, and length of syllables, using Arabic prosodic terminology. The results for Proverbs 31:10-31. The average length of the feet, and how they are joined.

1292.   Camp, Claudia V. *Wisdom and the Feminine in the Book of Proverbs*. Sheffield (JSOT P), 1985.

Combination of literary, anthropological, sociological, historical, and canonical methods in order to ask, "How are we to understand the function of a highly-exalted female figure [Woman Wisdom] in a canon that is patriarchal in source and monotheistic in perspective?" We must presuppose that Wisdom should be studied by methods appropriate to poetry; that literature forms part of any religious tradition; that literary and religious forms in turn have a historical-sociological context. "Woman Wisdom" is a metaphor. Personified wisdom within and outside of Israelite religion, and in relation to female roles in the HB. Proverbs is a literary work with Woman Wisdom as its unifying force.

1293. Camp, Claudia V. "Wise and Strange: An Interpretation of the Female Imagery in Proverbs in Light of Trickster Mythology," in #229, pp. 14-36.

Compares "various manifestations of the trickster figure from comparative myth and folklore with the presentation of personified Wisdom and the Strange Woman in ... Proverbs." Such a reading "undercut[s] the book's most obvious message of absolute opposition between good and evil as represented in the female figures...."

1294. Collins, John J. "Proverbial Wisdom and the Yahwist Vision." *Semeia* 17 (1980), 1-17.

Contrary to recent arguments, proverbial wisdom, though predominantly constructive, contains debunking tendencies because of its concern for human transience and the limitations of knowledge.

1295. Crenshaw, James L. "Impossible Questions, Sayings, and Tasks." *Semeia* 17 (1980), 19-34.

The literary form of Proverbs is related to the riddle, to numerical proverbs and question/answer dialogues. Examples from Proverbs 6 and II Esdras 4.

1296. Dahood, Mitchell. "Poetic Devices in the Book of Proverbs," in Yitschak Avishur and Joshua Blau, eds., *Studies in Bible and the Ancient Near East* (Jerusalem: E. Rubenstein, 1978), 7-17.

The bearing of Canaanite poetic structure on biblical poetry in Proverbs, especially on overlooked devices such as meristic parallelism.

1297. Gilchrist, Margaret Odell. "Proverbs 1-9: Instruction or Riddle? *PEGL* 4 (1984), 131-143.

The female and sexual imagery of Proverbs 1-9 can be better understood if we see that its intention is "to point toward complexity and ambiguity in the quest for wisdom." The difficulty of getting wisdom, this imagery tells us, is that doing so is a matter of the will and the heart. "... while Proverbs 1-9 may be rooted in the genre of instruction, it functions quite differently."

1298.   Glück, J.J. "The Figure of 'Inversion' in the Book of Proverbs." *Semitics* 5 (1977), 24-31.

Inversion is commonly encountered but seldom discussed in Proverbs. It reverses accepted syntax for the sake of variety or emphasis, though not needed to accommodate meter or rhyme scheme.

1299.   Irwin, William H. "The Metaphor in Prov 11,30." *Biblica* 65 (1984), 97-100.

Failure to recognize the metaphor in the second verset of Proverbs 11:30 has made a deliberate contradiction seem to be a textual corruption; thus the meaning of the verse is often missed.

1300.   Leeuwen, Raymond C. van. *Context and Meaning in Proverbs 25-27.* Atlanta (Scholars P), 1988.

A synchronic approach is needed to solve the problem of how to understand the contexts within and outside of Proverbs which help create the meaning of chapters 25-27. "Structural (post-Saussarian), poetic, and semantic methods" to address the issue of the extent to which these seemingly self-contained chapters are part of a larger literary composition.

1301.   Lichtenstein, Murray H. "Chiasm and Symmetry in Proverbs 31." *CBQ* 44 (1982), 202-211.

This chapter consists of two distinct poems: verses 1-9, and verses 10-31, having "thematic and verbal links" as well as "striking stylistic and structural analogies.... [B]oth poems artfully exploit chiasm as a means of articulating and highlighting their own particular kinds of symmetry."

*   Murphy, Roland E. *Wisdom Literature: Job, Proverbs, Ruth, Canticles, Ecclesiastes, and Esther.* See #1234.

1302.   Murphy, Roland E., O. Carm. "Wisdom's Song: Proverbs 1:20-33." *CBQ* 48 (1986), 456-460.

Characteristics of "song" in Proverbs 1. Certain nuances have been passed over by previous critics, notably verse 23: "turn aside in my reproof" as interpretive key.

1303.   Newsom, Carol A. "Woman and the Discourse of Patriarchal Wisdom: A Study of Proverbs 1-9," in Peggy L. Day, ed.,

Gender and Difference in Ancient Israel (Minneapolis: Fortress P, 1989), 142-160.

The "explicit self-consciousness [of Proverbs 1-9] about the central role of discourses in competition provides an internal basis for questioning its own claims.... For the reader who does not take up the subject position offered by the text, Proverbs 1-9 ceases to be a simple text of initiation and becomes a text about the problematic nature of discourse itself." This is accomplished through the role played by sexual difference "in this symbolic world ... making men's speech possible but at the same time rendering it problematic...."

1304.   Robertson, David. "The Book of Proverbs." *Hudson Review* 38 (1986), 570-579.

Proverbs examined from the viewpoint of Robert P. Armstrong's aesthetic theory of synthetic (organic) and syndetic (accumulative) works of art. Proverbs is syndetic, and thus not a book with "an" overall philosophy of life. Syndetic works proceed by accretion, repetition, accumulation, and proliferation. Proverbs is "an additive list without a sum."

1305.   Thompson, John Mark. *The Form and Function of Proverbs in Ancient Israel.* The Hague and Paris (Mouton), 1974.

In the ancient Near East, the form of a proverb was poetic, its function philosophical. The wisdom tradition was not a late and foreign addition to Israelite culture, but had an influence on the prophets, and probably the law as well as Exodus and elsewhere. Hebrew religion was marked by skepticism.

1306.   Trible, Phyllis. "Wisdom Builds a Poem: The Architecture of Proverbs 1:20-33." *JBL* 94 (1975), 509-518.

These verses have a chiastic structure of four concentric circles. Detailed analysis of this pattern show that wisdom's homiletic, advisory, didactic and prophetic dimensions "have their being in this poetic form."

1307.   Williams, James G. "The Power of Form: A Study of Biblical Proverbs." *Semeia* 17 (1980), 35-58.

Artistic forms and methods in Proverbs as examples of aphoristic speech. There are three aspects of this art: juxtaposition of images and sentences; patterns of sound; and common assumptions and artistry of popular and intellectual proverbs.

1308.   Williams, James G. "Proverbs and Ecclesiastes," in #33, pp. 263-282.

These are the two chief works of the wisdom tradition. Wisdom by "articulating a sense of order.... [D]epicts a vital order informed by retributive justice and given human expression in wise utterance.... Ecclesiastes both presupposes and attacks the conventional wisdom represented by Proverbs."

1309.   Williams, James G. *Those Who Ponder Proverbs: Aphoristic Thinking and Biblical Literature.* Sheffield (Almond P), 1981.

"... aphoristic discourse [comprises] ... nonnarrative modes of reflection and poetic expression that arise out of the deeply felt ontic tension between order and disorder that are employed either to reaffirm a tradition or articulate a counter-order ... based in experiences not validated by the tradition." Proverbs is an example of order, while Qohelet and the sayings of Jesus are examples of counterorder. **

1310.   Yee, Gale A. "An Analysis of Prov 8:22-31 According to Style and Structure." *ZAW* 94 (1982), 58-66.

The Wisdom Hymn analyzed according to Hebrew rhetorical conventions reveals a highly artistic poem governed by antithetical and synonymous parallelism and (in the third strophe), chiasmus.

See also: #s 4, 11, 12, 117, 166, 175, 177, 178, 215, 252, 307, 322, 380, 397, 402, 403, 433, 435, 469, 479, 1087, 1092, 1386, 1418.

RUTH

1311.   Bal, Mieke. "Heroism and Proper Names, or the Fruits of Analogy," in #304, pp. 68-88.

The book of Ruth demonstrates "Boaz's awareness of the indispensable part of women in history."

1312.   Bernstein, Moshe J. "Two Multivalent Readings in the Ruth Narrative." *JSOT* 50 (1991), 15-26.

Two examples (in 3 and 4:11-12) of the narrator's art in Ruth which illustrate its ambivalence or ambiguity, "the conscious employment of multiple levels of meaning in the narrative"—one on the lexical, the other on the contextual, level. The function of the lexical is to "create a tension in the text which reflects a tension in the episode"; that of the contextual is to employ language with one meaning for characters but two for readers—thus indicating to readers divine blessing on the union.

1313. Bertman, Stephen. "Symmetrical Design in the Book of Ruth." *JBL* 84 (1965), 165-8.

Elements of content counterbalance one another to produce this design: e.g., large sections of chapter 2 matching large parts of chapter 3, and smaller portions of chapters 1 and 4. Symmetrical design can also be observed in the Homeric epic.

1314. Black, James. "Ruth in the Dark: Folktale, Law and Creative Ambiguity in the Old Testament." *LT* 5 (1991), 20-36.

Analyzing Ruth as a folktale or as finished narrative art need not conflict. Folktale elements in Ruth, especially the "bride in the dark" trick patterned on the narrator's obvious knowledge of Leah and Tamar. "The narrative of Ruth's adventures is especially notable for its presentation of intricate relationships and creative tensions between patriarchal law and feminine resourcefulness."

*   Bos, Johanna W.H. "Out of the Shadows: Genesis 38; Judges 4:17-22; Ruth 3." See #608.

1315. Campbell, Edward F. "The Hebrew Short Story: A Study of Ruth," in Howard N. Bream, et al., eds., *A Light Unto My Path: Old Testament Studies in Honor of Jacob M. Myers* (Philadelphia: Temple UP, 1974), 83-101.

The Hebrew short story was a distinct form, with its own rules and partly poetic style; it could be both entertaining and edifying, and was probably invented in the early monarchy period. The author of Ruth wished to combine realism with God's purposes, and correlate God's will inextricably with human action. Plot timing, tempo, use of detail, repetition of key words.

1316. Chertok, Haim. "The Book of Ruth—Complexities Within Simplicity." *Judaism* 35 (1986), 290-295.

Various well-known cruxes of characterization and plot in Ruth: e.g., Ruth the virtuous seductress, the unerring behavior of Boaz, Genesis 38 as forerunner, isolation of Boaz and Naomi, Boaz as an allegorized God, and why Tob is not chosen as Ruth's wife.

1317. Coxon, Peter W. "Was Naomi a Scold? A Response to Fewell and Gunn." *JSOT* 45 (1989), 25-37.

Their analysis [in #1322] seriously misjudges the character of Naomi; and their interpretation of the literary allusions in Ruth is forced. Their literary emphasis is helpful, but it should have been more nonrepresentational. Answered by #1321.

1318.   Feeley-Harnik, Gillian. "Naomi and Ruth: Building Up the House of David";
Greenstein, Edward L. "On Feeley-Harnik's Reading of Ruth," in #230, pp. 163-191.

Ruth depicts the transition from Judges to Kings "against the background of the transition from bondage as Pharaoh's slaves to freedom as the Lord's slaves in Exodus. As Exodus 1-2 explained the birth of the Israelites out of Egypt, so ... Ruth explains the birth of Israelite monarchy out of Moab. The point of the parallel conveyed in Ruth is that King David's monarchy is not a faithless, lawless recreation of Egypt in Canaan." Greenstein: The difficulty of placing Feeley-Harnik's literary work in a historical and anthropological context is a concern.

1319.   Fewell, Danna Nolan, and David M. Gunn. "Boaz: Pillar of Society: Measures of Worth in the Book of Ruth." *JSOT* 45 (1989), 45-59.

Boaz is trapped by, and mocks, the patriarchal system. The narrator's use of the phrase, "pillar of society" to describe Boaz is therefore deliberate and ironic. Sequel to #1322.

1320.   Fewell, Danna Nolan, and David Miller Gunn. *Compromising Redemption: Relating Characters in the Book of Ruth.* Louisville (Westminster/John Knox P), 1990.

A retelling of Ruth "as we think it might appear to other readers who are rereading the biblical story, carefully and imaginatively—and in light of our particular analysis." A literary-critical reading of Ruth focusing on the three leading characters, in terms of characterization, plot, story world, reader response to gaps, and "multivalent language."

1321.   Fewell, Danna Nolan, and David M. Gunn. "Is Coxon a Scold? On Responding to the Book of Ruth." *JSOT* 45 (1989), 39-43.

Responds to #1317; defense of their characterization of Naomi in Ruth; Coxon is "careless" in his logic and his analysis of structure.

1322.   Fewell, Danna Nolan, and David M. Gunn. "'A Son is Born to Naomi!': Literary Allusions and Interpretation in the Book of Ruth." *JSOT* 40 (1988), 99-108.

Attention to literary allusion in Ruth can help us understand the character of Naomi. These allusions help construct the narrative's world-view, and illuminate attitudes and motivations of characters. The starting-point is the work of Phyllis Trible (in #221), though her portrayal of Naomi is flawed.

1323. Fisch, Harold. "Ruth and the Structure of Covenant History." *VT* 32 (1982), 424-437.

Structuralists have difficulty with the historical dimension of Ruth. Its literary structure is "loaded with the sense of history." The book seems ideally suited to the categories employed by Roland Barthes and Claude Lévi-Strauss. A synchronic analysis comes first; this must then be applied diachronically. Intertextuality shows us that Ruth is a meta-linguistic sign for redemption in the HB.

1324. Fuchs, Esther. "Status and Role of Female Heroines in the Biblical Narrative." *The Mankind Quarterly* 33 (1982), 149-160.

Although there are many generic and structural differences between the books of Ruth and Esther, as actors both main characters are agents rather than free actants—i.e., both are excluded from the central action of the climactic chapter, and both lack the complexity of male characters in their respective books. These are stories told by and for a man's world; they are, in other words, very patriarchal stories.

1325. Globe, Alexander. "Folktale Form and National Theme, With Particular Reference to Ruth," in #179, pp. 127-132.

How to read folktale plots in the HB, for modern readers who find such plots too predictable and the characters too superficial or improbable. The application of Vladimir Propp's model of "moves" and "ring structure" to Ruth.

1326. Gow, Murray D. "The Significance of Literary Structure for the Translation of the Book of Ruth." *BT* 35 (1985), 309-320.

Ruth consists of four episodes, each in turn subdivided into three sections. This thematic division does not precisely correspond with the chapter division. However, grasping it is crucial to successful translation because the sections and subsections are elaborately chiastic—which fact clarifies both theme and theology in the book.

1327.   Green, B. "The Plot of the Biblical Story of Ruth." *JSOT* 23
        (1982), 55-68.

The author of Ruth uses plot as one of several devices with
which to communicate his basic meaning. The carefully-arranged
nuptials make this more than a simple love story; it is in reality the
nuptials of the Lord and His people.

1328.   Hongisto, Leif. "Literary Structure and Theology in the
        Book of Ruth." *AUSS* 23 (1985), 19-28.

Ruth exhibits two chiastic patterns: one in chapter 1, the other
embracing the entire book. It also uses devices common to Hebrew poetry. These chiasms reinforce various theological motifs in
the book, including those of providence and redemption.

1329.   Hyman, Ronald T. "Questions and Changing Identity in the
        Book of Ruth." *USQR* 39 (1984-5), 189-201.

Four groups of "identity questions" in the book of Ruth all point
to a central theme: that of changing identity.

1330.   Kariv, Avraham. "The Message of Naomi," in Israel Cohen
        and B.Y. Michali, eds., *An Anthology of Hebrew Essays in Two
        Volumes*, Vol. I (Tel Aviv: Institute for the Translation of
        Hebrew Literature and Massada Publishing Co., Ltd.,
        1966), 117-123.

Naomi is a more important character in Ruth than is usually assumed. The book contains two life cycles: Ruth's and Naomi's, and
they are interlinked. "Not every woman can be a Ruth, but every
weary woman can become a Noami if she manages to transmit to
some other person the inner treasure of her spirit."

1331.   Keller, Joseph. "Biblical Literary Criticism: Logical Form
        and Poetic Function." *Journal of Religious Studies* 13
        (undated), 15-24.

The nature of man-woman relationships in the HB in the light
of literary criticism and linguistics, especially those in Ruth and I
Samuel 18. Loving relationships among humans are the "working
out in literary forms of the deep biblical conviction that the sacrificial reciprocity of human love entails and is entailed by God's love
for his children."

1332.   Loretz, Oswald. "The Theme of the Ruth Story." *CBQ* 22
        (1960), 391-9.

Any work of art must be seen in the context of the intellectual atmosphere of its own day. In the case of Ruth, the context is family history and what threatens it.

1333. de Moor, Johannes C. "The Poetry of the Book of Ruth." *Orientalia* n.s. 53 (1984), 262-283; 55 (1986), 16-46.

The distinction between poetry and prose in ancient Hebrew literature is still disputed. The role of parallelism in ancient literature. If we examine the language and structure of Ruth carefully we can see that the entire text is poetry, since its parallelism is too obvious to ignore.

* Murphy, Roland E. *Wisdom Literature: Job, Proverbs, Ruth, Canticles, Ecclesiastes, and Esther.* See #1234.

1334. Rauber, D.F. "The Book of Ruth," in #39, pp. 163-176.

Previous literary criticism has undervalued the "high art" and subtle nature of the book of Ruth. Sensitivity to patterns is the key to understanding biblical narrative art. The author of Ruth intended to "explore within specific situations of his story potent memories of major themes in the grand Hebraic tradition." Examples of such themes are the stranger among the Hebrews, and harvest versus barrenness. (JM)

1335. Rauber, D.F. "Literary Values in the Bible: The Book of Ruth." *JBL* 89 (1970), 27-37.

Biblical critics should welcome literary critics into their midst, however ignorant of biblical scholarship the latter may be. The OT is not yet treated seriously as literature. Analysis of Ruth shows that sensitivity to pattern is the key to reading Hebraic literature.

1336. Robertson, Edward. "The Plot of the Book of Ruth." *BJRL* 32 (1941), 207-228.

We must expect to find fictional elements and "much embellishing of facts to produce effect" in a book like Ruth. How the incidents of the plot of Ruth fit together.

1337. Rossow, Francis C. "Literary Artistry in the Book of Ruth and its Theological Significance." *Concordia Journal* 17 (1991), 12-19.

God works through language, rather than apart from or in spite of it. The four major episodes in Ruth and the symmetry they produce through organization; parallelism of theme and plot; irony; and skillful characterization.

1338.   Sacon, Kiyoshi K. "The Book of Ruth—Its Literary Structure and Theme." *AJBI* 4 (1978), 3-22.

Various structural devices in Ruth. Previous work on the theme of the book has not centered enough on the connection between the history of a family and that of the history of Israel.

1339.   Sasson, Jack M. "Ruth," in #33, pp. 320-328.

Literary analysis of Ruth "differs significantly," depending on whether we treat it as a folktale from oral tradition or examine its "literate narrative art." "... even among the artful narratives of Scripture, Ruth stands out in the power of its concentration, in the limpidity of its vocabulary, in the versatility of its language, in the balanced proportion of its scenes, and above all, in the vividness and integrity of its main characters."

1340.   Sasson, Jack M. *Ruth: A New Translation with a Philological Commentary and a Formalist-Folklorist Interpretation.* Baltimore (Johns Hopkins UP), 1979.

We need a new approach to the problem of the literary genre of Ruth. Of the various potential solutions provided by structuralism, that of Vladimir Propp is preferable. The narrative style of Ruth in the light of its rhetorical elements and the analysis of Erich Auerbach.

1341.   Tollers, Vincent L. "Narrative Control in the Book of Ruth," in #48, pp. 252-9.

The importance of Naomi as a key to understanding Ruth; in terms of Valdimir Propp and A.J. Greimas, she is "the principal actant in every scene—whether or not she actually appears in it." When a son is born to Naomi near the end, "the story's sender, object, subject, and receiver are one—thus weaving together its threads to our aesthetic satisfaction."

1342, 1343.   Trible, Phyllis. "Two Women in a Man's World: A Reading of the Book of Ruth." *Soundings* 59 (1976), 251-279; revised as chapter 6 of #221, and as "A Human Comedy: The Book of Ruth" in #40, pp. 161-190.

The story of Ruth is structured around relationships: male to female, and God to human beings. The characterization of the women in the book is developed through these relationships. "All together they are women in culture, women against culture, and women transforming culture. What they reflect, they challenge. And that challenge is a legacy of faith to this day for all who have ears to hear the stories of women in a man's world." (BD)

* Whiton, James M. "Ruth and Esther." See #1445.

1344. Wojcik, Jan. "Improvising Rules in the Book of Ruth."
PMLA 100 (1985), 145-153.

Ruth is about language and literature as well as about love.
"Boaz, Ruth, and Naomi draw on a rich common store of literary
allusions and laws derived from Hebrew literary tradition to create
a happy ending for the sterile stories of their individual pasts." The
book is not intended to be historical, but "celebrates the creative
improvisations religious rules are meant to inspire in any time or
place."

See also: #s 4, 7, 12, 17, 27, 166, 176, 178, 182, 187, 221, 252, 254,
304, 306, 307, 309, 315, 322, 324, 327, 335, 337, 711, 826, 1434.

SONG OF SONGS

1345. Barrett, Cyril. "The Language of Ecstasy and the Ecstasy of
Language," in #1517, pp. 205-221.

How are we to understand ecstatic language in the Bible? Are
religious sages "perhaps intoxicated by language, just as poets
sometimes are?" Poetry does not have to be empirically verifiable
to be valuable or true. Such utterances as Song of Songs 4, Psalm
19 and Revelation 21 are more than referential, but not just indul-
gence in language for language's sake. The poem itself is the experience, not merely an account of it.

1346. Boyarin, Daniel. "The Song of Songs: Lock or Key? Intertextuality, Allegory and Midrash," in #45, pp. 214-230.

One particular midrash on Song of Songs is a rare reflection by
the rabbis on their hermeneutical method, as well as an interpretation of the book which sees it as a key to unlocking the Torah.
The rabbis' reading method is not allegorical but rather intellectual: relating signifier to signifier.

1347. Brenner, Athalya. "'Come Back, Come Back the Shulam-
mite' (Song of Songs 7.1-10): A Parody of the *Wasf*
Genre," in #231, pp. 251-275.

There are three *wasf*-type poems in Song of Songs: 4:1-5, 5:10-16,
and 7:1-10. The final of these three examples also introduces fresh
material, "motivated by insights into the comic elements of the
dancing woman's figure." It is thus a parody, a tongue-in-cheek

treatment of the *wasf* genre. This probability reinforces the theory that the author is a female, since it offers a parody of the male lover's voice.

1348.   Brettler, Marc. "Sensual or Sublime: On Teaching the Song of Songs," in #179, pp. 133-5.

Song of Songs is a complex, difficult book. A teacher should concentrate on questions about how ancient Near Eastern poets in fact thought about love and sex in relation to God. Both allegorical and non-allegorical approaches to Jewish and to Christian literature have something to offer, though no one interpretation can be completely satisfying.

1349.   Broadribb, Donald. "Thoughts on the Song of Solomon." *Abr Nahrain* 3 (1961-2), 11-36.

The structure, diction, patterns of repetition, figures, and date of composition of Song of Songs in relation to the rest of the HB. All these considerations demonstrate that it is a unified poem, though probably not a love or wedding poem. Rather, it seems to have originated in certain nature rituals.

1350.   Cannon, William Walter. *The Song of Songs Edited as a Dramatic Poem.* Cambridge (Cambridge UP), 1913.

The purpose of analyzing Song of Songs as a dramatic poem is to enable readers to understand and enjoy "its force and significance as a piece of ancient literature." It is a unified poem, secular and dramatic in character. Various theories about its thematic intention; a possible structure; likely authorship and date; why an allegorical reading is unsatisfactory. Translation with textual notes.

*   Cook, Albert. *The Root of the Thing: A Study of Job and the Song of Songs.* See #1205.

1351.   Dorsey, David A. "Literary Structuring in the Song of Songs." *JSOT* 46 (1990), 81-96.

There is still no consensus on the unity or structure of Song of Songs. The analyses of J. Cheryl Exum and William Shea [#s 1352, 1387] are most convincing. The overall structure of the book seems to be chiastic.

1352.   Exum, J. Cheryl. "A Literary and Structural Analysis of the Song of Songs." *ZAW* 85 (1973), 47-79.

There has been insufficient attention to the stylistic and rhetorical devices in Song of Songs which comprise and elucidate the overall structure. It consists of six poems, with #1 and 6 forming an inclusio, with and within which 2-5 are in chiastic order. This proves that it is not an anthology nor a drama but a highly sophisticated and complex love poem.

1353. Falk, Marcia. *Love Lyrics from the Bible. A Translation and Literary Study of the Song of Songs.* Sheffield (Almond P), 1982.

Previous interpretations of Song of Songs as allegory, drama, liturgy, wedding cycle, and unified love poem are all inaccurate; it is probably an anthology of love poems. Six types of lyrics to be found in the book, and how each defines the "I-Thou" relationship. The role and importance of the *wasf* in the book, and the absence of sexism. The contexts of cultivated and wild countryside, interior environments, city streets. The themes of becoming, banishing, search for the beloved, self in a hostile world, and praise of love.

1354. Falk, Marcia. *The Song of Songs: A New Translation and Interpretation.* New York and San Francisco (HarperCollins), 1990.

The strengths and weaknesses of major literary interpretations of the work. It is a collection of thirty-one poems. Types of love lyrics. The similarities and differences between the *wasf* and Song of Songs, and the failure of scholars to perceive the function of metaphor in the book. Contexts, themes, and motifs, with interpretive notes.

1355. Fichman, Yaacov. "The Song of Songs," in Israel Cohen and B.Y. Michali, eds., *An Anthology of Hebrew Essays in Two Volumes.* Vol I. (Tel Aviv: Institute for the Translation of Hebrew Literature, and Massada Publishing Co., Ltd., 1966), 86-96.

The book is "utterly unlike" other ancient Hebrew poetry. Scholars cannot agree about its genre and structure, but its unified theme and tone are unmistakable. It inevitably attracted allegorization. The most plausible reading is that it is "a kind of festive drama, acted out ... by the groom, his bride, and her companions ... who constituted a chorus, rather as in the Greek drama." Ultimately, however, it "eludes the normal classifications of poetry. It flows rather through all channels and exploits all forms."

1356. Fox, Michael V. "Love, Passion, and Perception in Israelite and Egyptian Love-Poetry." *JBL* 102 (1983), 219-228.

For Egyptians, love was a way of feeling, remaining within the individual soul; love in Song of Songs is not only feeling, but a confluence of souls, and thus best expressed by tightly interlocking dialogue. Love is a mode of perception communicated through imagery of praise; it looks outward, a way of seeing and creating a world.

1357.   Fox, Michael V. *The Song of Songs and Ancient Egyptian Love Songs.* Madison (U of Wisconsin P), 1985.

Literary unity and style of Song of Songs; function of love songs in Hebrew and Egyptian cultures. The drama, especially use of monologue and dialogue, and major themes of the book.

*   Gordis, Robert. *Poets, Prophets, and Sages: Essays in Biblical Interpretation.* See #375.

1358.   Gordis, Robert. *The Song of Songs and Lamentations. A Study, Modern Translation and Commentary.* New York (KTAV), 1974.

Poetic form, unity, rhetorical devices, and leading theories of interpretation of the two books.

1359.   Griffis, William Elliot. *The Lily Among Thorns: A Study of the Biblical Drama Entitled The Song of Songs.* Boston and New York (Houghton, Mifflin) and Cambridge, Mass. (Riverside P), 1897 [copyright 1889].

The fact that the allegorical interpretation of Song of Songs is untenable should not make Christians forsake this book, since criticism in the nineteenth century has revealed its literary beauty and power. Its Solomonic background; its place in the poetic tradition of the ancient Near East; its dramatic structure; history of its interpretation. Close reading of its character development, verse form, and structure.

1360.   Griffis, William Elliot. "The Love-Song of the Bible," in #32, pp. 125-134.

Close attention to the literary structure, diction, dialogues and speeches shows Song of Songs to be a drama with three principal characters, structured in five acts of a total of fourteen scenes. The purpose of the book is to exalt human love as a reflection of divine love.

1361.   Gros Louis, Kenneth R.R. "The Song of Songs," in #40, pp. 243-258.

The two major obstacles to understanding Song of Songs as literature are the large number of allegorical interpretations, and the opposite tendency to see the work as entirely secular. It is rather somewhere in between; it describes the basic tensions of country versus court, and lover versus king. Its main image pattern is one of "enclosure" in which the writer implies that we may become too closed off from life and from nature. (BD)

1362. Grossberg, Daniel. "Canticles 3:10 in the Light of a Homeric Analogue and Biblical Poetics." *BTB* 11 (1981), 74-6

The interpretive crux of Solomon's love couch is clarified by comparing 3:10 to a parallel in classical Greek literature, as well as by being sensitive to Hebrew poetic style: e.g., in Amos 5:12 and Jeremiah 2:8 where a similar literary device is used. The couch, like that of Odysseus, is embellished both literally and figuratively; thus we should not just look for the "one correct meaning" of such an image.

1363. Grossberg, Daniel. "A Centrifugal Structure in Biblical Poetry." *Semiotica* 58 (1986), 139-150.

Song of Songs "exhibits a particularly diffuse structure with ... a mosaic of dazzling images; anti-teleological structure; polyphony of voices; abrupt shifts; peculiar and exotic elements, ambiguity and repetitions.... [T]he concerted use of the several devices ... warrant our fixing Song of Songs at the centrifugal extreme of the centripetal/centrifugal continuum."

* Grossberg, Daniel. *Centripetal and Centrifugal Structures in Biblical Poetry.* See #1179.

1364. Hyde, Walter Woodburn. "Greek Analogies to the Song of Songs," in Wilfred H. Schoff, ed., *The Song of Songs: A Symposium* (Philadelphia: Commercial Museum, 1924), 31-42.

Song of Songs is a unified poem, but it is of Greek, not Hebraic spirit. It is probably a collection of love lyrics such as those which Meleager and Philodemus compiled in the first century BC.

1365. Ibbotson, Joseph D. "The Song of Songs—A Secular Poem." *The Biblical World* 41 (1913), 314-321.

Song of Songs is a collection of Hebrew love songs, such as have been sung at weddings and festivals for thirty centuries in the middle east. Seeing them this way clears up certain interpretive puzzles, and helps explain why they got into the canon in the first place: Jewish reverence for Solomon.

1366. Kessler, R. *Some Poetical and Structural Features of the Song of Songs.* Leeds University Oriental Society Monograph Series #8 (July, 1965).

Specific poetic features which are prominent in Song of Songs but also present in other parts of the HB include most notably repetition, either for stylistic, thematic, or structural purposes. While it was probably a collection of originally independent poems, on balance the evidence favors seeing it as a unified, single-author composition.

1367.   Kinlaw, Dennis. "Charles Williams' Concept of Imaging Applied to the Song of Songs." *Wesleyan Theological Journal* 16, #1 (Spring, 1981), 85-92.

The traditional solution to the apparent lack of theology in Song of Songs is allegorical interpretation. The work of Charles Williams and Samuel Taylor Coleridge help us to see it instead as a celebration of human love.

1368.   Kramer, Samuel Noah. "The Biblical 'Song of Songs' and the Sumerian Love Songs." *Expedition* 5 (1962), 25-31.

Just as the Sumerian love songs all relate to the "joyous sacred marriage rites" of an ancient cult, so the songs in Song of Songs "must originally have been cultic in character.... [T]he imagery found in the songs ... [and the figurative language] bespeak court poetry rather than idyllic love lyrics between a man and a maid." Song of Songs is far superior aesthetically to its "stilted, repetitive, and relatively unemotional Sumerian forerunners," but its source must be Sumerian.

1369.   Landsberger, Franz. "Poetic Units within the Song of Songs." *JBL* 73 (1954), 203-216.

Various artistic devices in the work; the probable separate units or poems; relationship between poems; use of motifs. When we interpret Song of Songs, we should emphasize its delicacy, playfulness and grace as much as its passion and pathos.

1370.   Landy, Francis. "Beauty and the Enigma: An Inquiry into Some Interrelated Episodes of the Song of Songs." *JSOT* 17 (1980), 55-106.

"... a close reading of four of the most difficult passages in the Song of Songs, endeavouring to show that the difficulty ... is in fact part of the meaning, and contributes greatly to the mysterious and indefinable beauty of the Song." The four separate episodes are linked through imagery and theme.

1371.   Landy, Francis. "Eros and Hieros in the Song of Songs." *HJ* 24 (1983), 301-7.

The Song of Songs is valuable because "Love—the erotic drive in the world—is then God, pitted against and drawing its strength from Death, Sheol, and Chaos, and striving to integrate those contraries."

1372. Landy, Francis. *Paradoxes of Paradise: Identity and Difference in the Song of Songs.* Sheffield (Almond P), 1983

A close reading of the aesthetic dimensions of the Song of Songs shows that "The theme ... is the process of fusion and differentiation, the paradise that only exists in the world through being inaccessible to it, or is only accessible outside its limits, through imaginative transcendence."

1373. Landy, Francis. "The Song of Songs," in #33, pp. 305-319.

Imagery and metaphor in Song of Songs. It is a discourse of love, not sex. "... the dominance and initiative of the Beloved are the poem's most astonishing characteristics. Metaphorically aligned with a feminine aspect of divinity, associated with the celestial bodies, the land, and fertility, the Beloved reverses the predominantly patriarchal theology of the Bible. Male political power is enthralled to her." The poem is ambivalent about love: it is "the bond of a vital society, [but] it also threatens social order."

1374. Landy, Francis. "The Song of Songs and the Garden of Eden." *JBL* 98 (1979), 513-528.

Songs of Songs is a comment on the Garden of Eden myth, though not consciously and directly dependent on it. Genesis and Song of Songs use the same terms to discuss the same themes. Still, this echo of paradise is only one of many inter-biblical echoes in Song of Songs, even on the topic of love.

1375. Longxi, Zhang. "The Letter or the Spirit: The *Song of Songs*, Allegoresis, and the *Book of Poetry*." *Comparative Literature* 39 (1987), 193-217.

The history of arguments over the place of Song of Songs in the canon. The way Christians have allegorized the book in order to justify its presence in the Bible "bears striking similarities to the way many traditional Chinese scholars read part of the Confucian canon, *Shi Jing* or the *Book of Poetry*." Just as the decline of allegorizing after about 1750 marked an acceptance of secular poetry in the West, so "the dismantling of allegorical reading of the *Book of Poetry* likewise marked the decline of the Confucian tradition in Chinese history."

1376.   Mariaselvam, Abraham. *The Song of Songs and Ancient Tamil Love Poems: Poetry and Symbolism.* Rome (Editrice Pontificio Istituto Biblico), 1988.

History of literary study of Song of Songs; Hebrew meter, paral- lelism, and stanza-strophe form; symbolism, sound devices, rhetorical devices, and imagery in Song of Songs; historical study of classical Tamil literature. The similarities between the biblical and Tamil poetry occur in relationships of poems, themes, charac- terization, imagery, and diction. While there are also some dissimi- larities, the poems of Song of Songs can be classified according to Tamil categories. See also #1382.

1377.   Mazor, Yair. "The Song of Songs or the Story of Stories? 'The Song of Songs' Between Genre and Unity." *Scandi- navian Journal of the Old Testament* 1 (1990), 1-29.

We can detect in the imagery, themes, structure and plot of Song of Songs evidence of the classical Aristotelian plot shape: it is "tightly causal, intricate and logical." The main plot and subplots are related "by an emotional-rhetorical pattern of the bride's con- stantly alternating state of mind," and by the appearance of the bride's brothers. In this poem, narrative and lyrical layers are one.

1378.   Meyers, Carol. "Gender Imagery in the Song of Songs." *HAR* 10 (1986), 209-223.

Imagery is more important in Song of Songs than in any other book of the HB. Many examples of its imagery run counter to the stereotypical gender conceptions (e.g., architectural, military, and faunal). Reasons why Song of Songs breaks with gender stereo- types.

1379.   Murphy, Roland, O. Carm. "Interpreting the Song of Songs." *BTB* 9 (1979), 99-105.

The work is characterized by dialogical structure and flow, fre- quent repetition, and certain stock themes, of which garden and blossom are central. The poem should not be too quickly allego- rized, as its literal content is harmonious with the sages: tender- ness, fidelity, and intimacy are to characterize human sexual love.

1380.   Murphy, Roland E. "The Structure of the Canticle of Can- ticles." *CBQ* 11 (1949), 381-391.

Song of Songs is essentially a parable or allegory of the relation- ship of the New Israel and Yahweh, with a scene-based structure and an "indifference to logical development."

1381.   Murphy, Roland E. "The Unity of the Song of Songs." *VT* 29 (1979), 436-443.

There is little consensus about the date, structure, or meaning of Song of Songs. At least we can say that the many repetitions in it make it a unity.

*   Murphy, Roland E. *Wisdom Literature: Job, Proverbs, Ruth, Canticles, Ecclesiastes, and Esther.* See #1234.

1382.   Rabin, Chaim. "The Song of Songs and Tamil Poetry." *SR* 3 (1973), 205-219.

The use of love themes to express the relations of man to God which are common in Tamil Shaivite poetry could have been known to, and therefore borrowed by, the author of Song of Songs. See also #1376.

1383.   Segal, Benjamin J. "Double Meanings in the Song of Songs." *Dor Le Dor* 16 (1988), 249-255.

Whatever allegory may be present in Song of Songs, we must explain the details as details first. Stylistic details of importance because they demonstrate unity of authorship include double entendres (perhaps as many as fifty) used throughout the book. For example, 8:8-10 and 6:2-3 show careful delineation of how male and female view the world differently.

1384.   Segal, Benjamin J. "The Theme of the Song of Songs." *Dor Le Dor* 15 (1986-7), 106-113.

The theme of Song of Songs is articulated chiefly through repetition; theme is as important as structure in understanding the work. Repeated use of word play echoing with the "sh-l-m" combination emphasizes the theme that this world is not complete, nor is Solomonic love complete. This is why the lovers are urged to flee across the hills together.

1385.   Segal, M.H. "The Song of Songs." *VT* 12 (1962), 470-490.

The theme of Song of Songs is "the celebration of the love between a damsel and her swain. It is undoubtedly a lawful love to be sanctioned by marriage." Detailed examination of the structure of the poem.

1386.   Sekine, Masao. "Lyric Literature in the Davidic-Solomonic Period in the Light of the History of Israelite Literature" in Tomoo Ishida, ed., *Studies in the Period of David and*

Solomon and Other Essays (Winona Lake: Eisenbrauns, 1982), 1-11.

Japanese history shows epic arising from national unity, and lyric from the maturing of the individual consciousness. In Judges 5, Proverbs 8, Psalm 18, II Samuel 1, and Song of Songs we can see the same process occurring in ancient Israel. The unity and literary character of Song of Songs. Its lyrical nature "is parallel to its secular nature as love poetry."

1387.   Shea, William H. "The Chiastic Structure of the Song of Songs." *ZAW* 92 (1980), 378-396.

The existence of smaller chiastic units in Song of Songs should not prevent us from seeing that the whole has a chiastic structure as well. This reinforces the minority view that Song of Songs is a literary unity, not a random collection of love poems.

1388.   Soulen, Richard N. "The *Wasfs* of the Songs of Songs and Hermeneutics." *JBL* 86 (1967), 183-190.

Literary criticism can help us understand the imagery of the *wasfs* in the Song of Songs. They are not a thought problem but "a celebration of the joys of life and love, ... an invitation to share that joy. Only from this perspective is the intent of the poet preserved...."

1389.   Waterman, Leroy. *The Song of Songs Translated and Interpreted as a Dramatic Poem.* Ann Arbor (U of Michigan P), 1948.

The wide range of sometimes contradictory interpretations of Song of Songs; the literary form and problems which the book raises. It is clearly an organic whole, a unity, and an anti-Solomonic poem.

1390.   Webster, Edwin C. "Pattern in the Song of Songs." *JSOT* 22 (1982), 73-93.

A macrostructure of Song of Songs on the basis of well-known rhetorical patterns in the HB. It is a balanced structure developed through parallelism of subject, not through the progress of the festivities.

1391.   White, John Bradley. *A Study of the Language of Love in the Song of Songs and Ancient Egyptian Poetry.* Missoula (Scholars P), 1978.

"... the language of love in the Hebrew Song of Songs is reminiscent of the language used to describe love in the corpus of ancient Egyptian love poetry." The cultural milieu of 18th dynasty

Egypt; the spirit of their love poetry; its themes and imagery compared to those of Song of Songs.

See also: #s 12, 17, 18, 27, 166, 175, 178, 221, 241, 285, 293, 370, 407, 421, 441, 991.

QOHELET (ECCLESIASTES)

1392. Crenshaw, James L. *Ecclesiastes: A Commentary.* Philadelphia (Westminster P), 1987.

Introduction: literary expression, tone, truth-statements, presence of genres including wisdom, parody, malediction and benediction, parable, autobiographical narrative, among others. "Literary Integrity and Structure": various theories of its structure—that it is chiastic, palindromic, parallelistic in sections, thematic (the most probable solution), or that it lacks any structure. Commentary: close reading with attention to style, theme, influence of wisdom literature.

1393. Forman, Charles C. "Koheleth's Use of Genesis." *JSS* 5 (1960), 256-263.

Genesis 1-11 represents "the most important single influence in the ideas of Ecclesiastes regarding the nature and destiny of man, the character of human existence, and the fact of God."

1394. Fox, Michael. "Frame-Narrative and Composition in the Book of Qohelet." *HUCA* 48 (1968), 83-106.

It is not often recognized that Qohelet is a narrative. It is a unity, using interplay of voice as a deliberate literary device for rhetorical and artistic purposes. The most important point is to distinguish a frame-narrator and an implied author. Qohelet, that is, is a persona, not necessarily the author.

1395. Fox, Michael V. *Qohelet and His Contradictions.* Sheffield (Almond P), 1989.

The best way to read Qohelet is to interpret its contradictions, rather than trying to eliminate them. These contradictions for Qohelet are not paradoxes, as they are in Zen. They are "the lens through which to view life," the mark of his world view and the "substance of [his] thought." Thus we need to know what conclusions he draws from them. Important themes include those of toil and pleasure, wisdom and knowledge, justice and theodicy. The

unity of the book lies in "the constant presence of a single brood-
ing consciousness."

1396. Fox, Michael V., and Bezalel Porten. "Unsought
       Discoveries: Qohelet 7:23–8:1a." *HS* 19 (1978), 26-38.

       Through the interplay of inclusio, word pairs, key words and al-
       lusions, "the tone and texture of the work emerges and at the
       same time propositional content is conveyed to the audience."
       Qohelet's reversal of customary word-pair order signals and
       underlines his discovery that his (and humankind's) search for
       abstract truth only leads back to where he started.

1397. Fredericks, Daniel C. "Chiasm and Parallel Structure in
       Qoheleth 5:6–6:9." *JBL* 108 (1989), 17-35.

       The lack of consensus regarding the structure of Qohelet. The
       interpretational emphasis on bemoaning of riches misses the point
       that enjoyment of possessions is a true blessing of God. Chiastic
       pattern in the book reinforces this argument.

1398. Gammie, John G. "Stoicism and Anti-Stoicism in Qoheleth."
       HAR 9 (1985), 169-185.

       Parallels between ancient Greek stoicism and Qohelet lead to
       the conclusion that stoicism (along with other Greek philosophical
       schools) had an impact on Qohelet in its specific ideas about di-
       vine causation, and in its forms of argumentation.

1399. Ginsberg, H. Lewis. "The Structure and Contents of the
       Book of Koheleth." *VT* Supplement 3 (1955), 138-149.

       Qohelet has a quadripartite structure. Summary of its teachings;
       evaluation of Qohelet's orthodoxy, date, and authorship.

1400. Good, Edwin M. "The Unfilled Sea: Style and Meaning in
       Ecclesiastes 1:2-11," in John G. Gammie, et al., eds., *Israelite
       Wisdom* (Missoula: Scholars P, 1978), 59-73.

       We need to follow a text through its own process, pursue its lin-
       earity in order to uncover the meaning progressively as the text
       presents it. This enables us to elicit meaning better and more
       completely through process of presentation, methods of discourse,
       and stylistic devices. Since narrative is a literary mode where linear-
       ity is essential, we let the text have its own way.

1401. Gros Louis, Kenneth R.R. "Ecclesiastes," in #39, pp. 267-82

       A literary approach to Ecclesiastes will de-emphasize its pes-
       simism and deal more with the questions and reflections posed by
       the book. The "Preacher" is probably a literary device for the pur-

pose of more fully exploring life's meaning, through proverbs and questions as well as through feelings of despair and agnosticism. The inconsistencies in the book are not errors in editing nor later inclusions, but the extremes we encounter as we ponder life. (JM)

1402. Horton, Ernest, Jr. "Koheleth's Concept of Opposites." *Numen* 19 (1972), 1-21.

Koheleth's world view compared with those found in the Gilgamesh epic, the Greek philosophers, early Taoism, and Babylonian wisdom literature. Koheleth addresses much the same questions as are addressed in many ancient writings of the third to fifth centuries, BC, though his answers differ somewhat from theirs.

1403. Levine, Etan. "Qohelet's Fool: A Composite Portrait," in #231, pp. 277-294.

Qohelet induces both laughter and tears in his readers by dealing with the disparities between hope and reality. We all act like fools at times, he maintains, though we firmly believe in the possibility of growing from folly to wisdom. Qohelet's tactic is to attempt to root out folly. "Comedy is criticism because it exposes human beings for what they are in contrast to what they are or profess to be," which is the comic foundation of Qohelet.

1404. Loader, J.A. *Polar Structures in the Book of Qohelet.* BZAW 152. Berlin and New York (Walter de Gruyter), 1979.

Polar structures are the "patterns of tension created by the counterposition of two elements to one another"; they are the outstanding characteristic of Qohelet. Survey of stylistic figures (mainly parallelism and chiasmus), of polar thought-patterns, and of the position of Qohelet in the development of OT wisdom. The polarity of style reflects Qohelet's theological outlook: a distant God separated by a wide gap from humankind. The so-called contradictions of Qohelet are in fact intended polar structures in a "delicate and complex literary product."

1405. Loader, J.A. "Qohelet 3:2-8—A 'Sonnet' in the Old Testament." *ZAW* 81 (1969), 240-42.

These verses show an exceptional use of chiasmus and parallelism in Qohelet. "... purely formally and by way of comparison, we have here an exact parallel to the Petrarchan sonnet by taking Hebrew stylistics into account."

1406. Mulder, J.S.M. "Qoheleth's Division and Also Its Main Point," in W.C. Delsman, et al., eds., *Von Kanaan bis Ker-*

ala.... (Vluyn: Butzon and Bercker Kevelaer, 1982), 149-159.

Reconsideration of the work of Addison G. Wright [#1421] and others on the structure of Qohelet. Wright can be accepted with modification: the key divisions are at 4:6 and 8:17, the key theme argued in 3:1–4:6 and 8:1-17.

1407.   Murphy, Roland E. "The *Pensées* of Coheleth." *CBQ* 17 (1955), 304-14.

Qohelet is not a dramatic dialogue as is Job; rather it belongs to the genre of Pascal's *Pensées*: the reflections and jottings of a mature man on the meaning of life, edited by a disciple. Thus a satisfactory outline of the book is impossible.

*   Murphy, Roland E. *Wisdom Literature: Job, Proverbs, Ruth, Canticles, Ecclesiastes, and Esther.* See #1234.

1408.   Nichols, Francis W. "Samuel Beckett and Ecclesiastes on the Borders of Belief." *Encounter* 45 (1984), 11-22.

A comparison between Beckett's *Waiting for Godot* and Qohelet helps illuminate how the latter deals with problems of doubt and skepticism.

1409.   Ogden, Graham. *Qoheleth.* Sheffield (JSOT P), 1987.

A literary-thematic and theological treatment of the book. "... a programmatic question about humanity's *yitrôn* or 'advantage' (1.3), together with its answer (negative), and the response which flows from that, provide the framework for understanding Qohelet's structure." These features form the framework of chapters 1-8, which are designed to provide the setting for the final discourse of chapters 9-12.

1410.   Ogden, Graham S. "Qoheleth IX:1-16." *VT* 32 (1982), 158-169.

Detailed analysis of chapter 9 shows that form and content point us back to the basic question which Qohelet undertook to investigate in the beginning: the mystery of our common fate in death. Thus chapter 9 represents a major turning-point or change in the book.

1411.   Ogden, Graham S. "Qoheleth IX 17–X 20: Variations on the Theme of Wisdom's Strength and Vulnerability." *VT* 30 (1980), 27-37.

The basic issue in delimiting thought units in Qohelet is the miscellaneous collection of proverbial matter versus a thematic arrangement. Analysis of 9:17–10:20 shows the presence of *inclusiones* which hold the seemingly disparate matter together thematically.

1412.   Ogden, Graham S. "Qoheleth XI:1-6." *VT* 33 (1983), 222-230.

These verses can be isolated as a distinct literary unit. Their theme is the balance between what the sage can and what he cannot know. This in turn balances the confidence of chapter 9.

1413.   Ogden, Graham S. "Qoheleth XI:7–XII:8: Qoheleth's Summons to Enjoyment and Reflection." *VT* 34 (1984), 27-38.

The structure of these chapters as a clue to meaning, and in relation to the entire book. They argue that the call to enjoyment and concurrent reflection on the inevitability of death is the central theme of Qohelet.

1414.   Payne, Michael. "The Voices of Ecclesiastes." *College Literature* 15 (1988), 262-8.

Ecclesiastes as an undercutting of OT orthodoxy. It follows the form of the dramatic monologue. Its voices, theme of vanity versus vitality, place in the transition from the spoken to the written word.

1415.   Ranston, Harry. *Ecclesiastes and the Early Greek Wisdom Literature.* London (The Epworth P; J. Alfred Sharp), 1925.

It is mistaken to look for evidence of Greek influence on Ecclesiastes among the Greek philosophers; we should instead look for it among the writers between Homer and Aeschylus. Major examples of such influence would be Hesiod and Theognis, with lesser influence detectable from the Gilgamesh epic and the *Phokylidea.* There are also occasional parallels with the early Greek lyric poets. Contrary to previous critics, Solon, the early drama, Menander, the Seven Sages and Xenophanes did not influence Ecclesiastes at all.

1416.   Viviano, Pauline A. "The Book of Ecclesiastes: A Literary Approach." *The Bible Today* 22 (1984), 79-84.

Ecclesiastes resembles most closely the literary form called "The Royal Testament," as is found, e.g., in ancient Egypt. Its internal structure reinforces the theme that "all is vanity."

1417.   de Waard, Jan. "The Structure of Qoheleth." *PWCJS* 8
        (1982), 57-64.

        Formal discourse analysis of Qoheleth confirms a "chiastic the-
        matic arrangement" of the book. The structure of a work will be
        conditioned by the type of discourse to be presented.

1418.   Whybray, R.N. *Ecclesiastes.* Sheffield (JSOT P), 1989.

        A summary of current literary-critical and theological thinking
        about the author, times, language, style, structure, and characteris-
        tic ideas of the book.

1419.   Whybray, R.N. "The Identification and Use of Quotations in
        Ecclesiastes." *VT* Supplement 32 (1980), 435-451.

        Did Qohelet regard himself as an exponent of "wisdom" in the
        same sense as the author of Proverbs? Did he wish to oppose or to
        modify such wisdom teaching? He gave some traditional sayings
        absolute approval, others relative, guarded, or ambiguous ap-
        proval. He did regard himself as a wisdom writer, though he used
        even the sayings he approved of for less optimistic purposes. His
        use of Proverbs is confined to secular matters.

*   Williams, James G. "Proverbs and Ecclesiastes." See #1308.

1420.   Williams, James G. "What Does It Profit a Man? The Wis-
        dom of Koheleth." *Judaism* 20 (1971), 179-193; rpt James
        L. Crenshaw, ed., *Studies in Ancient Israelite Wisdom* (New
        York: KTAV, 1976), 375-389.

        "According to Koheleth, there is no profit for man in his exis-
        tence, but there is, nevertheless, a 'portion,'... a 'share' in the
        world which cannot be preserved, but simply enjoyed at the right
        time, as God gives the right time in an inscrutable way."
        Ultimately, for all his unorthodoxy, Qohelet fits into the Hebrew
        tradition.

1421.   Wright, Addison G. "The Riddle of the Sphinx: The Struc-
        ture of the Book of Qoheleth." *CBQ* 30 (1968), 313-334;
        rpt James L. Crenshaw, ed., *Studies in Ancient Israelite Wis-
        dom* (New York: KTAV, 1976), 245-266.

        The principle underlying the maze is not multiple authorship or
        dialectic mode or Qohelet's vacillation, but structure. The key to
        the structure lies in the patterns of verbal repetition in 1:12–11:6.
        Thus the book speaks more clearly, but says less than, we thought.
        Its theme is the impossibility of understanding what God has done.
        The various proverbs which Qohelet arranges are there to be re-
        futed, not accepted.

1422. Wright, Addison G., S.S. "The Riddle of the Sphinx Revisited: Numerical Patterns in the Book of Qoheleth." *CBQ* 42 (1980), 38-51.

Reception of #1421; more evidence enables us to conclude that "the message of the numbers may be the same as the literary message of the book—that everything is at sixes and sevens (precisely 36's and 37's)."

See also: #s 7, 12, 166, 175, 178, 182, 205, 209, 211, 215, 309, 370, 435, 1087, 1092, 1309.

LAMENTATIONS

1423. Cross, Frank M. "Studies in the Structure of Hebrew Verse: The Prosody of Lamentations 1:1-22," in Carol Myers and M. O'Connor, eds., *The Word of the Lord Shall Go Forth* (Winona Lake: Eisenbrauns, 1983), 129-155.

The presence in Lamentations 1 of the complex verse form called "Qinah" meter, which uses two basic building blocks of Hebrew poetry, 3-stress and 2-stress cola. Repetitions of words, phrases, and themes occur in cyclic structures.

1424. Durlesser, James A. "The Book of Lamentations and the Mesopotamian Laments: Experiential or Literary Ties." *PEGL* 3 (1983), 69-84.

The Sumerian lamentations bewailing the fall of cities compared to Lamentations, using the techniques of rhetorical criticism. While there are striking similarities in content, the best explanation is probably commonality of experience and not literary indebtedness.

* Gordis, Robert. *The Song of Songs and Lamentations: A Study, Modern Translation and Commentary.* See #1358.

* Grossberg, Daniel. *Centripetal and Centrifugal Structures in Biblical Poetry.* See #1179.

1425. Gwaltney, W.C., Jr. "The Biblical Book of Lamentations in the Context of Near Eastern Lament Literature," in William W. Hallo, et al., eds., *Scripture in Context II: More*

Essays on the Comparative Method (Winona Lake: Eisenbrauns, 1983), 191-211.

We can help explain the structure and poetry of Lamentations by comparing it to the lament genre in the ancient Near East. We find that the two share many poetic techniques, but that their structure and organization are dissimilar.

1426.   Hillers, Delbert R. "History and Poetry in Lamentations." *Currents in Theology and Mission* 10 (1983), 155-161.

Even where Lamentations seems to be conveying historical fact and information, it is not; it is instead participating in a poetic and religious tradition in which history was always interpreted, not just reported.

1427.   Johnson, Bo. "Form and Message in Lamentations." *ZAW* 97 (1985), 58-73.

Lamentations has a carefully designed structure. The five chapters are constructed on an elaborate play on the Hebrew alphabet as well as on a chiastic pattern. The main point of the book occurs at the center of chapter 3 (i.e., at the point of the chiasm): the distress felt by the Israelites is a punishment aimed at rehabilitation, not definite rejection.

*   Kaiser, Barbara Bakke. "Poet as 'Female Impersonator': The Image of the Daughter of Zion as Speaker in Biblical Poems of Suffering." See #949.

1428.   Lanahan, William F. "The Speaking Voice in the Book of Lamentations." *JBL* 93 (1974), 41-9.

We should concern ourselves with the persona (mask assumed by the poet) of Lamentations, not with who actually wrote the book. There are a total of five personae: the city of Jerusalem, the objective reporter, plus three distinct voices in chapters 3-5. The book is the product of a unique spiritual consciousness which can realize itself only by projecting its grief onto a different persona for each stage of that grief.

1429.   Landy, Francis. "Lamentations," in #33, pp. 329-334.

Lamentations "marks, with untempered immediacy, the focal calamity of the Bible, the destruction of Jerusalem in 586 BCE. The lyric discharges the cumulative emotions suppressed in the narrative and anticipated or recalled in the Prophets. The alienation ... of the Prophets suddenly becomes a collective experience.... [T]he descriptive voice is direct, unenigmatic, as if the scene spoke for itself, and uses rhetorical techniques—repetition, metaphor, personification, ... in the service of negation."

1430. Owens, Pamela Jean. "Personification and Suffering in Lamentations 3." *Austin Seminary Bulletin* 105, #2 (Spring, 1990), 75-90.

If we "chart Lamentations 3 for revealing grammatical parallelism," we also find paronomasia and personification as well (though the latter is handled differently here from other parts of the HB). The chapter expresses anguish but not resignation.

1431. Provan, Iain W. "Reading Texts against an Historical Background: The Case of Lamentations 1." *SJOT* (1990, #1) 130-143.

Historical critics must ask two questions if they decide to take the literary character of biblical texts seriously. "First, are some texts, particularly poetic texts, quite so susceptible to dating as is often assumed? Secondly, does it matter ... if we cannot date such texts precisely?" Lamentations 1 as an example of the difficulty in reading poetic texts historically. "It is not always desirable, even if it is possible."

1432. Renkema, Johan. "The Literary Structure of Lamentations" [four separate articles], in #382, pp. 294-396.

Literary analysis confirms the concentric structure of Lamentations, and "strongly confirms" the unity of the book—a unity which is not redactional; for example, the structure of chapter 3 has been used by the poet to structure the other chapters or songs.

1433. Shea, William H. "The *qinah* Structure of the Book of Lamentations." *Biblica* 60 (1979), 103-7.

"Qinah" or "lament" meter is the key to the structure of Lamentations. This structure proceeds in progressively larger units, and helps us see the unity of the book.

See also: #s 175, 376, 435, 437, 443, 458, 1454.

ESTHER

* Alter, Robert. "Biblical Imperatives and Literary Play." See #553.

1434.   Berg, Sandra Beth. *The Book of Esther: Motifs, Themes and Structure.* Missoula (Scholars P), 1979.

Dominant motifs in Esther; certain themes are primary; the structure is chiastic, and the whole book is a literary unity. Esther may be compared with Genesis 37-50 because both are "historical novels," and because it has been argued that both share a common set of themes, which suggests that Genesis influenced Esther. Direct borrowing, however, is unlikely. Esther also has similarities with other post-Exilic narratives, e.g., Daniel, Ruth, Jonah and Judith.

1435.   Clines, David J.A. "Reading Esther from Left to Right: Contemporary Strategies for Reading a Biblical Text," in #35, pp. 31-52.

Formalist analysis of Esther reveals the narrator's attitudes to power, violence and law, and shows that the story is less naive than is usually assumed. Actantial and semantic approaches to the book are probably the most promising. Feminist analysis sensitizes us to the possibility that the female's triumph may be less than complete. Materialist (socio-economic) approaches "point up the fragility of the stance toward power" in the book. Deconstruction shows "that a text shorn of the bogus claims of its reverers can become more effectual, even attractive."

*   Fuchs, Esther. "Status and Role of Female Heroines in the Biblical Narrative." See #1324.

1436.   Goldman, Stan. "Narrative and Ethical Ironies in Esther." *JSOT* 47 (1990), 15-31.

Typology of "multiple narrative ironies": rhetorical, generative, and intuitive in Esther offers new insights into the ethics of the book, and into how irony functions as a narrative device and an ethical value in the story.

1437.   Gordis, Robert. "Religion, Wisdom and History in the Book of Esther—A New Solution to an Ancient Crux." *JBL* 100 (1981), 359-388.

The unique (and to some readers troubling) characteristics of Esther may be explained by recognizing that it is written in the form of a chronicle of the Persian court by a supposedly gentile scribe who was a consummate literary artist.

1438.   Gordis, Robert. "Studies in the Esther Narrative." *JBL* 95 (1976), 43-58.

The literary unity of Esther; its outstanding literary characteristics, including its structure.

1439. Jones, Bruce William. "Two Misconceptions About the Book of Esther." *CBQ* 39 (1977), 171-181.

Misconceptions about the book of Esther, and resulting objections to it, can be cleared up if we recognize the humor, irony, and hyperbole of this obviously fictional narrative.

1440. McBride, William T. "Esther Passes: Chiasm, Lex Talio, and Money in the Book of Esther," in #318, pp. 211-223.

In its overall chiasm, Esther "tempts its readers to find a certain symmetry, balance, and cancellation without residue." However, the chiastic narrative is a "prismatic refraction," not a "mirror-like reflection." Xerxes as putative center of the chiasm is in fact an absence, a deferral of meaning. A "rather more profound center" would be the meeting of Mordechai and Haman in 5:9 which finally results in an "excess" of memory in the exchange of pogrom for Purim.

* Murphy, Roland E. *Wisdom Literature: Job, Proverbs, Ruth, Canticles, Ecclesiastes, and Esther.* See #1234.

1441. Radday, Yehuda T. "Esther with Humour," in #231, pp. 295-313.

Esther is "frightening and funny at the same time." Various humorous and satiric elements in the book, including humor in its overall structure, the movement from humor to near disaster to felicitous ending, and humor in various plot reversals and coincidences.

1442. Rossow, Francis C. "Literary Artistry in the Book of Esther and its Theological Significance." *Concordia Journal* 13 (1987), 219-223.

The excellent literary artistry of Esther is the primary vehicle for its theology. Its stylistic mastery, superb structure with careful symmetry, dramatic foreshadowing, irony, peripeteia, and fairy tale motifs. This artistry contains a subtle thesis about the design of God's universe.

1443. Sasson, Jack M. "Esther," in #33, pp. 335-342.

The narrative and stylistic techniques of Esther include alternation of action and description with little dialogue; a chatty, vernacular style and vocabulary; masterful juxtaposition of simultaneous activities within a single verse; and its sometimes caricatured characterization. The banquets are the key to the structure of the book.

1444.   Talmon, Shemaryahu. "'Wisdom' in the Book of Esther." *VT* 13 (1963), 419-455.

History of the argument over the historicity of Esther versus its being a "novel," as well as over its sources and redaction. We should classify it as a "historicized wisdom-tale," enacting standard "wisdom" motifs present in all wisdom literature. It is a book steeped in the wisdom tradition.

1445.   Whiton, James M. "Ruth and Esther," in #32, pp. 61-73.

Appreciation of the tightly-woven plots and interesting characterizations in these two books. On Esther, "The open questions of the origin of the Purim feast, and of the historical probabilities of the narrative, do not affect the literary or the moral value of the book."

*   Wills, Lawrence M. *The Jew in the Court of the Foreign King: Ancient Jewish Court Legends.* See #1467.

See also: #s 27, 166, 175, 178, 187, 241, 289, 315, 322, 335, 337, 370.

DANIEL

1446.   Baldwin, Joyce G. "Some Literary Affinities of the Book of Daniel." *TB* 30 (1979), 77-99.

In style and form, Daniel resembles Babylonian prophecies, and therefore may originate, as it claims, in the sixth century, rather than later as scholars have often assumed.

1447.   Boogart, T.A. "Daniel 6: A Tale of Two Empires." *Reformed Review* 39 (1986), 106-112.

The structure of Daniel 6 analyzed from the perspectives of plot and time. The author made the drama of the chapter emblematic of the drama of world history. Its apocalyptic origin gives evidence of the literary unity of Daniel.

1448.   Collins, John J. "Apocalyptic Genre and Mythic Allusions in Daniel." *JSOT* 21 (1981), 83-100.

"... any interpretation of the visions of Daniel must take into account the broader context of apocalyptic genre, and that the mythological imagery characteristic of that genre must be recognized as an integral factor in the message of the book...."

1449.   Collins, John J. *Daniel. With an Introduction to Apocalyptic Literature.* Grand Rapids (Eerdmans), 1984.

Definitions and illustrations of the various characteristics of apocalyptic literature: style, setting, scenes, related genres. Typical outline of the genre; setting and purpose of each chapter or section of Daniel; comparison with other apocalyptic books or passages in the HB.

1450.   Collins, John J. "The Jewish Apocalypses." *Semeia* 14 (1979) [#36], 21-59.

Defining the literary genre of Jewish Apocalypse; classification of types according to historical/cosmic/personal categories. Daniel 7-12, plus examples from apocryphal books written up to the first century, CE.

1451.   Collins, John J. "Jewish Apocalyptic against its Hellenistic Near Eastern Environment." *American Schools of Oriental Research Bulletin* #220 (December, 1975), 27-36.

The more conspicuous features which Jewish apocalyptic shares with its Hellenistic Near Eastern environment include differentiation from prophecy, periodization, end of the world expectation, belief in an after-life, esoteric symbolism, and dualism. There is some evidence of direct influence on Daniel of motifs and ideas from Near Eastern apocalyptic. See also #163.

1452.   Collins, John J. "The Symbolism of Transcendence in Jewish Apocalyptic." *BR* 19 (1974), 5-22.

Northrop Frye has taught us that myth is itself one literary mode among others, not an escape from literature. If we see it as a "model of transcendence," then it can point beyond its own symbols. Thus we should not be puzzled that it is resorted to in Daniel and elsewhere.

1453.   Coxon, Peter W. "The 'List' Genre and Narrative Style in the Court Tales of Daniel." *JSOT* 35 (1986), 95-121.

How does the writer of Daniel extend the "list" technique of Daniel 2-6 into the texture of his prose to develop repetition patterns? He has a tendency to produce tripartite lists of words and phrases, and repetition for rhetorical effect, so that the narrative proceeds by patterns of associated imagery. Lists are memorable here just as in Homer; they are pleasurable, expressing the writer's sense of immanent cosmic order.

1454.   Di Lella, Alexander A. "Daniel 4:7-14: Poetic Analysis and Biblical Background," in A. Caquot and M. Delcor, eds., *Mélanges Bibliques et Orientaux en L'honneur de M. Henri Cazelles* (Kevelaer: Butzon and Bercker, and Neukirchen-Vluyn: Neukirchener Verlag, 1981), 247-258.

Outline of a "suggestive structure" of Daniel 4 in six stanzas or strophes divided into bi- and tricola, based on the presence of inclusio, carefully-placed repetitions, and chiastic echoes. Literary devices include formulaic pairs, word- and word-root repetitions, alliteration and assonance. Parallels to this structure in Psalms, Hosea, Isaiah, Jeremiah, Lamentations and Ezekiel. The structure shows the essential theological argument of both the chapter and the book to be the power of God to destroy even the most powerful earthly kings.

1455.   Fewell, Danna. *Circle of Sovereignty: A Story of Stories in Daniel 1-6.* Sheffield (Almond P), 1988.

New Criticism's close attention to the language and structure of the text of Daniel 1-6; structuralism (Daniel 1-6 as description of court life in the story world of Daniel); deconstruction (the instability of the divinely-established world in these chapters, and its potential to produce ever new readings); and reader-response (the reader fills in the gaps).

1456.   Goldingay, John. "The Stories in Daniel: A Narrative Politics." *JSOT* 37 (1987), 99-116.

"Whatever historical value [the stories] may have, they are literary artifacts which blend the forms of court contest, ... confessor legend and prophetic legend, and (among others) aretalogy, midrash, pesher, and literary psalmody, into artful narratives which carry a vision of how life in politics may be lived, and on what basis."

1457.   Good, Edwin M. "Apocalyptic as Comedy: The Book of Daniel." *Semeia* 32 (1985) [#228], 41-70.

If we accept Northrop Frye's definition of comedy, we can argue that the plot line and major parts of Daniel are comic, each presenting "both a comedy in miniature and moments of humor." The "visions" chapters, however, are more ambiguous.

1458.   Gooding, David W. "The Literary Structure of the Book of Daniel and its Implications." *TB* 32 (1981), 43-79.

The structure of Daniel shows the book to be a literary unity in which every part is carefully positioned. Such complexity must be the work of one authorial mind.

*   La Sor, William Sanford. "Samples of Early Semitic Poetry." See #438.

*   Milne, Pamela J. *Vladimir Propp and the Study of Structure in Hebrew Biblical Narrative.* See #317.

1459.   Porter, Paul. *Metaphors and Monsters: A Literary-Critical Study of Daniel 7 and 8.* Lund (Gleerup; Liber Förlag), 1983.

Three interrelated aspects of animal metaphors in Daniel 7 and 8. Application of the "interaction" view of metaphor to these chapters shows the images to be semantically important. "The evocative power of the animal anomalies in Daniel 7 and 8 ... [stems] ... from their stylistic associations with Mesopotamian omen traditions." A "root-metaphor" model for grouping the animal images better accounts for their identity, function, and political symbolism. This root metaphor is that of the king as shepherd. Daniel 7 and 8 in the context of lamentation literature in the HB.

1460.   Raabe, Paul R. "Daniel 7: Its Structure and Role in the Book." *HAR* 9 (1985), 267-275.

To "demonstrate that Daniel 7 in its present form has a coherent literary structure and to show how the chapter acts as a hinge which binds together chapters 1-6 and 8-12."

1461.   Shea, William H. "Further Literary Structures in Daniel 2-7: An Analysis of Daniel 4." *AUSS* 23 (1985), 193-202.

Large-scale chiastic structures in Daniel 2-7 have already been noted by other scholars. Now we can look for smaller-scale ones, as for example those found in chapter 4.

1462.   Shea, William H. "Further Literary Structures in Daniel 2-7: An Analysis of Daniel 5, and the Broader Relationships Within Chapters 2-7." *AUSS* 23 (1985), 277-295.

Like chapter 4, chapter 5 of Daniel is chiastic, though it differs in significant ways from the one in chapter 4. For example, there is no prologue and epilogue; and there are thematic and content differences. Diagram of their position within chapters 2-7.

1463.   Shea, William H. "Poetic Relations of the Time Periods in Dan 9:25." *AUSS* 18 (1980), 59-63.

Differences among translations of this passage can be resolved
through poetic analysis. Separation of the verses into bi- and tricola shows the presence of thematic parallelism, and supports the
rendering of the King James version, as against those of the RSV,
NEB, and AB.

1464.   Soesilo, Daud. "Translating the Poetic Sections of Daniel 1-
         6." *BT* 41 (1990), 432-5.

"All of the four poems in Daniel 1-6, and the doxological poem
as well, have similar linguistic elements, form, and function. They
bear a close resemblance to the consistent forms of the book of
Psalms, and function as the theological summary of the main
thrust of the narrative texts."

1465.   Stefanovic, Zdravko. "Thematic Links Between the Histori-
         cal and Prophetic Sections of Daniel." *AUSS* 27 (1989),
         121-7.

Contrary to the usual scholarly opinion, there are a number of
overlappings between Daniel 1-6 and 7-12 which "provide an additional supporting argument for the unity of the book...."

1466.   Talmon, Shemaryahu. "Daniel," in #33, pp. 343-356.

"The linguistic and literary diversity of Daniel reveals a composite structure." Chapters 1-6, written in narrative style, are six court
tales; chapters 7-12 are quite different in style and outlook: four
units of apocalyptic dreams and visions. Nevertheless, the book has
a conceptual unity. Style, imagery, motifs, structural/numerical
patterns; type-plot of the "successful exile" (much like Joseph, Esther, and Ezra-Nehemiah). It is a fictional tale, with evidence of
"late biblical historiography."

1467.   Wills, Lawrence M. *The Jew in the Court of the Foreign King:
         Ancient Jewish Court Legends.* Minneapolis (Fortress P),
         1990.

The stories in Genesis 37-50, Esther, and Daniel 1-6, among others, are "examples of a literary tradition which presented ideals of
popular wisdom in a narrative form." Historical criticism, folklore
studies, and literary criticism can be successfully combined to analyze this material. Strikingly similar legends are also found in ancient Near Eastern and Greek literatures. Such a "concentration of
stories about wisdom in one time and place presents a remarkable
historical datum...."

1468.   Wilson, Gerald H. "Wisdom in Daniel and the Origin of
         Apocalyptic." *HAR* 9 (1985), 372-381.

Despite the work of Gerhard von Rad, and the presence of wisdom terms in chapters 8-12, there is insufficient evidence of sapiential influence on Daniel.

See also: #s 17, 27, 163, 166, 175, 216, 888, 1434.

EZRA-NEHEMIAH

1469.   Bliese, Loren F. "Chiastic Structures, Peaks and Cohesion in Nehemiah 9.6-37." *BT* 39 (1988), 208-215.

The presence of key words, and "the importance of analyzing structure in understanding Hebrew chiastic poems" both argue for a chiastic structure.

1470.   Breech, Earl. "These Fragments I Have Shored Against My Ruins: The Form and Function of 4 Ezra." *JBL* 92 (1973), 267-274.

The line from T.S. Eliot's poem can remind us that Ezra 4 "was composed by an author of considerable literary skill whose community's religious orientation was challenged by the destruction of Jerusalem. The author, under the stress of the consciousness that Jerusalem had once again been wasted, took up the broken fragments of the community's traditions and, drawing upon ancient patterns of consolation, constructed a literary work in a form or a pattern that might dispel the community's religious confusion."

*   Collins, John J., ed. *Semeia 14. Apocalypse: The Morphology of a Genre.* See #36.

1471.   Eskenazi, Tamara C. "Ezra-Nehemiah: From Text to Actuality";
Clines, David J.A. "The Force of the Text: A Response to Tamara C. Eskenazi's 'Ezra-Nehemiah: From Text to Actuality," in J. Cheryl Exum, ed., *Signs and Wonders: Biblical Texts in Literary Focus* [no city or publisher] (Scholars P?, 1989), 165-215.

"Ezra-Nehemiah [not only] ... highlight[s] the significance of texts through descriptions such as the public reading from the Torah (Nehemiah 8). The book also exemplifies the primacy of texts by its overall structure and its innovative use of genres such as letters and memoirs.... Ezra-Nehemiah ... combines form and content to articulate a central theme: the actualization of the written text in the life of the community." Clines: Eskenazi's argument is made "cogently, with enviable lucidity and force." However, how do we know that Ezra-Nehemiah is in prose? Does the text also restrain actuality? How are readers affected by the truth or falsity of texts? Do they sometimes do harm as well as good?

1472. Eskenazi, Tamara Cohn. *In An Age of Prose: A Literary Approach to Ezra-Nehemiah.* Atlanta (Scholars P), 1988.

We need more discourse-oriented studies of Ezra-Nehemiah. The unity of the book; its structure as articulation of its distinctive ideology; themes of the centrality of the people, expansion of the house of God, and the primacy of writing as vehicle for authority; characterization, point of view, and repetitions.

1473. Fitzmyer, Joseph A., S.J. "Some Notes on Aramiac Epistolography." *JBL* 93 (1974), 201-225.

Typical formulae found in ancient Aramiac letters, and their characteristic structure. These findings bear on the study of James and I Peter in the NT, but more importantly on certain OT passages which contain Aramaic epistolography: e.g., Ezra and Daniel.

* Solomon, Anne M. "The Structure of the Chronicler's History: A Key to the Organization of the Pentateuch." See #1481.

1474. Talmon, Shemaryahu. "Ezra and Nehemiah," in #33, pp. 357-64.

Like Chronicles, Daniel, and Esther, Ezra and Nehemiah sought to adapt the rich literary traditions from the monarchal era "to shape the social and religious awareness of their contemporaries." Ezra and Nehemiah are probably by two different authors, though they constitute "one literary complex." There are three constituent blocks to the structure of this complex, all with similar outline and composed of the same types of sub-units. The prose narration is vivid, and the author (unlike those of other books of the HB), records events of which he had immediate knowledge.

See also: #s 166, 187, 206, 336, 700, 711, 1481.

CHRONICLES

1475. Altink, Willem. "I Chronicles 16:8-36 as Literary Source for Revelation 14:6-7." *AUSS* 22 (1984), 187-196.

Similarities in key words, in use of words, and in structure all suggest I Chronicles 16 as a source for Revelation 14. Seeing this relationship enables us to understand certain themes in Revelation better.

1476. Dillard, Raymond B. "The Literary Structure of the Chronicler's Solomon Narrative." *JSOT* 30 (1984), 85-93.

The presentation of Solomon in II Chronicles 1-9 as a chiastic narrative, with some implications for interpretation. Why we should look for chiasm in biblical narrative, and how to do so.

1477. Duke, Rodney K. *The Persuasive Appeal of the Chronicler: A Rhetorical Analysis.* Sheffield (Almond P), 1990.

Application of classical rhetoric to Chronicles reveals it to be "persuasive historical narrative," using "artistic means of persuasion." It can be classified specifically as deliberative speech. Its *logos* employs a balance of enthymeme and example; its *ethos* centers on good sense, good character and good will, and creates reliability by "a mosaic of authoritative witnesses"; its *pathos* is unambiguous and heroic.

* Eslinger, Lyle. "Josiah and the Torah Book: Comparison of 2 Kgs 22:1–23:28 and 2 Chr 34:1–35:19." See #878.

1478. Hill, Andrew E. "Patchwork Poetry or Reasoned Verse? Connective Structure in I Chronicles XVI." *VT* 33 (1983), 97-101.

I Chronicles 16:8-36 is a composite psalm derived from Psalms 96, 105, and 106. All these psalms were chosen for the similarity of vocabulary with the immediate context of the narrative in Chronicles. The Chronicles passage exhibits "a deliberate and skillful poetic arrangement."

1479. Miscall, Peter D. "For David's Sake: A Response to David M. Gunn," in J. Cheryl Exum, ed., *Signs and Wonders: Biblical Texts in Literary Focus* [no city or publisher] (Scholars P? 1989), 153-163.

Response to #780. David M. Gunn's picture of David is essentially accurate, but if we contrast it with the "consistent image of

David" presented in Chronicles, we find that "The Chronicler can
be equal to or in conflict with Samuel-Kings. In 1 Kings the Lord
shows his freedom to shift...."

1480.   Snyman, Gerrie. "Fictionality and the Writing of History in
         1 Chronicles 13." *OTE* n.s. 3 (1990), 171-190.

The Constance school of reception theory shows that the reading process of fiction and of historical narrative are the same because both require "fictionality"—i.e., the image-forming ability of
the mind. In this sense the Chronicler "fictionalizes" a Samuel text
about the return of the Ark. "The Book of Chronicles ... [is based
on] his aesthetic experience during the reading process.... [I]t can
be described as a performance by the Chronicler.... Chronicles reveals fictionality on the part of the Chronicler as reader turned author...." I Chronicles 13.

1481.   Solomon, Anne M. "The Structure of the Chronicler's His-
         tory: A Key to the Organization of the Pentateuch." *Semeia*
         46 (1989), 51-64.

The Chronicler's work—i.e., I and II Chronicles, Ezra and Nehemiah—shows a fivefold structural pattern derived from the organization of the Pentateuch. They used a "common grid" for organizing the traditions they wrote about.

1482.   Talmon, Shemaryahu. "1 and 2 Chronicles," in #33, pp. 365-
         372.

"Altogether, Chronicles exhibits the chronological breadth
which characterizes biblical historiography and is unequalled in
the literatures of the ancient Near East...." The author's bias is, like
that in Psalms but unlike that in 1 Samuel to 2 Kings, strongly pro-
David. Historical scope, structure, possible authorship and date of
composition.

1483.   Wright, John W. "The Legacy of David in Chronicles: The
         Narrative Function of 1 Chronicles 23-27." *JBL* 110
         (1991), 229-242.

I Chronicles 23-27 is not an intrusion into the Chronicler's narrative, but "functions as the most significant part of the Davidic
narrative by providing the narrative basis for the establishment of
temple personnel" at crucial times in the book. "This legacy also
legitimates the rule of David himself. A comparison of [this] ...
motif to autobiographical writings of the Persian period suggests
that the passage functions to further the idealization of David in
Chronicles."

See also: #s 187, 711, 788, 1113, 1742.

THE NEW TESTAMENT

Books

1484. Anderson, Bernhard W., ed. *The Books of the Bible II: The Apocrypha and the New Testament.* New York (Scribners), 1989

Essays on each book or small groups of books of the apocrypha and the NT by a variety of different scholars, giving considerable space to literary-critical matters.

1485. Aune, David E., ed. *Greco-Roman Literature and the New Testament. Selected Forms and Genres.* Atlanta (Scholars P), 1988.

Vernon K. Robbins, "The Chreia"; David L. Balch, "Household Codes"; William Stegner, "The Ancient Jewish Synagogue Homily"; Stanley K. Stowers, "The Diatribe"; John L. White, "Ancient Greek Letters"; David E. Aune, "Greco-Roman Biography"; Ronald F. Hock, "The Greek Novel." Each essays discusses parallels in one or more NT books to demonstrate imitation or influence.

1486. Aune, David E. *The New Testament in its Literary Environment.* Philadelphia (Westminster P), 1987.

NT literary forms and genres compared with those found in the ancient Mediterranean world, especially in Hellenism. Gospels compared to ancient biographical literature (both Greco-Roman and Israelite-Jewish); Luke-Acts to ancient historiography; NT letters to Greco-Roman, Aramaic, and Jewish epistolography; Revelation to ancient apocalypses.

*   Barr, David L. *New Testament Story: An Introduction.* See #168.

1487.   Beardslee, William A. *Literary Criticism of the New Testament.*
         Philadelphia (Fortress P), 1969.

         The basics of literary criticism, and how it might work on the NT
         as a religious text. Micro- and macro-literary forms in the NT, e.g.,
         gospel, proverb, historiography, apocalyptic. Literary history of the
         synoptic gospels. How literary criticism and theological under-
         standing interact.

1487a.   Black, David Alan, and David S. Dockery, eds., *New
         Testament Criticism and Interpretation.* Grand Rapids (Zon-
         dervan Publishing House), 1991.

         Nineteen essays on various issues in, and methods of, interpret-
         ing the NT. Relevant are: Aida B. Spencer, "Literary Criticism"
         (pp. 227-251); Bill Stancil, "Structuralism" (pp. 319-344); and
         Craig L. Blomberg, "The Diversity of Literary Genres in the New
         Testament" (pp. 507-532). Each essay defines the method or issue
         and evaluates its usefulness for, or relevance to, NT study.

1488.   Douglas, Claude C. *Overstatement in the New Testament.* New
         York (Henry Holt), 1931.

         There is a great deal more hyperbole in the Bible than in any
         other ancient literature. Because it is literature, confusion results
         when we ignore fundamental literary principles in reading the
         Bible. Much of the NT, in fact, is hyperbole. This is probably be-
         cause otherwise our emotions could never be stirred to accept the
         truth.

1489.   Farrer, Austin. *The Glass of Vision* (*The Bampton Lectures*).
         London (Dacre Press), 1948; rpt 1966.

         Various interactions between theology and poetry and meta-
         physics, "the form of divine truth in the human mind." Imagery,
         archetypes, prophecy and the NT. "Poetry and divine inspiration
         have this in common, that both are projected in images which
         cannot be decoded, but must be allowed to signify what they sig-
         nify of the reality beyond them."

1490.   Funk, Robert W. *Language, Hermeneutic, and Word of God: The
         Problem of Language in the New Testament and Contemporary
         Theology.* New York (Harper and Row), 1966.

         Biblical language, like all language, is caught in the paradox
         that it mediates, and thus controls, reality. Since history itself
         comes to us in language, how are we to read the historical claims
         of the Bible? Language seems to have made traditional theology
         no longer viable. Theories of language in the twentieth century.
         The parable as metaphor, especially Matthew, Luke 10 and 14. A

phenomenology of NT language; the form of the Pauline letter; ways into Paul's thought through his "particular and diverse language." **

1491.   Grant, Patrick. *Reading the New Testament.* Grand Rapids (Eerdmans), 1989.

The NT and the literary reader. Literary readings of the gospels, I and II Corinthians, Hebrews, and Revelations. Mark, e.g., "is both imaginative and self-reflexive," with "no easy consolation, no finally secure interpretation of faith."

1492.   Jasper, David. *The New Testament and the Literary Imagination.* Atlantic Highlands (Humanities), 1986; London (Macmillan), 1987.

"... our primary response must be to [the NT texts] ... as language, as structures of words...." Literary criticism may get us "closer to the mystery which drove and inspired them." The NT sense of history; importance of imagination and metaphor; nature of NT narrative; use of proverb, poetry, and fiction.

1493.   Johnson, Alfred M., Jr., ed. and tr. *The New Testament and Structuralism.* Pittsburgh (Pickwick P), 1976.

Essays by French scholars on methods of A.J. Greimas; problems of narrative semiology in the Bible; structural analyses of NT "short stories" including the passion narratives, etc.

1494.   Jónsson, Jakob. *Humour and Irony in the New Testament Illuminated by Parallels in Talmud and Midrash.* Reykjavík (Bókaútgáfa Menningarsjóðs), 1965; rpt Leiden (E.J. Brill), 1984.

The authors of the NT were influenced by the rabbinic humor and prophetic irony of the OT, and possibly also by the use of humor and irony in Hellenistic culture. NT writers were educated in a milieu where ridiculing opponents and laughter in general as a means of instruction were not uncommon. Three main types of NT humor: the synoptic gospels' derives from Talmud and Midrash; John uses "divine irony"; and the Pauline letters use socratic irony. The 1984 reprint: searching for humor in the NT does not threaten theology, but provides through literary criticism a way into the heart of the NT.

1495.   Juel, Donald, with James S. Ackerman and Thayer S. Warshaw. *An Introduction to New Testament Literature.* Nashville (Abingdon P), 1978.

Broad survey of NT writings heavily based on literary-critical assumptions about structure, thematic analysis, characterization, plot and narrational strategies.

1496.   Keegan, Terence J. *Interpreting the Bible. A Popular Introduction to Biblical Hermeneutics.* New York and Mahwah (Paulist P), 1985.

New methods, e.g., literary criticism offer new understandings of how to read the Bible, and of how it has been read in the past. Biblical critics have always borrowed secular analytic techniques. Advantages of synchronic over older diachronic methods; definitions of structuralism and reader-response approaches, with sample analysis of Matthew; canonical criticism. Examples almost entirely from the NT. **

1497.   Kennedy, George A. *New Testament Interpretation Through Rhetorical Criticism.* Chapel Hill and London (U of North Carolina P), 1984.

Rhetorical criticism applied to Matthew 5-7 and Luke 6-7 (deliberative rhetoric); John 13-17 (epideictic rhetoric); the general rhetoric of the gospels. Acts as "classical historical monograph" as shown by its speeches; general rhetorical practices in Thessalonians, Galatians, and Romans.

1498.   Kinneavy, James L. *Greek Rhetorical Origins of Christian Faith: An Inquiry.* New York and Oxford (Oxford UP), 1987.

Not a direct literary-critical approach to the NT, but providing valuable information and arguments concerning the extensive influence of classical rhetoric on NT gospels and letters. "... a substantial part of the concept of faith found in the New Testament can be found in the rhetorical concept of persuasion, which was a major meaning of the noun *pistis* (faith or persuasion) and the verb *pisteuein* in the Greek language at the period the New Testament was written." Semantic, historical, and analytical evidence for this conclusion. **

1499.   Knight, G. Wilson. *The Christian Renaissance.* Revised edition. London (Methuen and Co.), 1962 [Original 1933].

As an art form, the NT's subject is both life and death, since like all poetry it offers a marriage of heaven and earth, life and death. It fuses poetry and history, since both are "creative abstractions from reality." The NT is close to myth, and therefore is more poetry than biography. To ask whether the NT is historically accurate is to miss the point. The symbolism in the Pauline letters.

1500.   Lund, Nils Wilhelm. *Chiasmus in the New Testament: A Study in Formgeschichte.* Chapel Hill (U of North Carolina P), 1942.

History of study of form in the NT. Seven laws governing chiastic structure therein. Chiasm in OT as background to its study in NT. Chiasm in Jesus' discourses; in I Corinthians, Ephesians, Colossians, Philippians, Philemon,, Romans, and Revelation. Although chiasm appears also in Homer and other ancient pagan writing, its most sophisticated literary and theological development came in Hebrew writing; this is why it is so common in the NT.

1501.   Mack, Burton L. *Rhetoric and the New Testament.* Philadelphia (Fortress P), 1990.

An "introduction to the recent scholarship in rhetorical criticism." Basics of classical rhetorical theory and practice; its connection with and influence on the gospels, Pauline letters, other letters, and Acts. Matthew 5-7; Mark 2, 8, 10; Luke 3, 12; John 5; Acts 2; I Corinthians 9, 13, 15; II Corinthians 9; Galatians; Hebrews 11, 12. The future of rhetorical criticism of the NT. **

1502.   Malherbe, Abraham J. *Moral Exhortation, A Greco-Roman Sourcebook.* Philadelphia (Westminster P), 1986.

Reprints of, and comments on, a number of pagan philosophical writings, both private and public, which illustrate various themes and approaches to moral exhortation. Each section or type related to NT passages. Stylistic and literary conventions of this writing.

1503.   Patte, Daniel. *Structural Exegesis for New Testament Critics.* Philadelphia (Fortress P), 1989, 1990.

An "inductive approach" to explaining structural analysis of the NT. Analyzing "religious discourse units" in John 3 through six repeatable steps. Exercises in structural exegesis of John 4 and Luke 10. Structuralism is capable of elucidating the different "faith-patterns" of NT texts.

1504.   Patte, Daniel. *What is Structural Exegesis?* Philadelphia (Fortress P), 1976.

The basic principles of structuralism, and how it differs from diachronic methods. One must first identify the system of signs within the text, and the sequence of narrative elements. The "deep structures" of mythological texts in general, and of Galatians 1:1-10 specifically. Narrative and mythic structures in Luke 10.

1505.   Perrin, Norman. *Jesus and the Language of the Kingdom. Symbol and Metaphor in New Testament Interpretation.* Philadelphia (Fortress P), 1976.

Gives "deliberate attention to literary factors" when investigating the concept of the Kingdom of God in Jesus' teachings. The kingdom is a symbol rather than a conception, and seeing it thus solves several basic problems. The literary dimension is important whether we are discussing the problem historically or as it applies to contemporary audiences. Jesus' "kingdom" is a "symbol of cultural range," and a "symbol evoking a myth." Considerable attention to the parables.

1506.   Petersen, Norman. *Literary Criticism for New Testament Critics.* Philadelphia (Fortress P), 1978.

Basic problems with historical criticism; why literary critics do respect history, despite their having problems with the specifics of the historical-critical method. A literary-critical model for biblical critics based on the work of Roman Jakobson and Claude Lévi-Strauss. "Story time and plotted time" in Mark; "narrative world and real world" in Luke-Acts.

1507.   Petzer, J.H., and P.J. Hartin, eds. *A South African Perspective on the New Testament: Essays by South African New Testament Scholars.* Leiden (E.J. Brill), 1986.

Literary essays on the NT generally, and on Matthew 22, John, Pauline letters, I Corinthians 13, and Galatians, analyzed separately as #s 1527, 1698, 1925, 1993, 2081, 2088, 2125, 2144, and 2163.

1508.   Petzer, J.H., and P.J. Hartin, eds. *Text and Interpretation: New Approaches in the Criticism of the New Testament.* Leiden (E.J. Brill), 1991.

Sixteen essays exploring a variety of new methods of analyzing the NT. Eight use some form of literary criticism; these are analyzed separately as #s 1835, 1838, 1863, 2004, 2034, 2035, 2107, and 2177.

1509.   Pritchard, John P. *A Literary Approach to the New Testament.* Norman (U of Oklahoma P), 1972.

Surveys of stylistic features, structure, arguments, and literary influence of each gospel, Acts, Pauline letters, other letters, and Revelation.

1510. Reese, James M., O.S.F.S. *Experiencing the Good News: The New Testament as Communication.* Wilmington (Michael Glazier, Inc.), 1984.

"When studied from a semiotic perspective, ... the discourse of the New Testament is the normative part of a complex, ongoing, expanding 'universe of discourse' centering around the Christ event...." Communication event, discourse analysis, language and NT culture; religious language and the imagination.

1511. Ryken, Leland. *Words of Life: A Literary Introduction to the New Testament.* Grand Rapids (Baker Book House), 1987.

The NT is "a book of the imagination in which religious truth is more often embodied in ... story, metaphor and symbol than it is expressed in theological abstraction.... [I]t is not a collection of essays, nor a theological outline with proofs attached, but an anthology of literary genres...." The gospel as a literary form; literary features of the parables; Acts as story; literary aspects of the letters. Presence of poetry and oratory in the NT, and literary approaches to Revelation.

1512. Sands, P.C. *Literary Genius of the New Testament.* Oxford (Clarendon P), 1932; rpt Westport (Greenwood P), 1970.

It is important to learn how to appreciate the literary beauty of the NT narratives and letters, since these writings could not have been so influential without their literary quality. Techniques and artistic qualities of each gospel; parables and sayings; Acts; Pauline and other letters; and Revelation.

1513. Silberman, Lou H., ed. *Semeia 39. Orality, Aurality and Biblical Narrative.* Decatur (Scholars P), 1987.

Essays on the relationship between oral communication criticism and literary criticism of the NT by Silberman, Walter J. Ong, Thomas J. Farrell, Thomas E. Boomershine, Gilbert L. Bartholomew, Werner H. Kelber, and Herbert N. Schneidau. NT passages treated include Mark, and John 21.

* Trawick, Buckner B. *The Bible as Literature: The New Testament.* See #188.

1514. Tuckett, Christopher. *Reading the New Testament: Methods of Interpretation.* Philadelphia (Fortress P), 1987.

Chapters 10 and 11 explain and evaluate structuralist and New Critical approaches to the NT. Structuralism is useful because it provides detailed justification for interpretations which we simply assumed before were true. The New Criticism is useful mainly on the parables. Historical criticism, while lacking in certain respects as a tool, cannot be abandoned.

1515.   Turner, Nigel. *A Grammar of New Testament Greek, Vol. IV: Style [Begun by James Hope Moulton].* Edinburgh (T. and T. Clark), 1976.

Chapters on each gospel; Pauline letters; pastoral letters; Hebrews; James; I Peter; Johannine letters; Jude and II Peter; and Revelation. Word order, use of figures, sentence construction, influence of Hebrew and pagan writing, etc. Comparison of the styles of various NT books with each other; evaluations of the stylistic success of each book.

1516.   Via, Dan O., Jr. *Kerygma and Comedy in the New Testament: A Structuralist Approach to Hermeneutic.* Philadelphia (Fortress P), 1975.

Theories of comedy applied to Mark and several Pauline letters. Attempted synthesis of structuralist, phenomenological, and existential methods of interpretation. For Paul, the paradigm of the death and resurrection of Jesus "is continuous with other comic syntagms...." I Corinthians 1-2; Romans 9-10; various genre possibilities for, and structuralist analysis of, Mark. Incorporates #2113.

1517.   Warner, Martin, ed. *The Bible as Rhetoric: Studies in Biblical Persuasion and Credibility.* London and New York (Routledge), 1990.

Eleven essays by scholars in rhetoric, literature, and biblical studies, of which nine are literary: two on the Bible as a whole, analyzed separately as #s 121 and 1345; two on the HB, analyzed separately as #s 681 and 1280; and five on the NT, analyzed separately as #s 1646, 1785, 1970, 2000, and 2069. **

1518.   Wilder, Amos N. *Early Christian Rhetoric: The Language of the Gospels.* Cambridge (Harvard UP), 1971. [Originally published 1964: New York: Harper and Row, with title and subtitle interchanged]; Chapter V rpt in #1669.

The forms of NT writings and their essential similarities to and differences from those of Classical literature. Three fundamental literary patterns observable in the NT: drama, narrative, and poem. Image, symbol, and myth are so pervasive in the NT that they form its very fabric and mode of perceiving reality. **

1519.   Wilder, Amos N. *The New Voice: Religion, Literature, Hermeneutics.* New York (Herder and Herder), 1969.

The narrative mode in both NT and modern literature is "a combination of myth, saga, and history" which orients humans to the mysteries of time and existence and to "the structures of a human order against chaos." The domain of myth and archetype, and of dreams, ecstatic and mystical experience are the "deeper determinants" which shape NT imagery and give it power. Ways of reading modern literature in the light of theological understandings gained from the NT.

Articles

1520. Beardslee, William A. "New Testament Apocalyptic in Recent Interpretation." *Interpretation* 25 (1971), 419-435.

Apocalyptic literature has not been much studied because it was thought to be theologically secure. Now that this is no longer the case, we do not know what to do with its symbolism. How apocalyptic has been studies over the centuries. Its characteristics include the otherness of God; faith that the end is at hand; a sense of existence in time; and esoteric revelation. We still do not know if it derived from prophecy or wisdom, whether its roots are Judaeo-Christian or Hellenistic.

1521. Black, C. Clifton II. "Rhetorical Criticism and the New Testament." *PEGL* 8 (1988), 77-92.

How rhetorical criticism works, with examples of how it applies to certain NT passages. Its most promising aspects are its ability to bridge the gap between the historical and the literary methods (partly because classical rhetoric was both literary and historical); its "distinctive, clear, systematic, and thorough" character; its power to place us more firmly into first century minds; and its value as a tool for reexamining tantalizing and intractable scholarly problems.

1522. Black, C. Clifton II. "Rhetorical Questions: The New Testament, Classical Rhetoric, and Current Interpretation." *Dialog* 29 (1990), 62-3, 66, 68-70.

Appraisal of the rhetorical method on the NT. Some recent books have left "rhetoric" too fuzzily defined; have failed to define adequately how it actually works in an NT setting; and have sometimes forced a classical rhetorical structure on an NT book. Its benefits are that it ties together the literary and historical methods, illuminates authorial intention, conceptualizes to a high degree, and accounts better for the power of NT texts.

1523. Botha, Jan. "On the 'Reinvention' of Rhetoric." *Scriptura* 31 (1989), 14-31.

The current definition of rhetoric as the use of stylistic figures to evoke emotional response differs significantly from the ancient definition. The reinvention of rhetorical interpretation of the NT "needs to affect both the practice of New Testament interpretation itself, and the institutionalizing of New Testament scholarship...." Rhetorical criticism brings us into contact with the power of texts, not just their contents.

1524. Botha, J. Eugene. "Style, Stylistics and the Study of the New Testament." *Neotestamentica* 24 (1990), 173-184.

Various twentieth century approaches to NT style, all of which have proven inadequate. A redefinition would offer a greater sense of the purpose of such study, identify the underlying text theory, and recognize the relevance of the functional, and not just the formal, approach to style.

1525. Bovon, Francois. "French Structuralism and Biblical Exegesis," in Roland Barthes, et al., *Structural Analysis and Biblical Exegesis: Interpretational Essays,* tr Alfred M. Johnson, Jr. (Pittsburgh: Pickwick P, 1974), 4-20.

The theological debate which structuralism will bring is welcome as a synchronic corrective to the dominance of diachronic methods heretofore. The fruitfulness of the theories of Claude Lévi-Strauss and Roland Barthes as they affect reading the NT. The method applied to Acts 10-11 and John 1. The functions of "parole" and "langue" in the realm of faith.

1526. Brunt, John C. "More on the *Topos* as a New Testament Form." *JBL* 104 (1985), 495-500.

There are additional problems with using the Greco-Roman *topos* form to explain Paul's rhetoric, beyond those identified by Terence Y. Mullins [see #1545].

1527. Combrink, H.J.B. "The Changing Scene of Biblical Interpretation," in #1507, pp. 9-17.

Surveys and comments on recent contributions to NT scholarship by literary critics and sociologists.

1528. Doty, William G. "The Classification of Epistolary Literature." *CBQ* 31 (1969), 183-199.

A background for more adequate study of the epistolary genre in the NT can be provided by reviewing the distinction between "epistle" and "letter" and proposing a more comprehensive schema once this has been done. All letters are literary. In the Hellenistic world, letters could be classified as fairly intimate, "less private," public, non-real, discursive and "other" (poetic, consolatory, etc.).

1529.   Doty, William G. "Fundamental Questions About Literary-Critical Methodology: A Review Article." *JAAR* 40 (1972), 521-7.

Various issues which are most relevant to "the methodological predicaments of contemporary New Testament literary criticism as I understand them" from the work of Erhart Güttgemanns—generic, structuralist, and sociological.

1530.   Doty, William G. "Linguistics and Biblical Criticism." *JAAR* 41 (1973), 114-121.

Follow-up to #1529. Review of the work of the "Generative Poetics" team headed by Erhart Güttgemanns. Two positions underlie their work: generative transformational grammar, and the "absolute linguistic givenness of the aesthetic work." They wish to decipher the linguistic rules followed by NT writers, and find the function of the "iconic signs" in the NT.

1531.   Elsom, Helen. "The New Testament and Greco-Roman Writing," in #33, pp. 561-578.

The later history of Christianity suggests that its climb to dominance was aided "by the fact that its sacred texts were written in Greek, and in literary forms which, if not Greek themselves, could be understood in Greek terms, popular as well as learned." Three new literary genres arose: biography, prose fiction, and biographical romance, all of which provided means of exploring the character and experiences of historical figures. So, too, NT letter writers followed conventions of Greco-Roman letter writing.

1532.   Filson, Floyd V. "How Much of the New Testament is Poetry?" *JBL* 67 (1948), 125-134.

Current critical discussion of this question is clouded by the use of vague criteria. When these are sharpened, we will undoubtedly find that much less of the NT is poetry than we now think.

1533.   Fischel, Henry A. "The Use of Sorites (*Climax, Gradatio*) in the Tannaitic Period." *HUCA* 44 (1973), 119-151.

Various NT passages "reflect the fashionableness, variety, structure, and function which the sorite possessed in Greco-Roman rhetoric and rhetorical literature of this period and are, with some exceptions, dependent upon the Greco-Roman models." Classification and definitions of various types.

1534. Funk, Robert W. "Saying and Seeing: Phenomenology of Language and the New Testament." *Journal of Bible and Religion* 34 (1966), 197-213.

We are beginning to see the importance of the "voices and linguistic contexts of the New Testament." How a phenomenology of language addresses these matters, especially the voice of Jesus in the parables and of Paul in his letters. Phenomenology is the "shelter of pre-established significations, as that which gives what is to be seen."

1535. Funk, Robert W. "The Significance of Discourse Structure for the Study of the New Testament," in James W. Flanagan and Anita Weisbrod Robinson, eds., *No Famine in the Land.* Missoula (Scholars P, 1975), 209-221.

Discourse structure will enable the NT critic to analyze narrative structures with greater precision and, "as a consequence, to develop a more vigorously controlled typology of narrative forms."

* Gammie, John G. "Paraenetic Literature: Toward the Morphology of a Genre." See #250.

1536. Jasper, David. "The New Testament and Literary Interpretation." *Religion and Literature* 17, #3 (1985), 1-10.

The historical criticism which wants ultimately only facts, and in the process becomes divorced from the kinds of questions which scripture demands, is inadequate. The New Testament is not just information, but address.

1537. Jennrich, Walter A. "Rhetoric in the New Testament." *Classical Journal* 44 (1948), 30-32.

Modern critics need to take up classical rhetoric as a tool for analyzing the New Testament. Early Christianity understood the importance of rhetoric for interpreting their scripture, but it has long since been forgotten.

1538. Kermode, Frank. "Introduction to the New Testament," in #33, pp. 375-386.

Various definitions of "gospel"; how and why the genre developed; how the differences among them were dealt with early on; their comparative styles and emphases, and the apparent influence of one on another. The dates, function, organization and style of Acts, and of the various New Testament letters and of Revelation.

1539. Krieg, Robert A. "Karl Adam's Christology: Towards a Post-Critical Method." *HJ* 25 (1984), 456-474.

Adam's christology in the light of the history of narrative approaches to the Bible; illustrations from the work of Hans Frei, Norman Perrin, Norman Petersen, and others who take a literary-critical approach to the NT.

1540. Lambrecht, Jan. "Rhetorical Criticism and the New Testament." *Bijdragen* 50 (1989), 239-253.

Definitions of classical and of modern rhetoric. The main contributions to and advances in rhetorical criticism of the Bible lie in matters of genre, language, concept of the work as a discourse, nature of persuasion, and identifying social context. Rhetorical criticism is not an independent, self-sufficient method, but is valuable nonetheless.

1541. Leach, Edmund. "Fishing for Men on the Edge of the Wilderness," in #33, pp. 579-599.

Demonstration of biblical exegesis deriving from structural anthropology, especially the work of Claude Lévi-Strauss, and "closely related to the typological style of argument employed by the majority of early Christian writers." This method is part of a "literary-aesthetic" approach to biblical books which takes the text in its present form as being a whole and of value. It worries not about historical accuracy of the Bible but about symbolic, internal dynamics.

1542. Louw, Johannes P. "Discourse Analysis and the Greek New Testament." *BT* 24 (1973), 101-118.

The importance of semantic discourse analysis for understanding and translating the NT. Examples from Luke 9 and Romans 5 show that the type of discourse employed is a clue to the structure of a passage, and therefore to its meaning.

1543. Macky, Peter W. "The Coming Revolution: The New Literary Approach to the New Testament." *The Theological Educator* 9 (1979), 32-46; rpt Donald K. McKim, ed., *A Guide to Contemporary Hermeneutics: Major Trends in Biblical Interpretation* (Grand Rapids: Eerdmans, 1986), 263-279.

For too long we have believed that the Bible is a window to facts and events. The move from historical to literary in biblical studies is a change of eras, a paradigm shift of fundamental importance. The literary approach does not deny the authority of the Bible as word of God. The assumptions of the literary approach about language, form, effect on the reader, figures and symbolism.

1544.   Man, Ronald E. "The Value of Chiasm for New Testament
        Interpretation." *B Sac* 141 (1984), 146-157.

        Various examples illustrating the contention that seeing chiastic
        arrangement in the NT helps us in attempting to understand its
        themes and its purpose.

1545.   Mullins, Terence Y. "Topos as a New Testament Form." *JBL*
        99 (1980), 541-7.

        The formal elements of the "topos"; various classical and NT ex-
        amples which require modification of the arguments in David G.
        Bradley's 1953 article on the subject [#2060]. "Topos" has three
        essential elements: injunction, reason, and discussion, with op-
        tional elements of analogy and refutation. Its purpose was to urge
        a type of behavior. It was popular with Stoic and Cynic philoso-
        phers, and occurs frequently in the NT.

1546.   Nielsen, Kirsten. "Intertextuality and Biblical Scholarship."
        SJOT (1990, #2), 89-95.

        "... some consequences of the post-structuralist emphasis on
        'intertextuality' ... [combining] Harold Bloom's idea of the anxi-
        ety of influence with the notion of intertextuality, and ... how ...
        the NT temptation narrative grapples with Deuteronomy 6-8 and
        Genesis 32."

1547.   Patte, Daniel. "'Love Your Enemies'—'Woe to You, Scribes
        and Pharisses': The Need for a Semiotic Approach in New
        Testament Studies," in Theodore W. Jennings, ed., *Text
        and Logos: The Humanistic Interpretation of the New Testament*
        (Atlanta: Scholars P, 1990), 81-96.

        A "semio-structural approach" to the seeming contradiction
        from Matthew quoted in the title asks, "What is, for the readers of
        ... Matthew, the meaning-effect of polemics against their ene-
        mies?" Traditional criticism tries to compromise, and thus "fails to
        [assess] ... the ways in which a discourse conveys meaning."
        Matthew's intended message is not anti-Jewish, but his gospel does
        have the effect of conveying such a message to his implied readers.

1548.   Petzer, J.H. "Author's Style and the Textual Criticism of the
        New Testament." *Neotestamentica* 24 (1990), 185-197.

        "... the complex literary origin of the New Testament docu-
        ments makes it impossible to expect a consistent use of linguistic
        and stylistic features.... [Therefore], consistency of style cannot
        easily serve as a basis for the analysis of language and style...."

1549.   Poland, Lynn. "The New Criticism, Neoorthodoxy, and the New Testament." *JR* 65 (1985), 459-477.

Recent alliances between neoorthodoxy and modern literary criticism appear to be a "union of kindred spirits, ... a marriage between partners who share certain theoretical assumptions, a cultural context, and some common preoccupations."

1550.   Porter, Stanley E. "Why Hasn't Reader-Response Criticism Caught On in New Testament Studies?" *LT* 4 (1990), 278-292.

There are several reasons for the failure of reader-response criticism to take firm hold in NT interpretation: many scholars are not certain what it is; claims by some to be using it seem erroneous or disappointingly vague; many using it are unwilling to free themselves from historical criticism; it is widely misunderstood as a reading strategy; and no significant, cohesive group practicing it has emerged. **

1551.   Reinhartz, Adele. "The New Testament and Anti-Judaism: A Literary Critical Approach." *Journal of Ecumenical Studies* 25 (1988), 524-537.

Literary criticism shows us that the question is not so much whether the authors of the NT were "intentionally and objectively anti-Jewish but whether reading it can produce feelings of hostility toward Jews on the part of Christian readers." Reader-response criticism demonstrates that the answer is yes, though also that the gospels in particular encourage the opposite view as well.

1552.   Ricoeur, Paul. "Interpretative Narrative," in #45, pp. 237-257.

"These are narratives in which the ideological interpretations these narratives wish to convey is not superimposed on the narrative by the narrator but is, instead, incorporated into the very strategy of the narrative.... [They] can have an interpretative function in relation to [their] own kerygmatic intention...." Examples mainly from Mark.

1553.   Segert, Stanislav. "Semitic Poetic Structures in the New Testament." *Aufstieg und Niedergang der Römischen Welt* 25, #2 (1984), 1434-1462.

The present state of research on the subject; the features of Semitic poetry, especially during the Roman period; the character of poetic passages and features in the NT. We may establish three categories of NT books based on how closely they follow Semitic poetic practices. On occasion we find that NT passages imitate or adapt the styles and techniques of OT verse.

1554.   Snyman, Andreas H. "On Studying the Figures (*schēmata*) in the New Testament." *Biblica* 69 (1988), 93-107.

The new rhetoric of Perelman and Olbrechts-Tyteca provides a fresh way of studying NT figures, where the traditional method of classification is vague and abstracted from the rhetorical situation, the requirements of argumentation and the role of the audience.

1555.   Stancil, Bill. "Structuralism and New Testament Studies." *SWJT* 22, #2 (Spring, 1980), 41-59.

The theory of structuralism, how it has been applied recently to the NT, and its limitations. It is a helpful approach, but due to its complexity its use may be limited to the most informed interpreters only.

1556.   Thimmes, Pamela. "The Biblical Sea-Storm Type-Scene: A Proposal." *PEGL* 10 (1990), 107-122.

The sea-storm type-scene is found primarily in the NT, deriving both from life around the Mediterranean and Greco-Roman literature. NT authors retain enough of the conventions to enable readers to identify with the stories, while introducing the authors' own implications: e.g., that God, not fate, wills the outcome. This type-scene "can be pointedly didactic or purely functional."

1557.   Thiselton, Anthony C. "Structuralism and Biblical Studies: Method or Ideology?" *ET* 89 (1978), 329-335.

The origins and basic aims of structuralism; how it is used in NT studies; its strengths and weaknesses when so applied. There is tremendous divergence, even disagreement, on both the ideology and the method of structuralism among its practitioners. Its weaknesses include its tendency to ignore history; its obsession with science and thus its arbitrary application of method; and its abstraction of code from message. It does bring, however, a freshness of insight.

1558.   van Unnik, Willem. "First Century A.D. Literary Culture and Early Christian Literature." *The Center for Hermeneutical Studies in Hellenistic and Modern Culture: Protocol of the First Colloquy: 25 April 1970* (Berkeley, 1975), 1-13; responses pp. 14-28.

The writers of the NT were undoubtedly influenced by the pagan literary culture around them in their handling of sources, standards of rhetorical excellence, genre theory, and sense of literary form. We have only begun to investigate these possibilities, and need to do much more.

1559. van Unnik, W.C. "First Century A.D. Literary Culture and Early Christian Literature." *Nederlands Theologisch Tijdschrift* 25 (1971), 28-43.

Characterization of the serious and the popular literary cultures of Rome at the time of Christ. It is important to realize that historiography was regarded as a branch of rhetoric, and that for various reasons this culture must have influenced the writing of the NT.

1560. Vorster, J.N. "Toward an Interactional Model for the Analysis of Letters." *Neotestamentica* 24 (1990), 107-130.

We can no longer stop at structural analysis of NT letters, but must "take cognizance of aspects of conversational analysis and rhetoric. That an interactional model rather than a structural approach should be adopted...is required from the letter genre itself." NT scholars still do not study the rhetorical situation enough; such analysis is built on speech act theory. The *inventio* stage of the rhetorical process is where the analysis must concentrate.

1561. Watson, Nigel. "The 'Intentional Fallacy' and Biblical Exegesis," in Eric Osborn and Lawrence McIntosh, eds., *The Bible and European Literature* (Melbourne: Academia P, 1987), 186-196.

Already by the 1920's the search for authorial intention, the cornerstone of the historical-critical method, was being called into doubt as "the intentional fallacy." However, we should be careful about abandoning authorial intention altogether. The more a biblical text is stamped with the author's personality (as is often the case in the NT, especially in the Pauline letters), the more we are irresponsible in ignoring authorial intention.

1562. Wilder, Amos N. "Scholars, Theologians, and Ancient Rhetoric." *JBL* 75 (1956), 1-11.

Proper interpretation, especially of ancient mytho-poetic texts, requires recognizing the kind of literature being dealt with. We need to know not only what was believed, but how. We need to deal with symbols in scripture, but the usual tools for doing so lack cogency. Literary criticism can give us help in this task.

1563. Wuellner, Wilhelm. "Hermeneutics and Rhetorics." *Scriptura* Special Issue S3: 1989.

The history of the interaction of hermeneutical and rhetorical criticism from Antiquity to the present. "... modern rhetorics is more than, if not other than, one of the literary 'arts' or 'technique.' Instead, it is one of the forms of modern literary theory, which includes the theory of reading."

1564.   Wuellner, Wilhelm. "Where is Rhetorical Criticism Taking Us?" *CBQ* 49 (1987), 448-463.

The place of rhetorical criticism in biblical studies; its distinction from literary criticism is that it is concerned both with text and context. A number of its current practitioners, especially George Kennedy; his model applied to I Corinthians 9. Rhetorical criticism can help bridge the gap between historical and purely literary criticism, while avoiding the extremes of both.

See also: #s 168, 187, 300, 1657, 2061.

THE GOSPELS

Books

1565.   Boomershine, Thomas E. *Story Journey: An Invitation to the Gospel as Storytelling.* Nashville (Abingdon P), 1988.

To understand the gospels, and to "enter more deeply into a relationship with Jesus' journey from his birth," we must first experience them as stories, in their original medium of oral narrative. Matthew 14, Mark 1, 2, 7, 10, 14, 15, Luke 15.

1566.   Burney, C.F. *The Poetry of Our Lord. An Examination of the Formal Elements of Hebrew Poetry in the Discourses of Jesus Christ.* Oxford (Clarendon P), 1925.

The formal characteristics of Hebrew poetry (chiefly parallelism, rhythm, and stress-accentuation) show up repeatedly in the words of Jesus recorded in the gospels. Jesus even used rhyme—probably as a mnemonic device—which, while rare in the HB, is present in the folk poetry Jesus would have known.

1567. Crossan, John D., ed. *Semeia 10. Narrative Syntax: Translations and Reviews.* Missoula (Scholars P), 1978.

Responses to Erhardt Güttgemanns' articles on generative poetics [#s 1612, 1613] by Claude Bremond and Vladimir Propp; reviews by Brian Kovacs, Edgar Mc Knight, Daniel Patte, and Robert Detweiler.

1568. Culbertson, Diana. *The Poetics of Revelation: Recognition and the Narrative Tradition.* Macon (Mercer UP), 1989.

Part III: "a conversation between secular literature and the gospel narratives." A "poetics of revelation" would attempt "to describe how God's self-communication is apprehended in history and how literature models that apprehension." Mark; John; "Audience Response and the Gospel Narrative."

1569. Freyne, Sean. *Galilee, Jesus, and the Gospels: Literary Approaches and Historical Investigations.* Philadelphia (Fortress P), 1988.

The present state of literary and socio-historical knowledge of the gospels, particularly with regard to their Galilean references. Galilean elements in the settings, characters, and plots of each of the gospels.

1570. Funk, Robert W. *The Poetics of Biblical Narrative.* Sonoma (Polebridge P), 1989.

"Examines the surface structures of narrative texts [in the gospels and Acts] to discover how the reader constructs plot, character, and perspective from signals embedded in the discourse."

1571. Gerhart, Mary, and James G. Williams, eds. *Semeia 43: Genre, Narrativity, and Theology.* Atlanta (Scholars P), 1988.

Essays on questions of genre in the gospels, paired with responses, by Werner H. Kelber and Dan O. Via (Mark); Mary Gerhart and Robert Detweiler; Charles H. Talbert and David P. Moessner; James G. Williams; John D. Crossan and Robert C. Tannehill; general responses by Adela Yarbro Collins and Frank Kermode.

1572. Helms, Randel. *Gospel Fictions.* Buffalo (Prometheus Books), 1988.

Although Jesus himself really lived, the gospels are not historical accounts but essentially literary fictions based almost entirely on OT texts. All four of the gospels show clear signs of their authors' literary dependence upon the OT instead of upon actual historical materials about Jesus. This can be most clearly seen in the narratives about Jesus' birth, miracles, passion and resurrection.

1573.   Mack, Burton L., and Vernon K. Robbins. *Patterns of Persuasion in the Gospels.* Sonoma (Polebridge P), 1989.

Discussion of "early traditions about Jesus in the light of rhetorical theory and practice common to the Hellenistic culture of the time" in order to "demonstrate rhetorical composition in clusters of sayings not normally regarded as patterned, much less as patterned in forms of argumentation that were current in conventional discourse of the first century." Pronouncement stories studied alongside the conventions of Hellenistic rhetoric demonstrate that these stories in the synoptic gospels are Hellenistic *chreiai.*

1574.   Marin, Louis. *The Semiotics of the Passion Narrative: Topics and Figures,* tr Alfred M. Johnson, Jr. Pittsburgh (Pickwick P), 1980.

Multiple analyses of the systems of the texts from a semiotic-structuralist standpoint, emphasizing "the opposition which the narrative finds necessary to be told and the mediation by which it overcomes that opposition."

1575.   Moore, Stephen D. *Literary Criticism and the Gospels: The Theoretical Challenge.* New Haven and London (Yale UP), 1989

An "analytic discussion of representative books and essays in the literary criticism of the Gospels, gradually leading into an interrogation of some of the grounding assumptions of biblical studies in general." Various forms of recent composition and narrative criticism of the gospels (as distinguished from traditional form and redaction criticism). Critics need to have an openness toward various forms of "demythologizing" criticism, including deconstruction. **

1576.   Patte, Daniel, ed. *Semeia 29: Kingdom and Children.* Chico (Scholars P), 1983.

Gospel pronouncement stories about the kingdom and children (Mark 10, Matthew 18, 19, Luke 18) from a structural (Daniel Patte) and rhetorical/form-critical (John D. Crossan and Vernon K. Robbins) perspective, with shorter responses by others.

1577.   Powell, Mark Alan. *What is Narrative Criticism?* Minneapolis (Fortress P), 1990.

The growth of interest in a literary criticism of the gospels, especially structuralism, rhetorical, reader-response and narrative criticisms. The basics of narrative theory, plot, characterization and setting. Plot in Matthew; setting in Mark; characters in the synoptic gospels. How we may answer the most common objections made by some theologians to the whole literary enterprise.

1578. Sanders, E.P., and Margaret Davies. *Studying the Synoptic Gospels.* London (SCM P) and Philadelphia (Trinity P International), 1989.

The nature of the "synoptic problem" in detail; how form, redaction, rhetorical criticism, structuralism, and deconstruction offer answers to this problem; how the influence of the OT and of sources in Hellenistic literature provide further insight.

1579. Smith, Dennis E., ed. *Semeia 52: How Gospels Begin.* Atlanta (Scholars P), 1990 (c. 1991).

Gospel beginnings and general theory of narrative openings in ancient and modern writings. Additional essays on Mark and on the gospel birth stories, analyzed separately as #s 1749, 1824, 1932, and 2018.

1580. Talbert, Charles H. *What is a Gospel? The Genre of the Synoptic Gospels.* Philadelphia (Fortress P), 1977.

The gospels are biographies. They show structural, functional and attitudinal similarities to Greco-Roman biographies: e.g., they are controlled by the same myths; they have cultural connections, as well as similar attitudes toward the world.

1581. Tannehill, Robert C. *The Sword of His Mouth.* Philadelphia and Missoula (Fortress P; Scholars P), 1975.

The "significance of forceful and imaginative language" is that it is often paradoxical and tense, that the imagination (and therefore imaginative language) is an essential part of being human. Formal analysis of a biblical (or any) text must not separate form and content, and must consider both narrative structure and reader's response. "Pattern and tension" in sayings in Matthew 5-7, 10, 11, 19; Mark 3, 7, 8, 10, 12; Luke 6, 9, 12, 17.

1582. Vanhoozer, Kevin J. *Biblical Narrative in the Philosophy of Paul Ricoeur: A Study in Hermeneutics and Theology.* Cambridge (Cambridge UP), 1990.

Poetic language transcends the dichotomy of real and imaginary; narrative has power to "invent" (discover and create) reality through the faculty of the imagination. Thus texts are never just their original historical referents nor purely linguistic structures. Ricoeur's work is an extension of Kant and Heidegger. "The gospels achieve their theological importance in Ricoeur as works of the creative imagination [in which] ... it is primarily the meaning of the accounts rather than their factuality that is of greatest human value."

1583.   Votaw, Clyde Weber. *The Gospels and Contemporary Biographies in the Greco-Roman World.* Philadelphia (Fortress P), 1970; originally published in *American Journal of Theology* 19 (1915), 45-73, 217-249.

Despite clear differences, there are also important similarities between Greco-Roman biographies of philosophers, e.g., Socrates and Epictetus and the canonical gospels.

1584.   Winton, Alan P. *The Proverbs of Jesus: Issues of History and Rhetoric.* Sheffield (JSOT P), 1990.

There is no reliable method for reconstructing Jesus' speech. How the wisdom tradition bears on understanding the gospels; how we classify and analyze proverbial sayings structurally; what issues previous literary-rhetorical and historical approaches to Jesus' shorter proverbial sayings have raised. The rhetoric of these sayings, and their significance within the synoptic gospels.

Articles

1585.   Aichele, George, Jr. "Biblical Miracle Narratives as Fantasy." *ATR* 73 (1991), 51-8.

"... Matthew, Luke, and John have eliminated or significantly reduced the indeterminacy of the Markan miracles—the element of the fantastic—by explaining them as powerful supernatural works.... Thus they neutralize Mark's fantastic reversal of the Hebrew prophetic miracle tradition and as a result their accounts are not nearly as paradoxical and ambiguous as are Mark's." We must remember that fantasy, in Tolkien's theory, is not anti-realistic.

1586.   Aichele, George, Jr. "The Fantastic in the Parabolic Language of Jesus." *Neotestamentica* 24 (1990), 93-105.

The contemporary theories of Todorov and Rabkin applied to the parables of Jesus. Matthew and Luke "eliminate the element of the fantastic in favour of theological coherence," whereas John "reverses this tendency and 're-fantasizes' the sayings material," but at the same time disarms it.

1587. Aichele, George, Jr. "Literary Fantasy and the Composition of the Gospels." *FFF* 5, #3 (September, 1989), 42-60.

In the synoptic gospels, "the narrator is also the narrated," where Mark "deconstructs" the sayings genres and Matthew and Luke in turn "reconstruct" Mark. John then "deconstructs" Matthew and Luke, and "Christology itself becomes self-referential and fantastic. In this very move ... the narrative potential of the genre was exhausted."

1588. Anderson, Janice Capel. "Mary's Difference: Gender and Patriarchy in the Birth Narratives." *JR* 67 (1987), 183-202.

Matthew and Luke embody male conceptions of females. In Matthew, the superscription and genealogy establish this immediately, where not only Mary's role is subordinate to patriarchy, but so are her four immediate predecessors. Luke also both celebrates and domesticates female difference. There is more emphasis on Mary in Luke, and she has partial independence from patriarchy, as is not the case in Matthew.

1589. Aune, David S. "The Gospels as Hellenistic Biography." *Mosaic* 20, #4 (Fall, 1987), 1-10.

The older consensus that the gospels did not derive from ancient biography is now disintegrating. There is wide disagreement, however, over which type of ancient biography they most resemble generically. How Greco-Roman biography differed from its modern counterpart, and how the gospels reflect those differences. They form a recognizable sub-type of Hellenistic biography, with their content being Judaeo-Christian, their form Hellenistic.

1590. Aune, David E. "The Gospels—Biography or Theology?" *Bible Review* 6 (1990), 14-21, 37.

In their literary structure, the gospels belong to the genre of biography, comprising Jewish background, Christian message, and Hellenistic form—i.e., they are a sub-type of Greco-Roman biography.

1591. Baker, Dom Aelred. "Form and the Gospels." *The Downside Review* 88 (1970), 14-26.

History of *Formgeschichte* and of redaction criticism on the gospels. Both kinds of criticism have something to offer, but they miss the probability that Mark, e.g., also genuinely cared about telling a story aesthetically as well.

1592. Beardslee, William A. "Narrative Form and Process Theology." *Encounter* 36 (1975), 301-15.

"Story" is becoming once again an important consideration in theology. To appreciate what it means, we must understand the function of symbols, and how narratives represent history and myth intertwined. The function of story (i.e., gospel minus parable) among early Christians. Kinds of narrative, and how we enter a narrative world.

1593.   Beardslee, William A. "Uses of the Proverb in the Synoptic Gospels." *Interpretation* 24 (1970), 61-73.

Wisdom literature has greatly influenced the NT because the wisdom tradition served to bridge the gap between faith and secular experience. This was especially true of practical wisdom (proverbs), as versus speculative wisdom. Proverb and parable are where these show up in the NT. The chief characteristics of the NT proverb are paradox, hyperbole, and intensification.

1594.   Brewer, Derek. "The Gospels and the Laws of Folktale. A Centenary Lecture, 14 June 1978." *Folklore* 90 (1979), 37-52

If we examine the gospels as if they were folktales, we can see evidence of oral tradition in them. Traditional narratives are by nature re-told (we note four gospels) because repetition is valued. Thus no one gospel supersedes any other. They each have an internal, recognizable, variable structure. They cannot be grasped unless we see them as traditional narratives.

1595.   Butts, James R. "The Chreia in the Synoptic Gospels." *BTB* 16 (1986), 132-8.

Jesus' sayings are related to Hellenistic *chreiai* in various ways: their use of number of examples is stereotypical; and the gospel writers knew several compositional techniques taught by first-century rhetoricians.

1596.   Chance, J. Bradley. "Fiction in Ancient Biography: An Approach to a Sensitive Issue in Gospel Interpretation." *PRS* 18 (1991), 125-142.

The presence of fictional elements in the gospels need not trouble believers. They probably entered because of the changing situation of the church and the "increasing specificity in Christian confession." Like other ancient Greco-Roman biographers and historians, the gospel-writers "refused to draw the line" between fact and fiction.

1597.   Comstock, Gary. "Truth or Meaning: Ricoeur versus Frei on Biblical Narrative." *JR* 66 (1986), 117-140.

Contrary to what some assume, Paul Ricoeur and Hans Frei are in basic conflict. "Ricoeur's is the more appropriate hermeneutic theory for narrative theology [because] ... it identifies literary and philosophical principles that cohere with a narrative interpretation of the Gospels."

1598. Cox, Roger L. "Tragedy and the Gospel Narratives." *Yale Review* 57 (1968), 545-570; rpt in #47, pp. 298-317.

Contrary to received opinion, "*everything* which is essential to the Christian actually *does* emerge in the tragic narrative which we have in the four gospels.... This analysis does not pretend ... that literary Christian tragedy does exist.... It merely shows that the arguments advanced to support the contention that 'no genuinely Christian tragedy can exist' are basically unsound."

1599. Craddock, Fred B. "The Gospels as Literature." *Encounter* 49 (1988), 19-35.

Definition of the literary method of reading the gospels (especially narrative and reader-response criticism), and its advantages and disadvantages. Biblical critics employing literary criticism need to be careful not to lose sight entirely of theological and historical concerns.

1600. Culpepper, R. Alan. "Story and History in the Gospels." *Review and Expositor* 81 (1984), 467-478.

The gospels studied as narratives represents a profound break with the historical-critical approach. Literary criticism teaches us that meaning is created in the experience of reading. We must ask what the text meant originally as a narrative.

1601. Dihle, Albrecht. "The Gospels and Greek Biography," in Peter Stuhlmacher, ed., *The Gospel and the Gospels* (Grand Rapids: Eerdmans, 1991), 361-386.

"... for the first time in the Greek language, the historiographic potential of the life-story of an individual was realized by way of a literary genre—gospel—that developed over a period of several generations, as it did among the Romans as well. However, while among the Romans the influence of the established forms of the traditions of Greek literature is undeniable, a similar statement cannot be made about the literature of the gospels."

1602. Downing, Gerald F. "Compositional Conventions and the Synoptic Problem." *JBL* 107 (1988), 69-85.

We can in fact tell with some certainty what compositional procedures for making use of existing writings were readily available in the first century. We must conclude that Matthew and Luke used a lost *Q* because that is the only likely literary strategy in the first-century Mediterranean world. It fits best with what we know about first-century language, culture, education, society, etc.

1603.   Droge, Arthur J. "Call Stories in Greek Biography and the Gospels." *SBLSP* 1983, pp. 245-257.

If we compare the gospel call stories with similar accounts in Greco-Roman religious and philosophical biographies we find that the gospel stories "have been shaped by a pre-existing literary schemata whose roots can be traced to cynic philosophy. The literary models for these narratives were supplied by the biographical anecdotes (*chreiai*) about Socrates and Diogenes in which the act of becoming a disciple is characterized as a decisive and paradoxical event."

1604.   Fowler, Robert M. "Using Literary Criticism on the Gospels." *The Christian Century* (May 26, 1982), 626-9.

Literary criticism represents a "significant shift in perspective" away from historical criticism. In fact, source, form, and redaction criticism almost inevitably mutate into literary criticism of the Bible. Redaction criticism of the gospels in particular has now reached an impasse. Mark 6 and 8 can be used as illustrations of this situation.

1605.   Freyne, Sean. "Our Preoccupation with History: Problems and Prospects." *Proceedings of the Irish Biblical Association* 9 (1985), 1-18.

We can give priority to literary methods in studying the gospels, but we should not thereby ignore historical studies. "In a word, by starting with a literary reading of the gospels while at the same time keeping our historical judgments alive and operative, our gospels become *both* windows *and* mirrors for all of us."

1606.   Frye, Roland Mushat. "The Jesus of the Gospels: Approaches Through Narrative Structure," in Dikran Y. Hadidian, ed., *From Faith to Faith: Essays in Honor of Donald G. Miller on His Seventieth Birthday* (Pittsburgh: Pickwick P, 1979), 75-89.

If we are to understand the message of the gospels, literary-critical approaches are a very important tool—particularly the techniques of analyzing narrative structures.

1607.   Frye, Roland M. "Literary Criticism and Gospel Criticism." *TT* 36 (1979), 207-219.

The problem with current biblical criticism is that it tends to disintegrate the gospels, as can be shown by Matthew 22, Luke 14, and parallel examples from the secular literature of various centuries. We cannot possibly separate Jesus' "real words" from the later additions of "redactors." "What I see as immensely hopeful is the prospect that the Gospels should be analyzed with the standard techniques ... employed in the study of other literature."

1608. Frye, Roland M. "The Synoptic Problems and Analogies in Other Literatures," in William O. Walker, ed., *The Relationships Among the Gospels: An Interdisciplinary Dialogue* (San Antonio: Trinity UP, 1978), 261-302.

We need to use literary criticism on the gospels, particularly the patterns and functions of symbols, contribution to meaning of various rhetorical devices, interrelationship of themes, patterns of imagery, etc. Analogies from other literatures illuminate the situation of the gospel writers; e.g., in language: the use of Norman French in England, Black English in America; in length: *Piers Plowman* and *Hamlet*; in conflation of sources: Old English poems, and Shakespeare's plays. One conclusion from this must be that Matthew came first, Luke used him, and Mark used Luke.

1609. Funk, Robert W. "The Form of the New Testament Healing Miracle Story." *Semeia* 12 (1978), 57-96.

We need to develop a "supersentential grammar for narrative," and then to inventory the formal narrative components of NT healing miracle stories. That is, we need a typology of such stories.

1610. Gerhardsson, Birger. "The Narrative Meshalim in the Old Testament Books and in the Synoptic Gospels," in Maurya P. Horgan and Paul J. Kobelski, eds., *To Touch the Text: Biblical and Related Studies in Honor of Joseph A. Fitzmyer, S.J.* (New York: Crossroad, 1989), 289-304.

Synoptic *meshalim* are primarily aphoristic or narrative. Characteristics of the latter as found in the OT, compared to those found in the synoptics. There are many more in the gospels, and they show considerably more artistic skill than those in the OT. The typical structure of a synoptic *mashal* is much less obtrusive than its OT counterpart.

1611. Gundry, Robert H. "Recent Investigations into the Literary Genre, 'Gospel,'" in Richard Longenecker and M.C. Tenney, eds., *New Dimensions in New Testament Study* (Grand Rapids: Zondervan, 1974), 97-114.

Review of a number of books and articles in biblical studies shows the limitations of form criticism of the gospels. There is no genre, "gospel," nor can one be found in the influence of ancient Greco-Roman models.

1612. Güttgemanns, Erhardt. "Introductory Remarks Concerning the Structural Study of Narrative." *Semeia* 6 (1976), 23-125.

The history of structural theory of narrative from Aristotle to Vladimir Propp; progress we have made in recent years toward "an international and interdisciplinary study of narrative." Application of two "motifeme sequences" to (among many other examples), Mark 1-3, 11, 12, 15; Matthew 4; Luke 4. Continued by #1613.

1613. Güttgemanns, Erhardt. "Narrative Analysis of Synoptic Texts." *Semeia* 6 (1976), 129-179.

Analysis of specific pericopes (mostly parables), using the theory in #1612. Mark 12; Matthew 18, 20, 21, 22, 25; Luke 10, 12, 14, 15, 16, 18, 19, 20.

1614. Helms, Randel. "The Study of the Gospels as Literary Fiction," in Paul Kurtz, ed., *Building a World Community: Humanism in the 21st Century* (Buffalo: Prometheus Books, 1989), 237-243.

"Much of the future of biblical studies lies in the secular world, particularly the secular universities; such a future is the consequence of the recognition that the Bible is a human book ... produced by imaginative human writers, a literary text that can be read with the same skills we bring to any other text." Fundamentalists' objections to this essentially literary approach "will become increasingly peripheral" to serious Bible study in the next century. "That the outline of the gospel story is mythological and the content ... legendary, at least to some extent, is now the majority view among serious biblical scholars."

*   Hilkert, M.C. "Retelling the Gospel Story: Preaching and Narrative." See #176.

1615. Hollenbach, Bruce. "Lest They Should Turn and Be Forgiven: Irony." *BT* 34 (1983), 312-321.

If translators are alert to gospel irony, e.g., in Mark 4 and John 12, they will not only translate better but will resist the temptation to include clues to guide their audience when Jesus sometimes meant to conceal meaning.

1616.   Kee, Howard C. "Aretalogy and Gospel." *JBL* 92 (1973), 402-22.

Is the genre of gospel an adaptation of the ancient literary form of the miracle story of a divine man? Previous attempts to answer this question faltered because of imprecise definitions of "aretalogy," as well as because they lacked systematic, basic parallels with the gospels. Even pagan writers of the time freely adapted the form rather than slavishly imitating previous examples. While the gospel writers probably did draw on such stories (as well as on other literary currents), we should look more to the figure of an eschatological deliverer in Jewish apocalyptic literature for the answer.

1617.   Kelber, Werner H. "Gospel Narrative Theory and Critical Theory." *BTB* 18 (1988), 130-136.

A "hermeneutical slice of our recent history of reading the gospel narratives" reveals that there are five modes, organized around the construction or deconstruction of meaning: historical, literary-formalist, receptionist aesthetics, structuralist, and postmodern. Each method makes different, and often competing epistemological and theological claims.

1618.   Kennedy, George A. "An Introduction to the Rhetoric of the Gospels." *Rhetorica* 1, #2 (Autumn, 1983), 17-31.

Since gospel writers sought to persuade, they practiced rhetoric. Since they were educated in the Greco-Roman world, whose curriculum included systematic study of rhetoric, they must have absorbed and used its principles. Assessment of the role of rhetoric in the gospels and in Paul, and in the arrangement of books in the NT. Recommended ways of approaching the purpose, audience, and situation of the gospel texts.

1619.   Kermode, Frank. "Two Instances of Interpretation." *HUSLA* 11 (1983), 1-19.

"Two examples of stories which vary and persist and carry a changing freight of interpretation": the temptation in the wilderness (synoptics), and the entry into Jerusalem (all four gospels). Their narrative similarities and differences as related to their theological purposes; how some interpretations die out; how stories function.

1620.   Lund, N.W. "The Influence of Chiasmus Upon the Structure of the Gospels." *ATR* 13 (1931), 27-48.

Chiasmus is a mnemonic device in the gospels. Examples, together with other kinds of symmetry and their centripetal tendencies.

1621.   Marin, Louis. "The Women at the Tomb: A Structural Analysis Essay of a Gospel Text," in Alfred M. Johnson, ed., *The New Testament and Structuralism* (Pittsburgh: Pickwick P, 1976), 73-96.

Semiotic and structuralist analysis of Matthew 28, Mark 16, and Luke 24, especially indebted to the "functional and mythical actantial model" of A.J. Greimas and others.

1622.   McCaughey, J.D. "Literary Criticism and the Gospels: A Rumination." *ABR* 29 (1981), 16-25.

Historical criticism is valuable, but literary criticism can reveal the former's weaknesses. We need to take both seriously while distinguishing between them; be open to literary criticism reinvigorating biblical studies because it can tell us things about the gospels as whole texts which historical criticism cannot.

1623.   McKnight, Scot. "Literary Criticism of the Synoptic Gospels." *Trinity Journal* 8 (1986), 57-68.

Literary criticism of the gospels is bad in several ways: it undermines the historicity and referentiality of the texts; it is misleading to compare ancient and modern works; it seeks to find techniques where they don't exist. However, it is good in that it contributes new understandings of text and author.

1624.   Moore, Stephen D. "Are the Gospels Unified Narratives?" *SBLSP* 1987, pp. 443-458.

A central assertion of narrative criticism is that the gospels are unified narratives—a paradigm shift, in effect, from the earlier "fragmentation" paradigm. But appeal to literary criticism as an *a priori* legitimation of the holistic approach is not viable because the discipline has no consensus which supports such an appeal. In addition, the literary criticism of the gospels as currently practiced is not exactly like secular literary criticism. Narrative criticism is highly selective, and deconstruction undermines the whole notion of a text being "out there." **

1625.   Moore, Stephen D. "Doing Gospel Criticism As/With a 'Reader.'" *BTB* 19 (1989), 85-93.

Reader-oriented gospel criticism is "at least, ... a critical simulation," yet also "a highly artificial construct which must be sharply distinguished from any actual reader, ancient or modern." The divorce between "real" readers of the gospels and criticism has been an unfortunate development. It is just as difficult to say what is actually in the reader's experience as it is to say what is actually in the text.

1626. Murphy-O'Connor, Jerome. "What Really Happened at the Transfiguration?" *Bible Review* 3 (1987), 3-21.

Various difficulties with historical and anti-historical interpretations of the Transfiguration. As literary critics we must conclude that the gospel writers were not so much concerned to record the past as they were "to make the tradition a vital force in the present."

1627. Newman, J.K. *"Esse Videatur* Rhythm in the Greek New Testament *Gospels* and *Acts of the Apostles."* *Illinois Classical Studies* 10 (1985), 53-66.

Contrary to the claims of another critic, writers of formal Hellenistic prose did pay attention to prose rhythms. The gospels are most carefully constructed examples of Greek dialogic literature, as the early Fathers understood, and show the same prose rhythms as does pagan literature. The purpose of *"esse videatur"* is to convey a sense of excitement and agitation at key points.

1628. Perkins, Pheme. "Crisis in Jerusalem? Narrative Criticism in New Testament Studies." *Theological Studies* 50 (1989), 296-313.

Discussion, evaluation, and comparison of the results of historical and literary criticism of the gospels, to show how each emphasizes something which the other ignores. "... narrative criticism cannot provide a short cut around the older elements of historical criticism."

1629. Perrin, Norman. "The Evangelist as Author: Reflections on Method in the Study and Interpretation of the Synoptic Gospels and Acts." *BR* 17 (1972), 5-18.

We need to reflect on our methods in biblical studies, and on their history. We are coming to realize that the evangelists were authors, with all that means—e.g., exercising creative freedom. Beyond a concern for source and form, we should care about protagonists, plots, and theme.

1630. Resseguie, James L. "Defamiliarization in the Gospels." *Mosaic* 21, #s 2 and 3 (Spring, 1988), 25-35.

"Defamiliarization" is a Russian Formalist term which can be used to classify and describe some of the "estranging forms" in the gospels. Explanation of defamiliarization on the levels of rhetoric, characterization, point of view, and plot. It "makes a familiar world seem chaotic ... [an] estrangement from the familiar and habitual that is, as much as its paraphrasable content, the message of the biblical text."

1631. Resseguie, James L. "Reader-Response Criticism and the Synoptic Gospels." *JAAR* 52 (1984), 307-324.

Description of the critical assumptions and strategies of the "Iser-Fish" school of reader-response criticism, which emphasizes the interaction of reader and text. Illustration of "the critical moves of reader-response criticism with material from the synoptic gospels."

1632. Robbins, Vernon K. "Picking Up The Fragments: From Crossan's Analysis to Rhetorical Analysis." *FFF* 1, #2 (June, 1985), 31-64.

John D. Crossan's *In Fragments* [#1654] on Jesus' sayings breaks valuable new ground, but its weakness is treating the aphorisms in isolation from each other and from their social context. Literary scholarship "must now learn the function of socio-rhetorical criticism" when it examines the Bible.

1633. Robbins, Vernon K. "Pronouncements Stories from a Rhetorical Perspective." *FFF* 4, #2 (June, 1988), 3-32.

The value of rhetorical analysis having moved away from form criticism toward "an environment of social analysis." We need more study of the process of writing in Greek for first century writers and audiences. Current knowledge of Greco-Roman rhetoric as it affects gospel pronouncement stories reveals that "the gospels contain stories and sayings that result from a mixture of rudimentary, elementary, and advanced rhetorical skills."

1634. Robinson, James M. "The Gospels as Narrative," in Frank McConnell, ed., *The Bible and the Narrative Tradition* (New York and Oxford: Oxford UP, 1986), 97-112.

Perhaps literary criticism can "provide biblical scholarship with ... decisive reconceptualizations and imaginative insights that would ... recast the discipline into an exciting, informative and progressive area of research...." Redaction criticism has failed to show us how the gospels differed, as well as how they absorbed their sources.

1635. Schneidau, Herbert. "Literary Relations Among the Gospels." *Studies in the Literary Imagination* 18, #1 (Spring, 1985), 17-32.

Most readers make a "gospel paste," ignoring the rich differences among the four gospels. The quest for the "real" Jesus "behind" the gospels is increasingly recognized as a chimera. The gospels "startingly illuminate each other," and each is important as a work of art. First we must seek to recover Mark as a gospel without contamination of our minds from the other gospels. We can see then how much Matthew and Luke have changed Mark. Thus an adversary model of the relations among the gospels may be more accurate. **

1636. Sheeley, Steven. "The Narrator in the Gospels: Developing a Model." *PRS* 16 (1989), 213-223.

None of the recent work on the problem of the narrator in the gospels is holistic—i.e., none takes into account point of view, narrative presence, commentary, and authority. Such a holistic model can, however, be found in Shlomith Rimmon-Kenan's book, *Narrative Fiction* (London, 1983).

1637. Shuler, Philip. "Genre Criticism and the Synoptic Problem" in William R. Farmer, ed., *New Synoptic Studies: The Cambridge Gospel Conference and Beyond* (Macon: Mercer UP, 1983), 467-480.

The gospels would have been received by their original readers as some sort of biography. They conform to a type of narrative designed to "enlist the reader's praise response in the form of acceptance or enlightenment ... to persuade the reader of the praiseworthiness of their heroes." They generally employ the *topoi* and literary techniques common to the encomium—not for historical but for rhetorical purposes. The gospels followed the encomium form closely.

1638. Shuler, Philip L. "The Genre(s) of the Gospels," in David L. Dungan, ed., *The Interrelations of the Gospels* (Leuven: Leuven UP, 1990), 459-483.

Review of the renewed debate over what genre the gospels belong to. The shift from individual sources to story form was a genre decision; there is no evidence that the resulting gospels could have been a "completely unique literary form"; they were "no doubt received as popular 'lives' of Jesus; and they are probably best viewed as being Hellenistic encomium biography.

1639.   Sider, John W. "The Meaning of *Parabole* in the Usage of the
        Synoptic Evangelists." *Biblica* 62 (1981), 453-470.

        The principle of analogy in studying the parables has been
        largely ignored because it assumed that the evangelists misunder-
        stood the parables, and because "parable" designates no set form.
        The tradition of *mashal* and *parabole* in the OT show three modes
        of analogy. The gospels modified the original meanings of these
        two OT terms.

1640.   Tannehill, Robert C. "Attitudinal Shift in Synoptic Pro-
        nouncement Stories," in Richard Spencer, ed., *Orientation
        by Disorientation* (Pittsburgh: Pickwick P, 1980), 183-197.

        Definition of the pronouncement story. We need to pay more
        attention to the movement from the provoking occasion for such
        stories to the response they evoke, and the resulting tension. A
        suggested typology of subtypes. The daring and imaginative origi-
        nality shown by these storytellers must somehow be recovered.

1641.   Tannehill, Robert C. "Introduction: The Pronouncement
        Story and Its Types." *Semeia* 20 (1981), 1-13.

        Study of "the relation between the stimulating occasion and the
        response" in each story gives us a typology of correction, commen-
        dation, objection, quest, inquiry, and description stories.

1642.   Tannehill, Robert C. "Tension in Synoptic Sayings and Sto-
        ries." *Interpretation* 34 (1980), 138-150.

        Careful study of the language of Jesus and of the evangelists
        shows that they were seeking something more than intellectual ac-
        ceptance and legalistic obedience. More concern for literary form
        in the gospels helps us here. Literature is an imaginative world;
        therefore we should try to avoid domesticating the forceful and
        imaginative language of the gospels; i.e., we should not study the
        sayings apart from their narrative settings.

1643.   Tannehill, Robert C. "Varieties of Synoptic Pronouncement
        Stories." *Semeia* 20 (1981), 101-119.

        Five out of six recognizable types of pronouncement stories are
        represented in the synoptic gospels. The function of each type.
        They are stories with narrative tension and movement, not just say-
        ings with settings that can be ignored.

1644.   Thiering, Barbara. "Opening and Closing Narratives in the
        Gospels and Acts." *Abr Nahrain* 4 (1963-4), 50-55.

        The endings of all five of these books pose one kind of problem
        or another. The writers of the gospels and Acts may have echoed

or imitated openings and closings from the HB, e.g., Genesis 1-4, I Samuel–II Kings, among others.

1645.　Tolbert, Mary Ann. "The Gospel in Greco-Roman Culture," in #45, pp. 258-275.

The problem of deciding to what genre the gospels belong may be partially solved by exploring Greek popular culture in the first century, given that the language of the gospels seems to be everyday Greek. What popular literary techniques, then, did they use? The ancient novel is a possible source or influence, since we find many of the conventions of that genre present also in the gospels. Examples mainly from Mark.

1646.　Trigg, Roger. "Tales Artfully Spun," in #1517, pp. 117-132.

Literary approaches to the Bible are objectionable when they insist on the incompatibility of ancient and modern ways of defining truth, and therefore conclude that we can have either the "meaning" of the gospels or their "truth," but not both. The NT writers both use rhetoric *and* make claims of historical accuracy. "... we cannot ... suspend our belief in what actually happened and still be guided by the 'message' of the putative events."

1647.　Tyson, Joseph. "Sequential Parallelism in the Synoptic Gospels." *NTS* 22 (1976), 276-308.

Descriptions of gospel parallels are faulty because they begin with an assumption that one gospel or another has priority, and are therefore not objective. A neutral analysis of the issue does not give solid support to any one hypothesis about the priority or the existence of given pre-gospel documents.

1648.　Vorster, Willem, James Voelz, Jean Delorme, and Ellen van Wolde. "Theoretical Reflections [on Intertextuality in Biblical Writings]," in #38, pp. 15-49.

Vorster: The main difference between intertextuality and redaction criticism is that the former "takes the fact that authors produce texts seriously and that readers react to those texts by assigning meaning to them." Voelz: Intertextuality is better as text- or receptor-oriented criticism than is source or author criticism. Delorme: Ways in which several passages in Mark about the identity of Jesus may be "opened" to other texts. van Wolde: Intertextuality "does not focus on causality ... but on *iconicity*, ... denot[ing] the principle that phenomena are analogous or isomorphic."

1649.　Wallis, Ethel. "Four Gospels, Four Discourse Genre." *Evangelical Journal* 1 (1983), 78-91.

Robert Longacre's discourse analysis assumes that "the viewpoint of the writer ... of a discourse is the crucial factor in determining its purpose, and ultimately its structure as well." Based on
this theory, John is "procedural discourse," where "Mark alone exhibits classical *climactic narrative* structure. Matthew is *expository*,
Luke *hortatory*...." John, i.e., is a "handbook on how to believe,"
with many structural contrasts with the synoptics.

1650.   Wright, T.R. "Regenerating Narrative: The Gospels as Fic-
         tion." *Religious Studies* 20 (1984), 389-400.

The gospels as fiction does not require abandoning all concern
for "history" or "truth," which are themselves "two other fictions
essential for faith." The contributions of Frank Kermode in *The
Genesis of Secrecy* [#1859] to this debate. We can accept the fictive
element shown us by post-structuralism without abandoning Newman's "real assent."

See also: #s 1, 3, 8, 17, 188, 435, 1486, 1497, 1500, 1657, 1758, 1806,
    1825, 1859.

THE PARABLES

Books

1651.   Blomberg, Craig L. *Interpreting the Parables.* Downers Grove
         (Intervarsity P), 1990.

"New literary and hermeneutical methods" of reading the Bible
include metaphor, structuralism, deconstruction, and reader-response. Various ways in which they affect our sense of the authenticity of the parables.

1652.   Boucher, Madeleine. *The Mysterious Parable: A Literary Study.*
         Washington, D.C. (Catholic Biblical Association of Amer-
         ica), 1977.

We need a sound definition of parable as verbal construct, an
ability to set it within Semitic tradition of "mysterious speech," and
knowledge of its place in Markan theology. Critics are mistaken to
accept Adolf Jülicher's classification of the parables and his incorrect definitions of parable and allegory. The parable as a literary

category and tradition. Figurative language in parables. The Markan theory of parables and the Markan theme of mystery argue that we must see parables in their larger context of an entire gospel.

1653.   Crossan, John D. *Cliffs of Fall: Paradox and Polyvalence in the Parables of Jesus.* New York (Seabury), 1980.

Parables as narrative form and metaphorical process. They are polyvalent because they mirror the mind that reads them; paradoxical because Jesus stands for the fact that God cannot be contained in language. The new reader-response and deconstructionist theories help us see that the parables are self-reflexive; they are "writerly" rather than "readerly" texts. We need a "metamodel of play," since the parables are ludic, not mimetic.

*   Crossan, John D. *The Dark Interval.* See #309.

1654.   Crossan, John Dominic. *In Fragments: The Aphorisms of Jesus* San Francisco (Harper and Row), 1983.

The aphoristic tradition of Jesus is more difficult to control than other Jesus traditions, because there are many more aphorisms than parables. A "transmissional analysis" for each of the 133 aphorisms chosen, to form a "basic generative model for the aphoristic tradition." The genre, its core, its appearance in sayings, compounds, clusters, conclusions, dialogues, and stories.

1655.   Crossan, John D. *In Parables: The Challenge of the Historical Jesus.* New York (Harper and Row), 1973.

Largely a form-critical examination of the parables, though chapter 1, expanded from #1677, argues the identity of the poetic and the religious imaginations, and the importance of understanding the parables as metaphors.

1656.   Crossan, John D. *Raid on the Articulate: Comic Eschatology in Jesus and Borges.* New York (Harper and Row), 1976.

Comedy, not tragedy, is the superior literary mode because it is capable of seeing itself objectively, and therefore of avoiding an "idolatry of language" which tends to dilute and circumscribe scripture. Application of this theory to the parables of Jesus. The gospel writers often sought to domesticate the parables, to rob them of their iconoclastic, paradoxical nature.

1657.   Entrevernes Group, The. *Signs and Parables: Semiotics and Gospel Texts.* Tr Gary Phillips. Pittsburgh (Pickwick P), 1978.

Deconstructing the parables in order to reconstruct them in terms of our relationship to them. General theory of the relationships of parables to miracle stories and to other NT narratives. Mark 6; Luke 5, 10, 15.

1658.   Funk, Robert W. *Parables and Presence: Forms of the New Testament Tradition.* Philadelphia (Fortress P), 1982.

The parable and the letter appear at critical points in the development of the language tradition that came to fruition in the NT. The great narrative parables have a common structure, which makes possible an evaluation of the rhetorical strategies as literary devices. Parables were new, while letters were an established literary form which Paul turned into a major theological form. General structuralist analysis of the parables, and of specific ones, e.g., Luke 15; of the letters of Paul and John.

1659.   Jones, Geraint Vaughan. *The Art and Truth of the Parables: A Study in their Literary Form and Modern Interpretation.* London (SPCK) and Naperville (Allenson), 1964.

A "pointer to the way in which the parables, as a form of art, may be read as pictures of the human situation." History of parables interpretation since the early nineteenth century. Some parables are certainly allegorical, while others certainly are not. Their closeness to the rabbinic (extra-scriptural) tradition of moral exhortation. Like all great art, the power of the parables resides in their symbolism, and like all great art they are apocalyptic. We should classify them not thematically but by their degree of applicability outside their original *sitz im leben.* **

1660.   Kjärgaard, Mogens Stiller. *Metaphor and Parable: A Systematic Analysis of the Specific Structure and Cognitive Function of the Synoptic Similes and Parables qua Metaphors.* Leiden (E.J. Brill), 1986.

Examination of the form of metaphor in the light of various theories shows that context determines form. Metaphor has a specific cognitive function, preventing its reduction to literal usage. Major scholarly examinations of the relationship between metaphor and the "simile narratives" of the synoptic gospels. NT similes and parables are in fact metaphors.

1661.   Lundin, Roger, Anthony C. Thiselton, and Clarence Walhout. *The Responsibility of Hermeneutics.* Grand Rapids (Eerdmans) and Exeter (Paternoster P), 1985.

The history of hermeneutics in America. A model of literature as action is preferable to the one popular among many literary critics of literature as language. The importance of reader-response criticism for interpreting the parables *if* it follows the action model.

1662.   Patte, Daniel, ed. *Semiology and Parables: Exploration of the Possibilities Offered by Structuralism for Exegesis.* Pittsburgh (Pickwick P), 1976.

Essays on the parables in general, and on specific examples. Includes essay by Susan Wittig which proposes a model "to account for the polysemy of language in general and of the parables in particular"; by Daniel Patte (#1948); and by J.D. Crossan which argues that "Paradox is to parable as proverb is to example. And the generic trajectory of parable, as narrative paradox, as paradox formed into the story, extends, for instance, from Jonah through Jesus to Kafka."

1663.   Scott, Bernard Brandon. *Hear Then the Parable: A Commentary on the Parables of Jesus.* Minneapolis (Fortress P), 1989.

How the parables "structure meaning"; how they "set conditions for [their] own performance." Analysis of each parable proceeds "from extant versions to narrative structure to parabolic effect."

1664.   Stoneburner, Tony, ed. *A Meeting of Poets and Theologians to Discuss Parable, Myth and Language.* Washington, D.C. (Church Society for College Work), n.d. [1968].

Essays and discussions/responses by Samuel Laeuchli, Denise Levertov, Robert Duncan, James M. Robinson, Robert W. Funk, Stephen D. Crites and others on the interrelationship of poetry, myth, scripture, and theology.

1665.   Te Selle, Sallie McFague. *Speaking in Parables: A Study in Metaphor and Theology.* Philadelphia (Fortress P), 1975.

We need a new kind of theology grounded in metaphor and parable, which takes the form of poem and story. "A theology that takes its cue from the parables never reaches its object, but in language, belief, and life as metaphor, story, and living engagement we are sent off in its direction."

1666.   Tolbert, Mary Ann. *Perspectives on the Parables: An Approach to Multiple Interpretations.* Philadelphia (Fortress P), 1979.

The problem with the parables is that they are at once culturally alien and canonically authoritative. We wonder why they are so amenable to multiple interpretations. Does the form itself contribute to this situation? How important is the gospel context of parables? Two models for the parable form: semiotic and rhetorical, and how they explain polyvalence. Narrative structure, rhetorical style, and realism in the parables. The advantages of clustering them by manner of discourse. Application of some of these considerations to Luke 15.

1667.   Via, Dan Otto, Jr. *The Parables: Their Literary and Existential Dimension.* Philadelphia (Fortress P), 1967.

Analysis of the parables as "tragic" or "comic" from a literary-existentialist perspective. The parables are literary in the strict sense, "and because of this they are not just illustrations of ideas and cannot have the immediate connection with Jesus' historical situation which is customarily attributed to them.... [The parables have] a certain autonomy ... and present a configuration of action and meaning which is a more fundamental form of expression than are theological concepts."

1668.   Westermann, Claus. *The Parables of Jesus in the Light of the Old Testament.* Edinburgh (T.T. Clark) and Minneapolis (Fortress P), 1990.

Various figures (metaphor, simile, allegory, symbol, etc.) found throughout the OT. Such figures are an essential part of both OT and NT, occurring not at random but only in dialogical texts. The parables in the gospels show many of the same characteristics, proving how deeply rooted Jesus' teachings were in the OT.

1669.   Wilder, Amos N. *Jesus' Parables and the War of Myths: Essays on Imagination in the Scripture.* Ed. James Breech. Philadelphia (Fortress P), 1982.

Editor: Wilder's approach seeks to combine historical with literary and phenomenological methods because interpretation should be concerned with the interdependence of the text and the world which produced it. Essays on the nature of biblical rhetoric, eschatological imagery, including reprints of #s 163, Chapter V of 1518, and 1696.

Articles

1670.   Beardslee, William A. "Parable, Proverb, and Koan." *Semeia* 12 (1978), 151-177.

We can clarify parables and proverbs found in the gospels by comparing them with Buddhist koans and with the sayings of the desert Fathers. Such comparison reveals that the traditional approaches to the parables are too static theologically.

1671. Beavis, Mary Ann. "Parable and Fable." *CBQ* 52 (1990), 473-498.

In our concern to relate the parables to the Hebrew *mashal* and to various Greco-Roman literary genres, we have neglected their resemblance to Greek fables since Adolf Jülicher first mentioned the possibility. The synoptic parables compared to fables in the Aesopian tradition which narrate human activities or the relationship of humans to the gods. The general similarities in theme, structure, use of irony, and moral argues that fable, parable, and *mashal* descended from a common Near East ancestor.

* "Symposium: Paul Ricoeur and Biblical Hermeneutics." See #1204.

1672. Blackman, E.C. "New Methods of Parable Interpretation." *Canadian Journal of Theology* 15 (1969), 3-13.

New literary approaches to the parables compared with more traditional methods. The newer methods are important because the parables are always capable of revealing new levels of meaning.

1673. Blomberg, Craig L. "Interpreting the Parables of Jesus: Where Are We and Where Do We Go From Here?" *CBQ* 53 (1991), 50-78.

In assessing the situation we need to distinguish between indispensable and implausible perspectives in the "new consensus" which combines historical and literary approaches. There is a movement toward allegorical interpretation; a questioning of the form-critical classification of the parables; and there are weaknesses in the redaction approach. The strength of structuralist and post-structuralist methods is that they have identified a triadic design in many parables. The differences among triadic, dyadic, and monadic parables.

1674. Carlston, Charles E. "Parable and Allegory Revisited: An Interpretive Review." *CBQ* 43 (1981), 228-242.

Discussion and evaluation of recent dissertations which apply literary theory to the problem of allegory in the parables. From these dissertations we can conclude that metaphor is important in the parables for its own sake; that allegory can never be completely ruled out; that purely aesthetic treatment of the parables is just as simplistic as traditional theological criticism is; and that even if allegory was present in some parables in their original form, that does not mean it couldn't have been added to others later on.

1675.   Champion, James. "The Parable as an Ancient and Modern Form." *LT* 3 (1989), 16-39.

Recent literary-critical work on the parables has been generally revealing. Consideration of Luke 10 as illustration of the differences between ancient and modern parables.

1676.   Crossan, John Dominic. "Parable as History and Literature." *Listening* 19 (1984), 5-18.

There is a "necessary interplay between historical reconstruction and literary criticism" of the parables. Parable as metaphor and allegory. A "historical and hermeneutical relationship" among versions of the same parable in different gospels. Historical and literary critics need each other's insights if the parables are to be understood.

1677.   Crossan, John Dominic. "Parable as Religious and Poetic Experience." *JR* 53 (1973), 330-358.

Jesus' parables are not didactic metaphors but poetic ones. Such metaphors contain and verbalize experience "so that the hearer or reader is able to participate thereby in that experience for himself." Such participation can occur only at the figurative, never at the literal level. Jesus' parables are "extended metaphors" which "articulate his own experience of God's advent."

1678.   Crossan, John D. "The Servant Parables of Jesus." *Semeia* 1 (1974), 17-62.

There are nine "servant" parables in the gospels. Structural examination of these shows that they are the linguistic embodiment of Jesus' teaching about eschatology.

1679.   Davis, Christian R. "Structural Analysis of Jesus' Narrative Parables: A Conservative Approach." *GTJ* 9 (1988), 191-204.

Structuralist criticism can reveal the "deep meanings" of the parables, and the need not to rest on "naturalistic" assumptions as does so much of recent criticism of the parables. Examination of twenty-seven parables in terms of actantial schemata, with classification of these into four categories.

1680.   Doty, William G. "The Parables of Jesus, Kafka, Borges, and Others, with Structural Observations." *SBLSP* 1973, pp. 119-141.

Study of the parables of such modern authors as Franz Kafka, Jorge Luis Borges, John Hawkes and Robert Coover helps us identify several features of parables in general which are especially relevant for comparative study. Examples include the use of paradox and reversal; secularity; revaluation of tradition; universality; application; and the creation of a narrative world—all of which are characteristic of the gospel parables.

1681. Funk, Robert W. "The Narrative Parables: The Birth of a Language Tradition." *St. Andrew's Review* 2 (1974), 299-305.

The major narrative parables were carefully composed, as is shown when they are studied on the levels of diction, scene construction, repetition, and variation. Creativity "has been inscribed into the parables both on the surface and at the depths."

1682. Funk, Robert W. "Parable, Paradox, Power: The Prodigal Samaritan." *JAAR Thematic Studies* 48, #1 (1981), ed. Mark L. Taylor, 83-97.

Definition of "narrative parable"; their characteristic structure; the function of Luke 10 as metaphor.

1683. Gerhardsson, Birger. "If We Do Not Cut the Parables Out of Their Frames." *NTS* 37 (1991), 321-335.

"Nor do I think that we remain ourselves within the limits of sound exegesis if we cut the narrative meshalim out of their frames in the gospels and treat them as wild texts designed to function as naked narratives with indeterminable messages."

1684. Hawkins, Peter S. "Parable as Metaphor." *Christian Scholar's Review* 12 (1983), 226-236.

A parable is a story "whose literal level must be taken seriously in its entirety, not as a direct description of spiritual truth, but as a disorienting redescription of everyday reality which is designed to reorient us to a new way of thinking." Matthew 13:44 as example. See also #1751.

1685. McKenna, Andrew J. "Biblioclasm: Joycing Jesus and Borges." *Diacritics* 8, #3 (1978), 15-29.

Review-essay growing out of John D. Crossan's *Raid on the Articulate* [#1656]. Crossan's semiotic-structural analysis of the Bible promises to renew it for us, returning us to the "semio-clasm" of original Christianity.

1686.   Parsons, Mikeal C. "'Allegorizing Allegory': Narrative Analy-
         sis and Parable Interpretation." *PRS* 15 (1988), 147-164.

         We need to heed Norman Perrin's call for a new approach to
         the parables combining historical and literary concerns for the in-
         teraction of author, text, and reader. Allegorizing the parables is
         all right, but it has not gone far enough behind the text (history)
         or in front of it (reader concerns). "Only by reading the parables
         in their historical, narrative, and interpretive contexts" will we suc-
         ceed.

1687.   Perrin, Norman. "Historical Criticism, Literary Criticism,
         and Hermeneutics: The Interpretation of the Parables of
         Jesus and the Gospel of Mark Today." *JR* 52 (1972), 361-
         375.

         The three approaches discussed in turn; all three must be per-
         formed on any given text. How each one works, and what each
         contributes to total understanding.

1688.   Perrin, Norman. "The Parables of Jesus as Parables, as
         Metaphors, and as Aesthetic Objects: A Review Article." *JR*
         47 (1967), 340-47.

         Important books on the parables by Joachim Jeremias, Robert
         W. Funk, Dan O. Via, Amos Wilder, and others. There are serious
         weaknesses in each of their literary approaches.

1689.   Ricoeur, Paul. "Biblical Hermeneutics." *Semeia* 4 (1978), 29-
         148.

         We can clarify the formal structure of the parables on the basis
         of the structural semiotics already being applied to non-biblical
         texts by Valdimir Propp, A.J. Greimas, and Roland Barthes, some-
         times called "Biblical semiotics." The work of Dan O. Via is the
         starting point.

*   Sider, John W. "The Meaning of *Parabole* in the Usage of the
         Synoptic Evangelists." See #1639.

1690.   Sider, John W. "Proportional Analogy in the Gospel Para-
         bles." *NTS* 31 (1985), 1-23.

         Proportional analogy (a:b = c:d) and its function in a number of
         the parables. "Fear of mistaking a part of a parable for the whole
         should make exegetes consider all the parts carefully, not proceed
         as if they did not exist." The greater danger lies in assuming that
         each parable embodies one simple idea; since they are extended
         figures, they are automatically allegorical.

1691.   Sider, John W. "Rediscovering the Parables: The Logic of the Jeremias Tradition." *JBL* 102 (1983), 61-83.

There is a conflict between gospel studies (looking through the text to the history behind), and literary studies (looking at the text itself). Joachim Jeremias' inferences about the original form of the parables is not as reliable as those based on more fully informed literary principles.

1692.   Sitterson, Joseph C., Jr. "Will to Power in Biblical Interpretation," in #48, pp. 45-53.

"... biblical hermeneutics should be skeptical of what much recent secular theory has to offer it. I believe that an influence should flow in the other direction, that biblical hermeneutics offers us a chastening perspective on our role in the creation of textual meaning, secular or sacred." How the situation of the parables as part of a "complex speech act" makes unworkable much postmodern criticism of them because it tends to evade the tension inherent in our relationship to texts.

1693.   Via, Dan O., Jr. "Parable and Example Story: A Literary-Structuralist Approach." *Semeia* 1 (1974), 105-133.

Largely a response to article by John D. Crossan in same issue [#1938] urging more use of "formal literary considerations," i.e., an integration of form and content which Crossan seems to neglect when studying the parables.

1694.   Via, Dan O. "The Relationship of Form to Content in the Parables: The Wedding Feast." *Interpretation* 25 (1971), 171-184.

The importance of plot in the parables, and of a philosophy of plot in which meaning depends as much on form as it does on content. Comic versus tragic plots in the parables, and specifically in "The Wedding Feast." How Matthew and Luke change the meaning of this parable by altering its structure; how it differs from others by emphasizing the unchangeable divine rather than the changeable human.

1695.   Vincent, Marvin R. "The Parables," in #32, pp. 237-256.

The parables have many "picturesque and dramatic features, ... [much] simplicity and vividness." However, because they are "suggestive rather than exhaustive," they cannot be understood simply as sermons making a straightforward theological point.

1696.   Wilder, Amos N. "The Parable of the Sower: Naivete and
        Method in Interpretation." *Semeia* 2 (1974), 134-151; rpt
        in #1669, pp. 89-100.

        The key issue of this parable is: What holds the reader's atten-
        tion? The appeal of a good story is determined by both its narra-
        tive structure and the structures of consciousness in its readers.
        The Sower "engages primordial responses involving man's com-
        merce with nature and the anguish of his ventures and striving." It
        proffers a vision of Israel's "archetype of election."

1697.   Wittig, Susan. "A Theory of Multiple Meanings." *Semeia* 9
        (1977), 75-103.

        Why do we get multiple meanings from multiple readings of the
        parables? The semiotic and reader-response models explain the
        general answer, and specifically that all of those meanings can be
        valid at the same time. Perhaps the purpose of the parables is not
        to convey a single meaning, "but to direct our attention to the na-
        ture of meaning itself."

See also #s 4, 12, 40, 87, 132, 177, 1309, 1505, 1534, 1707, 1821,
    1938, 1959.

INDIVIDUAL GOSPELS

MATTHEW

1698.   van Aarde, A.G. "Plot as Mediated Through Point of View.
        MT 22:1-14—A Case Study," in #1507, pp. 62-75.

        Plot and point of view as part of narrative theory, applied to
        Matthew 22. It is "an illustration of Matthew's 'plotted time' in a
        nutshell." Thus, the distinction between allegory and parable
        proper will not hold up.

1699.   van Aarde, Andries G. "Resonance and Reception: Inter-
        preting Mt 17:24-27 in Context." *Scriptura* 29 (1989), 1-12.

        Concepts of "resonance," "frequency," and "vacancy" in narrato-
        logical and "reception-ethical" terms. The Temple-tax discourse of

Matthew 17 "resounds not only with other temple pericopes in Matthew's narrative, but also with extra-textual effects."

1700. Akin, Daniel L. "A Discourse Analysis of the Temptation of Jesus Christ As Recorded in Matthew 4:1-11." *OPTAT* 1, #1 (January, 1987), 78-86.

Attempts to draw out the macrostructure of this Matthean episode end up with the Markan account. The discourse-type of Matthew 4 "appears to be narrative"; the paragraph type is "temporal sequence, with embedded simple dialogue(s), which could constitute a compound dialogue." It also helps to be aware of the mindset of first-century readers, especially their tendency to draw parallels between Jesus and Moses, Jesus and the Israelite nation.

1701. Anderson, Janice Capel. "Double and Triple Stories, the Implied Reader, and Redundancy in Matthew." *Semeia* 31 (1985), 71-90.

These are episodes which are essentially repeated two or three times. The repetition, arrangement, and location of the stories have a part in shaping the reading process, playing an integral role in development of plot and character in Matthew. The concept of redundancy from information theory may help explain this reading process.

1702. Anderson, Janice Capel. "Matthew: Gender and Reading." *Semeia* 28 (1983) [#46], 3-27.

"... the usefulness of certain literary approaches for a feminist exegesis of the Gospel of Matthew." The "symbolic significance of gender" in Matthew, especially the presence of females in the genealogy; this fact and the birth story following it are "attempts to come to terms with female difference." Role of the implied reader vis à vis a feminist understanding of Matthew, especially in scenes where women are prominent. The speeches of Jesus show a tension between patriarchal and non-patriarchal values.

1703. Anderson, Janice Capel. "Matthew: Sermon and Story." *SBLSP* 1988, pp. 496-507.

Reader-response criticism demonstrates that the Sermon on the Mount has several intimate connections with, an integral role in, the whole gospel. That is, it is not simply a self-contained repository of teachings inserted at a certain place. Implications for the historical critic who pays attention to the role of author and reader. Questions which this analysis raises about Matthew's strategy.

1704.   Barr, David L. "The Drama of Matthew's Gospel: A Recon-
        sideration of its Structure and Purpose." *Theology Digest* 24
        (1976), 349-359.

        A "purely formal" outline of the structure of Matthew shows that
        the five sections so long assumed are there, and that narrative and
        discourse sections alternate. The discourse sections act as connec-
        tors, not dividers, which explains many puzzles which theologians
        have failed to solve.

1705.   Bauer, David R. "The Literary Function of the Genealogy in
        Matthew's Gospel." *SBLSP* 1990, pp. 451-468.

        The structure of the genealogy, including the interruptions, and
        ways in which it "introduces the reader to the narrative of the
        Gospel." It has three main units, arranged chiastically. The narra-
        tive world of Matthew may illuminate the meaning of the breaks in
        that they discuss the women's powerlessness—a forecast of the
        theme of concern for the poor and powerless in Matthew. The ge-
        nealogy establishes Matthew's point of view.

1706.   Bauer, David R. *The Structure of Matthew's Gospel: A Study in
        Literary Design.* Sheffield (Almond P), 1988.

        Matthew was constructed according to four rhetorical elements:
        repetition of comparison (Jesus and disciples); repetition of con-
        trast (Jesus and opponents); repetition leading to climax; and rep-
        etition of climax with inclusio. Thus the traditional theory that the
        structure consists of five discourses (sections) based on the Penta-
        teuch is erroneous; instead, the overall structure is preparation
        (1:1-4:16), proclamation (4:17-16:20), and passion-resurrection
        (16:21-28:20), each section of which repeats the four rhetorical el-
        ements.

1707.   Beal, Timothy Kandler. "Bringing Out the New and the
        Old: An Interactive Approach to Reading the Parable In-
        stanced in Matthew 13:51-52," in John H. Morgan, ed.,
        Church Divinity 1989/1990 (Bristol, Indiana: Graduate
        Theological Foundation), 106-122.

        The parables of Jesus are "interactive metaphors of rhetorical
        power [which] engage the reader at her/his mythicopoetic core in
        the imaginative redescription of human reality. Thus they radically
        relativize all human models of meaning." The structure of
        Matthew 13 "resists final substitutionary interpretation by its many
        levels of interactive tension, radically redefining the concept of
        discipleship in the kingdom of heaven, as well as established pat-
        terns of biblical criticism.

1708. Boonstra, Harry. "Satire in Matthew." *CL* 29, #4 (Summer, 1980), 32-45.

The Jesus-Pharisee controversy as satire and polemic. Satire undercuts both antagonism and pomposity, and is a means of subduing pride. This works whether we consider Jesus' words to be historical, or to have been supplied later by Matthew as part of an ongoing feud between Christianity and Judaism.

1709. Bourke, Myles. "The Literary Genus of Matthew 1-2." *CBQ* 22 (1960), 160-175.

Matthew 1-2 is haggadic midrash, which means that it uses legendary materials but may still have a historical basis. The term means not "fictitious narrative" but "reflection upon the scriptures." In general, Matthew used midrashic traditions about OT characters: the star at birth (Abraham); Jesus as the new Israel (Jacob); Jesus as the new Moses.

1710. Brooks, Oscar S., Sr. "Matthew xxviii 16-20 and the Design of the First Gospel." *JSNT* 10 (1981), 2-18.

The concluding pericope of Matthew controls the design of the entire gospel. Its two main themes of "authority" and "teaching" are consistently emphasized throughout Matthew, "so as to support the thesis and prepare the reader for the concluding paragraph." Thus Matthew was able to produce a gospel with a unified design.

1711. Burnett, Fred W. "Characterization in Matthew: Reader Construction of the Disciple Peter." *McKendree Pastoral Review* 4 (1987), 13-43.

Reader-response criticism and discourse analysis help us "see how the reader is guided in the construction of the character 'Peter.'" He is largely a type of the disciples, though at certain moments we are allowed to see him as an individual who transcends type through such devices as his double name, his obvious opinions, the excess of information about him which is unnecessary to the plot, and the contrasts with the other disciples.

1712. Burnett, Fred W. "Prolegomenon to Reading Matthew's Eschatological Discourse: Redundancy and the Education of the Reader in Matthew." *Semeia* 31 (1985), 91-110.

Matthew is redundant on both story and discourse levels. Such redundancies help create an aesthetic experience when readers' expectations about Jesus are unfulfilled. However, the overall effect of redundancies is to create a stable narrative world: the unfolding plan of God.

1713.   Calloud, Jean. *Structural Analysis of Narrative.* Tr Daniel
         Patte. SBL Semeia Supplement 4. Philadelphia (Fortress
         P) and Missoula (Scholars P), 1976.

         Actantial and syntactic-semantic analysis applied to Matthew 4
         (with some use of Luke 4): the Temptation in the Wilderness
         story. Structuralism applied to the Bible has weaknesses as well as
         strengths, but works well overall.

1714.   Combrink, H.J.B., et al. *Structure and Meaning in Matthew 14-
         28* [*Neotestamentica* 16: 1982].

         Eight separate essays unified by discourse analysis of individual
         chapters or groups of chapters in the last half of Matthew, or (in
         one case) of the whole gospel. Addendum illustrates each essay
         with Greek text of that portion of Matthew diagrammed according
         to each critic's argument.

1715.   Combrink, H.J. Bernard. "The Structure of the Gospel of
         Matthew as Narrative." *TB* 34 (1983), 61-90.

         Once we have a sense of the formal structure, we must continue
         to a "deeper understanding of the values and message of the nar-
         rative." A structural "narrative paradigm" for analyzing gospels;
         detailed analysis of Matthew based on the paradigm.

1716.   Crossan, John Dominic. *Finding Is the First Act: Trove Folktales
         and Jesus' Treasure Parable.* Missoula (Scholars P) and
         Philadelphia (Fortress P), 1979.

         The structure of the parable of the hidden treasure (Matthew
         13:44) by mapping its plot against the tradition of Jewish treasure
         stories and ones in world folklore. This parable is a "metaparable,"
         a "paradoxical artifact" which succeeds because it fails.

1717.   Edwards, Richard A. *Matthew's Story of Jesus.* Philadelphia
         (Fortress P), 1985.

         Brief and basic analysis of Matthew in terms of reader-response
         criticism. The narrator's techniques for guiding the reader toward
         a certain understanding of and response to the plot and the char-
         acters.

1718.   Edwards, Richard A. "Reading Matthew: The Gospel as Nar-
         rative." *Listening* 24 (1989), 251-261.

         A reader-response approach to discussing ways that the narrator
         "shapes readers' expectations, controls reactions to characters, and
         employs suspense (*gar* clauses)...."

1719.   Edwards, Richard A. "Uncertain Faith: Matthew's Portrait of the Disciples," in Fernando F. Segovia, ed., *Discipleship in the New Testament* (Philadelphia: Fortress P, 1985), 47-61.

Because Matthew is a story, we should see the disciples as characters in a narrative. Reader-response criticism helps us understand Matthew's concept of discipleship by following our response to Matthew's clues and gaps. Importance of the pattern of the ambivalence of the disciples versus the stability of Jesus and God.

1720.   Fenton, J.C. "Inclusio-Chiasmus in Matthew," in Kurt Aland, et al., eds., *Studia Evangelica I: Papers Presented to the International Congress on "The Four Gospels in 1957"* (Berlin: Akademie-Verlag, 1959), 174-9.

We can distinguish between accidental and purposeful appearances of inclusio and chiasmus in Matthew; there are some of each instance in the gospel.

1721.   Funk, Robert W. "Beyond Criticism in Quest of Literacy: The Parable of the Leaven." *Interpretation* 25 (1971), 149-170.

Phenomenological analysis can help "clear away the debris" of previous attempts which succeeded only partially in recovering the parable as parable, which obfuscated as much as they clarified. We must find a way to let the words and sentences of this parable (Matthew 13, Luke 13, Thomas 96) have their own say; we start with the inseparability of form and content. So Jesus' language of the kingdom must be hidden and mysterious because that is the nature of the kingdom. How the early church often lost the likely original meaning(s) of the parables.

1722.   Green, H.B. "The Structure of St. Matthew's Gospel," in Frank L. Cross, ed., in *Studia Evangelica IV: Papers Presented to the Third International Congress on New Testament Studies. Part I: The New Testament Scriptures* (Berlin: Akademie-Verlag, 1968), 47-59.

Matthew's fondness for chiasmus and inclusio show what a conscious literary artist he was. Older theories of the structure of Matthew are inadequate because they deal only with content. A different theory will more satisfactorily explain the integration of form and content in Matthew.

1723.   Gros Louis, Kenneth R.R. "The Jesus Birth Stories," in #40, pp. 273-284.

The birth narratives in Matthew and Luke are "surprisingly different." These differences appear not just in details, but "in essen-

tials, in structure, in emphases, in point of view toward the birth
and those concerned with it." Part of the difference is one of the
sensibility of the narrators, since Luke is much more self-conscious
as an author; part of it is the more developed characterization in
Luke.

1724.   Harnisch, Wolfgang. "The Metaphorical Process in Matthew
          20: 1-15." *SBLSP* 1977, pp. 231-250.

          What consitutes the parabolic content of a story, and how much
          is it able to call attention to itself so that the hearer grasps that the
          parable points to something beyond what is said? The semantics of
          the metaphor may give us fresh access to the nature of parabolic
          speech, as, e.g., in the subtle metaphorical process of 20:1-15.

1725.   Heil, John Paul. "The Blood of Jesus in Matthew: A Narra-
          tive-Critical Perspective." *PRS* 18 (1991), 117-124.

          Literary and narrative criticism help us see that the theme of the
          blood of Jesus in Matthew has an additional meaning: the Jewish
          people calling Jesus' blood down upon their heads and their chil-
          dren's is for Matthew their willingness to share his atoning blood,
          and thus in the salvation it effects.

1725a.   Heil, John Paul. "The Narrative Structure of Matthew
          27:55–28:20." *JBL* 110 (1991), 419-438.

          The scenes that conclude Matthew "are arranged in an inter-
          locking network of literary sandwiches in which each successive
          scene is contrastingly framed by two other mutually related
          scenes." This narrative structure is designed to have a specific
          rhetorical effect on the implied reader: a progression through the
          "a" scenes of reliable witnesses to faith and resurrection, and si-
          multaneously through the "b" scenes of "powerless and fraudulent
          authority" of Jesus' opponents. The positive experience of the "a"
          scenes equips the reader to overcome the negative experience of
          the "b" scenes."

1726.   Howell, David B. *Matthew's Inclusive Story: A Study in the Nar-
          rative Rhetoric of the First Gospel.* Sheffield (JSOT P), 1990.

          We must assume the integrity of Matthew, the indispensability of
          point of view, and the role of the reader in the production of
          meaning. The most important dimension of reader-text interac-
          tion is temporal, not spatial; reading has a social dimension. The
          narrative rhetoric of the plot of Matthew; its implied author, narra-
          tor, and implied reader. Reader-response critique of the use of
          "salvation history" in interpreting the gospel.

1727.   Kermode, Frank. "Matthew," in #33, pp. 387-401.

Matthew's dependence on the HB may reveal clues to the way his imagination worked, and thus how to read him. For him, the HB has sanctity and force, but is not complete in itself. His view of the relation of old and new is typological, something like the parallelism of Hebrew poetry transformed from semantic technique into thematic argument: an excess of B (Matthew) over A (the HB). His themes are "excess, transformation, and the authority by which excess is demanded and transformation achieved," his emphasis always on fulfillment.

1728.   Kidder, S. Joseph. "'This Generation' in Matthew 24:34." *AUSS* 21 (1983), 203-9.

To relate this puzzling verse to the rest of the chapter, we first need to notice that chapters 23-25 form a significant chiasm, with its apex or pivotal point at 24:15. Apparently Matthew warns his readers against conflating two distinct events: the destruction of Jerusalem and the coming of Christ at the end of the age.

1729.   Kingsbury, Jack Dean. "The Developing Conflict between Jesus and the Jewish Leaders in Matthew's Gospel: A Literary-Critical Study." *CBQ* 49 (1987), 57-73.

The story-line of the Jewish leaders; characterization in detail, especially as they relate to Jesus in a developing conflict.

1730.   Kingsbury, Jack Dean. "The Figure of Jesus in Matthew's Story: A Literary-Critical Probe." *JSNT* 21 (1984), 3-36.

The phrase "Son of Man" does not function "confessionally" to inform the reader of "who Jesus is," but instead characterizes Jesus as "the man," or "the human being (this man, or this human being)." Nonetheless, it is also a christological title.

1731.   Kingsbury, Jack Dean. "The Figure of Jesus in Matthew's Story: A Rejoinder to David Hill." *JSNT* 25 (1985), 61-81.

Defense of #1730. Literary analysis cannot be under the control of source and redaction criticism, since a story is a story. Evaluative point of view is from God, not Jesus, as other critics would have it.

1732.   Kingsbury, Jack Dean. *Matthew as Story*. Philadelphia (Fortress P), 1986.

Narrative theory of plot, character, point of view, setting, and implied author and reader applied to the overall gospel of Matthew, then to the different foci of the plot; the community of Matthew's gospel; and the Matthean concept of Jesus as "Son of Man" as it affects our understanding of the plot.

1733. Kingsbury, Jack Dean. "The Parable of the Wicked Husbandman and the Secret of Jesus' Divine Sonship in Matthew: Some Literary-Critical Observations." *JBL* 105 (1986), 643-655.

The secret of Jesus' divine sonship, contrary to the opinions of most scholars, is a major motif in Matthew, and the parable of the wicked husbandman plays a critical role in developing this motif. It is the first point in Matthew where the Jewish leaders confront Jesus' claim to be son of God, and so has a major effect on the rest of the action. The motif serves two purposes: pointing toward the mission to the Gentiles, and toward important knowledge his followers everywhere must have.

1734. Kingsbury, Jack Dean. "The Place, Structure and Meaning of the Sermon on the Mount." *Interpretation* 41 (1987), 131-143

Structure and themes of Matthew 5-7. The notion of the implied reader is more crucial for grasping these chapters than is that of the actual hearers of the historical Jesus. The implied reader is the real recipient of the teachings.

1735. Kingsbury, Jack Dean. "Reflections on 'The Reader' of Matthew's Gospel." *NTS* 34 (1988), 442-460.

Peculiar to historical, redaction, and literary (narrative) criticism is that all contain a model of readership that dictates who is the "primary reader" of a gospel. Who this reader is in each school and what role he plays. Redaction criticism is superior to historical, and literary to redaction, because of the increasing accessibility of the implied reader to scholarly discussion. Scrutinizing the world of the story is essential preparation for examining the world of the evangelist.

1736. Kotze, P.P.A., et al. "The Structure of Matthew 1-13: An Exploration into Discourse Analysis." *Neotestamentica* 11 (1977), 1-9.

Discourse analysis—a method of analyzing linguistic utterances longer than a single sentence—applied to individual chapters or pairs of chapters in the first half of Matthew by ten different scholars.

1737. Lahurd, Carol Schersten. "Rhetorical Criticism, Biblical Criticism and Literary Criticism: Issues of Methodological Pluralism." *PEGL* 5 (1985), 87-101.

Several critical methods can be combined, and in fact the text often seems to call for precisely this interdisciplinary approach.

Sometimes conclusions will clash, as discussions of Matthew 5-7 by Jeremias and Kennedy demonstrate. However, the various methods can "check and balance," even complement each other if theological presuppositions each brings to the debate are clearly understood.

1738. Lincoln, Andrew T. "Matthew—A Story for Teachers," in #35, pp. 103-125.

From the relatively disappointing literary-critical work done so far on Matthew, we may conclude that such analysis will have more potential if it focuses more on the role of the disciples and less on Jesus, since the situation of the implied reader is more similar to that of the disciples. Such an approach integrates the various emphases in the narrative. "... Matthew's gospel should be read as a story for would-be teachers. The implied author is in effect saying to the implied reader, 'So you want to be a teacher? Let me tell you a story.'"

1739. Lohr, Charles H. "Oral Techniques in the Gospel of Matthew." *CBQ* 23 (1961), 403-435.

How Matthew adapted to the stereotyped style of the oral tradition. He uses formulaic devices, e.g., inclusio, refrain, foreshadowing and retrospection to elaborate his unifying themes. To arrange his structure he alternates narrative and discourse materials to arrive at an overall symmetry: grouping like materials and repeating key words. Matthew's gospel may have been preferred early on because of the care with which he arranged his materials, compared to Mark.

1740. Lund, N.W. "The Influence of Chiasmus upon the Structure of the Gospel According to Matthew." *ATR* 13 (1931), 405-433.

We must assume a conscious aesthetic interest in the chiasmus found in Matthew, since he uses it for suspense, climax, and numerical arrangements in clusters of threes, fives, and sevens. In addition, he groups the sayings and doings of Jesus into chiastic order. Matthew was probably written for reading at public worship.

1741. Macky, Peter W. "Exploring the Depths of Biblical Metaphor." *PEGL* 8 (1988), 167-176.

"... some biblical metaphors are more appropriately approached as artistic works than as expository ones." Criteria for distinguishing the two kinds, for seeing how they appeal to readers differently, and for analyzing metaphors once distinguished. Illustrations from Matthew 11:28-30.

1742.   Malina, Bruce J. "The Literary Form and Structure of Matt.
         XXVIII.16-20." *NTS* 17 (1970), 87-103.

         Matthew 28:16-20 is the key to the whole gospel. Its literary
         structure and relationship to the beginning of the gospel. Matthew
         28:16-20 is parallel with II Chronicles 36:23—a classic proof-pat-
         tern from the OT—and is chiastic with the opening verses. It was
         designed to endow the gospel with an open-ended character.

1743.   Matera, Frank J. "The Plot of Matthew's Gospel." *CBQ* 49
         (1987), 233-253.

         Standard literary-critical techniques enable the modern reader
         to recognize Matthew's plot and then to understand it. Outline of
         six "kernels" and of narrative blocks in the gospel. "As a narrative,
         Matthew's gospel ... concerns Israel's rejection of the Messiah and
         the consequent movement of the gospel to the Gentiles."

1744.   Morosco, Robert E. "Matthew's Formation of a Commission-
         ing Type-Scene." *JBL* 103 (1984), 539-566.

         The HB contains a number of commissioning type-scenes. A
         lead role in shaping this tradition was taken by Exodus 3:1–4:17,
         which also influenced the shape of Matthew 9:35–11:1 (the com-
         missioning of the disciples). Matthew used the type-scene for two
         reasons: he wanted to stimulate a powerful reader response to his
         message, and he wanted to place Jesus in the same theater of holy
         history as Moses.

1745.   Patte, Daniel. *The Gospel According to Matthew: A Structural
         Commentary on Matthew's Faith.* Philadelphia (Fortress P),
         1987.

         A "non-technical" reading of Matthew, based on the semiotic
         theories of narrative semantic oppositions of A.J. Greimas. "The
         contribution of this commentary is limited to elucidating the con-
         victions that Matthew expresses in each passage and how they are
         expressed through the thematic features of that passage."

*   Patte, Daniel. "'Love Your Enemies'—'Woe to You, Scribes
         and Pharisees': The Need for a Semiotic Approach in
         New Testament Studies." See #1547.

1746.   Phillips, Gary A. "History and Text: The Reader in Context
         in Matthew's Parables Discourse." *SBLSP* 1983, pp. 415-
         437, and *Semeia* 31 (1985), 111-138.

         Matthew 13 "as intertextuality and discourse." The reader-lis-
         tener of (to) Matthew must have textual competence—i.e., must
         grasp Matthew's allegorizing of Jesus, must affirm his "place within

the larger tradition of which Jesus himself is a part." Interpretation in this sense is "an intertextual game, a serious game." Thus Matthew 13 is more than mimetic history, more than imaginative reconstruction; it is a "working template of how to be a competent scribe oneself."

1747. du Plessis, J.G. "Pragmatic Meaning in Matthew 13:1-23." *Neotestamentica* 21 (1987), 33-56.

The pragmatic principles of G.N. Leech and the scheme of narrative roles of W. Schmid applied to Matthew 13 shows that "the intended effect of the discourse is the strengthening of the interpersonal relationship between Jesus and his disciples.... The disciples (and the readers) are urged to adhere in a dependent attitude to Jesus." Jesus' remarks about the purpose of the parables "are a foil used by Jesus to illuminate the relationship between himself and his disciples."

1748. Pregeant, Russell. "The Wisdom Passages in Matthew's Story." *SBLSP* 1990, pp. 469-493.

Reader-response analysis of the "wisdom" passages in Matthew reveals their apparent identification of Jesus as "Wisdom incarnate." Readers might well take this commissioning in a future sense, especially since it might otherwise conflict with the virgin birth. Reader-response criticism shows that readers may respond "in more than one way without violating the text."

1749. Scott, Bernard Brandon. "The Birth of the Reader." *Semeia* 52 (1990), 83-102.

"The narratives of the first section of Matthew's Gospel provide the reader with an ideological orientation to the rest of the Gospel. These expose the fundamental values of the text, the way in which it organizes its narrative world." "Close analysis" of the "surface structure" of this ideology through reader-response techniques. Testing the ideological structure is a way of explaining other elements of Matthew.

1750. Shuler, Philip L. *A Genre for the Gospels: The Biographical Character of Matthew.* Philadelphia (Fortress P), 1982.

Despite our knowledge of the literary skill which they evince, the gospels' genre is still a problem. The nature of Greco-Roman laudatory biography; the difficulty of identifying genres except through rhetorical traditions of encomium biography. This genre offers the best generic classification because of its specific characteristics and the variety it allows. Matthew fits this category of *bios*, though it is more than that as well.

1751.   Sider, John W. "Interpreting the Hid Treasure." *Christian Scholar's Review* 13 (1984), 360-372.

Response to #1684. Disagrees both that the central feature of Matthew 13:44 is the unethical business deal, and that the mystery parable was the only way moral discourse could be carried on.

1752.   Tannehill, Robert C. "The 'Focal Instance' as a Form of New Testament Speech: A Study of Matthew 5:39b-42." *JR* 50 (1970), 372-385.

Religious language cannot be separated from other functions of language. The parallel syntax of Matthew 5:39b-42, and its use to create resemblances as well as contrasts and tensions; its openness to extending and adapting the patterns contained therein. The center of these language operations is the command which becomes a "focal instance" characterized by specifity and extremity.

1753.   Tilborg, Sjef Van. "Matthew 27.3-10: An Intertextual Reading," in #38, pp. 159-174.

Matthew 27 read against Jeremiah, as compared to the usual comparison with Zechariah 11. The reference to Jeremiah "remains problematic," but important nonetheless, as Matthew's allusions to Jeremiah come after he is through alluding to Zechariah. They emphasize Matthew's point that the Jewish leaders think that they have found an escape, but in fact have not.

1754.   Viviano, Benedict T., O.P. "The Genres of Matthew 1-2: Light From I Timothy 1:4." *Revue Biblique* 97 (1990), 31-53.

Matthew took the daring and dangerous step of writing a prologue which his Jewish readers would recognize as "a complex of Old Testament citations, allusions, and midrashim," and his Hellenistic readers would receive as "mythopoetic." In the "extreme brevity and sobriety" of the stereotyped literary units, "he has done as much as a narrative author can to signify to the reader that this is not ordinary history but a prehistory such as we find in Genesis 1-11." His is a "symbolic narrative representation of ... primal reality." The author of I Timothy failed to understand this, as have most readers since.

1755.   Weaver, Dorothy Jean. *Matthew's Missionary Discourse: A Literary Critical Analysis.* Sheffield (JSOT P), 1990.

The discourse is contained in 9:35–11:1, though analysis through the end of chapter 11 is warranted. The role of the implied reader in 1:1–9:34; how the structure and narrative discourse of 9:35–11:1 communicates to this reader; how the rest of Matthew "responds to the unresolved tensions of 9:35–11:1," and the role of this discourse in Matthew's overall narrative.

1756. Williams, James G. "Paraenesis, Ethics, and Excess: Matthew's Rhetoric in the Sermon on the Mount." *Semeia* 50 (1990), 163-187.

Explication of Matthew 5-7 using both anthropological and literary methods. The "central ethical-religious impulse" of Matthew is that the kingdom is less a place than an act of helping our neighbor." It "expresses itself in a rhetoric of excess" where a collection of sayings is "changed into a passionate discourse that could be read or heard as the teacher's farewell even before he and his followers embark on their mission."

1757. Wojcik, Jan. "The Two Kingdoms in Matthew's Gospel," in #39, pp. 283-295.

The patterns of emphasis in Matthew "makes Jesus' message about the two kingdoms, preached throughout the Gospel, seemingly shape the very narrative which carries the message." The two scenes in chapter 14—Herod's banquet and the murder of John the Baptist, versus the feeding of the 5000—are juxtaposed in Matthew in order to underscore the stark choice facing his readers: an earthly kingdom leading to death, or a heavenly one leading to life. The theme thus enunciated then shows up repeatedly in Matthew.

See also: #s 135, 313, 532, 533, 1490, 1491, 1497, 1501, 1565, 1573, 1576, 1581, 1607, 1612, 1613, 1621, 1839, 1904, 1906, 1912, 2118.

MARK

1758. Aichele, George, Jr. "Poverty and the Hermeneutics of Repentance." *Cross Currents* 38 (1988-9), 458-467.

Fantastic stories are "anti-mythic, para-doxical, ... dangerous and even anti-human. Yet they also question the meaning and value of survival itself, and thus they are creative." The fantasy "operates in significant ways in ... the canonical gospel of Mark [in that] ... the conjoining of repentance of belief, and of astonishment and entry into the kingdom, is fantastic." Later gospels remove the fantastic and substitute the mythic.

1759.   Best, Ernest. "Mark's Narrative Technique." *JSNT* 37 (1989), 43-58.

Mark is the one true storyteller among the gospel writers. His gospel contains elements of biography, history or sermon, and narrative. His knowledge of how to do narrative may have been instinctual, so rhetorical analysis does not prove that he was educated in rhetoric. Facts and suppositions about his narrative techniques and early audience, signs of oral composition and how that affected the structure of the gospel. Many of his techniques may have in fact been inherent in his material.

1760.   Bilezikian, Gilbert G. *The Liberated Gospel: A Comparison of the Gospel of Mark and Greek Tragedy.* Grand Rapids (Baker), 1977.

Mark borrowed "compatible literary devices ... from ... Greek tragedy," because he felt it appropriate to use techniques already familiar to his audience. Mark shows the influence of Greek notions of plot, style, characterization, dramatic irony, and dialogue. "By casting the Gospel in a gentile cultural mold totally foreign to Jewish ... concerns, Mark powerfully demonstrated that the story of Jesus explodes the narrow categories popularly ascribed to it and that it really belongs to all mankind."

1761.   Bishop, Jonathan. "*Parabole* and *Parrhesia* in Mark." *Interpretation* 40 (1986), 39-52.

Careful attention to the regular patterns of contrast in Mark: parable and explanation, mystery and interpretation, crowd and disciples, gives new insight into Mark's structure and purpose.

1762.   Boers, Hendrikus. "Reflections on the Gospel of Mark: A Structural Investigation." *SBLSP* 1987, pp. 255-267.

The unity of Mark on the basis of its internal text-syntactic structure, rather than from theological motif or rhetorical forms. We may then grasp more fully not so much what Mark means, as how he means it. The possible meanings of various Greek terms in Mark. The gospel as a story for worship, a cult story, its lack of character development, actor roles, and the meaning of suffering.

*   Boucher, Madeleine. *The Mysterious Parable: A Literary Study.* See #1652.

1763.   Breytenbach, Cilliers. "The Gospel of Mark as Episodical Narrative." *Scriptura* Special Issue S4 (1989).

The interrelationship of the small independent narratives in Mark and its "narrative macro-structure." The consequences of its episodic nature for understanding its structure. Its several levels of narration.

1764. Burch, Ernest W. "Tragic Action in the Second Gospel: A Study in the Narrative of Mark." *JR* 11 (1931), 346-358.

Mark can be classified as a Greek tragedy, since it has the requisite recognition scene, exposition, plot leading to a climax, a tragic hero (Jesus), and it arouses pity and fear.

1765. Calloud, Jean. "Toward a Structural Analysis of the Gospel of Mark." *Semeia* 16 (1979), 133-165.

Elementary categories of signification, and networks of semantic relations applied to Mark, for the purpose of discovering its "structured totality."

* Collins, John J., ed. *Semeia 14. Apocalypse: The Morphology of a Genre.* See #36.

1766. Dewey, Joanna. "Mark as Interwoven Tapestry: Forecasts and Echoes for a Listening Audience." *CBQ* 53 (1991), 221-236.

The disagreements and difficulties in making a satisfactory outline of Mark. "... Mark does not have a single structure made up of discrete sequential units but rather is an interwoven tapestry or fugue made up of multiple overlapping structures and sequences, forecasts of what is to come and echoes of what has already been said.... [It] was still very close to oral composition, ... composed with the needs of a listening audience in mind." Therefore, we should study aural more than linear-print norms in order to grasp its plot.

1767. Donahue, John R., S.J. "Jesus as the Parable of God in the Gospel of Mark." *Interpretation* 32 (1978), 369-386.

The whole of Mark is itself intended as a narrative parable of the meaning of the life and death of Jesus. This can be shown through analysis of Mark's use of metaphor, irony and paradox.

1768. Drury, John. "Mark," in #33, pp. 402-417.

Mark closely resembles folktale in its lack of digressions, its "lean, close and complex ... articulation," its formulaic nature which demands close attention from the reader. It occupies "a threshold between the evanescent spoken word and the more permanent and fixed written word." Its structure; its semi-hidden OT codes and the patterns they make in the narrative; principles

of characterization; the function of clothes; various themes including that of bread, particularly in 6:35-44 and 8:1-10.

1769.   Edwards, James R. "Markan Sandwiches: The Significance
         of Interpolations in Markan Narratives." *Nov T* 31 (1989),
         193-216.

         Mark's habit of inserting a second, seemingly unrelated story in
         the middle of another one serves both theological and literary
         purposes; is done much more by Mark than by the other gospel
         writers; and is done by him with subtlety and sophistication.

1770.   Ellis, Peter F., C.S.S.R. "Patterns and Structures of Mark's
         Gospel," in Miriam Ward, ed., *Biblical Studies in Contempo-
         rary Thought* (Burlington: Trinity College Biblical Insti-
         tute; Somerville: Greeno, Hadden and Co., 1975), 88-103.

         Previous attempts to elucidate the structure of Mark have failed
         "to recognize the full significance of Mark's summaries at the be-
         ginning of each ... section as *introductory* summaries combined
         with a failure to grasp the importance of Mark's use of inclusion
         and climaxes in Part I and a failure to extrapolate from the
         parallel triads in parts I and II to the possibility of a similar
         arrangement of parallel triads in part III...."

1771.   Enslin, Morton S. "The Artistry of Mark." *JBL* 66 (1947),
         385-399.

         Analysis of the themes and structure of Mark show a single au-
         thor, not a redactor, and one who consciously shaped his narrative
         in a sophisticated style which served his purposes well.

1772.   Fowler, Robert M. "Irony and the Messianic Secret in the
         Gospel of Mark." *PEGL* 1 (1981), 26-36.

         "... there is no such thing as the Messianic Secret *in the text of
         Mark*; the Markan secret is ... to be found ... *in the experience of
         reading* the text of Mark.... [T]he Markan secret is the reader's ex-
         perience of *irony* as he or she reads a story about a messiah whose
         messiahship is virtually always hidden or misunderstood."

1773.   Fowler, Robert M. *Loaves and Fishes: The Function of the Feed-
         ing Stories in the Gospel of Mark.* Chico (Scholars P), 1981.

         Redaction and literary-critical examination, especially reader-re-
         sponse criticism. The doublets in chapters 4-8 function quite well
         as integral components of the gospel as a whole. Form criticism
         does violence to these stories, since repetition in them is inten-
         tional. Redaction critics miss evidence of the implied author of

Mark except where he is obvious; it can tell us "what," but not "why."

1774. Fowler, Robert M. "The Rhetoric of Direction and Indirection in the Gospel of Mark." *Semeia* 48 (1989), 115-134.

Rhetorical strategies of direction and indirection in Mark, examined from a reader-response position. Mark "is designed less to *say* something to the reader than to *do* something to the reader." The analyst's goal should be to understand "the workings of ... the rhetorical moves made by the narrator."

1775. Fowler, Robert M. "The Rhetoric of Indirection in the Gospel of Mark." *PEGL* 5 (1985), 47-56.

"Much ambiguity and opacity persists to the end of the narrative and beyond. The experience of reading this Gospel is the experience of encountering and wrestling with a whole spectrum of indirect rhetorical moves, ranging from opacity, at one extreme, to paradox, at the other. In the middle, and the driving force of Mark's rhetoric of indirection, is irony, which shares both the ambiguity of one side of the spectrum, and the persistent and reverbatory incongruity of the other side."

1776. Fowler, Robert M. "Thoughts on the History of Reading Mark's Gospel." *PEGL* 4 (1984), 120-130.

"... the history of reading Mark's gospel is the history of its being read through the distorting lenses we call Matthew, Luke, and John." We need to read Mark knowing that these lenses tend to block out certain features of Mark, and try to remove the lenses.

1777. Fowler, Robert M. "Who is 'the Reader' of Mark's Gospel?" *SBLSP* 1983, pp. 31-53.

The theory of reader-response criticism. Wayne Booth's "rhetoric of irony" is helpful in understanding the feeding stories in Mark, as is the work of Leonard Thompson [#187]. Mark provides "a great deal of stable, coherent guidance for the reader."

1778. Gros Louis, Kenneth R.R. "The Gospel of Mark," in #39, pp. 296-329.

All of Mark's major themes are introduced in his first four chapters: the mystery of Jesus; his healing powers; his secrecy; his roles as breaker of rules and as bridegroom; his hearers' lack of understanding; the development of the disciples. The development of these themes is greatly enhanced by the parables which Mark includes. If we ask why a given episode is placed where it is, we open up the literary approach to the gospel.

1779.   Hedrick, Charles W. "Narrator and Story in the Gospel of Mark: *Hermeneia* and *Paradosis.*" *PRS* 14 (1987), 239-258.

Narrative devices called "hermeneia" (i.e., asides) enable the implied author "to exercise better interpretive control of the story." Their appearance in Mark; how to classify them; how they characterize the narrator.

1780.   Hedrick, Charles W. "What is a Gospel? Geography, Time, and Narrative Structure." *PRS* 10 (1983), 255-268.

We need to describe the structure of Mark based on formal narrative features rather than on theological ones. Thus, literary theory shows us that chapters 1-13 are different from chapters 14-16; that the author went out of his way to keep the ministries of John and Jesus separate; that the usual explanations of the ending are inadequate. We will not grasp Mark's theology if we do not first understand his literary-structural principles.

1781.   van Iersel, B.M.F. "The Gospel According to St. Mark: Written for a Persecuted Community?" *Nederlands Theologisch Tijdschrift* 34 (1980), 15-36.

Semantic-linguistic analysis of Mark encourages us to read any portion of a gospel with the whole work in mind. When we do so, we are forced to conclude that Mark was addressing himself to readers for whom persecution was a real possibility.

1782.   van Iersel, Bas. "Locality, Structure, and Meaning in Mark." *LB* 53 (1983), 45-54.

A reading of the "topographical structure" of Mark on both the surface and deep structure levels.

1783.   van Iersel, B.M.F. "The Reader of Mark as Operator of a System of Connotations." *Semeia* 48 (1989), 83-114.

The reader-response model of Roland Barthes applied to the question of the messianic secret in Mark finds it to be "a central element of connotative layer of meaning" as found in the feeding stories, parables of the seed and the vineyard, and the last supper.

1784.   van Iersel, Bas. *Reading Mark.* Tr W.H. Bischeroux. Edinburgh (T. and T. Clark), 1989.

We must assume that Mark "constitutes a unified whole whose parts cannot be read separately without violating the book as well as the parts concerned." It must further be read as a narrative, and therefore has a narrator, narratee, characters, and an implied reader—in sum, the story world which Mark creates, and the ways in which it creates and conveys meanings beyond that world.

1785. Jasper, David. "'In the Sermon Which I Have Just Completed, Whenever I Said Aristotle, I Meant Saint Paul' (attrib. Revd. William A. Spooner)," in #1517, pp. 133-152.

Religious rhetoric is distinctive in pursuing authoritative proclamation rather than rational persuasion. Given this, there are two possible interpretations of the rhetoric of Mark: that it is a "rhetoric of power" and authority, "fearful of irony," born of the community's anxiety at the threat of alienation; or that it is a more "pauline" rhetoric—that of a communal project capable of embracing the shock of radical discontinuity in a radical newness. The latter is probably the less inadequate model.

1786. Jasper, David. "St. Mark's Gospel and the Interpretive Community." *Religion and Intellectual Life* 6 (1989), 173-81.

"... the rhetorical demands of this text have developed out of this newly-established community wishing to assert its identity and sense of mutual interdependence by an act of self-entextualizing—asserting the 'content' of its being in the 'form' of a rhetorical construct which both realizes and enacts its necessary moment of power and authority." It was a community "powerfully bound together by their specific, furtively repressed anxieties."

1787. Kelber, Werner. *Mark's Story of Jesus.* Philadelphia (Fortress P), 1979.

Mark is a "dramatically plotted journey of Jesus." We should approach it as we do any other story: read beginning to end; observe the interplay of characters; watch for plot clues; identify scenes of crisis and recognition; view the resolution in terms of its antecedent logic. That is, see Mark as one whole gospel, rather than either fragmented into verses, or only in the light of the other gospels.

1788. Kingsbury, Jack Dean. *Conflict in Mark: Jesus, Authorities, Disciples.* Minneapolis (Fortress P), 1989.

Analysis of Mark based on narrative considerations of plot and the story lines within it; setting; characters, both individuals and in groups. "Jesus' conflict with Israel and especially the religious authorities is the pivot on which the plot of Mark's story turns."

1789. Loudon, John. "Good News, Mostly." *Parabola* 4 (1979), 97-100.

A review of Alec McCowen's recitation of Mark on the London and New York stages. There is value in hearing the gospel as a whole—something rare for modern persons.

1790.   Malbon, Elizabeth Struthers. "Disciples/Crowds/Whoever:
        Markan Characters and Readers." *Nov T* 28 (1986), 104-
        130.

        Robert Tannehill is correct [see #1812] that the disciples may be
        problematic, "but potential models nonetheless." We can extend
        this analysis by examining the relationship between disciples and
        crowds, and the relationship of these Markan characters to Mark's
        readers. Mark is not an allegory with characters equivalent to some
        group beyond the narrative.

1791.   Malbon, Elizabeth Strothers. "Fallible Followers: Women
        Men in the Gospel of Mark." *Semeia* 28 (1983) [#46], 3-27.

        Literary analysis of Mark shows that his portrait of Jesus' follow-
        ers includes the crowds and women. We should ask two questions:
        How do these women characters shed light on what it means to
        follow Jesus? And, Why are these characters especially appropriate
        for illuminating followership? "... by providing a complex and
        composite image of followers, ... the author of the Markan gospel
        is able to communicate clearly and powerfully to the reader a
        twofold message: anyone can be a follower, no one finds it easy."

1792.   Malbon, Elizabeth Struthers. "Galilee and Jerusalem: His-
        tory and Literature in Marcan Interpretation." *CBQ* 44
        (1982), 242-255.

        The significance of the Marcan spatial designations of Galilee
        and Jerusalem from a literary-critical point of view. The effect of
        this designation "for its narrative space as a system of relation-
        ships." In this device there is "a movement toward the mediation
        of chaos and order."

1793.   Malbon, Elizabeth Struthers. "The Jewish Leaders in the
        Gospel of Mark: A Literary Study of Marcan Characteriza-
        tion." *JBL* 108 (1989), 259-281.

        Mark seems typical of ancient literature in its characterization by
        types: good and bad. Nevertheless, he increases the complexity
        and subtlety of his characterization by using flat and round charac-
        ters, and by resisting stereotyping.

1794.   Malbon, Elizabeth Strothers. "Mark: Myth and Parable."
        BTB 16 (1986), 8-17.

        What are the connections between myth and parable in Mark?
        Are they distinguishable? Myth is not a genre, but an underlying
        structure. Mark is organized by spatial oppositions. It is a "parable-
        myth," even though these two impulses are distinctive, and even
        opposing.

1795. Malbon, Elizabeth Struthers. *Narrative Space and Mythic Meaning in Mark.* San Francisco (Harper and Row), 1986.

Structural exegesis is a way of learning about Mark and about narrative space. Spatial framework of the gospel: geopolitical, topographical, and architectural space, and how we might integrate them into a holistic view. The overall spatial arrangement of Mark, illustrating fundamental oppositions, e.g., order versus chaos, familiar versus strange, topography as promise versus as threat, architecture as profane versus as sacred.

1795a. Marshall, Christopher D. *Faith as a Theme in Mark's Narrative.* Cambridge (Cambridge UP), 1989.

Narrative criticism can cope adequately with the literary and theological unity of Mark as redaction criticism has been unable to do. It reveals the "central role faith occupies in [Mark's] narrative world," and helps us see that the "messianic secret" is not as dominant in Mark as we have hitherto thought.

1796. Osborne, William L. "The Markan Theme of 'Who is Jesus.'" *Asia Journal of Theology* 3 (1989), 302-314.

Literary/thematic analysis of Mark enables us to outline the structure of his gospel and to elucidate his themes. Most likely his purpose was to throw a "pre-emptive strike" on "some generalized heresy."

1797. Perrin, Norman. "The Christology of Mark: A Study in Methodology." *JR* 51 (1973), 173-187.

Current theological thinking about the problem of Markan christology can be confirmed and validated by using literary-critical tools to examine plot movement, roles of the protagonist, and literary structure, because Mark is a literary text.

* Perrin, Norman. "Historical Criticism, Literary Criticism, and Hermeneutics: The Interpretation of the Parables of Jesus and the Gospel of Mark Today." See #1687.

1798. Perrin, Norman. "The Interpretation of the Gospel of Mark." *Interpretation* 30 (1976), 115-124.

Interpreting Mark requires a sophisticated, eclectic approach: a concern for the gospel as a totality, not just for authorial activity and theology. Some recent examples of such criticism. The basic features of a literary approach to Mark include literary genre, theme, structure, distinctive features, narrative levels, characterization, and meanings for Mark himself.

*   Petersen, Norman. *Literary Criticism for New Testament Critics.*
           See #1506.

1799.   Petersen, Norman R. "Point of View in Mark's Narrative."
           Semeia 12 (1978), 97-121.

           The notion of point of view enables us to isolate evidence prov-
           ing that Mark is a "carefully and integrally composed narrative,"
           and that it must be read that way. Its literary nature is mainly guar-
           anteed by "the intrusive omniscience of the narrator."

1800.   Rhoads, David, and Donald Michie. *Mark as Story: An Intro-
           duction to the Narrative of a Gospel.* Philadelphia (Fortress
           P), 1982.

           Mark has a final unity, consistency of point of view, coherent
           plot, and resolution of conflicts. Role of the narrator; style; narra-
           tive patterns. The settings "as a dynamic context for the action."
           Plot events, especially Jesus versus nature, the authorities, and dis-
           ciples. The role of characterization. At times, Jesus as protagonist
           is powerless to control events, and so must resort to flight, verbal
           evasion, etc.

1801.   Rhoads, David. "Narrative Criticisms and the Gospel of
           Mark." *JAAR* 50 (1982), 411-434.

           Story world, narrative and rhetorical techniques in Mark. We
           must shift our perspectives from fragmentation to wholeness, and
           from history to fiction. Grasping the autonomy of the story world is
           of fundamental importance. These principles applied to plot,
           characterization, etc., in Mark, with questions which literary criti-
           cism raises for future study of the gospel.

*   Ricoeur, Paul. "Interpretative Narrative." See #1552.

1802.   Robbins, Vernon K. *Jesus the Teacher: A Socio-Rhetorical Inter-
           pretation of Mark.* Philadelphia (Fortress P), 1984.

           Mark in the cultural setting of late Mediterranean antiquity re-
           veals a blend of narrative models of the teacher-disciple relation-
           ship from biblical, Jewish literary, and Greco-Roman traditions. A
           semiotic, socio-rhetorical approach via Kenneth Burke's concept
           of four kinds of form: progressive, repetitive, conventional, and
           minor (e.g., folklore). Mark, despite being 99% repeated by
           Matthew and Luke, was preserved because it "played a significant
           role within early Christianity by successfully meeting Jewish mes-
           sianic expectations with role enactment that was widely known and
           esteemed in popular Greco-Roman culture."

1803.   Robbins, Vernon K. "Mark as Genre." *SBLSP* 1980, pp. 371-399.

Review of generic analyses of Mark by pre-1920 form and redaction critics. The "extrinsic-intrinsic" approach as practiced by structuralists, mythicists, and literary critics. Mark may be "eschatological memorabilia," integrating Jewish and Greco-Roman genres.

1804.   Robbins, Vernon K. "Summons and Outline in Mark: The Three-Step Progression." *Nov T* 23 (1981), 97-114.

"The three-step progressions that cover two or three pericopes form interludes in the narrative that establish the basic outline for the Marcan narrative." They are characterized by "rhetorical progression," and "establish an image of Jesus that mediates between Israelite traditions about Yahweh and the prophets and Graeco-Roman traditions about disciple-gathering teachers."

1805.   Roth, Wolfgang. *Hebrew Gospel: Cracking the Code of Mark.* Oak Park (Meyer Stone Books), 1988.

Mark is basically patterned "by a narrative of similar plot, cast, and volume present in ... the Hebrew Scriptures," specifically the "conceptual-narrative paradigm" of the Elijah-Elisha part of I Kings 17–II Kings 13. Mark re-creates the plot and theme as a whole and in specific detail, transforming it into a John/Jesus story. The remaining unique features of Mark may be imitations of Haggadic midrash and/or Greco-Roman writing.

1806.   Sandmel, Samuel. "Prolegomena to a Commentary on Mark." *Journal of Bible and Religion* 31 (1963), 294-300.

The gospels are not evidence of a historical Jesus, but of each other. To know the other gospels, and the rest of the NT, one must know Mark first, and then the interrelationship of the gospels. We must above all study Mark through Mark, and not through the other evangelists.

1807.   Scott, M. Philip, O.C.S.O. "Chiastic Structure: A Key to the Interpretation of Mark's Gospel." *BTB* 15 (1985), 17-26.

Mark subordinates history to presenting his ongoing and gradual development of implicit meaning made explicit in 14:62. Various large and small chiasms in the gospel, and their relationship to linear patterns. It also has an overall chiastic structure.

1808.   Stock, Augustine, O.S.B. *Call to Discipleship: A Literary Study of Mark's Gospel.* Wilmington (Michael Glazier), 1982.

Concepts of implied reader and implied author, dramatic narrative, story and discourse, and closure applied to Mark demonstrate that his purposes were "to lead his readers through a particular story in which they could discover themselves and thereby change," and to exclude resurrection so as to make it impossible to separate resurrection and suffering.

1809.   Stock, Augustine, O.S.B. "Chiastic Awareness and Education in Antiquity." *BTB* 14 (1984), 23-27.

There is extensive chiasmus in Mark, which was to be expected, given the nature of Greco-Roman education, where awareness of and sensitivity to it were universal. Chiasm was especially important in a setting where much learning proceeded orally.

1810.   Stock, Augustine, O.S.B. "Hinge Transitions in Mark's Gospel." *BTB* 15 (1985), 27-31.

The presence of chiasm reinforces matters of geography and content in answering what the structure of Mark is. It has a five-part topographical framework, giving an overall concentric structure. Review of recent literary-critical work on "keywords," "links," and "hinges" in the structure of Mark.

1811.   Stone, Jerry H. "The Gospel of Mark and *Oedipus the King*: Two Tragic Visions." *Soundings* 67 (1984), 55-69.

The tragic elements in Mark provide fresh insights into that gospel. It is not so different from classical Greek tragedy as has been supposed; the presence of comedy in Mark does not preclude its being a tragedy. Its similarities with tragedy as exemplified in *Oedipus*, and answers to criticisms of such a position.

1812.   Tannehill, Robert C. "The Disciples in Mark: The Function of a Narrative Role." *JR* 57 (1977), 386-405.

Recent narrative and reader-response theory applied to Mark's selective emphasis on and evaluation of the disciples and their "narrative role" throughout the gospel. The relationships among characters, implied author, and response anticipated from the implied reader. Mark hints that his readers are like the disciples, and should therefore change.

1813.   Tannehill, Robert C. "The Gospel of Mark as Narrative Christology." *Semeia* 16 (1979), 57-95.

Mark displays more unity and more art than is commonly recognized if we study it as narrative, especially the techniques of characterization. How Mark controls his readers' responses through narrative patterns, especially delayed disclosure, irony, and paradox.

1814. Tolbert, Mary Ann. *Sowing the Gospel: Mark's World in Literary-Historical Perspective.* Minneapolis (Fortress P), 1989.

The gospel of Mark "within the literary currents of its own historical milieu," since it cannot be read simply by modern narrative methods. The typical patterns of popular Greek writing. Hypotheses about the "genre, stylistic conventions, and narrative strategies" in Mark. The resemblance of Mark to the ancient popular novel, with explication of its rhetorical structure. Mark is "a typological, episodic, rhetorically-molded religious tract, ... an apocalyptic message in a popular narrative framework, replete with all the 'helps for hearers' an ancient audience needed and would have expected."

1815. Vorster, W.S. "Characterization of Peter in the Gospel of Mark." *Neotestamentica* 21 (1987), 57-76.

"Peter is both a Helper and also an Opponent in the development of the plot.... This ambiguity in his role is basic to his characterization.... The semantic function of the characterization of Peter should be seen in terms of the theme of following." The reader identifies with Peter as fallible follower, and "the portrayal of Peter both repels and attracts the reader."

1816. Vorster, W.S. "The Function of the Use of the Old Testament in Mark." *Neotestamentica* 14 (1981), 62-72.

The author of Mark "used the Old Testament as a 'literary' means to put across a narrative point of view. Old Testament quotations and allusions in Mark function at the same level as other narrative techniques like narrative commentary, characterization and plot.... [I]t establishes perspectives through which the reader is presented with this story.... Mark is not only a collector or a redactor of traditions. He creates a story with the help of transmitted material," even altering his OT quotations to suit his purpose.

1817. Vorster, W.S. "Mark: Collector, Redactor, Author, Narrator?" *JTSA* #31 (June, 1980), 46-61.

Review of twentieth century scholarship on this question. "If Mark is taken seriously as narrator, and the text he created as a narrative with its own narrative world, a new world of interpretation and understanding of his text opens before us."

*   Vorster, Willem, James Voelz, Jean Delorme, and Ellen van
         Wolde. "Theoretical Reflections [on Intertextuality in
         Biblical Writings]." See #1648.

1818.   Wallace, Mark I. "Parsimony of Presence in Mark: Narratol-
         ogy, the Reader and Genre Analysis in Paul Ricoeur." *SR*
         18 (1989), 201-212.

         Ricoeur's importance "lies in his insistence that a narratological
         approach to the Bible must include a complete sensitivity to the
         role of the audience and the variety of discourses at work in the
         formation of the Bible's literary and theological world.... [His work
         preserves] both the poststructuralist concern for difference and
         the narrative theologians' interest in coherence...."

1819.   Walsh, Richard G. "Tragic Dimensions in Mark." *BTB* 19
         (1989), 94-99.

         Mark is not pure tragedy, but "does exhibit tragic dimensions:"
         passion and fate, e.g., though *hamartia* and *peripety* are absent.
         Jesus is not a tragic hero, but other characters in Mark resemble
         undeveloped tragic figures. "The text embodies a tragic vision as
         many characters choose not to accept the comic perspective of
         Jesus."

1820.   Weeden, Theodore J. *Mark—Traditions in Conflict.* Philadel-
         phia (Fortress P), 1971.

         The keys to understanding Mark lie in putting ourselves into the
         situation of his first-century readers, and in recognizing that such
         readers came to narrative/didactic texts with specific kinds of lit-
         erary training in the schools. Such readers would have concen-
         trated on the characters and the events in which they act in order
         to discover the author's message and viewpoint. Mark dramatizes a
         fierce christological dispute, with the disciples in his account serv-
         ing as surrogates for Mark's theological opponents.

1821.   Williams, James G. *Gospel Against Parable: Mark's Language of
         Mystery.* Sheffield (JSOT P), 1985.

         Wishes "to suggest the richly ambiguous relationships of [gospel
         and parable] in Mark's narrative.... 'Against' has three meanings:
         in conflict with, in contact with, and having as background." The
         style of narrative thinking in Mark; his way of writing was insepara-
         ble from his theology: silence, discontinuity, allusion, and
         narrative openness. There is a noticeable tension between the
         parables and their function in the gospel narrative because they
         are the product of two "fields of meaning: biography (myth,

character and his virtuous deeds) and parable (realism, metaphor."

See also: #s 15, 43, 1491, 1513, 1516, 1552, 1568, 1571, 1581, 1591, 1622, 1645, 1652, 1904.

Mark 1-8

1822. Bassler, Jouette M. "The Parable of the Loaves." *JR* 66 (1986), 157-172.

Parable defined as metaphor. Recent developments in literary criticism applied to Mark 6-8 justify our calling the story in these chapters a parable. Reader-response criticism shows chapters 6-8 to have many unexpected turns, clashes in perspectives, negations and omissions. The text uses such puzzles at crucial points to further its christological message.

1823. Beavis, Mary Ann. *Mark's Audience. The Literary and Social Setting of Mark 4.11-12.* Sheffield (JSOT/JSNT P), 1989.

Reader-oriented approach to analyze the persuasiveness of the echo in Mark 4:11-12 of Isaiah 6:9-10, in both its literary and social settings. We can counter the ahistoricism of this approach by recognizing that Mark is a Hellenistic literary text. Mark 4:11-12 is an epitome of Markan motifs: e.g., the gospel is seen to fit what a Greco-Roman reader would expect; it was meant to be read aloud; the verses in question have many verbal and thematic echoes in the rest of the gospel; and they hold it together.

1824. Boring, M. Eugene. "Mark 1:1-15 and the Beginning of the Gospel." *Semeia* 52 (1990), 43-81.

Mark "is a narrative structured with some care, divided into a bipartite outline determined by the author's Christology.... The variety of textual readings and syntactical options, as well as Mark's purpose, are best understood by construing Mark 1:1 as the title to the whole narrative, with the introduction extending through 1:15. The introduction is itself carefully structured into two sections parallelling ... [and] simultaneously subordinating John to Jesus.... [It] functions to introduce the main themes of the narrative as a whole, to focalize the narrative, and to relate the time of the Gospel to that of the reader"

1825.   Broek, Lyle D. Vander. "Literary Context in the Gospels."
        Reformed Review 39 (1986), 113-117.

        Illustration of the value of literary concerns in understanding
        the gospels through specific examples from Mark 8 and 11—
        picked because they are usually misunderstood when their literary
        context is ignored.

1826.   Clark, David J. "Criteria for Identifying Chiasm." *LB* 35
        (1975), 63-72.

        Review of the work of Joanna Dewey [#1828] on the structure of
        Mark 2:1–3:6, to ask whether it can be applied to 1:16–3:12. Chi-
        asm does seem to be present in this extended passage; it is an im-
        portant device, but the question of whether it is deliberate is mis-
        leading because we use structures unconsciously on all levels of
        language.

1827.   Detweiler, Robert, and William G. Doty, eds., *The Daemonic
        Imagination. Biblical Text and Secular Story.* Atlanta (Schol-
        ars P), 1990.

        Fifteen essays on Mark 5 and Margaret Atwood's short story,
        "The Sin Eater"—some on each narrative separately, the majority
        comparing them. The two narratives are examples of "moments in
        the history of Western culture showing apocalyptic asserting and
        reasserting itself against the momentum of mimesis." Reader-re-
        sponse, narratology, deconstruction, canonicity, and "open" versus
        "closed" text theories applied to Mark 5.

1828.   Dewey, Joanna. "The Literary Structure of the Controversy
        Stories in Mark 2:1–3:6." *JBL* 92 (1973), 394-401.

        How this section of five stories fits naturally into the overall
        structure of Mark—which in turn determines the shape of individ-
        ual pericopes. The passage has a chiastic structure which helps de-
        termines Mark's handling of his individual episodes. He intended
        2:1–3:6 to be seen as a literary unit.

1829.   Dewey, Joanna. *Markan Public Debate. Literary Technique, Con-
        centric Structure, and Theology in Mark 2:1–3:6.* Chico
        (Scholars P), 1980.

        There are three steps to literary analysis of Mark 2-3: describe
        the occurrence of literary devices, e.g., word and motif repetition,
        symmetry, etc; interpret how each device functions in the expres-
        sion; see what light this rhetorical understanding may shed on our
        grasp of the meaning and theology of the passage. The passage is
        concentric, which affects its message, and that of the gospel as a
        whole.

1830. Dewey, Joanna. "Point of View and the Disciples in Mark." *SBLSP* 1982, pp. 97-106.

The implied reader of Mark 2-3 would identify in some ways with the disciples, in other ways with Jesus. The theories of Gérard Genette applied to the problem the narrative portrayal of the disciples presents for the implied reader; the usefulness of this theory for understanding Mark.

1831. Drury, John. "Understanding the Bread: Disruption and Aggregation, Secrecy and Revelation in Mark's Gospel," in #318, pp. 98-119.

"The aim of today's gospel scholars must be the sort of cultural reconstruction so brilliantly achieved for Holland's golden age by Simon Schama's *The Embarrassment of Riches.*" The riddle about the leaven of the Pharisees in Mark, and the miraculous feeding in Mark 8, can be clarified if we see Mark's intended parallel with David's eating of the sacred bread while fleeing from Saul, and if we recognize the importance of all of the eating episodes (including the Last Supper) in Mark and in ancient Mediterranean society.

1832. Fay, Greg. "Introduction to Incomprehension: The Literary Structure of Mark 4:1-34." *CBQ* 51 (1989), 65-81.

Proposes a seven-part concentric structure for Mark 4 "in which the interpretation of the parable of the sower functions as the center terms and introduces the motif of the incomprehension of the disciples." This passage marks the beginning of the shift toward disapproval of the disciples, which becomes obvious by chapter 8.

1833. Fowler, Robert M. "The Feeding of the Five Thousand: A Markan Composition." *SBLSP* 1979 Vol. I, pp. 101-4.

Rather than trying to isolate "pre-Markan cycles" in chapters 6 and 7, we should note evidence that Mark composed the feeding and linked it deliberately with the sea story. It shows a typical Markan boat motif. Chapters 6 and 7 "have been carefully constructed by an author; they are not a jumble of tradition."

* Fowler, Robert M. "Using Literary Criticism on the Gospels." See #1604.

1834. Girard, René. "Scandal and the Dance: Salome in the Gospel of Mark";
Meetzer, François. "A Response to René Girard's Reading of Salome." *New Literary History* 15 (1984), 311-332.

The complex interweaving of ritual, desire, dance, and theme of sacrificial death in Mark 6. Meetzer: Girard's interpretation is unsatisfactory because he reads his own ideology back into the biblical story.

1835.   Hartin, P.J. "Disseminating the Word: A Deconstructive Reading of Mark 4:1-9 and Mark 4:13-20," in #1508, pp. 187-200.

"Reading the text of Mark 4:1-9 with the intertext of Mark 4:13-20 as well as other synoptic intertexts of Matthew 13:1-9, Luke 8:4-8 and Matthew 13:18-23 and Luke 8:11-15 allows one to view certain aspects of the deconstruction activity in operation." Where historical criticism seeks meaning within the text, deconstruction argues that meaning is constantly deferred as each evangelist rewrites the parable in his own focus. In deconstruction, the reader must become not just a hearer but a doer of the word in ever new contexts.

1836.   La Hurd, Carol Schersten. "Reader Response to Ritual Elements in Mark 5:1-20." *BTB* 20 (1990), 154-160.

A "methodological synthesis" of rhetorical, reader-response, and ritual studies criticisms applied to the place of Mark 5:1-20 in Mark 1-5. "... the gradual release of information to the implied audience, challenges to audience expectation, and the probable effect of textual ritual elements.... [H]ow the text guides audiences toward the episode's eschatological significance, challenges readers' attitudes toward 'clean' and 'unclean,' and invites them to accept for themselves the commissioning Jesus extends to the healed demoniac."

1837.   Leenhardt, Franz-J. "An Exegetical Essay: Mark 5:1-20," in Roland Barthes, et al., *Structural Analysis and Biblical Exegesis: Interpretational Essays*, Tr Alfred M. Johnson, Jr. (Pittsburgh: Pickwick P, 1974), 85-109.

Why did the writer of the Gerasene demoniac show such delight in telling this anecdote? Why this "literary abundance" of picturesque detail? The story needs to be seen as a unity, and in turn part of a larger literary unity; and, we must enter into the spirit of its socio-cultural atmosphere, since otherwise our presuppositions determine what the story will "mean." The demoniac's cure illustrates how all converts "go to Jesus" in order then to be "sent by Jesus" into the world.

1838.   Maartens, P.J. "'Sign' and 'Significance' in the Theory and Practice of Ongoing Literary Critical Interpretation with

Reference to Mark 4:24 and 25: A Study of Semiotic Relations in the Text," in #1508, pp. 63-81.

"... our knowledge of the meaning of a text is always perspectival. The various perspectives ... reveal the polymorphous character of the meaning of the text." Structural analysis of Mark 4:24-25 "highlights the opposition between the disciples ... and the Jews, Pharisees and scribes...." Only when the proverb is seen as an eschatological sign can the metaphoric signifier and its representation lead to an interpretation. Only a hermeneutic of literary-critical dialogue can guide interpretation between the extremes of functionalism and pluralism.

1839.   Ringe, Sharon H. "A Gentile Woman's Story," in #44, pp. 65-72.

The woman whose story is told in Mark 7 and Matthew 15 shows how the poor (and females) could enable Jesus to see his mission in a new way—contrary to the traditional interpretation which argues that it is simply a story of Jesus healing a woman and her daughter.

1840.   Robbins, Vernon K. "Mark 1.14-20: An Interpretation at the Intersection of Jewish and Gracco-Roman Traditions." *NTS* 28 (1982), 220-236.

We may hope to establish the structure of these verses "by exploring the merger of Jewish and Graeco-Roman conventions and traditions ... presupposing that the gospel of Mark contains a mixture of religious and cultural traditions similar to other literature written during the Hellenistic period ... Jesus' role in the narrative results from a merger of Jewish prophetic/apocalyptic traditions and Graeco-Roman teacher-disciple traditions."

1841.   Starobinski, Jean. "An Essay in Literary Analysis—Mark 5:1-20." *Ecumenical Review* 23 (1971), 377-397.

The structure of Mark 5 as a piece of discourse, not as a historical text. What is the "internal temporality implicit in what the text itself says?" Who speaks; who is addressed; whether the text indicates its own role (the scene may be Mark's symbol of his own activity); the spatial structure; who the characters are. The theme is the opposition of possessions and health—of recognizing or rejecting Jesus.

1842.   Starobinski, Jean. "A Struggle with Legion: A Literary Analysis of Mark 5:1-20." *New Literary History* 4 (1973), 331-356; rpt as "The Gerasene Demoniac" in Roland Barthes, et al., *Structural Analysis and Biblical Exegesis: Interpretational Essays* (Pittsburgh: Pickwick P, 1974), 57-84.

Revision of #1841, considering the passage also as parable.

1843.   Tannehill, Robert C. "Reading it Whole: The Function of Mark 8:34-35 in Mark's Story." *Quarterly Review* 2, #2 (Summer, 1982), 67-78.

"Narrative methods reveal that Mark's story is a weapon for tearing apart and tearing open our comfortable assurance that we are adequate disciples."

1844.   Wright, John. "Spirit and Wilderness: The Interplay of Two Motifs Within the Hebrew Bible as a Background to Mark 1: 2-13," in Edgar W. Conrad and Edward G. Newing, eds., *Perspectives on Language and Text* (Winona Lake: Eisenbrauns 1987), 269-298.

The development of the motifs of wilderness and of the spirit through the HB, which were brought together by Deutero-Isaiah in a new and creative manner. For Mark as well, the wilderness was a symbol in itself, a motif, a "model for desolation" rather than a literal place.

See also: #s 3, 10, 16, 1501, 1506, 1573, 1615, 1657, 1768.

Mark 9-16

1845.   Auerbach, Erich. "Fortunata," in *Mimesis: The Representation of Reality in Western Literature* (Princeton: Princeton UP, 1953), 24-49.

Comparison of three first-century narrators: in Tacitus' *Annals,* Petronius' *Satyricon,* and Mark. Classical narrative was unable to represent everyday life and reality seriously (i.e., without comedy). On the other hand, the betrayal of Jesus by Peter in Mark shows Peter as "the image of man in the highest and deepest and most tragic sense"—a thing incompatible with the classical sublime. To the Greeks and Romans, reality was static and fixed, while to Christians it was dynamic and in process. Thus the Bible made realistic writing inevitable; its view of reality was revolutionary. **

1846.   Barton, Stephen C. "Mark as Narrative: The Story of the Annointing Woman (Mk 14:3-9)." *ET* 102 (1991), 230-34.

There are many stories in Mark where women are leading actors. In exploring the structure of Mark 14, we note the framing of verses 3-9 by 1-2 and 10-11; how chapter 13 is framed by stories contrasting exemplary women and villainous men. We also notice many thematic parallels in the setting, and an archetypal quality to the plot and characters. Verses 3-9 epitomize the meaning of discipleship in Mark.

1847.   Beavis, Mary Ann. "The Trial before the Sanhedrin (Mark 14: 53-65): Reader Response and Greco-Roman Readers." *CBQ* 49 (1987), 581-596.

Mark's account of the trial before the Sanhedrin structurally resembles four other Markan pericopes. These similarities and their implications would have been recognized by Greco-Roman readers because of the way they were taught to read.

1848.   Blackwell, John. *The Passion as Story: The Plot of Mark.* Philadelphia (Fortress P), 1986.

Mark 14-16 in the context of the rest of the gospel. Mark's role as composer of the story he tells—selecting and arranging scenes. "To suggest that the Passion is story, as opposed to a mere repetition of historical facts, is to suggest that the Passion is the imaginative communication of truth. It is composed, formed, and shaped by an author ... [and is therefore] capable of forming or shaping the community of today."

1849.   Boomershine, Thomas E. and Gilbert L. Bartholomew. "The Narrative Technique of Mark 16:8." *JBL* 100 (1981), 213-223.

Mark employs the same narrative technique in 16:8 as that used to end earlier stories in his gospel; and he uses it in 16:8 in a concentrated and climactic manner. Therefore, purely from the standpoint of narrative style, it is probable that Mark did intend to end his gospel there.

1850.   Bush, Roger Anthony. "Mark's Call to Action: A Rhetorical Analysis of Mark 16:8," in John H. Morgan, ed., *Church Divinity 1986* (Notre Dame: Graduate Theological Foundation) 22-30.

Analysis of Mark's style using Aristotelian rhetoric shows that 16:8 must have been Mark's intended conclusion, leaving the actual task of carrying out the young man's instructions to the audience. This final verse helps readers accept their task and consti-

410   *The New Testament*

tutes a "well-developed call to action" rather than being (as is usually thought) abrupt and incomplete.

1851.   Cosby, Michael R. "Mark 14:51-52 and the Problem of
        Gospel Narrative." *PRS* 11 (1984), 219-231.

        Judgments as to Mark's literary ability vary widely; this passage
        can form a test case. The naked youth fleeing symbolizes for Mark
        the flight of the disciples.

1852.   Culpepper, R. Alan. "Mark 10:50: Why Mention the Gar-
        ment?" *JBL* 101 (1982), 131-2.

        The garment which blind Bartimaeus casts aside when he goes
        to meet Jesus is an instance of a literary motif whose function is de-
        fined by its context, and by other Markan references to garments.
        This and other such references are narrative devices—important
        as a symbol of conversion.

1853.   Danker, Frederick W. "The Literary Unity of Mark 14:1-25."
        JBL 85 (1966), 467-472.

        The primary clue to the unity of this passage is its possible refer-
        ence to Psalm 40; previous critics have noticed but handled it in-
        adequately. The themes of Psalm 40, and how Mark uses them to
        unify his narrative.

1854.   Fetters, Pamela. "The Irony of Mark." *McKendree Pastoral Re-
        view* 2, #3 (December, 1985), 11-17.

        "Mark deliberately leaves the reader with a sense of unfulfill-
        ment at the end of the story. Irony has doubled back on the reader
        making him feel like one of the failed disciples."

1855.   Girard, René. "Peter's Denial and the Question of Mimesis."
        Notre Dame English Journal 14 (1982), 177-189.

        In discussing the relationship of Mark to mimesis, Erich Auer-
        bach [#1845] misses the point that imitation in Mark is not a sepa-
        rate theme, but permeates the relationships among all the charac-
        ters. The gospels show a "gigantic but still misunderstood advance
        beyond the platonic concept of mimesis." This advance must be
        explored further if it is to have maximum use for biblical criticism.

1856.   Heil, John-Paul. "Mark 14, 1-52: Narrative Structure and
        Reader-Response." *Biblica* 71 (1990), 305-332.

        The nine scenes of Mark 14 "are arranged in a pattern of literary
        sandwiches in which each successive scene is contrastingly framed
        by two other mutually related scenes." The rhetorical effect on the
        implied reader is a reassurance of Jesus' ultimate triumph.

* Josipovici, Gabriel. "Interpretation vs. Reading: From Meaning to Trust." See #619.

1857. Juel, Donald. "The Function of the Trial of Jesus in Mark's Gospel." *SBLSP* 1975, Vol. 2, pp. 83-104.

The function of this unit in the gospel; its location within the plot or narrative structure; themes linking it with its literary context. The OT language in this and other units is not independent of the story, but part of it. That is, Mark is narrating his story on two levels. The clues lie in Jesus' three death predictions, and in the various charges brought against him. Only here is he called "Messiah" or "King" by anyone; thus the darkest moments are also the most revealing. Questions all this raises about the audience of Mark.

1858. Juel, Donald. *Messiah and Temple: The Trial of Jesus in the Gospel of Mark.* Missoula (Scholars P), 1977.

The trial scene in Mark is best approached on the literary level, within the context of the passion story and of Mark as a whole. In this scene, Mark chooses to introduce themes of particular importance for the account which follows: rejection of the Messiah, and vindication. The scene depends on a two-level narration, and on irony.

1859. Kermode, Frank. *The Genesis of Secrecy: On the Interpretation of Narrative.* Cambridge, Mass. and London (Harvard UP), 1979.

Various constraints make the interpretation of texts both "necessary and virtually impossible." One of these constraints, the secrecy of the insiders, is symbolized by the boy in the shirt who flees naked at the arrest of Jesus. Narratives acquire opacity, making the distinguishing of a central meaning from other possible meanings very difficult.

1860. Magness, J. Lee. *Sense and Absence: Structure and Suspension in the Ending of Mark's Gospel.* Atlanta (Scholars P), 1986.

The problem of the ending of Mark is a very significant one. Literary investigation based on the hypothesis that Mark affirms resurrection without narrating it—a "suspended ending." Theories about such endings in ancient pagan, Hebrew, and Christian literatures. Mark's narrative technique in the miracle, transfiguration, and passion stories place fear and silence in a positive light, imply proclamation outside the text, and foreshadow the fulfillment of 16:7. That is, modern literary criticism helps us understand openness and its meaning-effects.

1861.   Patte, Daniel and Aline. *Structural Exegesis: From Theory to Practice. Exegesis of Mark 15 and 16; Hermeneutical Implications.* Philadelphia (Fortress P), 1978.

A "fully operational" method of structural exegesis appears to be too complex, but actually is not. Difference between "informational" and "symbolic" dimensions of meaning of a text or language; the goal of structural exegesis is the latter. The relationships among the narrative, mythical, and semantic structures of Mark 15 and 16.

1862.   Petersen, Norman R. "When is the End Not the End? Literary Reflections on the Ending of Mark's Narrative." *Interpretation* 34 (1980), 151-166.

We may be dissatisfied with the ending of Mark, but that does not mean we can substitute our own. We should read the rest of Mark in the light of 16:8, not vice versa. We must read this verse ironically to make any sense of it.

1863.   du Plessis, J.G. "Speech Act Theory and New Testament Interpretation with Special Reference to G.N. Leech's Pragmatic Principles," in #1508, pp. 129-142.

Speech act theory as a refinement of exegesis applied to specific NT passages, especially Mark 12:1-12 (the Parable of the Vineyard). Leech's "politeness principle" as a means of interpreting Mark 12 shows it to be an incomplete part of the discourse, being completed by the discourse as a whole, including the quotation from Psalm 118. Jesus' "provocative and outrageous" flouting of the politeness principle in facing the Jewish authorities leaves them aware of "the dark and sombre purpose of judgement."

1864.   Smith, Stephen H. "The Literary Structure of Mark 11:1–12:40." *Nov T* 31 (1989), 104-124.

Argues a structure for Mark 11-12 based on a re-evaluation of internal clues, and its relationship to other sections of the gospel. In each of the narratives "Jesus is presented as the judge who indicts his people through symbolism and parable."

1865.   Via, Dan O., Jr. "Mark 10:32-52—A Structural, Literary and Theological Interpretation." *SBLSP* 1979, Vol. II, pp. 187-203.

How structuralism and related literary-critical approaches illuminate the plot sequences of Mark 10, as older historical biblical criticism could not. Theologically, the four-fold structure of this chapter shows a mandate concerning "repeated eschatological opportunities" given, refused, given again, and accepted.

1866. Vorster, W.S. "Literary Reflections on Mark 13:5-37: A Narrated Speech of Jesus." *Neotestamentica* 21 (1987), 203-224.

The fact that Mark 13 is a narrated speech of Jesus means that it has a narrative, not a historical, function within Mark's story of Jesus. It is comparable to the parables because both "receive their messages ... from their narrative context of communication." The function of narrative time and context in Mark, as well as point of view and apocalyptic (Jesus as reliable character). Chapter 13 is a mixture of apocalyptic imagery and paranesis, leaving the reader "with a strong expectation of an imminent parousia."

See also: #s 619, 1501, 1565, 1573, 1576, 1613, 1621, 1825, 2118, 2234.

LUKE-ACTS

Note: This section lists and annotates those items which treat Luke-Acts as a single work, or which analyze passages from both books. Items discussing Luke or Acts alone may be found in separate sections so labelled below.

1867. Ades, John I. "Literary Aspects of Luke." *Papers on Language and Literature* 15 (1979), 193-199.

Luke's "distinctly literary" treatment of material appearing also in the other synoptic gospels (Luke 4 and 24); his unique material also given literary treatment (Luke 15); and an incident in Acts 26 where a problem can be clarified "by viewing the text with the eye of a literary critic."

1868. Balch, David L. "The Genre of Luke-Acts: Individual Biography, Adventure Novel, or Political History?" *SWJT* 33 (1990), 5-19.

Luke-Acts is neither biography nor ancient novel, but ancient history. The author's model was Dionysius of Halicarnassus' *Roman Antiquities*, written more as rhetoric than as history. Various parallels between the devices and "problematic historical ideas" of Dionysius and Luke-Acts. Extensive review of #s 1580, 1893, and 2049.

1869. Barr, David L., and Judith L. Wentling. "The Conventions of Classical Biography and the Genre of Luke-Acts: A Preliminary Study," in Charles H. Talbert, ed., *Luke-Acts:*

New Perspectives from the S.B.L. Seminar (New York: Crossroad, 1984), 63-88.

The conventions of classical biography compared with those used in Luke-Acts. "On several points (kind of hero, appropriate language, internal organization, point of view, to some extent aesthetic mode), Luke can be successfully related to biography. On other points ... serious questions arise...."

1870.   Brawley, Robert L. *Centering on God: Method and Message in Luke-Acts.* Louisville (Westminster/John Knox P), 1990.

Analyzing Luke-Acts through Roland Barthes' notion that "texts are woven out of at least five voices": the hermeneutic, semiotic, proairetic, cultural, and symbolic. According to Barthes, varieties of interpretation originate in the various ways these five voices can be integrated. The hermeneutical voice deals with truth in the narrative world of Luke-Acts; the semiotic voice with logic; the proairetic voice with characterization; the cultural voice with shared presumptions; and the symbolic voice with "ambiguous borders." How these are synthesized, as seen in analysis of Luke 15.

1871.   Brodie, Thomas Louis. "Greco-Roman Imitation of Texts as a Partial Guide to Luke's Use of Sources," in Charles H. Talbert, ed., *Luke-Acts: New Perspectives From the Society of Biblical Literature Seminar* (New York: Crossroad, 1984), 17-46.

Greco-Roman practices of literary imitation offer "at least a partial guide to Luke's way of reworking and transforming various texts, especially the Old Testament."

1872.   Cadbury, Henry J. *The Making of Luke-Acts.* New York (Macmillan), 1927; rpt London (SPCK), 1961.

Amid much form criticism, extensive discussion of conventions of popular literature of Luke's day, and of the style and purpose and authorship of Luke-Acts.

1873.   Callan, Terence. "The Preface of Luke-Acts and Historiography." *NTS* 31 (1985), 576-581.

The preface to Luke-Acts resembles those for histories more than for biographies or any other ancient prose writings. Specifically, it resembles a new kind of history done by Sallust and Josephus; thus, they are a clue to what Luke thought he was doing.

1874.   Dawsey, James M. "The Literary Unity of Luke-Acts: Questions of Style—a Task for Literary Critics." *NTS* 35 (1989), 48-66.

Does saying that Acts was written as a sequel to Luke mean that sequence equals narrative unity? The case for unity beginning with the work of Henry Cadbury. Similarities and differences between the vocabulary, style, grammar, and formulae of Luke and Acts. These results create some difficulties for the unity theory, but more work especially on style is needed.

1875. Hubbard, Benjamin. "Commissioning Stories in Luke-Acts: A Study of their Antecedents, Form and Content." *Semeia* 8 (1977), 103-126.

The possible influence of commissioning stories from the ancient Near East, and the certain influence of ones from the Septuagint version of the OT; they become a vehicle of Luke's theology. The typical form of these stories, of which three occur in Luke (1, 2, 24), and twelve in Acts (5, 9, 10, 16, 18, 22, 26, 27). Luke gave his own distinct shaping to the OT format.

1876. Johnson, Luke T. *The Literary Function of Possessions in Luke-Acts.* Missoula (Scholars P), 1977, 1985.

Luke's literary expansion and refinement of prophecy dictates the shape of his gospel more than it does Matthew's. Luke is a story, not a theological tract, rule of discipline, or liturgical formulary. Patterns of association connecting apostles, possessions, and the Jerusalem community. The pattern of "prophet and his people" gives Luke-Acts its coherence and color, wedding structure and content. Possessions play a key role in Luke's theme of continuity from Jewish to Christian prophetic mission, symbolically expressing the identity of God's people and the transmission of authority.

1877. Kurz, William S., S.J. "Hellenistic Rhetoric in the Christological Proof of Luke-Acts." *CBQ* 42 (1980), 171-195.

"... a definite set of rules known as the 'art of rhetoric' has profoundly influenced Luke's attempt to make a convincing case for the Christian message..... [H]is Christological proof is his Christian adaptation of the rhetorical form of deduction, the enthymeme as Aristotle had originally explained it."

1878. Kurz, William S., S.J. "Narrative Approaches to Luke-Acts." *Biblica* 68 (1987), 195-220.

Modern literary criticism can illuminate biblical texts if we are cautious how we apply it. How it can balance historical criticism of Luke-Acts. Insights into Luke-Acts from considering shifts in point of view, "showing versus telling," implied author, plot, gaps left by the abrupt endings of Acts and Mark; the use of "We" conventions.

1879.   Kurz, William S. "Narrative Models for Imitation in Luke-Acts," in David L. Balch, et al., eds., *Greeks, Romans, and Christians: Essays in Honor of Abraham J. Malherbe* (Minneapolis (Fortress P, 1990), 171-189.

"... the consensus about ancient paradigmatic uses of narratives holds also for the narrative of Luke-Acts." Many ancient narrative genres use narratives as exempla for imitations. The rhetorical emphasis on imitation in Luke-Acts relates to contemporary Hellenistic concern "for implicit moral exhortation to implied readers of narratives." Good examples of this are the death of Jesus in Luke 23 and of Stephen in Acts 7.

1880.   Maddox, Robert. *The Purpose of Luke-Acts*. Göttingen (Vandenhoeck and Ruprecht), 1982.

Luke-Acts is a unified work with a perceptible structure. How structure is revealed through Luke's treatment of Jews, Gentiles, and Christians, his picture of Paul, and his eschatology. The structure of Luke-Acts derives from the fact that the books is about the relationship of the church to Jesus and to Judaism. It is a "theological history."

1881.   Moessner, David P. *Lord of the Banquet: The Literary and Theological Significance of the Lukan Travel Narrative*. Minneapolis (Fortress P), 1989.

There is a "decisive clue" to problems of form and content in the central travel section of Luke in its many references to Jesus eating and drinking. This section is in turn the literary and theological key to the rest of Luke and ultimately to the whole of Luke-Acts. The Russian Formalists' distinction between story and plot helps us see Luke's "fourfold Exodus typology based on the calling and fate of Moses as a heuristic principle for the plotted story, ... " grounded in a literary study of "the prophet as the prime character model for the narrative world of Luke-Acts." The influence of Deuteronomic notions of prophets as well.

1882.   Nuttall, Geoffrey F. *The Moment of Recognition: Luke as Storyteller*. London (U of London: Athlone P), 1978.

Key moments in Luke and Acts which reveal Luke's power and techniques as a storyteller. Typical Lukan turns of phrase, imaginative re-creation of history, debt to Greco-Roman devices for character speech, characteristic use of repetition and anaphora. Luke was most fascinated by "the dialectic of men's ignorance and knowledge, of their blindness and the moment of recognition."

1883.   Parsons, Mikeal C. *The Departure of Jesus in Luke-Acts: The Ascension Narratives in Context.* Sheffield (JSOT P), 1987.

Historical-critical and literary (narratological) analyses of Luke 24 and Acts 1. In the former passage, Luke has employed certain closural strategies to resolve the plot tensions and to frame the portrait. Plot lines, suspense, point of view and relationship of narrator to reader are also important. In Acts 1, Luke's strategies to involve the reader include focalization, defamiliarization, and the "primacy effect." The function of pericopae, deliberate redundancy, and variation.

*   Petersen, Norman. *Literary Criticism for New Testament Critics.* See #1506.

1884.   du Plooy, Gerhard P.V. "The Author in Luke-Acts." *Scriptura* 32 (1990), 28-35.

The "authorial meaning cannot be separated from a text" since "in the experience of reading, the reader is confronted with an authorial consciousness which influences the process of reading." Test cases of the presence of an implied author in Luke-Acts are the prologue and the "we" speeches. This implied author "is traceable both as formal textual structure, and as creator of the value structure and the total narrative world of Luke-Acts."

1885.   Praeder, S.M. "Luke-Acts and the Ancient Novel." *SBLSP* 1981, pp. 269-292.

Previous comparisons of Luke-Acts with the ancient novel have been too narrow, perhaps because we feared calling the work "fiction." Genres are never absolutely uniform. In Luke-Acts, historical and fictional events are embedded in fictional sequence, and Luke represents salvation through both means. The similarities in setting, point of view, chronological sequence, literary references, etc., mean that Luke-Acts is an adaptation of a popular pagan literary form—the form most widely read.

1886.   Richardson, W. "A Motif of Greek Philosophy in Luke-Acts," in F.L. Cross, ed., *Studia Evangelica II*, Part One (Berlin: Akademie-Verlag, 1964), 628-634.

Because the author of Luke-Acts was concerned to reach educated as well as proletarian Greeks and Romans, he interprets the life of Jesus and of the early church "in terms of this historic quest for the Sage Philosopher-King" in Greco-Roman philosophy.

1887.   Robbins, Vernon K. "Prefaces in Greco-Roman Biography and Luke-Acts." *PRS* 6 (1979), 94-108.

"The oratorical and epistolary features in the Lucan prefaces are more common to biography than to historiography. The language and style of the prefaces are characteristic of didactic biography," which Luke was using as a defense of Christianity. These prefaces are restrained but direct.

1888.   Schenk, Wolfgang. "Luke as Reader of Paul: Observations on his Reception," in #38, pp. 127-139.

The crucial importance for the formation of early Christianity of Luke's forcing Paul's theology into a Lukan mold.

1889.   Schmidt, Daryl, et al. "Toward a Comprehensive Approach to Understanding the Contribution to Gospel Studies Made by Joseph B. Tyson in His Book, *The Death of Jesus in Luke-Acts.*" *Perkins Journal* 40, #2 (April, 1987), 31-50.

Review discussions by Schmidt, "Tyson's Approach to the Literary Death of Luke's Jesus"; David L. Balch, "Comparing Literary Patterns in Luke and Lucian"; Philip L. Shuler, "Questions of an Holistic Approach to Luke-Acts"; Joseph B. Tyson, "Further Thoughts on *The Death of Jesus in Luke-Acts.*"

1890.   Schubert, Paul. "The Structure and Significance of Luke 24" in *Neutestamentliche Studien für Rudolf Bultmann* (Berlin: Alfred Töpelmann, 1957), 165-186.

The "prominent and unmistakable ... close literary transition from volume I (Lc 24:50-53) to volume II (Acts 1:1-4)." Both Luke 24 and Acts 28 constitute conscious literary as well as theological conclusions/climaxes to their respective books, and in fact these two concluding chapters are "deliberate and close parallel[s], structurally, formally and materially."

1891.   Sheeley, Steven M. "Narrative Asides and Narrative Authority in Luke-Acts." *BTB* 18 (1988), 102-107.

Narrators of Luke and Acts establish personal relationships with the reader largely through the technique of narrative asides. After this relationship is established, other asides cultivate the reader's dependence on the narrator, thus establishing the narrator's authority over the reader.

1892.   Stockhausen, Carol L. "Luke's Stories of the Ascension: The Background and Function of a Dual Narration." *PEGL* 10 (1990), 251-263.

Luke's compositional redundancy, as instanced in his dual narration of the ascension (Luke 24 and Acts 1), and Luke-Acts "as a repetitive, or redundant, mode of communication." Luke fre-

quently employs "narrative echoes" (repeated stories) of actual
events described by Paul in his letters, each time communicating
something different. The ascension stories are also echoes of II
Kings 2—a third level of communication.

1893. Talbert, Charles H. *Literary Patterns, Theological Themes, and
the Genre of Luke-Acts.* Missoula (Scholars P), 1974,5.

Parallels and correspondences between Luke and Acts, and chiasmus in Luke 10-18 and Acts 15-21 must all have been intended
by the author. Possible thematic functions of the structure of the
books. Luke-Acts follows, or belongs to, the genre of ancient biography of a philosopher-founder and accounts of his successors.

1894. Tannehill, Robert C. "Israel in Luke-Acts: A Tragic Story."
JBL 104 (1985), 69-85.

Luke-Acts as a unified narrative. Use of a narrator, characterization, plot, tragic theory, and representative thematic patterns all
demonstrate that Luke fashioned the problem of the Jews' rejection of Jesus as a tragic story. We can trace a steady downward slide
in Luke's portrait of Israel from the beginning of Luke to the end
of Acts. Although Luke feels anguish, pity, and sorrow for Israel,
he is not anti-Semitic.

1895. Tyson, Joseph B. *The Death of Jesus in Luke-Acts.* Columbia (U
of South Carolina P), 1986.

Four literary-critical devices in Luke-Acts: the initial receptivity
to and later rejection of Jesus and Paul by the Jewish public; division of the Jewish leaders into Pharisees and Chief Priests corresponding to responsibility for Jesus' death; ambivalence toward
Jerusalem and the Temple; and dominant themes during the trial.
Luke's use of these themes and devices is distinctive when compared to the other synoptics. Contains revisions of #s 1896 and
1958.

1896. Tyson, Joseph B. "The Jewish Public in Luke-Acts." *NTS* 30
(1984), 574-583.

We may not know Luke's sources for his treatment of the Jewish
public, but literary criticism helps reveal his tactics anyway. His
treatment of the subject is more complex in Acts than in Luke,
though still following the pattern of initial acceptance followed by
rejection as developed in Luke. Seeing this pattern helps clarify
apparent inconsistencies in both books. Revised as part of #1895.

1897. Wallis, Ethel E. "Aristotelian Echoes in Luke's Discourse
Structure." *OPTAT* 2, #2 (1988), 81-88.

The overall structure of Luke bears a "startling resemblance" to Aristotle's notion of the relationship between parts of a drama . This resemblance carries over also to the opening section of Acts. Indeed, Acts is a "dependent" structure, technically an "embedded discourse" as defined by linguists such as Robert Longacre.

1898. Weren, W.J.C. "Psalm 2 in Luke-Acts: An Intertextual Study," in #38, pp. 189-203.

"... explicit and implicit quotations from Psalm 2 play an important role in Luke-Acts. Luke re-interprets the Psalm christologically, since in his view Jesus opened the Old Testament to his disciples as never before." Thus, Luke applies Psalm 2 to Jesus' death and resurrection in Acts 4 and 13, though without much justification from the text.

1899. Wolfe, Kenneth R. "The Chiastic Structure of Luke-Acts and Some Implications for Worship." *SWJT* 22, #2 (Spring, 1980), 60-71.

Theory of the structure of Luke-Acts and how utilizing it in the author's worship services has restored "drama" to them.

See also: #s 1486, 1491, 1506, 1910.

LUKE

Note: The reader should also consult the section above on "Luke-Acts" for additional items on the Gospel of Luke.

1900. Bailey, Kenneth E. *Poet and Peasant: A Literary Cultural Approach to the Parables in Luke.* Grand Rapids (Eerdmans), 1976.

Types of literary structures in the NT including inversion (chiasm), parallelism, parabolic ballad form, and their usefulness in studying the Lukan parables. Four parables and two poems in the "Travel Narrative" (Luke 9-19); in chapter 16 (parable of the Unjust Steward); in the poem on God versus Mammon; the Friend at Midnight and the poem on the Father's Gifts (chapter 11); the parables of the Lost Sheep and Lost Coin (chapter 15).

1901. Carpenter, S. *Christianity According to S. Luke.* London (SPCK), and New York (Macmillan), 1919.

Part III, "The Workmanship": chapters on Luke the psychologist and artist. His masterful style, use of contrast, climax, characterization, irony, and sophisticated structure.

1902.   Dawsey, James M. *The Lukan Voice: Confusion and Irony in the Gospel of Luke.* Macon (Mercer UP), 1986.

Considerable differences in style, vocabulary, and viewpoint exist between Luke's narrator and Luke's Jesus. These differences naturally cause confusion for the reader. Various possible explanations for the differences, and for the irony that Luke wrote his gospel for the very class from whom Jesus argued the kingdom was to be hidden. Luke's purpose was to force a re-encounter within the early church with the humiliated, suffering Jesus. **

1903.   Dawsey, James M. "What's in a Name? Characterization in Luke." *BTB* 16 (1986), 143-7.

The trial of Jesus in Luke "works so well because of the secret knowledge shared by the readers and the unearthly beings."

1904.   Drury, John. "Luke," in #33, pp. 418-439.

Luke is master of the long view, of "space, light, and long perspective." "Lucid articulation of historical process is Luke's skill.... The historical presupposition that runs through and energizes his whole work [is that] time's structure consists of prophecies made and fulfilled." His historical source is, of course, the Septuagint OT. "Pattern, pace, ... language, characters and actual events" all derive from that source. The importance of the opening and closing chapters. Luke's parables compared with those of Mark and Matthew; Luke's concept of good and evil.

1905.   Drury, John. *Tradition and Design in Luke's Gospel: A Study in Early Christian Historiography.* London (Darton, Longman and Todd) and Atlanta (John Knox P), 1976.

Luke's deep roots in OT historiography; the OT sense of time and the *midrash* tradition of writing history by grafting one text on another. As historian (which other gospel writers are not), Luke is much more tied to time, more concerned with putting things "in order," with hierarchy and settled middle-class values. Jesus in Luke is at the middle of time, not as in Matthew and Mark, at the end. Thus Luke is not the Gentile gospel which many have assumed: he omits Mark's Gentile journeys and his gospel is full of Septuagint echoes.

1906.   Farmer, William R. "Luke's Use of Matthew: Literary Inquiry." *African Journal of Biblical Studies* 2 (1987), 7-24.

Both Matthew and Luke "are examples of popular religious biography aimed to praise." Luke made skillful use of Matthew, selecting and modifying it with considerable authorial freedom, though Luke "is compositionally dependent on the sequential arrangement of the Matthean pericopes...."

1907.   Gowler, David B. "Characterization in Luke: A Socio-Narratological Approach." *BTB* 19 (1989), 54-62.

We need both literary criticism and "the cultural scripts inherent in the texts" (cultural anthropology) if we are to understand the NT characters. Luke does not attempt to be unbiased; his "cultural scripts" include honor/shame and the dyadic personality, and the concept of limited good.

1908.   Hadas, Moses, and Morton Smith. *Heroes and Gods: Spiritual Biographies in Antiquity.* New York (Harper and Row), 1965.

Definition of "aretalogy" as an ancient biographical writing which is "a formal account of the remarkable career of an impressive teacher that was used as a basis for moral instruction." The gospel of Luke is an aretalogy.

1909.   Kingsbury, Jack Dean. *Conflict in Luke: Jesus, Authorities, Disciples.* Minneapolis (Fortress P), 1991.

The "world of the story" in Luke in terms of settings, characterization (including the narrator and Jesus) and plot. "... the three chief story lines, ... that of Jesus, of the religious authorities, and of the disciples."

1910.   Marshall, I. Howard. "Luke and His 'Gospel,'" in Peter Stuhlmacher, ed., *The Gospel and the Gospels* (Grand Rapids: Eerdmans, 1991), 273-292.

We must take the unity of Luke-Acts seriously if we wish to grasp the purpose of the gospel of Luke itself, his conscious aims, the unconscious factors shaping his work and the occasion of writing. Luke did not write in a "gospel" genre, since to him Matthew and Mark had written "accounts," not gospels. His "main purpose was to confirm the kerygma/catechetical instruction heard by people like Theophilus with a fuller account of [its] ... basis in the story of Jesus" and in the founding of the early church.

1911.   Parsons, Mikeal C. "Narrative Closure and Openness in the Plot of the Third Gospel: The Sense of an Ending in Luke 24:50-53." *SBLSP* 1986, pp. 201-223.

The narrator of Luke employs certain strategies of closure, particularly circularity and parallelism, to resolve the plot tensions. These devices draw a circle around the narrative. The plot lines, developed by such strategies as conflict, prophecy-fulfillment, and journey, are now framed by these signals to the reader.

1912. Powell, Mark Allan. "The Religious Leaders in Luke: A Literary-Critical Study." *JBL* 109 (1990), 93-110.

We lack a "sweeping character study" of Luke—specifically a literary analysis of the religious leaders as characters—e.g., that provided by Jack Dean Kingsbury's article on Matthew [#1729]. We should "determine the intended literary effect of Luke's portrayal on the implied reader of his narrative." Traits Luke attributes to the leaders; their human standards of evaluation; the "story-line" for them which Luke develops. In Matthew the leaders are to be hated; in Luke, they are to be pitied.

1913. Smith, Dennis E. "Table Fellowship as a Literary Motif in the Gospel of Luke." *JBL* 106 (1987), 613-628.

Table fellowship is a prominent literary motif for Luke. He would have inherited some references and symbols from the tradition, but he has greatly expanded the possibilities. He expects his readers to catch his literary references to meal symbolism—both from popular and from Christian writing. His meal imagery is rich, imaginative and complex, making a significant contribution to the central themes of the book.

1914. Tannehill, Robert. *The Narrative Unity of Luke-Acts: A Literary Interpretation, Vol. I: The Gospel According to Luke.* Philadelphia (Fortress P), 1986.

Luke is a narrative unity despite being episodic, which is typical of ancient Greco-Roman narrative. The controlling objective—explaining God's purpose—provides the unity. Its size and complexity make this unity difficult to grasp without help. The major roles in the narrative lie "on the borderline between character and plot." The plot emerges from the roles of Jesus as preacher/healer; the oppressed; the crowd; the authorities; the disciples.

1915. Wojcik, Jan. *The Road to Emmaus: Reading Luke's Gospel.* West Lafayette (Purdue University Press), 1989.

An "outsider's" reading of Luke, on the analogy of gnosticism. The implied reader, ambiguity, "writtenness," and relationship of author, narrator and reader in the gospel. A literary-critical reading of Luke "should celebrate the Christian scriptures as exquisite artifacts of human language."

1916.   York, John O. *The Last Shall Be First: The Rhetoric of Reversal in Luke.* Sheffield (Sheffield Academic P), 1991.

"Luke exhibits a pattern of double or 'bi-polar' reversal which is not as prevalent in the other Gospels." This pattern is a "repetitive form in Luke which communicates a theme in the Lukan narrative." The examples "present a unified form rhetorically," and most often show a chiastic structure as a way of achieving this reversal. Narrative clues tell the reader how and when to expect reversals, emphasizing especially the values of honor versus shame. These passages reinforce the "now-not yet" eschatology of the rest of Luke. Both Jewish and Greco-Roman readers could have found precedents for this thematic pattern in their respective cultures.

Luke 1-9

1917.   Alexander, Loveday. "Luke's Preface in the Context of Greek Preface-Writing." *Nov T* 28 (1986), 48-74.

Examination of Greek prose prefaces from the fourth century BC to the second century AD shows that Luke's models in terms of function were undoubtedly Greek scientific treatises, as instanced by Luke's respect for manual labor and for the master-disciple tradition. Syntactic evidence is also suggestive in this regard.

*   Anderson, Janice Capel. "Mary's Difference: Gender and Patriarchy in the Birth Narrative." See #1588.

1918.   Bailey, Kenneth E. "The Song of Mary: Vision of a New Exodus (Luke 1:46-55)." *The Near East School of Theology Theological Review* 2, #1 (April 1979), 29-35.

Awareness of the carefully-composed structure of Luke 1:46-55 makes its theological significance clearer. It is a two-stanza poem using inverted parallelism, with the lowliness-exaltation theme forming the climax of each stanza.

1919.   Brodie, Thomas L. "The Departure for Jerusalem (Luke 9,51-56) as a Rhetorical Imitation of Elijah's Departure for the Jordan (2 Kgs 1,1-2, 6)." *Biblica* 70 (1989), 96-109.

Luke "abbreviates, fuses, and improves" two separate OT texts—a typical ancient rhetorical practice—to make a theological point that Jesus surpassed Elijah. His technique is a "deliberate literary procedure," its history assimilated to literature.

1920. Brodie, Thomas L., O.P. "Luke 7,36-50 as an Internalization of 2 Kings 4,1-37: A Study in Luke's Use of Rhetorical Imitation." *Biblica* 64 (1983), 457-485.

Luke is indebted to the Septuagint throughout his gospel, but especially in 7:1–8:3, which is based on OT accounts of Elijah and Elisha. Almost every element of I Kings 4 "may be found in abbreviated or transferred shape in [Luke 7:36-50]." Luke used the common Hellenistic practice of rhetorical imitation and all its particular devices.

1921. Brodie, Thomas Louis. "Towards Unravelling Luke's Use of the Old Testament: Luke 7.11-17 as an *Imitatio* of 1 Kings 17.17-24." *NTS* 32 (1986), 247-267.

The relationship of Luke 7 to I Kings 17 is literary, "to be understood in light of the Hellenistic literary practice known as *imitatio*, and ... the practice of *imitatio* may be an important clue in detecting and unravelling other areas of Luke's sources."

1922. Combrink, H.J.B. "The Structure and Significance of Luke 4: 16-30." *Neotestamentica* 7 (1973), 27-47.

This passage is "a well-structured organic whole" which reiterates all of Luke in miniature. It shows a circular structure, and appears to have been placed quite deliberately at the beginning of the narrative of the work of Jesus: "a witness to Luke's stylistic and literary ability."

1923. Davis, Charles Thomas III. "The Literary Structure of Luke 1-2," in #34, pp. 215-229.

Luke 1-2 is structured literarily around the three angel visits, with the actual birth of Jesus "treated only as a detail within the framework of a much larger narrative.... The narrative focuses upon the incursion of the divine into time and space for the accomplishment of creative and *original* acts," subordinating the hero's life and character to this central concern.

* Gros Louis, Kenneth R.R. "The Jesus Birth Stories." See #1723.

1924. Kozar, Joseph Vlcek. "The Function of the Character of Elizabeth as the Omniscient Narrator's Reliable Vehicle in the First Chapter of the Gospel of Luke." *PEGL* 10 (1990), 214-222.

Luke uses Elizabeth as a foil to Zechariah, a "Spirit-filled spokesperson," and as "surprising example of the reversals that will characterize the Lucan narrative," for which she prepares the reader in chapter 1.

1925.   Louw, J.P. "Macro Levels of Meaning in LK 7:36-50," in #1507, pp. 128-135.

A semiotic approach to discourse analysis is necessary since a discourse is more than words and sentences; it is also a speech-act, a socio-linguistic event with more than one level of meaning. Luke 7:36-50 shows three levels of interpretation: declarative (revealing Luke's selectivity as author); structural (revealing the theme that forgiveness is in direct relationship to love); and intentional (revealing Luke's ironic message).

1926.   Mather, P. Boyd. "The Search for the Living Text of the Lucan Infancy Narrative," in Dennis E. Groh and Robert Jewett, eds., *The Living Text: Essays in Honor of Ernest W. Saunders* (Lanham: U P of America, 1985), 123-140.

"It is extremely interesting to me that the brightest future today seems to be in the direction of reading Luke 1-2 as fictionalized history, in appreciation of the story telling of Luke."

1927.   McKnight, Edgar V. *Meaning in Texts: The Historical Shaping of a Narrative Hermeneutics.* Philadelphia (Fortress P), 1978.

The structural study of narrative related to NT hermeneutics. The latter is neither historical nor theological; it can engage the NT more fruitfully by adopting the insights and methods of structuralism. Luke 5:1-11 used as examples of application of the method to an NT text.

1928.   Moessner, David P. "Luke 9:1-50: Luke's Preview of the Journey of the Prophet Like Moses of Deuteronomy." *JBL* 102 (1983), 575-605.

Luke in the journey follows the fourfold Moses-Deuteronomic typology, and the larger Deuteronomistic history as well. Jesus recapitulates and consummates the Exodus drama as the prophet like Moses of Deuteronomy as this drama is "pre-viewed" in chapter 9.

1929.   Resseguie, James L. "Automatization and Defamiliarization in Luke 7:36-50." *LT* 5 (1991), 137-150.

"[Victor] Shklovsky's concept of defamiliarization is useful for literary analyses of the New Testament gospels, for it helps define … the qualities that make them literary.… In Luke 7, defamiliarization encourages the reader to voice his or her own automatized views, and then ... it reveals their strangeness. Hence the 'power' of the subtle, yet forceful, narrative lies in its 'literariness' which 'makes strange' the reader's automatized perception of reality."

1930. Talbert, Charles. "Prophecies of Future Greatness: The Contribution of Greco-Roman Biographies to an Understanding of Luke 1:5–4:15," in James Crenshaw and Samuel Sandmel, eds., *The Divine Helmsman* (New York: KTAV, 1980), 129-142.

Greco-Roman readers would have been conditioned by the biographies of heroes to expect certain specific items, and these Luke supplies. Thus we can speak of a genre of pre-public careers of great men in Mediterranean antiquity.

1931. Tannehill, Robert C. "The Magnificat as Poem." *JBL* 93 (1974), 263-275.

Certain features of the poetic form of the "Magnificat" in Luke 1 and their significance for understanding the passage. Various patterns of repetition bind the whole in a complex interaction of parts. This enables us to see the mother and baby as signs, but only if we first see them as human.

1932. Tyson, Joseph B. "The Birth Narratives and the Beginnings of Luke's Gospel." *Semeia* 52 (1990), 103-120.

The place and literary function of the birth narratives in Luke 1:5–2:52 have been questioned, with some arguing that 3:1 was probably the first beginning of Luke. However, literary analysis of the birth narratives, using the work of Boris Uspensky, leads us to conclude that these narratives "function as an effective framing device and may be compared with the way in which the prologue functions in certain Greek dramas."

1933. Vogels, Walter. "A Semiotic Study of Luke 7:11-17." *ETh* 14 (1983), 273-292.

How Luke 7 is currently understood in the light of semiotic theory which analyzes the parts of narrative syntax in their "schema"; the discursive syntax to find oppositions and themes; and the link between these two forms of analysis.

1934. Wren, Malcolm. "Sonship in Luke: The Advantage of a Literary Approach." *Scottish Journal of Theology* 37 (1984), 301-311.

The gospels as "told stories" is the basic source of their meaning. Why Luke juxtaposes two birth narratives; the "magnificat" as conclusion to this scene; the nativity scenes as preparation for the "recognition-epiphany narrative" of chapter 4. Luke's creative concept of "Son of God" can only be presented in narrative.

See also: #s 18, 46, 190, 364, 1497, 1501, 1504, 1542, 1573, 1612, 1657, 1658, 1682, 1713, 1875.

Luke 10-24

1935.   Byrne, Brendan, S.J. "Parable in Context: Reading Luke 16 as a Literary Whole," in Eric Osborn and Lawrence McIntosh eds., *The Bible and European Literature* (Melbourne: Academia P, 1987), 207-218.

The Parable of the Rich Man and Lazarus (verses 19-31) and the rest of the chapter mutually illuminate each other. The Parable of the Unjust Steward is connected with it by the theme of the wise and foolish uses of wealth—not in contrast as is usually thought, but in parallel, as both parables teach that we should be free to dispose of it vigorously, in order to gain eschatological blessings. The great difficulty in converting the rich unites the stories.

*   Champion, James. "The Parable as an Ancient and Modern Form." See #1675.

1936.   Craig, Kerry M., and Margret A. Kristjansson. "Women Reading as Men/Women Reading as Women: A Structural Analysis for the Historical Project." *Semeia* 51 (1990), 119-136.

Feminist biblical criticism needs to become conscious "of the patriarchal ideology implicit in feminism's own thought. Feminist exegesis must be prepared to read suspiciously both pro-women and anti-women biblical texts in the effort to discern underlying structures and thus to challenge the ubiquitous logic of patriarchy." Structuralism and deconstruction applied to Luke 11:14-32 as "not an exercise in method for its own sake but a liberating praxis for both women and men."

1937.   Crossan, John D., ed. *Semeia 2: The Good Samaritan.* Missoula (Scholars P), 1974.

Contents: Daniel Patte, "An Analysis of Narrative Structure and the Good Samaritan"; Georges Crespy, "The Parable of the Good Samaritan: An Essay in Structural Research"; Robert W. Funk, "Structure in the Narrative Parables of Jesus" and "The Good

Samaritan as Metaphor" (both revised as part of #1658); John D. Crossan, "The Good Samaritan: Towards a Generic Definition of Parable."

1938. Crossan, John D. "Parable and Example in the Teaching of Jesus." *NTS* 18 (1971-2), 285-307; rpt *Semeia* 1 (1974), 63-104.

The tension between the story and its present interpretive frames in Lukan parables in general, and particularly The Good Samaritan. "... the acceptance of parables as examples ... shows a very fundamental misunderstanding of the parable as poetic art and most effectively blunts the perennial challenge of the parable itself. The parable does not belong to the realm of didactic tools and pedagogic tactics but comes from the world of poetic metaphors and symbolic expressions." It is therefore essentially different from Rabbinic usage.

1939. Crossan, J.D., ed. *Semeia 9: Polyvalent Narration* [in the Parable of the Prodigal Son]. Missoula (Scholars P), 1977.

Contents: Two essays explaining the theory of polyvalent narration by Susan Wittig and John D. Crossan; essays on the Prodigal son from a psychoanalytic perspective by Mary Ann Tolbert; from a Jungian perspective by Dan O. Via; from a structuralist perspective by Bernard Scott.

1940. Farrell, Hobart K. "The Structure and Theology of Luke's Central Section." *Trinity Journal* 7 (1986), 33-54.

Granting the chiastic structure of Luke, examines in detail the lengthy chiasm of chapters 13-18. This central chiasm develops seven different themes or scenes as it unfolds in two directions: death, relationship to the kingdom, call to discipleship and repentance, warnings about Hell and wealth, coming of the kingdom, eternal life, and following Jesus. Through all this we see Luke's literary care, the relationship of each theme or scene with those around it, which underscore what Luke thought important: a total commitment to Christ and his message.

* Funk, Robert W. "Beyond Criticism in Quest for Literacy: The Parable of the Leaven." See #1721.

1941. Funk, Robert W. "The Old Testament in Parable: A Study of Luke 10:25-37." *Encounter* 26 (1965), 251-267.

The parable is that mode of language most appropriate to the incarnation because the kingdom itself is a language event. Scripture is the text for which parable is the exposition. As the Good

Samaritan shows, shattering the tradition that obscured the Law required the enigma of parable.

*   Funk, Robert W. "Parable, Paradox, Power: The Prodigal Samaritan." See #1682.

1942.   Goulder, M.D. "The Chiastic Structure of the Lucan Journey," in F.L. Cross, ed., *Studia Evangelica II*, Part One (Berlin: Akademie-Verlag, 1964), 195-202.

The Lukan travel narrative (10:23–18:30) is structured chiastically within a context of Luke's use of Deuteronomy just before and after the journey.

1943.   Heil, John Paul. "Reader-Response and the Irony of Jesus Before the Sanhedrin." *CBQ* 51 (1989), 271-284.

Reader-response analysis of the impact that dramatic irony in the "key Lucan scene" of 22:66-71 has on the implied reader. This reader is required to hold together two contradictory levels of meaning: the Sanhedrin's evidence that Jesus is the fake Messiah in fact proves that he is the true one; and the fact that the evidence for condemning him is the same as the evidence for believing him. The reader thus balances the tragic story of Israel's rejection of Jesus against the paradox that this rejection was necessary.

*   Hilkert, M.C. "Retelling the Gospel Story: Preaching and Narrative." See #176.

1944.   Karris, Robert J. *Luke: Artist and Theologian. Luke's Passion Account as Literature.* New York, Mahwah, and Toronto (Paulist P), 1985.

Luke's artistry as a vehicle for his theology. His major motifs are the faithful God, justice, and food, with many subthemes developing from these three. All the themes come together in chapter 23, "a recapitulation of Luke's motifs [which] forms a vast tapestry of meaning."

1945.   Kurz, William S., S.J. "Luke 22:14-38 and Greco-Roman and Biblical Farewell Addresses." *JBL* 104 (1985), 251-268.

"... how a collection of traditional sayings of Jesus combines in Luke 22:14-38 to form a farewell speech ... this speech [compared] to other farewell addresses in Greco-Roman and biblical traditions, regarding both its forms and its functions.... Luke imitates farewell speeches in the biblical tradition for readers in a Hellenistic culture."

*   Moessner, David P. *Lord of the Banquet: The Literary and Theo-
        logical Significance of the Lukan Travel Narrative.* See #1881.

1946.   Noël, Timothy. "The Parable of the Wedding Guest: A Nar-
        rative-Critical Interpretation." *PRS* 16 (1989), 17-27.

        The continuity between Luke 14:7-11, its immediate context in
        the rest of the chapter, and its larger context in the rest of Luke.
        Such a narratological reading shows verbal, characterization, plot
        and setting contacts with the rest of Luke.

1947.   O'Toole, Robert F., S.J. "The Literary Form of Luke 19: 1-
        10." *JBL* 110 (1991), 107-116.

        "Most probably Luke 19:1-10 constitutes a diptych," which allows
        Luke to tell his story, "each of whose panels ended with and
        stressed the words of Jesus." Robert Tannehill is correct to see it as
        a quest story (a type of the pronouncement story), and the diptych
        helps us discover that.

1948.   Patte, Daniel. "Structural Analysis of the Parable of the
        Prodigal Son: Toward a Method," in #1662, pp. 71-149;
        responses by Robert Culley and William Doty, pp. 151-
        178.

        An attempt "to find a model which can represent the relation of
        the narrative (metonymic) structure ... with the mythic structure."
        The relationship between the mythic structure as conceived by
        Lévi-Strauss and Carl Jung's archetypal theory in this and other
        parables.

*   Patte, Daniel. *Structural Exegesis for New Testament Critics.* See
        #1503.

1949.   Patte, Daniel. "Structural Network in Narrative." *Soundings*
        58 (1975), 221-242; rpt Susan Wittig, ed., *Structuralism: An
        Interdisciplinary Study* (Pittsburgh: Pickwick P, 1975), 77-
        98.

        Luke 10 is terms of the theories of A.J. Greimas and Claude Lévi-
        Strauss: cultural structures, structures of enunciation (constraints
        imposed by the author and his concrete situation), and deep struc-
        tures (narrative and mythic) in The Good Samaritan. The
        "semantic effect" of this Lukan parable (as versus the effect of Je-
        sus' parable) "deeply challenges the traditionally religious: as long
        as they do not venture outside their religiously ordered world and
        become irreligious, they ... do not belong to the Kingdom."

1950.   Perpich, Sandra Wackman. *A Hermeneutic Critique of Struc-
        turalist Exegesis with Specific Reference to LK 10.29-37.* Lan-
        ham (U P of America), 1984.

        A "bivalent," "structural" literary criticism must be the ground-
        ing for any hermeneutical activity. The work of Karl Rahner, e.g.,
        can be the model for this combining of textual structures and
        "mystery-referential" levels of understanding. These theories, and
        those of Claude Bremond, A.J. Greimas, and Tsvetan Todorov ap-
        plied to Luke 10, with help from Paul Ricoeur's theory of
        parabolic discourse.

1951.   Porter, Stanley E. "The Parable of the Unjust Steward (Luke
        16.1-13): Irony *is* the Key," in #35, pp. 127-153.

        Many of the attempts to solve the problem of why the unjust
        steward is commended by Jesus are unconvincing because they rest
        on shaky textual or cultural grounds. Irony is the key because it
        enables us to see that Jesus is using the steward as an example of
        the impossibility of serving both God and mammon. This is the
        only reading which is internally consistent, contextually consistent
        with the parables in Luke 15, and consistent with Jesus' other re-
        marks to the Pharisees throughout Luke.

1952.   Ramsey, George W. "Plots, Gaps, Repetitions, and Ambigu-
        ity in Luke 15." *PRS* 17 (1990), 33-42.

        Narrational concepts applied to the Prodigal Son, e.g., methods
        of revealing character, the narrator's use of gaps to enhance
        meaning, repetition as a means of characterization, and
        generation of ambiguity, are all crucial to the meaning of this
        parable.

1953.   Resseguie, James L. "Point of View in the Central Section of
        Luke (9:51-19:44)." *JETS* 25 (1982), 41-7.

        The problem of the purpose of this parable is solved by examin-
        ing point of view. We notice two diametrically opposed points of
        view, with the narrator of Luke clearly endorsing one and oppos-
        ing the other. Examination of characterization in the parable sup-
        ports this interpretation.

1954.   Robbins, Vernon K. "Structuralism in Biblical Interpreta-
        tion and Theology." *Thomist* 42 (1978), 349-372.

        The move from a historical to a linguistic paradigm in biblical
        criticism, illustrated on Luke 10. We move then "from narrative
        structure to mythical and semantic structure (Dan O. Via and
        Daniel Patte), and then "from structural exegesis to theology."

While there are different kinds of structural analysis, biblical critics can no longer ignore it.

1955. Scott, Bernard Brandon. "How to Mismanage a Miracle: Reader Response Criticism." *SBLSP* 1983, pp. 439-449.

The relationship between audience and text in Luke 12:16-20 and in the Gospel of Thomas. The surface structure of the parable; its "reading performance," the purpose of which is to observe the "interaction between story and hearer/audience and the development of plot and characterization."

1956. Steele, E. Springs. "Luke 11:37-54—A Modified Hellenistic Symposium?" *JBL* 103 (1984), 379-394.

Analysis of Luke 7:36-50 and 14:1-24 shows that they are editorially imposed and belong to a modified Hellenistic symposium genus; a significant number of the same features are present in 11:37-54 as well. In all three pericopes the Lucan redactor has organized traditional material to create an appropriate setting based on the model of these symposia.

1957. Tolbert, Mary Ann. "The Prodigal Son: An Essay in Literary Criticism from a Psychoanalytic Perspective." *Semeia* 9 (1977), 1-20.

Literary-critical tools and methodologies can aid in relating ancient texts to contemporary situations. Analysis of the content of Luke 15 by psychoanalytic categories, and of the form of this parable by rhetorical anaylsis of surface structure. The unity of the narrative, and the correspondence between theme and structure.

1958. Tyson, Joseph B. "Conflict as a Literary Theme in the Gospel of Luke," in William R. Farmer, ed., *New Synoptic Studies: The Cambridge Gospel Conference and Beyond* (Macon: Mercer UP, 1983), 303-327.

Recent work on the genre of the gospels shows their authors' success in creating a unified narrative. The themes of conflict and opposition in Jesus' teaching in the Temple. This episode is an intentional and dramatic shift by Luke because the Temple itself was a major issue in the debate between Jesus and the Pharisees. Revised as part of #1895.

1959. Via, Dan O. "The Parable of the Unjust Judge: A Metaphor of the Unrealized Self," in #1662, pp. 1-32.

In what way can parable as narrative be viewed as a metaphor of the self? Models for the narrative and archetypal structures of this parable based on the theories of Claude Bremond, A.J. Greimas, and Carl Jung. "In Jesus' narrative parables in general, the story it-self is a concrete vehicle for a mysterious tenor, God's reign."

1960.   Vogels, Walter. "*Having or Longing*: A Semiotic Analysis of Luke 16:19-31." *ETh* 20 (1989), 27-46.

Discursive/narrative-syntactic analysis of Luke 16 suggests that "the text speaks of something much deeper than" the selfishness of the rich man. It speaks not just of a sharing, but of the need for poverty on the believer's part.

1961.   Welzen, Huub. "Loosening and Binding: Luke 13.10-21 as Programme and Anti-Programme of the Gospel of Luke," in #38, pp. 175-187.

The parables of verses 18-21 are really part of the argument in verses 10-17. The connections between chapter 13 and the rest of Luke are figurative, narrative and structural, not just theological.

See also: #s 7, 10, 135, 1490, 1501, 1504, 1565, 1573, 1576, 1613, 1657, 1658, 1666, 1875, 1879.

JOHN

1962.   Bowen, Clayton R. "The Fourth Gospel as Dramatic Material." *JBL* 49 (1930), 292-305.

Unlike the synoptics, John is in no sense a narrative. It fails to tell us a "straight ahead story," and its succession of events "has no relation to the sequences of a life-experience or the development of a plot." It is rather a drama—not a finished one but "a miscellany of material conceived dramatically, a set of dramatic symbols," to be seen or heard rather than read; perhaps on the order of what today we call a pageant.

1963.   Brown, Schuyler. "John and the Resistant Reader: The Fourth Gospel After Nicea and the Holocaust." *Journal of Literary Studies* 5 (1989), 252-261.

John's polemic against the Jews has been appropriated by Christians and thus "has made a sinister contribution to the Holocaust." Nicean definitions of Christology "have opened up a 'divinity gap' between the reader and the central figure in the narrative." Instead, an "archetypal reading [of John] ... makes possible an encounter with the author's imaginal world, without being put off by the offensive rhetoric."

1964. Connick, C. Milo. "The Dramatic Character of the Fourth Gospel." *JBL* 67 (1948), 159-169.

Careful examination of John's techniques shows unmistakable dramatic characteristics: in form and plot, concentrated action, dramatic contrast and synmmetry, irony and dialogue.

1965. Culpepper, R. Alan. *Anatomy of the Fourth Gospel: A Study in Literary Design.* Philadelphia (Fortress P), 1983.

John as a narrative text, "what it is and how it works." "The character of this particular narrative and gospel genre more generally, ... [and] how the narrative components of the gospel interact with each other and involve and affect the reader." Narrator's point of view; narrative time; plot; characterization; implicit commentary and the implied reader. The plot of John is "propelled by conflict between belief and unbelief as responses to Jesus." Characters in John have two functions: to draw out Jesus' character, and to represent alternative responses for the reader. **

1966. Deeks, David. "The Structure of the Fourth Gospel." *NTS* 15 (1968-9), 107-128.

There is no general agreement on the structure of John. We may argue that the structure of John is similar to that successfully shown for I John and Revelation. That is, it is a chiastic, quadripartite, and generally parallel structure.

1967. Dodd, C.H. *The Interpretation of the Fourth Gospel.* Cambridge (Cambridge UP), 1970; originally published 1953.

There are twelve "leading ideas" in John, including "truth," "faith," "light," and "logos." The importance of its symbolism. How the argument of John is structured; the relationship between its narratives and its discourses.

1968. Domeris, W.R. "The Johannine Drama." *JTSA* #42 (March, 1983), 29-35.

There is a "need to examine the Gospel [of John] in the light of the Greek plays." Analysis of the Prologue, discourses, dialogues, names of characters, and use of direct speech are evidence that John's intentions were to use the techniques of Greek drama to present his material.

1969. Duke, Paul D. *Irony in the Fourth Gospel.* Atlanta (John Knox P), 1985.

"Local irony" in isolated passages of John as a means of identifying the characteristics of John's style; these include questions, repetition, double meaning, and use of sarcasm by characters.

"Extended" and "sustained" irony are also found in such chapters as 9 and 18-19, and in the gospel as a whole. John's irony is unique, important, always polemical, and relevant to his purpose.

1970.   Edwards, Michael. "The World Could Not Contain the Books," in #1517, pp. 178-194.

"John is clearly organizing history into a constraining literary form, whose inordinate ambition is to relate heaven to earth...." History in John "is already elaborated as narrative by a more than human story-teller who writes events as humans write tales." John confronts the whole of past scripture, claiming to fulfill and absorb them as Jesus does, binding all previous works into a single work, penetrating to origin and concluding with a prophecy.

1971.   Ellis, Peter F. *The Genius of John: A Composition-Critical Commentary on the Fourth Gospel.* Collegeville (Liturgical P), 1984.

The gospel of John (as John Gerhard argued) is a unified work with one author, "written according to the laws of parallelism rather than the laws of narrative." His literary techniques are mostly those of the dramatist: scenes, dialogue and monologue, misunderstanding which requires characters to explain themselves, irony, foreshadowing, ring composition and chiasm, among others. Chiastic parallelism is the key to the structure of John, with its elaborate attention to artistic detail.

1972.   Enz, Jacob J. "The Book of Exodus as a Literary Type for the Gospel of John." *JBL* 76 (1957), 208-215.

The typology of Exodus in John is extensive and complex: the unrecognized deliverer, the serpent in the wilderness, the use of "sign," the devotion of the later chapters of the gospel to Israel's own. Parallels between Exodus and John occur in the larger structure as well.

1973.   Foster, Donald. "John Come Lately: The Belated Evangelist," in Frank McConnell, ed., *The Bible and the Narrative Tradition* (New York and Oxford: Oxford UP, 1986), 113-131.

"The writer of the Gospel of John ... is disquieted by his belatedness, by the fact that he comes after Matthew, Mark, and Luke.... John's purpose is not to add one more to a growing heap of apocryphal Gospels, ... but rather to provide the world ... with the true Gospel of Jesus Christ. John wishes to clarify the message of a badly misunderstood Son of God. And, in the process, he does more than a little campaigning on his own behalf as belated evangelist."

1974. Giblin, Charles H., S.J. "The Tripartite Narrative Structure of John's Gospel." *Biblica* 71 (1990), 449-468.

We must avoid assuming that only one literary structure of a given work is possible. The older proposed bipartite structure for John nevertheless makes the narrative, plot line and theology of John less clear. There is a three-part structure 1:19-4:54, 5:1-10:42, and 11:1-20:29, with chapter 21 as supplement. Seeing such a structure also helps clarify some of John's motifs.

1975. Hitchcock, F.R.M. "The Dramatic Development of the Fourth Gospel." *The Expositor*, 7th Series, #21 (September, 1907), 266-279.

In every respect: plot, characterization, dialogue, etc., John is a work of supreme dramatic art, to set beside the greatest ancient Greek tragedies.

1976. Hitchcock, F.R.M. "Is the Fourth Gospel a Drama?" *Theology* 7 (1923), 307-317.

John is constructed as a five-act drama, which fact accounts for its unity. Where the scene boundaries are; how characterization develops; how the plot advances and builds to a climax.

1977. Kelber, Werner H. "The Authority of the Word in St. John's Gospel: Charismatic Speech, Narrative Text, Logocentric Metaphysics." *Oral Tradition* 2 (1987), 108-131.

In John, "a substantial measure of oral ethos has become absorbed into the written narrative. Yet the overall function of this gospel is not to produce an unedited version of oral verbalization, but to recontextualize orality, and to devise a corrective against it." This corrective is the privileging of the *Logos* so that it dominates and subsumes the *logoi* of the text.

1978. Kermode, Frank. "John," in #33, pp. 440-466.

The relationship of the prologue to the rest of the narrative; style and theology of the prologue; John's use of signs and allegorical "parables"; symbolism in key narrative sequences, e.g., the wedding at Cana; structural and thematic relationships among episodes; the relationship of John's passion narratives to those in the other gospels.

1979. Kermode, Frank. "St. John as Poet." *JSNT* 28 (1986), 3-16.

"... the literary relations between the proem and the narrative that follows are strong. The axis of the proem ... is also the axis of the book.... [T]his antithesis [between 'being' and 'becoming'] animates the whole, which is why one ought to think of the Prologue as the paradigm of the narrative."

1980. Kotzé, P.P.A. "John and the Reader's Response." *Neotestamentica* 19 (1985), 50-63.

Wolfgang Iser's phenomenological analysis applied to John. Important stylistic devices "used by the writer to accommodate text-reader interaction" include ambiguity, misunderstanding of Jesus by his opponents, and resulting belief or disbelief. Iser's theories also show us three levels or directives in the gospel: Jesus' works and words, authorial comment, and characterization.

1981. Louw, J.P. "On Johannine Style." *Neotestamentica* 20 (1986), 5-12.

Johannine (or any) style is more than Semitisms and figures: it involves all the author's verbal choices, and moves beyond sentences to total discourse. John's stylistic devices are commonly found in ancient Greek writing; these include close synonyms, different meanings for the same word, increasingly lengthy phrases as a pericope proceeds, careful structuring of discourse, and devices promoting repetition and "shift in expectancy."

1982. Maier, John. "Johannine Myth and the New Trinity," in #48, pp. 329-346.

Examination of two important "literary deconstructive" readings of John [one included here as #1977] as offering two quite different interpretations of Jacques Derrida. If we try to use the other one (by Joseph Stephen O'Leary in *Questioning Back*) we find that the mistakes we make can be corrected by reading Gail R. O'Day [#1987].

1983. Malina, Bruce J. *The Gospel of John in Sociolinguistic Perspective.* Berkeley (Center for Hermeneutical Studies in Hellenistic and Modern Culture 48th Colloquy): 11 March 1984.

Sociolinguistics helps us see how and why John is so different from the other gospels in a more testable, empirical way than the "usual intuitive and impressionistic approaches" allow. It can explain John's distinct ways of describing God, and man's relationship with the divine; his community's "self-distancing from their original mooring," and its "highly creative" ways of making sense of the meaning of human existence. Responses by, and dialogue with, E.A. Judge, Stephen Reid, and Herman C. Waetjen.

1984. Mlakuzhyil, George. *The Christocentric Literary Structure of the Fourth Gospel.* Rome (Editrice Pontificio Istituto Biblico), 1987.

A "new literary structure" of John can be based on literary criteria, dramatic techniques, and structural patterns of parallelism, chiasm, concentric and spiral structure. This new theory accounts for previously unexplained peculiarities of John and integrates the findings of other scholars.

1985. Muilenberg, J. "Literary Form in the Fourth Gospel." *JBL* 51 (1932), 40-53.

Various earlier arguments illustrating literary and artistic qualities in individual scenes or verses in John. Evidence of careful attention to form is "most striking" in the gospel. The author "has a powerful dramatic sense." There is much climactic arrangement within these scenes. The narratives are not so much historical accounts as "literary moulds embodying a theological theory."

1986. Myers, Doris E. "Irony and Humor in the Gospel of John." *OPTAT* 2, #2 (1988), 1-13.

A reader trained in literary analysis but who knows nothing about theology soon notices that "the failure to see is the archetypal ironic plot" of John, and that "the relationship of the author to his story is ironic." This irony is often achieved by presenting two different accounts of the same episode. In sum, "our archetypal graduate student ... finds it humorous, ironic, and unified where many scholars and theologians find it mystical, dogmatic, and somewhat disarranged."

1987. O'Day, Gail R. "Narrative Mode and Theological Claim: A Study in the Fourth Gospel." *JBL* 105 (1986), 657-668.

Bultmann's "what" categories are inadequate because they fail to take into account the ways in which literary characteristics of John shape the Johannine portrait of Jesus and his theology. We should substitute the "how" of revelation, since we cannot separate form and content, and studies ignoring this consideration plus the style will always fall short. Irony is the best way into the "how" of John, since he used it as a revelatory language, forcing readers to make judgments. John is not just a portrait of Jesus as revealer, but allows readers to experience Jesus' revelation for themselves.

1988. O'Day, Gail R. *Revelation in the Fourth Gospel: Narrative Mode and Theological Claim.* Philadelphia (Fortress P), 1986.

We can attempt "to arrive at an understanding of the interface between *narrative mode* and *theological claim* in the study of revelation" in John. It is important to define irony and how it functions in this gospel. John 4 as a test case, with movement outward to the whole gospel. John's goal is to get the reader to participate in the narrative, and irony is a means for doing that.

1989.   Ostenstad, Gunnar. "The Structure of the Fourth Gospel: Can It Be Defined Objectively?" *Studia Theologica* 45 (1991), 33-55.

Only recently was the "most essential structural element" of John discovered: that it is "composed *concentrically* in seven main sections, symmetrically oriented around chapters 8:12–12:50." This thesis can be confirmed by the presence of an elaborate inclusion at that point, by a "concentric heptad on the theme of *Jesus—the Light and Life of the World,*" and by many forward and backward-looking cross-references throughout. This elaborate chiastic outline underscores the integrity of hitherto doubtful chapters.

1990.   Pamment, Margaret. "Focus in the Fourth Gospel." *ET* 97 (1985-6), 71-4.

John can be elucidated under three headings: recounting/representation, perspective, and voice, in keeping with narrative theory. "Recounting" shows that John (like all biblical authors) was more concerned with what is said than with what happens. "Perspective" shows how omniscient point of view operates in John to carry both straight and ironic meaning; and "voice" shows the reliability of the narrator.

1991.   Pratt, Rev. D. Butler. "The Gospel of John From the Standpoint of Greek Tragedy." *The Biblical World* n.s. 30 (1907), 448-459.

While we may not be able to prove that John is a Greek tragedy, "there is a close parallelism of form and method between it and the great Greek tragedies." We can even lay out an act-scene division of the gospel.

1992.   du Rand, J.A. "The Characterization of Jesus as Depicted in the Narrative of the Fourth Gospel." *Neotestamentica* 19 (1985), 18-36.

John is a "coherent witnessing story about the protagonist Jesus." Reader-response criticism helps us understand John's characterization of Jesus within the point of view and plot of the gospel. We see, e.g., the difference between Jesus' emotional responses here and in the other gospels, as well as his "professional distance and aloofness" in John. He remains "in many ways ... a mysterious figure to the reader."

1993. du Rand, J.A. "Plot and Point of View in the Gospel of John," in #1507, pp. 149-169.

Elements of plot and narrative point of view in John—the latter from temporal, psychological, spatial and ideological perspectives.

1994. Rhees, Rush. "The Fourth Gospel," in #32, pp. 281-297.

John is neither a biography of Jesus nor a theological treatise, but a highly personal reminiscence by the author, whose intention is to "lift up his Master" to his readers. The Prologue is not at all like the rest of the gospel.

1995. Richard, E. "Expressions of Double Meaning and their Function in the Gospel of John." *NTS* 31 (1985), 96-112.

"... John's vision and method is dialectical. Reality in a human context is ambiguous and therefore all symbolism is inadequate by nature." The double meaning is a function of John's desire that the reader consider both the earthly and the heavenly reality.

1996. Rogers, Thomas F. "The Gospel of John as Literature." *Brigham Young University Studies* 28, #3 (Summer, 1988), 67-80.

If we view and describe John aesthetically, we find it to be "richly poetic"; its "precepts strike with ... force ... like compelling music." It is "basically lyric," and characterizes through dialogue with "remarkable skill." Its narrative structure is powerfully dramatic.

1997. Smith, Robert Houston. "Exodus Typology in the Fourth Gospel." *JBL* 81 (1962), 329-342.

John's Exodus typology differs from that of the synoptics because he limited his to the death and resurrection of Jesus, whereas the other gospels extended theirs to the life of the early church. John evidently thought of his use of the OT as a structural typology for his whole gospel, but didn't quite bring that idea to reality. John is interested in Moses as revealer of signs, more than as a leader through the wilderness.

1998. Staley, Jeffrey L. *The Print's First Kiss: A Rhetorical Investigation of the Implied Reader in the Fourth Gospel.* Atlanta (Scholars P), 1988.

The "rhetorical levels" of John: real and implied authors and reader, narrator and narratee. It has a concentric structure, plot, and implied reader all built on the implied reader. The implied author of John uses rhetorical strategy of "reader victimization" to form and reform the text's implied reader.

1999.   van Tilborg, S. "The Gospel of John: Communicative Pro-
        cesses in a Narrative Text." *Neotestamentica* 23 (1989), 19-
        31.

        John exhibits three devices typical of narrators: the communica-
        tion among characters in the story; the indirect communication
        between narrator and readers; and their direct communication as
        well.

*   Wallis, Ethel E. "Four Gospels, Four Discourse Genre." See
        #1649.

2000.   Warner, Martin. "The Fourth Gospel's Art of Rational Per-
        suasion," in #1517, pp. 153-177.

        John shows sophisticated rhetorical use of *ethos* and *pathos*, ap-
        proximating the mythopoeic shape of a quest in which we as read-
        ers learn gradually to increase our trust in Jesus. However, unless
        we can be persuaded (*logos*) that Jesus was not guilty as charged,
        the ethical and pathetic appeals will not move us. John integrates
        these three appeals through categories drawn from Wisdom litera-
        ture, especially Job: both books offer a "radically subversive" wis-
        dom—a liberating truth which readers are invited to join; in the
        case of John, the paradox of the cross as glory.

2001.   Wead, David W. *The Literary Devices in John's Gospel.* Basel
        (Friedrich Reinhardt Kommissions-verlag), 1970.

        Some of John's literary devices can also be found in Homer and
        Aristotle; others John would have invented for the occasion. They
        include point of view: those who participated, but mainly those
        who came after; the sign: intended to produce faith, with John
        choosing miracles in accordance with this requirement; double
        meanings; irony; and metaphor: especially the "I Am" passages,
        since the Christian message is both reliant upon background and
        unique. These devices "become the modes of thought in which he
        wished to convey his message."

2002.   Webster, Edwin C. "Pattern in the Fourth Gospel," in #34,
        pp. 230-257.

        John "as a literary whole, is meticulously constructed on the ba-
        sis of a symmetrical design and balanced units." Such patterns are
        analogous to the parallelism of Hebrew poetry. John, heir to this
        poetic tradition, employs a balancing of incident against incident,
        theme against theme; triadic arrangements of paired units which
        are sometimes chiastic; parallel sequences; word repetition; and
        balance of length in complementary units.

2003. Wyller, Egil A. "In Solomon's Porch: A Henological Analysis of the Architectonic of the Fourth Gospel." *Studia Theologica* 42 (1988), 151-167.

The compositional structure of John, "looked upon as a coherent literary work." The literary type of John is a "dramatic dialogue," and can therefore be illuminated using Aristotle's theory of drama. The basic division is between chapters 1-12 and 13-21, with each part having thematic unity. Detailed outline of the chiastic structure (though we must recognize that other outlines of the structure of John make sense as well).

See also: #s 3, 60, 1491, 1494, 1568, and 2236.

John 1-10

2004. van Aarde, A.G. "Narrative Criticism Applied to John 4:43-54," in #1508, pp. 101-128.

The poetics of the gospel form as narrative include its being a closed narrative world, a projection of the early church onto the world of Jesus, and an open-ended form. Point of view, surface structure, narrated time, and deep structure in John 4. The ideological/theological perspective of the protagonist (Jesus) coincides with that of the narrator, and the implied reader is manipulated to associate with the action of the royal official and dissociate from the Jewish citizens.

2005. Bishop, Jonathan. "Encounters in the New Testament," in #40, pp. 285-294.

One important form of characterization in John is changes in characters as a result of encounters with Jesus. The change in the blind beggar in John 9 is an example. (BD)

2006. Boers, Hendrikus. "Discourse Structure and Macro-Structure in the Interpretation of Texts: John 4:1-42 as an Example." *SBLSP* 1980, pp. 159-182.

Despite its puzzling outline, and the appearance of containing separate texts, John 4 is shown by discourse and macro (surface and deep structure) analysis to be unified. Ultimately, the entire gospel of John might be read as a single macro-sentence.

2007. Boers, Hendrikus. *Neither On This Mountain Nor In Jerusalem: A Study of John 4.* Atlanta (Scholars P), 1988.

A semiotic/structuralist analysis of John 4, beginning with the "syntactic component" (surface and deep structures); then the "semantic component" (discourse structure and themes); finally the "generative trajectory." The meaning of this chapter in light of the structuralist analysis.

2008.   Botha, J. Eugene. "Reader 'Entrapment' as Literary Device in John 4:1-42." *Neotestamentica* 24 (1990), 37-47.

In John, "implied readers are manipulated and entrapped mercilessly by the implied author. They are subjected to tension, apprehension and suspense. They are cast now as outsiders now as insiders, and caught wrong-footed time and again.... All these manipulations are very functional, however, since they are designed to enhance the communication between author and reader."

2009.   Cahill, P. Joseph. "Narrative Art in John IV." *Religious Studies Bulletin* 2 (1982), 41-48.

We can suggest a literary structure for John 4 which will enlarge both its theological significance and the dimensions of its literary continuity between OT and NT. John 4 shows various repetitive devices, motifs, a type scene and a chiastic structure, all of which reveal continuity with OT narrative.

2010.   Crossan, John Dominic. "It Is Written: A Structuralist Analysis of John 6." *SBLSP* 1979, pp. 197-213; rpt *Semeia* 26 [#2023] (1983), 3-21.

An "exercise in structuralist imagination rather than the detailed application of a deductive method." We explore *how* the text means in order to see *what* it means, how it holds together as a whole. Its motif is first of all physical consumption, then spiritual consumption.

2011.   Crossan, John D. "A Structuralist Analysis of John 6," in Richard Spencer, ed., *Orientation by Disorientation* (Pittsburgh: Pickwick P, 1980), 235-249.

We look at how the text means as a unity, in order to see what the text means. Analysis of John 6 in terms of its "narrative actants" and "discourse actants."

2012.   Culbertson, Diana. "'Are You Also Deceived?' Reforming the Reader in John 7." *PEGL* 9 (1989), 148-160.

John 7 is a "crucial narrative unit in John's attempt to describe the identity of Jesus and the mystery of his presence in the world." The psychoanalytic reader-response theory of Marshall Alcorn and Mark Bracher can help us understand John's narrative strategy.

John "is directed especially to implied readers (and by implication real readers) who want to *see* in order to strengthen their belief." This is accomplished partly through groups of characters who objectify appropriate or inappropriate beliefs.

2013. Dockery, David S. "John 9:1-41: A Narrative Discourse Study." *OPTAT* 2, #2 (1988), 14-26.

Extensive thematic parallels and a chiastic structure reinforce the themes of revelation and judgment as dramatized in the episode of the man born blind. We notice the irony of the man who moves progressively toward sight while the Pharisees move toward blindness.

2014. Eslinger, Lyle. "The Wooing of the Woman at the Well: Jesus, the Reader and Reader-Response Criticism." *LT* 1 (1987), 167-183.

"... reader-response criticism is able to shed new light on the literary devices such as the type-scene and the double-entendres that are employed in [John 4]...."

2015. Giblin, Charles Homer, S.J. "Two Complementary Literary Structures in John 1:1-18." *JBL* 104 (1985), 87-103.

We can read the Prologue as a well-integrated literary introduction to John and at the same time take seriously the process of its final stages of composition. The Prologue exhibits a twofold structure based on verbal correlations and use of imagery. It is a "meditative, appreciative reflection on the eschatological theophany effected through the Word, ... and also as a literary and thematic introduction to John's narrative (when one reads it according to its chiastic structure)."

2016. Henaut, Barry W. "John 4:43-54 and the Ambivalent Narrator. A Response to Culpepper's *Anatomy of the Fourth Gospel.*" *SR* 19 (1990), 287-304.

A combined literary and historical-critical analysis of John 4 shows us that Culpepper is inconsistent and himself ambivalent in applying his own exclusively literary approach to John. A "tension or ambivalence towards signs" lies at the heart of John 4; therefore literary criticism is most helpful if used alongside of, rather than in place of, historical criticism.

2017. Hoffman, Joy J. "Unmasking the Drama: The Rhetoric of John 9," in John H. Morgan, ed., *Church Divinity 1984* (Notre Dame: Graduate Theological Foundation), 113-127.

"Rhetorical analysis shows John's gospel moving in two directions simultaneously: it serves the insiders in the Johannine community while proclaiming the good news of Jesus to those outside the in-group." John 9 especially shows considerable rhetorical and literary skill and power, revealing the author's use of the machinery of comic drama: "the blind man here plays *eiron* to the *alazon* of Pharisaic Judaism." We also find in this chapter the tension between old and new, satire with dialogue, puns and sarcasm.

2018.　Kelber, Werner H. "The Birth of a Beginning: John 1:1-18." *Semeia* 52 (1990), 121-144.

"Broadly viewed, the prologue signals a double gesture. In keeping with the ethos of beginnings, it affirms authoritative primordiality. Its *Logos* signifies the quintessential logocentric gesture. Once in place, the transcendental authority is compelled to dislodge itself from its origin so as to engender textual and incarnational consecutiveness. In a second gesture, therefore, the prologue enacts a decentering, a deconstruction of the *Logos*' ontotheological foundation. Transcendental and earthly beginnings, this double gesture of centering and decentering, constitute the prologue's program which creates the central predicament for the subsequent narrative. Whether this problem is perceived in terms of flesh versus glory, the earthly versus the heavenly, the literal versus the metaphorical, or the signifier versus the signified, it resists any demonstrable narrative resolution."

2019.　Menken, M.J.J. *Numerical Literary Techniques in John: The Fourth Evangelist's Use of Numbers of Words and Syllables.* Leiden (E.J. Brill: *Nov T* Supplement 55), 1985.

Analysis of the structure or "individual shape" of John "as created by its author and perceptible to its readers." Numerical analysis of number of of syllables and words in John 1, 5, 6, 9, 17. Combined with conventional analysis of literary structure, and similar to analysis of surface structure by structuralists, such numerical analysis may refine and concretize literary criticism of the Bible. It may also be useful as internal evidence for textual analysis as well.

2020.　Moore, S.D. "Rifts in (a Reading of) the Fourth Gospel, or: Does Johannine Irony Still Collapse in a Reading That Draws Attention to Itself?" *Neotestamentica* 23 (1989), 5-17.

Deconstruction can act as a corrective to compositional and narrative criticism of passages such as John 4, 7, and 19. It annuls Johannine irony by recognizing its liminality, since the audience cannot detect this irony without awareness of a spirit/matter, figural/literal hierarchical separation.

2021. Nida, Eugene A. "Rhetoric and the Translator: With Special Reference to John 1." *BT* 33 (1982), 324-8.

Knowledge of rhetoric as defined and practiced by literary critics is vital for the translator because the rhetorical level of communication is distinct and important: ideas related to other ideas, and ideas related to reality. John 1 is one of the most intricately organized chapters rhetorically in the entire Bible.

2022. Olsson, Birger. *Structure and Meaning in the Fourth Gospel: A Text-Linguistic Analysis of John 2:1-11 and 4:1-42*. Lund (C.W.K. Gleerup), 1974.

Application of the subfield of linguistics dealing with semantic structures, discourse analysis and textual problems applied to John 2 and 4. The former is a "narrative" text, the latter a "dialogue" text; each has its own event structure, its own spatial and temporal orientation appropriate to that structure.

2023. Patte, Daniel, ed. *Semeia* 26: *Narrative Discourse in Structural Exegesis: John 6 and I Thessalonians*. Chico (Scholars P), 1983.

Essays on John 6 by John Crossan and Gary A. Phillips, analyzed separately as #s 2010, 2024; by Elizabeth Malbon and Daniel Patte, analyzed separately as #s 2169, 2171.

* Patte, Daniel. *Structural Exegesis for New Testament Critics*. See #1503.

2024. Phillips, Gary A. "'This is a Hard Saying. Who Can Be a Listener to It?': Creating a Reader in John 6." *SBLSP* 1979, pp. 185-195; rpt *Semeia* 26 (1983) [#2023], 23-56.

A reading of John 6 "in terms of its nature and function as discourse and its capacity to create a reader.... The work of John 6 as text is, in part, the performative act of creating a world in which the scriptive reader/hearer becomes a 'you' for Jesus through the proffering of various models of narrative speaking and hearing."

2025. du Rand, Jan A. "A Syntactical and Narratological Reading of John 10 in Coherence with Chapter 9," in Johannes Beutler and Robert T. Fortna, eds., *The Shepherd Discourse of John 10 and its Context* (Cambridge: Cambridge UP, 1991), 94-115.

John 10 as a "syntactic co-text" of John 9, and as a "narratological co-text" of John 5-10. That is, "the unfolding of the plot in chapters 9-10 is given relief against the unfolding in chapters 5-8." These chapters build the "belief versus unbelief" theme toward its climax in 9-10, where the contrast between healed blind man and "blind" Jewish leaders is forced upon the reader.

2026. Resseguie, James L. "John 9: A Literary-Critical Analysis," in #40, pp. 295-303.

"The imagery, the structure, the movement of the plot, and the characterization all work together to form a tightly knit narrative." Outline of the structure of the chapter. The comic plot of the blind man going toward sight deliberately contrasts with the tragic downward movement of the Pharisees toward spiritual blindness.

2027. Roth, Wolfgang. "Scriptural Coding in the Fourth Gospel." *BR* 32 (1987), 6-29.

John is a selective and inverted narrative rewriting of the Law and the Prophets. The key lies in six "signals": John 2:13, 5:1, 6:4, 7:2, 10:22, and 11:55, which contain coded references to, and rewritings of, Deuteronomy, Numbers, Leviticus, Exodus, Genesis, and I Kings 17–II Kings 13. All of these texts from the HB served as John's compositional model.

2028. Staley, Jeff. "The Structure of John's Prologue: Its Implications for the Gospels' Narrative Structure." *CBQ* 48 (1986), 241-264.

The relationship between the prologue and the rest of John. The gospel exhibits a symmetrical, concentric structure built upon the structure of the prologue.

2029. Talbert, Charles H. "Artistry and Theology: An Analysis of the Architecture of Jn 1,19–5,47." *CBQ* 32 (1970), 341-366

John 1:19–5:47 forms an elaborate chiasm; thus the author should be seen as a great literary artist, as well as a great theologian.

2030. Topel, L. John. "A Note on the Methodology of Structural Analysis in *Jn* 2:23–3:21." *CBQ* 33 (1971), 211-220.

Existing proposals for structural analysis of John 2-3 are faulty. Any such analysis must be checked against thematic words and aesthetic forms, e.g., here the use of dialogue.

2031. Wahlde, Urban C. Von. "Literary Structure and Theological Argument in Three Discourses with the Jews in the Fourth Gospel." *JBL* 103 (1984), 575-584.

A curious structural feature of John 6:31-59, 8:13-59, and 10:22-39 is their parallel structures, which occur in John only at these places. Their literary and theological function seems to be to present grounds for belief so that proofs become clear and persuasive for the reader. Thus the rejection of Jesus by the Jews is for John the crucial event in his ministry.

See also: #s 117, 135, 1501, 1513.

John 11-21

2032. Kurz, William S. "The Beloved Disciple and Implied Readers." *BTB* 19 (1989), 100-107.

Gaps in the narrative about the beloved disciple "suggest that he has a typological relationship with the implied readers of [John]." Historical criticism has distanced modern readers from identifying with this disciple, whereas narrative criticism can restore this identification.

2033. Malatesta, Edward. "The Literary Structure of John 17." *Biblica* 52 (1971), 190-214.

The themes of John 17 are woven together "with astonishing variety and subtle repetition." The literary characteristics of the chapter as a clue to its structure.

* Moore, S.D. "Rifts in (a Reading of) the Fourth Gospel, or: Does Johannine Irony Still Collapse in a Reading That Draws Attention to Itself?" See #2020.

* Roth, Wolfgang. "Scriptural Coding in the Fourth Gospel." See #2027.

2034. van Tilborg, S. "Ideology and Text: John 15 in the Context of the Farewell Discourse," in #1508, pp. 259-270.

"Ideology is a system that lies at the base of any concrete textual expression...." John 15, like any text, divides "on the base of ideological coherences," and requires the reader to reconstruct that ideology. John 15 "creates space for the otherwise suppressed and not-heard word of the weak and losing party.... [E]ven the narrator of John's gospel—always seemingly so sure of himself—is subject to ambiguity."

2035.   Wuellner, W. "Rhetorical Criticism and Its Theory in Cul-
         ture-Critical Perspective: The Narrative Rhetoric of John
         11," in #1508, pp. 171-185.

    The history of rhetoric in relation to biblical hermeneutics. The
    basics of modern rhetorical theory, and differences between it and
    post-modern rhetoric. We should not attempt to reduce rhetoric
    to one of its constituent parts. Argumentative coherence and strat-
    egy in John 11 is manifested in the apparent gaps, surpluses, and
    allusions to other texts within the chapter. The importance of our
    reading of John 1-10 in making sense of John 11.

See also: #s 1497, 1513, 1615.

ACTS OF THE APOSTLES

*Note: Additional items on Acts may be found in the "Luke-Acts"
section above.*

*   Ades, John I. "Literary Aspects of Luke." See #1867.

2036.   Balch, David L. "Acts as Hellenistic Historiography." *SBLSP*
         1985, pp. 429-432.

    The speeches, periodization of history, and scheme of divine
    promise and fulfillment all point to first-century Roman historical
    practices as easily as they do to deuteronomistic practices.

2037.   Barthes, Roland. "The Structural Analysis of a Narrative
         from Acts X-XI," in Alfred Johnson, ed., *Structuralism and
         Biblical Hermeneutics* (Pittsburgh: Pickwick P, 1979), 109-
         139; rpt in Barthes, *The Semiotic Challenge* (New York: Hill
         and Wang, 1988), 217-245.

    The origins of structural analysis, its general principles, and the
    structural problems in Acts 10-11, e.g. its various codes. The
    "subject" of Acts 10-11 is the idea of the message itself, making use
    of language and communication—a theme of Pentecost itself.

2038.   Black, C. Clifton II. "The Rhetorical Form of the Hellenistic
         Jewish and Early Christian Sermon: A Response to
         Lawrence Wills." *HTR* 81 (1988), 1-18.

    "... the benefits of regarding Hellenistic-Jewish and early Chris-
    tian sermons in concert with, rather than as innovative departures

from, Greco-Roman oratory are obvious. From such a standpoint, we can better understand the devices of ... argument being employed. The rhetorical function of certain exhortations in building transitional bridges between arguments, and the role played by repetitions of, and deviations from, established patterns of argument."

2039. Brawley, Robert L. "Paul in Acts: Aspects of Structure and Characterization." *SBLSP* 1988, pp. 90-105.

We can use structuralism to locate Paul in the "antithesis of the narrative." Modern literary theory can then aid us in studying Luke's characterization of Paul. Ultimately, we need a synthesis; do the methods combine to enrich interpretation?

2040. Brehm, H. Alan. "The Significance of the Summaries for Interpreting Acts." *SWJT* 33 (1990), 29-40.

Literary criticism is fruitful for NT interpretation because it investigates genres, paying careful attention to every detail of a text and how parts fit together to make a whole. Luke used two distinct types of summaries in Acts: the "summary narrative" (in 2:42-7, 4:32-5, 5:12-16), and the "summary statement" (6:7, 9:31, 12:24, 16:5, 19:20).

2041. Brodie, Thomas L., O.P. "Towards Unravelling the Rhetorical Imitation of Sources in Acts: 2 Kgs 5 as One Component of Acts 8, 9-40." *Biblica* 67 (1986), 41-67.

Acts 8:9-40 is "modelled largely, but not exclusively, on the OT story of Naaman and Gehazi (2 Kgs 5)." Luke's adaptation is an example of *imitatio*, and it presents a "partial clue" to the old problem of the use of sources in Acts. In doing this, the author was following a common Greco-Roman procedure.

2042. Dibelius, Martin. *Studies in the Acts of the Apostles*. London (SCM P), 1956; originally published 1951.

"The Speeches in Acts and Ancient Historiography": Luke did not report his speeches from life, but invented them, influenced by Greco-Roman historiography. He was thus a conscious literary artist.

* Funk, Robert W. *The Poetics of Biblical Narrative.* See #1570.

2043. Horsley, G.R. "Speeches and Dialogues in Acts." *NTS* 32 (1986), 609-614.

The author of Acts "has embraced the convention of formal, set speeches ... [which] is to be seen as one way he chose to display his literary craftsmanship.... [T]he comparatively heavy, and diverse, use of direct discourse in Acts is likely to be due to the author's stylistic concern to lighten the narrative, and to vivify it."

2044.   Marin, Louis. "A Structural Analysis Essay of Acts 10:1–11:18," in Alfred M. Johnson, ed., *Structuralism and Biblical Hermeneutics* (Pittsburgh: Pickwick P, 1979), 145-177.

The narrative structure of Acts may be explained in terms of "pairs of narrative discourses" (surface structure); and archetype, codes, and "circuits of exchange" (deep structure). The fundamental problem in Acts is articulating and combining two orientations: verbality and orality, speaking and eating. Peter's itinerary inscribes this problem into the textuality of the narrative.

2045.   Mealand, David L. "Hellenistic Historians and the Style of Acts." *ZNW* 82 (1991), 42-66.

"... Acts is closer to major Hellenistic historians than has often been granted.... [W]ords and phrases widely considered to be 'alien to non-Biblical Greek' or strange or rare, do in fact have their antecedents in the work of writers like Polybius."

2046.   Miesner, Donald R. "The Missionary Journeys Narrative: Patterns and Implications," in Charles H. Talbert, ed., *Perspectives on Luke-Acts* (Edinburgh: T. and T. Clark, 1978), 199-214.

Acts 12-21 has a chiastic structure. Various implications of this structure for understanding Luke's placing of some of the events and sermons in Acts.

2047.   Neyrey, Jerome. "The Forensic Defense Speech and Paul's Trial Speeches in Acts 22-26: Form and Function," in Charles H. Talbert, ed., *Luke-Acts: New Perspectives from The S.B.L. Seminar* (New York: Crossroads, 1984), 210-224.

"... the trial speeches of Paul in Acts deserve to be described formally as forensic defense speeches according to the models presented in the rhetorical handbooks."

2048.   Palmer, D.W. "The Literary Background of Acts 1.1-14." *NTS* 33 (1987), 427-438.

Luke has drawn on four main literary forms in composing the opening paragraph of Acts: prologue, epiphany, farewell scene, and assumption. He found these forms in Hellenistic pagan literature as well as in the HB.

2049. Pervo, Richard I. *Profit with Delight: The Literary Genre of the Acts of the Apostles.* Philadelphia (Fortress P), 1987.

The usual comparison of Acts with ancient historiography is misplaced, since Acts is not a learned treatise. Rather, it is a "popular entertainment," modelled on the ancient novel—specifically the "edifying historical novel." The structures, themes, cultural settings, and modes of a number of ancient pagan, Jewish and Christian historical novels, and their resemblance to Acts.

2050. Praeder, Susan Marie. "Acts 27:1–28:16: Sea Voyages in Ancient Literature and the Theology of Luke-Acts." *CBQ* 46 (1984), 683-706.

The theological relationship of Acts 27-28 to the rest of Luke-Acts will remain unresolved unless we see the literary relationship between the sea voyages in Acts 27-28 and those in ancient literature; it is obvious that Luke was famnilar with this material and used it as a model.

2051. Praeder, Susan Marie. "The Problem of First Person Narration in Acts." *Nov T* 29 (1987), 193-218.

Various redaction and literary-critical studies of this problem have not solved it. An alternative approach could be based on unexplained features, e.g., anonymity, inconsistent use of the first person, a plurality of narrators, and intermixing of first and third person in the same passages. Literary critics have so far failed to show convincing parallels with pagan sea-voyage narratives.

2052. Robbins, Vernon K. "The We-Passages in Acts and Ancient Sea Voyages." *BR* 20 (1975), 5-18.

The "we-passages" in Acts are a stylistic device borrowed from, or influenced by, Greco-Roman sea stories.

2053. Robinson, James M. "Acts," in #33, pp. 467-478.

Acts shows "a lack of concern for normal historical treatment and thereby emphasize[s] the primacy of [Luke's] literary concern." Luke exhibits in Acts a "subtle, pervasive politicizing"; he changed Christianity from an otherworldly to a this-worldly religion.

2054. Schierling, Stephen P., and Marla J. Schierling. "The Influence of the Ancient Romances on *Acts of the Apostles*." *Classical Bulletin* 54 (1978), 81-8.

While Acts is not in itself an ancient romance, it shows the definite influence of the genre. In all, nine of the twelve basic characteristics of the ancient romance show up in Acts, including travel, miracles (e.g., miraculous rescue), heroes who are "images of perfection" and sometimes taken for gods, dreams and visions with purposes similar to those found in the romances, trials of endurance and a happy ending.

2055.   Tannehill, Robert C. "The Composition of Acts 3-5: Narrative Development and Echo Effect." *SBLSP* 1984, pp. 217-240.

The repetitive patterns in Luke-Acts have various kinds of significance. They are a means of emphasis, of jogging memory, and relieving boredom; they help readers anticipate a climactic instance of a familiar pattern; they preserve a sense of unity and purpose; they encourage interaction between the reader's experiences, creating a "resonance" in the text; etc.

2056.   Tannehill, Robert C. *The Narrative Unity of Luke-Acts: A Literary Interpretation. Volume 2: The Acts of the Apostles.* Minneapolis (Fortress P), 1990.

The book "is not a monograph arguing a single, central thesis that Luke-Acts is a unified narrative. It presents much evidence of unity in Luke-Acts and shows how unity is maintained through narrative developments, but it neither argues that this unity is perfect nor focuses on this issue as its sole concern."

*   Thiering, Barbara. "Opening and Closing Narratives in the Gospel and Acts." See #1644.

2057.   Tyson, Joseph B. "The Problem of Food in Acts: A Study of Literary Patterns with Particular Reference to Acts 6:1-7." *SBLSP* 1979, Vol. I, pp. 69-85.

A typical narrative pattern in Acts is the threatening situation followed by a solution. This pattern in Acts 6 can help us see how the resolution fits the problem of the gentile widows and the sacrificial meal which unites the community.

2058.   Zweck, Dean. "The *Exordium* of the Areopagus Speech, Acts 17.22-23." *NTS* 35 (1989), 94-103.

The exordium in Hellenistic rhetoric. In Acts 17, the exordium is for a deliberation on religion. The closest parallel is the *Olympic Discourse* of Dio Chrysostom, written in the year 97. Luke portrays Paul as a rhetor, "skilfully bridg[ing] the gap between hellenistic religiosity and the topic on which he would speak...."

See also: #s 7, 18, 135, 1497, 1501, 1525, 1538, 1629, 1875, 1878, 1881.

THE PAULINE LETTERS

Notes:

(a) No attempt has been made to differentiate between "genuine" and "pseudo" Pauline letters, since which letters to assign to which category is still a matter of some dispute in scholarly circles. In this bibliography, all NT letters except Hebrews through Jude are regarded as Pauline.

(b) A few NT letters have no, or almost no, entries under their separate headings in this bibliography. This does not mean that literary critics have not addressed the issues which arise in those letters, only that such criticism is more likely to be found in items listed under the general headings of "Pauline" or "Other" letters.

2059. Bahr, Gordon J. "Paul and Letter Writing in the First Century." *CBQ* 26 (1966), 465-477.

We must know the literary procedures which Paul followed in his letter writing if we are to understand them. On several occasions he probably used someone else to write for him. This was common in Roman times, as was having a secretary to save time. Shorthand was in use by the mid first century, and a secretary might even compose a letter; forgery was a danger, as was co-authorship. Since we do not know how Paul used his secretary, it is possible that some Pauline terminology and theology is not in fact Paul's.

* "Symposium: Paul Ricoeur and Biblical Hermeneutics." See #1204.

2060. Bradley, D.G. "The Topos as a Form in the Pauline Paranaesis." *JBL* 72 (1953), 238-246.

Paul himself admits to using many traditional materials in his letters. Examples of the *topos* in Hellenistic ethical writing, especially Stoic and Cynic philosophy, with parallel examples from Paul's letters.

* Brunt, John C. "More on the *Topos* as a New Testament Form." See #1526.

* Doty, William G. "The Classification of Epistolary Literature." See #1528.

2061. Doty, William G. *Letters in Primitive Christianity.* Philadelphia
       (Fortress P), 1973.

       The aspects of Greco-Roman letter-writing relevant to Christian-
       ity. Similarities and differences between Greco-Roman and Pauline
       letters. The "sub-units found within primitive Christian letters" in-
       clude stylistic, rhetorical, and structural features. How post-Pauline
       letters fit these characteristics.

2062. Fiore, Benjamin, S.J. "The Hortatory Function of Paul's
       Boasting." *PEGL* 5 (1985), 39-46.

       Paul undoubtedly "knew and was consciously using rhetorical
       principles and strategems such as those outlined by Plutarch and
       ... Quintilian. Examples from I and II Corinthians and
       Philippians.

2063. Fischer, James A. "Pauline Literary Forms and Thought Pat-
       terns." *CBQ* 39 (1977), 209-223.

       We must presume that Paul is in the mainstream that flows from
       OT wisdom to the rabbinic writings. A "crude tool" for under-
       standing Pauline form consists of dividing off the introductory
       formula; looking for the *mot crochet* and for antithesis; the *Sitz im
       Leben*; analyzing the antithesis as the "operative literary form" for
       the whole thought pattern; and looking for the theological mes-
       sage.

2064. Fredriksen, Paula. "Paul and Augustine: Conversion Narra-
       tives, Orthodox Traditions, and the Retrospective Self."
       JTS n.s. 37 (1986), 3-34.

       Conversion accounts are both anachronistic and apologetic: "a
       condensed, or disguised description of the convert's *present,* which
       he legitimates through his retrospective creation of a past and a
       self.... [T]he conversion narrative ... can reveal ... only the retro-
       spective moment, and the retrospective self."

*   Funk, Robert W. *Parables and Presence: Forms of the New Testa-
       ment Tradition.* See #1658.

2065. Gale, Herbert M. *The Use of Analogy in the Letters of Paul.*
       Philadelphia (Westminster P), 1964.

       Paul's analogies are central to the formulation of many of the
       most important Christian theological ideas and doctrines. His
       analogies show Hebraic rather than Greek influence. He tends to
       focus on a single element within his analogies; his applications of
       them are not always traditional, and not always systematic. Exam-
       ples from most of the Pauline letters.

2066.   Goulder, Michael. "The Pauline Epistles," in #33, pp. 479-
         502.

   Which letters are currently thought genuine. The purpose of letters to communities. A model from II Maccabees upon which Paul
   may have drawn. Each letter in its presumed chronological order:
   its structure, theology, theme and mood, with concentration on
   the agreed-upon authentic letters: I Thessalonians, I Corinthians,
   Galatians, Romans, II Corinthians, possibly Ephesians, Philippians,
   Romans, and Philemon.

2067.   Hays, Richard B. *Echoes of Scripture in the Letters of Paul.* New
         Haven and London (Yale UP), 1989.

   Paul's use of scripture approached not historically in terms of
   the first-century church "but by reading the letters as literary texts
   shaped by complex intertextual relations with Scripture." Intertextual echoes in Romans; discussions of Galatians and II Corinthians;
   the theological ramifications of literary-critical readings of Paul's
   intertextual practices.

2068.   Judge, E.A. "Paul's Boasting in Relation to Contemporary
         Professional Practice." *ABR* 16 (1968), 37-50.

   The place of rhetoric in ancient education. Evidence that Paul
   knew and used this rhetoric is inconclusive, but it needs thorough
   investigation, since the NT is, after all, a Greek and not a Hebrew
   work.

2069.   Kennedy, George. "'Truth' and 'Rhetoric' in the Pauline
         Epistles," in #1517, pp. 195-202.

   "Saint Paul's statements about 'truth' and his attitude toward
   rhetoric can be examined as ... a rhetorical attempt to claim external validation for subjective experience." Paul avoids the historical and rhetorical terms available in classical civilization, a fact
   which is itself "a feature of his rhetoric: a way of setting himself
   and his community off from secular society...." He assumes that
   both nature and history (and if not those, then inner experience)
   will validate his rhetoric over that of the pagans. This is true likewise of the deutero-Pauline and the pastoral epistles.

2070, 2071. Not used.

2072.   Kim, Chan-Hie. *Form and Structure of the Familiar Greek Letter
         of Recommendation.* Missoula (Scholars P), 1972.

   Letters of recommendation from the third century BC to the
   sixth century AD, including non-biblical Christian examples. Relationship of this type of letter to NT letters and passages of com-

mendation. The "Pauline commendation formula" in Philemon, I
Thessalonians 5, I Corinthians 16, and Philippians 4. We should
not isolate the NT letter from its contemporary setting, even
though we must also recognize its differences from other pagan
letters of the time.

2073.   Lund, N.W. "The Presence of Chiasmus in the New Testa-
        ment." *JR* 10 (1930), 74-93.

        Intensive use of chiasmus in the NT makes these devices much
        more than "minor literary flourishes." The history of awareness of
        biblical chiasmus since the late eighteenth century. Examples, with
        discussion, from Colossians 3, Ephesians 4, 5, 6, I Corinthians 12,
        and II Corinthians 1 and 14. The use of it in the NT probably is
        derived from its use in the OT.

2074.   Marks, Herbert. "Pauline Typology and Revisionary Criti-
        cism." *JAAR* 52 (1984), 71-92.

        Following the literary theories of Harold Bloom on the "anxiety
        of influence," we see that "Paul's subordination of the Jewish
        scriptures to their 'spiritual' understanding is a paradigmatic in-
        stance of revisionary power realized in the process of overcoming a
        tyranny of predecession."

2075.   Mullins, Terence Y. "Disclosure: a Literary Form in the New
        Testament." *Nov T* 7 (1964), 44-60.

        "Disclosure" is a literary form usually recognized by its function
        as terminating the Pauline thanksgiving. We need sharper defini-
        tions of formulae in the letters in order to study their function.

2076.   Mullins, Terence Y. "Greeting as a New Testament Form."
        JBL 87 (1968), 418-426.

        Types of greetings from the ancient world as revealed in Greco-
        Roman papyri; how Paul used these in his letters.

2077.   Mullins, Terence Y. "Petition as a Literary Form." *Nov T* 5
        (1962), 46-54.

        Elements of the petition as a literary form in the ancient world,
        and their function. Classification of types.

2078.   O'Brien, Peter Thomas. *Introductory Thanksgivings in the Let-
        ters of Paul.* Leiden (E.J. Brill), 1977.

        Examination of these passages shows their "deep pastoral and
        apostolic concern for the addressees," a didactic function, a para-
        netic and an epistolary function as introducing the main themes of
        the letters. Style, vocabulary, and the influence of the HB's liturgi-

cal language on the introductory thanksgivings in Philippians, Philemon, Colossians, I and II Corinthians, I and II Thessalonians and Romans. They are not meaningless devices but "integral parts of their letters, setting the tone and themes of what is to follow."

2079. Patte, Daniel. *Pauls's Faith and the Power of the Gospel: A Structural Introduction to the Pauline Letters.* Philadelphia (Fortress P), 1983.

A structural reading of Paul's letters on an elementary level for those without previous training in biblical or structural studies. The task is to reconstruct Paul's "system of convictions" on the basis of structural elements discovered in his letters. In the process of doing so, we must be careful to distinguish between faith and theology.

2080. Pfitzner, Victor C. *Paul and the Agon Motif: Traditional Athletic Imagery in the Pauline Literature.* Nov T Supplement 16. Leiden (E.J. Brill), 1967.

Athletic imagery is frequent in Paul's letters, and serves important motifs. There is a striking correspondence between Paul's *agon* motif and that found in the diatribe, Cynic-Stoic literature, and Hellenistic Judaism; in fact, such a motif was universal in the Greek diaspora. In Paul, *agon* refers to self-renunciation and training, the goal of the contest being the victory of the gospel. It also refers to exertion and will; our wrestling against the temptation to give up; our physical suffering as a result, and our heavenly victory as reward if we stay the course. Paul completely changed the scope of the pagan *agon*: it has for him "paradigmatic character for the contest of all believers." I Corinthians 9, Philippians 3, I and II Timothy.

2081. Roberts, J.H. "Transitional Techniques to the Letter Body in the *Corpus Paulinorum*," in #1507, pp. 187-201.

"It would appear that ... the function of the transitory techniques are to create a sympathetic relationship between author and reader which will allow successful communication and to lay a foundation for the argument/s or admonition/s to follow."

2082. Roetzel, Calvin J. *The Letters of Paul: Conversations in Context.* 2nd edition. Atlanta (John Knox P), 1982.

The religious and cultural world of Paul in late first-century Greco-Jewish context. The "anatomy" of the letters as Paul "constrains to his own use the epistolary conventions of his time." The letters as extended conversations with his intended readers; Paul and his "myths"; the anatomy and purpose of the deutero-Pauline letters, and the history of their interpretation.

460   *The New Testament*

2083.   Sanders, Jack T. "The Transition from Opening Epistolary
        Thanksgivings to Body in the Letters of the Pauline Cor-
        pus." *JBL* 81 (1962), 348-362.

        Formal constructions present in Paul's letters which go far be-
        yond the contemporary conventions for openings and closings.

2084.   Schubert, Paul. *Form and Function of the Pauline Thanksgiv-
        ings. BZNW* 20. Berlin (Töpelmann), 1939.

        Almost all Pauline letters have a thanksgiving, and all of those
        thanksgivings show "certain identical and readily observable func-
        tional and formal features." The extent and significance of these
        resemblances, and the function of the thanksgivings. All Greco-
        Roman epistolary papyri "attest a wide-spread conventional use of
        ... introductory thanksgiving," whose function is always "to intro-
        duce the vital theme of the letter." Paul's letters lie halfway be-
        tween epigraphical (i.e., public) documents and private, intimate
        letters.

2085.   Spencer, Aida Besançon. *Paul's Literary Style: A Stylistic and
        Historical Comparison of II Corinthians 11:16–12.13, Romans
        8:9-39, and Philippians 3:2–4:13.* Jackson (Evangelical
        Theological Society), 1984.

        "... Paul adapted his style to the mood of his readers or
        hearers." In II Corinthians 12, Paul "employed an 'indirect' style
        because the Corinthians were not especially receptive to him and
        to his values." The interrelationship of stylistic and historical
        approaches. Analysis of style "through the performance of ten
        stylistic operations.... All three passages have similar subjects,
        exemplify the epistolary genre, discuss similar opponents, and
        address similar situations." Philippians expressive, direct, complex;
        Romans and Corinthians indirect, cautious, rhetorical and
        defensive.

2086.   Stanley, Christopher D. "Paul and Homer: Greco-Roman
        Citation Practice in the First Century C.E." *Nov T* 32
        (1990), 48-78.

        Paul's techniques of citation of, and quotation from, the OT
        conforms not so much to Jewish practice but to the Greco-Roman
        practice of using Homer: a combined/conflated citation, with
        faithfulness to narrative context, and selective and modified quota-
        tion. Paul and his pagan contemporaries show "a near identity of
        conceptions regarding the acceptable parameters for citing literary
        texts."

2087.   Stevens, George B. "The Epistles of Paul as Literature," in #32, pp. 301-317.

Paul's literary style derives not from Greco-Roman rhetorical practice but from his rabbinic training. The allegorical method of reading scripture Paul also got from the rabbinical schools—a fact which somewhat restricts his arguments. More important than stylistic devices, however, is "the vigor and intensity with which he enters into his subject."

2088.   du Toit, A.B. "Hyperbolical Contrasts: A Neglected Aspect of Paul's Style," in #1507, pp. 178-186.

Definition of hyperbolical contrast and its two distinguishable subtypes. Attention to this device helps us interpret otherwise difficult passages in Paul's letters.

2089.   White, John Lee. *The Form and Function of the Body of the Greek Letter: A Study of the Letter-Body in the Non-Literary Papyri and in Paul the Apostle.* Missoula (Scholars P), 1972.

Structural analysis of the body of the Pauline letter as part of a broader literary analysis of the letter. The phraseology, form and function of the private Greek letter, of the Pauline letter, and comparison of the two. There is a variety of opening, middle, and closing formulae in both. Paul's are longer, have additional subdivisions, a more sharply-focused middle, and an additional closing element: the "confidence" formula.

2090.   White, John L. "Introductory Formulae in the Body of the Pauline Letter." *JBL* 90 (1971), 91-7.

To contribute further to the formal identification of the body of the Pauline letter, building on the work of Schubert and Sanders [#s 2083, 2084]. "By observing where the first introductory formula begins and where the last terminates in the body of the Pauline letters," we may provisionally identify the introductory sections of Philemon, Galatians, Romans, I Thessalonians, Philippians, and I and II Corinthians. We may presume that the body of the Pauline letter will in future be analyzed by its formulae as have other parts.

2091.   White, J.L. "New Testament Epistolary Literature in the Framework of Ancient Epistolography." *Aufstieg und Niedergang der Römischen Welt* II 25.2 (1984), 1730-1756.

Definition of different kinds of the ancient letter; their formulae for each part. The typical structure of a Pauline letter and its relationship to his purposes in writing. Greco-Roman influence on Paul, and his influence in turn on other NT letters.

See also: #s 1, 4, 12, 23, 46, 177, 188, 210, 246, 545, 1486, 1490, 1494, 1499, 1500, 1515, 1516, 1528, 1534, 1561, 1888, 2178, 2237.

ROMANS

2092. Aageson, James W. "Scripture and Structure in the Development of the Argument in Romans 9-11." *CBQ* 48 (1986), 265-289.

"... Paul's use of Scripture and the literary structure ... in Romans 9-11 are inseparable and ... together they form the interlacing that binds the discourse into a unity." To investigate these characteristics, then, only theologically "is to obscure Paul's manner of scriptural argumentation...."

2093. Achtemeier, Paul J. "Romans 3:1-8: Structure and Argument." *ATR* Supplementary Series Eleven (March, 1990), 77-87.

The "dialogic-diatribal form" of Paul's argument as well as the rhetorical pattern of these verses, which has hitherto been unnoticed. "Its intention is to educate, not refute...." and it is not, despite previous critics, an *ad hominem* argument.

2094. Biays, Paul M. *Parallelism in Romans.* Fort Hays, Kansas [no publisher given], 1967.

The influence of OT parallelism on Romans, and the most commonly-used kinds. Examples from Romans 4 and 8. We cannot avoid concluding that "parallelism is the major literary characteristic of the epistle to the Romans."

2095. Black, David Alan. "The Pauline Love Command: Structure, Style, and Ethics in Romans 12:9-21." *Filologia Neotestamentaria* 2 (1989), 3-22.

Through a judicious use of such literary techniques as anaphora, asyndeton, isocolon and paronomasia, Paul sought to help "validate [his] ... claim that those who are saved do not perpetuate evil by adding to it but rather demonstrate that faith in Christ goes hand in hand with love toward all the saints and indeed toward all men."

2096. Boguslawski, Steven R. "Romans 15:30-33," in John H. Morgan ed., *Church Divinity 1982* (Notre Dame: Graduate Theological Foundation), 1-15.

Greco-Roman rhetorical theory helps us see that "Paul's use of rhetorical argumentation is indeed powerful and calculated," and that 15:30-33 "is not the conclusion to Romans but rather the 'pathos section' of the peroration."

2097. Donfried, Karl Paul. "False Presuppositions in the Study of Romans." *CBQ* 36 (1974), 332-355.

Attention to the classical literary background of the Pauline letters is important, though it is questionable whether such a genre as the "diatribe" ever existed. We may have in Romans a classical "letter essay," so rhetorical analysis does bear fruit when studying Romans if we use it appropriately.

2098. Elliott, R. Neil. *The Rhetoric of Romans.* Sheffield (Sheffield Academic P), 1990.

Romans is not primarily either an anti-Jewish polemic nor a "source lode" for systematic Pauline theology. It has specific paranetic and rhetorical goals related to the universal gentile church and the specific Roman audience. Paul's argumentative strategy resembles forensic rhetoric of the classical handbooks, especially in its handling of legal and juridical issues. Its beginning and ending correspond to *exordium* and *peroratio*, and its overall deep structure corresponds to the "once-but now" scheme of early Christian paranesis.

2099. Fiore, Benjamin, S.J. "Friendship in the Exhortation of Romans 15:14-33." *PEGL* 7 (1987), 95-103.

"The mode, content, and aim of argumentation in the paranetic section of Romans" are based on the 'friendship' *topos* of classical rhetorical theory. In this way Paul hopes to underscore the importance of mutual love in overcoming nagging divisions in the Christian community."

2100. Fiore, Benjamin, S.J. "Invective in Romans and Philippians." *PEGL* 10 (1990), 181-9.

Romans 2-3 and Philippians 3 use invective, a standard feature in classical oratory, as outlined by Cicero and Quintilian. The point of Pauline invective is not to attack a particular group but "to arouse a common feeling of shocked awareness of universal sinfulness...."

2101.   Fiore, Benjamin, S.J. "Romans 9-11 and Classical Forensic Rhetoric." *PEGL* 8 (1988), 117-126.

"Romans 9-11 is a defense of God's trustworthiness, whose careful elaboration reflects the norms of forensic oratory like those detailed in Quintilian in his *Institutio Oratoria.*" The sermonic style is more intense and sustained here than elsewhere in Romans, partly because of the forensic purpose; when this purpose has been fulfilled, Paul moves on in later chapters to a more hortatory discourse.

2102.   Fraikin, Daniel. "The Rhetorical Function of the Jews in Romans," in Peter Richardson, ed., *Anti-Judaism in Early Christianity, Vol. I: Paul and the Gospels* (Waterloo: Wilfrid Laurier UP, 1986), 91-105.

Romans should be placed in the epideictic rhetorical genre because Paul knows he is addressing an unconvinced audience (Jews, where relevant), and tries to force a new definition of Judaism on them which they would reject. His ambiguity toward them is the result of his awareness of this situation.

2103.   Heil, John Paul. *Paul's Letter to the Romans: A Reader-Response Commentary.* New York and Mahwah (Paulist P), 1987.

"The audience we meet in Romans is not a real ... Roman audience but an implied or intended epistolary audience created ... by the author Paul through the text.... Although Paul meant to address a real, historical Roman Christian audience, he did so by ... imagining ... them in certain rhetorical positions.... [We should be] concerned to determine not how the actual, historical Roman audience may have responded, ... but how the imaginary, implied audience is required or meant to respond to the Letter's rhetorical communication."

2104.   Jewett, Robert. "Following the Argument of Romans." *Word and World* 6 (1986), 382-9.

Romans is a situational letter rather than a doctrinal treatise, and therefore rhetorical method is the most promising way of "grasp[ing] the structure of the argument within the context of the peculiar purpose of the letter so that the rhetoric can be understood on its own terms...." Romans is cast in an Aristotelian form known as "demonstrative rhetoric whose aim is to strengthen the ethos of an audience in a particular direction."

2105.   Jewett, Robert. "Romans as an Ambassadorial Letter." *Interpretation* 36 (1982), 5-20.

We can find in Romans structures of several subtypes of epideictic rhetoric: speech upon disembarking, paranetic and hortatory speech, and the ambassador's speech.

2106. Kirby, John T. "The Syntax of Romans 5.12: A Rhetorical Approach." *NTS* 33 (1987), 283-6.

Rhetorical criticism demonstrates that the usual assumption about 5:12 being a disruptive digression where Paul never resumes his train of thought is inadequate.

2107. Lategan, B.C. "Reception: Theory and Practice in Reading Romans 13," in #1508, pp. 145-169.

Stylistic features and argumentative strategies in Romans 13, as revealed by reader-response criticism. Samples of previous readings compared to discourse analysis theory about reading strategies: actual readings begin to diverge where ambiguities and gaps in the text appear; readings tend to be either "affirmative" or "resistant" in terms of the argument of the chapter.

2108. Scroggs, Robin. "Paul as Rhetorician: Two Homilies in Romans 11," in Robert Hamerton-Kelly and Robin Scroggs, eds., *Jews, Greeks and Christians: Religious Cultures in Late Antiquity* (Leiden: E.J. Brill, 1976), 270-297.

"Not only stylistically but structurally, the rhetorician Paul has been informed by his Jewish and Greek heritages." In verses 1-4 and 9-11 he reworks ancient Jewish patterns, and in verses 5-8 he uses the diatribe structure. Both sections may reflect original appeals in sermon form to Jewish and Hellenistic audiences respectively.

2109. Snyman, A.H. "Style and the Rhetorical Situation of Romans 8.31-39." *NTS* 34 (1988), 218-231.

The function of certain stylistic techniques in meeting the rhetorical situation of Romans 8. The work of George Kennedy as example of the promise of this kind of study for biblical criticism. It can lead to appreciation of the "practical and powerful aspects of religious texts."

* Spencer, Aida Besançon. *Paul's Literary Style: A Stylistic and Historical Comparison of II Corinthians 11:16–12:13, Romans 8:9-39, and Philippians 3:2–4:13.* See #2085.

2110. Stein, Robert H. "The Argument of Romans 13:1-7." *Nov T* 31 (1989), 325-343.

Romans 13:1-7 is "carefully and even meticulously constructed.... [It has] a carefully worked out logical construction, a chiasmic summary in 13:5, a poetic parallelism in 13:7, and an inclusio of imperatives introducing and concluding the passage."

2111.   Stowers, Stanley Kent. *The Diatribe and Paul's Letter to the Romans.* Chico (Scholars P), 1981.

Romans shows a form of address like the diatribe, as well as objections, false conclusions and dialogue which derive from that form. Paul's use of this style is deliberate, and central to his message. He may have adapted it for purely literary purposes, or he may have also employed it in his teaching.

2112.   du Toit, A.B. "Persuasion in Romans 1:1-17." *Biblische Zeitschrift* 33 (1989), 192-209.

Various reasons why we may conclude that Paul was influenced by Greco-Roman rhetoric. Romans 1:1-17 shows a three-part division; its implications for understanding the rest of the letter.

2113.   Via, Dan O., Jr. "A Structuralist Approach to Paul's Old Testament Hermeneutic." *Interpretation* 28 (1974), 201-220.

Paul's use of Deuteronomy 30:11-14 in Romans 9:30-10:21, and his partial misinterpretation of it. The structure of the Romans passage is shaped by Paul's articulation in a comic genre: awareness of the rhythm of upset and recovery. We should remember that comedy is a structure of the human mind.

2114.   Wuellner, Wilhelm. "Paul's Rhetoric of Argumentation in Romans: An Alternative to the Donfried-Karris Debate ...," in Karl Donfried, ed., *The Romans Debate* (Minneapolis: Augsburg P, 1977), 152-174.

The debate over whether Romans requires a specific situation to explain it is unfruitful. Rather, we should study the rhetorical nature of Paul's argumentation as the best way to account for the logical, dialectical, literary and social dimensions of the Romans. Romans seems to belong to the epideictic genre, with the handling of proofs being especially important. Attempts to fit Paul's letters into the ancient letter genres is inferior to the rhetorical approach.

See also: #s 117, 1497, 1500, 1516, 1542, 2065, 2067, 2072, 2078.

I CORINTHIANS

2115. Bailey, Kenneth E. "Paul's Theological Foundation for Human Sexuality: I Cor 6:9-20 in the Light of Rhetorical Criticism." *The Near East School of Theology Theological Review* 3, #1 (April, 1980), 27-41.

I Corinthians 6:9-20 "becomes Paul's all-inclusive foundation for Christian sexual ethics. When seen in its rhetorical form the passage no longer appears 'somewhat disjointed and obscure'.... Rather it surfaces as a literary and theological masterpiece."

2116. Bailey, K.E. "Recovering the Poetic Structure of I Cor i 17-ii 2: A Study in Text and Commentary." *Nov T* 17 (1975), 265-296.

The elaborate chiastic structure of this passage shows it clearly to be a poem, with semantic and other parallelisms as well. Probably Paul borrowed these devices from Aramaic/Syriac poetry. How the various thematic repetitions reveal Paul's theological intent in these verses.

2117. Betz, Hans Dieter. "The Problem of Rhetoric and Theology According to the Apostle Paul," in A. Van Hoye, ed., *L'Apôtre Paul: Personnalité, Style, et Conception du Ministère* (Leuven: Leuven UP, 1986), 16-48.

In I and II Corinthians, I and II Thessalonians, and Galatians, Paul faced a typical Greek problem: the relationship of rhetoric to theology. It was a particularly Corinthian problem which tended to disappear in his later letters. The effectiveness and purpose of the rhetorical formulae in these five letters.

2118. Farla, Piet. "'The Two Shall Become One Flesh': Gen. 1.27 and 2.24 in the New Testament Marriage Texts," in #38, pp. 67-82.

"... the allusion to Genesis 1-3 is conspicuous in Paul's fundamental position with regard to sexuality, [especially in I Corinthians 7].... His point of view is rooted in the Jewish tradition of the creation," as found in Genesis. In Mark 10, "both Genesis texts undergo ... a radical change of meaning, but as quotations ... they bring about a world of meaning in Mark." Matthew 19 brings in a new, non-Markan theme: justice in the church. Ephesians 5 shows Genesis 1-3 having the same meaning as in the gospels: "the ideal of mutual love between husband and wife is founded on God's plan of creation."

2119.   Fiorenza, E.S. "Rhetorical Situation and Historical Recon-
        struction in I Corinthians." *NTS* 33 (1987), 386-403.

        By using rhetorical criticism on I Corinthians, we can help form
        a new critical paradigm out of a combination of literary critical,
        hermeneutical, and socio-political approaches. We do this by fo-
        cusing on the rhetorical situation of a given work. We find this sit-
        uation in reader-response concepts of the implied author and im-
        plied reader.

2120.   Lampe, Peter. "Theological Wisdom and the 'Word About
        the Cross': The Rhetorical Scheme in I Corinthians 1-4."
        Interpretation 44 (1990), 117-131.

        "Thus, as the rhetoric suggests, the *schema* of I Corinthians 1:18-
        2:16 hides a 'ticklish' message behind a seemingly 'harmless' text."
        The Greco-Roman rhetorical rule called for replacing a specific,
        dangerous thought with a general, perhaps "irrelevant" one, which
        is exactly what Paul does. Paul's readers would have known of
        Quintilian's schema and its purpose in his *Institutio Oratoria* 9.2
        and have applauded their own cleverness in detecting the con-
        cealed meaning.

2121.   Lund, N.W. "The Literary Structure of Paul's Hymn to
        Love." *JBL* 50 (1931), 266-276.

        The extent to which chiasmus has shaped the structure of I
        Corinthians 13, and its intimate connections with chapters 12 and
        14. The chiasm is elaborate and intricate, constantly reinforcing
        and expressing the theme and balance of the chapter; in fact, chi-
        asm determines the disposition of material itself.

2122.   Malherbe, Abraham J. "The Beasts at Ephesus." *JBL* 87
        (1968), 71-80.

        I Corinthians 15:32 offers a notorious interpretive crux, as to
        whether to take it literally or figuratively. We are better off
        noticing that some characteristics of the Cynic-Stoic diatribe
        appear in this verse, concentrated to an unusually high degree.
        Paul appropriated its characteristics to his own style.

2123.   Plank, Karl. *Paul and the Irony of Affliction.* Atlanta (Scholars
        P), 1987.

        Paul as a rhetorical poet and a "specific instance of his dis-
        course, his self-description of affliction in 1 Corinthians 4:9-13....
        Paul's language of affliction here embodies a thorough and fun-
        damental irony." The rhetorical situation is both apologetic and
        homiletic: "the way of the cross and the way of irony are one way."
        The purpose of Paul's irony is to restore and enlarge vision, not

destroy it. Paul's language of affliction is forceful and imaginative rather than plain, and makes the reader "vulnerable to the ... power of his paradoxical gospel." **

2124. Smit, J. "The Genre of I Corinthians 13 in the Light of Classical Rhetoric." *Nov T* 33 (1991), 193-216.

Rhetorical analysis of the style, selection, sequence of topics, and rhetorical strategy of I Corinthians 13 shows that it follows the rhetorical handbooks' rules for the genus "demonstrativum." If we recognize its purpose as a devaluation of the charismata, then we can see how it functions in the larger argument of chapters 12-14.

2125. Snyman, A.H. "Remarks on the Stylistic Parallelismus in I Corinthians 13," in #1507, pp. 202-213.

The semiotic meaning of Paul's rhetorical devices "in respect to two relations which they serve to mark"—i.e., parts of a text to each other, and the text to the "participants in the communication." Stylistic analysis of chapter 13 in terms of semantics, rhetorical features and principles in Hellenistic and modern culture.

2126. Templeton, Douglas A. "Paul the Parasite: Notes on the Imagery of 1 Corinthians 15:20-28." *HJ* 26 (1985), 1-4.

Paul was "almost innocent of poetic gifts," but "is parasitic on a poetic tradition" of Xenophanes and Job, thus "making Pauline theology metaphorical by definition." I Corinthians 15 as example.

2127. Wuellner, Wilhelm. "Greek Rhetoric and Pauline Argumentation," in William R. Schoedel and Robert L. Wilken eds., *Early Christian Literature and the Classical Intellectual Tradition* (Paris: Editions Beauchesnes, 1979), 177-188.

Paul's use of digressions in I Corinthians is part of what makes him "self-consciously Greek." The digressions are more than evidences of his style; they are "functionally determined by the rhetorical situation." I Corinthians specifically belongs in the epideictic category.

2128. Wuellner, Wilhelm. "Paul as Pastor: The Function of Rhetorical Questions in First Corinthians," in A. Van Hoye, ed., *L'Apôtre Paul: Personnalité, Style, et Conception du Ministère* (Leuven: Leuven UP, 1986), 49-77.

Paul's rhetorical questions in I Corinthians as related to the rhetorical situation. Their function, the "typology of audiences/readers," appeal to codes and shared values; use of specific argumentative and rhetorical techniques including syllogism and induction. Paul's rhetoric was innovative in three ways: it broke with the status and function of Greco-Roman education; with that system's social patronage; and with its self-esteem and boasting. See also #2068.

2129. Zaas, Peter S. "Catalogues and Context: I Corinthians 5 and 6." *NTS* 34 (1988), 622-9.

Paul's catalogs of vices are not just repetitions from Greco-Roman sources, but specific to each context in which he gives them. They relate his prior moral instruction to the issues taken up in that specific chapter. They are "artfully constructed rhetorical devices."

See also: #s 3, 117, 192, 1491, 1500, 1501, 1516, 1564, 2062, 2065, 2072, 2073, 2078, 2080.

II CORINTHIANS

2130. Belleville, Linda L. "A Letter of Apologetic Self-Commendation: 2 Corinthians 1:8–7:16." *Nov T* 31 (1989), 142-163.

How the epistolary structure of these chapters of II Corinthians fit with the Hellenistic letter tradition. They have an overall chiastic structure; only seeing them as apologetic self-commendation can account for the "movement from disclosure... [to] request...." There are many formal and stylistic parallels with earlier and contemporary rhetorical examples of letters of recommendation; the differences are that Paul speaks from his office, and that his credentials are derivative.

2131. Betz, Hans Dieter. *2 Corinthians 8 and 9: A Commentary on Two Administrative Letters of the Apostle Paul*, ed. George W. MacRae. Philadelphia (Fortress P), 1985.

These chapters are separate, complete Pauline letters showing the literary form, internal structure, and argumentative rhetoric appropriate to ancient letters: exordium, narratio, propositio, probatio, and peroratio.

*   Betz, Hans Dieter. "The Problem of Rhetoric and Theology According to the Apostle Paul." See #2117.

2132. Duff, Paul Brooks. "Metaphor, Motif, and Meaning: The Rhetorical Strategy Behind the Image 'Led in Triumph' in 2 Corinthians 2:14." *CBQ* 53 (1991), 79-92.

Paul's use of the processional metaphor in this verse is an *insinuatio,* one of two recognized strategies for introducing an apologetic text. He even follows the rhetoricians' advice about how to begin this portion of the *prooemium*: he wants "an image which will both adequately account for and vividly portray his suffering."

2133.   Fitzgerald, John T. "Paul, the Ancient Epistolary Theorists, and 2 Corinthians 10-13: The Purpose and Literary Genre of a Pauline Letter," in David L. Balch, et al., eds., *Greeks, Romans, and Christians: Essays in Honor of Abraham J. Malherbe* (Minneapolis: Fortress P, 1990), 190-200.

The hortatory character of II Corinthians 10-13 has not received sufficient emphasis. Its apologetic character cannot be traced to the Socratic model, but belongs in the "broader rhetorical tradition of self-defense," characterized by "accusation" and "reproach" letters in Greco-Roman culture. It was also influenced by the "ironic" and "provoking" letter types.

2134.   Forbes, Christopher. "Comparison, Self-Praise and Irony: Paul's Boasting and the Conventions of Hellenistic Rhetoric." *NTS* 32 (1986), 1-30.

"The close application of the rhetorical conventions of comparison, self-praise and irony to the analysis of II Corinthians 10-12 allows us to understand far more clearly Paul's rhetoric and 'boasting,' and hence his self-understanding in the midst of one of the great crises of his career."

2135.   Patte, Daniel. "A Structural Exegesis of 2 Corinthians 2: 14–7:4 with Special Attention on 2:14–3:6 and 6:11–7:4." *SBLSP* 1987, pp. 23-49.

Semiotics allows us to distinguish among several dimensions of meaning in a text and to see how they interact. Structural exegesis of these chapters of II Corinthians shows us how all its dimensions work together, and bring out Paul's metaphors.

2136.   Sampley, J. Paul. "Paul, His Opponents in 2 Corinthians 10-13, and the Rhetorical Handbooks," in Jacob Neusner, et al., eds., *The Social World of Formative Christianity and Judaism* (Philadelphia: Fortress P, 1988), 162-177.

The standard rhetorical handbooks of Cicero and Quintilian applied to II Corinthians 10-13 to see if Paul "uses the specific rhetorical devices that the handbooks ... advise for winning good will for oneself and undercutting one's opponents." They help explain why he presses his case so hard, why he writes as if expressing himself as madman or fool. In 13, however, he departs from the handbook because he separates his fate from that of the Corinthians.

* Spencer, Aida Besançon. *Paul's Literary Style: A Stylistic and Historical Comparison of II Corinthians 11:16–12:13, Romans 8:9-39, and Philippians 3:2–4:13.* See #2085.

2137. Spencer, Aida Besançon. "The Wise Fool (and the Foolish Wise): A Study of Irony in Paul." *Nov T* 23 (1981), 349-360.

In II Corinthians 11:16–12:13, Paul is sardonic, bitterly ironic—a tone achieved through metaphor, irony, and parallelism. It is difficult to reduce Paul's sentences to their propositions due to the difficulty of reducing metaphors and rhetorical questions to statements.

See also: #s 1491, 1501, 2062, 2065, 2067, 2073, 2078.

GALATIANS

2138. Betz, Hans Dieter. *Galatians: A Commentary on Paul's Letter to the Churches in Galatia.* Philadelphia (Fortress P), 1979.

A commentary organized around categories of Greco-Roman rhetoric and epistolography. Galatians is "an apologetic letter" in that tradition; it consists of exordium, narratio, propositio, probatio, and exhortatio. **

2139. Betz, Hans Dieter. "The Literary Composition and Function of Paul's Letter to the Galatians." *NTS* 21 (1974-5), 353-379.

Galatians can be analyzed according to Greco-Roman rhetoric and epistolography. How such rhetoric and epistolography—especially that recommended by Quintilian—illuminates various questions of organization, allegory, theme, and theology. Galatians falls into the "magical letter" category.

* Betz, Hans Dieter. "The Problem of Rhetoric and Theology According to the Apostle Paul." See #2117.

2140. Bligh, John. *Galatians in Greek: A Structural Analysis of St. Paul's Epistle to the Galatians with Notes on the Greek.* [Detroit] (U of Detroit P), 1966.

The Greek text of Galatians, with English translation opposite, laid out as a "primary chiasm." Diagram subdivides the letter into three "secondary chiasms," each in turn subdivided into "tertiary" and then into "quartan" chiasms. Paul employed chiastic composition "with care and skill," and (like other ancient authors) did so "both from sheer delight in verbal artistry and as a mnemonic device."

2141. Briggs, Sheila. "'Buried with Christ': The Politics of Identity and the Poverty of Interpretation," in #45, pp. 276-303.

In the light of Marxist literary theory, the problem of how Paul's claims that Christianity dissolves traditional social class, gender, and power distinctions were understood by early Christians. With Galatians 3:28 as starting point, we may conclude that there is an intimate link between interpreting a text and understanding (and changing) social relationships. This is true even if we can never know how ancient Christians understood Galatians 3, nor can ever liberate them ourselves.

2142. Brinsmead, Bernard Hungerford. *Galatians—Dialogical Response to Opponents.* Chico (Scholars P), 1982.

The dialogical nature of Galatians as literature, the structure of its arguments, and its genre. Externally, it is a "dialogical response to opponents," and internally its unity of argument is shown by its themes and its antitheses (diatribe). Galatians follows the standard structure of a Greco-Roman argument in opposing the opponents' traditions about apostleship, Abraham, law, sacraments, and ethics.

2143. Calloway, Joseph Sevier. "Paul's Letter to the Galatians and Plato's *Lysis.*" *JBL* 67 (1948), 353-5.

The "patent similarity in ideas and even the language" of Galatians and of *Lysis* seems noteworthy; it suggests the possibility that Paul was "dimly remembering" Plato.

2144. Cronje, J. Van W. "Defamiliarization in the Letter to the Galatians," in #1507, pp. 214-227.

"Reading the *Letter to the Galatians* from a stylistic point of view, one is struck by the impact achieved by various stylistic devices or techniques.... [T]he special effect of this letter is achieved due to the fact that most of its special stylistic features have one common denominator: the unexpected."

2145.   Hall, Robert G. "The Rhetorical Outline for Galatians: A Reconsideration." *JBL* 106 (1987), 277-287.

Galatians fits squarely into the "deliberative" species of classical rhetoric. Seeing this permits a grasp of Paul's unified purpose in the letter.

2146.   Hansen, G. Walter. *Abraham in Galatians: Epistolary and Rhetorical Contexts.* Sheffield (JSOT P), 1989.

We cannot resolve interpretive cruxes in Galatians until we understand its rhetorical structure and the development of its argument. The Abraham references in 3:6-29 and 4:21-31 are the key to the letter.The significant shift from forensic to deliberative rhetoric at 4:12, and the chiastic structure of 3:1–4:11 both help clarify Paul's themes. We must modify existing methods of epistolary and rhetorical analysis of Galatians, since we find evidence of argument by authority, definition, dissociation, enthymeme and transitivity—all influences from pagan Greek letters of the "rebuke-request" type.

2147.   Hays, Richard B. *The Faith of Jesus Christ: An Investigation of the Narrative Substructure of Galatians 3:1–4:11.* Chico (Scholars P), 1983.

"... Paul returns repeatedly to a narrative structure which operates as a constant factor in his efforts to wrestle through the practical and theological issues raised by the Galatians crisis.... In the shape and sequence of this story, Paul finds warrants which authorize his theological statements and constraints which pose limits to the logic of his argument."

2148.   Hester, James D. "The Rhetorical Structure of Galatians 1:11–2:14." *JBL* 103 (1984), 223-233.

Hans D. Betz's explanation of the rhetorical structure of Galatians 1-2 as "heavenly letter" may need modification. If we see that 2:11-14 serves as a digression (which in ancient rhetoric can be a distinct section) after the narratio, then it is "structurally and functionally separate from 1:15–2:10." This in turn means that the narratio is closer to having the brevity which classical rhetoricians require.

2149.   Hester, James D. "The Use and Influence of Rhetoric in Galatians 2:1-14." *TZ* 42 (1986), 386-408.

What the tradition of Greco-Roman rhetoric tells us about generic problems in Paul's letters. Rhetorical criticism needs to be concerned with much more than style. "We must take more seriously the possibility that Paul understood the dynamic of his letters as speeches." The argumentative situation of Galatians; topoi and figures in the narratio (1:15-2:10) and the digressio (2:11-14). "We must take into account the interplay of situation, topoi, figures, tropes, semantics, syntax, grammar and vocabulary" to understand how they function to persuade readers.

2150.   Koptak, Paul E. "Rhetorical Identification in Paul's Autobiographical Narrative. Galatians 1.13–2.14." *JSNT* 40 (1990), 97-113.

The literary-rhetorical method of Kenneth Burke applied to "the relationships that Paul portrays and creates with the Jerusalem apostles, his opponents, and the Galatians...." How Paul depicted these relationships within the autobiographical narrative as a way of enhancing his ties with the Galatians: he depicted a "community created by a common response to the gospel," forced them to choose, and used the principle of identification.

2151.   Kraftchick, Steven J. "Why do the Rhetoricians Rage?" in Theodore W. Jennings, ed., *Text and Logos: The Humanistic Interpretation of the New Testament* (Atlanta: Scholars P, 1990), 55-79.

Review of various recent contributions to the study of rhetoric of and in Galatians. Most fruitful for future study is Perelman's "new rhetoric" as exemplified in his *Realms of Rhetoric.* It will move us closer to the core convictions of his [Paul's] thought."

2152.   Lategan, Bernard C. "Levels of Reader Instructions in the Text of Galatians." *Semeia* 48 (1989), 171-184.

Four levels of the text which contain instructions to the reader in Galatians: syntacto-rhetorical, cultural code, semantic universe of the text, and development of a participatory ethics.

2153.   Smit, Joop. "The Letter of Paul to the Galatians: A Deliberative Speech." *NTS* 35 (1989), 1-26.

A theory of the structure of Galatians based on the rhetorical requirements of the deliberative speech in Greco-Roman rhetoric: a speech which set forth what course of action should be followed.

See also: #s 1497, 1501, 1504, 2065, 2067.

EPHESIANS

2154.   Cameron, P.S. "The Structure of Ephesians." *Filologia Neotestamentaria* 3 (1990), 3-17.

"Ephesians is constructed on an extraordinarily intricate pattern, ... [consisting] of eight pairs of parallel panels, enclosed within a palistrophic envelope ...; one of each pair of parallel panels is also constructed palistrophically; and the letter as a whole itself forms a palistrophe." This intricate structure suggests that Ephesians is not (as is usually charged) diffuse, repetitive, and undisciplined; it bears on our theological understanding of the book as well.

See also: #s 1500, 2073, 2118.

PHILIPPIANS

2155.   Alexander, Loveday. "Hellenistic Letter-Forms and the Structure of Philippians." *JSNT* 37 (1989), 87-101.

Philippians seems to have been particularly influenced by the "family letter" form identified by John L. White. By chapter 3, however, Paul has moved beyond secular letter forms. This analysis "provides an indispensable framework for understanding the progression of thought in chapters 1 and 2, ... signals the centrality of 1.12 to the main message ... [and reveals] a deep unity of thought between chapter 2 and chapter 3...."

2156.   Combrink, H.J. Bernard, Detlev Dormeyer, and James W. Volz. [Responses to Wolfgang Schenk, *Die Philiperbriefe des Paulus*]. *Semeia* 48 (1989), 135-169.

Schenk's reader-response approach to Philippians is valuable in breaking new ground, but clings too much to traditional text-centered analysis.

2157.   Dalton, William J. "The Integrity of Philippians." *Biblica* 60 (1979), 97-102.

Philippians is not a compilation; and even if we could prove that it was, it was read early on as a unity, and therefore we should read it that way.

*   Fiore, Benjamin, S.J. "Invective in Romans and Philippians." See #2100.

2158.   Garland, David E. "The Composition and Unity of Philippians: Some Neglected Literary Factors." *Nov T* 27 (1985), 141-173.

Review of arguments for and against seeing Philippians as a unity. Recognizing the presence of *inclusio* and *digressio* helps us see that it is indeed a unity.

2159.   Robbins, Charles J., C.P.P.S. "Rhetorical Structure of Philippians 2:6-11." *CBQ* 42 (1980), 73-82.

"Phil 2:6-11 could have been written according to the principles of classical rhetoric, since it conforms to all the principles of periodic structure set forth by the classical authors themselves."

2160.   Russell, Ronald. "Pauline Letter Structure in Philippians." *JETS* 25 (1982), 295-306.

There is as much irregularity as there is regularity in the Pauline letter form. He adapts the Greek letter to unique Christian purposes. The working model must be flexible for Paul because he does not adhere rigidly to one form; that is a natural concomitant to letter-writing.

*   Spencer, Aida Besançon. *Paul's Literary Style: A Stylistic and Historical Comparison of II Corinthians 11:16-12:13, Romans 8:9-39, and Philippians 3:2-4:13.* See #2085.

2161.   Watson, Duane F. "A Rhetorical Analysis of Philippians and its Implications for the Unity Question." *Nov T* 30 (1988), 57-88.

Rhetorical criticism can make important contributions to understanding the unity of Philippians. Outline of the exordium, narratio, probatio, etc., shows that they all are in accordance with ancient rhetoric, despite apparent discontinuities.

See also: 1500, 2062, 2065, 2072, 2078, 2080.

COLOSSIANS

2162. Baugh, Steven M. "The Poetic Form of Col 1:15-20." *WTJ* 47 (1985), 227-244.

The overall pattern of Colossians 1:15-20 is a simple chiasm like much OT poetry and prose. Other explanations of its structure and why they are less satisfactory. Comparison with Hellenistic verse shows that the Colossians passage is not Greek. Thematic and formal elements of chapter 1.

2163. Botha, Jan. "A Stylistic Analysis of the Christ Hymn (Colossians 1:15-20)," in #1507, pp. 238-251.

Detailed analysis of this passage "confirms its hymnic character" and its "aesthetic and emotional quality." The poetic structure of the passage emphasizes theme, creates aesthetic attraction, and communicates ideas in ways that prose could not.

2164. Pickering, Wilbur. *A Framework for Discourse Analysis*. Dallas (Summer Institute of Linguistics), 1978, 1980.

Outline of a framework of discourse analysis in terms of hierarchy, cohesion, prominence, style, strategy, and medium, language and culture. Application of the framework to Colossians and a "complete and precise display of the hierarchical structure of the text."

2165. van der Watt, J.G. "Colossians 1:3-12 Considered as an Exordium." *JTSA* #57 (December, 1986), 32-42.

Explanation of the exordium in classical rhetoric. "Paul's letter to the Colossians reflects the two main stylistic 'techniques' associated with the exordium by Aristotle," and knowing this makes his theological points clearer.

2166. Wright, N.T. "Poetry and Theology in Colossians 1.15-20." *NTS* 36 (1970), 444-468.

This passage exhibits a clear poetic structure; read as a poem, it "exhibits a characteristically Pauline form of ...Christological monotheism.... [T]he poem clearly transfers to Christ language and predicates which had ... belonged in Judaism to Wisdom and Torah."

See also: #s 1500, 2073, 2078.

I THESSALONIANS

* Betz, Hans Dieter. "The Problem of Rhetoric and Theology According to the Apostle Paul." See # 2117.

2167. Jewett, Robert. *The Thessalonian Correspondence: Pauline Rhetoric and Millenarian Piety.* Philadelphia (Fortress P), 1986.

A "well-disguised audience hypothesis is required to explain the peculiar context of the Thessalonian letters." The detailed rhetorical structure of I and II Thessalonians is tightly organized by Greco-Roman standards and expectations. Historical/theological as well as literary-critical.

2168. Johanson, Bruce C. *To All The Brethren: A Text-Linguistic and Rhetorical Approach to I Thessalonians.* Stockholm (Almqvist and Wiksell International), 1987.

I Thessalonians as an act of communication from the standpoint of rhetoric, literary theory and textlinguistics. Its "rhetorical-persuasive function" dominates other functions. Its unity is demonstrated through the overall rhetorical coherence of the text. It shows evidence of "rich intertextuality of overlapping structures and functions common to ancient Greek letters and to rhetorical-persuasive discourse...."

2169. Malbon, Elizabeth Struthers. "'No Need To Have Anyone Write?' A Structural Exegesis of 1 Thessalonians." *SBLSP* 1980, pp. 301-335; rpt *Semeia* 26 (1985) [#2023], 57-83.

Explanation of both syntagmatic and paradigmatic structure of the letter. Narrative and epistolary texts are basically similar as texts; I Thessalonians "suggests that communication is an ongoing action, not a static state...."

2170. Olbricht, Thomas H. "An Aristotelian Rhetorical Analysis of 1 Thessalonians," in Daniel L. Balch, et al., eds., *Greeks, Romans, and Christians: Essays in Honor of Abraham J. Malherbe* (Minneapolis: Fortress P, 1990), 216-236.

As applied to I Thessalonians, Aristotelian rhetoric involves proofs, style, and arrangement. Rhetorical influence on Paul is more likely to have been Greek than Roman. Paul started from Aristotle, but in effect invented from him a new genre, "church rhetoric." He works "in the classic Aristotelian manner," using very little *pathos*, much *logos*. On balance, some stylistic elements of this letter are Aristotelian, some are not.

2171.   Patte, Daniel. "Method for a Structural Exegesis of Didactic Discourses. Analysis of 1 Thessalonians." *Semeia* 26 (1986) [#2023], 85-129.

A method "aimed at elucidating the 'system of convictions' ... of didactic texts, such as Paul's letters." Characteristics of didactic (as opposed to narrative) discourses; the methodology applied to I Thessalonians. This letter is representative of the type of didactic discourse Paul writes, but we should not necessarily expect that all such discourses will involve the same manipulations of syntactic and semantic structures.

See also: #s 1497, 2065, 2072, 2078.

II THESSALONIANS

*   Betz, Hans Dieter. "The Problem of Rhetoric and Theology According to the Apostle Paul." See #2117.

2172.   Hughes, Frank Witt. *Early Christian Rhetoric and 2 Thessalonians*. Sheffield (Sheffield Academic P), 1989.

The problems of authorship and purpose of II Thessalonians. It is best understood as a pseudopauline letter. How traditional Greco-Roman rhetoric influenced the writing of ancient letters; how we may understand II Thessalonians according to these rhetorical and structural traditions. The rhetoric of the book is a polemical response to theological conflict following Paul's death.

*   Jewett, Robert. *The Thessalonian Correspondence: Pauline Rhetoric and Millenarian Piety*. See #2167.

2173.   Sumney, Jerry L. "The Bearing of a Pauline Rhetorical Pattern on the Integrity of 2 Thessalonians." *ZNW* 81 (1990), 192-204.

"Since 2 Thessalonians 1,3–3,5 does fit the A B A pattern, we have a positive argument for its integrity.... Additionally, this pattern supports identifying 2,13–3,5 as the proper way to divide 2 Thessalonians rather than seeing the major break at 2,16 or 3,1. Since this rhetorical pattern is Pauline, its presence offers some support for the authenticity of 2 Thessalonians."

See also: #s 1497, 2078.

I TIMOTHY

2174. Bush, Peter G. "A Note on the Structure of 1 Timothy." *NTS* 36 (1990), 152-6.

A careful examination of the artistry, the literary and rhetorical devices of I Timothy shows its differences from Titus, its unity (against those who have denied it), and its structure based on the inclusio.

See also: #s 1754, 2080.

II TIMOTHY

See #2080.

TITUS

See #2174.

PHILEMON

2175. Church, F. Forrester. "Rhetorical Structure and Design in Paul's Letter to Philemon." *HTR* 71 (1978), 17-34.

In Philemon Paul "employed basic tactics of persuasion taught and widely practiced in his day," though it shows no trace of the dialogic style. Philemon belongs to deliberative (as versus epideictic or forensic) rhetoric.

2176. Petersen, Norman R. *Rediscovering Paul: Philemon and the Sociology of Paul's Narrative World.* Philadelphia (Fortress P), 1985.

We can integrate contemporary literary and sociological approaches to the Bible with traditional historical-critical method. We must recognize that letters have stories, and that events are "reemplotted" in the writing of the letters in rhetorically significant ways. Philemon as a point of departure for exploring Paul's "narrative world."

2177.   Snyman, A.H. "A Semantic Discourse Analysis of the Letter to Philemon," in #1508, 83-99.

Survey of various types of discourse analysis of biblical texts and their chief practitioners in the past two decades. Colon analysis, a branch of discourse analysis, can help us inquire about the cohesion of Philemon in order to outline the parts and describe the direction of the argument. We find in Philemon cola of introduction and conclusion, and four more which form the body of the letter, revealing an argument of basic statement and inference.

See also: #s 1500, 2065, 2072, 2078.

OTHER LETTERS

*   Cladder, H.J. "Strophical Structure in St Jude's Epistle." See #2224.

*   Doty, William G. "The Classification of Epistolary Literature." See #1528.

*   Doty, William G. *Letters in Primitive Christianity.* See #2061.

2178.   Fiore, Benjamin. *The Function of Personal Example in the Socratic and Pastoral Epistles.* Rome (Biblical Institute P), 1986.

Various stylistic, structural and formal features of the pastoral epistles. Rhetorical analysis identifies them as belonging to the hortatory genre, which is especially strong in antithesis and example. The theory of hortatory rhetoric in the Greco-Roman world, especially the use of example in the Socratic letters, in Paul, and in the pastoral epistles. These epistles "attest the capacity of Christianity to absorb the best of its surroundings in content as well as in form."

* Josipovici, Gabriel. "The Epistle to the Hebrews and the Catholic Epistles." See #2189.

See also: #s 177, 188, 1515, 1528, 1658, 2091.

HEBREWS

2179. Attridge, Harold W. "The Uses of Antithesis in Hebrews 8-10." *HTR* 79 (1986), 1-9.

Hebrews represents a "complex case of both the appropriation and the rejection of [the Jewish] heritage." This is shown by an analysis of the literary techniques by which Paul appropriates the Yom Kippur ritual.

2180. Attridge, Harold W. "The Uses of Antithesis in Hebrews 8-10," in George W.E. Nickelsburg and George W. MacRae, S.J., eds., *Christians Among Jews and Gentiles* (Philadelphia: Fortress P, 1986), 1-9.

"A striking feature" of Hebrews 8-10, as seen through analysis of its surface structure, is the use throughout of "certain fundamental antitheses." Surprisingly, at a decisive point in the letter, "there is a reversal in the polarity of the antithetical pattern and ... the spiritual ... is seen to be earthly as well as heavenly."

2181. Black, David Alan. "Hebrews 1:1-4: A Study in Discourse Analysis." *WTJ* 49 (1987), 175-194.

Modern linguistics contributes to biblical studies a renewed appreciation of the importance of context and situation for meaning. The first four verses of Hebrews "possess the most refined and literary piece of theological argument in the whole of the NT." Stylistic analysis and colon structure-based discourse analysis: semantic and syntactic, then rhetorical.

2182. Black, David Alan. "The Problem of the Literary Structure of Hebrews: An Evaluation and a Proposal." *GTJ* 7 (1986), 163-177.

The structure of Hebrews is uniquely complex. The traditional approach to the book divides it into doctrinal and practical matter; the detailed literary approach of A. Van Hoye, and the "patchwork" approach are two other ways of going about the analysis. Van Hoye's seems to be the preferable one: he finds Hebrews to be an "intricate theme woven in an intricate style."

2183.   Bligh, John. *Chiastic Analysis of the Epistle to the Hebrews.* Oxford (Athaeneum P of Heythrop College), 1966.

The Greek text of Hebrews laid out as a series of primary and secondary chiasms. Chapters and verses numbered; no translation of the text.

2184.   Bligh, John, S.J. "The Structure of Hebrews." *HJ* 5 (1964), 170-178.

Review and evaluation of "competing" theories about the structure of Hebrews.

2185.   Cosby, Michael R. *The Rhetorical Composition and Function of Hebrews 11 In Light of Example Lists in Antiquity.* Macon (Mercer UP), 1988.

"... the author of Hebrews consciously implemented artistic use of language in his efforts at persuasion...." Hebrews, especially chapter 11, in the light of ancient rhetoric—specifically the lists of famous or infamous people in Greco-Roman, Jewish, and first-century Christian literatures. Identification and analysis of such rhetorical techniques as anaphora, asyndeton, polysyndeton, antithesis, and hyperbole in Hebrews provides "new and valuable insights" into the author's intention.

2186.   Cosby, Michael R. "The Rhetorical Composition of Hebrews 11." *JBL* 107 (1988), 257-273.

"Through anaphora, asyndeton, polysyndeton, paronomasia, repeated clausal structure, rhetorical questions, and explicit assertions, the authors of these lists sought to make their evidence more persuasive.... [Thus, the] attention to careful selection and ordering of words is especially important in the study of Hebrews 11, whose original effectiveness depended heavily on the auditory impact of the ... eighteen exempla in 11:3-31."

2187.   Freyne, Seán. "Reading Hebrews and Revelation Intertextually," in #38, pp. 83-93.

"The new Jerusalem of Hebrews will be a lasting city, whereas that of Revelation will be without a temple. Both would appear to have the actual post-70 situation in view.... Thus, both works are grounded in a more general discursive exercise ... taking place both inside and outside Judaism in the wake of the crisis that the destruction of that 'famous city' had precipitated." That fact, plus the "performative intention of both works as revealed in their overall rhetorical strategies," shows the value of intertextual analysis.

2188. Horning, Estella B. "Chiasmus, Creedal Structure, and Christology in Hebrews 12:1-2." *BR* 23 (1978), 37-48.

These verses are pivotal ones in Hebrews, manifesting many characteristics of NT creedal formulae, as well as a chiastic structure used to intensify the focus.

2189. Josipovici, Gabriel. "The Epistle to the Hebrews and the Catholic Epistles," in #33, pp. 503-522.

"It is in Hebrews ... that we find the most powerful and inclusive attempts to read the Hebrew Scriptures from a particular point of view. No one, reading it, is ever likely to be able to read what comes before it in the Bible in quite the same way again.... [I]t ... mirrors for us what is involved in the reading and interpreting of any text." Hebrews seriously misreads the HB, "draining the vocabulary [of Hebrew culture] of its original meaning." Incidental references to the Catholic letters.

2190. Koops, Robert. "Chains of Contrasts in Hebrews 1." *BT* 34 (1983), 220-225.

Chains of contrasts are thematically important in Hebrews 1, though sometimes hidden or not clearly stated. Examples of such chains are "honor/submission" and "servant/ruler."

2191. Lindars, Barnabas. "The Rhetorical Structure of Hebrews." *NTS* 35 (1989), 382-406.

We must determine the class of rhetoric to which the book belongs, the intended effect upon its readers, and its essentially rhetorical character. The audience of Hebrews were probably converts from Hellenistic Judaism. Because the aim of the book is practical—to call the hearers back to apostolic faith—the climax occurs at chapters 10-12, not 7-10.

2192. Lowrie, Samuel T. "The Epistle to the Hebrews," in #32, pp. 321-339.

Hebrews has a "cultured style and literary form" probably derived from the stages of the ritual for the Great Day of Atonement as found in Leviticus 16. Since literary form "is necessarily determined by the public for whom it is meant," Hebrews appears to be addressed to Jewish Christians. It is "rhetorical, ... direct, ... and dramatic."

2193.   MacLeod, David J. "The Literary Structure of the Book of
        Hebrews." *B Sac* 146 (1989), 185-197.

        Of the various literary devices in Hebrews which scholars have
        identified, "announcements," "hook words," and "alternation of
        genres" seem to be primary. The structure contains five main sec-
        tions. In terms of diction, the author's use of comparatives, terms
        denoting finality, and a fortiori arguments are the main devices
        which make the message clear.

2194.   Miller, Merland Ray. "What is the Literary Form of Hebrews
        11?" *JETS* 29 (1986), 411-417.

        There are three literary elements common to Hebrews 11 and
        Jewish literature: historical summary, example series, and catch-
        word. The presence of all these shows that this chapter is an en-
        comium on Jesus.

2195.   Neeley, Linda Lloyd. "A Discourse Analysis of Hebrews."
        OPTAT 1, #s 3-4 (September, 1987), 1-146.

        Criteria for dividing Hebrews into embedded discourses and
        paragraphs, for differentiating "backbone" from "support" mate-
        rial, for creating objective summaries, for deciding the "overall
        constituent structure" of the book.

2196.   Rice, George E. "Apostasy as a Motif and its Effects on the
        Structure of Hebrews." *AUSS* 23 (1985), 29-35.

        Recent debate over the structure of Hebrews; a suggested new
        one based on factors previously overlooked. Despite some pres-
        ence of chiasm, the overall structure appears to be based on con-
        tent: specifically, the five "warning passages" about apostasy.

2197.   Robinson, D.W.B. "The Literary Structure of Hebrews 1:1-
        4." *Australian Journal of Biblical Archaeology* 2 (1972), 178-
        186.

        The structure of Hebrews 1:1-4 is chiastic; this, together with its
        allusions to Psalms 2 and 110 "firmly sandwich the whole section
        together," showing it to be a unity and careful prologue to the rest
        of the letter.

2198.   Swetnam, James. "Form and Content in Hebrews 1-6." *Bib-
        lica* 53 (1972), 368-385.

        The principal formal criteria peculiar to the content of chapters
        1-6 are "announcement," "genre," and "length." It divides itself
        into three sections: 1:5–2:18 is exposition: Christ as divine and
        human; 3:1–4:13 is exhortation: of Christ's divinity leading to faith;
        4:14–6:20 is exhortation: of Christ's humanity leading to hope.

2199. Swetnam, J. "Form and Content in Hebrews 7-13." *Biblica* 55 (1974), 333-348.

The three sections are: 7:1–10:18, 10:19–39, and 11:1–13:21. Based, as is #2198, on the assumption that intelligible patterns are not chance but design. The pattern influences our understanding of the content (so long as the patterns are really "there" for the intended first audience). The issue is not certainty, but rather what combination of form and content seems most plausible.

2200. Vanhoye, Albert, S.J. *Structure and Message of the Epistle to the Hebrews.* Rome (Éditrice Pontificio Istituto Biblico), 1989.

From the very first sentence of Hebrews, we can see how artistically balanced the work is, how concerned the author was with writing well. Its most obvious characteristic is its careful concentric structure, with the idea of Christ as high priest at its structural and thematic center (9:11-14), and a clear exordium and peroration. Includes a "structured translation" of the book.

See also: #s 4, 14, 117, 188, 1491, 1501, 1515.

JAMES

* Cladder, H.J. "Strophical Structure in St Jude's Epistle." See #2224.

* Fitzmyer, Joseph A., S.J. "Some Notes on Aramaic Epistolography." See #1473.

2201. Francis, Fred O. "The Form and Function of the Opening and Closing Paragraphs of James and I John." *ZAW* 61 (1970), 110-126.

"Scholarship must reassess the literary character of the epistles of James and I John in the light of what would appear to be carefully styled opening thematic statements, a recognizable epistolary close, and the rather substantial literary-thematic coherence of the epistles as a whole."

2202. Fry, Evan. "The Testing of Faith: A Study of the Structure of the Book of James." *BT* 29 (1978), 427-435.

The main themes of James and how they relate to each other. James is structured on an ABA pattern, and is thus not the unstructured book which many have supposed.

2203. Schökel, Luis Alonso. "James 5,2 [error for "5,6"?] and 4,6." *Biblica* 54 (1973), 73-6.

We need to recognize in James 4:6 a stylistic device called "thematic announcement"; it is echoed in 5:6. "Stylistically, a rhetorical question makes an excellent conclusion for the rhetorical speech...." and emphasizes and creates a powerful irony.

2204. Songer, Harold S. "The Literary Character of James." *Review and Expositor* 66 (1969), 379-389.

The literary character of James in terms of form and content. Major characteristics of hortatory speech appear in the book. James is parenetic in the tradition of Jewish and Greco-Roman moral teaching, and follows those characteristics. That is, it is typical of parenetic literature to stress what we do, not what we believe.

See also: #1515.

I PETER

2205. Achtemeier, Paul L. "Newborn Babes and Living Stones: Literal and Figurative in 1 Peter," in Maurya P. Horgan and Paul J. Kobelski, eds., *To Touch the Text: Biblical and Related Studies in Honor of Joseph A. Fitzmyer, S.J.* (New York: Crossroad, 1989), 207-236.

The consensus is now that I Peter "represents a literary unity with no particular relation to an earlier baptismal liturgy or homily...." The probable date and social situation of the letter; various figures (mainly metaphors and analogies) which illuminate the theme. Its structure is based on an antithesis between past and present.

2206. Brooks, O.S. "I Peter 3:21—The Clue to the Literary Structure of the Epistle." *Nov T* 16 (1974), 290-305.

I Peter is a baptismal tract or instructional sermon whose literary design is held together by 3:21. "Its literary design is to focus attention on baptism as that moment when the convert openly declares that he understands his new life...." It is carefully constructed to show the entire scope of the relationship between God and the convert.

2207. Combrink, H.J.B. "The Structure of 1 Peter." *Neotestamentica* 9 (1975), 34-63.

Discourse analysis of I Peter reveals a chiastic structure overall, with smaller chiasms within the separate sections. The theme leads us from "God gives everything," to a consideration of conduct and suffering, to "God gives us power."

* Fitzmyer, Joseph A., S.J. "Some Notes on Aramaic Epistolography." See #1473.

2208. Kendall, David W. "The Literary and Theological Function of 1 Peter 1:3-12," in Charles H. Talbert, ed., *Perspectives on First Peter* (Macon: Mercer UP, 1986), 103-120.

The literary and theological relationship between I Peter 1:3-12 and 1:13-5:11. The former passage serves to introduce the epistle as a whole, and is a foundation for its three exhortations: 1:13-2:10 (implications of Christian existence); 2:11-4:11 (ways in which holiness, love and election are to be expressed); and 4:12-5:11 (synthesis of main themes, and threefold reiteration of the author's instructions). Thus, verses 3-12 are a declaration about life in grace, while 1:13-5:11 is a parenesis about being God's people in a hostile world. This makes the epistle a unity, though not in the theme of baptism, as many critics have argued.

2209. Schutter, William L. *Hermeneutic and Composition in I Peter.* Tübingen (J.C.B. Mohr [Paul Siebeck]), 1989.

The literary design of I Peter as evidence for its methods of using the OT. Psalm 34 is less formative in the composition of I Peter than has been supposed. 1:13-2:10 seems dependent on contemporary Jewish homiletic midrash as its guide for reading the OT, while the holiness theme seems drawn from Leviticus 19:2ff. The "statement on Hermeneutics" of 1:10-12 has its origin "in sectarian Judaism with a decidedly apocalyptic orientation." The author also makes extensive literary use of Isaiah and Ezekiel.

2210. du Toit, A.B. "The Significance of Discourse Analysis for New Testament Interpretation and Translation: Introductory Remarks with Special Reference to 1 Peter 1:3-13." *Neotestamentica* 8 (1974), 54-79.

Values of discourse analysis for studying the NT are that it helps us demarcate pericopes more accurately while supplying correct captions for them; and gives us insights into syntactical composition, and into the overall arguments of a book. Such analysis shows I Peter 1:3-13 to be a definite pericope whose argument is: "You have received a glorious expectation of things to come: praise God and rejoice in spite of affliction."

See also: #1515.

II PETER

2211.   Watson, Duane Frederick. *Invention, Arrangement, and Style: Rhetorical Criticism of Jude and 2 Peter.* Atlanta (Scholars P), 1988.

Separate chapters on the two books. Implications of rhetorical criticism for the argument over the literary integrity of II Peter; dependency of both epistles on Greco-Roman rhetoric. While they both show extensive familiarity with this rhetoric, the rhetoric of II Peter "seems much more the product of study. He outshines Jude, both in inventional and in stylistic finesse." Rhetorical analysis shows some dependency of one epistle on the other, but does not enable us to say which one is prior.

See also: #1515.

I JOHN

2212.   Feuillet, Andre. "The Structure of First John." *BTB* 3 (1973), 194-216.

The problem of the relationship between the gospel of John and the letter, I John, can be illuminated if we compare their literary structures, which are strikingly alike. The structure of the latter has been much debated. Detailed explication of I John shows how similarity of form follows doctrinal similarities. The two works are alike in arguing for a certain conception of the Christian life; each helps explain the conundrums of the other.

*   Francis, Fred O. "The Form and Function of the Opening and Closing Paragraphs of James and I John." See #2201.

2213.   du Rand, J.A. "A Discourse Analysis of 1 John." *Neotestamentica* 13 (1979), 1-42.

Discourse analysis reveals the structure of I John as other methods have been unable to do. It has five main sections which accentuate the themes of certainty as "subjective moment," and fellowship as "objective moment," and of the leading motif of the possession of eternal life.

2214.   Thompson, P.J. "Psalm 119: A Possible Clue to the Structure of the First Epistle of John," in F.L. Cross, ed., *Studia Evangelica II, Part One* (Berlin: Akademie-Verlag, 1964), 487-492.

The author of I John consciously patterned the structure and themes of his epistle on Psalm 119, as evidenced by their shared use of key words, strophic structure, parallelism, subject matter, and the Pleroma.

2215.   Watson, Duane F. "I John 2.12-14 as *Distributio, Conduplicatio,* and *Expolitio*: A Rhetorical Understanding." *JSNT* 35 (1989), 97-110.

These verses form a rhetorical unit; rhetorical analysis reveals the repetitions and their purpose. We need to recognize the presence of these three rhetorical devices: they are there for purposes of "amplific," or "appeal to pity" and the development of topics; they show how it is to be done in a particular way.

See also: #s 117, 2217, 2219.

II JOHN

2216.   Funk, Robert W. "The Form and Structure of II and III John." *JBL* 86 (1967), 424-430. Rpt as chapter 8 of #1658.

Little has been achieved in establishing the form and structure of the early Christian letter, perhaps due to our failure to extend the study to the letters' relationship with papyri. Marks of the connection can be found in II and III John, especially the former, which conforms with the papyri in many structural and stylistic ways. III John is the most secularized book of the NT, though it is also more Pauline than II John.

2217.   du Rand, J.A. "Structure and Message of 2 John." *Neotesta-
        mentica* 13 (1979), 101-120.

        II John contains characteristics of a typical Hellenistic letter, and
        these "play a decisive role in the analysis." Discourse analysis re-
        veals five sections, each with various subsections. The theme is an
        argument concentrating on two concerns: confession that God be-
        came man, and the ethical requirement to love one another. Such
        structural analysis also shows a definite relationship between II
        John and I John.

2218.   Watson, Duane F. "A Rhetorical Analysis of 2 John Accord-
        ing to Greco-Roman Convention." *NTS* 35 (1989), 104-
        130.

        II and III John conform more closely to Greco-Roman epistolary
        format than do any other NT epistles. Following the rhetorical
        method of George Kennedy, we may outline the structure of II
        John as a deliberative speech and a paraenetic-advisory letter.

2219.   Wendland, E.R. "What is Truth? Semantic Density and the
        Language of the Johannine Epistles (with Special Refer-
        ence to 2 John)." *Neotestamentica* 24 (1990), 301-333.

        Deliberate ambiguity, or semantic density, is likely present in II
        John, as revealed by discourse analysis. Translators should try
        whenever possible to find equivalents for this composite meaning
        in the original. The semantic structure of II John can also be
        shown through propositional display, predicational display, and
        chiastic patterns.

III JOHN

*   Funk, Robert W. "The Form and Structure of II and III
        John." See #2216.

2220.   du Rand, J.A. "The Structure of 3 John." *Neotestamentica* 13
        (1979), 121-131.

        Christological and ethical themes are not as prominent in III
        John as they are in II John, as is shown by the former's syntactic
        structure. It is a "splendid example" of the classic form of the an-
        cient letter. Discourse analysis reveals six sections; a "dominant
        structural marker" shows the theme to be that of *alētheia*: the ethi-
        cal requirement of hospitality for missionaries.

2221.   Watson, Duane F. "A Rhetorical Analysis of 3 John: A Study in Epistolary Rhetoric." *CBQ* 51 (1989), 479-501.

Using the methodology of George Kennedy, we can isolate the rhetorical unit, define the rhetorical situation, determine the species of rhetoric (question, stasis, invention, arrangement, and style), and evaluate the rhetoric. This method shows III John to be an epideictic letter.

See also: #s 2218, 2219.

JUDE

2222.   Charles, J. Daryl. "Jude's Use of Pseudepigraphal Source-Material as Part of a Literary Strategy." *NTS* 37 (1991), 130-145.

"By means of strategic use of extra-biblical sources, incorporation of OT themes and characters, and a concise and pungent literary style, the writer mounts a sharp polemic against his opponents who are distorting the faith." The author uses various pseudepigraphal sources readily recognized by his audience. "As part of his literary strategy, Jude assumes and builds upon several themes fundamental to intertestamental literature."

2223.   Charles, J. Daryl. "Literary Artifice in the Epistle of Jude." *ZNW* 82 (1991), 106-124.

"By means of unusual verbal economy, apocalyptic force, strategic use of catchwords and word-play, ... parallelism, triadic illustration, and rhetorical skill, the writer applies a typological exegesis ... of ungodliness ... [to his opponents]." The literary Greek of Jude is of a very high order, a powerful tool for uniting form with content in this letter.

2224.   Cladder, H.J. "Strophical Structure in St Jude's Epistle." *JTS* o.s. 5 (1903-4), 589-601.

The oldest NT manuscripts hint that several of the Catholic epistles may have a poetical structure. A suggested structure for Jude, aligned with a Greco-Roman rhetorical division of the epistle. If we compare Jude with James, we conclude that recognizing the artistic skill of the writer should not make the letter lose any of its theological merit.

*   Watson, Duane Frederick. *Invention, Arrangement, and Style:*
       Rhetorical Criticism of Jude and 2 Peter. See #2211.

2225. Wolthuis, Thomas R. "Jude and the Rhetorician: A Dialogue
       on the Rhetorical Nature of the Epistle of Jude." *Calvin*
       Theological Journal 24 (1989), 126-134.

       An imaginary dialogue between Jude and Cicero exploring the
       extent to which the letter of Jude follows the dictates of Greco-
       Roman rhetoric. The possible cultural gaps between a Jew and a
       Roman in the first century should make us cautious about assum-
       ing that Jude was influenced only by the concern for form in clas-
       sical rhetoric.

See also: #1515.

REVELATION

*   Altink, Willem. "I Chronicles 16:8-36 as Literary Source for
       Revelation 14:6-7." See #1475.

2226. Aune, David E. "The Apocalypse of John and Graeco-Ro-
       man Revelatory Magic." *NTS* 33 (1987), 481-501.

       In Revelation, John has taken up selected Hellenistic magical
       traditions and fashioned them into an anti-magic polemic; that is,
       he has written an assault on Greco-Roman culture itself.
       Revelation 1:9-20 ("I am Alpha and Omega") and other passages as
       evidence.

2227. Aune, D.E. "The Form and Function of the Proclamations
       of the Seven Churches (Revelation 2-3)." *NTS* 36 (1990),
       182-204.

       "... to provide a more satisfactory intrinsic literary analysis of the
       seven proclamations themselves as well as to link them with regard
       to both form and function to the specific literary genre which
       served the author as a literary model." They were public proclama-
       tions, which is not typical of apocalypses. They are not like letters,
       but like royal edicts in structure; they also resemble early Christian
       "paraenetic salvation-judgment oracles."

2228.   Aune, David E. "The Influence of Roman Imperial Court Ceremonial on the Apocalypse of John." *BR* 28 (1983), 5-26.

Not only is John in Revelation openly hostile to Roman authority, but he took much of the imagery of the latter days directly from popular images of the court ceremonial of his time. Thus, the heavenly liturgy in Revelation is not depicting an earthly liturgy of western Asian Christians.

2229.   Barr, David L. "The Apocalypse as a Symbolic Transformation of the World: A Literary Analysis." *Interpretation* 38 (1984), 39-50.

The various dualisms in Revelation, and their use as a technique of reversal of the "real" world. To find its organizing principle, we must note three basic strategies: ecstatic incoherence, recapitulation, and intercalation. The plot is also structured in three scenes.

2230.   Barr, David L. "The Reader of/in the Apocalypse: Exploring a Method." *PEGL* 10 (1990), 79-91.

Wolfgang Iser's concept of the implied reader applied to Revelation reveals that the book "utilizes a broad array of response-inviting structures, from direct authorial address to surprise and negation." It constructs its implied reader through narrator-narratee dynamics, gaps, and surprises, and in expectation of the end. The implied reader of Revelation is thus superior to the seven churches.

*   Barrett, Cyril. "The Language of Ecstasy and the Ecstasy of Language." See #1345.

2231.   Blevins, James L. "The Genre of Revelation." *Review and Expositor* 77 (1980), 393-408.

The genre of Revelation is syncretistic, "setting forth a prophetic message in the form of Greek tragic drama." The author adapted Greek tragedy because "it was a vessel through which his community could interpret its experiences in a troubled time."

2232.   Bowman, John Wick. *The First Christian Drama: The Book of Revelation.* Philadelphia (Westminster P), 1955, 1968.

Revelation is in fact a drama on which the letter form has been superimposed. It can be analyzed by "acts" and "scenes," with a prologue and epilogue. (Largely theological approach.)

2233.   Bowman, John Wick. "The Revelation to John: Its Dramatic
         Structure and Message." *Interpretation* 9 (1955), 436-455.

         As a literary creation, Revelation is *sui generis*, a product of liter-
         ary genius. If it is related to anything at all, it would be to the OT
         prophets rather than to Judaeo-Christian apocalypses of 175 BC–
         100 AD. The clue to understanding the book is that its original de-
         sign is that of a drama in seven acts. Outline of this structure com-
         pared to the most prominent existing outlines of Revelation.
         John's hearers, as Greco-Romans, would have been familiar with
         the idea of a cosmic drama.

2234.   Collins, Adela Yarbro. "The Early Christian Apocalypses."
         Semeia 14 (1979) [#36], 61-121.

         Definition of the apocalypse within early Christian literature;
         definition of subtypes, using the typology of John Collins [see
         #1450]. Examples mainly from Revelation, also Mark 13, and apoc-
         ryphal NT writings through the third century.

*   Collins, John J., ed. *Semeia 14. Apocalypse: The Morphology of a
         Genre.* See #36.

2235.   Farrer, Austin. *A Rebirth of Images: The Making of St. John's
         Apocalypse.* London (Dacre P), 1949.

         Detailed study of Revelation giving considerable space to struc-
         ture, plot, symbolism, themes, and influence of the HB.

2236.   Feuillet, André. *The Apocalypse,* tr Rev. Thomas E. Crane,
         S.S.L. Staten Island (Alba House), 1965.

         Revelation is a unified literary work, not a collection of frag-
         ments (though of course the author may have used pre-existing
         documents). It is influenced by Jewish apocalyptic, the lack of co-
         herence in fact being a mark of the apocalyptic style; its peculari-
         ties have been exaggerated. The repetitions in the book are the
         key to its interpretation. Possible date of composition. We cannot
         rule out the John of the fourth gospel as the author, despite dif-
         ferences in style and content between the two books.

2237.   Fiorenza, Elisabeth Schüssler. "Composition and Structure
         of the Book of Revelation." *CBQ* 39 (1977), 344-366; re-
         vised as "Composition and Structure of the Apocalypse"
         in *The Book of Revelation: Justice and Judgment* (Philadel-
         phia: Fortress P, 1985), 159-180.

         "The unitary composition of Revelation does not result from a
         final redactor's arbitrary compilation but from the author's theo-
         logical conception and literary composition." Therefore, the in-

terpretation of Revelation must "show how he embodied his theology in a unique fusion of content and form." It is epistolary combined with apocalyptic genre, deriving authority through patterning itself after the Pauline letter form. Its structure is chiastic: ABCDC'B'A', with 10:1-15:4 as climactic center.

*   Freyne, Seán. "Reading Hebrews and Revelation." See #2187.

2238.   Gros Louis, Kenneth R.R. "Revelation," in #39, pp. 330-345.

Various difficulties which Revelation poses for modern readers, and in particular for teachers of literature. Yet, "it is a carefully and consciously wrought statement ... which contains passages of striking ... imaginative energy. The opening three chapters illustrate its careful artistry, certain thematic links in succeeding chapters substantiate this artistry, and the closing chapters finally confirm ... that Revelation is not a patchwork of ineffable, unrelated mystical visions, but a highly wrought and controlled work of art."

2239.   Kirby, John T. "The Rhetorical Situation of Revelation." *NTS* 34 (1988), 197-207.

Definition of a rhetorical situation; three kinds which occur in Revelation 1-3. The interplay of these situations is the key to the overall meaning of the book, since it follows classical rhetoric closely. Revelation functions for the reader as discourse, and therefore as primary rhetoric.

2240.   McGinn, Bernard. "Revelation," in #33, pp. 523-541.

Revelation is compelling even to those who try to avoid it. "... even today Revelation raises the question of how it is to be read in a more dramatic way than perhaps any other book of the New Testament." To grasp it, we must first understand the history of its interpretation. Its announced attention and apparent structure; the nature of apocalypses in the Hellenistic world; its use of mythological symbolism.

2241.   Payne, Michael. "Voice, Metaphor, and Narrative in the Book of Revelation," in #48, pp. 364-372.

Revelation has three essential characteristics: it is a book about books, with a "highly self-conscious author who wrestles with problems of textuality and inspirational authority"; its major metaphors "are abstract, tending toward the symbolic rather than the allegorical, and they retain their Judaic and pagan identity"; and the narrative "defies even those structured forms it invokes." At first it appears to have a standard biblical shape with framing devices; however, these are not "able to contain the vision of Revelation. Taken together, the narrative forms in Revelation suggest a process of semiological overloading...."

2242.   Shea, William H. "Chiasm in Theme and by Form in Revelation 18." *AUSS* 20 (1982), 249-256.

We can support Kenneth Strand's investigation of thematic chiasm in Revelation 18 [see #2249; also 2245, 2247, 2250] by arguing that there is a chiasm of form there as well. The seven hymns balance the seven seals within the broad chiastic structure of the entire book of Revelation.

2243.   Shea, William H. "The Parallel Literary Structure of Revelation 12 and 20." *AUSS* 23 (1985), 37-54.

The parallel (non-chiastic) structural forms in chapters 12 and 20 are found in similar positions within the overall structure of the book. They correspond by having similar tripartite literary structures including the use of inclusio and "reciprocal" themes."

2244.   Shea, William H. "Revelation 5 and 19 as Literary Reciprocals." *AUSS* 22 (1984), 249-257.

Parallels between these two hymns are evident from a number of angles: use of number, chiastic structure, shared words and phrases, and persons being addressed, among others. Even the contexts in which the hymns are found are similar. This forces us to conclude that the chapter 19 hymns are separate from those found in chapter 18.

2245.   Strand, Kenneth A. "Chiastic Structure and Some Motifs in the Book of Revelation." *AUSS* 16 (1978), 401-8.

Two existing literary analyses of Revelation either find a major break between chapters 11 and 12, or offer a concentric-symmetry model. The chiastic structure model, however, is a third possibility which finds the main division between chapters 14 and 15. It is based on thematic counterparts supported by the twofold theme of Revelation as a whole: Christ's return, and the presence of the Alpha and Omega.

2246.   Strand, Kenneth A. "The Eight Basic Visions in the Book of Revelation." *AUSS* 25 (1987), 107-121.

Revelation is a remarkably well-constructed literary piece with many neatly-intertwining patterns. The book is structured chiastically, with prologue and epilogue as counterparts and the intervening major prophetic visions paired in chiastic order as well. This structure reinforces the theological message of Christ as Alpha and Omega.

2247. Strand, Kenneth A. *Interpreting the Book of Revelation: Hermeneutical Guidelines, with Brief Introduction to Literary Analysis.* Worthington, Ohio (Ann Arbor Publishers), 1976.

We must first understand the literary structure and context of Revelation before we can deal with the book theologically. The nature of literary apocalypse and of biblical symbols. Various previous literary analyses of its structure. Revelation has an overall chiastic structure, with chapters 1-14 comprising a "historical series," and 15-22 an "eschatological series." Therefore it is important to note into which series a given passage falls for interpreting that passage. Appendix by Philip Payne outlines the chiastic structure of Zechariah.

2248. Strand, Kenneth A. "'Overcomer': A Study in the Macrodynamic of Theme Development in the Book of Revelation." *AUSS* 28 (1990), 237-254.

The "overcomer" theme is integral to the entire book of Revelation, giving evidence that the book "is indeed a beautifully crafted literary piece" whose macrodynamic theme development "is set forth most strikingly in its double aspect of prevailing against deception and coercion, even unto death itself...."

2249. Strand, Kenneth A. "Some Modalities of Symbolic Usage in Revelation 18." *AUSS* 24 (1986), 37-46.

Revelation is exceptionally rich not only in imagery and symbol, "but also in the variety of modalities it utilizes in drawing upon OT materials." Awareness of these modalities illuminates significant nuances in the book which we might otherwise miss, and increases our respect for the author's literary craftsmanship.

2250. Strand, Kenneth A. "Two Aspects of Babylon's Judgment Portrayed in Revelation 18." *AUSS* 20 (1982), 53-60.

The theme of chapter 18 is clarified when its literary structure is considered. The structure is chiastic by theme: the situation of Babylon, the appeal to them, and mourning at the judgment about them.

2251. Strand, Kenneth A. "The 'Victorious-Introduction' Scenes in the Book of Revelation." *AUSS* 25 (1987), 267-288.

[A follow-up to #2246.] There are eight of these "victorious introduction" scenes; each introduces one of the eight prophetic visions analyzed earlier. The first and eight have an "inclusio" structure, again probably for theological reasons.

2252. Terry, Milton S. "The Apocalypse of John," in #32, pp. 343-362.

Revelation "contains the elements of a great epic, and its elaborate structure has, by the inimitable art and genius of the author, appropriated nearly all its imagery from the Old Testament, and wrought it over to suit a purpose strikingly original ... while the language and style of this book are often rough and Hebraistic...."

2253. Thompson, Leonard L. "The Literary Unity of the Book of Revelation," in #48, pp. 347-363.

Three types of unity we may see in the biblical text: narrative, metaphoric, and mythic. "The seer's language does not simply flow in narrative or logical sequence; it plays on formal, thematic, metaphoric, symbolic, and auditory levels of association," all of which overlap.

2254. Vorster, W.S. "'Genre' and the Revelation of John: A Study in Text, Context and Intertext." *Neotestamentica* 22 (1988), 103-123.

Scholars working on Revelation may either continue to look for a theory of the genre of that book from within interpretive theory; or, they may turn to deconstruction, where genre disappears and intertextuality takes over. Both choices will work if we recognize that they rest on different epistemological grounds.

See also: #s 7, 12, 17, 27, 60, 163, 188, 1486, 1491, 1500, 1515, 1538.

Author Index